Anglo-Saxon Studies 39

THE DYNASTIC DRAMA OF *BEOWULF*

Anglo-Saxon Studies

ISSN 1475-2468

GENERAL EDITORS
John Hines
Catherine Cubitt

'Anglo-Saxon Studies' aims to provide a forum for the best scholarship on the Anglo-Saxon peoples in the period from the end of Roman Britain to the Norman Conquest, including comparative studies involving adjacent populations and periods; both new research and major re-assessments of central topics are welcomed.

Books in the series may be based in any one of the principal disciplines of archaeology, art history, history, language and literature, and inter- or multi-disciplinary studies are encouraged.

Proposals or enquiries may be sent directly to the editors or the publisher at the addresses given below; all submissions will receive prompt and informed consideration.

Professor John Hines, School of History, Archaeology and Religion, Cardiff University, John Percival Building, Colum Drive, Cardiff, Wales, CF10 3EU, UK

Professor Catherine Cubitt, School of History, Faculty of Arts and Humanities, University of East Anglia, Norwich, England, NR4 7TJ, UK

Boydell & Brewer, PO Box 9, Woodbridge, Suffolk, England, IP12 3DF, UK

Previously published volumes in the series are listed at the back of this book

THE DYNASTIC DRAMA OF *BEOWULF*

Francis Leneghan

D. S. BREWER

© Francis Leneghan 2020

All Rights Reserved. Except as permitted under current legislation
no part of this work may be photocopied, stored in a retrieval system,
published, performed in public, adapted, broadcast,
transmitted, recorded or reproduced in any form or by any means,
without the prior permission of the copyright owner

The right of Francis Leneghan to be identified as
the author of this work has been asserted in accordance with
sections 77 and 78 of the Copyright, Designs and Patents Act 1988

First published 2020
D. S. Brewer, Cambridge
Paperback edition 2022

ISBN 978-1-84384-551-5 (hardback)
ISBN 978-1-84384-629-1 (paperback)

D. S. Brewer is an imprint of Boydell & Brewer Ltd
PO Box 9, Woodbridge, Suffolk IP12 3DF, UK
and of Boydell & Brewer Inc.
668 Mt Hope Avenue, Rochester, NY 14620-2731, USA
website: www.boydellandbrewer.com

A CIP catalogue record for this book is available
from the British Library

The publisher has no responsibility for the continued existence or accuracy of
URLs for external or third-party internet websites referred to in this book, and
does not guarantee that any content on such websites is, or will remain, accurate
or appropriate

For my mother and father

Contents

Preface	viii
Acknowledgments	xi
Abbreviations	xii
Family Trees: The Dynasties of Beowulf	xv
Dramatis Personae	xviii
Introduction: Reading *Beowulf* as a Book of Kings	1
1 The Dynastic Life-Cycle and the Structure of the Poem	32
2 Shaping the Dynastic Drama	104
3 The Role of the Monsters in the Dynastic Drama	153
4 *Beowulf* and Biblical Kingship	195
Conclusion: Reading the Dynastic Drama in Anglo-Saxon England	236
Appendix A: Plot Summary of Skjöldunga saga	247
Appendix B: Plot Summary of Hrólfs saga kraka	251
Bibliography	256
Index	293

Preface

In an article published in the *Times Higher Education Supplement* in the year 2000 entitled 'Goodbye to *Beowulf*', Valentine Cunningham remarked:

> Kingsley Amis went too far, of course, in his spleen over what Oxford English involved him in ('the anonymous, crass, purblind, infantile, featureless HEAP OF GANGRENED ELEPHANT'S SPUTUM, "Barewolf"'), but his feelings about compulsory *Beowulf* have not been uncommon.[1]

Twenty years on, however, *Beowulf* is enjoying a period of unprecedented popularity, not only as a staple of undergraduate English courses worldwide, but also as the subject of countless translations, retellings and adaptations.[2] No longer routinely mocked as a relic of Dark Age primitivism, the poem is now widely recognized as one of the masterpieces of early medieval literature, a work of rare sophistication and supreme artistry. Equipped with digital reproductions of the manuscript and scholarly bibliographies, the modern *Beowulf*-scholar can now engage with the text from any number of critical and methodological perspectives. In recent decades, scholars have turned their attention to neglected areas of the work such as gender,[3] psychology and the representation of mental

---

[1] V. Cunningham, 'Goodbye to *Beowulf*', *Times Higher Education Supplement*, 12 May 2000, https://www.timeshighereducation.com/news/goodbye-to-beowulf/151563.article (accessed 29 January 2018). Amis's biographer, Zachary Leader, notes that 'he had very little to say in favour of any author on the English syllabus' (*The Life of Kingsley Amis* [London, 2007], p. 192), recording similarly dismissive remarks made in letters to Philip Larkin concerning the merits of Chaucer ('THE SODDING OLD *FOOL*'), Dryden, Johnson, Keats, Shelley and Milton (p. 193). Amis attained a first in English at Oxford in 1947, gaining high marks in Old English (β++) and Chaucer (α).

[2] For a study of verse translations up to Heaney, see H. Magennis, *Translating Beowulf: Modern Versions in English Verse* (Cambridge, 2011). The recent publication of J. R. R. Tolkien's prose translation, completed in 1926, has also attracted considerable media interest: *Beowulf: A Translation and Commentary, together with Sellic Spell*, ed. C. Tolkien (Boston, 2014) (subsequent references to the commentary-section of this volume are labelled simply 'Commentary'). For a recent assessment of the current revival of interest in *Beowulf* and Old English poetry more generally, see S. Irvine, 'Bawling and brawling', *Times Literary Supplement*, 16 February 2018, pp. 26–27. On film adaptations, see C. Jones, 'From Heorot to Hollywood: *Beowulf* in its Third Millennium', in *Anglo-Saxon Culture and the Modern Imagination*, Medievalism 1, ed. D. Clark and N. Perkins (Cambridge, 2010), pp. 13–30; and L. Neidorf, '*Beowulf*', in *Books to Film: Cinematic Adaptations of Literary Works*, Vol. I, J. Craddock (Detroit, 2018), pp. 21–24.

[3] See, for example, G. R. Overing, *Language, Sign, and Gender in* Beowulf

states,⁴ landscape,⁵ trauma,⁶ humour,⁷ and, most recently, intimacy, affect and erotics.⁸ Aided by new digital resources, specialist studies of style, prosody, metrics and linguistics are revealing new aspects of the poet's artistry and sharpening our sense of the work's position within the corpus of Old English literature.⁹ Recent archaeological discoveries, combined with the unearthing of new and meaningful analogues and possible sources, continue to enhance our knowledge of *Beowulf*'s literary and cultural background.¹⁰

(Carbondale and Edwardsville, 1990); and S. Klein, *Ruling Women: Queenship and Gender in Anglo-Saxon Literature* (Notre Dame, 2006), pp. 87–124. For a summary, see K4, pp. cxxvi–cxxvii.

⁴ See, for example, M. Lapidge, '*Beowulf* and the Psychology of Terror', in *Heroic poetry in the Anglo-Saxon period: studies in honor of Jess B. Bessinger, Jr.*, ed. H. Damico and J. Leyerle (Kalamazoo, MI, 1993), pp. 373–402; M. Lapidge, '*Beowulf* and Perception', *PBA* 111 (2001), 61–97; J. W. Earl, *Thinking about Beowulf* (Stanford, 1994); A. Harbus, *The Life of the Mind in Old English Poetry* (Amsterdam, 2002); A. Harbus, *Cognitive Approaches to Old English Poetry*, CSASE 18 (Cambridge, 2012); and B. Mize, 'Manipulations of the Mind-as-Container Motif in *Beowulf*, *Homiletic Fragment II*, and Alfred's *Metrical Epilogue to the Pastoral Care*', *JEGP* 107 (2008), 25–56.

⁵ See, for example, J. Neville, *Representations of the Natural World in Old English Poetry*, CSASE 27 (Cambridge, 1999); M. Gelling, 'The Landscape of *Beowulf*', *ASE* 31 (2002), 7–11; P. S. Langeslag, 'Monstrous Landscape in *Beowulf*', *ES* 96 (2015), 119–38.

⁶ T. Morrissey, *The* Beowulf-*Poet and his Real Monsters: A Trauma-Theory Reading of the Anglo-Saxon Poem* (Lampeter, 2013).

⁷ R. P. Tripp, Jr., 'Humor, Wordplay, and Semantic Resonance in *Beowulf*'; and E. L. Risden, 'Heroic Humor in *Beowulf*', both in *Humour in Anglo-Saxon Literature*, ed. J. Wilcox (Cambridge, 2000), pp. 49–70, 71–78.

⁸ *Dating Beowulf: Studies in Intimacy*, ed. D. C. Remein and E. Weaver (Manchester, 2019). For overviews and samples of recent critical approaches, see *The Postmodern* Beowulf: *A Critical Casebook*, ed. E. A. Joy and M. K. Ramsey, with the assistance of B. D. Gilchrist (Morgantown, WV, 2006); J. M. Hill, 'Current Trends in *Beowulf* Scholarship', *Literature Compass* 4 (2007), 66–88; and J. D. Niles, 'Changing Currents in *Beowulf* Studies', in his *Old English Literature: A Guide to Criticism with Selected Readings* (Chichester, 2016), pp. 20–31.

⁹ For analysis of the poet's mastery of a range of stylistic techniques, see *CCB*, pp. 57–97. For studies of the language, metre and text of *Beowulf* pertaining to the chronology of Old English verse, see R. D. Fulk, *A History of Old English Meter* (Philadelphia, 1992), pp. 348–92; M. P. Brown, '*Beowulf* and the Origins of the Written Old English Vernacular', *SELIM* 20 (2013–14), 81–120; and L. Neidorf, *The Transmission of Beowulf: Language, Culture and Scribal Behavior*, Myth and Poetics 2 (Ithaca, NY, 2017). The *Toronto DOE* has now reached the letter *I*, while Andy Orchard's ongoing Oxford-based ERC project, *A Consolidated Library of Anglo-Saxon Poetry* (*CLASP*), promises to reveal much about the relatively unexplored relationships between Old English and Anglo-Latin poetry, as well as between texts in both languages.

¹⁰ See esp. C. Rauer, *Beowulf and the Dragon: Parallels and Analogues* (Cambridge, 2000); and Bruce, *Scyld and Scef*. See further T. M. Andersson, 'Sources and Analogues', in Bjork and Niles (1997), pp. 125–48; and *CCB*, pp. 130–68. For new archaeological evidence with a bearing on the dating of Old English

Preface

Yet, despite these advances many fundamental questions about *Beowulf* remain unanswered. There is still no consensus, for example, on the poem's date and provenance, with recent arguments ranging from the seventh to eleventh centuries.[11] Nor can scholars agree on matters such as the work's genre, structure, or theme, while a number of passages are still regarded as suspicious or inauthentic.[12]

This book offers a new interpretation of *Beowulf* as a dynastic drama concerning the fluctuating fortunes of the great royal houses of Scandinavia in the fifth and sixth centuries.[13] It argues that the hero's three great monster-fights assume mythical significance within this dynastic context as portents of the fall of royal houses and nations. By shifting the focus away from the characterization of the hero himself and on to the wider social and familial structures within which he operates, *The Dynastic Drama of Beowulf* places the legends of the Scyldings, Scylfings and Hrethlings at the centre of the discussion. Situating the poem in an eighth-century context, when Germanic ideas about royal succession based on valour in battle were coming into conflict with Christian notions of dynasty and moral worthiness, it proposes that the poem served as an Anglo-Saxon Book of Kings, mythologizing the origins of dynastic kingship in the pre-Christian courts of southern Scandinavia.

---

biblical verse, see J. Hines, 'The *Benedicite* Canticle in Old English Verse: An Early Runic Witness from Southern Lincolnshire', *Anglia* 133 (2015), 257–77. For connections between *Beowulf* and the Staffordshire Hoard, see Conclusion, pp. 239–40.

[11] *The Dating of* Beowulf: *A Reassessment*, ed. L. Neidorf, Anglo-Saxon Studies 24 (Cambridge, 2014); H. Damico, *Beowulf and the Grendel-kin: Politics and Poetry in Eleventh-Century England*, Medieval European Studies XVI (Morgantown, 2015). For a survey of scholarship up to 1997, see R. E. Bjork and A. Obermeier, 'Date, Provenance, Author, Audiences', in Bjork and Niles (1997), pp. 13–34.

[12] One popular early view was that the poem is a *Fürstenspiegel* ('mirror for princes'); for references, see Bjork and Obermeier, 'Date, Provenance, Author, Audience', p. 33. Tolkien, however, termed it a 'heroic elegy' ('Monsters', p. 85). For the argument that *Beowulf* is a *summa* of Old English poetic genres, see J. Harris, '*Beowulf* in Literary History', *Pacific Coast Philology* 17 (1982), 16–23, repr. in *Interpretations of* Beowulf: *A Critical Anthology*, ed. R. D. Fulk (Bloomington, IN, 1991), pp. 235–41; and for a review of the standard position that the poem is a form of epic, see J. Harris, '*Beowulf* as Epic', *Oral Tradition* 15 (2000), 159–69. For criticism of the structure see K. Sisam, *The Structure of Beowulf* (Oxford, 1965). For a useful survey of the many competing theories, see T. A. Shippey, 'Structure and Unity', in Bjork and Niles (1997), pp. 149–74, at 154–58.

[13] I use the term 'drama' throughout this book in the sense of a 'series of actions or course of events having a unity like that of a drama, and leading to a final catastrophe or consummation' (*OED*, s. v. *drama* 3).

Acknowledgments

For generously reading part or all of this book in draft and sharing their insights, as well as saving me from many mistakes, I warmly thank Daniel Anlezark, Mark Atherton, Louise Nelstrop and Andy Orchard. The anonymous reader for Boydell & Brewer provided invaluable advice on the overall structure and direction of the book, as well as many points of detail, for which I am also very grateful. For assistance with proofreading, thanks go to Rachel Burns, Sally-Ann DelVino and Amy Faulkner. Any remaining errors are, of course, entirely my own fault.

For discussing various aspects of this book and sharing their expertise, I am particularly grateful to Helen Appleton, Hannah McKendrick Bailey, Marilina Cesario, Jim Earl, Sarah Foot, Susan Irvine, Hugh Magennis, Richard North, Heather O'Donoghue, Winfried Rudolf, Mercedes Salvador Bello, Hattie Soper, Roxanne Taylor and Daniel Thomas. At Trinity College Dublin, I was fortunate to have such inspirational teachers of Old and Middle English as the late Helen Cooney, Helen Conrad O'Briain, Gerald Morgan and John Scattergood, and it gives me great pleasure to register here my deep gratitude to them for setting me on this path. I am also thankful to my colleagues at the Faculty of English, St Cross College and St Peter's College, Oxford, especially Marina MacKay and Abby Williams, for their support and friendship. I would also like to thank my undergraduate and graduate students who have contributed to this book in so many ways over the years.

For hospitality and encouragement along the way, I thank Frank Armstrong, Tamara Atkin, Marc Brightman and Vanessa Grotti, Edward Clarke and Francesca Magnabosco, Jed Dale, Ann Kenny, Clare MacCumhaill and Rob Leach, Sinéad O'Hart, Malachy O'Neill and Helen Crawford, Barry Ryan, Sebastian Sergeant and Evelyn Léon, and Tara Stubbs and Avshalom Guissin.

For permission to reproduce images, I am grateful to The Potteries Museum and the Bodleian Library. For editorial and production assistance, I warmly thank Nick Bingham, Emily Champion, Elizabeth McDonald and Paul Pearson. Special thanks go to Caroline Palmer at Boydell for her enthusiasm for this project and for her patience and guidance throughout the publication process.

Abbreviations

ANQ	*American Notes and Queries: A Quarterly Journal of Short Articles, Notes and Reviews*
ARV	*ARV: Nordic Yearbook of Folklore*
ASE	*Anglo-Saxon England*
ASPR	*The Anglo-Saxon Poetic Records: A Collective Edition*, 6 vols, ed. George Phillip Krapp and Elliot Van Kirk Dobbie (New York: Columbia UP, 1931–55)
BAR	British Archaeological Reports
Bjork and Niles	*A Beowulf Handbook*, ed. Robert E. Bjork and John D. Niles (Exeter: University of Exeter Press, 1997)
B-T	*An Anglo-Saxon Dictionary Based on the Manuscript Collections of the Late Joseph Bosworth*, ed. Thomas Northcote Toller (Oxford: Clarendon Press, 1898); Supplement ed. Thomas Northcote Toller (Oxford: Clarendon Press, 1921); Revised and Enlarged Addenda, ed. Alistair Campbell (Oxford: OUP, 1972)
CASSS	Corpus of Anglo-Saxon Stone Sculpture, 12 vols <http://www.ascorpus.ac.uk/index.php>
CCB	Andy Orchard, *A Critical Companion to* Beowulf (Cambridge: D. S. Brewer, 2003)
CSASE	Cambridge Studies in Anglo-Saxon England
CCSL	Corpus Christianorum Series Latina, 201 vols (Turnhout: Brepols, 1953–2014); references are given to volume and page number(s)
DOE	*Dictionary of Old English: A to I online*, ed. Angus F. Cameron, Ashley Crandell Amos and Antonette diPaolo Healey (pubd online 2007) <http://tapor.library.utoronto.ca/doe/dict/index.html>
DOE Corpus	*Dictionary of Old English Web Corpus*, compiled by Antonette diPaolo Healey with John Price Wilkin and Xin Xiang (Toronto: Dictionary of Old English Project 2009)
DOML	Dumbarton Oaks Medieval Library
EETS, e.s.	Early English Text Society, extra series

Abbreviations

EETS, o.s.	Early English Text Society, original series
EETS, s.s.	Early English Text Society, supplementary series
EHR	*English Historical Review*
ELH	*English Literary History*
ELN	*English Language Notes*
EME	*Early Medieval Europe*
ES	*English Studies*
Garmonsway	G. N. Garmonsway and Jacqueline Simpson, trans., Beowulf *and its Analogues*, including 'Archaeology and *Beowulf*' by Hilda Ellis Davidson (New York: Littlehampton, 1971)
Gneuss and Lapidge	Helmut Gneuss and Michael Lapidge, eds, *Anglo-Saxon Manuscripts: A Bibliographical Handlist of Manuscripts and Manuscript Fragments Written or Owned in England up to 1100*, Toronto Anglo-Saxon Series 15 (Toronto/Buffalo/London: UTP, 2014)
JEGP	*Journal of English and Germanic Philology*
K2	Friedrich Klaeber, ed., Beowulf *and* The Fight at Finnsburg, 2nd edn (Boston: D. C. Heath and Company, 1922)
K3	Friedrich Klaeber, ed., Beowulf *and* The Fight at Finnsburg, 3rd edn (Boston: D. C. Heath and Company, 1936; supplemented 1941 and 1950)
K4	*Klaeber's* Beowulf *and* The Fight at Finnsburg, *Fourth Edition*, ed. R. D. Fulk, Robert E. Bjork and John D. Niles (Toronto: UTP, 2008)
Ker	Neil Ker, ed., *Catalogue of Manuscripts Containing Anglo-Saxon* (Oxford: The Clarendon Press, 1957)
MÆ	*Medium Ævum*
MGH	Monumenta Germaniae Historica
MLN	*Modern Language Notes*
MLR	*Modern Language Review*
MP	*Modern Philology*
NM	*Neuphilologische Mitteilungen*
NQ	*Notes and Queries*
OE	Old English
OED	*Oxford English Dictionary online* (pubd online 2009), http://www.oed.com

Abbreviations

ON	Old Norse
PASE	Prosopography of Anglo-Saxon England, http://www.pase.ac.uk (London: King's College London, 2010)
PBA	*Proceedings of the British Academy*
PG	*Patrologia Graeca*, ed. Jacques-Paul Migne *et al.*, 161 vols (Paris: Imprimerie Catholique, 1856–66). References are given to volume and column number(s)
PMLA	*Proceedings of the Modern Languages Association of America*
PL	*Patrologia Latina*, ed. Jacques-Paul Migne *et al.*, 221 vols (Paris Imprimerie Catholique, 1841–55). References are given to volume and column number(s)
PQ	*Philological Quarterly*
RES	*Review of English Studies*
Saga-Book	*Saga-Book of the Viking Society for Northern Research*
SELIM	*Journal of the Spanish Society for Medieval English Language and Literature*
Shippey and Haarder	Beowulf: *The Critical Heritage*, ed. T. A. Shippey and Andreas Haarder (Abingdon: Routledge, 1998)
SN	*Studia Neophilologica*
SP	*Studies in Philology*

Family Trees

The Dynasties of Beowulf

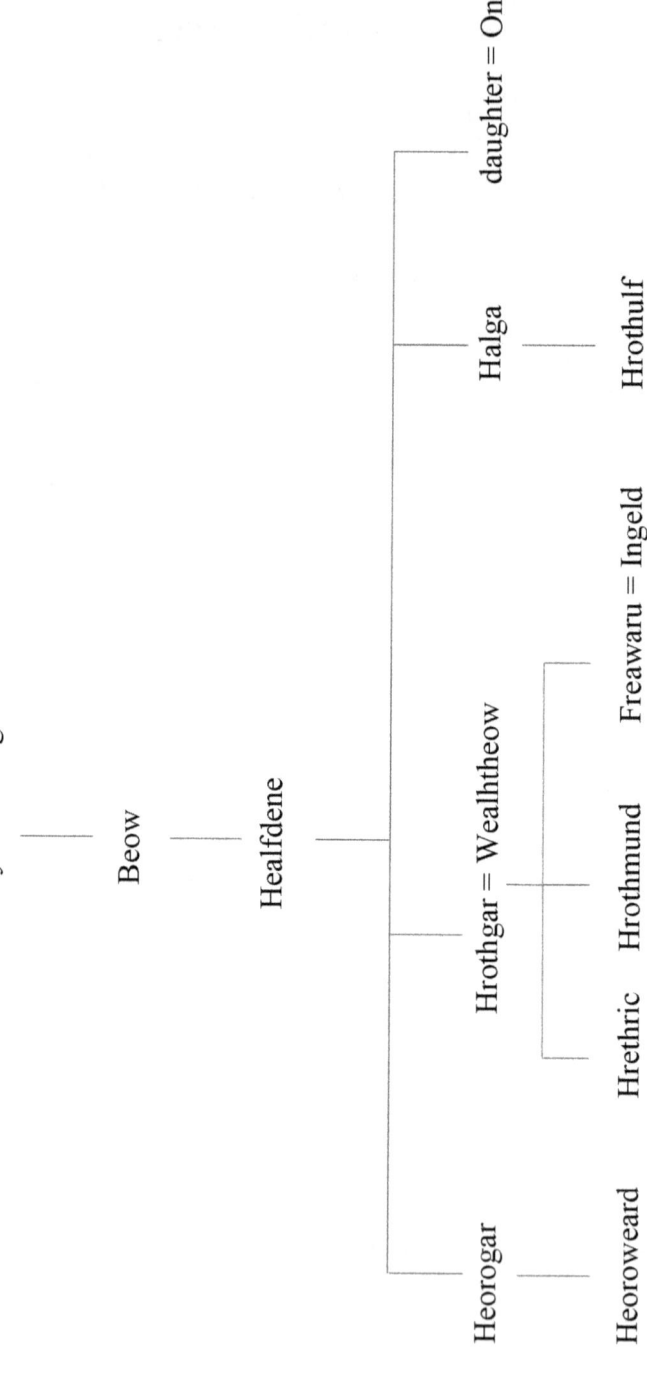

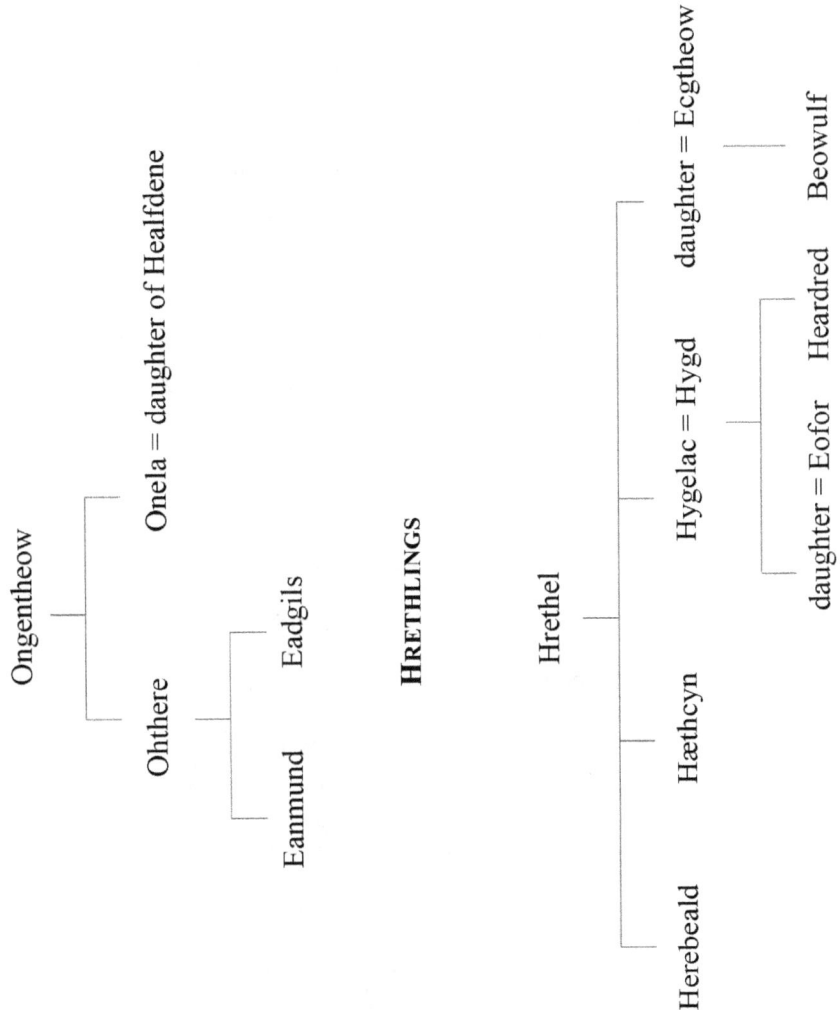

Lines of Royal Succession in Beowulf

Scyldings

Heremod
|
[interregnum]
|
Scyld Scefing (of unknown origin)
|
Beow (son of Scyld)
|
Healfdene (son of Beow)
|
Heorogar (son of Healfdene)
|
Hrothgar (brother of Heorogar)
|
Hrothulf (paternal nephew of Hrothgar, son of Halga)
|
Heoroweard (paternal cousin of Hrothulf, son of Heorogar)
|
Hrethric (paternal cousin of Heoroweard, son of Hrothgar)[14]

Scylfings

Ongentheow
|
Onela (son of Ongentheow)[15]
|
Eadgils (paternal nephew, son of Onela's brother, Ohthere)

Hrethlings

Hrethel
|
Hæthcyn (son of Hrethel)
|
Hygelac (brother of Hæthcyn)
|
Heardred (son of Hygelac)
|
Beowulf (maternal nephew of Hygelac, son of Hygelac's sister)

---

[14] Italics denote events which take place outside the narrative of the poem, inferred from other sources.
[15] It is unclear if Onela seized the throne from his brother, Ohthere, leading to the exile of the latter's sons among the Geats.

Dramatis Personae

Scyldings

Heremod	An early king of the Danes, deposed because of his greed
Scyld Scefing	A foundling who restores the Danes to glory and establishes a great line of kings, the Scyldings
Beow	Scyld's son and heir
Healfdene	Beow's son and heir
Heorogar	Healfdene's eldest son and heir
Hrothgar	Healfdene's second-born son; heir to Heorogar; builder of the royal hall, Heorot; husband to Queen Wealhtheow
Halga	Healfdene's third-born son
Healfdene's (unnamed) daughter	Queen to Onela, King of the Swedes
Heoroweard	Heorogar's son
Hrethric and Hrothmund	Hrothgar's sons
Hrothulf	Halga's son
Wealhtheow	Queen of the Danes; wife of Hrothgar; a Wulfing
Freawaru	Daughter of Hrothgar and Wealhtheow; betrothed to Ingeld, prince of the Heathobards
Unferth	King Hrothgar's advisor
Wulfgar	King Hrothgar's spokesman

Grendelkin

Grendel and his mother	Monstrous descendants of Cain; enemies of the Scyldings

Heathobards

Froda	King of the Heathobards; enemy of the Scyldings
Ingeld	Froda's son; betrothed to Freawaru, princess of the Scyldings

Dramatis Personae

Scylfings

Ongentheow	King of the Swedes
Ecgtheow	Brother of Ongentheow? Father of Beowulf; previously exiled at the court of King Hrothgar
Ohthere	Ongentheow's son
Onela	Ongentheow's son and successor; husband of Healfdene's (unnamed) daughter
Eanmund and Eadgils	Ohthere's sons; exiled among the Geats, under the protection of King Heardred

Hrethlings

Hrethel	Former King of the Geats
Herebeald	Hrethel's eldest son; killed in a shooting accident by his brother, Hæthcyn
Hæthcyn	Hrethel's second-born son and successor
Hygelac	Hrethel's third-born son; successor to Hæthcyn as King of the Geats
Hygd	Queen of the Geats; wife of Hygelac; mother of Heardred
Heardred	Son of Hygelac and Hygd; Hygelac's successor
Beowulf	Son of Ecgtheow; maternal grandson of King Hrethel; Heardred's successor; last of the Hrethlings

Wægmundings

Weohstan	A Wægmunding warrior; father of Wiglaf; slayer of Eanmund, son of Ohthere
Wiglaf	Son of Weohstan the Wægmunding; loyal to Beowulf

Others

Sigemund	A legendary dragon-slayer
Fitela	Sigemund's nephew (and son?) and partner-in-crime
Hildeburh	Daughter of Hoc; princess of the Half-Danes; married to Finn, king of the Frisians
Hnæf	Leader of the Half-Danes at Finnsburg
Hengest	Leader of the Danes at Finnsburg; possibly a Jute

Dramatis Personae

Finn	King of the Frisians
Offa	A king of the Angles; married to 'Modthryth'/'Fremu'[1]
Eomer	Offa's son
Eofor and Wulf	Geatish warriors loyal to Hygelac
A dragon	Hoarder of treasure

---

[1] Although editors have proposed the names (Mod)-Thryth and Fremu, the name of Offa's bride may be missing from the MS due to a copying error (as in the case of Healfdene's daughter) or simply omitted by the poet, as appears to have been the case with both Hygelac's daughter and Beowulf's mother. The absence of these names may reflect the fact that dynastic power passes through the male line in the world depicted in the poem. See pp. 18, 19, 25, 86, 206, 209, 210 n.72, 216.

Introduction:

Reading *Beowulf* as a Book of Kings

Achilles rings a bell, not Scyld Scēfing. Ithaca leads the mind in a certain direction, but not Heorot.

(Seamus Heaney).[1]

For the modern reader of *Beowulf*, the poet's frequent and casual allusions to legends of the Scyldings, Scylfings and Hrethlings can seem an unwelcome distraction from 'the main plot' of the hero's monster-fights. Even with the help of genealogies, plot summaries, explanatory notes and analogues, we struggle to grasp the significance of these obscure ancient dynasties.[2] Yet, as the opening lines make clear, the poem's original Anglo-Saxon audience was well-versed in this material:[3]

---

[1] S. Heaney, 'Introduction', Beowulf: *A New Verse Translation* (London, 1999; repr. New York, 2001), p. xii. All quotations from *Beowulf* are taken from K4. Other Old English poems are cited from ASPR unless otherwise stated. I have silently inserted vowel-length markers and hyphenated compounds. For the sake of convenience, and following convention, I refer to the anonymous *Beowulf*-poet (or poets) throughout with the singular male personal pronoun, though the possibilities of either a female author or multiple authors should not be discounted: see Bjork and Obermeier, 'Date, Provenance, Author, Audiences', pp. 30–31. For recent arguments in favour of a single author, see L. Neidorf, *Transmission* and L. Neidorf, M. S. Krieger, M. Yakubek, P. Chaudhuri and J. P. Dexter, 'Large-scale quantitative profiling of the Old English verse tradition', *Nature: Human Behaviour* 3 (2019), 560–67. Quotations from the Vulgate Bible are from *Biblia Sacra: Iuxta Vulgatam Versionem*, ed. R. Weber and R. Gryson, 5th edn (Stuttgart, 2007), with translations supplied from the Douay-Rheims, unless otherwise stated. Psalm quotations, however, are taken from the Romanum Psalter – rather than the Gallican which forms the basis of the Vulgate texts – as this remained the most popular version throughout the Anglo-Saxon period: *Le Psautier Romain et les autres anciens Psautiers latins*, Collectanea Biblica Latina X, ed. R. Weber (Rome, 1953).

[2] W. W. Lawrence, for example, devotes an entire chapter of his monograph to 'Tragedies of the Royal Houses' (Beowulf *and Epic Tradition* [Harvard, 1928], pp. 71–106), with the aim of allowing the modern reader 'to gain such a knowledge of the old stories about the Danes and Geats as the poet took for granted' (pp. 71–72). For a recent example of a similar approach, see K4, pp. li–lxvii.

[3] R. Frank, 'Germanic Legend in Old English Literature', in *The Cambridge Companion to Old English Literature*, 2nd edn, ed. M. Godden and M. Lapidge (Cambridge, 2013), pp. 82–100, at 91: 'Germanic legend was something people had to know, like chess, claret or cricket, if they wanted to be thought cultured.' Frank argues for the currency of Germanic legend in Viking-Age England,

Hwæt, *wē* Gār-Dena   in geār-dagum,
þēod-cyninga   þrym *gefrūnon*
hū ðā æþelingas   ellen fremedon.
(1–3). (Emphasis added).

[Listen! *We have learnt about* the might of the people-kings of the Spear-Danes in ancient times, how those princes attained glory.]

The placement of the nouns *þēod-cyninga*, 'people-kings', and *æþelingas*, 'princes, sons of nobles', in apposition in lines 2a and 3a points towards the distinctively dynastic nature of kingship as presented in the poem.[4] Moreover, as George Clark comments, the *Beowulf*-poet's worldview suggests that he was an insider at a royal court:

> This is a royalist's poem, its great hero is born a prince and dies a king still serving the memory of the beloved king of his youth. The characters of the poem are royals, courtiers, court poets, and aristocratic warriors; the poem's vision of history is dynastic and cyclical; royal families prove as mortal as royals themselves.[5]

---

on the grounds of renewed contact with Scandinavia. For the counter-argument that Germanic legends such as those known to the poet and his audience were popular in the early, pre-Viking period but were less well-known in later Anglo-Saxon England, see L. Neidorf, 'Germanic Legend, Scribal Errors and Cultural Change', in Neidorf (2014), pp. 37–57.

[4] On the etymology of the terms *cyning*, *þēod-cyning* and *æþeling*, see, pp. 24–26. On the meaning of these opening lines, see F. C. Robinson, *Beowulf and the Appositive Style* (Knoxville, 1985), pp. 27–28. The collocation of *gefrægn* (supplied)/ *gefrunon*, *þēod-cyning* and *ellen* occurs again in the description of how Wiglaf assisted Beowulf in his hour of need (2694–96); the alliterative collocation of *þēod-cyning* and *þrym* occurs in *Genesis A* 1965, during the description of how the kings of four peoples set out to seek Sodom and Gomorrah.

[5] G. Clark, *Beowulf*, Twayne's English Authors Series 477 (Boston, 1990), p. ix. Among the poem's few non-royal characters, we can number the Danish coastguard (234–319), the anonymous *þeow* ('slave') or *þeof* ('thief') who steals the cup from the dragon's hoard (2223b–31a) and, perhaps, the grieving Geatish woman at Beowulf's funeral (3150–55a). Cf. R. North, *The Origins of Beowulf: From Vergil to Wiglaf* (Oxford, 2007), p. 16: '*Beowulf* is about kings. [...] [T]his poet presents Danish royal history as the foundation of heroic narrative.' See below for the theory that *Beowulf* was composed as a 'mirror' for a prince or king, see pp. x, n. 12, 239, 243. For arguments that the poet was closely connected to a royal court, see, for example, P. Wormald, 'Bede, *Beowulf* and the Conversion of the Anglo-Saxon Aristocracy', in *Bede and Anglo-Saxon England: papers in honour of the 1300th anniversary of the birth of Bede, given at Cornell University in 1973 and 1974*, BAR 46, ed. R. T. Farrell (Oxford, 1978), pp. 32–95, repr. in P. Wormald, *The Times of Bede: Studies in Early English Christian Society*, ed. S. Baxter (Malden, 2006), pp. 30–105; M. Lapidge, '*Beowulf*, Aldhelm, the *Liber Monstrorum* and Wessex', *Studi Medievali* 3rd ser. 23 (1982), 151–92; and C. Davis, *Beowulf and the Demise of Germanic Legend in England* (New York, 1996), p. 90.

Introduction

Hence, the poem is book-ended by two magnificent royal funerals: the opening describes how the Danes honoured their great warrior king, Scyld Scefing, with a splendid ship-funeral (26–52),[6] while the closing lines relate how the Geats prepared a funeral pyre atop a sea-cliff for King Beowulf, praising him for his noble deeds:

cwædon þæt hē wǣre *wyruld-cyninga*
manna mildust ond monðwǣrust,
lēodum līðost ond lofgeornost.
(3180–82). (Emphasis added).

[They said that he was *of the kings of the world* the mildest of men and the gentlest, the kindest to the people and the most eager for glory.][7]

As Adrien Bonjour comments, the striking contrast between Scyld's funeral, which leaves 'an impression of brilliancy and splendour', with the 'more depressing and sorrowful' account of Beowulf's obsequies, is 'one of the finest artistic achievements in the poem'.[8] Underscoring the structural apposition of these two royal funerals are the contrasting dynastic legacies of Scyld and Beowulf: while the Danes mourn the departure of their beloved king, they are comforted by the knowledge that God has provided Scyld with a son and heir, Beow, *folce tō frōfre*, 'as a comfort to the people' (14a); King Beowulf, on the other hand, laments his own lack of a son in his dying speech to Wiglaf (2729–32a) and his own funeral-scene is framed with dire portents of a national disaster (2884–91, 2910b–3027, 3148b–55a). Scyld stands at the head of a great line of kings, the Scyldings; Beowulf is the last member of his own royal house, the Hrethlings.

---

[6] On the poet's muting of Scyld's death, see pp. 38, 40–46. For the standard emendation of MS *Beowulf* to Beow/Beo for Scyld's son, see p. 8. I follow K4 in printing the name as 'Beow'. For arguments in favour of *Bēo(w)* (for Anglian *Bio*) or *Beowe* (for *Biowi*), see R. D. Fulk, 'The Etymology and Significance of Beowulf's Name', Anglo-Saxon 1 (2007), 109–36; N. Goering, 'The linguistic elements of Old Germanic metre: phonology, metrical theory, and the development of alliterative verse' (Unpubl. doctoral dissertation, Univ. of Oxford, 2016), pp. 58–59, n. 59.

[7] This thematic link (or 'ring pattern') between the opening and closing lines is strengthened by a series of aural echoes. For example, the final stressed item in the poem is the palatal *g* of *geornost*, which creates a ring with the alliteration of palatal *g* and velar *g* in the first line: *Gār/ gēar* (cf. C. B. Kendall, *The Metrical Grammar of Beowulf*, CSASE 5 [Cambridge, 1991], p. 9). Similarly, the first and last sentences of the poem are linked through the use of end-rhyme, an unusual feature of Old English verse (2b and 3b: *gefrunon/ fremedon*; 3182b–83b: *monð-wǣrust/ lof-geornost*). See A. Orchard, 'Artful Alliteration in Anglo-Saxon Song and Story', Anglia 113 (1995), 429–63, at 451–63, for discussion of the high degree of inventive alliteration in the Scyld-prologue. For discussion of the interpretation of these lines, see Chapter Four, pp. 227–31.

[8] A. Bonjour, *The Digressions in* Beowulf, Medium Ævum Monographs 5 (Oxford, 1950; repr. 1965) pp. 9–10. See also G. R. Owen-Crocker, *The Four Funerals in* Beowulf *and the Structure of the Poem* (Manchester, 2000).

This pronounced interest in deaths of kings and princes is sustained throughout the narrative. Indeed, the hero's three great monster-fights are set within a complex network of overlapping royal tragedies, past and future.[9] Yet, despite the clear importance of the dynastic theme to the poem's conception and meaning, and the importance of royal legend to the work's overall structural and thematic design, this major area of the poem remains relatively unexplored. Tellingly, there is no mention of the dynastic theme in the section on 'Structure and Unity' in the standard modern scholarly edition of the poem.[10] This book therefore aims to help readers 'sharpen their perception' of the interlinked royal legends that underpin the action of *Beowulf* and give the hero's three great monster-fights meaning.[11]

Traces of the royal legends known to the original audience of *Beowulf* are preserved in a range of sources from across the medieval period. The popularity of Scandinavian royal tradition in early Anglo-Saxon England is attested by Old English poems, such as *The Finnsburg Fragment* and *Widsith*, as well as the Anglo-Latin *Liber monstrorum*.[12] Anglo-Saxon rulers proclaimed their descent from lines of ancient Scandinavian kings via elaborate royal genealogies that in several places overlap with royal traditions recorded in *Beowulf*.[13] Legends surrounding the Danish, Swedish and Geatish royal houses are also contained in a wide range of (much later) Scandinavian sources. Although the text of the twelfth-century *Skjöldunga saga* is no longer extant, an outline of the narrative survives in a Latin abstract made by the sixteenth-century Icelandic historian, Arngrímur Jónsson,[14] while related traditions are preserved in Saxo Grammaticus's

---

[9] Reflecting on the high number of royal deaths in the poem, James H. Morey comments: 'The poem could indeed be called a series of "sad stories on the death of kings" (*Richard II*, III.ii.156)' ('The Fates of Men in *Beowulf*', in *Source of Wisdom: Old English and Early Medieval Latin Studies in Honour of Thomas D. Hill*, ed. C. D. Wright *et al.* [Toronto, 2007], pp. 26–51, at 26).

[10] See K4, pp. lxxix–xci.

[11] J. D. Niles, 'Introduction: Beowulf, Truth, and Meaning', in Bjork and Niles (1997), pp. 1–12, at 10: 'If specialized scholarship has a mission, it is to help readers deepen their knowledge and sharpen their perceptions of every possible factor that can have a bearing on the understanding of texts and readerly events.'

[12] For recent debate surrounding the dating of *Widsith*, see L. Neidorf, 'The Dating of *Widsið* and the Study of Germanic Legend', *Neophilologus* 97 (2013), 165–83; E. Weiskott, 'The Meter of *Widsith* and the Distant Past', *Neophilologus* 99 (2015), 143–50; R. J. Pascual, 'Old English Metrical History and the Composition of *Widsið*', *Neophilologus* 100 (2016), 289–302. For discussion of the *Beowulf*-poet's reshaping of dynastic tradition, see Chapter Two.

[13] On connections between these genealogies and *Beowulf*, see esp. pp. 40–46, 143–47, 240–41, 245.

[14] See 'Danasaga Arngríms Lærða', ed. Bjarni Guðnason, in *Danakonunga Sogur: Skjoldunga Saga, Knytlinga Saga, Ágrip Af Sogu Danakonunga*, Islenzk Fornrit 35 (Reykjavik, 1982), pp. 3–38. Garmonsway, pp. 119–23, translates excerpts from

twelfth-century *Gesta Danorum* and the fourteenth-century Icelandic *Hrólfs saga kraka*. Early Swedish royal tradition is attested in the writings of the thirteenth-century Icelander Snorri Sturluson. Plot summaries of *Skjöldunga saga* and *Hrólfs saga kraka* are provided as appendices to this volume, while relevant sections of other sources pertaining to early Scandinavian royal legends are quoted in full in subsequent chapters.

The significance of these royal legends to what is conventionally regarded as the poem's 'main action' – that is, the hero's fights with three monsters – has long been a matter of controversy. For some early commentators, the poem's chief interest was the valuable light it shed on early Germanic kingship and Scandinavian royal history. For instance, W. P. Ker famously complained that the 'irrelevances' of the monster fights were an unwelcome distraction from the more 'serious things' half-buried in the so-called digressions, namely fragments of royal legends and other heroic tales.[15] All that was to change with J. R. R. Tolkien's paradigm-shifting 1936 lecture, 'The Monsters and the Critics', which emphatically rejected the attempts of Ker and others to read the poem as 'bad history' and defended the poet's decision to place the monsters at the centre.[16] Tolkien's interpretation of the poem as essentially a folktale with a historical setting echoes that of Klaeber, who comments:

> The subject-matter of *Beowulf* comprises in the first place, as the main plot, three fabulous exploits redolent of folk-tale fancy (the first two forming a closely connected series), and secondly a number of apparently historical elements which are introduced as a setting to the former and by way of more or less relevant digressions.[17]

---

these and other texts which are analogous to passages in *Beowulf*. See also A. M. Bruce, *Scyld and Scef: Expanding the Analogues* (New York, 2002), pp. 141–43. For discussion of its relation to *Beowulf* and other texts, see J. Benediktsson, 'Icelandic Traditions of the Scyldings', *Saga-Book* 15 (1957–61), 48–66; K3, pp. xxx–xlv; R. W. Chambers, Beowulf: *An Introduction to the Study of the Poem with a Discussion of the Stories of Offa and Finn*, 3rd edn with a supplement by C. L. Wrenn (Cambridge, 1959), pp. 13–16; Bruce, *Scyld and Scef*, pp. 66–68; and P. Acker, 'Part 1. "Fragments of Danish History" (*Skjöldunga saga*)', *ANQ* 20 (2007), 1–9. For a full translation of the Skjöldungr section of Arngrímur's *Rerum Danicarum Fragmenta*, see C. H. Miller, 'Fragments of Danish History', *ANQ* 20 (2007), 9–22.

[15] W. P. Ker, *The Dark Ages* (Edinburgh, 1923), pp. 252–53. For a re-evaluation of Ker's interpretation of the poem, see A. Haarder, Beowulf: *The Appeal of a Poem* (Viborg, 1975), pp. 118–56. Sisam, *Structure*, p. 66, acknowledges that it is 'unreasonable to apply to *Beowulf* classical standards which the audience and probably the poet could not know', but nonetheless judges the poem 'architecturally inferior to the *Odyssey*'.

[16] J. R. R. Tolkien, '*Beowulf*: The Monsters and the Critics', *PBA* 22 (1936), 245–95, repr. in *An Anthology of* Beowulf *Criticism*, ed. L. E. Nicholson (Notre Dame, 1963), pp. 51–103, at 85. All references are to this reprint.

[17] K3, pp. xlii–xliii. See also the contemporary comments of R. Girvan, Beowulf

Broadly speaking, this is the view of *Beowulf* that has come down to us, one in which the royal legends are relegated to a supporting role as 'background' to the monster-fights. As this book will argue, however, the full meaning of the hero's monster-fights only becomes clear when viewed within the context of the surrounding royal legends, as part of a wider dynastic drama concerning the fates of royal houses and nations. In other words, the dynastic material does not merely serve as 'background' but provides the essential context for the monster-fights, while the monster-fights themselves serve to dramatize dynastic legend.

The Origins of the Poem and its Manuscript

Although the matter of the origins of *Beowulf* remains unsettled, there is now an increasing body of linguistic, metrical and cultural evidence to support the view that the work originated in an Anglian-speaking region of Anglo-Saxon England, probably the central kingdom of Mercia, during the late-seventh or early-eighth century.[18] That being said, barring the discovery of another manuscript, the precise circumstances under which the work was composed, for whom, and why, are likely to remain shrouded in mystery. Compounding the difficulty is the fact that there are precious few tangible signs of the poem's circulation between the period of its composition and its copying in the Nowell Codex *c.* 1000. It is now generally agreed that the author of *Andreas*, an Old English verse saint's life contained in the Vercelli Book, borrowed certain elements of heroic phraseology and imagery from *Beowulf*.[19] Similar arguments have been advanced, albeit more tentatively, for the possible influence of *Beowulf* on the signed poems of Cynewulf, the Old English prose version of *Alexander's Letter to Aristotle* with which it now shares a manuscript, and the West-

---

and the Seventh Century (London, 1935; repr. 1971), p. 57.

[18] See esp. Fulk, *History of Old English Meter*, pp. 348–92; and Neidorf (2014). For earlier arguments in favour of a very wide range of dates, from the seventh to eleventh centuries, see *The Dating of Beowulf*, ed. C. Chase (Toronto, 1981). See further Conclusion, pp. 237–46.

[19] C. Schaar, 'On a New Theory of Old-English Poetic Diction', *Neophilologus* 40 (1956), 301–05; A. Riedinger, 'The Formulaic Relationship between *Beowulf* and *Andreas*', in *Heroic Poetry in the Anglo-Saxon Period: Studies in Honor of Jess B. Bessinger*, Studies in Medieval Culture 32, ed. H. Damico and J. Leyerle (Kalamazoo, MI, 1993), pp. 283–312; A. Powell, 'Verbal Parallels in *Andreas* and its Relationship to *Beowulf* and Cynewulf' (Unpubl. doctoral dissertation, Univ. of Cambridge, 2002); R. North and M. D. J. Bintley, eds, *Andreas: An edition* (Liverpool, 2016), pp. 57–81; A. Orchard, 'The Originality of *Andreas*', in *Old English Philology: Studies in Honour of R. D. Fulk*, ed. L. Neidorf, R. J. Pascual and T. Shippey (Cambridge, 2016), pp. 331–70. On connections between *Beowulf* and *Andreas*, see Conclusion, pp. 241–44.

Saxon royal genealogy.[20] A further hint of the text's circulation may be provided by what appears to be a pen-trial or doodle in a tenth-century Anglo-Saxon hand in MS BL Harley 208 reading *hwæt ic eall fela ealde sæge*, 'Listen, I [have heard] very many ancient tales'.[21] The resemblance between this inscription and the *Beowulf*-poet's description of the Danish court poet (*scop*), *sē ðe eal fela eald-gesegena/ worn gemunde*, 'the one who could remember from far back a great many ancient tales' (869–71a), may indicate that this scribe was recalling lines from the poem.[22]

Towards the end of the Anglo-Saxon period, around the year 1000, a version of *Beowulf* was copied into an eclectic anthology of vernacular prose and verse. The items in this collection are broadly linked, it seems, by their concern with the monstrous and the exotic.[23] This codex now forms the second part of MS BL Cotton Vitellius A.xv and is usually referred to either as the Nowell Codex, after the Dean of Lichfield, Laurence Nowell, who wrote his name on the first page in 1567, or simply 'the *Beowulf* manuscript'.[24] The manuscript was produced by two scribes (conventionally

---

[20] A. Orchard, 'Both Style and Substance: The Case for Cynewulf', in *Anglo-Saxon Styles*, ed. C. E. Karkov and G. Hardin Brown (Albany, NY, 2003), pp. 271–305; *CCB*, pp. 163–68; A. Orchard, *Pride and Prodigies: Studies in the Monsters of the Beowulf-Manuscript* (Cambridge, 1985; repr. Toronto, 2003), pp. 23–35; S. C. Thomson, *Communal Creativity in the Making of the* Beowulf *Manuscript: Towards a Reception History of the Nowell Codex*, Library of the Written Word 67 (Leiden, 2018), pp. 27–30. For links with the West Saxon royal genealogy, see Chapter Two, pp. 143–47, and Conclusion, pp. 241–46.

[21] The text is written beneath the text of one of Alcuin's letters on fol. 88r.

[22] See Ker §229; M. B. Parkes, '*Rædan, areccan, smeagan*: How the Anglo-Saxons Read', *ASE* 26 (1997), 1–22, at 19; A. Orchard, 'The Word Made Flesh: Christianity and Oral Culture in Anglo-Saxon Verse', *Oral Tradition* 24 (2009), 293–318, at 309; Thomson, *Communal Creativity*, pp. 256–59. If the scribe was indeed recalling *Beowulf* here, it is all the more interesting that he chose to paraphrase a passage directly concerned with the memorization of ancient poetry. For discussion of this passage and its function as a metaphor for the *Beowulf*-poet's own reshaping of tradition, see Chapter Two, pp. 106–11.

[23] Ker §216; Gneuss and Lapidge §399. The manuscript is conventionally dated to c. 1000, though Kiernan (*Beowulf Manuscript*), Thomson (*Communal Creativity*, pp. 65–83) and others have pushed for a slightly later date. For codicological studies and discussion of thematic links between the items, see K. Sisam, *Studies in the History of Old English Literature* (Oxford, 1953), pp. 61–96; K. Powell, 'Meditating on Men and Monsters: A Reconsideration of the Thematic Unity of the *Beowulf* Manuscript', *RES* 58 (2006), 1–15; Orchard, *Pride and Prodigies*; N. Howe, 'Books of Elsewhere: Cotton Tiberius B v and Cotton Vitellius A xv', in his *Writing the Map of Anglo-Saxon England* (New Haven, 2008), pp. 151–94; and Thomson, *Communal Creativity*. For the texts, see R. D. Fulk, ed. and trans., *The Beowulf Manuscript*, DOML 3 (Cambridge, MA, 2010).

[24] The Nowell Codex is preceded in Cotton Vitellius A.xv by an unrelated twelfth-century collection, the Southwick Codex. For a facsimile of the Nowell Codex, see K. Malone, *The Nowell Codex: British Museum Cotton Vitellius A. vx, Second MS*, Early English Manuscripts in Facsimile 12 (Copenhagen, 1963); for a digital reproduction, see K. Kiernan, *Electronic Beowulf: 4th edition* (London,

referred to as Scribes A and B) as well as several illustrators.²⁵ In its present state the Nowell Codex comprises three Old English prose texts, *The Passion of Saint Christopher* (missing its beginning), *The Wonders of the East*, also known as *The Marvels of the East* (illustrated), and *Alexander's Letter to Aristotle*, followed by the two poems, *Beowulf* and *Judith* (missing its beginning). All three prose texts are in the hand of Scribe A, who also copied up to line 1939 of *Beowulf*, at which point he was replaced by Scribe B, who also copied *Judith*. Examination of the codex, however, reveals that *Judith* in fact once stood before *Christopher*, meaning that *Beowulf*, the last pages of which are especially badly damaged, was originally the final item in the collection.²⁶ Judging by the ambitious nature of this project and the relatively poor standard of its execution, it seems likely that the Nowell Codex was produced for a moderately wealthy patron at a provincial scriptorium rather than a royal court or major ecclesiastic centre. Both scribes inconsistently adapted the Anglian spelling of their exemplar to the Late West Saxon dialect of their day. Like the modern reader, these scribes were at times baffled by the ancient royal names that are littered throughout *Beowulf*. Scribe A appears to have confused the name of Scyld's son, Beow, with that of the Geatish hero, Beowulf, at lines 18a and 53b.²⁷ Similarly, Scribe B garbles the phrase *Merewīoingas milts*, 'the mercy of the Merovingian' (2921), as *mere wio ingasmilts*, and later renders the genitive form of Ongentheow (*Ongenþeoes*) at line 1968b as four separate lexemes, thereby producing the meaningless *on gen þeo*

2015), http://ebeowulf.uky.edu/ebeo4.0/start.html (last accessed 21 March 2019). For the text of *Beowulf* alone, see J. Zupitza, ed. *Beowulf: Autotypes of the Unique Cotton MS. Vitellius A. XV in the British Museum, with a Transliteration and Notes*, EETS o.s. 245 (London, 1882), 2nd edn, containing a new reproduction of the manuscript, with an introductory note by N. Davis, EETS o.s. 245 (London, 1959; reprinted 1967).

[25] See K. S. Kiernan, Beowulf *and the* Beowulf *Manuscript* (New Brunswick, NJ, 1981), repr. with a new foreword by K. O'Brien O'Keeffe (Ann Arbor, MI, 1997); A. Orchard, 'Reading *Beowulf* Now and Then', *SELIM* 12 (2003–04), 49–81; Neidorf, *Transmission*; and Thomson, *Communal Creativity*.

[26] See P. J. Lucas, 'The Place of *Judith* in the *Beowulf*-manuscript', *RES* 41 (1990), 463–78. Based on his recent examination of the manuscript, Thomson suggests that the Nowell Codex originally comprised 'a missing religious poem, followed by *Judith*, followed by another religious text in either prose or poetry, followed by the full *St Christopher*, and then the texts as we have them now: *Wonders, Alexander*, and *Beowulf*' (*Communal Creativity*, p. 89).

[27] In the West-Saxon royal genealogy, Sceldwea (= Scyld) is succeeded by Beaw/Beow/Beo. See K3, pp. xxiii–xxix; Chambers, *Introduction*, pp. 41–47, 87–88, 291–304; K. Sisam, 'Anglo-Saxon Royal Genealogies', *PBA* 39 (1953), 287–346, at 317–20 and 339–45; E. A. Anderson, 'Beow the Boy-Wonder (*Beowulf* 12–25)', *ES* 89 (2008), 630–42; K4, p. 113; Neidorf, *Transmission*, pp. 73–74. For arguments in defence of the MS reading, see D. Whitelock, *The Audience of* Beowulf (Oxford, 1951), pp. 69–70; and Earl, *Thinking*, p. 8.

es.²⁸ To make matters worse, the Nowell Codex was badly damaged by fire in the early-eighteenth century. Nevertheless, despite its defects, it is this single, battered and error-strewn copy that provides our only complete witness to this extraordinary poem.

The Modern Recovery of the Text and its Critical Reception

Following the copying of the Nowell Codex, the text of *Beowulf* lay relatively undisturbed for much of the next millennium. Although some early-modern antiquarians evidently took an interest in the manuscript, it was not until the early-nineteenth century that *Beowulf* became the subject of sustained analysis.²⁹ With the rise of 'national philologies', scholars began to study the text in the hope that they might discover first-hand evidence of the languages and customs of the 'Germanic Heroic Age'.³⁰ Extensive efforts were made to excise the 'Christian elements' by a process of textual 'disintegration', in the hope of recovering the unadulterated pagan material that lay behind.³¹ Even with the gradual recognition that *Beowulf* is a work of art in its own right, rather than a mangled version of a series of earlier lays, unfavourable comparisons with the epics of ancient Greece and Rome nevertheless persisted. The generally low crit-

---

[28] See Neidorf, *Transmission*, pp. 88–89. Neidorf takes the scribes' evident unfamiliarity with royal names as indicative of the decline of Germanic legend in late Anglo-Saxon England (*Transmission*, pp. 96–101). Thomson, however, notes that these same scribes at times struggled to make sense of other types of personal names (e.g. biblical) elsewhere in the manuscript, while emphasizing that some of these transmission errors could have been a feature of their exemplar (*Communal Creativity*, pp. 34–35, 154–57, 216–23).

[29] The poem was catalogued and partially transcribed in 1705 by Humfrey Wanley. For a recent discussion of evidence of engagement with the manuscript by later medieval and early modern readers, see Thomson, *Communal Creativity*, pp. 9–10, 338–48. For samples of eighteenth-century interest in the text of *Beowulf*, see Shippey and Haarder, pp. 1–10, 75–90; and K4, p. xxvi.

[30] The classic critique of this approach is E. G. Stanley, *The Search for Anglo-Saxon Paganism* (Cambridge, 1975). See also T. A. Shippey, 'Kemble, *Beowulf*, and the Schleswig-Holstein Question', in *The Kemble Lectures on Anglo-Saxon Studies, 2005–08*, ed. A. Jorgensen, H. Conrad O'Briain and J. Scattergood (Dublin, 2009), pp. 64–80; L. Neidorf, '*Beowulf* as Pre-National Epic: Ethnocentrism in the Poem and its Criticism', *ELH* 85 (2018), 847–75. The Icelandic-Danish scholar, Grímur Jónsson Thorkelín, who oversaw the first modern transcription of the poem in the 1780s, termed it the *Scildingid*, proclaiming it 'truly Danish' (*De Danorum Rebus Gestis Seculis III et IV: Poema Danicum Dialecto Anglosaxonica* [Copenhagen, 1815], trans. in Shippey and Haarder, pp. 91–92).

[31] The most important exponent of this approach, known as *liedertheorie*, was Ernst Moritz Ludwig Ettmüller (1802–77); for a sample of his work, see Shippey and Haarder, pp. 231–34. For summaries of this method, and criticism of its underlying principles, see E. G. Stanley, *In the Foreground:* Beowulf (Cambridge, 1994), pp. 16–20; Shippey, 'Structure and Unity', pp. 154–58.

ical standing of the work prevailed until well into the twentieth century, as influential voices such as W. P. Ker complained of its thematic incoherence and structural inadequacies.[32] This view of the poem as essentially a botched job, the production of an ambitious author ill-suited to the task, characterizes the early phase of modern *Beowulf*-scholarship.

Tolkien's 1936 lecture, 'The Monsters and the Critics', signalled a sea-change in critical attitudes towards *Beowulf*. In response to Friedrich Klaeber's complaint of a 'lack of steady advance',[33] Tolkien insisted that 'the poem was not meant to advance, steadily or unsteadily'.[34] Although he was critical of the poet's abstract presentation of the dragon,[35] and sceptical about the integrity of certain passages, such as the *gif-stōl crux* (168–69) and the 'Christian excursus' (175–88), Tolkien's generally sympathetic treatment of the poet's compositional method paved the way for a series of post-war studies that highlighted the work's artistic sophistication.[36] Adrien Bonjour's 1950 monograph, *The Digressions in* Beowulf, set out to demonstrate that these contentious passages serve 'as a highly appropriate foil to the transcendental interest of the main theme'.[37] Another major advance came with Arthur Brodeur's 1959 book, *The Art of* Beowulf, which highlighted the work's richness of diction and the inventiveness and skill of its author. Comparing *Beowulf* with other long Old English narrative poems such as *Andreas*, *Exodus*, *Judith* and *Elene*, Brodeur maintained that 'none of them attains the dignity, the beauty, the nobility of thought of *Beowulf*; none exhibits its conscious mastery of form'.[38] Fred C. Robinson's 1985 monograph used the poetic technique of apposition, sometimes referred to as variation, whereby elements in a structure are

---

[32] See Chapter One, pp. 32–33.
[33] K3, p. lvii.
[34] Tolkien, 'Monsters', p. 81. Comparing *Beowulf* with classical epic, Tolkien comments: 'the real resemblance of the *Aeneid* and *Beowulf* lies in the constant presence of a sense of many-storied antiquity, together with its natural accompaniment, stern and noble melancholy. In this way they are really akin and together differ from Homer's flatter, if more glittering, surface' ('Monsters', p. 75, n. 21).
[35] Tolkien, 'Monsters', p. 66: 'the conception [...] approaches *draconitas* rather than *draco*: a personification of malice, greed, destruction (the evil side of heroic life), and of the undiscriminating cruelty of fortune that distinguishes not good or bad (the evil aspect of all life).'
[36] For discussion of the meaning of the *gif-stōl crux* in the dynastic drama, see Chapter Three, pp. 162–76.
[37] Bonjour, *Digressions*, p. 71. Bonjour distinguishes between digressions and episodes: 'Strictly speaking, an episode may be considered as a moment which forms a real whole and yet is merged in the main narrative, whereas a digression is more of an adjunction and generally entails a sudden break in the narrative' (p. xi). The first sensitive treatment of the poet's use of digressions and episodes was that of L. P. Schrøder, *Om Bjovulfs-drapen: Efter en række foredrag på folkehöjskolen i Askov* (Copenhagen, 1875).
[38] A. G. Brodeur, *The Art of* Beowulf (Berkeley, 1959), p. 5.

placed in a paratactical relationship, as a lens through which to examine the poem's broader themes, not least its balancing of Christian and pagan themes.[39] Owing to these and other foundational studies, the excellence of *Beowulf* and the sophistication of its blending of Christian and pagan themes are no longer in doubt.

The Problem of the Poem's Uniqueness

Beowulf is the most substantial witness to a 'lost tradition' of alliterative verse celebrating the deeds of legendary Germanic heroes that flourished in the centuries after the collapse of the Western Roman Empire.[40] Part of what may once have been an Old English epic poem or short lay on the feud between the Half-Danes and Frisians at the hall of King Finn was transcribed from a now-lost manuscript by George Hickes in 1705. Despite its brevity, the so-called *Finnsburg Fragment* provides an invaluable analogue for the 'Finnsburg Episode' in *Beowulf* (1068–1158).[41] Also surviving only in fragmentary form is another Old English heroic poem of unknown length, *Waldere*, celebrating the deeds of Walter of Aquitaine.[42] Further hints of the popularity of this material are provided by two short Old English '*scop* poems' preserved in the Exeter Book, *Deor* and *Widsith*, as well as lines from the Old High German *Hildebrandslied* copied on two blank leaves used as bindings for an early-ninth-century codex from Fulda.[43]

Although these texts overlap with *Beowulf* to some extent in terms of subject-matter, as Michael Lapidge comments, 'no extant medieval poem – in Latin or the vernacular – composed before *c*.1100 bears any resemblance to *Beowulf* either in its structure or in its narrative discourse.'[44]

---

[39] Robinson, *Appositive Style*. See further pp. 196, 243–44.
[40] For an overview, see R. M. Wilson, *The Lost Literature of Medieval England* (London, 1970), pp. 1–23.
[41] See J. R. R. Tolkien, *Finn and Hengest: The Fragment and the Episode*, ed. A. J. Bliss (New York, 1983). The fragment was part of MS London, Lambeth Palace Library 487.
[42] Two short fragments of *Waldere* are preserved in MS Copenhagen, Royal Library, Ny kongelige Samling 167b. For the text, see *The Old English Epic of* Waldere, ed. J. B. Himes (Cambridge, 2009). The related Frankish Latin verse epic, *Waltharius*, dating from the ninth or tenth century, survives in ten manuscripts dating from the eleventh to fifteenth centuries: for the text, see *Waltharius*, ed. and trans. A. Ring, Dallas Medieval Texts and Translations 22 (Louvain, 2016).
[43] MS Murhardsche Bibliothek 2o Theol. 54, fols 1r and 76v. The texts of *The Finnsburg Fragment*, *Waldere* and the fragment of *Hildebrandslied* are edited in K4, pp. 273–90, 337–41. See further C. E. Wright, *The Cultivation of Saga in Anglo-Saxon England* (Edinburgh, 1939).
[44] Lapidge, '*Beowulf* and Perception', 80. Cf. L. D. Benson, 'The Originality of

The uniqueness of *Beowulf* naturally problematizes attempts to judge the poem's merits or defects, or to assess its style, structure and form,[45] with the result that scholars have resorted to drawing analogies with other media, including visual art,[46] architecture,[47] music,[48] and 'pageant-drama'.[49] The full implications of the poet's abiding concern with the dynastic theme to the work's unusual structure and mode of narration has yet to be explored.

The Poem's Main Themes

Given the extent of these disagreements concerning the structure and style of *Beowulf*, it is unsurprising that attempts to identify something as nebulous as a single, overarching theme have proved even less conclu-

---

Beowulf, in *The Interpretation of Narrative: Theory and Practice*, Harvard English Studies 1, ed. M. W. Bloomfield (Cambridge, MA, 1970), pp. 1–43, repr. in *Contradictions: From* Beowulf *to Chaucer: Selected Studies of Larry D. Benson*, ed. T. M. Andersson and S. A. Barney (Aldershot, 1995), pp. 32–69, at 41: 'we have no Germanic heroic poem of this length (heroic lays are very brief), and there is no evidence that any other Germanic poet in the eighth century or before attempted a secular narrative poem of such dimensions.'

[45] On the difficulty of judging the aesthetic qualities of 'alliterative, low-information poetry' from a modern perspective, see T. Shippey, '"The Fall of King Hæðcyn": Or *Mimesis* 4a, the Chapter Auerbach Never Wrote', in *On the Aesthetics of* Beowulf *and Other Old English Poems*, ed. J. M. Hill (Toronto, 2010), pp. 247–66, at 265.

[46] J. Leyerle, 'The Interlace Structure of *Beowulf*', *University of Toronto Quarterly* 37 (1967), 1–17, repr. in Fulk (1991), pp. 146–67. See also A. P. Campbell, 'The Time Element of Interlace Structure in *Beowulf*', *NM* 70 (1969), 425–35; M. Bundy, 'Deciphering the Art of Interlace', in *From Ireland Coming*, ed. C. Hourihane (Princeton, 2001), pp. 183–210; A. C. Bartlett, *The Larger Rhetorical Patterns in Anglo-Saxon Poetry* (New York: 1935; repr. New York, 1966), p. 7; G. R. Owen-Crocker, 'Telling a Tale: Narrative Techniques in the Bayeux Tapestry and the Old English Epic *Beowulf*', in *Medieval Art: Recent Perspectives: A Memorial Tribute to C. R. Dodwell*, ed. G. R. Owen-Crocker and T. Graham (Manchester, 1998), pp. 40–59. For criticism of this analogy, see C. L. Wrenn, ed., *Beowulf with the Finnesburg Fragment*, 3rd edn fully revised by W. F. Bolton (Exeter, 1973), henceforth Wrenn-Bolton, p. 76; R. D. Stevick, 'Representing the Form of *Beowulf*', in *Old English and New: Studies in Language and Linguistics in Honor of Frederic G. Cassidy*, ed. J. H. Hall, N. Doane and D. Ringler (New York, 1992), pp. 3–14; U. Schaefer, 'Rhetoric and Style', in Bjork and Niles (1997), pp. 105–24, at 122.

[47] Tolkien, 'Monsters', pp. 83–84. See also J. D. Niles, Beowulf: *The Poem and Its Tradition* (Cambridge, MA, 1983), p. 160.

[48] Brodeur, *Art*, p. 79; J. A. Nist, 'The Structure of *Beowulf*', *Papers of the Michigan Academy of Science, Arts, and Letters* 43 (1958), 307–14, at 310–11; Owen-Crocker, *Four Funerals*, p. 134.

[49] A. E. Du Bois, 'The Unity of *Beowulf*', *PMLA* 49 (1934), 374–405, at 403.

Introduction

sive: suggestions have ranged from 'the ideal of kingship',[50] *sapientia et fortitudo*,[51] and 'the nature and use of power',[52] to 'the fatal contradiction at the heart of heroic society',[53] feuding,[54] community,[55] 'threats to the social order'[56] and 'lordlessness'.[57] The limitations of such a 'monothematic' approach have been highlighted by Kathryn Hume:

> thematic interpretations share, to a greater or lesser degree, one drawback: they tend to rest for supportive evidence on relatively few lines, and consequently the resultant readings [...] are wildly varied – indeed are often mutually exclusive – and none has gained general acceptance.[58]

Taking a less rigid approach to the question of the poem's meaning, several scholars in the second half of the twentieth century highlighted the interplay of major and minor themes or motifs across the narrative, in some cases highlighted through the poet's employment of chiastic 'ring structures'.[59] Indeed, as John Nist comments: 'The author does not introduce a theme, no matter how minor, without developing and varying it later on.'[60] Among the many themes that have been identified are the death of Hygelac,[61] visits to halls, the presentation of women as the bond of kinship, the pursuit and loss of treasure,[62] and scenes of arrival and

---

[50] L. L. Schücking, 'Das Köningsideal im *Beowulf*', *Bulletin of the Modern Humanities Research Association* 3 (1929), 143–54, repr. as 'The Ideal of Kingship in *Beowulf*', in Nicholson (1963), pp. 35–49; G. D. Schmidt, 'Unity and Contrasting Kingships in *Beowulf*', *Concerning Poetry* 17 (1984), 1–11.
[51] R. E. Kaske, '*Sapientia et Fortitudo* as the Controlling Theme of *Beowulf*', *SP* 55 (1958), 423–57, repr. in Nicholson (1963), pp. 269–310.
[52] M. J. Swanton, *Crisis and Development in Germanic Society 700–800:* Beowulf *and the Burden of Kingship* (Göppingen, 1982), p. 154.
[53] J. Leyerle, 'Beowulf the Hero and the King', *MÆ* 34 (1965), 89–102.
[54] J. L. N. O'Loughlin, '*Beowulf* – its Unity and Purpose', *MÆ* 21 (1952), 1–13; Brodeur, *Art*, pp. 71–87; T. E. Hart, 'Tectonic Design, Formulaic Craft, and Literary Execution; the Episodes of Finn and Ingeld in *Beowulf*', *Amsterdamer Beiträge zur älteren Germanistik* 2 (1972), 1–61, at 15–21.
[55] Niles, *Beowulf*, pp. 224–34.
[56] K. Hume, 'The Theme and Structure of *Beowulf*', *SP* 72 (1975), 1–27, at 5.
[57] E. G. Stanley, '*Beowulf*: Lordlessness in Ancient Times is the Theme, as Much as the Glory of Kings, if not More', *NQ* 52 (2005), 267–81.
[58] Hume, 'Theme and Structure', 5.
[59] On the repetition of formulas, see K. O'Brien O'Keeffe, 'Diction, Variation, the Formula', in Bjork and Niles (1997), pp. 85–104; Schaefer, 'Rhetoric and Style', p. 119; Robinson, *Appositive Style*; and *CCB*, pp. 57–97. On repetition and variation of larger themes, see Bartlett, *Larger Rhetorical Patterns*, esp. pp. 108–16; Brodeur, *Art*, pp. 39–70; Leyerle, 'Interlace Structure'; and *CCB*, pp. 91–97. On ring structures, see H. W. Tonsfeldt, 'Ring Structure in *Beowulf*', *Neophilologus* 61 (1977), 443–52; and Niles, *Beowulf*, pp. 152–62.
[60] Nist, 'Structure of *Beowulf*', 311.
[61] Brodeur, *Art*, pp. 78–79.
[62] Leyerle, 'Interlace'.

departure pregnant with meaning.[63] Others have noted the recurrence of certain traditional type-scenes (sometimes referred to within oral-formulaic theory as 'themes') such as 'the beasts of battle' and 'the hero on the beach'.[64] This book will argue that the poet was guided throughout by the theme of kingship, and more specifically the dynastic principle. It is this theme, rather than the life of the hero, that governs the work's structure and provides the essential link between the royal legends contained in the poem and the hero's three great monster-fights. Broadly speaking, scholarship on Beowulfian kingship can be divided into studies that focus on the hero's own progression from warrior-prince to ruler and those which attempt to locate the poem's presentation of royal succession against the background of Anglo-Saxon and early Germanic practice. Before proceeding to the main thesis of this book, it will be helpful to summarize briefly these two approaches.

King Beowulf

The centrality of the figure of Beowulf to the work that now bears his name is one of the few matters about which scholars are in general agreement.[65] The hero is first introduced, however, not by his own name but that of his king and nation. Initially the narrator simply refers to him as *Higelāces þegn/ gōd mid Gēatum*, 'Hygelac's thane, a good one among (*or* from?) the Geats' (194b–95a), and then as *se yldesta*, 'the eldest', (258a), among the Geatish party arriving in Denmark, before the hero himself declares to the Danish coastguard on behalf of the same group:

Wē synt gum-cynnes   Gēata lēode
ond Higelālces   heorð-genēatas
(260–61).

[We are men of the nation of Geats, and Hygelac's hearth-companions.][66]

---

[63] J. M. Hill, *The Narrative Pulse of* Beowulf: *Arrivals and Departures* (Toronto, 2008).
[64] F. P. Magoun, Jr., 'The Theme of the Beasts of Battle in Anglo-Saxon Poetry', *NM* 56 (1955), 81–90; A. Bonjour, '*Beowulf* and the Beasts of Battle', *PMLA* 72 (1957), 563–73; M. S. Griffith, 'Convention and Originality in the Old English "Beasts of Battle" Typescene', *ASE* 22 (1993), 179–99; D. K. Crowne, 'The Hero on the Beach: An Example of Composition by Theme in Anglo-Saxon Poetry', *NM* 61 (1960), 362–72. For a useful list of recurring themes in *Beowulf* with bibliography up to 1990, see J. M. Foley, *Traditional Oral Epic: The* Odyssey, Beowulf, *and the Serbo-Croatian Return Song* (Berkeley, 1990), pp. 331–32. The dynastic theme is not included in this list.
[65] Cf. Tolkien, 'Monsters', p. 85; P. Clemoes, 'Action in *Beowulf* and Our Perception of It', in *Old English Poetry: Essays on Style*, ed. D. G. Calder (Berkeley and Los Angeles, 1979), pp. 147–68.
[66] On Beowulf as a fictional double or poetic variation of his legendary uncle, see

Introduction

In his subsequent address to the coastguard, the hero announces that he is the son of the late Ecgtheow, whom he describes as a famous leader of warriors (262–66). No record survives of this Ecgtheow, however, outside of the poem.[67] Information concerning Beowulf's mother is even thinner on the ground. On the two occasions when she is mentioned in the poem, both times by Hrothgar, she goes unnamed (374–75a, 942b–46a), and all we learn is that she was the only daughter of King Hrethel, ruler of the Geats, who gave her in marriage to Ecgtheow (374–75). This means that Beowulf is a Hrethling by birth, albeit through the weaker, maternal line, and a nephew of King Hygelac. Despite the fact that he was brought up at King Hrethel's court alongside his uncles (2428–34), Beowulf's relatively lowly status within his own royal house, as well as the revelation that the Geats had held him in little regard while he was still a youth (2183b–88),[68] makes him an unlikely candidate for kingship in his homeland. However, in the course of the poem a series of figures judge Beowulf worthy of kingship, including the Danish people and their king, Hrothgar, and Hygelac's widow, Queen Hygd. Having rejected two previous offers of kingship, Beowulf finally comes to rule the Geats after the death of his cousin, Heardred.

Critics have long debated whether Beowulf's career as king matches up to his achievements as a young warrior.[69] In the view of many early commentators, King Beowulf is a model of lordly generosity, loyalty and courage, with some even comparing him with Christ in his final act of laying down his life for his people.[70] While this positive interpretation of the hero as an ideal ruler still finds the occasional supporter,[71] a markedly

---

Chapter Two, pp. 121–39.

[67] For debate as to whether Ecgtheow is either a Geat, Swede or Wægmunding, or any combination of these three, see pp. 18 n.84, 87, 187 n.114.

[68] See pp. 81 n.174, 103, 120 n.44.

[69] For an overview, see G. Clark, 'The Hero and the Theme', in Bjork and Niles (1997), pp. 271–90.

[70] Schücking, 'Ideal of Kingship'; Schmidt, 'Unity and Contrasting Kingships'; Kaske, '*Sapientia et Fortitudo*'. For comparisons with Christ, see F. Klaeber, 'Die christlichen Elemente im *Beowulf*', *Anglia* 35 (1911–12), 111–36, 249–70, 453–82; *Anglia* 36 (1912), 169–99, trans. by P. Battles as 'The Christian Elements in *Beowulf*', *Old English Newsletter*, Subsidia 24 (Kalamazoo, MI, 1997); M. B. McNamee, '*Beowulf*: An Allegory of Salvation?', *JEGP* 59 (1960), 190–207; A. Cabannis, '*Beowulf* and the Liturgy', *JEGP* 54 (1955), 195–201, repr. in Nicholson (1963), pp. 223–32. See further, Chapter Four, pp. 231–35.

[71] See E. B. Irving, Jr., *A Reading of* Beowulf (New Haven, CT, 1968), p. 246; Niles, *Beowulf*, p. 236; J. A. Burrow, *The Poetry of Praise* (Cambridge, 2008), pp. 2, 13, 29–60; J. Neville, 'Redeeming Beowulf and Byrhtnoth: The Heroic Idiom as Marker of Quality in Old English Poetry', in *Narration and Hero: Recounting the Deeds of Heroes in Literature and Art of the Early Medieval Period*, Ergänzungsbände zum Reallexikon der Germanischen Altertumskunde 87, ed. V. Millet and H. Sahme (Berlin, 2014), pp. 45–69. For a recent discussion of the problems inherent in reading modern conceptions of irony into Old English

less sympathetic view of King Beowulf began to take hold following the publication of John Leyerle's 1965 article, 'Beowulf the Hero and the King'. Leyerle's central thesis is that, while Beowulf meets with great success in his youth due to his superhuman strength, he fails in his duties as ruler owing to his lack of wisdom.[72] In 1970, Margaret Goldsmith substantially developed this negative assessment of the hero into a full-blown Augustinian allegory in which the ageing king succumbs to the sin of *cupiditas* in his foolhardy pursuit of gold in the dragon's cave.[73] While stopping short of direct criticism of the hero's conduct as king, Andy Orchard nevertheless argued in 2003 that the copying of *Beowulf* alongside Christian and classical monster-tales in the Nowell Codex provides a moral lesson on how 'prodigious pride can make monsters of men'.[74] Such negative assessments of King Beowulf tend to view the work's closing lines, in which twelve Geatish *æþelinga bearn*, 'sons of æthelings' (3170a), praise the hero, as ironic, if not tragic, with the poem's last word, *lofgeornost*, 'most eager for fame' (3182b), dramatically undercutting what comes before.[75]

In his 2008 monograph, Scott Gwara proposed a compromise position, emphasizing the work's essential ambiguity and foregrounding the manner in which characters themselves frequently offer contradictory assessments of Beowulf's conduct.[76] It is not difficult to imagine that the *Beowulf*-poet, with his fondness for contrast and the continual variation of themes, might have expected his audience to debate the very same questions that have so divided modern critics. Is Beowulf in the right in choosing to fight the dragon single-handed? Or does he eventually succumb, like Heremod, to the sin of *ofer-hygd*?[77] Is it right for kings to fight in the vanguard and thereby risk their own lives – and the future safety of their people – in pursuit of treasure? What are the qualities required of a *gōd cyning*? That the poet chose not to provide simple

---

verse, see E. Louviot, *Direct Speech in* Beowulf *and Other Old English Narrative Poems* (Cambridge, 2016), pp. 223–50.

[72] Leyerle, 'Beowulf the Hero and the King'.

[73] M. E. Goldsmith, *The Mode and Meaning of* Beowulf (London, 1970). Equally critical is Michael Swanton, who in 1982 argued that kingship is a burden which Beowulf struggles to bear, before eventually succumbing to pride in his final battle by relying on strength alone rather than God (*Crisis and Development*, p. 140).

[74] Orchard, *Pride and Prodigies*, p. 171. Orchard takes a more neutral view in his subsequent essay, '*Beowulf*', in Godden and Lapidge (2013), pp. 137–58, at 140: 'The manuscript itself seems a self-conscious collection of texts about monsters, both man-shaped and otherwise, with *Beowulf* as the last word.'

[75] For a summary, see Chapter Four, pp. 228–30.

[76] S. Gwara, *Heroic Identity in the World of* Beowulf, Medieval and Renaissance Authors and Texts 2 (Leiden, 2008), pp. 12–21.

[77] For the suggestion that Beowulf succumbs to *ofer-hygd* by refusing to take a troop with him to face the dragon, see pp. 16, 190, 195, 220 n.102, 228–30, 243–45.

answers to these and many other questions, and even sought to complicate them whenever possible, should not surprise us. *Beowulf* is, after all, a poem, not a political tract, and as such it embraces those very qualities of ambivalence and ambiguity that so trouble critics who would prefer it to *mean* simply one thing or another.[78] This book argues that while the work as a whole expresses a deeply ambivalent vision of the institution of kingship itself, it nonetheless presents in the figure of Beowulf an image of a pre-Christian ruler in whom the qualities of Germanic warrior-kingship are merged with the virtues of mildness, generosity and kindness associated with the *basileus*.[79]

Rather than attempting to pin down the elusive nature of the hero's character, a number of scholars have concentrated on the poem's rich and varied accounts of social rituals, such as feasting and gift-giving, as well as its recurrent emphasis on courtly decorum and hospitality.[80] Others still have explored the underlying political structures within which the hero operates, either with a view to situating the poem within a specific moment in Anglo-Saxon cultural history or to explaining the significance of certain passages. As Brian Murdoch notes, like many other Germanic heroes Beowulf does not fight solely for *dōm* or *lof*, 'glory, fame', or *māþmas*, 'treasures', vitally important though these factors are, but also to preserve the reputation of his family and the safety of his people.[81] Hence, in his youth, Beowulf is motivated by loyalty to his lord and uncle, King

---

[78] Cf. A. Scheil, '*Beowulf* and the Emergent Occasion', *Literary Imagination* 11 (2008), 83–98, at 98: 'this most puzzling and unexpected of poems offers no easy answers – only a stark, enigmatic view of time, history, and change.' See further J. Köberl, *The Indeterminacy of* Beowulf (Lanham, MD, 2002). *CCB*, pp. 263–64, makes a similar point: 'We can still argue (as I suppose we are supposed to) over the significance of the cursed treasure, or what precisely it means to be *lofgeornost* […]. [A]ny all-embracing solution to the poem's mysteries remains, for the moment at least, clearly beyond its critics.' See also G. Overing, '*Beowulf*: A Poem in Our Time', in *The Cambridge History of Early Medieval English Literature*, ed. C. Lees (Cambridge, 2012), pp. 309–31.

[79] See esp. Chapter Four, pp. 227–35.

[80] H. Magennis, *Images of Community in Old English Literature*, CSASE 18 (Cambridge, 1996), pp. 60–81; H. Magennis, *Anglo-Saxon Appetites: Food and Drink and Their Consumption in Old English and Related Literature* (Dublin, 1998), pp. 51–84; J. M. Hill, 'Beowulf and the Danish Succession: Gift Giving as an Occasion for Complex Gesture', *Medievalia et Humanistica* 11 (1982), 177–97; J. M. Hill, *The Cultural World in* Beowulf, 2nd edn (Toronto, 2015); J. M. Hill, *Narrative Pulse*; P. Baker, *Honour, Exchange and Violence in* Beowulf (Cambridge, 2013); F. L. Michelet, 'Hospitality, Hostility and Peacemaking in *Beowulf*', *PQ* 94 (2015), 23–50. Andrew Scheil notes that the hero-centric approach is reinforced by the title bestowed on the poem by modern editors and suggests that it could just as easily have been named 'Ancient Deeds of the North' ('The Historiographic Dimensions of *Beowulf*', *JEGP* 107 [2008], 281–302, at 298).

[81] See B. Murdoch, *The Germanic Hero: Politics and Pragmatism in Early Medieval Poetry* (London, 1996), p. vii.

Hygelac, to whom he and the poet constantly refer; in his dying words, Beowulf takes comfort in having protected the Geats from invasion for fifty years (2723–36a).[82] Indeed, while the actions of Beowulf as warrior and king dominate the action, the poem cannot in any sense be considered a *bildungsroman*.[83] On the contrary, the poet weaves the narrative of Beowulf's heroic deeds into a rich tapestry of overlapping dynastic traditions which must have held the attention of his audience. The poem therefore begins not with the Geat's own ancestry but with a lengthy *encomium* on the origins of the Scyldings, rulers of the Danes (3–85). Grendel's attacks on Heorot take place during a period of uncertainty over the Danish succession. Similarly, the account of King Beowulf's death in the dragon's cave, arguably the main action of the final section of the poem, is repeatedly interrupted by a series of lengthy digressions on the fates of the royal houses of the Geats and Swedes. The hero himself is something of an outsider in both the Danish and Geatish ruling dynasties, with no blood ties to the Scyldings and only a distant claim, via his mother, to the Hrethling throne. Indeed, as we shall see, it appears that his closest family ties are in fact with another royal house, the Swedish Scylfings.[84] The story of Beowulf's adventures, and his own protracted rise to kingship, can only be fully understood within this dynastic context.

The Theme of Royal Succession

In the past few decades, a number of scholars have explored the poem's pronounced interest in the matter of royal succession. In a 1983 article, Stephanie Hollis argued that the poet actively sought to promote the principle of primogeniture through the hero's responses to two dynastic crises.[85] The first of these situations arises when the Danish king, Hrothgar, attempts to adopt Beowulf as his son (1175–80a) after the hero's

---

[82] On Beowulf and Hygelac, see Chapter Two, pp. 121–39.
[83] See Chapter One for theories about the hero's life-cycle.
[84] See below, Chapter Three. On the possible Swedishness of Beowulf's father, see E. E. Wardale, '*Beowulf*: The Nationality of Ecgtheow', *MLR* 24 (1929), 322; and E. M. Shaull, 'Ecgþeow, Brother of Ongenþeow, and the Problem of Beowulf's Swedishness', *Neophilologus* 101 (2017), 263–75. Shaull argues that Ecgtheow is a brother of the Swedish king, Ongentheow, on the basis of the shared second element *-theow* in their names and vocalic alliteration with the names of the other Scylfings (Ongen-*theow*, Ecg-*theow*, Ohthere, Onela, Eanmund, Eadgils). Similarly alliterative naming practice can be observed among the Scyldings – omitting the probably fictional Scyld Scefing and Beow – (Here-mod, Healfdene, Heoro-gar, Hroth-gar, Halga, Heoro-weard, Hreth-ric, Hroth-mund) and Hrethlings (Hrethel, Here-beald, Hæth-cyn, Hyge-lac, Heard-red). On history and fiction in the poem, see Chapter Two.
[85] S. Hollis, '*Beowulf* and the Succession', *Parergon* 1 (1983), 39–54.

victory over Grendel. Hrothgar appears to make public his desire to have Beowulf succeed him as king of the Danes by rewarding the Geat with the armour of his brother and predecessor, King Heorogar (2155–62). Later, after the premature death of King Hygelac, Queen Hygd offers the Geatish throne to Beowulf ahead of her only son, Heardred (2370b–73).[86] Significantly, in both these situations, Beowulf rejects the opportunity to become king when there are other candidates available with more direct blood-ties to the current ruler, that is via the privileged male line. Hence, Hrothgar's queen, Wealhtheow, advises her husband to abandon his plans to adopt Beowulf, instructing him to leave the Danish throne to his own kin (1175–80a). Beowulf subsequently leaves the Danes and, in a display of loyalty, presents his own king, Hygelac, with Heorogar's armour (2155–62). Then, in response to Queen Hygd's offer of the Geatish throne, Beowulf chooses to act as protector to the young Heardred until he comes of age (2367–79a). It is only when Heardred is killed by the Scylfings that Beowulf, as the last surviving Hrethling, finally takes the Geatish throne (2387–90). As this pattern of behaviour makes plain, Beowulf is deeply respectful of the primacy of royal blood and cannot be accused of having designs on either the Danish or Geatish thrones. His failure to secure the royal succession through the provision of a son is something he regrets as he lies dying (2729–32a).[87] However, it is questionable whether the practice of primogeniture, as opposed to simply the dynastic principle, serves as the main motivating factor behind Beowulf's cautious approach to the succession. The early Germanic period seems, in fact, to have been unaffected by primogeniture, as the many instances of fraternal and other forms of collateral succession, including uncle-to-nephew, in the poem and in Anglo-Saxon culture attest.[88]

---

[86] For discussion of both these passages, see Chapter One, pp. 84–85, 91–92.
[87] On Beowulf's conferral of his arms to Wiglaf as an act of non-succession, see below, pp. 98–102.
[88] See G. Morgan, 'The Treachery of Hrothulf', ES 53 (1972), 23–39, at 29; B. Mitchell, 'Literary Lapses: Six Notes on *Beowulf* and Its Critics', RES 43 (1992), 1–17, at 13; and J. D. Niles, 'Myth and History', in Bjork and Niles (1997), pp. 213–32, at 226. On uncle-nephew relations in *Beowulf* and elsewhere, see R. H. Bremmer, Jr., 'The Importance of Kinship: Uncle and Nephew in *Beowulf*', *Amsterdamer Beiträge zur älteren Germanistik* 15 (1980), 22–38. See further, below, pp. 49, 64–66, 70, 95, 121–39. Examples of fraternal succession from within *Beowulf* include Hrothgar's accession after the death of his elder brother Heorogar ahead of the latter's son, Heoroweard, and Hygelac's accession to the Geatish throne after the death of his brother Hæthcyn. Heorogar's priority is to be inferred both from the order in which the sons of Healfdene are named, *Heorogār ond Hrōðgār ond Hālga til* (61), and Hrothgar's subsequent reference to Heorogar as *min yldra mæg* (468a). See further, Chambers, *Introduction*, pp. 14–15. After Hygelac's death, Queen Hygd offers the throne to her nephew Beowulf ahead of her own son, Heardred, though the hero rejects her offer, respectful of the priority of royal blood; see further pp. 91–93.

In what remains the sole book-length study of the theme of royal succession in *Beowulf*, Michael Swanton argued in 1982 that *Beowulf* reflects a 'pregnant moment of poise' between the old Germanic system of royal succession by popular election from members of the *nobilitas*, 'itself not a closed group but accessible from lower ranks of society' (*vox populi*), and the new Christian system of succession limited to the royal kin and ratified by divine grace (*vox dei*) – a moment which he would locate in the late-eighth century.[89] This tension comes to the fore in these same two moments of dynastic crisis outlined above, in both of which the hero resists the impulse towards the election of kings on the basis of prowess and advocates instead a new system in which ancestry is paramount.

Taking a broadly similar approach to Swanton, Frederick M. Biggs has argued in a series of articles that the *Beowulf*-poet carefully juxtaposes two competing systems of royal succession in order to evaluate their relative strengths and weaknesses.[90] In his reading, the model of succession practised by the Scyldings reflects the old pagan, Germanic system, in which any male member of the dynasty is eligible for the throne, whereas the Hrethlings practise the new Christian model, which limits the succession to the legitimate sons of the dynastic founder. Over the course of the poem, Biggs argues, both models of succession are shown to be flawed: the Germanic model resulting in a proliferation of rival claimants and, therefore, a contested succession, while the Christian model is found to be too restrictive, meaning that the royal line of Hrethel will die out with Beowulf. One difficulty with this argument is that Beowulf himself succeeds to the Geatish throne despite the fact that he is descended from the dynastic founder, Hrethel, only via his unnamed mother.[91] However

---

[89] Swanton, *Crisis and Development*, pp. 34, 152–53. Swanton cites Alcuin's Letter to Charlemagne of 798, in which he prioritizes 'vox dei' over 'vox populi' as the deciding factor in kingship (p. 12). For discussion of the poem's date and its relationship to Anglo-Saxon royal succession, see Conclusion, pp. 236–46.

[90] F. M. Biggs, 'The Naming of Beowulf and Ecgtheow's Feud', *PQ* 80 (2001), 95–112; 'Beowulf's Fight with the Nine Nicors', *RES* 53 (2002), 311–28; 'Hondscioh and Æschere in *Beowulf*', *Neophilologus* 87 (2003), 635–52; '*Beowulf* and some fictions of the Geatish succession', *ASE* 32 (2003), 55–77; 'The Politics of Succession in *Beowulf* and Anglo-Saxon England', *Speculum* 80 (2005), 709–41; '*The Dream of the Rood* and *Guthlac A* as a Literary Context for the Monsters in *Beowulf*', in *Text, Image, Interpretation: Studies in Anglo-Saxon Literature and its Insular Context in Honour of Éamonn Ó Carragáin*, ed. A. Minnis and J. Roberts (Turnhout, 2007), pp. 289–301; and 'History and Fiction in the Frisian Raid', in Neidorf (2014), pp. 138–56. Biggs agrees with Swanton that this approach to succession fits best with the early Anglo-Saxon period ('History and Fiction', p. 156).

[91] As recently noted by Shaull, 'Ecgþeow, Brother of Ongenþeow', 272. See Biggs, 'Politics of Succession', 741.

we interpret the matter, it is certainly the case, as Biggs maintains, that the theme of succession is 'at the centre of the poem'.[92]

A number of other scholars have offered equally pessimistic assessments of the presentation of royal succession in *Beowulf*. In 1995, for example, Raymond P. Tripp, Jr. argued that the poem paints a gloomy picture of 'dynastic decay' in which sons are presented as weak links in succession, 'whose collective inadequacies and excesses suggest that familial transmission of society through boys is no longer working.'[93] In 2007, James H. Morey found that while the majority of the Scylfings and Hrethlings die violent deaths, the fates of the Scyldings are either peaceful or 'unexplicit'.[94] Echoing Hollis's view that the poem advocates primogeniture, Morey accounts for breaches of this principle, such as Hrothgar's apparently uncontested succession ahead of his elder brother Heorogar's son, Heoroweard, and Hygd's offer of the throne to her nephew Beowulf ahead of her own son, Heardred, as 'disruptions of and threats to usual practice that generate the drama of the poem'.[95] In the same year, Michael D. C. Drout argued that systems of inheritance in *Beowulf* based on blood, deeds or both all result in failure: 'the tragedy of the cultural world of *Beowulf* is that it inevitably will end through the failure of inheritance.'[96] The extent to which the poem's 'cultural world' comes to an end with the death of Beowulf himself and, implicitly, the end of the Hrethling line, is, however, far from clear. Although Germanic legend may have become less popular in later Anglo-Saxon England, in the earlier period there appears to have been a fashion among English monks for adopting the names of continental heroes celebrated in *Beowulf* and other related tales.[97]

---

[92] Biggs, '*Beowulf* and some fictions of the Geatish succession', 74.

[93] R. P. Tripp, Jr., 'Fathers and Sons: Dynastic Decay in *Beowulf*', *In Geardagum* 16 (1995), 46–60, at 46.

[94] Morey, 'Fates of Men', p. 26. Morey counters Bruce Mitchell's argument that the presence of such violations of primogeniture in the poem suggests that 'direct succession from father to son was not automatic' (Mitchell, 'Literary Lapses', 13).

[95] Morey, 'Fates of Men', p. 34.

[96] M. D. C. Drout, 'Blood and Deeds: The Inheritance System in *Beowulf*', *SP* 104 (2007), 199–226, at 226. Other discussions of the theme of succession in the poem include J. M. Hill, '*Beowulf* and the Danish Succession'; J. M. Hill, *Narrative Pulse*, pp. 5–9, 43–64; T. D. Hill, 'Scyld Scefing and the *Stirps Regia*: Pagan Myth and Christian Kingship in *Beowulf*', in *Magister Regis: Studies in Honor of Robert Earl Kaske*, ed. A. Groos (New York, 1986), pp. 37–47; R. J. Schrader, 'Succession and Glory in *Beowulf*', *JEGP* 90 (1991), 491–504; and M. R. Kightley, 'The Brothers of *Beowulf*: Fraternal Tensions and the Reticent Style', *ELH* 83 (2016), 407–29. Stacy Klein notes the poem's 'obsessive interest' in succession (*Ruling Women*, p. 116).

[97] On the fashion for Germanic legendary names in early Anglo-Saxon England, as witnessed primarily by the Durham *Liber vitae*, see P. Wormald, '*Beowulf*: the Redating Reassessed', published as an appendix to 'Bede, *Beowulf* and the Conversion of the Anglo-Saxon Aristocracy', in his *The Times of Bede: Studies*

Moreover, as we shall see, throughout the Anglo-Saxon period the royal houses of Kent, Mercia and Wessex, among others, continued to claim descent from dynasties that feature in *Beowulf*.[98] The poem's cyclical structure implies that another royal house will eventually arise to govern the Geats after the fall of the Hrethlings, just as Scyld Scefing had previously rescued the Danes after a long period of lordlessness.[99]

The Dynastic Theme

As Guy Halsall has commented, aside from the widespread (though not universal) tradition of claiming descent from Woden, nothing can be said with any certainty about a distinctively 'Germanic' model of kingship, dynastic or otherwise.[100] The theory that dynastic kingship, in which royal succession was limited to those who could claim direct descent from an ancestral founder-figure, was a widely established custom among the Germanic tribes east of the Rhine prior to the collapse of the Western Empire rests almost entirely on the famous statement of the first-century Roman historian, Tacitus: *rex ex nobilitate, duces ex virtute sumunt*, 'their kings are taken for their nobility, their chiefs for their courage' (*Germania*, VII).[101] The distinction that Tacitus draws between the roles of the *rex* and *dux* has been explained in terms of the dual nature of primitive kingship, a feature observed in many cultures: the king's role is priestly, sacral and associated with ritual and judicial duties; the chief's role is to fight and gain plunder. However, it seems likely that there was a degree of permeability between these two roles, if indeed such an arrangement was ever in place among the early Germanic peoples. As Patrick Wormald comments, 'A *dux ex virtute* appointed in an emergency might thus acquire the permanence of a *rex* for himself and his family; a *rex* might indeed achieve the role of a *dux*.'[102] It has long been recognized, however, that Tacitus probably did not have any direct knowledge of the practices of the early Germanic peoples.[103] His statements about the nature of early Germanic kingship are, therefore, now largely discredited.

---

in *Early English Christian Society*, ed. S. Baxter (Malden, 2006), pp. 30–105, at 71–81, 98–100. For the argument that such names – and the legends associated with them – were relatively unproductive in the late Anglo-Saxon period, see L. Neidorf, 'Beowulf before *Beowulf*: Anglo-Saxon Anthroponymy and Heroic Legend', *RES* 64 (2013), 553–73; and Neidorf, 'Germanic Legend'.
[98] See pp. 140 n.101, 143–46, 237–46.
[99] See Chapter One, *passim*, and pp. 138, 231–35, 24.
[100] G. Halsall, *Barbarian Migrations and the Roman West, 376–568* (Cambridge, 2007), p. 494.
[101] See further Wallace-Hadrill, *Early Germanic Kingship*.
[102] Wormald, 'Kings and Kingship', p. 592.
[103] See, for example, A. Gudeman, 'The Sources of the Germania of

Introduction

The claims of Tacitus aside, there is little evidence of fully-developed hereditary monarchy – in other words, the dynastic principle – in the early medieval West prior to the Romanization and Christianization of the Germanic-speaking peoples.[104] During the third to sixth centuries, the gradual emergence of powerful, migratory war-bands disrupted earlier tribal groupings, as warriors gathered around powerful military leaders who could reward their loyalty with plunder.[105] The leaders of these multi-ethnic groups became epicentres around which formed new tribal identities or confederations.[106] Many Germanic tribes had no kings at all, and among those that did rulers might be elected solely for the length of a military campaign from a pool of aristocratic families.[107] According to Bede, this practice of temporary kingship persisted among the Old Saxons until as late as the eighth century.[108] Between the fourth and sixth centuries, the most successful of these Germanic rulers began to found dynasties of their own, often claiming descent from a god or an ancient line of rulers. As Ian Wood notes, the emergence of these new Germanic dynasties was facilitated by the 'social and territorial dislocation' of peoples following the breakdown of Roman rule.[109] Paradoxically, however, the main catalyst for the foundation of these dynasties was exposure to the ruler ideology of the Empire itself and its newly-adopted Christian faith.[110] From the fourth century, Christian notions of dynastic succession and royal morality increasingly came to shape ideas of rulership both within the Empire itself and in its surrounding regions. It is now recognized, for example,

---

Tacitus', *Transactions and Proceedings of the American Philological Association* 31 (1900), 93–111.

[104] Patrick Wormald cites evidence for the early respect of royal blood among the Heruli and the Goths in the writings of the fourth-century Roman historians Ammianus Marcellinus and Procopius ('Kings and Kingship', in *The New Cambridge Medieval History, Volume 1, c. 500–c. 700*, ed. P. Fouracre [Cambridge, 2005], pp. 571–604, at 593). See further J. M. Wallace-Hadrill, *Early Germanic Kingship in England and on the Continent: The Ford Lectures Delivered in the University of Oxford in Hilary Term 1970* (Oxford, 1971).

[105] L. Hedeager, trans. J. Hines, 'Kingdoms, Ethnicity and Material Culture: Denmark in a European Perspective', in *The Age of Sutton Hoo: The Seventh Century in North-Western Europe*, ed. M. Carver (Woodbridge, 1992), pp. 279–300, at 280–82.

[106] Wallace-Hadrill, *Early Germanic Kingship*, pp. 14–15; Wormald, 'Kings and Kingship', p. 592.

[107] I. N. Wood, 'Kings, Kingdoms and Consent', in *Early Medieval Kingship*, ed. P. H. Sawyer and I. N. Wood (Leeds, 1977), pp. 6–29, at 7. See further R. Abels, 'Royal Succession and the Growth of Political Stability in Ninth-Century Wessex', *The Haskins Society Journal: Studies in Medieval History* 12 (2002), 83–97.

[108] Bede, *HE*, v.10, refers to these temporary Saxon leaders as *satraps*.

[109] Wood, 'Kings, Kingdoms and Consent', pp. 7–9.

[110] As emphasized by Halsall, *Barbarian Migrations*, pp. 118–23. For a discussion of *Beowulf* and biblical kingship, and the growth of the dynastic principle in the medieval West, see below, Chapter Four.

that the elaborate royal genealogies created in this period for the Gothic, Frankish and Anglo-Saxon royal houses are clerical fictions, inspired by biblical and classical models, rather than genuine records of pre-Christian dynastic roots.[111] This hybrid form of kingship, with its blend of Germanic, Judeo-Christian and Roman influences, came to pertain in early Anglo-Saxon England and found its expression in *Beowulf*.[112]

The increasingly dynastic or familial nature of post-Roman barbarian kingship, the product of contacts between Germanic-speaking peoples and imperial and Christian models of rule, is itself reflected in the most common Old English term for a king, *cyn-ing*, literally 'descendant/son of the people/kin', from Proto Germanic **kuningaz*.[113] The compound *cyne-cynn*, 'royal family, royal lineage, royal race' (*DOE*), appears occasionally in Alfredian texts, and then with increasing frequency in late manuscripts of the *Anglo-Saxon Chronicle* and the writings of Ælfric, who uses it to refer to the royal line of David and Christ.[114] In all but one instance, *cyne-cynn* is restricted to prose, and in the single exception, from the Old English *Metres of Boethius* (Met. 26.38), the term is itself carried over from the Old English prose translation of the *Consolation of Philosophy*. The related compound *cyning-cyn*, 'royal family', is restricted to manuscripts of the Old English *Bede*, usually rendering the Latin terms *regio genere/originem*, while *eald-hlāford-cyn*, 'of noble family', appears just once in the prefatory section of the Old English *Boethius*, in a passage which has no basis in the Latin.[115] Nevertheless, it is clear that Anglo-Saxon kingship was dynastic from an early date in the sense that royal power was, at least in theory, limited to

---

[111] Sisam, 'Anglo-Saxon Royal Genealogies'.

[112] For a recent overview of the development of early Anglo-Saxon kingship, see K. McCann, *Anglo-Saxon Kingship and Political Power: Rex gratia dei* (Cardiff, 2018), pp. 17–45.

[113] *DOE*, s. v. *cyning*: 'king, monarch, male sovereign'. See further H. M. Chadwick, *The Origin of the English Nation* (Cambridge, 1907), pp. 315–16; W. A. Chaney, *The cult of kingship in Anglo-Saxon England: The transition from paganism to Christianity* (Manchester, 1970; repr. 1999), p. 21; D. H. Green, *Language and history in the early Germanic world* (Cambridge, 1998), pp. 121–40, esp. 130–34.

[114] *DOE* cites examples of *cyne-cynn* in Old English *Orosius*, Old English *Bede* and *Metres of Boethius*. This term is frequently used by Ælfric, but makes its earliest appearance in the probably ninth-century Old English prose Life of Guthlac in reference to the ancestry of King Æthelbald: *wæs sum foremæara man æþelan kynekynnes on Myrcna rice* (cf. Felix, *Vita Guthlaci* 40, 124: *de inclita Merciorum prole*). *DOE Corpus* lists one further attestation in Blickling Homily II (Quinquagesima Sunday): *and hwæþere hie wæron of Dauides cynnes strynde, þæs riht-cyne-cynnes*, 'and whether they were descended from David's kin, the true royal line' (*The Blickling Homilies of the Tenth Century*, EETS 73, ed. and trans. R. Morris [London, 1880], pp. 22–23). See *A Thesaurus of Old English*, ed. J. Roberts and C. Kay, with L. Grundy, 2 vols (London, 1995), I, p. 543: '12.01.01.06.07.01 *A royal race*: cynecynn. *A rightful royal line*: ealhdhlāfordcynn. *Royally born*: cyneboren.'

[115] *DOE*, s. v. *cyning-cyn*.

those *æþel-ingas*, literally 'sons of nobles',[116] who could claim *riht-fæder-en-cynn*, 'legitimate *or* direct paternal descent',[117] from another member of the ruling family. As this last term implies, the paternal line was considered the stronger: hence, as a rule, Anglo-Saxon genealogies only provide lists of royal fathers.[118] Indeed, the term *æþel-ing* is etymologically related to *cyn-ing* in that both convey the sense of royalty in terms of origins: Old English *æþele*, 'noble', is related to Old English *ēðel*, 'homeland', so an *æþel-ing* is someone who can trace their origins to the land, just as a *cyn-ing* is a 'son of the people'.[119]

The *Beowulf*-poet's fascination with the ancestry of rulers – in other words, their dynastic credentials – is indicated by his frequent and prominent use of the rare compound *þeod-cyningas*, as well as the related hapax *lēod-cyning* used to refer to Beow son of Scyld (54a). Both terms are usually translated as 'kings of the nation' or 'people-kings' but may also have originally meant something like 'dynastic kings', or 'kings of the royal kin', that is, kings whose right to rule was connected with their ancestry.[120] Moreover, in the poem, royal succession is determined by paternal

---

[116] *DOE*, s. v. *æþeling* A.1: 'lord; prince, ruler'. See D. N. Dumville, 'The ætheling: a study in Anglo-Saxon constitutional history', *ASE* 8 (1979), 1–34.

[117] This term appears in the entry for 755 (= 757) in the *Anglo-Saxon Chronicle* (*ASC*), MS A in the genealogy of the West Saxon king Cynewulf and his rival, Cyneheard. For the meaning of this term, see F. Leneghan, 'Royal Wisdom and the Alfredian Context of *Cynewulf and Cyneheard*', *ASE* 39 (2009), 71–104, at 100–03.

[118] A notable exception is Asser's genealogy for King Alfred, which includes both paternal and maternal lines, an echo of the paternal and maternal genealogies of Christ in the opening of the Gospels of Matthew and Luke respectively (Mat. 1.1–17, Luke 3.23–38).

[119] *DOE*, s. v. *æþele*: 'noble, famous, glorious, holy, splendid, magnificent'; cf. 1.c: specifically: noble, well-born; *æþele cynn / (ge)byrd* 'noble lineage'; *æþele on gebyrdum* 'well-born'; *(of) æþel(r)e gebyrde / of æþelum cynrene / (of) æþel(r) e strynde / æþeles gestreones* 'of noble descent'; *DOE*, s. v. *ēþel* 1: 'one's own country, one's true home; often in collocation with *eard* 'dwelling-place', and contrasted with 'exile' variously expressed. 1.a. home, homeland, land of one's birth, (hereditary) land, (ancestral) domain.'

[120] K4, s. v. *þēod-cyning*: '*King of a people, king (over wide dominions)*' (p. 445). Cf. B-T, s. v. *þeód-cyning*: 'I. the king of a whole nation, a monarch, an independent sovereign. II. the king of all nations, the monarch of the world, the Deity.' The same compound appears twice in *Genesis A*, in reference to Pharoah (1869) and the four kings who set out to attack Sodom and Gomorrah (1965; cf. Gen. 14.1: *Thadal, rex gentium*, 'Tidal, king of nations'). Elsewhere in verse this compound is used to refer to earthly kings in a broad sense (*Judgement Day II*, 162; *Riddle 67*, 1; *Death of Edward*, 34) and to kings more generally. In *Beowulf* it is used to refer to Hrothgar (2144), Ongentheow (2970) and Beowulf (2157, 2694, 3007, and possibly in 3084a, where *þeod-cyning* is usually supplied in lines to compensate for the lack of an alliterating item). In prose, *þeod-cyning* occurs only in the Nowell Codex text *Alexander's Letter* (ch. 11), where it is used to expand Latin *gentes* (ed. Orchard, *Pride and Prodigies*, p. 230). Orchard notes the commonality of this term – and other heroic compounds – to *Beowulf* and the *Letter* (*Pride and*

ancestry, hence the frequent references to fathers in a dynastic context – rather than mothers, who in several cases remain unnamed – as well as Heremod's failure to inherit *fæder-æþelu*, 'paternal rank' (911b), and, ironically, the importance attached to the mythical narrative of Cain's slaying of his own brother and *fæderen-mæg*, 'paternal kinsman', Abel (1263a).

This book will argue that the distinctly dynastic model of kingship presented in *Beowulf* reflects the merging of Germanic warrior kingship with Christian models of dynastic rule that pertained in early Anglo-Saxon England.[121] The great importance attached to lineage as a qualifying factor for royal succession in the poem is indicated by the frequency of the familial suffix *-ing*, 'descendant' and the noun *eafora/eafera*, 'son, successor, heir', in the text,[122] as well as the recurrence of familial names such as *Scyld-ing*, *Scylf-ing* and *Hreþl-ing*.[123] Indeed, so close is the bond in the poem between a ruling dynasty and its subjects that dynastic titles are sometimes used to refer to a people as much as the royal house itself.[124] Hence, for example, in the opening lines of the poem we learn that Scyld Scefing, a *gōd cyning*,

---

Prodigies, p. 136, n. 122) and suggests that the author of the *Letter* made use of *Beowulf* (ibid., pp. 23–35).

[121] For the influence of biblical kingship on *Beowulf*, see Chapter Four.

[122] K4 glosses *eafora/eafera* as 'offspring, son, descendant' (p. 366). B-T, s. v. *eafora*: 'An offspring, successor, heir, son', glossing the Latin terms 'prōles, successor, filius' (p. 266). *DOE*, s. v. *eafora*, records 'ca. 90 occ. (mainly in poetry)' and gives the primary meaning as 'offspring, child; descendant', with the additional primary senses '1.a. offspring in the first degree, in relation to either or both of the parents; child. 1.a.i. without specific reference to sex.' However, *DOE* cites *Beo* 375b–76a (*is his eafora nū/ heard hēr cumen*) as an example of the sense '1.a.ii. specifically: son', and *Beo* 1547a (*āngan eaferan*) as an example of '1.a.ii.a. [...] only son'. A search of the *DOE* Corpus reveals that the vast majority of the occurrences of *eafora* are in *Genesis A* and *B* (x43) and *Beowulf* (x18). Given the preoccupation of these texts with the theme of patriarchal/royal succession, it is possible that this term may also have had the narrower sense of 'successor, heir'. For sense '1.b. in plural [i.e. *eaforum*]: offspring in near or distant degree; descendants, heirs', *DOE* cites *Andreas*, Prose Psalms and Ælfric; for '1.b.i. specifically of mortals as the (literal and spiritual) descendants of Adam and Eve', examples are given from *Genesis B*, *Guthlac B* and *Phoenix*; and for '1.b.ii. *eaforan manna* "children of men", either referring to the descendants of Seth (if in variation with *bearn Godes*) or to the descendants of Cain (if in variation with *wīf*)', a single example is given from *Genesis A*. The related noun *yrfe-weard*, '(Guardian of an inheritance), heir' (K4, p. 463) appears twice in *Beowulf*, at lines 2453a, where the *gomelum ceorle* cares not for his other heirs after the hanging of his son, and at line 2731a, where the dying King Beowulf laments his own lack of an heir. See below, Chapter One, pp. 88–90 and 100–02, for discussion of these passages. On the prevalence of patronymics in the poem, see *CCB*, pp. 170–71.

[123] *Hreþling-as* (1923, 2925, 2960), *Scylding-as* (30, 53, 58, 148, 170, 229, 274, 291, 351, 371, 428, 456, 500, 597, 663, 778, 913, 1019, 1069, 1108, 1154, 1166, 1168, 1183, 1321, 1418, 1563, 1601, 1653, 1675, 1710, 1792, 1871, 2004, 2026, 2052, 2101, 2105, 2159), *Scylfing-as* (63, 2205, 2381, 2487, 2603, 2927, 2968, 3005). Cf. *Wylfing-as* (461, 471), *Mere-wioing* (2921).

[124] See *CCB*, pp. 171–72.

'good king' (11b), of obscure ancestry, rescued the Danes from a period of lordlessness (3–52) by founding a royal line of *Scyld-ingas*, 'descendants of Scyld', through ensuring the succession of his son, *Bēow Scyldinga* (53b). This pattern of father-to-son succession is repeated as Beow passes the throne to Healfdene, who in turn produces three sons and a daughter, the last of whom will marry into another powerful dynasty, the Scylfings, rulers of the Swedes (53–63).[125] These Scylfings will play a prominent role in the final third of the poem, as long-standing adversaries of Beowulf's own dynasty, the Hrethlings, kings of the Geats. The flourishing of the house of Scyld continues until the latter years of King Hrothgar's reign, when the external threat of the Heathobards and the possibility of an internal power-struggle between Healfdene's grandsons combine to place the future of the Danish royal house in jeopardy (82b–188).

The dynastic theme sounded in the opening section remains a constant motif throughout the narrative via a series of major and minor variations, all of which can be said to stand in apposition to the Scyld-prologue.[126] The final movement of the poem, during which the hero dies in combat with a great dragon, is dominated by images of dynastic decline as two royal houses, the Scylfings and the Hrethlings, are decimated by a series of disasters. King Beowulf's death marks the end of the Hrethlings and the final elaboration of the dynastic theme.[127] As the table below demonstrates, the outlying dynastic drama of the rise of the Scyldings and fall of the Hrethlings forms a chiastic structure, within which Beowulf's own protracted accession serves as the 'kernel':

A: Scyld founds a dynasty, rescuing the Danes from lordlessness (3–25)
  B: The funeral of King Scyld (26–52)
    C: The Scylding dynasty flourishes and the Danes prosper (53–67a)
      D: The Scyldings face a crisis over the succession (83b–5, 1008b–19)
        E: Hrothgar offers Beowulf the Danish throne (946b–49a, 1175–80a)
          F: Beowulf rejects Hrothgar's offer of the throne (2155–62)

            G: Beowulf becomes king of the Geats (2200–10a)

          F/E: Beowulf rejects Hygd's offer of the Geatish throne (2354b–79a)
      D/C: The Hrethlings face crises (2379–2409, 2910–3027)
  B: The funeral of King Beowulf (3137–82)
A: The Geats are lordless and vulnerable to attack (2999–3027, 3148b–55).[128]

---

[125] See pp. 47–49, 83, 180.
[126] See below, Chapter One, pp. 38–46. On the fundamental importance of the principle of contrast and apposition at all levels of Old English poetry (including metre, language and theme), see Robinson, *Appositive Style*.
[127] Cf. Bonjour, *Digressions*, p. 9: 'We may say that if the rise of the Scyldings is the prologue to the epic, its counterpart, the fall of the Geats (announced by Beowulf's death) is in a way an epilogue.'
[128] See below, Chapter Three, for discussion of how the monster fights and other

Evidently the structure is somewhat imbalanced, with considerably more space being devoted to the gradual rise of Beowulf from *æþeling* to *cyning* than to his reign and death. Indeed, as Richard North has recently suggested, 'The poet's true theme is Beowulf's rise to kingship.'[129] This book will argue that the hero's own rise to the throne is part of a wider dynastic drama concerning the fates of three great royal houses.

The Argument and Structure of this Book

Instead of imposing a hypothetical literary and cultural context onto the poem, the first three chapters of this book concentrate on the internal evidence of the text of *Beowulf* itself, while Chapter Four and the Conclusion broaden the focus to consider a range of potential theological and literary contexts that arise from this close reading.[130] Chapter One offers a new explanation of the poem's unusual structure in terms of the life-cycle of an archetypal dynasty. In a series of close readings of key passages, including the Scyld-prologue, the Finnsburg Episode, allusions to the future of Healfdene's grandsons, the story of Offa's bride, and Beowulf's long speech at Hronesnæss before facing the dragon, this chapter argues that the poet explores different stages in the dynastic life-cycle, sequentially charting its progression from birth to youth and maturity, through to old age and death.

Chapter Two explores how the poet adapted various royal traditions, fusing disparate moments in the histories of three great royal houses of the north, and introducing a number of new, original elements to bring this dynastic drama alive in the imaginations of his audience. Central to this chapter is the argument that the poet shaped his narrative around the popular legend of King Hygelac's untimely fall in Frisia, from which he elaborated the figure of Beowulf, son of Ecgtheow, transforming a figure previously famous only for his swimming prowess into a great monster-slayer and the last of the Hrethlings. This chapter further argues that the poet balanced this account of dynastic decline by fashioning a mythical account of the foundation of the royal house of the Scyldings,

---

narrative elements are integrated into this structure.

[129] R. North, 'Gold and the Heathen Polity in *Beowulf*', in *Gold in der Heldensage: Tagungsband*, ed. W. Heizmann, V. Millett and H. Sahm (Berlin, 2018), pp. 72–114, at 111.

[130] For studies which begin by situating the poem within a specific literary or cultural context, see Girvan, *Seventh Century*; W. F. Bolton, *Alcuin and* Beowulf: *An Eighth-Century View* (New Jersey, 1986); W. G. Busse and R. Holtei, '*Beowulf* and the Tenth Century', *Bulletin of the John Rylands Library* 63 (1981), 285–329; and, most recently, Damico's *Beowulf and the Grendelkin*, which reads the Danish part of the poem within an eleventh-century Anglo-Danish context.

Introduction

which he opportunistically inserted into an interregnum between the legendary Scylding kings Heremod and Healfdene.

Chapter Three focuses on how the poet dramatized these episodes in dynastic history through the introduction of the monsters. Grendel is read as an illegitimate usurper who attempts to seize power during a moment of uncertainty over the Scylding succession; Grendel's mother is then considered alongside the poem's prominent royal women and the ongoing discourse concerning the consequences of feud and revenge, factors which threaten the survival of dynasties. This chapter is rounded off with a discussion of the relationship between the hero's last fight with the dragon and surrounding accounts of dynastic wars between the Scylfings and Hrethlings. It is argued that, through the artful interlacing of these seemingly disconnected narrative threads, the poet weaves together a series of personal, dynastic and national tragedies. The dynastic elements are therefore to be viewed as fundamentally *dramatic*, in the sense that they inform and shape the action of the hero's final battle.

The debt of *Beowulf* to the traditions of the Old Testament, especially the Book of Genesis, is widely recognized, and a number of studies have drawn attention to the way the poet utilizes biblical paradigms to invest his narrative with mythical significance.[131] Eleazar Meletinsky distinguishes mythological thought from scientific thought, and emphasizes the function of myth in explaining origins through narrative:

> The creation of models is the specific function of myth [...] the fundamental characteristic of myth consists in linking the essence of events and objects to their origins. *In myth, to explain the structure of something means narrating the manner in which it was formed.*[132] (Emphasis added).

---

[131] See, for example, M. Godden, 'Biblical Literature: the Old Testament', in Godden and Lapidge (2013), pp. 214–33, at 223–24; Anlezark, *Water and Fire*, pp. 291–374; and T. Major, *Undoing Babel: The Tower of Babel in Anglo-Saxon Literature* (Toronto, 2018), pp. 239–44.

[132] E. M. Meletinsky, *The Poetics of Myth*, trans. G. Lanoue and A. Sadetsky (New York, 2000), pp. 157–59. Cf. *OED*, s. v. *myth* 1.a. 'A traditional story, typically involving supernatural beings or forces, which embodies and provides an explanation, aetiology, or justification for something such as the early history of a society, a religious belief or ritual, or a natural phenomenon.' On the cyclical nature of 'mythical time', see C. Lévi-Strauss, 'The Structural Study of Myth', *Journal of American Folklore* 68 (1955), 428–44. On the distinction between myth, legend and folktale, see W. Bascom, 'The forms of folklore: prose narratives', *The Journal of American Folklore* 78 (1965), 3–20, at 4: '[Myths are] prose narratives which, in the society in which they are told, are considered to be truthful accounts of what happened in the remote past [...]. Myths are the embodiment of dogma; they are usually sacred, and they are often associated with theology and ritual [...]. [Legends] are prose narratives which, like myths, are regarded as true by the narrator and his audience, but they are set in a period less remote, when the world was much like it is today. Concerned with such things as wars, chiefs and kings, heroic deeds, and dynastic successions, legends are like our

Scholars have identified a large number of mythical patterns underlying the structure of *Beowulf*, ranging from the struggle between chaos and order or nature and civilization to the changing of the seasons.[133] Although such approaches are typically associated with the nineteenth-century school of folklore studies, two recent examples are Nicholas Howe's *Migration and Mythmaking in Anglo-Saxon England* (1989) and Daniel Anlezark's *Water and Fire: The Myth of the Flood in Anglo-Saxon England* (2006). Howe argues that Anglo-Saxon authors drew imaginatively on the biblical Exodus as a means of understanding their own migration from the 'ancestral homeland' of Germania to the island of Britain. Emphasizing the poem's role as a conduit of 'the memory of cultural continuity between continent and island', Howe proposes that *Beowulf* invites its audience to make an 'imaginative journey back to the continental homeland'.[134] Anlezark, on the other hand, argues that the biblical paradigm of the two floods of water and fire underpins the poem's structure: Beowulf's fights against the Grendelkin echo the destruction of the giants in Noah's watery Flood; his death in the dragon's cave evokes the conflagration that will come on Judgement Day.[135] These two studies serve as timely reminders of the profound influence of the mythical narratives of the Old Testament on *Beowulf*.

Building on these studies, Chapter Four explores parallels between the 'succession narrative' of the Books of Kings and *Beowulf*, arguing that the poet utilized this biblical paradigm in order to transform the legends of the Scyldings, Scylfings and Hrethlings into a myth concerning the origins of dynastic kingship. The scriptural text charts the development of earthly kingship from a charismatic office based on valour to a dynastic institution contingent on wisdom, through to its demise. This chapter proposes that the poet saw the noble, pre-Christian rulers of the Danes, Swedes and Geats as *figurae* of the flawed but admirable kings of the Old Testament. Situating *Beowulf* within the broader narrative of the development of dynastic kingship in early medieval Europe, this chapter also suggests ways in which the poem may have served as a mirror to the political realities of early Anglo-Saxon England.

The Conclusion briefly considers how the dynastic drama of *Beowulf* might have been read in Anglo-Saxon England during three key stages

---

"history" in their content, if not in their science. The third category, folktales, consists of entertaining stories not told as truths, nor in the social or ritual contexts that suppose they are.' On the complex melding of myth, legend and folktale in the poem, see Chapter Two.

[133] For an overview, see Niles, 'Myth and History', pp. 218–24.
[134] N. Howe, *Migration and Mythmaking in Anglo-Saxon England* (New Haven, 1989), pp. 174, 176.
[135] D. Anlezark, *Water and Fire: The Myth of the Flood in Anglo-Saxon England* (Manchester, 2006), pp. 291–374.

Introduction

of the poem's transmission history. First, it explores the possibility that the poem was composed during the age of Bede, a time when the Church sought to reform English kingship, by bringing it into line with Christian teaching. Second, it discusses the reception of the poem during the age of King Alfred (r. 871–99), during which the Anglo-Saxons began to develop a new form of Christological kingship. Finally, it considers the poem's copying into the Nowell Codex during the age of Æthelred II (978–1013, 1014–16) and Cnut (1016–34), a time of great dynastic upheaval and renewed Scandinavian contact.

Across these four chapters, this book offers a holistic reading of *Beowulf* in which the hero's fights against the monsters are viewed as integral parts of a wider dynastic drama. Many aspects of the poem that have often puzzled critics, notably the unusual structure and the inclusion of various seemingly otiose digressions and episodes, can be accounted for by the poet's preoccupation with the dynastic theme. While we can never fully recover the royal legends known to the original audience, by placing the dynastic material at the centre of the discussion we can gain a fuller sense of the poet's artistry and a clearer picture of the work's significance in Anglo-Saxon England.

1

The Dynastic Life-Cycle and the Structure of the Poem

Critics have long expressed frustration with the structure of *Beowulf*. In the assessment of Kenneth Sisam, 'the poem has enough high qualities without the claim to structural elegance'.[1] Jan de Vries praised the poet's 'noble dignity' of style, but added:

> On the other hand, one wonders at the strange, weak structure. What truly epic poet would have hit on the idea of making a hero tell a story afresh from the beginning that he has just told circumstantially, by making him report on his adventures to the king? The fight with Grendel and that with the dragon do not form a logical whole; they are two independent deeds of Beowulf's, the former from his youth, the latter from his old age.[2]

Such negative opinions of the structure are broadly representative of nineteenth and early-twentieth-century scholarship.[3] Earlier commentators such as Levin Schücking had taken the view that the present text represents what were originally two separate works, with 'Beowulf's Return' serving as a bridge.[4] However, for the most part scholars now accept that the poem is a unified work of art, albeit distinctly uneven in its parts.[5]

---

[1] See Sisam, *Structure*, p. 50.
[2] J. de Vries, *Heroic Song and Heroic Legend* (London, 1963), p. 59.
[3] See, for example, H. M. Chadwick, *The Heroic Age* (Cambridge, 1912), p. 116; R. W. Chambers, '*Beowulf* and the "Heroic Age" in England', in his *Man's Unconquerable Mind: Studies of English Writers, from Bede to A. E. Housman and W. P. Ker* (London and Toronto, 1939), pp. 53–59; K3, pp. liv–lv; B. S. Phillpotts, 'Wyrd and Providence in Anglo-Saxon Thought', *Essays and Studies* 13 (1928), 7–28, reprinted in Fulk (1991), pp. 1–13, at 8–10. For the views of W. P. Ker, and Tolkien's response, see pp. 5, 10.
[4] L. L. Schücking, *Beowulfs Rückkehr: Eine kritische Studie*, Studien zur englischen Philologie 21 (Halle, 1905), summarized in Shippey and Haarder, pp. 506–11. See also K3, pp. cvi–cvii, li–lii, and 121. For recent studies which treat the text as in some way two separate works, see Kiernan, *Beowulf Manuscript*; and Damico, *Beowulf and the Grendelkin*. In Kiernan's view, Scribe B is to be equated with 'the *Beowulf*-poet'.
[5] R. E. Bjork, 'Speech as Gift in *Beowulf*', *Speculum* 69 (1994), 993–1022, has highlighted differing patterns of speech in the Danish and Geatish sections as well as the absence of clear biblical allusions in the latter. See further J. M. Hill, *Narrative Pulse*, pp. 80–83; S. Newton, *The Origins of* Beowulf *and the Pre-Viking Kingdom of East Anglia* (Cambridge, 1993), p. 55; and D. Cronan, 'Narrative

This view can largely be traced back to Tolkien, who famously identified the bipartite structure with the sequence of the hero's own youth and age:

> It is essentially a balance, an opposition of ends and beginnings. In its simplest terms it is a contrasted description of two moments in a great life, rising and setting; an elaboration of the ancient and intensely moving contrast between youth and age, first achievement and final death.[6]

Tolkien's elegant assessment of the structure remains a pivotal moment in *Beowulf*-studies, informing almost all subsequent readings of the poem.[7] There are, nevertheless, some significant problems with Tolkien's theory.[8] Perhaps the most significant objection is that, despite his stated intention to restore the monsters to the centre of the poem, Tolkien has remarkably little to say about Grendel's mother. In 1955, H. L. Rogers advanced the theory of a tripartite structure revolving around the hero's three great fights, with Grendel's mother assuming the central role.[9] Rogers's theory

---

Disjunctions in *Beowulf*, *ES* 99 (2018), 459–78. In Chapter Three, I propose that the apocryphal tradition of the Fall of the Angels lies behind *Beowulf* 168–69 (pp. 162–76), while Chapter Four identifies a series of parallels between the Beowulfian rulers and the biblical kings, Saul, David and Solomon. Others have argued that the greater lengths to which the poet goes to explain the traditions of the Scylfings and Hrethlings might indicate that these particular royal legends were less well-known to the audience than those concerning the Scyldings: see Niles, *Beowulf*, pp. 184–85; E. B. Irving Jr., 'Christian and Pagan Elements', in Bjork and Niles (1997), pp. 175–92, at 186–87; J. W. Earl, 'The Swedish Wars in *Beowulf*', *JEGP* 114 (2015), 32–60; *CCB*, pp. 142–49. However, as we shall see in this and the next chapter, the densely allusive narration of the Geatish-Swedish wars suggests that, if anything, these stories were even better known than those of the Scyldings.

6   Tolkien, 'Monsters', p. 81. Tolkien divides the text into 'two opposed sections, different in matter, manner, and length: A from 1 to 2199 (including an exordium of 52 lines); B from 2200 to 3182 (the end)' ('Monsters', p. 81). See also Tolkien, 'Commentary', pp. 312–13. See further Chambers, *Introduction*, pp. 117–20; T. M. Gang, 'Approaches to *Beowulf*', *RES* 33 (1952), 1–12. Anlezark argues for a bipartite structure based on the underlying myth of the two biblical floods of water and fire (*Water and Fire*, pp. 291–367).

7   See, for example, K4, p. lxx: 'It is thus the person of the hero that holds the two parts together, and the change of character encountered in him (and the turn toward a more somber narrative mood) after the passage of so many years (2327–32) serves to reinforce the impression of the poem's structure as contrastive.'

8   For a measured critique of this and other aspects of Tolkien's lecture, see Niles, *Old English Literature*, pp. 23–29.

9   See H. L. Rogers, 'Beowulf's Three Great Fights', *RES* 6 (1955), 339–55, repr. in Nicholson (1963), pp. 233–56; Sisam, *Structure*, pp. 4–5; Niles, *Beowulf*, pp. 249–53; J. Chance, 'The Structural Unity of *Beowulf*: the Problem of Grendel's Mother', in *New Readings on Women in Old English Literature*, ed. H. Damico and A. H. Olsen (Bloomington, IN, 1990), pp. 248–61. In an influential application of oral-formulaic theory to the text, Francis P. Magoun, Jr. divided the poem into three parts: A (1–2009a: Beowulf's exploits in Denmark), A' (2009b–2176:

was accepted by Sisam, who a decade later commented that the structure is suggestive of 'a serial in three instalments'.[10] More recently, Gale Owen-Crocker has argued for a four-part structure revolving around funeral set-pieces.[11]

A further difficulty with Tolkien's theory lies with its emphasis on the structural and thematic importance of the hero's own life-cycle. As Sisam notes, Beowulf's ability to fight monsters is in fact relatively unaffected by his age.[12] Moreover, John Burrow has pointed out that the young Beowulf is shown to possess the qualities of the *iuvenis senex*, while in old age he is presented as a *senex fortis* who retains the strength and bravery of the young warrior.[13] Hence, for example, Hrothgar announces to the young Beowulf in Heorot: *ne hȳrde ic snotlicor / on swā geongum feore guman þingian*, 'I have never heard a wiser speech from such a young man' (1842b–43), just as the old Beowulf reflects that he has no reason to doubt his *eafoð ond ellen*, 'strength and valour' (2349a). As the narrator comments, up to this point Beowulf had never tasted defeat in battle:

Swā hē nīða gehwane genesen hæfde,
slīðra geslyhta, sunu Ecgðiowes,
ellen-weorca [...].
(2397–99a).

Beowulf's return) and B (2177–3182: Beowulf's death) ('*Béowulf A*': a Folk-Variant', *ARV* 14 [1958], 95–101; and '*Béowulf B*: A Folk-Poem on Beowulf's Death', *Early English and Norse Studies Presented to Hugh Smith in Honour of His Sixtieth Birthday*, ed. A. Brown and P. Foote [London, 1963], pp. 127–40). North, 'Heathen Polity', pp. 95–96 and 111, cautions against breaking the poem in two at line 2200 (at the point of Beowulf's accession), emphasizing 'narrative flow'. In support of Tolkien's approach to the structure, see A. Bonjour, 'Monsters Crouching and Critics Rampant: or the *Beowulf* Dragon Debated', *PMLA* 68 (1953), 304–12, repr. in his *Twelve* Beowulf *Papers* (Neuchâtel, 1962), pp. 97–113; and Brodeur, *Art*, pp. 71–87.

[10] Sisam, *Structure*, p. 4.
[11] Owen-Crocker, *Four Funerals*, acknowledges the 'triple structure' revolving around the monster-fights (p. 134), but argues for the structural importance of the royal funerals of Scyld (26–52), the kin of Hildeburh (1107–24) and Beowulf (3137–82) as well as a fourth 'funeral' embedded in the 'Lay of the Last Survivor' (2247–66) (p. 1). E. V. K. Dobbie, ed. Beowulf *and* Judith, ASPR IV (New York, 1954), p. xxxiii, also breaks the poem down into four sections, but here the divisions correspond to thematic and structural breaks, with prominence given to the various stages of the hero's career: 1–85 (introduction), 86–1887 (Beowulf's fights with Grendel and Grendel's mother), 1888–2199 (Beowulf's return to Geatland) and 2200–3182 (Beowulf's kingship and death).
[12] Sisam, *Structure*, p. 24.
[13] J. A. Burrow, *The Ages of Man: A Study in Mediaeval Writing and Thought* (Oxford, 1986), pp. 123–34. See also L. Abraham, 'The Decorum of *Beowulf*', *PQ* 72 (1993), 267–87.

[So the son of Ecgtheow had survived every struggle, hostile encounters, through glorious deeds.]

Evidently, the poem is not primarily concerned with the effects of ageing on the character of Beowulf, nor is the contrast between the hero's youth and age the main factor determining the poem's structure.[14]

One alternative approach to the structure is to concentrate on the intersection between the hero's career and larger historical processes.[15] Of particular relevance to this discussion is Robert Hanning's description of the poem as a form of 'biographically centred' heroic history, in which the story of the hero's life is presented 'in a much more complex context of *social organisms* moving in time toward their own destiny, over which the hero does not exercise complete control' (emphasis added).[16] The term 'social organism' was coined by the nineteenth-century English philosopher Herbert Spencer to refer to a social group or culture that has its own organic quality, for example its own life-cycle and system of reproduction.[17] Throughout the poem, the principal social organism that the hero interacts with is that of the royal dynasty. While accepting that the structure is indeed contrastive, as Tolkien had argued, this chapter will demonstrate that the central contrast is not between the youth and age of the hero but between the various stages in the life-cycle of an archetypal dynasty.

Narratives concerning the fortunes of individual peoples and their ruling dynasties enjoyed great popularity in the early middle ages. The *historiae* of Jordanes, Gregory of Tours, Paul the Deacon and Bede each relate the origin and conversion of an individual 'barbarian' *gens*.[18] Similarly,

---

[14] In his recent study of the Nowell Codex, however, Simon Thomson notices that a hand resembling Scribe A has marked up a passage on the youth and age of rulers in the text of *Alexander's Letter* (*Communal Creativity*, p. 343), perhaps indicating his interest in the youth-age theme.

[15] See L. Tennenhouse, '*Beowulf* and the Sense of History', *Bucknell Review* 19 (1971), 137–46; A. Hardy, 'Historical Perspective and the *Beowulf* Poet', *Neophilologus* 63 (1979), 431–49; R. Frank, 'The *Beowulf* Poet's Sense of History', in *The Wisdom of Poetry: Essays in Early English Literature in Honour of Morton W. Bloomfield*, ed. L. D. Benson and S. Wenzel (Kalamazoo, MI, 1982), pp. 53–65; Scheil, '*Beowulf* and the Emergent Occasion'; Scheil, 'Historiographic Dimensions'. For a recent argument that the poem accurately reflects the social conditions of sixth-century Scandinavia, notably in its portrayal of a number of small neighbouring royal dynasties vying for power, see T. A. Shippey, 'Names in *Beowulf* and Anglo-Saxon England', in Neidorf (2014), pp. 58–78, at 74–78. For comparison with the political realities of Northumbria and Mercia in the late-seventh and early-eighth centuries, see Conclusion, pp. 237–40.

[16] R. W. Hanning, '*Beowulf* as Heroic History', *Medievalia et Humanistica* 5 (1974), 77–102, at 84.

[17] For the use of this term in modern sociology, see W. M. Simon, 'Herbert Spencer and the "Social Organism"', *Journal of the History of Ideas* 21 (1960), 294–99.

[18] See, for example, W. Goffart, *The Narrators of Barbarian History (A.D. 550–800):*

a range of Scandinavian sources provide accounts of the fortunes of an individual dynasty, often tracing its origins back to a Norse god. Among these we can number dynastic sagas of a historical nature (*forneskjusögur*) which were mainly written down in Iceland and Norway in the twelfth to fourteenth centuries, such as *Skjöldunga saga* and *Ynglinga saga*,[19] and the later sagas of ancient times which incorporate more legendary and fantastical elements (*fornaldarsögur*), notably the fourteenth-century *Hrólfs saga*.[20] *Beowulf*, however, stands apart from both the Latin *historia* genre and the various forms of Scandinavian dynastic legends in that, instead of relating the fortunes of one particular dynasty or people, it draws together legends of three separate royal houses, the Scyldings, Scylfings and Hrethlings, to create a narrative charting the life-cycle of a single archetypal dynasty.[21]

Although both cyclical and linear conceptions of time operate alongside each other in the Old Testament, it is the cyclical model that prevails, at least in the historical books.[22] In Christian thought, the transition from cyclical or mythic time to teleological or linear time, moving towards the Second Coming, is brought about through the birth of Christ: *at ubi venit plenitudo temporis misit Deus Filium suum factum ex muliere factum sub lege*, 'But when the fulness of the time was come, God sent his Son, made of a woman, made under the law' (Gal. 4.4). As the narrator of *Beowulf* repeatedly reminds his Christian audience, the characters of his poem, living *in gēar-dagum*, 'in ancient times' (1b), effectively lived *before* Christ: *metod hīe ne cūþon*, 'they did not know the Measurer' (180b).[23] As Nicholas Howe has shown, the Anglo-Saxons viewed their conversion as

---

Jordanes, Gregory of Tours, Bede, and Paul the Deacon (Princeton, 1988; repr. Notre Dame, 2005).

[19] See Ármann Jakobson, 'Royal Biography', in *A Companion to Old Norse-Icelandic Literature and Culture*, ed. R. McTurk (Oxford, 2005), pp. 388–402; and M. Clunies Ross, *The Cambridge Introduction to Old Norse-Icelandic Saga* (Cambridge, 2010), pp. 84–89. On the distinction between *forneskjusaga* and *fornaldarsaga*, see Andersson, 'Sources and Analogues', p. 146; Acker, '"Fragments of Danish history"', 7.

[20] See below, Chapter Two, pp. 114–18.

[21] See Tripp, 'Fathers and Sons'. For discussion of the concept of entropy in medieval literature (including *Beowulf*), see S. S. Morrison, *The Literature of Waste: Material Ecopoetics and Ethical Matter* (New York, 2015). For comparison with Boethian and Orosian conceptions of time, see Conclusion, pp. 241.

[22] For a useful discussion of the prevalence of cyclical, as opposed to teleological or eschatological conceptions of time in the Old Testament, see M. Brettler, 'Cyclical and Teleological Time in the Hebrew Bible', in *Time and Temporality in the Ancient World*, ed. R. M. Rosen (Philadelphia, 2004), pp. 111–28.

[23] Cf. P. Cavill, 'Christianity and Theology in *Beowulf*', in *The Christian Tradition in Anglo-Saxon England: Approaches to Current Scholarship and Teaching*, ed. P. Cavill (Cambridge, 2004), pp. 15–40, at 38: 'The Danes could be unaware of the later historical events of Christian faith and history, as the poet knew they were, but he himself did not or could not imagine a world that was not poised between the heaven and hell of revelation.'

a direct consequence of the migration from the 'continental homeland', the world in which *Beowulf* is set, to the island of Britain.[24] I will argue that the ending of *Beowulf*, however, returns us to its beginning by presenting a people still waiting for redemption in a world as yet without Christ.[25]

Read in this light, the Old Testament character of the poem takes on added significance, inviting the Christian audience to reflect on their relationship with – and distance from – their pagan ancestors. Just as the Old Testament 'setting' of the poem, with its allusions to Creation, Cain and Abel and the Flood, points towards the revealed knowledge of the New Testament known to the audience, so the poem's cyclical rising and falling of pagan dynasties implies the possibility of a more stable form of kingship in the Christian Anglo-Saxon present, a theme to which I will return in Chapter Four and the Conclusion. Augustine famously divided the history of the world into six ages, corresponding to the life of man.[26] Another approach, more generally relevant to the period, is the threefold scheme of the life-cycle: *pueritia* (childhood), *iuuentus* (young adulthood), and *senectus* (old adulthood).[27] In recent years, a number of scholars have demonstrated the usefulness of this scheme as a lens for approaching Old English literature.[28] It is within this framework, therefore, that this chapter examines the poem's mythical account of the dynastic life-cycle.

---

[24] See Howe, *Migration and Mythmaking*.

[25] For Christological themes in the poem, see Chapter Four, pp. 231–35.

[26] (1) *infantia*, from Creation to Flood; (2) *pueritia*, from the Flood to the time of Abraham; (3) *adolescentia*, from Abraham to the reign of David; (4) *iuuentus*, from David and the kings of Israel to the captivity; (5) *gravitas*, corresponding to the decline of the Israelites after the Babylonian captivity to the coming of Christ; (6) *senectus*, from the coming of Christ and the destruction of the temple to the apocalypse. Following the sixth age, a seventh age of 'sempiternal rest' awaits the good Christian. See P. Archambault, 'The Ages of Man and the Ages of the World: A Study of Two Traditions', *Revue d'Études Augustiniennes et Patristiques* 12 (1966), 193–228; Burrow, *Ages of Man*, pp. 12–21; E. Sears, *The Ages of Man: Medieval Interpretations of the Life-cycle* (Princeton, 1986), pp. 54–79, 174–83. For discussion of the applicability of the six-ages scheme to *Beowulf*, see Anlezark, *Water and Fire*, p. 296.

[27] I. Cochelin, 'Introduction: Pre-Thirteenth Century Definitions of the Life Cycle', in *Medieval Life Cycles: Continuity and Change*, ed. I. Cochelin and K. Smyth (Turnhout, 2013), pp. 1–54, explains that each of these three stages was itself often subdivided into (1) *infantia* and *pueritia*; (2) *adolescentia* and *iuuentus*; and (3) *senectus* and *senium* or *decrepita aetas*.

[28] H. Soper, '*Eald æfensceop*: Poetic Composition and the Authority of the Aged in Old English Verse', *Quaestio Insularis: Selected Proceedings of the Cambridge Colloquium in Anglo-Saxon, Norse and Celtic* 17 (2016), 74–100; H. Soper, '*A Count of Days*: The Life Course in Old English Poetry' (Unpubl. doctoral thesis, University of Cambridge, 2018); T. Porck, *Old Age in Early Medieval England: A Cultural History*, Anglo-Saxon Studies 33 (Cambridge, 2019). See also J. Sánchez-Martí, 'Age Matters in Old English Literature', in *Youth and Age in the Medieval North*, ed. S. Lewis-Simpson (Leiden, 2008), pp. 205–26; P. Semper, '*Byð se ealda man ceald and snoflig*: Stereotypes and Subversions of the Last Stages of the Life-

In a recent study of the deaths of kings in *Beowulf*, James H. Morey expressed puzzlement at the poet's relative reticence about the fates of the Scyldings, contrasting this with the care with which he subsequently details the deaths of so many Scylfings and Hrethlings.[29] Morey accounts for this discrepancy by proposing that (a) the poet could rely on the audience's prior knowledge of the fates of the Scyldings, and (b) he felt the need to describe the violent deaths of all five Hrethlings in order to dispel any suspicion that Beowulf himself might have committed treachery on his way to the throne.[30] As this chapter will demonstrate, however, this silence can be more readily accounted for by the poet's consistent use of what Clare Kinney has called 'narrative foregrounding', a technique by which certain themes are alternately emphasized or muted depending on the 'needs of the discrete narrative moment'.[31] Hence, in description of the birth of a dynasty with which the poem opens (lines 1–67) the poet suppresses details of royal deaths and contested successions among the Scyldings while emphasizing the flourishing of young princes.[32] Then, during the second, longest phase of the dynastic life-cycle (lines 68–1887), the hero's victories over Grendel and his mother are juxtaposed with cautionary tales of the deaths of princes and hints of the disasters that lie ahead for the Scyldings. In the third and final section of the poem (lines 1888–3182), the hero's fight with the dragon becomes entangled with accounts of the premature deaths of young and old members of the Scylfing and Hrethling dynasties. With the death of the childless Beowulf, the dynastic life-cycle is complete and the poem reaches its conclusion.

PUERITIA: THE BIRTH OF A DYNASTY

haec est hereditas Domini filii mercis fructus ventris
sicut sagittae in manu potentis ita filii excussorum
(Ps. 126.3–4).

Cycle in Old English Texts and Anglo-Saxon Contexts', in *Medieval Life Cycles*, ed. Cochelin (2013), pp. 287–318; and *Childhood and Adolescence in Anglo-Saxon England*, ed. S. Irvine and W. Rudolf (Toronto, 2018).

[29] Morey, 'Fates of Men', p. 36. As Morey notes, the exception is the account of the funeral of the quasi-mythical Scyld Scefing.
[30] Morey, 'Fates of Men', pp. 36–44.
[31] C. Kinney, 'The Needs of the Moment: Poetic Foregrounding as a Narrative Device in *Beowulf*', *SP* 82 (1985), 295–314, at 302. See Chapter Three, pp. 180–94, for discussion of how the contrapuntal narrative strands of the increasingly distant past of the Scylfing-Hrethling wars and the narrative present of the hero's fight with the dragon converge in the deaths of Beowulf and the dragon and the demise of the Hrethlings.
[32] For the argument that lines 1–52 – an unnumbered section in the manuscript – constitute a prologue to the main action, see below, pp. 39–46, and Chapter Two, pp. 139–52.

[Behold the inheritance of the Lord are children: the reward, the fruit of the womb. As arrows in the hand of the mighty, so the children of them that have been shaken.]³³

Scyld Scefing and Beow

The opening phase of the dynastic life-cycle comprises the so-called 'Scyld-prologue' (1–52), followed by brief sketches of the subsequent reigns of Beow and Healfdene (53–67).³⁴ The relationship between lines 1–52, in particular, and the rest of the poem has long been viewed as problematic, not least because the genealogy provided is not, as we might expect, that of the Geatish hero, but rather of a line of Danish kings descended from the mythical figure of Scyld Scefing.³⁵ The nineteenth-century practitioners of *liedertheorie*, for example, generally regarded this section as an interpolation.³⁶ Part of the reason for this suspicion is that this section

---

³³ Psalms are numbered according to the Septuagint system, as used in the Vulgate Bible.
³⁴ Cf. A. A. Lee, *Gold-Hall and Earth-Dragon:* Beowulf *as Metaphor* (Toronto, 1998), p. 30; Biggs, 'Geatish succession', 58–60. Scholars have typically referred to lines 1–52 as the 'prologue' on the grounds that this section constitutes an unnumbered fitt or section of the manuscript and (superficially) appears to have little connection with what follows. Klaeber, for example, terms lines 1–52 an 'introductory canto' (K3, p. c), while Tolkien calls it an 'exordium' ('Monsters', p. 81). Others have referred to the passage as a 'proem' (Irving, *A Reading of Beowulf*, p. 44; Kiernan, *Beowulf Manuscript*, p. 16); and an 'episode' (C. Tolley, '*Beowulf*'s Scyld Scefing Episode: some Norse and Finnish Analogues', *ARV* 52 [1996], 7–48). C. B. Pasternack, *The Textuality of Old English Poetry*, CSASE 13 (Cambridge, 1995), p. 151, defines a prologue as a passage which 'establishes the theme of the sequence and acts as an opening frame for the following text, which the conclusion of the sequence may echo'. For further discussion of this passage, see Sisam, 'Anglo-Saxon Royal Genealogies', 317–20 and 339–45; Bonjour, *Digressions*, pp. 1–11; T. D. Hill, 'Scyld Scefing'; A. L. Meaney, 'Scyld Scefing and the Dating of *Beowulf*—Again', *Bulletin of the John Rylands University Library of Manchester* 71 (1988), 7–40, at 21–22; A. L. Meaney, 'Postscript to "Scyld Scefing and the Dating of *Beowulf*—Again"', in *Textual and Material Culture in Anglo-Saxon England: Thomas Northcote Toller and the Toller Memorial Lectures*, ed. D. G. Scragg (Cambridge, 2003), pp. 54–73; J. King, 'Launching the Hero: the Case of Scyld and Beowulf', *Neophilologus* 87 (2003), 453–71; D. Clark, 'Relaunching the Hero: the Case of Scyld and Beowulf Re-opened', *Neophilologus* 90 (2006), 621–42; E. R. Anderson, 'Beow the Boy-Wonder' (*Beowulf* 12–25)', *ES* 89 (2008), 630–42.
³⁵ See R. E. Bjork, 'Digressions and Episodes', in Bjork and Niles, pp. 193–212, at 201.
³⁶ See, for example, K. Müllenhoff, *Beovulf: Untersuchungen über das angelsächsische Epos*, ch. 3, trans. in Shippey and Haarder, pp. 346–54, at 348. See also the comments of the anonymous reviewer of Thorkelín, thought to be P. E. Müller, *Dansk Litteratur-Tidende* (1815), trans. in Shippey and Haarder, pp. 98–107, at 99; J. Grimm, *Die deutsche Mythologie* (Göttingen, 1835), trans. in Shippey and Haarder, pp. 200–02, at 201.

of the poem appears to contradict other accounts of the inception of the Danish royal house. In the surviving Scandinavian records, the figure corresponding to Scyld (ON Skjöldr) is usually succeeded by Frötho, a hero associated with a dragon-slaying legend.[37] Moreover, as we have seen, Scribe A appears to have confused the names of Beow, son of Scyld, and Beowulf, son of Ecgtheow, at lines 18a and 53b.[38] On these grounds, Henry Bradley proposed in 1910 that the 'curiously irrelevant prologue' had been grafted onto a poem about a Geatish dragon-slayer, also named Beowulf.[39] An alternative, equally ingenious theory was advanced in 1912 by Richard Boer, who argued that the passage that now serves as a prologue was originally positioned in the middle of the text, before Beowulf's dragon-fight.[40]

Sisam's argument that the Scyld-prologue is an interpolation on the basis of its parallels with the West Saxon genealogy was revived in 1988 by Audrey Meaney, while others have continued to question its relationship to the poem that follows.[41] Nevertheless, most scholars now generally accept Bonjour's argument that this passage prefigures in a general sense the movement of the poem.[42] As this discussion will demonstrate, when approached from the perspective of the dynastic life-cycle, the structural integrity of the prologue and its thematic connection to the narrative as a whole become clear. In this short, introductory section, the poet foregrounds his first major theme – the birth of a royal dynasty – by presenting a series of images of royal births and the development of young

---

[37] For discussion of the genealogies, see Chapter Two, pp. 143–46, and Conclusion, pp. 240–44. In *Beowulf*, Froda is presented as King of the Heathobards, a neighbouring tribe, and father of Ingeld, who is promised in marriage to Hrothgar's daughter, Freawaru.

[38] See Introduction, p. 8.

[39] H. Bradley, '*Beowulf*', in *Encyclopedia Britannica*, 29 vols (London & New York, 1910–11), III, pp. 758–61, at 759. For a critique of Bradley's interpretation, see Chambers, *Introduction*, pp. 91–97.

[40] Boer, *Die altenglische Heldendichtung. 1: Beowulf*. Boer suggests that the last in a series of 'compilers' transferred the Danish dragon fight to the land of the Geats and placed the remodelled prologue at the beginning of the entire poem. See, however, K3, p. ciii; Bonjour, *Digressions*, p. 2; and Chambers, *Introduction*, pp. 424–30. Klaeber also had his doubts about the integrity of this passage (see K3, p. cvii). See also Schücking, *Beowulfs Rückkehr*, p. 72.

[41] Sisam, 'Genealogies', 339; Meaney, 'Scyld Scefing and the Dating of *Beowulf*— Again', 39; King, 'Launching the Hero', 454. See also Irving, *A Reading of Beowulf*, p. 45.

[42] See Bonjour, *Digressions*, pp. 1–11; Owen-Crocker, *Four Funerals*, pp. 11–42, 217–40. For a critique of Bonjour's interpretation of the prologue, see J. C. Van Meurs, '*Beowulf* and Literary Criticism', *Neophilologus* 39 (1955), 114–30, at 123–25. See further Bonjour's reply, '*Beowulf* and the Snares of Literary Criticism', *Études Anglaises* 10 (1957), 30–36, repr. in his *Twelve Beowulf Papers*, pp. 121–28.

The Dynastic Life-Cycle and the Structure of the Poem

princes.[43] In the course of the poem, this theme will undergo a series of minor and major variations culminating in the magnificent funeral of the childless King Beowulf. At the heart of this opening section is the poem's first major set-piece, the so-called 'funeral' of Scyld Scefing. As we shall see, however, in order to foreground the theme of the birth of a dynasty, the poet deals with Scyld's death and funerary rites in a decidedly euphemistic manner, while also muting details of the deaths of various other early Danish rulers and glossing over instances of contested succession.[44] The poem's opening section presents dynastic kingship in the earliest phase of its life-cycle as a dynamic institution in which old rulers work together with their young heirs for the benefit of their subjects.

In the first of a series of dramatic reversals of fortune (*edwenden*),[45] the poet juxtaposes Scyld Scefing's might as an adult ruler with his former vulnerability as an abandoned child:[46]

> Oft Scyld Scēfing   sceaþena þrēatum,
> monegum mægþum   meodo-setla oftēah,   5
> egsode eorlas,   syððan ǣrest wearð
> fēa-sceaft funden. He þæs frōfre gebād:
> *wēox under wolcnum,   weorðmyndum þāh*
> oð þæt him æg-hwylc   þāra ymb-sittendra
> ofer hron-rāde   hȳran scolde,   10
> gomban gyldan.   Þæt wæs gōd cyning.
> (4–11). (Emphasis added).

[Often Scyld Scefing dragged away the mead-benches of many tribes, troops of enemies, terrified the warriors, since in the beginning he was found destitute. He received consolation for that, *grew under the skies, flourished with honours*, until each of the neighbouring peoples over the whale-road had to obey him, tender tribute. That was a good king.]

Scyld's remarkable transformation from destitute infant to mighty king is made manifest through his ability to strike fear into the neighbouring

---

[43] See above, pp. 29–30 for discussion of myths as tales concerning origins.
[44] See below, pp. 44–45.
[45] On reversals in *Beowulf*, see Bonjour, *Digressions*, pp. 5–6; T. A. Shippey, *Old English Verse* (London, 1972), pp. 38–41; P. R. Brown, 'Cycles and Change in *Beowulf*', in *Manuscript, Narrative, Lexicon: Essays on Literary and Cultural Transmission in Honor of Whitney F. Bolton*, ed. R. Boenig and K. Davis (Lewisburg, 2000), pp. 171–92, at 183–86; and Scheil, '*Beowulf* and the Emergent Occasion', 93–94.
[46] Although Scioldus appears as a son of Odinus (ON Odin, OE Woden) and early king of the Danes in *Skjöldunga saga* (ch. 1) (see Appendix A), there is no trace of the legend of Scyld Scefing's watery arrival among the Danes in Scandinavian tradition. For the argument that this story is largely the poet's invention, see Chapter Two, pp. 139–51. See Chapter Two, pp. 150–51, for the relationship between the Scyld story and the legend of Heremod, a Danish king whose career follows the opposite trajectory.

peoples and to force them to pay tribute (9–11). We are left in no doubt of the narrator's admiration for this model of aggressive, warrior-kingship: *þæt wæs gōd cyning*, 'that was a good king' (11b).[47]

Significantly, the identity of those who sent him out as a child, alone over the waves, in a boat laden with treasures (43–46) is never revealed, just as Scyld's own origins are silently omitted.[48] The designation 'Scefing' would seem to indicate that Scyld is the 'son of Scef', though in narrative terms he effectively has no father; we hear nothing about this Scef in the poem and, as we shall see in Chapter Two, the linking of these two name elements is in fact more suggestive of ritualistic associations of the shield and the sheaf than of a patronymic.[49] In the light of the great significance attached to royal ancestry throughout the poem, the poet's reticence over the matter of Scyld's ancestry might initially seem puzzling. However, this problem soon disappears with the recognition that Scyld is a manifestation of the folktale motif of the 'stranger king', or the 'king from overseas', a figure traditionally taken in and nursed by the people who goes on to establish a dynasty, usually by violent means.[50] Scyld Scefing, the 'stranger king', with his mysterious origins and violent nature, is presented as the true founder of the Scylding dynasty, even though we later learn that there were in fact other 'Scylding' kings before him.[51]

[47] King, 'Launching the Hero', 460–62, tentatively raises the possibility that this phrase might be meant ironically. Owen-Crocker, *Four Funerals*, p. 37, n. 28, notes that the interpretation of this phrase as an ironic assessment of Scyld's aggression on the grounds that such a reading 'supposes a pacifism in the Anglo-Saxon audience which is not justifiable'. See further Niles, *Beowulf*, p. 201. For comparison with the last half-line of *Andreas*, see Conclusion, pp. 242–43.

[48] In the West-Saxon genealogies preserved in the *ASC*, Heremod appears as the immediate ancestor of Sceldwa/Scyld (see below, pp. 109, 143–44). Paul Beekman Taylor therefore proposes that it was in fact the exiled Heremod who sent his 'son' Scyld back to the Danes in a boat accompanied by royal treasures to signify his pedigree in order to continue the royal line ('The Language of Sacral Kingship in *Beowulf*', *Studia Neophilologica* 66 [1994], 129–45, at 139).

[49] See below, pp. 146–47.

[50] See the recent discussion of D. Graeber and M. Sahlins, 'Theses on kingship', in their *On Kings* (Chicago, 2017), pp. 1–22, esp. p. 5. Cf. M. Sahlins, 'The Stranger-King: Or Dumézil among the Fijians', *Journal of Pacific History* 16 (1981), 107–32. On the tradition of the people as nursemaids of the king in central Madagascar, see Graeber, in Graeber and Sahlins (2017), pp. 249–344. While there is no suggestion that Scyld had ever committed crimes typically associated with the 'stranger king', such as incest, fratricide or patricide, prior to his arrival among the Danes – and his youth would certainly seem to count against this – his subsequent terrorizing of the local *eorlas* fits the pattern of violent behaviour characteristic of the 'stranger king'.

[51] For the argument that the name 'Scyld' is a back-formation from the dynastic name 'Scylding', see Chapter Two, pp. 139–52. Busse and Holtei note that the story of Scyld's transformation provides 'a model of social rise' from inauspicious origins to beloved ruler which is then amplified in the career of Beowulf

However, despite his great success as a war leader, Scyld's most lasting contribution to the Danes comes in the form of his son and heir, Beow, whose birth ensures that the Danes do not suffer an equally swift reversal of their fortunes after his death:[52]

> Ðǣm *eafera wæs   æfter cenned*
> *geong in geardum,*   þone God sende
> folce tō frōfre;[53]   fyren-ðearfe ongeat —
> þæt hīe ǣr drugon   aldor-lēase   15
> lange hwīle. Him þæs līf-frea
> wuldres wealdend   worold-āre forgeaf;
> Bēow wæs brēme   – *blǣd wīde sprang* –
> *Scyldes eafera*   Scede-landum in.
> (12–19). (Emphasis added).

[To him *a son was born to follow after, young in the courts,* whom God sent as a comfort to the people. He [i.e. God] recognized their terrible need, that they before had suffered lordlessness for a long time; the Lord of Life, Ruler of Glory, gave worldly comfort to them; Beow was famous – *his reputation spread far and wide* – *Scyld's son* in Scedeland.]

Significantly, the poet chooses the moment at which the theme of dynastic succession is first introduced to foreground God's omnipotent and yet simultaneously detached role in human history.[54] Hence it is *God*, rather than Scyld himself, who 'recognized the terrible need' (*fyren-ðearfe ongeat*) of the Danes, by sending to Scyld a son and heir as a comfort to the people. Underscoring God's status as supreme ruler and King of Kings are the Cædmonian variants *līf-frea*, 'lord of life', and *wuldres wealdend*, 'ruler of glory'. While Scyld had himself received *frōfre*, 'comfort' (7b), as a boy, the vulnerable Danes are now comforted by God (13b–14a) with the gift of a stable ruling dynasty.[55]

Complementing the references to youth (*geong in geardum*) and offspring (*eafera* x2) are a series of playful agricultural puns: *Scēf*, 'sheaf', *Bēow*, 'wheat', *wēox under wolcnum*, 'grew under the skies' (8b), and *blǣd wīde sprang*, 'glory sprang up far and wide' (18b).[56] Moreover, just as

---

('*Beowulf* and the Tenth Century', 301). On Beowulf's 'unpromising youth' see below, pp. 81 n.174, 103, 120 n.44, 132–33.

[52] On the absence of primogeniture and the tolerance of fraternal and other forms of succession in Anglo-Saxon England, see pp. 18–21, 237–40. For discussion of a 'two-generational' model of kingship in *Beowulf*, see J. M. Hill, *Narrative Pulse*, p. 6.

[53] See Chapter Four, pp. 231–34, for the Christological implications of this term in other Old English texts.

[54] See Chapter Four for discussion of *Beowulf* and biblical kingship.

[55] See Chapter Four, pp. 231–35, for connections with Christ.

[56] See J. Harris, 'The Dossier on Byggvir, God and Hero: *Cur deus homo*', *ARV* 55 (1999), 7–23; *CCB*, p. 104, n. 41. For discussion of agricultural imagery and the

Scyld's aggressive foreign policy was held up by the poet as an example of good kingship, so Beow's generosity towards his retainers while still in his father's protection (*on fæder bearme*) is now presented as a model of princely conduct:

> Swā sceal *geong guma*   gōde gewyrcean,
> fromum feoh-giftum   *on fæder bearme*,
> þæt hine *on ylde*   eft gewunigen
> wil-gesīþas,   þonne wīg cume,
> lēode gelæsten [...].
> (20–25a). (Emphasis added).

> [So *a young man* should bring it about with goodness, with splendid gifts of treasure *while still in the father's protection*, so that afterwards *in old age*, when war comes, loyal companions will stand by him, support the prince.]

Again, youth and age are shown to work harmoniously within a dynastic framework. The young ætheling, Beow, is protected by his father and king, Scyld; later when Beow himself is old, he too will be supported by loyal retainers. It is through Beow's generous distribution of gifts while still in his youth that the prince ensures both his own safe passage from youth to age and, by implication, the flourishing of the royal line.

With the succession now secure, the focus shifts to the preparations for Scyld's ship funeral.[57] Significantly, however, Scyld's death is dealt with in a circumlocutory manner, while the description of the funeral itself is, as Bonjour notes, dominated by images of progress and movement:[58]

> Him ðā Scyld gewāt   tō gescæp-hwīle
> *fela-hrōr fēran*   on frēan wǣre.
> (26–7). (Emphasis added).

> [Then Scyld took himself away at the appointed time, *journeyed far, very strong*, into the Lord's keeping.]

Sustaining the impression of dynastic progression, oblique references to Scyld's death (26–27) and old age (29–31) are carefully balanced by allusions to his vigour when he was still a youth, with the description of the king's final journey into the embrace of the sea echoing that of his equally mysterious arrival among the Danes as an infant:[59]

---

theme of creation in ON literature, see M. D. J. Bintley, *Trees in the Religions of Early Medieval England* (Woodbridge, 2015), pp. 129–52. For echoes of this passage in the Finnsburg Episode, see below, pp. 68–72.

[57] On connections with Beowulf's funeral, see p. 3.

[58] Bonjour, *Digressions*, pp. 9–10.

[59] For discussion of the prevalence of water and flood-imagery in the early parts of the poem, and its correspondence with Augustine's first age of the world, from Creation to Flood (*infantia*), see Anlezark, *Water and Fire*, pp. 298–323.

The Dynastic Life-Cycle and the Structure of the Poem

Hī hyne þā ætbǣron   tō brimes faroðe,
swǣse gesīþas,   swā hē selfa bæd
þenden wordum wēold.
(28–30a).

[They carried him to the water's edge, loyal retainers, as he himself had instructed when he held the power of words.]

Nalæs hī hine lǣssan   lācum tēodan,
þēod-gestrēonum,   þonne þā dydon,
þē hine æt *frum-sceafte*   forð onsendon
ǣnne ofer ȳðe   *umbor-wesende*.[60]
(43–46). (Emphasis added).

[Not at all did they provide him with lesser treasures, treasures of the people, than did those who, *in the beginning*, sent him forth alone over the waves *while still a child*.]

DOE suggests that the term *frum-sceaft*, literally 'first formation, beginning', should be taken here to mean 'birth'.[61] However, this is the only example cited of this sense and the term is most frequently used throughout the Old English corpus, both in prose and verse, to refer to the biblical account of the beginning of the world. Most famously, it appears as a translation of the Latin *Canta principium creaturarum* (Bede, *HE* IV.24) in the Old English *Bede*'s account of Cædmon: *Sing me frum-sceafte*, 'Sing to me of Creation!'[62] Indeed, it is in precisely this biblical sense that the term *frum-sceaft* is used only fifty lines later, on its sole further appearance in *Beowulf* during the Danish *scop*'s 'Song of Creation': *Sægde sē þe cūþe/frum-sceaft fīra feorran reccan*, 'He spoke, he who knew how to recount from afar the creation of men' (90b–91). Moreover, on each of the four occasions where the collocation *æt frum-sceafte* occurs in verse outside of *Beowulf*, it is always used in the specific biblical sense of 'at the time of the Creation'.[63] I would suggest, therefore, that the poet gives his audience to

---

[60] For discussion of the unusual term *umborwesende*, see S. Irvine and W. Rudolf, 'Introduction', in Irvine and Rudolf (2018), pp. 3–14, at 4.

[61] *DOE*, s. v. *frumsceaft* 1.b. K4 has 'creation, beginning, origin' (p. 381) for both lines 45 and 91.

[62] *DOE*, s. v. *frumsceaft*: '1. first formation, beginning [...] 1.a. beginning of the world, creation'. On this connection, see P. Dean, '*Beowulf* and the Passing of Time', *ES* 75 (1994), 193–209, 293–302, at 197. The term *fruma* is often used to refer to God in OE: for example, *frum-sceafta frea* ('Lord of Creation') (*Exodus*, 274a), *fæder frum-sceafta/ frum-sceafta fæder* ('Father of Creation') (*Christ I*, 472a; *Vainglory*, 66a); *līfes ord-fruma* ('Starting Point of Life') (*Christ I*, 227a), *sigores fruma* ('Chief of Victory'), *ēce ēad-fruma* ('Eternal Origin of Blessings') (*Christ I*, 532a). OE *frum-sceaft* is used to translate Lat. *primogenitum* (first born) in the Anglo-Saxon glossed psalters.

[63] *Soul and Body II* (74a), *Andreas* (797a), *Metres of Boethius* 26 (7a), *Exeter Book*

understand that Scyld's miraculous appearance among the Danes took place in 'Mythic Time', 'in the beginning', through the use of the biblically charged term *frum-sceaft*.[64]

Much later in the poem, it is revealed that the Danes had in fact been ruled before Scyld by King Heremod, whom they had subsequently rejected as ruler due to his wicked behaviour and his refusal to share out treasures with his retainers (901–15, 1709–24a).[65] It seems likely, therefore, that the state of lordlessness in which the Danes find themselves prior to Scyld's arrival was the direct result of Heremod's deposition. The omission of the story of Heremod's fall from the opening section of the poem allows the poet to present Scyld's reign as effectively the beginning of dynastic kingship among the Danes.[66] As we shall see, the poet postpones the introduction of Heremod into the narrative until the next stage in the dynastic life-cycle, during which he first begins to emphasize threats to the survival of royal houses.[67]

Riddle 3 (14a). On the close relationship between *Andreas* and *Beowulf*, see below, Conclusion. On the importance of the theme of Creation in the Exeter Book riddles more generally, see R. Wehlau, *The Riddle of Creation: Metaphor Structures in Old English Poetry* (New York, 1997). Cf. references to the Creation and Incarnation in *Christ I* (225b and 234: *æt fruman/æt frymðe*). On the possible Christological implications of the Scyld Scefing-Beow story, see Chapter Four, pp. 231–35.

[64] On further biblical parallels to this story, in particular with the tale of Moses in the reeds, see below, Chapter Two, pp. 147–48. Hanning, 'Beowulf as Heroic History', 86, identifies Scyld and Beowulf as 'displaced Christ figures' who intersect with 'a world living in time'. See also K3, pp. l–li; Niles, *Beowulf*, p. 181; T. D. Hill, 'Scyld Scefing', p. 37; Niles, *Beowulf*, pp. 182–85. For comparison of the poem's temporal setting and the time of the biblical patriarchs, see C. Donahue, '*Beowulf*, Ireland and the Natural Good', *Traditio* 7 (1949–50), 263–78; M. Bloomfield, 'Patristics and Old English Literature: Notes on Some Poems', *Comparative Literature* 14 (1962), 36–43, repr. in *Studies in Old English Literature in Honor of Arthur G. Brodeur*, ed. S. B. Greenfield (Eugene, OR, 1963), pp. 36–43. For discussion of the transformation of Scyld Scefing, the founder of the Scyldings, into Scef/Sceaf, the ark-born son of Noah, in the West Saxon royal genealogy, see below, pp. 143–44. Niles locates the biblical stories that accompany the construction of Heorot and Beowulf's fights with the Grendelkin in the 'Mythic Past' (*Beowulf*, pp. 189–96).

[65] On the position of Heremod as Scyld's ancestor or predecessor in the West Saxon royal genealogy, see pp. 140–43. On Heremod's career as king, see pp. 104, 106–09, 150–51; for parallels with Saul, see Chapter Four, pp. 210–23.

[66] As T. D. Hill notes, the poem opens with 'a mythical digression which explicitly concerns the origin of one of the great royal families of the north and implicitly the institution of kingship itself' ('Scyld Scefing', p. 37).

[67] As Richard J. Schrader notes, earlier Danish rulers such as Heremod and Hnæf 'are not mentioned until other themes require them: here the poet has established a *translatio gloriae* in which they have no part' ('Succession and Glory in *Beowulf*', 491).

Healfdene and his Children

Having sketched the earliest and smoothest phase in the life-cycle of the dynasty in the prologue, the poet varies this theme of father-to-son succession in the brief summary of the succeeding generations of Scyldings. Like his father before him, Beow will grow to become a great *lēod-cyning*, 'king of the people', enjoying a long and successful reign and providing the Danes with a single, worthy heir, Healfdene, to succeed him as ruler (53–56a). The close connection between the fortunes of the ruling dynasty and its subjects is suggested now by the use of the term 'Scylding' to refer first to Beow himself (53b: *Bēow Scyldinga*, 'Beow of the Scyldings') and then to the Danish people (58b: *glæde Scyldingas*, 'gracious Scyldings'). Under Healfdene, the royal line of Scyld, and hence the Danish nation, continues to prosper with the birth of three more royal sons and a daughter:

> Ðǣm fēower bearn   forðgerīmed
> in worold wōcun,   weoroda rǣswan,
> Heorogār ond Hrōðgār   ond Hālga til;
> hȳrde ic þæt [.......] wæs On]elan[68] cwēn,
> Heaðo-Scilfingas   heals-gebedda.
> (59–63)
>
> [Four children were counted up, born into the world, for the leader of troops, Heorogar and Hrothgar and Halga the Good; I heard that (...) was Onela's queen, the bed companion of the War-Scylfings.]

Significantly, no details are provided of the deaths of either Beow or Healfdene, allowing the focus to remain on the flourishing of a young dynasty and the transference of royal power across the generations. Similarly glossed over is the reign of Hrothgar's elder brother, Heorogar. As with the case of Heremod, the poet delays mentioning Heorogar's reign until a more apposite moment in the narrative – in this case, several

---

[68] Most editors emend MS *hȳrde ic þæt elan cwēn* to *hȳrde ic þæt Yrse wæs Onelan cwēn* on metrical grounds. See K4, pp. 117–18; Neidorf, *Transmission*, p. 77. In both *Skjöldunga saga* (chs 10–11) and *Hrólfs saga* (chs 1, 6–17), however, Halfdanus (ON Halfdan) has one daughter named Signya (ON Signy), while Yrsa is the incestuous daughter and wife of Helgo (ON Helgi, OE Halga) and mother of Rolfo (ON Rolf, OE Hrothulf). Alfred Bammesberger has proposed that the entirety of lines 62–63 are in fact an interpolation derived from a gloss ('Hidden Glosses in Manuscripts of Old English Poetry', *ASE* 13 [1984], 43–49, at 49). See further K. Malone, 'The Daughter of Healfdene', in *Studies in English Philology: A Miscellany in honor of Frederick Klaeber*, ed. K. Malone and M. B. Ruud (Minneapolis, 1929), pp. 135–58; N. E. Eliason, 'Healfdene's Daughter', in *Anglo-Saxon Poetry: Essays in Appreciation, for John C. McGalliard*, ed. L. E. Nicholson and D. W. Frese (London and Notre Dame, 1975), pp. 3–13.

hundred lines later, as Hrothgar recalls to Beowulf the circumstances of his accession and his brother's early death (465–69). Heorogar is absent from the Scandinavian accounts of the Scyldings, in which Halfdan (OE Healfdene) only has two sons, Roas (OE Hrothgar) and Helgo (OE Halga). Moreover, the figure presented in *Beowulf* as Heorogar's son, Heoroweard (ON Hjorvard), appears in these texts as the great-grandson of Healfdene (ON Halfdan) via marriage to Skuld, daughter of Hrothulf (ON Hrolf). We must wait until Beowulf's own recount of this same speech to Hygelac to learn that Heorogar gave his armour – and, by implication, the throne – to his more mature and experienced brother, Hrothgar (2155–62), rather than his own son, Heoroweard.[69] Hollis has argued that, by assuming power ahead of Heoroweard, Hrothgar violated the code of primogeniture.[70] Yet, as we have seen, there is in fact no evidence that primogeniture was a factor in early Germanic kingship or that Hrothgar ever took the throne by force from either Heorogar or Heoroweard. Furthermore, when Hrothgar later recalls to Beowulf the circumstances of his accession, he speaks of his elder brother in terms more suggestive of sincere affection than rivalry:

> ðā ic furþum wēold   folce Deniga
> ond on geogoðe hēold   ginne rīce,
> hord-burh hæleþa,   ðā wæs Heregār dēad,
> mīn yldra mæg   unlifigende,
> bearn Healfdenes;   sē wæs betera ðonne ic!
> (465–69).

> [Then I ruled the Danish people, and in my youth possessed a broad kingdom, treasure-hoard of warriors, when Heorogar was dead, my elder brother unliving, son of Healfdene; he was better than I!]

It appears, therefore, that Heorogar designated his brother rather than his son as his successor on the grounds that Hrothgar had already established his reputation as the head of a thriving *young* warband:[71]

> Þā wæs Hrōðgāre   here-spēd gyfen,
> wīges weorð-mynd,   þæt him his wine-māgas
> georne hȳrdon,   oðð þæt *sēo geogoð gewēox,*
> *mago-driht micel.*
> (64–67a). (Emphasis added).

---

[69] See further pp. 19 n.88, 84.
[70] Hollis, '*Beowulf* and the Succession', 42.
[71] For discussion of Queen Hygd's offer of the Geatish throne to Beowulf ahead of her relatively inexperienced son, Heardred, see pp. 19, 21, 91–92, 206. Beowulf's rejection of Hygd's offer need not imply that Hrothgar acted improperly in succeeding his brother, as the two dynastic situations are quite different: Hrothgar is the brother of the deceased ruler and therefore a perfectly good candidate for election; Beowulf's claim to the Geatish throne is much weaker, coming through his mother, who is Hygelac's sister.

[Success in war was granted to Hrothgar, honour in battle, so that his dear companions eagerly obeyed him, until the *young warriors grew, a great band of young men.*]⁷²

Aside from another brief and euphemistic reference to Scyld's death (55b–56a), the poet continues to foreground the Scylding dynasty's vitality and momentum, presenting a proliferation of royal births (*onwōc, wōcun*) and carefully balancing references to age (*gamol ond gūð-rēouw*) with images of youth (*fēower bearn*).

Just as the poet had witheld information about Heorogar and Heoroweard in order to foreground the theme of dynastic progression, so he now glosses over the career of Healfdene's third son, Halga. In later accounts of the legend, notably *Skjöldunga saga* (chs 10–11) and *Hrólfs saga* (chs 5–17), the brothers Helgi (OE Halga) and Roas (OE Hrothgar) are presented as co-rulers, with the former establishing his royal seat at Lejre in Denmark and the latter in England, where he marries a Northumbrian queen. With no figure corresponding to Heorogar in the Scandinavian records of the Skjöldungs, Roas becomes sole ruler after the death of Helgi.⁷³ It is possible that in the version of the Scylding legend known to the *Beowulf*-poet and his original audience, Halga died before he was old enough to rule, leaving his only son, Hrothulf, the famous Hrólfr Kraki of Norse legend, in the protection of his uncle Hrothgar.⁷⁴ Either way, the poet deems it fitting to leave out details of Halga's career, with the result that the narrative remains focused on the royal house's steady progression. Further evidence of the careful planning of the poem is provided by the brief allusion at lines 62–63 to the marriage of Healfdene's daughter to a Scylfing prince. This detail anticipates the prominent role that royal women will subsequently play in the dynastic drama as well as foreshadowing the wars between the Swedish and Geatish royal houses that will come to dominate the final third of the poem.⁷⁵

---

⁷² As we shall see, the Geatish hero's own subsequent military success against Grendel will result in his public proclamation as a future king by the Danes. See below, pp. 60–61.

⁷³ For summaries see appendices, pp. 248–49, 251.

⁷⁴ In *Ynglinga saga*, Helgi (OE Halga) dies leaving an eight-year-old son. See Newton, *Origins*, p. 94; Garmonsway, pp. 141–55, 218–20. On Hrothgar and Hrothulf, see pp. 64–66.

⁷⁵ On royal women in *Beowulf*, see J. Chance, *Woman as Hero in Old English Literature* (Syracuse, 1986), pp. 1–12 (on peaceweavers), and pp. 95–108 (on Grendel's mother as antitype of the Virgin and Queen); J. L. Sklute, '*Freoðuwebbe* in Old English Poetry', in Damico and Olsen (1990), pp. 204–10; A. H. Olsen, 'Gender Roles', in Bjork and Niles (1997), pp. 311–24, at 313–14; A. Hall, 'Hygelac's only daughter: a present, a potentate and a peaceweaver in *Beowulf*, SN 78 (2006), 81–87; L. Neidorf, 'Hildeburh's Mourning and *The Wife's Lament*', SN 89 (2017), 197–204. On Grendel's mother as antitype of the poem's other royal women,

Through this consistent suppression of royal deaths and details concerning complicated successions, the poem's opening section presents the Danish royal house as a dynamic social organism transcending generational boundaries. A succession of suitable male heirs ensures that the death of an individual king need not have any long-lasting impact on the well-being of either the dynasty itself or its subjects. However, relations between young and old members of royal families become increasingly complex and ambiguous from this point onwards in the dynastic life-cycle.[76]

IUUENTUS: DYNASTIES IN CRISIS

dixitque Cain ad Abel fratrem suum egrediamur foras
cumque essent in agro
consurrexit Cain adversus Abel fratrem suum et interfecit eum
(Gen. 4.8).

[And Cain said to Abel his brother: Let us go forth abroad. And when they were in the field, Cain rose up against his brother Abel, and slew him.]

The Future of the Scyldings

The construction of King Hrothgar's great hall, Heorot, marks the end of the first phase of the dynastic life-cycle. As the royal seat of the Scyldings, Heorot provides a stable centre from which the king can distribute the treasures granted to him by God. By extending his generosity to both young and old members of his court, Hrothgar consolidates his authority over a broad kingdom. The poet now casts Hrothgar as both *rex iuustus* and *sapiens architectus* in terms that echo Genesis 1 and, more specifically, *Cædmon's Hymn*.[77] As Niles notes, the link with Cædmon is strengthened by the *scop*'s song of Creation that follows shortly after:[78]

Him on mōd bearn
þæt heal-reced   hātan wolde,
medo-ærn micel   men *gewyrcean*

---

see Chapter Three, pp. 177–80. On Wealhtheow, see below, pp. 72–76. On the Scylfing-Hrethling wars, see pp. 82–102, and Chapter Three, pp. 180–93.

[76] As we shall see in Chapter Three, this breakdown in kinship is dramatically realized through the advent of Grendel, pp. 159–62.

[77] On connections between Hrothgar and Solomon, see Chapter Four, pp. 216–19.

[78] Niles, *Beowulf*, pp. 78–79. Cf. Abimelech's injunction to Abraham in *Genesis A* (2825b–31), which also features the rare term *folc-scearu*. See further below, pp. 51–52. On parallels with the construction of the Tower of Babel, see Major, *Undoing Babel*, pp. 241–44.

The Dynastic Life-Cycle and the Structure of the Poem

þonne *yldo bearn*   ǣfre gefrūnon,
ond þǣr on innan   eall gedǣlan
geongum ond ealdum   swylc him God sealde,
būton folc-scare   ond feorum gumena.
(67b–73). (Emphasis added).

[*It came into his mind* that he would order a hall-building to be *constructed* by men, the greatest mead-hall that *the children of men* had ever heard of, and inside there he would deal out everything that God had given him to young and old alike, *except for the nation (?) and the lives of men*.]

Nū sculon herian   heofon-rīces weard
metudes myhte,   ond his mōd-geþanc,
wurc wuldor-fæder,   swā hē wundra gehwilc,
ēce drihten,   or *āstealde*.
Hē ǣrest *sceōp*   *ylda bearnum*
heofon tō *hrōfe*, hālig scyppend;
þā middan-geard   man-cynnes weard,
ēce drihten, æfter *tēode*,
firum on foldan   frēa ælmihtig.[79]
(*Cædmon's Hymn*, 1–8). (Emphasis added).

[Now we must praise the Guardian of the Heaven-kingdom, the might of *the Measurer* and his intention, the *work* of the Glory-Father, as he in the beginning *established*, Eternal Lord, each wonder. First he *made* heaven as a *roof for the children of men*, Holy Shaper, then the Guardian of Mankind, Eternal Lord, afterwards *made* the middle-earth, *for men* on the land, Lord Almighty.]

In both texts, rulers are praised for purposing (*Beo*: *Him on mōd bearn*, *Cæd*: *mōd-geþanc*) to have a great *weorc* built for the benefit of 'the children of men' (*Beo*: *yldo bearn*; *Cæd*: *ylda bearnum*). The precise meaning of the compound *folc-scare* (73a) is unclear, with suggestions ranging from 'public land' to land granted in perpetuity (i.e. *folc-land*).[80] However, in all the eight other instances of this compound in the poetic corpus, *folc-scare* denotes 'nation' or 'people', as does its once-occurring cognate *lēod-scearu* (*Exodus*, 337).[81] It is possible, then, that the *Beowulf*-poet may have used

---

[79] West-Saxon *ylda* recension, cited from *Cædmon's Hymn: a multimedia edition and archive*, ed. D. O'Donnell (Cambridge, 2005), http://people.uleth.ca/~daniel.odonnell/caedmon/html/htm/edition/ylda/index.htm (accessed 29 December 2018).

[80] See E. John, 'Folkland reconsidered', in his *Orbis Britanniae and Other Studies*, Studies in Early English History 4 (Leicester, 1966), pp. 64–127, at 118–21; S. Jurasinski, *Ancient Privileges: Beowulf, Law, and the Making of Germanic Antiquity* (Morgantown, WV, 2006), pp. 49–77.

[81] *DOE*, s. v. *folc-scearu*: land, country; nation, people. Cf. *Andreas* 684; *Genesis A*, 1781, 1872, 2479, 2681, 2830; *Elene*, 402, 967. The term *scearu* (BT: 'a share') also occurs as the second element in the compounds *hearm-scearu* (*DOE*: '[what is

this term in order to indicate that Hrothgar was in some way prohibited from conferring the rule of the nation on an appointed successor without the consent of the *witan*.[82] It has already been established that Hrothgar has two brothers, Heorogar and Halga, both of whom, we later learn, have sons of their own. As we shall see, the combined presence of so many young Scyldings within Heorot will significantly complicate the next stage in the Danish succession.

With the Scyldings now facing an uncertain future, the dynastic life-cycle now enters its second stage. The trouble lying ahead for the Scyldings is first hinted at immediately after the account of the building of Heorot:[83]

>   Sele hlīfade
> hēah ond horn-gēap;   heaðo-wylma bād,
> lāðan līges –   *ne wæs hit lenge þā gēn,*
> *þæt se ecg-hete   āþum-swēoran*
> *æfter wæl-nīðe   wæcnan scolde.*
> (81b–85). (Emphasis added).

[The hall towered, high and horn-gabled – *it was not long after* that the sword-hatred between father-in-law and son-in-law would awaken after deadly slaughter.]

With this proleptic allusion to the family feud that will soon destroy the royal seat of the Scyldings, the poet presents for the first time a scenario in which young and old members of the royal kin come into conflict.[84] The origins of this feud between son-in-law and father-in-law are never explored in the poem, presumably because the audience was already familiar with the legend. In Beowulf's own version of events, delivered much later in the narrative during his long report to Hygelac, the hero predicts

---

appointed as] punishment, penalty', appearing only in *Genesis B* and cognate with Old Saxon *harm-skara*), *land-scearu* (BT: 'share, division, or portion of land', found in the Metrical Epilogue to the Old English *Pastoral Care* [18], *Andreas* [1231], and in charters) and *sceap-scearu* ('sheep-shearing'), which appears twice in the Old English Heptateuch (translation of Genesis). A. Bammesberger, 'The meaning of Old English *folcscaru* and the compound's function in *Beowulf*', *NOWELE: North-Western European Language Evolution* 72 (2019), 1–10, has recently suggested the following translation for line 73: 'with the exception of his men's clan and (their) lives' (8).

[82] K4, p. 119.
[83] See K3, pp. xxxiv–xxxvi, 129–30; N. E. Eliason, 'The Burning of Heorot', *Speculum* 55 (1980), 75–83. The legend of the heroic defence of Heorot by Hrothgar and his nephew, Hrothulf, against the Heathobards is alluded to in *Widsith* 45–49.
[84] DOE notes that the hapax *āþum-swēoran* (84b) is 'almost universally taken as a so-called dvandva compound meaning "son-in-law and father-in-law" in the dative plural […]; the basis of the supposed compound is *āþum* "son-in-law" and *swēor* "father-in-law" (cf. *Jul.* line 65: *swēor ond āþum*)'. On Ingeld, Hrothgar and the Scylding-Heathobard feud, see further Chapter Two.

The Dynastic Life-Cycle and the Structure of the Poem

that Hrothgar will later give his daughter, Freawaru, as a 'peace-weaving' queen to the young Heathobard prince, Ingeld, son of King Froda, in a doomed attempt to broker a truce (2020–69a).[85] Attempts to reconstruct the details of this story are hampered by the fact that the extant Scandinavian sources offer conflicting accounts.[86] Nonetheless, it is generally agreed that the battle at Heorot between the Scyldings and Heathobards alluded to in *Beowulf* lines 81b–85 and also described in *Widsith* lines 45–49 is a direct consequence of the re-awakening of this feud.

It is within this tense dynastic atmosphere that the monster Grendel is first introduced into the narrative.[87] With Grendel now effectively 'ruling' in Heorot, the Scyldings are unable to sustain the rapid growth of previous generations. Whereas in the first stage of the dynastic life-cycle the harmful effect of old age on kings was offset by the youthful vigour of sons and heirs, here the aged Hrothgar cannot rely on his sons and nephews for help:

---

[85] See further below, pp. 80, 81, 130–31.
[86] Freawaru is not mentioned in the Scandinavian sources, though a figure corresponding to her appears in Saxo Grammaticus's *Gesta Danorum* (vi.6–vii.1), which recounts how the Danish king, Frotho (OE Froda), was murdered by a Saxon warrior named Sverting (Latin Swertingus); Frotho's son, Ingiald (Lat. Ingellus; OE Ingeld), married Sverting's daughter, angering Starkath (Lat. Starcardus), a warrior loyal to Frotho; during a banquet held with the sons of Sverting, Starkath confronts Ingiald, and incites him to kill the sons of his father's slayer and divorce his bride. This last scene clearly resembles Beowulf's prediction of the fight that will break out after the wedding of Freawaru and Ingeld (2024b–69a). In *Skjöldunga saga* (chs 9–10), Frodo IV is the father of both Halfdanus (OE Healfdene) and Ingialldus (OE Ingeld), though they are born of different mothers; Halfdanus's mother is the kidnapped daughter of Iorundus, the King of Sweden, while Ingialldus's mother is the daughter of Sverting, a Swedish baron; Frodo is murdered by Iorundus (the father of Halfdanus's mother), after which the half-brothers ruled together for a time, before Ingialldus, 'out of greed for the kingdom, led a surprise attack with his army against Halfdanus and killed him' (trans. Miller, 'Fragments of Danish History', 16), marrying his half-brother's widow, Sigrida; once Halfdanus's sons, Roas (OE Hrothgar) and Helgo (OE Halga) had come of age, they avenged their father's death and killed Ingialldus; Helgo and Roas then ruled together, before the latter eventually married the daughter of the King of England and came to rule there. In Sven Aggessen's account, Haldanus is the slayer of Frothi. In *Hrólfs saga* (ch. 1), Ingeld plays no part in the legend: Frodi and Halfdan are brothers and co-rulers; jealous of Halfdan's success, Frodi attacks and kills him in his hall; as in *Skjöldunga saga*, Halfdan's two sons, Hróar and Helgi, avenge their father's death and kill Frodi once they have come of age. For the texts, see Garmonsway, pp. 124–27 and 238–47. See further Chambers, *Introduction*, p. 21; K3, pp. xxxv–xxxvi; K4, pp. lv–lvi. For plot summaries of the relevant sections of *Skjöldunga saga* and *Hrólfs saga*, see the appendices to this volume.
[87] In Chapter Three, I discuss how all three of Beowulf's major monstrous adversaries are carefully woven into the dynastic drama, to serve as portents of impending royal crises and manifestations of internal and external threats to royal families.

> Mǣre þēoden,
> æþeling ǣrgōd, unblīðe sæt,
> þolode ðrȳð-swȳð, þegn-sorge drēah,
> syðþan hīe þæs lāðan lāst scēawedon,
> wergan gāstes; *wæs þat gewin tō strang,*
> *lāð ond longsum.*
> (129b–34a)
>
> [...]
>
> Swā *rīxode* ond wið rihte wan,
> āna wið eallum, oð ðæt īdel stōd
> hūsa sēlest. *Wæs sēo hwīl micel:*
> *twelf wintra tīd torn geþolode*
> *wine Scyldinga, wēana gehwelcne,*
> *sīdra sorga.*
> (144–59a)
>
> [...]
>
> Swā ða *mǣl-ceare* maga Healfdenes
> *sin-gāla sēað*; ne mihte snotor hæleð
> wēan onwendan; *wæs þæt gewin tō swȳð,*
> *lāþ ond longsum,* þē on ðā lēode becōm,
> *nȳd-wracu nīþ-grim, niht-bealwa mǣst.*
> (189–93). (Emphasis added).

[The famous prince, the noble good-of-old, sat miserably, *suffered a great pain, endured thane-sorrow,* after they examined the tracks of that loathsome one, cursed spirit. *That struggle was too great, hateful and long.* [...] So a certain one *held sway* against all, and fought against righteousness, until the best of houses stood empty. *That was a long time, twelve years,* that the friend of the Scyldings *endured suffering, each and every affliction, deep sorrows.* [...] So the kinsman of Healfdene *endured a time of sorrow, continually;* nor could the wise warrior expect a change; *that struggle was too great, hateful and long,* that had befallen the prince, *cruel afflictions, the greatest of night-sorrows.*]

This moving description of a once-mighty ruler rendered impotent by a powerful adversary stands in stark contrast to the preceding portrait of Scyld, who despite losing the power of speech (29b–30a) nevertheless remained *fela-hrōr*, 'very-strong' (27a), at the time of his death.[88] A series of lexical variations on the theme of Hrothgar's grief across these three linked passages suggests both the seemingly endless, cyclical nature of the old king's sorrow and a loss of momentum on the part of the dynasty over which he presides.

---

[88] Likewise, the great age of Hrothgar's ancestors, Beow (54: *lēof lēod-cyning longe þrāge*) and Healfdene (58: *gamol ond gūð-rēouw*), is, as we have seen, balanced by the youth of their sons.

Again help arrives for the Danes in the unexpected form of a hero from across the water:

> Þæt fram hām gefrægn   Higelāces þegn
> gōd mid Gēatum,   Grendles dǣda;   195
> sē wæs moncynnes   mægenes strengest
> on þǣm dæge   þysses līfes
> æþele ond ēacen.   Hēt him ȳðlidan
> gōdne gegyrwan;   cwæð, hē gūð-cyning
> ofer swan-rāde   sēcean wolde,   200
> mǣrne þēoden,   þā him was manna þearf.
> (194–201). (Emphasis added).

[From home Hygelac's thane, a good one among the Geats, heard about that, Grendel's deeds; *he was possessed of the greatest strength of all mankind in that day of this life, noble and prodigious.* He ordered them to make for him a good wave-traverser; he said that he would seek out the famous prince over the swan's riding, *since he was in need of men.*]

While the aged *gūð-cyning* sits fretting over the ruin of his royal hall, the young Geat is all action and determination. Acting on the advice of the old Geatish counsellors (202b: *snotere ceorles*), the headstrong prince's decisiveness is indicated by a series of active verbs as he orders a boat to be made and handpicks his own band of men: *Hēt him* [...] *gegyrwan; cwæð, hē* [...] *sēcean wolde; Hæfde* [...] *gecorone; hē* [...] *findan meahte* (188–201, 205–08a).[89] This strong sense of motion and intent that surrounds Beowulf in this passage is sustained in the compact and vivid description of his sea journey (210–18). Upon their arrival on the Danish shore, Beowulf's men disembark quickly (224b: *hraðe*), with their mail coats ringing out (224–27a).

Reversing the conventional association of age with wisdom, Beowulf declares that he can offer advice to Hrothgar, many years his senior, about how best to overcome the crisis of Grendel:[90]

> Ic þæs Hrōðgār mæg
> þurh rūmne sefan   rǣd gelǣran,
> hū hē *frōd ond gōd*   fēond oferswȳðeþ [...].
> (277b–79). (Emphasis added).

---

[89] This appears to contradict the narrator's subsequent statement that Hygelac had in fact tried to dissuade Beowulf from travelling to Denmark (1994b–97b), unless, of course, Hygelac was not one of the *snotere ceorlas*. See Chapter Two, p. 131.

[90] See Burrow, *Ages of Man*, pp. 123–34, on 'transcendence themes' which 'serve to mute contrasts between youth and age' in *Beowulf*. Porck, *Old Age*, pp. 177–211, argues that *Beowulf* is 'a mirror for elderly kings'.

[*I can offer Hrothgar counsel about that* (i.e. Grendel), *through a generous spirit, how he, old and wise, might overcome the enemy.*]

Underlining the hero's outsider-status in Denmark, both the coastguard and Hrothgar's *ār ond ombiht*, 'servant and herald' (336a), Wulfgar, treat the new arrival with circumspection, both inquiring of his lineage: *Nū ic ēower sceal/frum-cyn witan*, 'Now I must know of your ancestry' (251b–52a); *æfter æþelum frægn*, 'he inquired about (their) pedigree' (332b).[91] Speaking on behalf of his group, the hero identifies their tribe and allegiance, before revealing his own paternal ancestry:

> Wē synt gum-cynnes   Gēata lēode
> ond Higelāces   heorð-genēatas.
> Wæs mīn fæder   folcum gecȳþed
> æþele ord-fruma   Ecgþēow hāten;
> *gebād wintra worn   ǣr hē on weg hwurfe*
> *gamol of geardum*;   hine gearwe geman
> witena wēl-hwylc   wīde geond eorþan.
> (260–66). (Emphasis added).

[*We are of the race of the Geatish people and hearth-companions of Hygelac. My father was known to the people as a noble war-chief, called Ecgtheow, he experienced a great many winters before he departed on the journey, old from the courts, he is readily remembered by each of the wise ones throughout the wide earth.*]

We learn more about the hero's status within the Geatish ruling house from Hrothgar himself once Beowulf has finally been granted access to the presence of the Danish king:

> Hrōðgār maþelode,   helm Scyldinga:
> 'Ic hine cūðe   *cniht-wesende*;
> wæs his *eald-fæder*   Ecgþēo hāten,
> ðǣm tō hām forgeaf   Hrēþel Gēata
> āngan dohtor;   is his *eafora* nū
> heard hēr cumen,   sōhte holdne wine. [...].'
> (371–76). (Emphasis added).

[*Hrothgar made a speech, Protector of the Scyldings: "I knew him when he was still a child; his old father was called Ecgtheow, to whom Hrethel of the Geats gave his only daughter in marriage; his son is now come bravely here, to seek out a dear friend. [...]."*]

From these two short biographies we learn the essential details about Beowulf's paternal and maternal lineage. As a descendant of the dynastic

---

[91] J. M. Hill, *Narrative Pulse*, pp. 21–42, provides a sensitive analysis of the various tensions, spoken and unspoken, arising from Beowulf's arrival in Denmark.

founder, Hrethel, via the weaker, maternal line, Beowulf is an unlikely candidate for the Geatish throne.[92] The fact that no other character in the poem has their ancestry explained with such care may be suggestive of the introduction of a new, fictional character into a legendary framework.[93]

The rapid development of Beowulf's relationship with Hrothgar on what appears to be his second visit to Denmark, and the implications this will have for the future of the Scylding house, provide the main impetus for this section of the dynastic drama. In place of the relatively straightforward model of father-to-son succession exemplified in the opening lines, we now find a decidedly more complex scenario with multiple royal *eaforan* ('sons, offspring, descendants') in the Danish court. Although Beowulf's stated mission is to help the Danish king by ridding his court of the menace of Grendel, his presence in Heorot only serves to further complicate the dynastic situation. Having formerly acted as Beowulf's protector during a vulnerable period of his youth, the aged Hrothgar himself now stands in desperate need of the young Geat's help.[94] Yet, in gratefully accepting Beowulf's offer of help and taking the extraordinary measure of turning over control of Heorot to an outsider, Hrothgar is effectively conceding that the once-mighty Scyldings are no longer able to defend their own territory. As we shall see, the king's decision to entrust the protection of the royal hall to a foreign prince with no blood-ties to the dynasty will give prominent members of the court cause for concern.

Beowulf's outsider status among the Scyldings is first brought to the fore by the drunken and jealous outburst of Unferth (409–528). Though apparently not a member of the royal family, this complex and much-discussed figure enjoys an influential position in Heorot as Hrothgar's *þyle*, 'orator, spokesman' (1165, 1465).[95] It is unclear what role, if any, Unferth played in Scylding legend. Indeed, the absence of an equivalent figure in extant Scandinavian accounts may suggest that Unferth is another innovation of the *Beowulf*-poet, designed to serve simply as a foil for Beowulf.[96] In

---

[92] Much later we learn that Beowulf was fostered at Hrethel's court from the age of seven and treated with equal respect to the three young Hrethlings (2426–34).

[93] See Chapter Two, pp. 105, 118–21, 126–39, on Beowulf's fictionality.

[94] In another case of role-reversal, again suggestive of deliberate patterning on the poet's part, Beowulf himself will later act as protector – in the capacity of vice-regent – to the young Hrethling king, Heardred, following the premature death of his father, King Hygelac. On the possibility that Hrothulf acted as regent to Hrethric and Hrothmund after Hrothgar's death, see p. 73 n.149.

[95] On the characterization of Unferth and references to the wealth of criticism on this topic, see *CCB*, pp. 245–49. See also now L. Neidorf, 'Unferth's Ambiguity and the Trivialization of Germanic Antiquity', *Neophilologus* 101 (2017), 439–54.

[96] See J. D. A. Ogilvy, 'Unferth: Foil to Beowulf?' *PMLA* 79 (1964), 370–75; R. D. Fulk, 'Unferth and his Name', *MP* 85 (1987), 113–27. G. R. Wieland, 'The Unferth Engima: The *þyle* between the Hero and the Poet', in *Fact and Fiction:*

addition to providing a spur to the hero's own recount of his superhuman swimming exploits with Breca, Unferth also plays a significant role in the dynastic drama as an embodiment of the sin of fratricide (587–89) at the very centre of the court: *æt fōtum sæt frēan Scyldinga*, 'sat at the feet of the Lord of the Scyldings' (500, 1166a). In this way, Unferth provides a human link between the inner workings of the Danish court and the Cainite monster, Grendel, whose nightly attacks have reduced the Scyldings to their present state of misery and fear.[97]

Following Beowulf's public rebuke of Unferth, harmony is temporarily restored in the royal hall as now Queen Wealhtheow, in a carefully stage-managed scene, rises to distribute the drinking-cup among the warriors:

Ðǣr wæs hæleþa hleahtor, hlyn swynsode,
word wǣron wynsume. Ēode Wealhþēo forð,
cwēn Hrōðgāres *cynna gemyndig*,
grētte gold-hroren guman on healle,
ond þā frēolic wīf ful gesealde   615
ǣrest Ēast-Dena ēþel-wearde,
bæd hine blīðne æt þǣre bēor-þege,
lēodum lēofne; hē on lust geþeah
symbel ond sele-ful, sige-rōf kyning.
Ymbēode þā ides Helminga   620
duguþe ond geogoþe dǣl ǣghwylcne,
sinc-fato sealde, oþ þæt sǣl ālamp
þæt hīo Bēowulfe, bēag-hroden cwēn
mōde geþungen *medo-ful ætbǣr;*
grētte *Gēata lēod*, Gode þancode   625
wīs-fæst wordum þæs ðe hire se willa gelamp
þæt hēo on ǣnigne eorl gelȳfde
fyrena frōfre.
(611–28a). (Emphasis added).

[There was laughter of warriors, the clamour resounded, the talk was joyful, Wealhtheow went forth, Hrothgar's queen, *mindful of kin (or customs?)*, decorated in gold, greeting the warriors in the hall, and *that generous woman gave*

From the Middle Ages to Modern Times, Essays Presented to Hans Sauer on the Occasion of his 65th Birthday, Part II, Münchner Universitätsschriften, vol. 37, ed. R. Bauer and U. Krischke (Frankfurt, 2011), pp. 35–46, suggests that Unferth may have assisted Hrothgar in a power struggle against the latter's elder brother Heorogar, during which he was compelled to commit fratricide out of loyalty to his lord – the only scenario in which such a deed could be tolerated. However, as we have seen, there is no clear indication of any such struggle between Hrothgar and Heorogar over the Danish succession either in *Beowulf* or in wider Scandinavian tradition. On Heorogar's absence from the Scandinavian sources, see above, pp. 48–49.

[97] On Grendel and the devil, see Chapter Three, pp. 162–73.

the cup first to the homeland-protector of the East-Danes, bade him to be joyful at that beer-taking, beloved prince; he happily received the feast and hall-cup, courageous-in-victory king. Then *the lady of the Helmings went around the old and young retainers*, gave a portion of the drinking-cup to each, *until that time came that she*, ring-adorned queen, excellent in mind, *carried the mead-cup to Beowulf.* She greeted *the prince of the Geats*, thanked God with secure-in-wisdom words that her wish had been fulfilled, *that she might trust any warrior to bring about relief for the crimes.*]

In offering the mead first to her king, Hrothgar, and then in turn to the company of old and young men before finally presenting it to the newcomer, Beowulf, the queen demonstrates her respect for decorum while at the same time reasserting Danish authority within the hall. The symbolic distribution of the mead-cup by a royal woman (*ides*) as a display of courtly etiquette and social cohesion is, of course, a familiar trope in Old English poetry, and *DOE* accordingly translates *cynna gemyndig* here as 'mindful of what is fitting, proper behaviour'.[98] However, given the more common use of the term *cynn* throughout the poem to denote 'family, race or people', and the special attention given to Wealhtheow's concern for the future of the young Scyldings, it is possible that the phrase could have a double meaning in this instance, as both 'mindful of customs *and* kin'.[99] Implicit in this passage is the queen's lack of faith in the abilities of the various *eorlas* assembled in Heorot, including her own sons and nephews, to protect Heorot against Grendel. In her courteous but guarded welcome of the young Geat, we see the first hint of the queen's heightened sensitivity to the dynastic implications of the presence of this powerful outsider in the Scyldings' midst.

In contrast to the queen's decidedly circumspect treatment of Beowulf, Hrothgar wastes little time in declaring his absolute faith in this brave young warrior, whom he had fostered as a boy. Having handed Beowulf temporary control of Heorot, the king departs, leaving Beowulf in his stead (655–61):

Đā him Hrōþgār gewāt[100] mid his hæleþa gedryht,
eodur Scyldinga   ūt of healle;
wolde wīg-fruma   Wealhþēo sēcan,

---

[98] *DOE*, s. v. *cynn* adj.: 'b.i. *cynna gemunan / gemyndig beon* ('to be mindful of what is fitting, proper behaviour'); 5.e.: 'to be mindful of social distinction', cf. *Genesis A*, 2431: *cynna gemunde riht and gerisno.*' See also K4, p. 362, s. v. *cyn(n)*, (adj. &) nja.: '*proper procedure, etiquette, courtesy.*' For an overview of the trope, see M. J. Enright, *Lady with a Mead Cup: Ritual, Prophecy and Lordship in the European warband from La Tène to the Viking Age* (Dublin, 1996).

[99] Cf. *eotena cyn* (421a), *Wedera cyn* (461b), and the sole other instance of *cynn* as a genitive plural in the poem: *līf ēac gesceōp / cynna gehwylcum*, 'he created all life, every kind of living thing' (97b–98a).

[100] Cf. 26a: *Him ðā Scyld gewāt*, 'Scyld then took himself away.'

> cwēn tō gebeddan.   *Hæfde kyning-wuldor*   665
> Grendle tōgēanes,   swā guman gefrugnon,
> *sele-weard āseted; sundor-nytte behēold*
> *ymb aldor Dena,*   eoton-weard ābēad.
> (662–68). (Emphasis added).

[*Then Hrothgar took himself away* with his lordly troop of warriors, *shelter of the Scyldings*, out of the hall; the war-chief wished to seek Wealhtheow, the queen, as a bed-companion. The *glory-king* had established against Grendel, as men have heard, *a hall-guardian*; the giant-guardian offered, *performed a special service for the lord of the Danes*.][101]

The dynastic implications of Hrothgar's relinquishing of authority within the hall to Beowulf only start to emerge once the hero's victory over Grendel is made known. With the hall cleansed (825: *gefǣlsod*), the Geatish prince now finds himself cast as the saviour of the Danes:

> Denum eallum wearð
> æfter þām wæl-ræse   willa gelumpen:
> hæfde þā gefǣlsod   sē þe ǣr feorran cōm,   825
> snotor ond swȳð-ferhð,   sele Hrōðgāres,
> genered wið nīðe.   Niht-weorce gefeh,
> ellen-mǣrþum.   Hæfde Ēast-Denum
> Gēat-mecga lēod   gilp gelǣsted,
> swylce oncȳþðe   *ealle gebētte*,   830
> *inwid-sorge   þe hīe ǣr drugon*
> *ond for þrēa-nȳdum   þolian scoldon,*
> *torn unlȳtel.*
> (823b–33a). (Emphasis added).

[He had fulfilled all the wishes of the Danes after that slaughter-rush, the one who had come from afar, wise and brave-hearted, saved the hall of Hrothgar against hostility. He rejoiced in the night's work, glorious deeds. The prince of the Geatish people had fulfilled his boast to the East-Danes and *completely remedied all their distress, deep sorrows that they previously suffered and because of terrible affliction had been forced to endure, a great deal of grief*.]

Close verbal parallels with the opening account of the establishment of the Scylding dynasty once more invite us to consider Beowulf as a new Scyld (14b–16a: *fyren-ðearfe ongeat / þæt hīe ǣr drugon aldorlēase / lange hwīle*, 'He recognized their terrible need, that they had suffered without a lord for a long time').[102] With the Scylding succession still unresolved, however, the introduction of this popular foreign champion adds a new dimension to the dynastic drama, namely the tension between popular election and

---

[101] On the ambiguous syntax of this passage, see the note in K4, p. 157.
[102] On Beowulf and Scyld, see above p. 55 and below, Chapter Two.

The Dynastic Life-Cycle and the Structure of the Poem

ancestry as qualifying factors in succession:[103]

> Ðǣr wæs Bēowulfes
> mǣrðo mǣned;   monig oft gecwæð
> þætte sūð nē norð   be sǣm twēonum
> ofer eormen-grund   ōþer nǣnig
> under swegles begong   *sēlra nǣre*   860
> *rond-hæbbendra,   rīces wyrðra.*
> Nē hīe hūru wine-drihten   wiht ne lōgon,
> glædne Hrōðgār,   ac þæt wæs gōd cyning.
> (856b–63). (Emphasis added).

[There Beowulf's glory was made known; many often said that, south nor north, between the seas, over the wide earth, under the expanse of the sky, *there was no better shield-carrier, worthier of a kingdom*. Nor did they in any way blame the beloved lord, gracious Hrothgar, for that was a good king.]

Despite the rejoinder that the Danes were not critical of their own king, this public proclamation of Beowulf as a future ruler threatens to undermine the position of both Hrothgar and the young Scylding princes.

Beowulf's future career as king is also an underlying theme in the Danish court-poet's ensuing song concerning the exploits of Sigemund, the legendary dragon-slayer, and Heremod, the poem's first example of bad kingship. Scholars have speculated as to why this *scop* should choose to introduce these two particular figures, both of whom are associated with crimes (879a: *fæhðe ond fyrena*, 'feuds and crimes'; 915b: *hine fyren onwōd*, 'evil entered him'), into his song in honour of Beowulf.[104] However, both legends are apposite when viewed from a dynastic perspective: it was Heremod's deposition that resulted in the interregnum before the arrival of Scyld Scefing and the (re-)foundation of the Scylding line, while Sigemund's dragon-slaying exploits anticipate Beowulf's own death, an event that will bring to an end the royal line of the Hrethlings. In this way, the legends of Sigemund and Heremod effectively provide the inspiration for the two major dynastic events that bookend the poem, the rise of the Scyldings and the fall of the Hrethlings.[105] The introduction of Heremod at this particular juncture in the narrative, rather than in his more natural chronological position before Scyld, provides further evidence of the poet's careful and deliberate foregrounding of themes pertinent to different stages of the dynastic life-cycle. Indeed, Heremod's failure to live

---

[103] See Swanton, *Crisis and Development*; and Biggs, 'Politics of Succession'.
[104] For a summary of the arguments, see *CCB*, pp. 104–14. See further Chapter Two, pp. 150, 159 n.23.
[105] See Chapter Two, pp. 106–09. Sigemund's legendary nephew, Fitela, may also have provided the inspiration for the figure of Wiglaf.

up to his early promise inverts the pattern of dynastic progress presented thus far:[106]

> Hē mid Ēotenum wearð
> on fēonda geweald   forð forlācen,
> snūde forsended.   Hine sorh-wylmas
> lemedon tō lange; *hē his lēodum wearð*   905
> *eallum æþellingum   tō aldor-ceare;*
> swylce oft bemearn   ǣrran mǣlum
> swīð-ferhþes sīð   snotor ceorl monig,
> *sē þe him bealwa tō   bōte gelȳfde,*
> *þæt þæt ðēodnes bearn   geþēon scolde,*   910
> fæder-æþelum onfōn,   folc gehealdan,
> hord ond hlēo-burh,   hæleþa rīce,
> ēþel Scyldinga.
> (902b–13a). (Emphasis added).

[He was betrayed into the power of enemies among the Jutes, swiftly dispatched. Sorrow-surgings oppressed him for a long time; *to his own people, to all the æthelings, he had become a great sorrow*; many a wise man often lamented in previous times his strong-minded ways, *those who had turned to him for a remedy from suffering, hoped that that prince's son would prosper*, inherit his father's nobility, protect the people, hoard and stronghold, kingdom of warriors, homeland of the Scyldings.]

In concluding his summary of the *scop*'s song of Heremod, however, the narrator emphasizes that his own hero, Beowulf, is not destined to repeat Heremod's mistakes:

> Hē þǣr eallum *wearð*,
> mǣg Higelāces,   manna cynne
> frēondum gefǣgra;   hine fyren onwōd.
> (913b–15). (Emphasis added).

[He (i.e. Beowulf) *became* a better friend to mankind, the kinsman of Hygelac; evil entered him (i.e. Heremod).][107]

Indeed, at King Beowulf's funeral, the Geats will praise their beloved ruler for his superlative mildness, kindness, generosity and love of fame

---

[106] Hrothgar will later echo the *scop*'s sentiment, lamenting Heremod's failure to fulfil his potential: *ne gewēox hē him tō willan ac tō wæl-fealle/ ond tō dēað-cwalum Deniga lēodum*, 'he did not grow as they wished, but for their slaughter, and to the deadly destruction of the people of the Danes' (1711–12). For the argument that the tale of Scyld and Beow is a poetic innovation, original to our poet, designed to serve as a counterpoint to the traditional tale of Heremod's decline, see Chapter Two, pp. 139–51.

[107] For the possibility that the object of this half-line could in fact be Beowulf, see *CCB*, p. 113.

The Dynastic Life-Cycle and the Structure of the Poem

(3180–82).[108] Nevertheless, the inclusion of this cautionary tale of a ruler who failed in his duty to his people at this particular juncture, immediately after the Danes have proclaimed Beowulf as a future king, serves as a timely reminder to the audience that not all promising young princes will develop into good kings.

In another major development in the dynastic drama, soon after the *scop*'s song of Sigemund and Heremod, the Danish king declares his intention to adopt Beowulf as his own son:

> Nū ic, Bēowulf, þēc,
> secg betesta, mē for sunu wylle
> frēogan on ferhþe; heald forð tela
> nīwe sibbe.[109]
> (946b–49a).

[Now I would have you as a son for myself, Beowulf, best of men, to cherish in my heart; from now on hold well this new relationship (*or* kinship).]

It was common practice in the early medieval period for young princes to be fostered at a foreign court, sometimes as royal 'hostages'.[110] Beowulf himself, we later learn, was reared from the age of seven at the court of his maternal grandfather, Hrethel, alongside his three uncles, Herebeald, Hæthcyn and Hygelac (2428–34). However, we might reasonably ask why King Hrothgar, who has two young sons of his own (Hrethric and Hrothmund) and two nephews (Heoroweard and Hrothulf), all of whom are legitimate contenders for the throne, should wish to further complicate an already potentially fraught succession by adopting Beowulf. One possibility is that Hrothgar may have taken this measure in order to reassert his own royal authority by making an ally of this rising young prince. Alternatively, the Danish king may have simply wished to resume the close relationship that he had with Beowulf during the period of Ecgtheow's exile.[111] A third possibility, and one supported by the following exchanges in court involving Wealhtheow, is that the king has by now come to see Beowulf as a potential heir.[112] Although the hero is in fact des-

---

[108] See below, pp. 227–31.
[109] On the meaning of *sibb*, see below, p. 65–66.
[110] See, for example, R. Lavelle, 'The use and abuse of hostages in later Anglo-Saxon England', *EME* 14 (2006), 269–96.
[111] As he departs from the Danes in order to confront Grendel's mother, Beowulf reminds Hrothgar that he had promised *ðū mē ā wǣre/ forðgewitenum on fæder stǣle*, 'you would always be like a father to me when I went forth (i.e. died)' (1478b–80); the hero then requests that, should he die in the mere, Hrothgar will look after his men and send his armour to Hygelac (1480–84).
[112] In a recent article, T. D. Hill highlights a parallel between the account of how Hrothgar *stōd on stapole* (926a) at the beginning of this speech and Saxo's account of the early Danish practice of standing on a stone to elect a king

tined to rule another kingdom, the poet uses Beowulf's brief appearance in the Danish court to explore the intrigues of the house of Scyld during a critical period in its history.[113]

The first hint of the troubles that await the Scyldings appears soon after Hrothgar has announced his plan to adopt Beowulf. During the same feasting scene in Heorot, we are presented with Hrothgar and Hrothulf, uncle and nephew, seated together in the hall and sharing the mead-cup in a scene of familial harmony:

>   fægere geþægon
> medo-ful manig   *māgas þāra*   1015
> swīð-hicgende   on sele þām hēan,
> Hrōðgār ond Hrōþulf.   Heorot innan wæs
> frēondum āfylled;   nalles fācen-stafas
> Þēod-Scyldingas   *þenden* fremedon.
> (1014b–19). (Emphasis added).

[Many a cup full of mead was passed with ceremony among the *kinsmen*, brave-hearted ones, in that high hall, Hrothgar and Hrothulf. Heorot was filled with friends; not at all did the People-Scyldings perform acts of malice *at that time*.]

Hrothulf's seniority among the group of young Scyldings is indicated by the prominent position he occupies in the court, next to the king himself. This friendly scene is overshadowed, however, by an allusion to future family discord.[114] Significantly, immediately after this passage we learn

---

(*History of the Danes* i. 2. 1; Friis-Jensen, I, pp. 20–21) ('Hrothgar's Speech of Adoption: A Danish-Latin Analogue', *NQ* 66 [2019], 163–66). As Hill notes, this analogue lends further support for the view that Hrothgar was indeed making public his intention to appoint Beowulf as the next king of the Danes, explaining Wealhtheow's subsequent anxiety about the future of her sons and nephew(s). See further G. P. Braccini, 'Perché Hrōðgar *Stod on Stapole* (*Beowulf* 926a)', in *Echi di Memoria: Scritti di varia filologia, critica e linguistica in recordo di Giorgio Chiarini*, ed. G. Chiappini (Florence, 1998), pp. 139–57; K4, pp. 172–73.

[113] On the intersection of originality and tradition in *Beowulf*, see Chapter Two.

[114] As Orchard notes, the unusual placement of the adjective *þenden*, 'at that time', as the headstave (i.e. the item that determines the alliteration) of line 1019 strongly implies that there will come a time when relations between the Scyldings – if not necessarily Hrothgar and Hrothulf – will not be so harmonious (*CCB*, pp. 245–46). Orchard compares the placement of *þenden* as the alliterating headstave in 1019b with the equally unusual – and therefore emphatic – stress placed on the demonstrative pronouns in the repeated formula *on þǣm dæge þysses līfes* (197, 790, 806). Orchard notes that out of fourteen instances in *Beowulf*, only here and perhaps in a parallel passage (284b: *þrēa-nyd þolað þenden þǣr wunað*) does *þenden* bear alliteration (*CCB*, p. 246, n. 28). However, 284b is a C-type line (Bliss, *Metre of Beowulf*, p. 141, scans this half line as a 2C2b-type), with the alliteration falling on *þǣr*, meaning that the alliterative stress on *þenden* in 1019b is indeed unique. On the contested meaning of the hapax *fācen-stafas*, see K4, p. 177. There is no evidence of discord between Hrólfr (OE Hrothulf)

that, in addition to various other treasures, Hrothgar gave Beowulf *brand Healfdenes*, 'Healfdene's sword', another dynastic token to complement Heorogar's battle-gear.[115] The poet does not register the reaction of the young Scyldings to their father's decision to bestow these family heirlooms on this foreign champion, though, as we shall see, the queen is firmly set against Hrothgar's planned adoption of Beowulf.[116]

A second allusion to future discord among the Scyldings occurs soon after the Danish *scop*'s song about Finn's sons – discussed in detail below – as Wealhtheow once more distributes the mead-cup to Hrothgar and Hrothulf:

> Þā cwōm Wealhþēo forð
> gān under gyldnum bēage   þǣr þā gōdan twēgen
> sǣton *suhterge-fæderan;   þā gȳt wæs hiera sib ætgædere,*
> ǣghwylc ōðrum trȳwe.[117]
> (1162b–65a). (Emphasis added).

[Then Wealhtheow came forth, advancing under her golden diadem, to where that goodly pair sat, *uncle-and-nephew; their kinship was still together at that time*, each true to the other.]

The poet uses similar temporal constructions elsewhere, such as *ne wæs hit lenge þā gen*, 'it was not long after' (83b), and *oð ðæt*, 'until that' (100b, 2116b, 2210b), in order to set up antitheses between present happiness and future strife.[118] Yet, much to the frustration of modern scholars, the poet refrains from providing any further details of this anticipated conflict between the Scyldings, relying on his audience's prior knowledge of the legend. Many have taken the headstave of 1164b, *sib*, to mean 'peace' or 'truce'.[119] However, given the alliteration of *sib* with *suhterge-fæderan*, a

---

and Roas (OE Hrothgar) in Scandinavian tradition. Most of the sources agree, however, in presenting Hjorvard (OE Heoroweard) as the killer of Hrólfr.

[115] The MS reading *brand Healfdenes* (1020b) is retained by the editors of K4, who take it to mean that Hrothgar gave Healfdene's sword (varying line 1023: *māþum-sweord*) to Beowulf, though previous editors had often emended to *bearn Healfdenes*, 'son of Healfdene (i.e. Hrothgar)', or taken *brand Healfdenes* to be a kenning for Hrothgar. For discussion of this crux, see K4, pp. 178–79.

[116] See below, p. 72–76.

[117] Given the unusual placement of alliterative stress on the term *þenden* in the first passage alluding to future discord among the Scyldings, it may be significant that this passage is also metrically irregular, occuring in the first of only two hypermetric sections in the poem (1163–68). Orchard describes this second passage as 'a self-contained vignette of the Danish court' (*CCB*, p. 67). The other, shorter, hypermetric passage occupies lines 1705–07, near the opening of Hrothgar's 'sermon'.

[118] On the structural importance of *oð ðæt* constructions in the poem, see Irving, *Reading*, pp. 31–42.

[119] B-T, s. v. *sibb*. III: 'peace, the opposite of war'. Liuzza, for example, renders this

rare dvandva compound meaning 'nephew (brother's son) and (paternal) uncle',[120] the alternative sense of 'kinship' seems if anything more suitable here.[121] Indeed, both terms are used in this sense in *Widsith*, again in collocation with *ætgædere/ætsomne*, in a passage referring to the same figures:[122]

> Hrōþwulf ond Hrōðgār   *hēoldon lengest*
> *sibbe ætsomne   suhtor-fæðran;*
> siþþan hȳ forwræcon   wīcinga cynn
> ond Ingeldes   ord forbigdan,
> forhēowan æt Heorote   Heaðobeardna þrym
> (*Widsith*, 45–9). (Emphasis added).

[Hrothulf and Hrothgar *held kinship together most closely, uncle and nephew*; then they avenged the viking host and withheld Ingeld's vanguard, cut down at Heorot the might of the Heathobards.]

The close verbal parallels between these two passages indicate that they are both derived from the same royal legend, in which Hrothulf and Hrothgar were close allies bound by ties of *sib*, 'kinship', rather than deadly enemies. The *Beowulf*-poet's statement that each was true to the other (1165a: *æghwylc ōðrum trȳwe*) is usually taken to refer directly to Hrothulf and Hrothgar. However, it should be noted that Wealhtheow herself uses the same construction soon after in a more expansive sense, with *ōþrum* as a collective singular, in reference to all the *eorlas* gathered in the hall: *Hēr is æghwylc eorl ōþrum getrȳwe*, 'here every warrior is true

---

half-line: 'their peace was still whole then' (p. 125). For occurrences of *sibb* in the sense of 'peace' in *Beowulf*, see lines 154b, 1857a and 2922b.

[120] K4, s. v. *suhterge-fæderan* (p. 437). The paternal element of this relationship is significant, in that it distinguishes Hrothulf and Hrothgar's kinship from that between Beowulf and his (maternal) uncle Hygelac. On the privileged nature of paternal uncle-nephew relations in early Germanic culture, see Bremmer, 'Uncle and Nephew in *Beowulf*'. See below, pp. 70, 95, 121–39.

[121] B-T, s. v. *sibb*. I: 'relationship'. Indeed, the editors of K4 give the primary sense of the term in the poem as 'kinship', before 'friendship, peace' (p. 433). Having announced that he wishes to adopt Beowulf as his son, Hrothgar instructs the hero to cherish their *nīwe sibbe*, 'new kinship' (949a). Similarly, when Beowulf recalls how, in his youth, his grandfather Hrethel *geaf mē sinc ond symbel, sibbe gemunde*, 'gave me treasure and feasting, mindful of (our) kinship' (2431). Finally, it is Wiglaf's sense of *sibb*, 'kinship' (2600b), with Beowulf that motivates him alone to come to the wounded king's aid, after the other *hand-gesteallan*, 'hand-picked comrades' (2596b), have fled to the woods in terror of the dragon.

[122] This is the only other appearance of *suhter/suhtor(ge)-fæderan* in the corpus. On the closeness of *Beowulf* and *Widsith*, see *CCB*, pp. 115–16. Orchard notes the commonality of *suhter/suhtor(ge)-fæderan* to *Beowulf* and *Widsith* (*CCB*, pp. 246–47), but does not comment on the collocation of this term with *sib* and *ætgædere/ætsomne* in both texts.

The Dynastic Life-Cycle and the Structure of the Poem

to the other' (1228).[123] It is possible, therefore, that lines 1164b–65a allude to a time when kin-relations will break down between other members of the dynasty, rather than to any conflict between this famous uncle-and-nephew pair who are elsewhere presented as close friends. Some have argued that Hrothulf later acted as a traitor, murdering Hrothgar's son, Hrethric, in order to seize the throne.[124] However, only in Saxo's paraphrase of *Bjarkamál* is King Rolf (OE Hrothulf) referred to as the killer of Røricus (OE Hrethric) (I.ii.7.14), and it is unclear what relationship, if any, this Røricus has with the Danish royal family: Saxo describes him as 'the son of Bøgi the miser' rather than as a son of Roar (OE Hrothgar) or cousin of Rolf.[125] Moreover, the theory that it was necessary for Hrothulf to kill Hrethric in order to take the throne after Hrothgar's death is predicated on the misconception that primogeniture was a factor in early Germanic succession.[126] Indeed, in all the extant Scandinavian versions of this legend, King Hrothulf (ON Rolf; Latin Rolvo) in fact succeeds his father, King Halga (ON Helgi; Latin Helgi), unopposed. Some years later, Heoroweard (ON Hjǫrvard; Latin Hiarwardus/Hiarvarthar), who is presented not as Hrothulf's paternal cousin but as the husband of his sister, Skuld (Latin Sculda), leads a revolt against Hrothulf, attacking him in his hall and killing him together with his warriors. Heoroweard is himself then slain by a warrior loyal to Hrothulf, with the result that, in some accounts, Hrethric takes the throne.[127] That the poet should choose to leave the fates of the Scyldings in the balance fits with this transitional phase of the dynastic life-cycle, in which conflicts between members of the royal kin take place either in the near future or, as in the tale of Finn's sons discussed below, in the legendary past.

---

[123] Cf. K4, p. 423.
[124] See Olrik, *The Heroic Legends of Denmark*, pp. 68–74; Malone, 'Hrethric', pp. 275–82; K3, p. 169; Chambers, *Introduction*, pp. 25–27. See also Newton, *Origins*, pp. 85–88; *CCB*, pp. 245–46.
[125] For the text, see Friis-Jensen, I, pp. 130–31. See further Lawrence, *Epic Tradition*, p. 76; Chambers, *Introduction*, pp. 21–29. This reference to 'Bøgi' is generally considered an error on Saxo's part, perhaps stemming from a misreading of ON *hnoggvandbaugi*, 'greedy for rings' (Friis-Jensen, I, p. 131, n. 12). William Cooke has argued that this 'Røricus' is in fact identical with the 'Rærecus' mentioned in *Skjöldunga saga* as the brother of Frodo, who helps the latter to kill Roas (OE Hrothgar) and eventually succeeds Hjorvard to the throne, rather than Roas/Hrothgar's son or cousin of Rolf/Hrothulf: 'Hrothulf: A Richard III or an Alfred the Great?', *SP* 104 (2007), 175–98, at 188. For the translated text, see Garmonsway, p. 207.
[126] See above, p. 19. See further Morgan, 'Treachery of Hrothulf'; Mitchell, 'Literary Lapses', 10–14.
[127] For plot-summaries of the major sources, see Appendices.

The Tale of Finn's Sons

The placement of the Danish court poet's recitation of the tale of Finn's sons, the so-called 'Finnsburg Episode' (1063–59a), during the feasting-scene in Heorot discussed above has important ramifications for the dynastic drama. Scholars have generally taken the view that this passage is included in order to introduce themes such as maternal grief, failed peaceweaving and revenge that are brought to the fore with the arrival of Grendel's mother (1255b–1306a).[128] However, the wedding of Hildeburh and Finn itself is not described in the episode and, as Peter Baker has recently observed, the poet is reticent with details of the feud between the Half-Danes and Frisians.[129] In the discussion that follows, I read the tragic tale of Finn's sons as a tragic variation on the opening account of the rise of the Scyldings and a further hint of the imminent breakdown in kinship that will threaten this same dynasty's survival.[130]

Through comparison with *The Finnsburg Fragment*, it is possible to reconstruct a rough outline of the legend, such as might have been known to the original audience of *Beowulf*:[131]

> Hildeburh, a princess of the Half-Danes, travels to Frisia to marry King Finn, perhaps in order to settle a feud between the two peoples; some years later, a party of Half-Danes led by Hnæf, visits Hildeburh and Finn; the Half-Danes are attacked by Finn's men; after bravely defending themselves in Finn's hall, the Half-Danes are overrun, with a large number of casualties on both sides, among them Hnæf; a great funeral is held for Hnæf and the others who fell in this battle; a truce is agreed, the terms of which allow the Danes, now led by Hengest, to remain in Finn's hall during the winter while the seas are frozen; once springtime comes, Hengest takes his revenge on Finn, killing him and many of his men, before returning home with Hildeburh, who has by now lost her husband and at least one son in the feud.[132]

---

[128] For an overview of the vast amount of scholarship on this passage and a detailed discussion of its themes and content, see *CCB*, pp. 173–87. On Hildeburh and peaceweaving, see Lawrence, *Epic Tradition*, p. 126; Sklute, 'Freoðuwebbe'; Neidorf, 'Hildeburh's mourning'. For a recent re-assessment of the critical construction of the figure of the 'peace-weaving queen', see Baker, *Honour*, pp. 103–38. Baker discusses this passage in the wider context of 'the perils of peacemaking' (pp. 167–99). M. Cavell, *Weaving Words and Binding Bodies: The Poetics of Human Experience in Old English Literature* (Toronto, 2016), pp. 280–95, suggests *freoðu-webbe* should be translated as 'peace-maker' rather than 'peace-weaver'.
[129] Baker, *Honour*, p. 169.
[130] See below, pp. 177–80, for the role of Grendel's mother.
[131] On the *Fragment*, see Introduction, p. 11.
[132] For a detailed discussion of the Finnsburg legend and comparison with *The Finnsburg Fragment*, see Tolkien, *Finn and Hengest*; K4, pp. 273–81.

The Dynastic Life-Cycle and the Structure of the Poem

The description of Hengest's party as Scyldings (1069b, 1108b, 1154a), Danes (1090b, 1158b) and Half-Danes (1069a) invites us to view them as ancestors of the current royal house.[133] The inclusion of the episode at this point allows the *Beowulf*-poet to foreground aspects of the dynastic drama previously suppressed in the narrative through the medium of the *scop*, specifically the premature deaths of royal fathers, sons, uncles and nephews. In addition to foreshadowing the attacks of Grendel's mother, the *scop*'s song thereby provides a cautionary tale for the audience of Scyldings gathered in Heorot, some of whom are likewise destined to fall in a family feud:[134]

> Þǣr wæs sang ond swēg   samod ætgadere
> fore Healfdenes   hilde-wīsan,
> gomen-wudu grēted,   gid oft wrecen,   1065
> ðonne heal-gamen[135]   Hrōþgāres scop
> æfter medo-benc   mǣnan scolde
> *Finnes eaferan*;[136]   ðā hīe se fǣr begeat,
> hæleð Healf-Dena,   Hnæf Scyldinga
> in Frēs-wæle   *feallan scolde*.   1070
> (1063–70). (Emphasis added).

[There was song and noise joined together in the presence of Healfdene's battle-leader, the joy-wood was plucked, stories often recited, when Hrothgar's *scop* had to recount along the mead-benches his hall-entertainment about *Finn's sons*; how quickly the warrior of the Half-Danes, Hnæf of the Scyldings, *had to fall* in the Frisian slaughter.]

---

[133] This link is consolidated by the reference to Hrothgar as *Healfdenes hilde-wīsan*, 'Healfdene's battle-chief' (1064), immediately before the description of Hengest's men as *hæleð Healf-Dena*, 'warriors of the Half-Danes' (1069a).

[134] Hrothgar is himself referred to twice as Healfdene's *sunu*, 'son' (1009b, 1040b), in the lines immediately preceding the tale of *Finnes eaferan*. Most editions, including K3, emend MS *brand Healfdenes* (1020b) to *bearn Healfdenes*; K4, however, retains the MS reading on grammatical grounds. Other references to Hrothgar as Healfdene's son (*sunu/bearn*) appear at lines 268a, 344b, 469a, 645a, 1652b, 1699a, and as Healfdene's kinsman (*maga/mago*) at lines 1474b, 1867a, 2011b, 2143b, 2147a.

[135] The editors of K4 treat MS *heal-gamen* as a personal name, the subject of *mǣnan scolde*. It is possible that Hrothgar's *scop* is named here, in the manner of the fictional poets Widsith and Deor. However, I follow the practice of early editors here in taking it as a noun meaning literally 'hall-game', varying *gid*; it would seem strange to name Hrothgar's *scop* here given that court poets are unnamed elsewhere in the text. For a list of named Anglo-Saxon poets, see E. V. Thornbury, *Becoming a Poet in Anglo-Saxon England*, Cambridge Studies in Medieval Literature 88 (Cambridge, 2014), pp. 243–47.

[136] MS *eaferum* is emended to *eaferan* in K4 and many other editions and is usually taken to mean 'sons' rather than 'men' on the grounds of similar usage elsewhere in the poem. Some editors also insert the preposition *be* at the beginning of the line; see K4, pp. 180–81.

In the long and vivid description of the cremation of Hildeburh's kin, the *scop* provides the present-day Scyldings, themselves on the brink of disaster, with a stark warning about the impact of feuding on royal families:[137]

> Ād[138] wæs geæfned   ond icge gold
> āhafen of horde;   *Here-Scyldinga*
> *betst beado-rinca   wæs on bǣl gearu.*
> Æt þǣm āde wæs   ēþ-gesȳne   1110
> swātfāh syrce,   swȳn eal gylden,
> eofer īren-heard,   *æþeling manig*
> wundum āwyrded;   sume on wæle crungon.
> Hēt ðā Hildeburh   æt Hnæfes āde
> *hire selfre sunu*   sweoloðe befæstan,   1115
> bān-fatu bærnan,   ond on bǣl don
> *ēame on eaxle.*[139]   Ides gnornode,
> geomrōde giddum.   Gūð-rēc āstāh,
> wand tō wolcnum;   wæl-fȳra mǣst
> hlynode for hlāwe.   Hafelan multon,   1120
> ben-geato burston   ðonne blōd ætspranc,
> lāð-bite līces;   līg ealles forswealg,
> gǣsta gīfrost,   þāra ðe þǣr gūð fornam
> bēga folces.[140]   Wæs hira blǣd scacen.
> (1107–24). (Emphasis added).

[A funeral pyre was prepared and (?)[141] gold taken from the hoard; *the best battle-warriors of the War-Scyldings were placed on the fire*. At that pyre it was easy to see the bloodstained mail-shirt, the boar-images all golden, the iron-fierce boar, *many an ætheling* dispatched by wounds; some had fallen in the slaughter. Hildeburh ordered *her own son(s)* to be placed on Hnæf's pyre, entrusted to the flame, to burn the bone-vessels, and on the fire placed *at his/ their uncle's side.*[142] The woman mourned, sang a sad song. The war-smoke rose up, dark under the clouds; the greatest of deadly fires roared around

---

[137] For detailed discussion of this cremation scene and its links to other funerals in the poem, see Owen-Crocker, *Four Funerals*, pp. 43–60.

[138] For discussion of the standard emendation from MS *āð*, 'oath', see K4, p. 185.

[139] Most editions, including K3 and K4, follow Holthausen in emending MS *earme*, 'wretched', to *ēame*, 'uncle'. Tolkien describes this as 'a typical scribal blunder' and favours the emendation to *ēame* (*Finn and Hengest*, pp. 110–11). Neidorf describes this error as an example of 'trivialization', a common feature of MS-copying, whereby scribes inadvertently distort the sense of the original 'authorial lexeme' (*Transmission*, p. 67). For arguments in defence of the MS reading, see G. A. Lester, '*Earme on eaxle* (*Beowulf* 1117a)', SN 58 (1986), 159–63; and *CCB*, p. 182.

[140] Compare with the two accounts of how Grendel ate the Geatish warrior, Hondscioh, in Heorot, at lines 739–45a and 2076–80.

[141] The meaning of *icge* is unknown; see note in K4, p. 185.

[142] On the importance of this relationship, see Bremmer, 'Uncle and Nephew in *Beowulf*'.

the corpses. Heads melted, bone-gates burst apart, then blood sprang out, from hateful bites of fire; the flame consumed all, the greediest of spirits, of those of both peoples whom war had taken away. *Their glory was gone.*]

This gruesome scene provides a tragic variation on Scyld's relatively peaceful, bloodless departure over the waves, while the slaughter of Finn's son (or sons) provides a striking contrast to the procession of young Scyldings in the opening section.[143] Echoes of the Scyld-prologue are sustained in the concluding lines of the Finnsburg episode, as the queen is taken back to the Danes in a treasure-laden boat:

    Đā wæs heal roden,[144]
fēonda fēorum, swilce Fin slægen,
cyning on corþre, ond sēo cwēn numen.
Scēotend Scyldinga tō scypon feredon
eal ingesteald eorð-cyninges,   1155
swylce hīe æt Finnes hām findan meahton
sigla searo-gimma. Hīe on sǣlāde
drihtlice wīf tō Denum feredon,
læddon to lēodum.
(1151b–59a)

[Then the hall was reddened with the blood of enemies; thus Finn was killed, the king in company, and the queen taken. The bowmen of the Scyldings carried to their ships all the ancient treasure of the earth-king, such as they could find at Finn's home of skilfully wrought gems and treasures. They took the lordly woman over the water to the Danes, led her to the people.]

While Scyld's departure across the waves ushered in a great line of Danish kings, Hildeburh leaves behind no dynastic legacy. Read in the context of the court setting, the *scop*'s cautionary tale of a royal family torn apart by feuding anticipates not only the imminent attack of Grendel's mother but also the troubled future of the young Scyldings and, less immediately, the dynastic wars between the Swedes and Geats that dominate the poem's final third. The Finnsburg episode thereby foreshadows the main themes that will come to dominate the final act of the dynastic drama, namely the

---

[143] *CCB*, p. 182, takes *sunu* (1115a) as plural, arguing that Hildeburh lost multiple sons (cf. 1068a: *Finnes eaferum*; 1074a: *bearnum ond brōðrum*). Others have argued that she only lost one son; for the arguments, see K4, pp. 185–86. Klaeber argues that *bearnum* (1074a) refers to 'Finn's men', and *brōðrum* (1074a) is a 'generic plural', on the grounds that Hildeburh only lost one brother, Hnæf, at Finnsburg (K3, p. 171). Orchard, on the other hand, reads both as plurals, commenting: 'It is true that Hildeburh herself only loses one brother, but of course her sons are brothers too' (*CCB*, p. 182, n. 67).

[144] MS *hroden*, 'decorated', is emended in K4 and most other editions on metrical grounds. See Neidorf, *Transmission*, pp. 65–66. For a defence of the MS reading, see *CCB*, p. 177, n. 54.

failure of promising æthelings to develop into kings, the human cost of feuding and the failure of royal lines.

Wealhtheow Centre Stage

Following the Finnsburg Episode, the narrative remains focused on the figure of the royal mother and queen as Wealhtheow, *ides Scyldinga*, 'lady of the Scyldings' (1168b),[145] is again depicted distributing the mead-cup to Hrothgar and Hrothulf (1159–64a).[146] With the threat of Grendel removed, the queen now gives voice to her concerns about the future of the Scyldings. In her estimation, Hrothgar's proposed adoption of Beowulf has implications for the Scylding succession, placing their two young sons, Hrethric and Hrothmund, in a vulnerable position.[147] She therefore advises Hrothgar to reconsider his plans for Beowulf and to restrict the Danish succession to the members of the house of Scyld:

> Mē man sægde,   þæt þū ðē for sunu wolde
> here-rinc habban.   Heorot is gefælsod,
> bēah-sele beorhta;   brūc þenden þū mōte
> manigra mēdo,   *ond þīnum māgum lǣf*
> *folc ond rīce*   þonne ðū forð scyle,
> metod-sceaft seon.
> (1175–80a). (Emphasis added).

> [Men have said to me that you would have the battle-warrior as a son. Heorot is cleansed, the brightest of ring-halls; enjoy for as long as you can many benefits, *and leave to your kin the people and kingdom* when you must go forth, to seek out your appointed fate.]

With the matter of the succession still in mind, Wealhtheow reminds the king of the future role she envisages for their nephew, Hrothulf:[148]

---

[145] On her first appearance in the poem, Wealhtheow is referred to as *ides Helminga*, 'lady of the Helmings' (620b); the young Scyldings are not directly mentioned in this scene. Helm is mentioned as a ruler of the Wulfings in *Widsith* line 21. On Wealhtheow's ethnicity and possible connections with the East Anglian royal house, see Newton, *Origins*, pp. 105–31. The term *ides*, 'woman, lady', is used elsewhere to refer to Hildeburh (1075b, 1117b), Grendel's mother (1259a, 1351a) and Wealhtheow (1649b), as well as to royal women more generally in the tale of Offa's bride (1941a). On the figure of the *ides* in Old English poetry, see Chance, *Woman as Hero*, pp. 1–11.

[146] A further link between this second portrait of family harmony among the Scyldings and the preceding tale of Finn's sons, in which brother is pitted against brother and father against son, is provided by the reference to Unferth, the fratricide, sitting at the king's feet (1165b–68). On the role of this character, see above, pp. 57–58.

[147] See further Mitchell, 'Literary Lapses', 13; and Drout, 'Blood and Deeds', 202.

[148] See Morgan, 'Treachery of Hrothulf'. For summaries of the major Norse

> Ic mīnne can
> glædne Hrōþulf, þæt hē þā geogoðe wile
> ārum healdan gyf þū ǣr þonne hē,
> wine Scildinga, worold oflǣtest;
> wēne ic þæt hē mid gōde gyldan wille
> uncran eaferan gif hē þæt eal gemon,
> hwæt wit tō willan and tō worðmyndum
> umborwesendum ǣr ārna gefremedon.
> (1180b–87).

> [I know that my gracious Hrothulf will protect the youths with honours, if you, Friend of the Scyldings, should take leave of the world before him; I expect that he will treat our sons with goodness, if he remembers it all, how we two treated him with kindness while he was a child.]

As we have seen, Hrothulf already occupies a prominent position in the court, sitting at Hrothgar's side. In the Scandinavian sources, it is this Hrólfr (OE Hrothulf) who will succeed his father, Helgo (OE Halga), and uncle, Roas (OE Hrothgar), after their deaths.[149] The queen's words in this scene are matched in their significance by her gestures, which further underline her commitment to the preservation of the dynasty. By contrast with her first appearance in Heorot, when Wealhtheow had welcomed Beowulf by passing him the cup before turning to take up her elevated seat beside her lord (620–40), now she turns protectively to the mead-benches where her sons (*byre* carrying the alliteration of line 1188) sit with Beowulf:[150]

> Hwearf þā bī bence, þǣr *hyre byre* wǣron,
> Hrēðric ond Hrōðmund, ond hæleþa *bearn*,
> *giogoð ætgædere*; þǣr se gōda sæt,
> Bēowulf Gēata be þǣm *gebrōðrum* twǣm.
> (1188–91). (Emphasis added).

> [She turned then to the bench, where *her sons* were, Hrethric and Hrothmund, and *the sons* of warriors, *the youth gathered together*; there sat the good one, Beowulf of the Geats, beside the two *brothers*.]

---

accounts, see the appendices to this volume.

[149] For the theory that Hrothulf killed Hrethric, see above, p. 67. For the recent suggestion that Hrothulf acted as regent after Hrothgar's death, and protector of Hrethric and Hrothmund, see R. North, 'Hrothulf's Childhood and Beowulf's: A Comparison', in Irvine and Rudolf (2018), pp. 222–43, at 228.

[150] See L. L. Schücking, 'Heldenstolz und Würde im Angelsächsischen, mit einem Anhang: Zur Charakterisierungstechnik im Beowulfepos', *Abhandlungen der Philologisch-historischen Klasse der sächsischen Akademie der Wissenschaften*, 42.5 (Leipzig, 1933), p. 41; J. M. Hill, 'Beowulf and the Danish Succession'; Hollis, '*Beowulf* and the Succession', 41; Biggs, 'Geatish succession', 55; *CCB*, pp. 219–22.

While some scholars have taken Wealhtheow's actions as those of a concerned mother who fails to grasp the complexity of the political situation,[151] others have credited the Danish queen with more diplomatic skill.[152] Viewed from a dynastic perspective, Wealhtheow certainly appears to have a much firmer grasp on the political situation than her husband, who is so impressed by this foreign prince that he is willing to violate the dynastic principle for his sake. Wealhtheow speaks and acts in this scene as a powerful queen who commands respect from the king and the court, rather than as a mere king's wife or royal concubine.[153]

This same alertness to the political implications of Hrothgar's plan to adopt Beowulf is on display in Wealhtheow's subsequent address to the young hero himself. The structural importance of this instructive speech is suggested by thematic and verbal links with Hrothgar's own subsequent, more celebrated 'sermon' to Beowulf (1700–84), and the closing lines of the poem in which the Geats praise Beowulf's virtues. Balancing her deep gratitude for the hero's great service to the Danes with stern warnings about his future conduct and mortality, the queen again moves to ensure the safety of her sons while highlighting the importance of loyalty in the court:[154]

> *Brūc* þisses bēages, Bēowulf lēofa,
> *hyse*, mid hǣle, ond þisses hrægles *nēot*,
> þēod-gestrēona, ond geþēoh tela,
> cen þec mid cræfte, ond þyssum cnyhtum wes

---

[151] Chance, *Woman as Hero*, p. 100; *CCB*, p. 220; Davis, *Demise of Germanic Legend*, pp. 126–28.

[152] Louviot, *Direct Speech*, p. 81. See further J. Hill, '*Þæt wæs geomoru ides!* A female stereotype examined', in Damico and Olsen, eds (1990), pp. 235–47, at 238; Overing, *Language, Sign and Gender*, pp. 88–100. On Wealhtheow's political role, see H. Damico, *Beowulf's Wealhtheow and the Valkyrie Tradition* (Madison, WI, 1984); Klein, *Ruling Women*, pp. 87–124.

[153] Despite the prevalence of polygamy among the early Germanic peoples, the rulers of *Beowulf* are strikingly monogamous. See M. Clunies Ross, 'Concubinage in Anglo-Saxon England', *Anglo-Saxon History: Basic Readings*, Basic Readings in Anglo-Saxon England 6, ed. D. A. E. Pelteret (New York, 2000), pp. 251–88; E. John, 'The Social and Political Problems of the Early English Church', in *Land, Church, and People: Essays Presented to Professor H. P. R. Finberg*, ed. J. Thirsk (Reading, 1970), pp. 39–63; and A. Davies, 'The Sexual Conversion of the Anglo-Saxons', in *A Wyf Ther Was: Essays in Honour of Paule Mertens-Fonck*, ed. J. D'or (Liège, 1992) pp. 80–102. On the absence of concubinage from *Beowulf*, and the biblical character of its presentation of kingship, see Chapter Four, p. 216. On queens as royal mothers, see Chance, *Woman as Hero*, p. 1; H. M. Jewell, *Women in Dark Age and Early Medieval Europe c. 500–1200* (London, 2007), p. 87.

[154] Orchard notes the high frequency of imperatives in this speech (*CCB*, p. 221). It is noteworthy, however, that Wealhtheow employs a similarly high number of imperatives in her previous speech to Hrothgar: *Onfōh, wes, spræc, swā sceal man don, Bēo, brūc, lǣf* (1169–87), suggesting that she occupies a highly respected position in the court.

> lāra līðe. Ic þē þæs lēan geman. 1220
> Hafast þū gefēred   þæt ðē feor ond nēah
> ealne wīde-ferhþ   weras ehtigað,
> efne swā sīde   swā sǣ bebūgeð,
> wind-geard, weallas.   *Wes* þenden þū lifige
> æþeling, ēadig. Ic þē an tela 1225
> sinc-gestrēona. *Bēo þū suna mīnum*
> *dǣdum gedēfe*, drēam-healdende.
> Hēr is ǣghwylc eorl   ōþrum getrȳwe,
> *mōdes milde*,   man-drihtne hold;
> þegnas syndon *geþwǣre*,   þēod eal gearo; 1230
> druncne dryht-guman   dōð swā ic bidde.[155]
> (1216–31). (Emphasis added).

[*Make use* of this neck-ring, dear Beowulf, *young warrior*, in good health, and *enjoy* this war-garment, treasure of the people, and *prosper* well; *may you be bold* with skill, and *be a gentle teacher to these young warriors*. I will remember to reward you for that. You have brought it about that far and near, for all time, men will praise you, even as far as the sea, home of the wind, embraces the shore. *Be* for as long as you live, nobleman, blessed. I wish you alone well in these treasures. *May you be generous in deeds* to *my sons*, holding them in joy. Here every man is loyal to his liege-lord, *mild in heart*, thanes are always *true*, the people together, the lordly troop united in beer-drinking; they do as I say.]

Noting the absence of a verbal response from either Hrothgar or Beowulf to either of the queen's speeches, Orchard concludes that 'none of Wealhtheow's words have hit home'.[156] Elise Louviot, on the other hand, has recently identified this passage as an 'isolated speech', that is a type of speech in which the speaker's status is elevated by virtue of the fact that they do not bother to wait for an answer.[157] Certainly, the fact that Hrothgar's plan to adopt Beowulf is never again mentioned suggests that Wealhtheow's words and deeds had their desired effect.[158] Beowulf's diplomatic response, in which he assures the court that Hrethric will receive

---

[155] Cf. *Beo* 3181–82: *manna mildust ond monð-wǣrust,/ lēodum līðost ond lof-geornost*. For discussion of the closing lines, see Chapter Four, pp. 228–31. For the arguments favoured by early editors that Wealhtheow's closing words should themselves be read as an imperative ('do as I say'), see K4, p. 196. See further Damico, *Wealhtheow*, pp. 144–45; Overing, *Language, Sign and Gender*, p. 90.

[156] *CCB*, pp. 221–22.

[157] Louviot, *Direct Speech*, p. 35. For further analysis of Wealhtheow's speeches, see pp. 80–82.

[158] It is unclear to what extent Wealhtheow was equally successful in persuading Hrothulf to act with kindness towards her sons after Hrothgar's death. For the debate as to Hrothulf's conduct, see above, p. 67. As Louviot notes, 'if Hrothulf is innocent, there can be no dramatic irony in Wealhtheow's words' (*Direct Speech*, p. 81).

a warm welcome among the Hrethlings should he ever wish to visit the Geats (1836–39), provides a further indication of the respect which the queen commands in the court.[159] In these court-scenes, we see Wealhtheow acting as both concerned mother and politically astute dynast during a precarious moment in the life-cycle of her own royal house.

Beowulf's Departure from the Danes

With the removal of the threat of Grendel and Grendel's mother and the abandonment of Hrothgar's planned adoption, the hero takes his leave of the Scyldings with the matter of the Danish succession unresolved. In Beowulf's departure-scene, Hrothgar accepts that the hero's royal destiny lies not with the Danes but in his own homeland:[160]

Gecyste þā cyning æþelum gōd,	1870
þēoden Scyldinga ðegn betestan	
ond be healse genam; *hruron him tēaras*	
blonden-feaxum. Him wæs bēga wēn	
ealdum infrōdum, ōþres swīðor,	
þæt hīe seoððan nō gesēon mōston,	1875
mōdige on meþle. *Wæs him se man tō þon lēof*	
þæt hē þone brēost-wylm forberan ne mehte,	
ac him on hreþre hyge-bendum fæst	
æfter dēorum men dyrne langað	
born wið blōde. Him Bēowulf þanan,	1880
gūð-rinc gold-wlanc græs-moldan træd	
since hrēmig; *sǣ-genga bād*	
āgend-frean, se þe on ancre rād.	
Þā wæs on gange gifu Hrōðgāres	
oft geæhted; þæt wæs ān cyning	1885
ǣghwæs orleahtre, oþ þæt hine yldo benam	
mægenes wynnum, sē þe oft manegum scōd.	
Cwōm þā tō flōde fela-mōdigra,	
hæg-stealdra hēap, hring-net bæron,	
locene leoðo-scyran. Land-weard onfand	1890
eft-sīð eorla, swā hē ǣr dyde;	

---

[159] See K. Malone, 'Hrethric', *PMLA* 42 (1927), 168–313, at 273. As J. M. Hill notes, any lingering suspicions that the hero may have harboured political ambitions among the Danes are dispelled when Beowulf later presents Heorogar's arms to Hygelac (2155–62) (*Narrative Pulse*, pp. 65–74). See also Hollis, 'Beowulf and the Succession', 45–47. Biggs argues that Beowulf uses this speech to gain political power among the Geats ('Politics of Succession', 726–34). For further discussion of 'Beowulf's Return', see Chapter Two, pp. 129–34.

[160] Hill, *Narrative Pulse*, p. 5, describes this departure scene as 'the most expansively promising in the poem'. See further pp. 61–64.

The Dynastic Life-Cycle and the Structure of the Poem

nō hē mīd hearme   of hliðes nōsan
gæstas grētte,   ac him tōgēanes rād,
cwæð þæt wil-cuman   Wedera lēodum
scaþan scīr-hame   tō scipe fōron.   1895
*Þā wæs on sande   sǣ-gēap naca
hladen here-wǣdum,   hringed-stefna
mēarum ond māðmum;*   *mæst* hlīfade
ofer Hrōðgāres   *hord-gestrēonum*.
Hē þǣm bāt-wearde   bunden golde   1900
swurd gesealde,   þæt hē syðþan wæs
on meodu-bence   māþme þȳ weorþra,
yrfe-lāfe.   Gewāt him on naca
drēfan dēop wæter,   Dena land ofgeaf.
(1870–1904). (Emphasis added).

[Then that good king, of noble ancestry, lord of the Scyldings, kissed the best of thanes, grasped him by the neck; *that grey-haired man shed tears*. That very wise and old man was in two minds – but he knew it most likely that they would never see each other again, brave in the meeting-place. *That man was so dear to him that he could not prevent the welling of his heart, but secure in the thoughts of his breast a deep and secret longing for that dear man burned against his blood*. From there Beowulf took himself away, trod the grassy earth, the battle-warrior rejoicing in gold, exulting in treasure; *the sea-goer awaited its lordly owner, the one who rested at anchor*. Then the gift of Hrothgar was often praised during the departure; that was a king without match, always blameless, until old age deprived him of the joys of strength, he who often injures so many.

Then they came to the water, many brave ones, a gathering of young warriors, carrying ring-nets, locked mail-shirts. The coastguard observed the return of the men, just as he did before; he did not greet the guests with insults from the edge of the cliff, but he rode towards them, and said that the warriors in their shining armour were welcome to travel to their ships, people of the Weders. *Then the sea-curved prow was on the sand, the ring-necked ship, laden with battle-gear, horses and treasures*; the *mast* towered above, over Hrothgar's *treasure-hoard*. He gave that boat-guardian a sword of bound gold, so that afterwards he was always the more honoured on the mead-benches because of the ancient heirloom. They went into the boat, drove across deep water, departed from the land of the Danes.]

A series of verbal parallels link this departure scene to the Scyld-prologue: Hrothgar's grief at Beowulf's departure recalls the mourning of the Danes as they watch Scyld's ship pass into the deep (*him wæs geōmor sefa,/ murnende mōd*, 49b–50a); Beowulf's awaiting ship, *hringed-stefna*, 'ring-prowed' (1897b), is *hladen here-wǣdum, [...] mēarum ond māðmum*, 'laden with battle-gear, horses and treasures' (1896–98a), its *mæst* towering over Hrothgar's *hord-gestrēonum* (1899b), just as Scyld's *hringed-stefna* vessel (32b) was loaded (*gelǣded*) and fitted (*gegyrwan*) with *mādma fela [...]/ hilde-wǣpnum ond heaðo-wǣdum,/ billum ond byrnum [...] þēod-gestrēonum* (36b–41a, 44a), in which the departing king himself lies, *mǣrne be mǣste* (36a).[161] This cluster of echoes serves to highlight the contrasting dynastic legacies of these heroes from over the water: while Scyld had provided the Danes with a son and heir to rule after him, Beowulf's departure is overshadowed by hints of *fācen-stafas*, 'acts of malice', and of a breakdown in *sib*, 'kinship', between the four grandsons of Healfdene. There is no textual evidence to support Mary Dockray-Miller's view of Hrothgar's *dyrne langað*, 'secret longing' (1879b), for Beowulf as homoerotic.[162] On the contrary, as David Clark argues, 'it is much more likely that the illicit longing here is for Beowulf to remain as Hrothgar's heir.'[163] However, as we have seen, for Beowulf to succeed Hrothgar would violate of the dynastic principle as well as endangering the future of the young Scyldings; Queen Wealhtheow is unwilling to countenance either possibility. The hero's departure from the Scyldings therefore marks a major juncture in the dynastic drama. From this point on, the poet directs his attentions to the Hrethlings, rulers of the Geats, and their own cross-generational wars with their Swedish neighbours, the Scylfings. As soon becomes clear, Beowulf is destined to play a key role in both of these dynasties.

The Tale of Offa's Bride

Before the poet can turn his full attentions to the matter of Beowulf's protracted rise to the Geatish throne, we encounter another inset-story tangential to the main narrative, in the mould of the Finnsburg Episode.[164] Further developing the portrait of royal women, the tale of Offa's bride (1931b–62) utilizes the folktale of 'The Taming of the Shrew' in order to describe the transformation of a once-violent princess into a gracious queen and mother.[165] The story begins somewhat abruptly with an account of a woman who reacted violently to the attentions of men (1931b–43), before marriage brought her unqueenly conduct to an end:[166]

---

[161] See further F. Leneghan, 'The Departure of the Hero in a Ship: the Intertextuality of *Beowulf*, Cynewulf and *Andreas*', SELIM 24 (2019), 105–34.
[162] M. Dockray-Miller, 'Beowulf's Tears of Fatherhood', *Exemplaria* 10 (1998), 1–28.
[163] D. Clark, *Between Medieval Men: Male Friendship and Desire in Early Medieval English Literature* (Oxford, 2009), p. 132.
[164] See further F. Leneghan, 'The Poetic Purpose of the Offa Digression in *Beowulf*', RES 60 (2009), 538–60.
[165] See K4, p. 222. See Chapter Two, pp. 105, 111–18, 120 n.44, 146, 149, for the poet's use of other folktale-motifs in service of the dynastic drama.
[166] It seems likely that some material, perhaps including the bride's name, has been lost. At lines 1931b–32a the MS reads: *mod þryðo wæg/ fremu folces cwen*.

> Hūru þæt onhōhsnode   Hemminges mæg:
> ealo-drincende   ōðer sædan,   1945
> þæt hīo lēod-bealewa   læs gefremede,
> inwit-nīða,   syððan ærest wearð
> gyfen gold-hroden   geongum cempan,
> æðelum dīore,   syððan hīo Offan flet
> ofer fealone flōd   be fæder lāre   1950
> sīðe gesōhte   ðær hīo syððan well
> in gum-stōle,   gōde mære,
> līf-gesceafta   lifigende brēac,
> hīold hēah-lufan   wið hæleþa brego,
> ealles mon-cynnes   mīne gefræge   1955
> þone sēlestan   bī sæm twēonum,
> eormen-cynnes;   forðām Offa wæs
> geofum ond gūðum,   gār-cēne man,
> wīde geweorðod,   wīsdōme hēold
> ēðel sīnne   1960
> (1944–60a).

[However, Hemming's kinsman [i.e. Offa] put a stop to that, men drinking ale said that she performed fewer terrors to the people, wicked deeds, after she was given, gold-adorned, to the young champion, dear prince, since she sought Offa's hall, far over the fallow flood, at her father's bidding. Afterwards she prospered there on the throne, famous for gifts, enjoyed living her fated life, held high in love by the lord of warriors, who was, as I have heard, the best of all mankind between the seas; for this Offa, the spear-brave man, was widely famed for gifts and wars, he ruled his homeland with wisdom.]

Completing this idealized portrait of a royal marriage is the birth of a male heir, Eomer, whose martial prowess makes him a worthy successor:

> þonon Ēomēr[167] wōc
> hæleðum tō helpe,   Hemminges mæg,
> nefa Gārmundes,   nīða cræftig.
> (1960b–62). (Emphasis added).

The editors of K4 take the bride's name to be *Fremu* (p. 65). See also R. D. Fulk, 'The Name of Offa's Queen: *Beowulf* 1931–3', *Anglia* 122 (2004), 614–39. Other suggestions include *Mōdþrȳðo* (K3, pp. 72, 198–99) and *Þrȳð*. See further K. Malone, 'Hygd', *MLN* 56 (1941), 356–58; Brodeur, *Art*, pp. 157–81. Norman E. Eliason proposes that Offa's bride was in fact a young Hygd, prior to her marriage to Hygelac ('The "Thryth-Offa Digression" in *Beowulf*', in *Franciplegius: Medieval and Linguistic Studies in Honor of Francis Peabody Magoun, Jr.*, ed. J. B. Bessinger Jr. and R. P. Creed [New York, 1965], pp. 124–38, at 126). See further Klein, *Ruling Women*, p. 111. For connections with Grendel's mother, see Chapter Three, pp. 177–80.

[167] Emended from MS *geomor*, 'sad', in order to provide alliteration with *eðel* in 1980, and on the basis of the Mercian royal genealogy.

[*Then Eomer was born*, as a help to warriors, Hemming's kinsman, grandson of Garmund, skilful in battle]

Scholars have long treated the so-called 'Offa digression' as an irrelevant interpolation on the grounds that it appears to have no organic connection either with 'Beowulf's Return' or the poem as a whole. Indeed, some have argued that the entire section was clumsily introduced into the text in order to flatter King Offa of Mercia.[168] However, as will be clear from the above summary, the story of Offa's bride provides another variation on the dynastic theme introduced in the Scyld-prologue, this time foregrounding the benefits of royal marriage to the individual, the court and society as a whole. Although its significance might not be immediately obvious, Eomer's birth can be seen as a pivotal moment in the dynastic drama: while it recalls the steady procession of royal births in the poem's opening movement,[169] it also proves to be the last such event mentioned in the poem, as the dynastic life-cycle moves towards its final phase.[170]

Soon after the tale of Offa's bride, Beowulf shares his own views on the topic of royal marriage. As noted above, during the course of his report to Hygelac, the hero predicts the failure of Hrothgar's plan to broker a truce with the Heathobards through the marriage of his daughter, Freawaru,

---

[168] See, for example, Shippey, 'Structure and Unity', p. 159; K4, p. lxxxv. For earlier doubts about the passage, see Chambers, *Introduction*, pp. 39, 104–05 and 540–43; K3, p. cvii; G. Bond, 'Links Between *Beowulf* and Mercian History', *SP* 40 (1943), 481–93; Sisam, *Structure*, pp. 48–49; Whitelock, *Audience*, p. 60; and Bonjour, *Digressions*, pp. 54–55. For a review of the genealogical evidence, see Leneghan, 'Offa Digression'. In that article, I argued that the compilers of the Mercian genealogy in the late-eighth century drew the names Eomer, Offa, Garmund (and possibly the title Angelþeow) from heroic traditions preserved in poems resembling *Beowulf*. Lapidge has suggested that a similar process lies behind the addition of the names Scyld, Scef and Beow to the West Saxon royal genealogy in the ninth century ('*Beowulf*, Aldhelm, the *Liber Monstrorum* and Wessex', 187). See also Tolley, '*Beowulf*'s Scyld Scefing Episode', 12; R. D. Fulk, 'An Eddic Analogue to the Scyld Scefing Story', *RES* 40 (1989), 313–22, at 320–22. Newton, *Origins*, p. 71, suggests that 'a version of *Beowulf* could have been known in Mercia in the late-eighth or ninth centuries, where it may have inspired royal name-giving, as may be suggested by the names of the Mercian kings at that time, such as *Beornwulf*, *Wiglaf* and *Wihstan*'. North, *Origins*, proposes that the poem was composed to honour the accession of King Wiglaf of Mercia in 827.

[169] See above, pp. 38–50.

[170] The formula *hæleðum tō helpe*, 'as a help to warriors' (1961a), used here to describe Eomer's career as king, echoes the earlier description of Beow, sent by God *folce tō frōfre*, 'as a comfort to the people' (14a). Similarly, Hrothgar says of Beowulf *Ðū scealt tō frōfre weorþan/ eal lang-twīdig lēodum þīnum,/ hæleðum tō helpe*, 'You will become a lasting comfort to your people, a help to warriors' (1707b–09a). For the possible Christological connotations of *folce tō frōfre*, see Chapter Four, pp. 231–34.

and Froda's son, Ingeld.[171] While the Danish king had considered this union good policy (2026–29a), in Beowulf's estimation such peaceweaving strategies are futile, regardless of the bride's excellence:[172]

> Oft seldan hwær
> æfter lēod-hryre   lȳtle hwīle
> bon-gār būgeð,   þēah sēo brȳd duge.
> (2029b–31).

> [But seldom anywhere, after the fall of a prince, does the deadly spear rest for a little while, even though the bride be good!][173]

Although the circumstances behind the marriages of Offa's bride and Freawaru are quite different, their relatively close juxtaposition in the narrative invites us to consider them together. While Freawaru's story highlights the obstacles to peaceweaving, the tale of Offa's bride demonstrates to the poem's audience, if not the hero, that royal marriages can succeed, even with the most unpromising bride. The positioning of this tale at this particular moment in the narrative can therefore be seen as particularly apposite, foreshadowing Beowulf's subsequent failure either to marry or to produce an heir during his fifty-year reign.[174]

Critics are divided over the import of Beowulf's lack of a queen: while Fred C. Robinson argues that 'Beowulf's marital status was of insufficient interest to warrant mention in the poem', Stacy Klein points out that this does not sit well with the fact that 'the poet appears deeply interested in the marital status of so many other male characters in the poem'.[175] Certainly in comparison with the other kings of the poem, Beowulf cuts

---

[171] See above, pp. 52–53.
[172] For debate as to the interpretation of this passage, see Chambers, *Introduction*, p. 21; Lawrence, *Epic Tradition*, p. 80; K. Malone, 'Time and Place in the Ingeld Episode of *Beowulf*', *JEGP* 39 (1940), 84–85; Bonjour, *Digressions*, pp. 56–63; Brodeur, *Art*, p. 158; CCB, pp. 241–43; Louviot, *Direct Speech*, p. 211.
[173] This is the same feud that the narrator had briefly hinted at much earlier, culminating in the destruction of Heorot (81b–85). For the argument that Beowulf's prediction of Freawaru's fate reflects his own disappointment that Hrothgar did not reward him for cleansing Heorot with her hand in marriage, see North, 'Heathen Polity'. On connections between Beowulf's story of Freawaru and his own lack of a bride, see S. Marshall, 'Digression, Coherence, and a Missing Cup in *Beowulf*', *Zeitschrift für Literaturwissenschaft und Linguistik* 48 (2018), 167–92.
[174] See further B. Moore, 'The Thryth-Offa Digression in *Beowulf*', *Neophilologus* 64 (1980), 127–33, at 132. Moore compares Beowulf with Offa, who according to other accounts also progressed from unpromising youth to respected king. For speculation as to the identity of the *geatisc meowle*, 'Geatish woman' (3150b), at Beowulf's funeral, see below, p. 92.
[175] F. C. Robinson, 'Teaching the Backgrounds: History, Religion, Culture', in *Approaches to Teaching* Beowulf, ed. J. B. Bessinger and R. F. Yeager (New York, 1984), pp. 107–22, at 119, cited in Klein, *Ruling Women*, p. 115.

a relatively solitary figure, with only his Wægmunding relative, Wiglaf, to accompany him in his final battle. As discussed below, the poet skirts around the subject of Beowulf's middle years, a time when a marriage alliance such as that achieved by Offa could have happened. In the next chapter, I argue that Beowulf's unmarried status and resultant lack of an heir stems not from any personal failing or oversight on the poet's part but is rather a by-product of his fictionality. Had the poet provided the hero with an heir, his death would not have marked the end of the Hrethling dynasty. By presenting King Beowulf as childless, the poet was able to present his demise and that of his royal line as the denouement of the dynastic drama.

SENECTUS: THE DEATH OF A DYNASTY

erunt enim ex hoc quinque in domo una divisi
tres in duo et duo in tres dividentur
pater in filium et filius in patrem suum
mater in filiam et filia in matrem
socrus in nurum suam et nurus in socrum suam
(Luke 12.52–53).

[Think ye, that I am come to give peace on earth? I tell you, no; but separation. For there shall be from henceforth five in one house divided: three against two, and two against three. The father shall be divided against the son, and the son against his father, the mother against the daughter, and the daughter against the mother, the mother-in-law against her daughter-in-law, and the daughter-in-law against her mother-in-law.]

As this chapter has so far demonstrated, in the first part of the poem kingship is presented as a dynamic institution transcending generational boundaries. During this first phase of the dynastic life-cycle, the provision of worthy and legitimate heirs ensures that the royal house itself and its subjects remain relatively untroubled by the death of an individual monarch. Towards the end of Hrothgar's reign, however, we saw that the issue of the Danish royal succession becomes increasingly uncertain, with a number of æthelings poised to contest the throne. As Chapter Three will argue, the arrival of Grendel and Beowulf on the Danish royal scene at this stage is no accident. In the third and final section of the poem (1888–3182), during which the hero confronts the dragon, dynastic tragedies previously only hinted at in retrospective digressions and proleptic allusions now start to emerge into the narrative foreground.[176] In order to bring about this tonal shift, and to universalize the dynastic drama, the poet leaves

---

[176] Indeed, as we shall see in Chapter Three, in this final section of the narrative the struggles of the Scylfings and Hrethlings are given precedence over what is usually considered the 'main action' of the dragon fight.

behind the Scyldings and turns instead to explore the cross-generational feud between the Geatish royal house, the Hrethlings, and their Swedish rivals, the Scylfings. These conflicts, typically referred to as the 'Swedish wars', are alluded to in a series of retrospective historical digressions of varying length. As many scholars have noted, far from simply serving as a historical dramatic backdrop to the dragon-fight, the Swedish wars at times crowd out the 'main action'.[177] This section will explore how King Beowulf's death is presented as the final act in a tightly constructed dynastic drama concerning the rise and fall of royal houses.

The audience has in fact already been primed for this shift in setting via a number of allusions to Scylfing and Hrethling legend scattered throughout the Danish section of the work. So, for example, we learn near the beginning of the poem that Healfdene's daughter was *[On]elan cwēn/ Heaðo-Scylfingas heals-gebedda*, 'Onela's (?) queen, the bed-companion of the War-Scylfing' (63b–64). Although Healfdene's daughter herself does not make another appearance in the work, Onela will play a vital role in Beowulf's rise to kingship. Similarly, the event that triggers the fall of the Hrethlings, namely Hygelac's death in Frisia, is twice alluded to in the Danish section, first during a treasure-giving scene in Heorot (1197–1214a), and then in Hrothgar's prediction that, should Hygelac ever suffer a violent death, the throne of the Geats will pass to Beowulf (1845b–54).[178] Combined with the sustained foregrounding or suppression of themes such as royal births and deaths at different points in the narrative as outlined above, these anticipatory allusions provide a further indication of the careful construction of the work around the life-cycle of dynasties.

The Fall of the Hrethlings

In marked contrast to the opening account of the progression of the Scylding line, in which the throne had passed uncontested over four generations from Scyld to Hrothgar, every stage in the Hrethling succession is determined by the violent death of a monarch. However, before describing the complicated series of events that will culminate in Beowulf's accession, the poet must disentangle the hero from the Scyldings once and for all. This realignment of Beowulf with his own royal house, the Hrethlings, is achieved during the long bridging passage known as 'Beowulf's Return'. In the course of this exchange between Beowulf and his uncle, King Hygelac, the hero reveals just how close he had come to the Danish

---

[177] Connections between this dynastic conflict and the narrative of the dragon-fight are explored in detail in Chapter Three, pp. 180–94.
[178] For discussion of the prominence of the theme of Hygelac's death throughout the poem, see Chapter Two, pp. 121–26.

throne. After relating how Hrothgar esteemed him with an honoured seat in the royal hall *wið his sylfes sunu*, 'opposite (*or* alongside?) his own sons' (2013a),[179] he then explains how he was rewarded for his victory with the gift of King Heorogar's suit of armour:

> Mē ðis hilde-sceorp Hrōðgār sealde,   2155
> snotra fengel; sume worde hēt
> þæt ic his ǣrest ðē   ēst gesǣgde;[180]
> cwæð þæt hyt hæfde Hiorogār cyning,
> lēod Scyldunga lange hwīle;
> nō ðȳ ǣr suna sīnum syllan wolde,   2160
> hwatum Heorowearde, þēah hē him hold wǣre,
> brēost-gewǣdu. Brūc ealles well!
> (2155–62).

[Hrothgar, the wise ruler, gave this battle-gear to me; he commanded in a particular speech that I first should tell you about the ancestry of his bequest (*or* that I should give you his good wishes); he said it had belonged to King Heorogar, lord of the Scyldings, for a long time; no sooner did he [i.e. Heorogar] wish to give it to his own son, brave Heoroweard, though he was dear to him, the breast-ornaments. Enjoy all of it well!]

As we have seen, a king's bestowal of ancestral armours such as these on a prince can symbolize the conferral of royal power.[181] Reinforcing this impression, Beowulf employs a range of rare terms in describing this prestigious gift. The first term, *hilde-sceorp* is a hapax, while the related compound *brēost-gewǣdu* is also unique to *Beowulf*, occurring on only one further occasion, in reference to the armour lost by King Hygelac on the Frisian raid (1211a).[182] Both compounds are suggestive of especially

---

[179] It is unclear whether Beowulf is referring here to his first appearance in Heorot or his return from Grendel's mere. Given the subsequent reference to Beowulf sitting alongside Hrethric and Hrothmund during the treasure-giving after the victory over Grendel (1188–91), the latter seems more likely. On this scene, and Wealhtheow's response to the seating arrangements, see above, pp. 72–76.

[180] On the interpretation of this problematic line, and the various possible meanings of *ēst*, see K4, p. 235.

[181] See pp. 19, 47–48, 128, for discussion of Heorogar's gift of the same armour to his brother, Hrothgar, rather than his son, Heoroweard, thereby signalling the former's succession.

[182] It should be noted that these same *brēost-gewǣdu* lost by Hygelac in Frisia may, like Heorogar's armour, also be a gift from the Danish royal house: in the same passage, Hygelac is said to be wearing the great *hring/bēah*, 'ring' (1202a, 1211b), that Wealhtheow gave as a gift to Beowulf, who himself later presented it to Queen Hygd in the exchange of treasures on his return from Denmark discussed above (2172–76). Another related compound, *hilde-geatwa*, occurs twice in *Beowulf*, in reference to presumably less prestigious (or regal) items of clothing, namely the hero's own armour as he undresses before preparing to fight Grendel (674b) and the plundered items that Beowulf brings back over the sea

high-status armour, such as might be worn by a king or given to a future ruler. The other term, *ēst*, bearing alliterative stress as the headstave in line 2157b, is used adverbially in *Beowulf* in the sense of 'generously' or 'bounteously' (1195a, 2378a) and as a noun in the sense of 'the grace of God' (3075a), or 'goodwill' (958b). Significantly, however, *ēst* again carries the alliteration immediately after Beowulf's speech, as the narrator describes how the hero gave four horses to Hygelac, together with Heorogar's arms: *hē him ēst getēah/ mēara ond māðma*, 'he (i.e. Beowulf) gave him (i.e. Hygelac) the gift of horses and treasures' (2165b–66).[183] With these extra details now supplied, we are left in no doubt that Hrothgar had indeed preferred Beowulf to any of the young Scyldings as his successor.[184] However, by presenting the Scylding arms to Hygelac immediately upon his return, Beowulf makes plain his allegiance to his own royal house.[185]

Recognizing the political implications of this gesture and pleased with his nephew's loyalty, Hygelac promptly rewards Beowulf with an ancestral treasure of the Hrethlings, as well as a large endowment of land and a hall, in a scene replete with dynastic significance:

Hēt þæt eorla hlēo in gefetian,	2190
heaðo-rof cyning Hrēðles lāfe	
golde gegyrede; næs mid Gēatum ðā	
sinc-māðþum sēlra on sweordes hād;	
þæt hē on Bīowulfes bearm ālegde,	
ond him gesealde seofan þūsendo,	2195
bold ond brego-stōl. Him wæs bām samod	
on ðām lēodscipe lond gecynde,	

---

from the raid on Frisia (2362a). Cf. OE *sceorp*, which occurs in two compounds, both hapaxes, in Exeter Book Riddles 12 (13a: *fyrd-sceorp*, 'war-gear') and 7 (5b: *hlēow-sceorp*, 'protecting garment').

[183] Some translators take *māðma* here to refer to the trappings of the horses mentioned in the preceding lines (2163–65a) (e.g. Liuzza, p. 185), but the term could equally refer to Heorogar's armour, itself clearly a 'treasure'.

[184] Cf. Baker, *Honour, Exchange and Violence*, p. 67: 'Beowulf's gift is symbolically nothing less than the kingdom of Denmark.' See further Chambers, *Introduction*, pp. 14–15; J. M. Hill, '*Beowulf* and the Danish Succession'. As he is dying, Beowulf gives his own armour to Wiglaf, though he appears to acknowledge that Wiglaf will not succeed him as king; see further below, pp. 98–102; and Biggs, '*Beowulf* and some fictions of the Geatish succession'. For discussion as to why Heorogar chose not to give his armour to his own son, Heoroweard, see above, p. 48; Hollis, '*Beowulf* and the Succession', 41; J. M. Hill, '*Beowulf* and the Danish Succession', 180–81; and A. L. J. Thieme, 'The Gift in *Beowulf*: Forging the Continuity of Past and Present', *Michigan Germanic Studies* 22 (1996), 126–43. That Hrothgar considers Beowulf a king in the making is later confirmed in his remarks prior to the hero's departure (1844–54), though by now it has become clear that he will rule the Geats; see above, pp. 76–78. On the possibility that Hrothgar was prohibited from nominating his successor, see above, pp. 51–52.

[185] On Beowulf's subsequent bestowal of his own arms on Wiglaf as an act of non-succession, see below, pp. 100–02.

eard ēðel-riht,   ōðrum swīðor
sīde rīce   þām ðǣr sēlra wæs.
(2190–99).

[The protector of warriors (i.e. Hygelac), the battle-glorious king, ordered that Hrethel's heirloom be fetched, gold-decorated; there was no better treasure-gift in the form of a sword among the Geats; he ordered that to be placed in Beowulf's lap, and gave him seven thousand hides of land, a hall and lordly throne. Together they both held inherited land among that people, home and land-rights, though the greater kingdom was reserved for the one higher in rank (i.e. Hygelac).]

With this gift of Hrethel's sword, Beowulf takes his first step towards the Geatish throne, despite his relatively weak claim via his mother. Indeed, Biggs suggests that by providing Beowulf with such a large grant of land and a hall, Hygelac effectively makes Beowulf a sub-king.[186] Nevertheless, the narrator takes care to emphasize Hygelac's continued seniority (*þām ðǣr sēlra wæs*), just as he had done previously when Hrothgar's authority had been threatened by the Danes' proclamation of the young Geat's throne-worthiness (863–64).[187] The hero's rise to the throne is in fact the consequence of a series of disasters that befall the Hrethlings.

The highly allusive manner in which the poet sketches the background to Beowulf's accession strongly suggests that the poem's original audience was, if anything, more familiar with Geatish – and indeed Swedish – royal legend than they were with Scylding tradition:[188]

Eft þæt geīode ufaran dōgrum	2200
hilde-hlæmmum, syððan Hygelāc læg,	
ond Heardrēde hilde-mēceas	
under bord-hrēoðan tō bonan wurdon,	
ðā hyne gesōhtan on sige-þēode	
hearde hild-frecan, Heaðo-Scilfingas,	2205
nīða genægdan nefan Hererīces:	
syððan Bēowulfe brāde rīce	
on hand gehwearf; hē gehēold tela	
fīftig wintra – wæs ðā frōd cyning,	
eald ēþel-weard –	2210
(2200–10a).[189]	

---

[186] Biggs, 'Politics of Succession', 731–32.
[187] See above, pp. 60–61.
[188] For the argument that Beowulf is a fictionalized elaboration of his legendary uncle, Hygelac, see Chapter Two, pp. 126–39. See also Chapter Two, pp. 104–05, for a summary of royal legends that may have been known to the audience.
[189] On connections between the circumstances of Beowulf's accession and the roots of the dragon-fight, see Chapter Three.

The Dynastic Life-Cycle and the Structure of the Poem

[Eventually it came to pass in later days, with the clashing of battles, after Hygelac lay dead, and war-blades became Heardred's slayer under the shield-wall, when they sought him out among the victory-people, fierce war-attackers, the nephew of Hereric (i.e. Heardred); then the broad kingdom came into the hands of Beowulf; he held it well for fifty years – that was an experienced king, old guardian of the people [...].]

Further equally casual references to the wars between the Scylfings and Hrethlings are scattered throughout the final section of the narrative. From these passages we gather that King Hrethel had three sons, Herebeald, Hæthcyn and Hygelac, and one daughter, who married Ecgtheow of the Wægmundings,[190] and bore a son, Beowulf. The hero himself describes how he was reared at the royal court from the age of seven by his grandfather, King Hrethel, who treated him as a son:[191]

Ic wæs syfan-wintre þā mec sinca baldor,
frēa-wine folca æt mīnum fæder genam;
hēold mec ond hæfde Hrēðel cyning,   2430
geaf mē sinc ond symbel, sibbe gemunde;
næs ic him tō līfe lāðra ōwihte,
beorn in burgum, þonne his bearna hwylc,
Herebeald ond Hæðcyn oððe Hygelāc mīn.
(2428–34). (Emphasis added).

[I was seven years old when the giver of treasures, friendly lord of the people, took me from my father, kept me and held me, king Hrethel, gave me treasure and feasting, remembered kinship; I was in no way more hateful to him, a young man in the courts, than any of his sons, *Herebeald and Hæthcyn, or my Hygelac*.]

A series of parallels with the Danish royal house suggest that the poet has manipulated royal traditions in order to place the Scyldings and Hrethlings in structural apposition, the one dynasty in its ascendancy, the other in terminal decline. This apposition underpins the structure of the dynastic drama. Hence, for example, Hrethel's fostering of Beowulf echoes Hrothgar's treatment of the infant hero during the period of Ecgtheow's exile as well as his subsequent attempts to integrate the young Geat into the Danish royal house. Hrethel also resembles Healfdene, who likewise produced three sons, *Heorogār ond Hrōðgār ond Hālga til* (61), and a daughter.[192] Indeed, as Thomas D. Hill notes, Beowulf's relationship to Hygelac,

---

[190] For speculation as to Ecgtheow's origins, see Wardale, 'The Nationality of Ecgðeow'; and R. P. Lehmann, 'Ecgþeow the Wægmunding: Geat or Swede?', *ELN* 31 (1994), 1–5. See further Chapter Three, pp. 18 n.84, 87, 187 n.114.
[191] See K3, p. xlv.
[192] In addition, the description of the young Beowulf as *beorn in burgum* (2433a) recalls the earlier reference to Scyld's son, Beow, as *geong in geardum* (13a).

as a nephew of the current ruler, is equivalent to Hrothulf and Hrothgar.[193] However, as Gerald Morgan notes, there is one major difference between these two æthelings in terms of dynastic status: while Hrothulf has a strong claim to the Danish throne because he can trace his ancestry directly back to the founder of the royal house via his father, Halga, Beowulf's descent from Hrethel comes through his mother, thereby weakening his claim.[194] Indeed, Beowulf's rise to the throne is only brought about through a series of disasters that befall the house of Hrethel.

Developing the theme of fratricide that hangs over the Danish royal house, in the final section the poet traces the roots of the fall of the Hrethlings back to the accidental slaying of Herebeald, King Hrethel's eldest son, by his own brother, Hæthcyn.[195] The story of Herebeald's death is related by Beowulf himself in a long speech at Hronesnæss as he prepares for what he knows will be his last battle.[196] In contrast with the poem's opening section, wherein images of old kings were balanced by those of flourishing princes, the aged King Beowulf now ponders the predicaments of two grief-stricken old men, Hrethel and an unnamed *gomelum ceorle*,[197] both of whom can only watch helplessly as the promise of youth is wasted:[198]

---

[193] T. D. Hill, 'Scyld Scefing', p. 44.
[194] Morgan, 'The Treachery of Hrothulf', 29–30.
[195] On links between this story and the Norse myth of the slaying of Baldr by Hoðr, see R. Frank, 'Skaldic Verse and the Date of *Beowulf*', in Chase, ed. (1981), pp. 123–49, at 132; North, *Origins*, pp. 199–202; H. O'Donoghue, 'What has Baldr to do with Lamech?', *MÆ* 72 (2003), 82–107; *CCB*, pp. 116–19. On Hermóðr and Heremod, see Chapter Two, pp. 108–09.
[196] G. Clark, 'The Hero and the Theme', p. 276, notes that the common labelling of this speech as a 'soliloquy' is problematic as the hero wishes his companions well in the preceding lines (2418): 'The representation of Beowulf is severely "dramatic". His part has no soliloquies; he addresses audiences within the poem, not us.' However, in its introspection and use of epic simile this speech stands apart from others in the poem. Although Louviot does not discuss this passage in her recent study of Beowulfian speeches, it would seem to fit into her category of 'isolated speeches' (pp. 35–38), that is speeches that leave no room for an answer and thereby elevate the status of the speaker. Louviot comments: 'To some extent, they function as icons of heroic culture, which may explain why they are represented as isolated set pieces' (*Direct Speech*, p. 35). For further discussion of this passage, see D. Whitelock, '*Beowulf* 2444–2471', *MÆ* 8 (1939), 198–204; L. Georgianna, 'King Hrethel's Sorrow and the Limits of Heroic Action in *Beowulf*', *Speculum* 62 (1987), 829–50; K4, pp. 245–48; *CCB*, pp. 229–33; Soper, *Count of Days*, pp. 200–05.
[197] For possible connections between the *gomelum ceorle* and Odin, who is often depicted as an old man and is associated with hanging, see *CCB*, p. 118.
[198] Georgianna contrasts the disorienting effect of Herebeald's death with the 'ceremonial epic grandeur' of Scyld's funeral ('King Hrethel's Sorrow', 834). For parallels with fathers' laments in other Germanic and ON texts, see J. Harris, 'A Nativist Approach to *Beowulf*: the Case of Germanic Elegy', in *Companion to Old English Poetry*, ed. H. Aertsen and R. H. Bremmer Jr. (Amsterdam, 1994),

Swā bið geōmorlīc   gomelum ceorle
tō gebīdanne,   þæt his byre rīde   2445
giong on galgan.   Þonne hē gyd wrece,
sārigne sang,   þonne his sunu hangað
hrefne tō hrōðre,   ond hē him helpe ne mæ
eald ond in-frōd   ǣnige gefremman,
symble bið gemyndgad   morna gehwylce   2450
eaforan ellor-sīð;   ōðres ne gȳmeð
tō gebīdanne   burgum in innan
yrfe-weardas,   þonne se ān hafað
þurh dēaðes nȳd   dǣda gefondad.
Gesyhð sorh-cearig   on his suna būre   2455
wīn-sele wēstne,   windge reste,
rēotge berofene;   rīdend swefað,
hæleð in hoðman;   nis þǣr hearpan swēg,
gomen in geardum,   swylce ðǣr iū wǣron.
Gewīteð þonne on sealman,   sorh-lēoð gæleð   2460
ān æfter ānum;   þūhte him eall tō rūm,
wongas ond wīc-stede.
                        Swā Wedra helm
æfter Herebealde   heortan sorge
weallinde wæg;   wihte ne meahte
on ðām feorh-bonan   fǣghðe gebētan;   2465
nō ðȳ ǣr hē þone heaðo-rinc   hatian ne meahte
lāðum dǣdum,   þēah him lēof ne wæs.
Hē ðā mid þǣre sorhge,   þē him sīo sār belamp,
gum-drēam ofgeaf,   Godes lēoht gecēas;
eaferum lǣfde,   swā dēð ēadig mon,   2470
lond ond lēod-byrig,   þā hē of līfe gewāt.
(2444–71). (Emphasis added).

[*So* an old man is sad when he has to live to see his young son ride on the gallows; then he must recite a sad tale, a sorrowful song, when his son hangs, as a comfort to the ravens, and he cannot offer him any help, old and wise. Every morning, continuously, he is reminded of his son's passing; he does not care to wait in the courts for another heir, when that one, through the compulsion of death, tasted evil deeds. He sees sorrowfully in his son's chamber the empty wine-hall, the windy bower, deprived of joy; the riders sleep, warriors in their graves; there is no joy of the harp, no games in the courts, such as there once was. He retires to the couch, sings a sorrow-song, one after the other, it all seems too empty to him, the fields and dwellings.

So the Protector of the Weders lamented in his heart after Herebeald, surging with sorrows; not at all could he settle that feud with that life-slayer; nor

---

pp. 45–62; and J. Harris, '*Homo necans borealis*: Fatherhood and Sacrifice in *Sonatorrek*', in *Myth in Early Northwest Europe*, ed. S. O. Glosecki (Tempe, AZ, 2007), pp. 153–73.

could he hate that battle-warrior for the loathsome deed, though he was not
dear to him. He then, with that sorrow that so sorely afflicted him, gave up
the joys of men, chose God's light; left land and stronghold to his sons, as a
blessed man does, when he departed from life.]

A series of verbal parallels link this speech with the Scyld-prologue, signalling another tragic variation on the dynastic theme. For example, while Scyld's son, Beow, was born *geong in geardum* [...] *folce tō frōfre* (13–14a), the *gomelum ceorle* must watch as his son is hanged *gīong on galgan* [...] *hrefne tō hrōðre, ond hē him helpe ne mæg* (2446–48).[199] Similarly, while *Scyldes eafera* (19a), Beow, becomes king once his father has departed (*fæder ellor hwearf*, 55b), the unnamed old man's first-born son (*se ān*, 2453b) departs from the world before his father (*eaforan ellor-sīð*, 2451a), reversing the normal pattern of succession. The sorrow of the Danes at the departure of their aged king Scyld (*murnende mōd*, 50a) is echoed by the grieving figures of the unnamed old man (2455–56a) and King Hrethel (*weallinde wæg*, 2464a), both of whom lament the loss of their respective sons. Hrethel's own death (*þā hē of līfe gewāt*, 2471b) recalls that of the aged Scyld (*Him ðā Scyld gewāt*, 26a). Reflecting on his own position at the end of this line of Hrethlings, Beowulf observes that despite the tragedy of Herebeald's death, Hrethel was nevertheless able to leave his kingdom to his two remaining sons, Hæthcyn and Hygelac: *eaferum læfde, swā dēð ēadig mon/ lond ond lēod-byrig* (2470–71a). Beowulf himself, as we soon discover, has not been blessed with sons of his own (2729b–32a), and his death therefore marks the end of the Hrethlings.[200]

While Beowulf's speech at Hronesnæss concentrates on the deaths of Herebeald and Hrethel, it is not until several hundred lines later, during the Geatish messenger's prophecy at the hero's funeral, that we learn of the circumstances that had led to the accession of Hygelac. In this passage, we discover that after the deaths of Herebeald and Hrethel, Hæthcyn ruled for a time before he was killed by the great Scylfing king, Ongentheow, at the Battle of Ravenswood (2924–25).[201] In another variation of the Scyld-

---

[199] Cf. *Judith* 296a: *fuglum tō frōfre*, 'to the comfort of birds'; the reference is to the corpses of the defeated Assyrian warriors, in a variant of the 'beasts of battle' motif.

[200] For speculation that Beowulf was homosexual, see J. M. Hill, *Cultural World*, p. 88; D. Clark, *Between Medieval Men*, pp. 130–43. For the counter argument, see Biggs, 'Geatish Succession', 72–73. North, 'Heathen Polity', p. 103, argues that Beowulf fails to provide for the future security of the Geats because 'he rules without the ideology to support his power'.

[201] For a more detailed discussion of these conflicts and their relationship with the dragon-fight, see Chapter Three, pp. 180–94. For the suggestion that the audience was less familiar with Geatish history than with stories concerning the Danes, see Grundtvig, in Shippey and Haarder, p. 148; Benson, 'Originality', p. 61; J. D. Niles, 'Locating *Beowulf* in Literary History', *Exemplaria* 5 (1993),

The Dynastic Life-Cycle and the Structure of the Poem

prologue, the Geats briefly find themselves *hlāford-lēase*, 'lordless' (2935a), during this battle, just as the Danes had prior to the arrival of the 'stranger king' Scyld. The Geats' saviour arrives now in the figure of Hygelac, Hrethel's only surviving son, who routs the Swedes (2941b–45) and succeeds his brother Hæthcyn to the throne. The description of Hygelac as a *geongne gūð-cyning*, 'young war-king' (1969a), at the time of Beowulf's return from Denmark suggests that he had not long assumed the throne after Hæthcyn's death.

Hygelac's own premature death in the Frisian raid results in another succession crisis for the Hrethlings. Herebeald and Hæthcyn both died without issue, leaving only Hygelac's young son, Heardred, with a direct paternal link to the dynastic founder. Given Hygelac's warlike career, the Geats find themselves vulnerable to attack from all sides and in urgent need of strong leadership. Fearing that Heardred is too young to rule on his own, Hygelac's widow, Queen Hygd, therefore takes the pragmatic step of offering the throne instead to her nephew, Beowulf, the sole survivor of the Frisian raid, despite his weaker claim in terms of ancestry.[202] With this proposal, Beowulf once more unexpectedly finds himself on the cusp of royal power. In refusing Hygd's offer, the hero demonstrates his respect for the dynastic principle, just as Wealhtheow had years before in Heorot.[203] Despite the entreaties of the Geats, Beowulf chooses to act as a protector to the young Heardred until he reaches his majority, echoing Wealhtheow's instructions to Hrothulf to safeguard her sons after Hrothgar's death (1180b–87).[204] The Geatish hero has learned from the political wisdom of the Danish queen:

> Oferswam ðā sio-leða bigong   sunu Ecgðeowes,
> earm ān-haga   eft tō lēodum;
> þǣr him Hygd gebēad   hord ond rīce,
> bēagas on brego-stōl;   bearne ne truwode,   2370
> þæt hē wið ælf-ylcum   ēþel-stōlas
> healdan cūðe,   ðā wæs Hygelāc dēad.
> Nō ðȳ ǣr fēa-sceafte   findan meahton
> æt ðām æðelinge   ǣnige ðinga,
> þæt hē Heardrēde   hlāford wǣre,   2375
> oððe þone cyne-dōm   cīosan wolde;
> hwæðre hē him on folce   frēond-lārum hēold,

79–109, at 100–01. See, however, pp. 33 n.5, 86. For connections with external sources, such as *Ynglinga saga*, see Chapter Two, pp. 125–27.

[202] See A. Bonjour, 'Beowulf and Heardred', *ES* 32 (1951), 193–200, repr. in his *Twelve Beowulf Papers*, pp. 67–76. On the problem of child-kings in the Merovingian dynasty, see Chapter Four, pp. 206.

[203] On Wealhtheow's respect for the dynastic principle, and her advice to Hrothgar concerning his plan to adopt Beowulf, see above, pp. 19, 72–76.

[204] For discussion of this passage, see above, pp. 74–75.

ēstum mid āre, oð ðæt hē yldra wearð,
Weder-Gēatum wēold.
(2367-79a).

[The son of Ecgtheow swam across the expanse of the seas, wretched solitary one, returned to the homeland; there Hygd offered him the hoard and kingdom, rings and gift-throne; she did not trust her son, that he knew how to hold the ancestral seat against foreign troops, now that Hygelac was dead. But in no way, despite her misery, could they prevail upon that ætheling that he (i.e. Beowulf) should be Heardred's lord, or that he should choose (to rule) the kingdom. Yet he (i.e. Beowulf) protected him (i.e. Heardred) among the people with friendly counsel, honoured him with grace, until he had come of age, he (i.e. Heardred) ruled the Weder-Geats.]

No sooner has Heardred come of age, however, than he too becomes a victim of the long-running feud with the Scylfings, falling prey to Ongentheow's son and heir, Onela, for harbouring the Swedish exiles Eanmund and Eadgils (2379b–86).[205] With Heardred's death, the path is finally cleared for Beowulf, as the only surviving member of the dynasty, to assume the Geatish throne, with the permission of Onela (2387–90).[206]

As the culmination of this series of royal tragedies, King Beowulf's own failure to produce an heir takes on heightened significance, bringing the dynastic life-cycle to its end.[207] With the extinction of the Hrethling line, the spectre of lordlessness with which the poem had begun now returns.[208] In the aftermath of Beowulf's death, the Geatish Messenger predicts the annihilation of the Geatish tribe (2999–3027), before at King Beowulf's funeral an unnamed *Geatisc meowle*, 'Geatish old woman' (3150b),[209] pre-

---

[205] See below, pp. 97–98, and Chapter Three, pp. 183–84, 188–91.
[206] See below, pp. 95–96.
[207] See Chapter Two, pp. 126–39, for the suggestion that Beowulf's death without issue is a poetic amplification of Hygelac's untimely demise in Frisia.
[208] On the importance of this theme, and its relevance to the Anglo-Saxons, see Stanley, 'Lordlessness'.
[209] K. Müllenhoff, 'Die innere Geschichte des Beowulfs', *Zeitschrift für deutsche Philologie* 14 (1869), 193–224, at 242, proposed that the *Geatisc meowle*, 'old woman' (3150b), was Beowulf's widowed queen. However, as Klaeber argues, the poet is unlikely to have introduced such an important character at such a late point in the story (K3, p. 230). Biggs notes that the poet raises the possibility of 'a sexual failing on Beowulf's part simply by including in the final fitt a woman who laments him' ('Geatish succession', 69). For the identification of royal sterility with sin among the Carolingian kings of the late-ninth century by the tenth-century chronicler, Regino of Prüm, see F. Leneghan, '*Translatio imperii*: The Old English *Orosius* and the Rise of Wessex', *Anglia* 133 (2015), 656–705, at 667–68. Others have identified this figure as Hygelac's widow, Hygd, as a traditional ritual mourner (for references, see K4, p. 270), or as one of Beowulf's concubines (North, 'Heathen Polity', pp. 103–04).

Dynastic Strife Among the Scylfings

dicts a miserable future for the Geats, *wæl-fylle worn werudes egesan*, 'a great many slaughters, warrior's terror' (3154).[210]

Contributing to the overall mood of dynastic decay, the Messenger's speech provides details of the family feud that has torn apart the royal house of the Geats' Swedish rivals, the Scylfings.[211] In contrast to the opening section of the poem, and in keeping with the parallel portrait of the Hrethlings, no details are provided of Swedish royal births, with the Messenger focusing entirely on the deaths of old kings and violently contested successions. At the head of this dynasty, occupying a position equivalent to Scyld and Hrethel, is the old and terrible figure of Ongentheow.[212] The Messenger relates how Ongentheow took vengeance on the Geats on account of their arrogant abduction of his queen, by killing their king, Hæthcyn, and then relentlessly pursuing the survivors to Ravenswood:[213]

```
             ac wæs wīde cūð
þætte Ongenðīo    ealdre besnyðede
Hæðcen Hrēþling   wið Hrefna Wudu,                    2925
þā for onmēdlan   ǣrest gesōhton
Gēata lēode   Gūð-Scylfingas.
Sōna him se frōda   fæder ōhtheres,
eald ond egesfull   ondslyht āgeaf,
ābrēot brim-wīsan,   brȳd āhredde,                    2930
gomelan iō-meowlan   golde berofene,
Onelan mōdor   ond Ōhtheres,
ond ðā folgode   feorh-genīðlan
oð ðæt hī oðēodon   earfoðlīce
in Hrefnes Holt   hlāfordlēase.                       2935
Besæt ðā sin-herge   sweorda lāfe
wundum wērge;   wēan oft gehēt
earmre teohhe   ondlonge niht,
cwæð, hē on mergenne   mēces ecgum
gētan wolde   sum on galg-trēowum                     2940
```

[210] The MS is badly damaged at this point; I follow the emendations of K4.
[211] For general discussion of the poem's presentation of the Swedish royal house, see R. T. Farrell, *Beowulf, Swedes and Geats* (London, 1972). The reader may find it helpful to consult the family tree in this volume at pp. xv–xvi.
[212] The origin of the dynastic name 'Scylfing' is obscure, though the first element, Scylf, may be connected to Old English *scielf, scylf*, and Old Norse, *skjálf*, 'peak, crag, pinnacle'; see K4, pp. 471–72.
[213] For thematic links between the abduction of Ongentheow's queen and the awakening of the feud with the dragon, see Chapter Three, pp. 185–88.

fuglum tō gamene.
(2923b–41a). (Emphasis added).

[But it was widely known that *Ongentheow ended the life of Hæthcyn son of Hrethel* at Ravenswood when the Geats arrogantly first sought out the War-Scylfings. Immediately *the old father of Ohthere* [i.e. Ongentheow], *ancient and terrible*, repaid that attack, chopped down the sea-captain [i.e. Hæthcyn], recovered the bride, *the old woman* deprived of gold, mother of Onela and Ohthere, and then pursued his deadly enemies to Ravenswood, lordless. He [i.e. Ongentheow] besieged the sword-leavings [i.e. the Geats], weary with wounds, with his standing army; he often threatened suffering to that miserable troop all through the night, saying that in the morning he would gut them with the edges of swords, and leave some on the gallows tree for the sport of birds.]

Ongentheow's violent death at the hands of two of Hygelac's men, Eofor and Wulf, has already been described in vivid detail by Beowulf in his speech at Hronesnæss, in which the hero places similar emphasis on the Scylfing's age:

Þā ic on morgne gefrægn   mǣg ōðerne
billes ecgum   on bonan stǣlan,   2485
þǣr Ongenþēow   Eofores nīosað;
gūð-helm tōglād,   *gomela Scylfing*
hrēas hilde-blāc;   hond gemunde
fǣhðe genōge,   feorh-sweng ne oftēah.
(2484–89). (Emphasis added).

[Then I heard in the morning that one kinsman became the slayer to another, with swords' edges, where Ongentheow attacked Eofor; war-helmet slipped, *the ancient Scylfing* staggered, battle-pale; the hand (of Eofor) remembered enough feuds, did not withold the life-blow.]

Following Ongentheow's death, the Swedish throne appears to have been contested between his two sons, Ohthere and Onela, who had previously fought side-by-side against Hæthcyn, as Beowulf reports:

Þā wæs synn ond sacu   Swēona ond Gēata
ofer wīd wæter   wrōht gemǣne,
here-nīð heardra,   syððan Hrēðel swealt,
oð ðe him *Ongenðeowes   eaferan* wǣran   2475
from fyrd-hwate,   frēode ne woldon
ofer heafo healdan,   ac ymb Hrēosna Beorh
eatolne inwit-scear   oft gefremedon.
(2472–78). (Emphasis added).

[Then there was strife and hostility between the Swedes and Geats across the wide water, a common quarrel, fierce battle-conflict, after Hrethel died, and *Ongentheow's sons* were brave and warlike, they did not wish to keep peace over the sea, but around Hreosnabeorh they continually performed hostile and deadly warfare.]

Details of the power-struggle between Ongentheow's sons are provided prior to the hero's speech at Hronesnæss in the narrator's brief summary of the circumstances leading to Beowulf's accession. Here we learn that Ohthere's two sons, Eanmund and Eadgils, had rebelled against their uncle, Onela. It is unclear what motivated their revolt, though it seems likely that it was connected with a struggle between Onela and Ohthere over the succession which had resulted in the latter's death. Such a scenario would explain why the now-vulnerable sons of Ohthere sought refuge with the young Geatish king, Heardred, despite the long-standing enmity between these two royal houses:

> Hyne wræc-mæcgas
> ofer sæ sōhtan,   suna Ōhteres;
> hæfdon hȳ forhealden   helm Scylfinga,
> þone sēlestan   sæ-cyninga
> þāra ðe in Swīo-rīce   sinc brytnade,
> mære þēoden.
> (2379b–84a).

[Wretched exiles sought him (i.e. Heardred) out over the sea, the sons of Ohthere; they had rebelled against the protector of the Scylfings (i.e. Onela), the best of sea-kings of those who distributed treasure in the Swedish kingdom, glorious prince.]

As the narrator goes on to explain, Heardred would pay a heavy price for offering sanctuary to these exiled Scylfing princes, incurring the wrath of Onela:

> Him þæt tō mearce wearð:
> hē þær for feorme   feorh-wunde hlēat,   2385
> sweordes swengum,   *sunu Hygelāces*;
> ond him eft gewāt   *Ongenðioes bearn*
> hāmes nīosan,   syððan Heardrēd læg,
> lēt ðone brego-stōl   Bīowulf healdan,
> Gēatum wealdan;   *þæt wæs gōd cyning*.[214]   2390
> (Emphasis added).

---

[214] Given the extensive praise of Onela in the preceding lines (2381b–84a) it seems more likely that this half-line refers to the Swedish ruler rather than Beowulf. If read this way, *þæt wæs gōd cyning* completes an envelope pattern that begins with *helm Scylfinga* (2381b), the subject of which is the great Swedish king, Onela. Either way, the temporary ambiguity here may be deliberate, in that it invites the audience to wonder whether Beowulf *was* indeed a good king, in much the same way that the syntax of line 915 creates temporary confusion over whether *fyren*, 'crime/evil', entered Beowulf or Heremod (see p. 159 n.23.

[That was deadly for him (i.e. Heardred); because of his hospitality he received a deadly wound, with the swinging of swords, *the son of Hygelac*; and afterwards *Ongentheow's son* returned to seek out his home, after Heardred lay dead, he let Beowulf hold the gift-throne, rule the Geats; that was a good king.]

Beowulf's accession to the Geatish throne is thereby shown to be the result not only of untimely deaths among members of his own royal house but also of feuding within their rival dynasty, the Scylfings. The vulnerability of the exiled Scylfing princes (*wræc-mæcgas*, 2381b; *fēa-sceaftum*, 2393a) and their young Hrethling protector, Heardred, laid low by *sweordes swengum*, 'the swinging of a sword' (2386a), stands in apposition to the flourishing of Danish princes that characterized the first, short phase of the dynastic life-cycle.[215]

This deadly conflict between two generations of Ongentheow's descendants, and the terrible consequences of Heardred's harbouring of the exiled Scylfings, recurs as a minor theme throughout the last phase of the dynastic life-cycle. Hence, during the hero's fight with the dragon, we learn of the slaying of Eanmund by Wiglaf's father, Weohstan, a warrior in the service of Onela:[216]

þæt wæs mid eldum   Ēanmundes lāf,
suna Ōhtheres; þām æt sæcce wearð,
wræccan wine-lēasum   Wēohstān bana
mēces ecgum,   ond his māgum ætbær
brūn-fāgne helm,   hringde byrnan,   2615
eald-sweord etonisc; þæt him Onela forgeaf,
his gædelinges   gūð-gewædu,
fyrd-searo fūslic – nō ymbe ðā fæhðe spræc,
þēah ðe hē his brōðor bearn   ābredwade.
(2611–19).

[That was known among men as Eanmund's heirloom, Ohthere's son; he (i.e. Eanmund) was killed in war, friendless exile, by Weohstan with the edges of that sword, and he (i.e. Weohstan) carried off to his kinsman (i.e. to Onela) the gold-decorated helmet, the ringed mailcoat, the gigantic ancient sword; in return for that Onela gave to him (i.e. Weohstan) the war-gear of his young kinsman (i.e. Eanmund), the splendid war-equipment; he (i.e. Onela) never spoke about the feud, although he (i.e. Weohstan *or* Onela?)[217] had killed his (i.e. Onela's) brother's son (i.e. Eanmund).]

---

[215] Like the exiled Swedish princes, the foundling Scyld was himself once *fēasceaft* (7a).

[216] Weohstan plundered Eanmund's sword and later passed it on to his son, Wiglaf. For further discussion of this passage, see Chapter Three, pp. 190–91.

[217] Compare the reference to Hygelac as *bonan Ongenþeoes*, 'Ongentheow's slayer' (1968a), despite the fact that this act was technically performed by Eofor and Wulf; see pp. 94, 130–31.

The Dynastic Life-Cycle and the Structure of the Poem

Onela's employment of Weohstan to kill *his brōðor bearn*, 'his brother's son' (2619), foregrounds the theme of kin-violence that had been repeatedly hinted at in the preceding sections of the poem.

Despite the fact that it was only with Onela's permission that Beowulf came to occupy the Geatish throne following Heardred's death, the hero then perhaps surprisingly sides with the surviving Scylfing exile, Eadgils, in a counter-attack against the Swedish king. What might appear disloyalty towards Onela on the hero's part can, however, be accounted for by Beowulf's overriding obligation to avenge the slayer of his own king and kinsman, Heardred:[218]

> Sē ðæs lēod-hyres lēan gemunde
> uferan dōgrum, Ēadgilse wearð
> fēa-sceaftum frēond; folce gestēpte
> ofer sǣ sīde sunu Ōhteres,
> wigum ond wǣpnum; hē gewræc syððan
> cealdum cear-sīðum, cyning ealdre binēat.
> (2391–96).

[He (i.e. Beowulf) did not forget that prince's (i.e. Heardred's) fall in later days, he (i.e. Beowulf) became a friend to the destitute Eadgils; he (i.e. Beowulf) supported the son of Ohthere (i.e. Eadgils) across the broad sea with warriors and weapons. Afterwards he (i.e. Beowulf *or* Eadgils?) took revenge with cold sorrow-journeys, deprived the king (i.e. Onela) of his life.]

As we have seen, in the earlier stages of the poem the narrator had merely alluded to future conflicts among the Scyldings.[219] With the dynastic life-cycle nearing its end, the poet now brings the principal threat to the survival of dynasties – the Cainite sin of kin-murder – into the narrative foreground by punctuating the narration of the dragon-fight with these repeated allusions to the wars between the Scylfings and the Hrethlings.

The impact of dynastic feuding on a ruler's subjects emerges into the foreground in the Geatish Messenger's speech at Beowulf's funeral. Despite Beowulf's assistance of Eadgils in his revolt against Onela, the Messenger predicts that the Swedes will now seek recompense for the actions of Hæthcyn, who over fifty years previously had arrogantly (2927a: *for onmēdlan*) sought out and attacked Ongentheow:[220]

---

[218] On kin-murder among the Scyldings, see pp. 52–53, 66–67. On the Hrethling prince Hæthcyn's accidental slaying of his brother, Herebeald, see pp. 88–90, 105, 183.

[219] See pp. 50–76.

[220] Beowulf claims to have ruled the Geats for fifty years after Heardred's death (2732b–33a). Hæthcyn's death at the Battle of Ravenswood took place prior to the reigns of Hygelac and Heardred.

> Nē ic te Swēo-ðēode sibbe oððe trēowe
> wihtne ne wēne, ac wæs wīde cūð
> þætte Ongenðīo ealdre besnyðede   2925
> Hæðcen Hrēþling wið Hrefna Wudu,
> þā for onmēdlan ǣrest gesōhton
> Gēata lēode Gūð-Scilfingas.
> [...]
> Þæt ys sīo fǣhðo ond se fēondscipe,
> wæl-nīð wera, ðæs ðe ic wēn hafo,   3000
> þē ūs sēceað tō Swēona lēoda,
> syððan hīe gefricgeað frēan ūserne
> ealdorlēasne, þone ðe ǣr gehēold
> wið hettendum hord ond rīce,
> æfter hæleða hryre, hwate Scilfingas,[221]   3005
> folc-rēd fremede, oððe furður gēn
> eorlscipe efnde.
> (2922–27, 2999–3007a).

[I do not expect peace or truce from the Swedish people at all, for it was widely known that Ongentheow deprived Hæthcyn, son of Hrethel, of life at Ravenswood, for the Geatish people arrogantly first sought out the War-Scylfings. [...] That is the feud and the fierce hostility, deadly slaughter of men, that I expect, after the Swedish people seek us out, once they discover that our lord is lifeless, he who before protected the hoard and kingdom against the hated ones, after the fall of warriors, the brave Scylfings, he worked for the people's benefit and, what is more, performed noble deeds.]

In the Messenger's bleak assessment of Geatish-Swedish relations, Beowulf's assistance of Eadgils will count for little given the latter's obligation to avenge the slaying of Ongentheow by Hygelac's warriors, Eofor and Wulf. Ironically, it was this same sense of loyalty to kin that had compelled Beowulf to join Eadgils in his attack on Onela. Through this tightening web of conflicting allegiances, the fates of these two royal houses are woven together, providing a narrative counterpoint to the unfolding conflict between the hero and the dragon.[222]

Wiglaf: the End of the Line?

At the beginning of this chapter, we saw how during the first phase of the dynastic life-cycle Beow generously distributed the treasures that his father had won in battle, thereby guaranteeing his own accession on the event of Scyld's death. The narrator stresses that conduct such as this will

---

[221] Emended in K4 (p. 102) from MS *scildingas*.
[222] See Chapter Three, pp. 180–94.

The Dynastic Life-Cycle and the Structure of the Poem

ensure that *wil-gesīþas*, 'willing retainers' (23a), support a prince when he too reaches old age and faces the prospect of war. In Beowulf's final struggle with the dragon, however, we are presented with the reverse situation, in which a king's subjects fail to repay his generosity with loyalty:[223]

> Nealles him on hēape hand-gesteallan,
> æðlinga bearn ymbe gestōdon
> hilde-cystum, ac hȳ on holt bugon,
> ealdre burgan.
> (2596–99a).

> [Not at all did his hand-picked companions, sons of æthelings, stand around him in a troop with warlike courage, but they fled to the forest, protected their lives.]

The sole exception to this cowardly betrayal of King Beowulf is Wiglaf, a young warrior of the Wæmundings, the tribe of Beowulf's father, Ecgtheow. As mentioned above, Wiglaf's own father, Weohstan, had played an important role in the Swedish wars as the slayer of Eanmund, on behalf of King Onela (2611–19).[224]

This Wiglaf certainly provides the youthful vigour that the aged Beowulf now lacks.[225] Indeed, the poet repeatedly emphasizes Wiglaf's youth, referring to him as a *geongan cempan*, 'young warrior' (2626a),[226] *geongum gār-wigan*, 'young spear-warrior' (2674a, 2811a), *se maga geonga*, 'the young kinsman' (2675a), and *guman unfrōdum*, 'an inexperienced warrior' (2821b), while simultaneously highlighting Beowulf's age (e.g. 2817a: *gomelan*, 'old man').[227] This aspect of their relationship comes to the fore in the fight with the dragon, during which Beowulf's old sword, Nægling, breaks, leaving the king powerless:

> Byrne ne meahte
> *geongum gār-wigan* gēoce gefremman,

---

[223] Beowulf's superlative generosity is commemorated by his own men in the poem's final line: *lēodum līðost*, 'the kindest to the people' (3182a).

[224] See above, pp. 96–97. On Wiglaf's name, which means literally 'war-remnant', see P. Portnoy, *The Remnant: Essays on a Theme in Old English Verse* (London, 2005), pp. 90–91. For discussion of Wiglaf's relationship to the Hrethlings, see Biggs, 'Geatish succession', 71–74.

[225] Orchard comments: 'in the absence of a dynamic and positive Beowulf in the second part of the poem, the heroic mantle falls on Wiglaf' (*CCB*, p. 261).

[226] The same collocation is used to describe the young Offa (1948b) and the young Danish warrior taunted by the old Heathobard in Beowulf's prediction of the failed marriage of Ingeld and Freawaru (2044b). Beowulf is himself referred to as a *cempa* several times (1312b: *æþele cempa*; 1551b: *Geata cempa*; 1585a: *rēþe cempa*; 1761a: *mǣre cempa*).

[227] The term *gamol* is also used by Beowulf to refer to the nameless *gomelum ceorle* (2444b) who sees his son hanged on the gallows.

ac *se maga geonga* under his mæges scyld 2675
elne geēode, þā his āgen wæs
glēdum forgrunden. Þā gēn guð-cyning
mōd gemunde, mægen-strengo slōh
hilde-bille, þæt hyt on heafolan stōd
nīþe genȳded; *Nægling forbærst,* 2680
geswāc æt sæcce sweord Bīowulfes
gomol ond græg-mæl. Him þæt gifeð ne wæs
þæt him īrenna ecge mihton
helpan æt hilde; *wæs sīo hond tō strong,*
sē ðe mēca gehwane mīne gefræge 2685
swenge ofersōhte þonne hē tō sæcce bær
wæpen wundum heard; næs him wihte ðē sēl.
(2673b–87). (Emphasis added).

[The mail-coat could not bring about help for *the young spear-warrior*, but *the young warrior* achieved glory under his kinsman's shield, when his own was completely consumed with flames. Still, the war-king recalled glory, dealt a mighty blow with his war-blade, so that it stuck into the head, driven in by hatred; *Nægling shattered, Beowulf's sword fell apart in battle, ancient and gray*. It was not granted to him that the edges of irons might help him at battle; *the hand was too strong*, he who, as I have heard, overtaxed every blade in the swinging when he carried to battle the weapon, fierce with wounds; it was no help to him at all.]

In this scene, images of youth and age are juxtaposed in the context of a deadly struggle, echoing the earlier encounter between the young Beowulf and the aged Hrothgar, for whom the *gewin* (struggle) with Grendel was *tō strang* [...] *tō swȳð*, 'too strong [...] too great' (133b, 191b). Wiglaf is thus presented as the last in a line of youthful counterparts to ageing kings, stretching back to Beow and the young Beowulf himself. In terms of prowess, this young Wægmunding warrior might, therefore, seem an ideal candidate to succeed Beowulf on the Geatish throne. The possibility of Wiglaf's accession appears to move a step closer as the dying Beowulf laments his own lack of a son, while pondering what to do with the Hrethling arms that he wears:[228]

Nū ic suna mīnum syllan wolde
gūð-gewædu, þær mē gifeð swā
ǣnig yrfe-weard æfter wurde
līce gelenge.
(2729–32a).

[228] On this passage, see Biggs, 'Geatish succession', 55–56. See also above, p. 19. On Beowulf's lack of kin as a by-product of his largely fictional status, see Chapter Two, p. 119.

[Now I would give my war-gear to my son, if any successor had been granted to me, surviving after my body.]

We saw above how kings in *Beowulf* signal their intended successor through the bestowal of ancestral armour.[229] In the absence of a son, or indeed brother or cousin who can claim direct paternal descent from Hrethel, Beowulf presents his armour to his Wægmunding relative, Wiglaf, who alone had fought beside him to the last:

> Dyde him of healse   hring gyldenne
> þīoden þrīst-hȳdig   þegne gesealde,   2810
> *geongum gār-wigan*   gold-fāhne helm,
> bēah ond byrnan,   hēt hyne brūcan well:
> 'Þū eart ende-lāf   ūsses cynnes,
> Wægmundinga;   ealle wyrd forswēop
> mīne māgas   tō metod-sceafte,   2815
> eorlas on elne;   ic him æfter sceal.'
> Þæt wæs *þām gomelan*   gingæste word
> brēost-gehygdum,   ǣr hē bǣl cure,
> hāte heaðo-wylmas;   him of hraðre gewāt
> sāwol sēcean   sōð-fæstra dōm.   2820
>   Ðā wæs gegongen   *guman unfrōdum*
> earfoðlīce,   þæt hē on eorðan geseah
> þone lēofestan   *līfes æt ende*
> blēate gebǣran.
> (2809–24a). (Emphasis added).

[He took from his neck a golden ring, the bold-minded prince, gave it to the thane, *the young spear-warrior*, the gold-adorned helmet, ring and mail-coat, ordered him to make good use of them: 'You are the last of our kin, of the Wægmundings; fate has swept away all of *my family* at the appointed time, warriors in glory; I must follow after them.' That was the final word of *that old man* from the thoughts of his heart, before he chose the fire, hot battle-surges; from his body his soul departed to seek out the judgement of the firm-in-truth.

Then it came to pass dreadfully for *the young warrior* that he saw on the earth that most beloved one *at the end of his life*, faring so wretchedly.]

However, despite this gesture's dynastic implications, the possibility that Wiglaf will ever succeed Beowulf as ruler of the Geats is never seriously entertained, presumably on account of his lack of Hrethling blood.[230]

---

[229] For Heorogar's conferral of the Scylding armour to his brother, Hrothgar, see pp. 48–49; for the journey of these same treasures from Hrothgar to Beowulf and subsequently to Hygelac, see pp. 84–85, 132–33.

[230] For the suggestion that Wiglaf did indeed succeed Beowulf, see Glosecki,

Indeed, as Biggs notes, the presentation of Wiglaf as the closest thing the hero has to a son only serves to highlight Beowulf's lack of an heir in the strict dynastic sense.[231] In referring to Wiglaf as the last of *ūsses cynnes* (2813b) (i.e. the Wægmundings), as well as alluding more generally to the deaths of *mīne māgas* (2815a), the hero movingly evokes the demise of both his maternal and paternal family-lines. In Beowulf's death-scene, the poet has thereby carefully fashioned a scene of non-succession, in which an old king confers his arms onto a warrior who, brave though he is, has no ancestral claim to the throne.[232] The contrast with the prologue, in which Scyld was succeeded without incident by his son, Beow, is striking.[233]

Of Wiglaf's future career, the poet has nothing to say; his primary concern is with the fall of the Hrethlings. Nevertheless, the Geatish Messenger's prediction that the Swedes, now presumably ruled by Eadgils, will attack once news of Beowulf's death is made known (2999–3007a) places Wiglaf in a precarious position, given the involvement of his father, Weohstan, in the killing of Eanmund. Indeed, Wiglaf is not named among the twelve *æþelinga bearn*, 'sons of æthelings' (3170a), who ride around Beowulf's barrow in the poem's final scene. As Biggs notes: 'These sons of nobles […] like the sons who follow their fathers to the throne in the opening genealogy, focus attention on Beowulf's lack of a son of his own.'[234] Moreover, given the vital importance attached to royal blood in matters of succession throughout the poem, the absence of a single *cyninges bearn*, 'king's son', from this party of twelve is telling. With the last of the Hrethlings gone, the borders that Beowulf had protected from attack for fifty years (2732b–39a) are suddenly vulnerable. The likelihood of a violent struggle over the throne between these æthelings makes the future of the Geats seem even more uncertain. In this way, the poem weaves together the fates of princes, kings, royal houses and their subjects within a carefully structured framework of dynastic rise and fall.

'*Beowulf* and the Wills'. For counter-arguments, however, see W. F. Bryan, 'The Wægmundings–Swedes or Geats?', *MP* 34 (1936), 113–18; N. E. Eliason, 'Beowulf, Wiglaf and the Wægmundings', *ASE* 7 (1978), 95–105; and Biggs, 'Geatish succession', 72–74.

[231] Biggs, 'Geatish succession', 71.

[232] See further Niles, 'Locating *Beowulf* in Literary History', 91; Biggs, 'Geatish succession', 72–73.

[233] On the political and theological implications of this contrast, see Chapter Four, pp. 227–35.

[234] Biggs, 'Geatish succession', 71.

Conclusion

This chapter has argued that the main structural contrast in *Beowulf* is not, as Tolkien argued, between the hero's youth and age but rather between three different phases in the life-cycle of an archetypal dynasty. The first, shortest stage in the dynastic life-cycle (1–67) describes the formation of a royal house – the Scyldings – before charting its early period of growth across three generations. Portraits of the aged Scylding rulers, Scyld, Beow and Healfdene, are balanced by their harmonious relations with young princes and successors. The much longer, second phase meditates on the fortunes of this same royal house as it reaches maturity, evenly poised between past achievements and future crises (68–1887). The third and final phase of the dynastic life-cycle takes as its subject the fall of Beowulf's own royal house, the Hrethlings (1888–3182).

Through acknowledging the structural significance of the dynastic life-cycle, we can better understand the poet's reticence on the subject of the hero's own childhood. In the first part of the poem, the main theme is not Beowulf's youth but the rise of the Scyldings.[235] It is only towards the end of the poem, by which stage the narrative has become dominated by images of the deaths of kings and princes, that we learn how Beowulf had once been despised as a youth, with the Geats considering *þæt hē slēac wǣre,/ æðeling un-from*, 'that he was slothful, an unpromising ætheling' (2187b–88a).[236]

By imaginatively setting legends of the rise of the Scyldings and the fall of the Hrethlings in structural apposition, the *Beowulf*-poet produced a political framework within which the hero's monster-fights were made meaningful for the work's original audience.[237] The next two chapters will explore in more detail how the poet developed the dynastic drama by embellishing royal legends through the re-arrangement of episodes and the introduction of new characters, themes and plots derived from folk-tale, myth and other sources.

---

[235] Though Scribe A seems to have mistakenly believed that Beowulf was the son of Scyld; see above, p. 8. It is unclear whether Hrothgar's statement, *Ic hine cūðe cniht-wesende*, 'I knew him while he was still a boy' (372), implies that he had met, or simply heard of, Beowulf during the period of Ecgtheow's exile (372–76).

[236] See K3, p. 196, n. 7; G. J. Engelhardt, 'On the Sequence of Beowulf's *Geogoð*', MLN 68 (1953), 91–95; N. E. Eliason, 'Beowulf's Inglorious Youth', SP 76 (1979), 101–08; Biggs, 'Politics of Succession', 724–26; and North, 'Hrothulf's Childhood and Beowulf's'. As Biggs argues, the term *un-from*, 'unpromising', may be suggestive of Beowulf's outsider-status in terms of the Hrethling succession, due to his descent from Hrethel via the weaker maternal line ('Politics of Succession', 725). See further above, pp. 19, 91.

[237] For discussion of possible audiences and contexts, see the Conclusion.

2
Shaping the Dynastic Drama

This chapter explores how the poet transformed the raw material of royal legend into a powerful and original dynastic drama. Given the highly allusive manner in which the poet introduces dynastic material throughout the work, it is safe to assume that his original audience was steeped in legends of the Scyldings, Scylfings and Hrethlings. A brief outline of the main Scandinavian royal traditions that lie behind the poem, such as might have been known to the audience, is therefore provided below. Sections in square brackets and italics denote legends that are not directly described in the poem but are corroborated or suggested by external sources:

Scylding tradition:

King Heremod was deposed because of his greed and wickedness, resulting in an interregnum during which the Danes suffered greatly; eventually, King Healfdene restored the kingdom, bringing stability to the Danes; Healfdene had three sons, Heorogar, Hrothgar and Halga, and a daughter, who married the Scylfing king Onela; Heorogar had a son, Heoroweard; Hrothgar had two sons, Hrethric and Hrothmund, and a daughter, Freawaru; Halga had one son, Hrothulf; Heorogar succeeded Healfdene; from Heorogar the throne passed to his brother, Hrothgar, who had proved himself a strong military leader; King Hrothgar's daughter, Freawaru, married the Heathobard prince, Ingeld, in an attempt to smooth relations between the two dynasties; the planned alliance failed, with the result that the Heathobards attacked and burned Heorot; [*King Hrothgar and his nephew, Hrothulf, son of Halga, heroically defended the hall; Hrothgar was succeeded by Hrothulf, who enjoyed a long and successful reign, but was attacked and killed by Heoroweard, son of Heorogar; Heoroweard briefly took the throne but he was soon killed by a warrior loyal to Hrothulf; Heoroweard was succeeded by Hrethric, son of Hrothgar.*][1]

Scylfing tradition:

King Ongentheow had two sons, Ohthere and Onela; the Scylfings, led by Ohthere and Onela, attacked the Hrethlings, rulers of the Geats, after King Hrethel's death; the Hrethlings, led by their young king, Hæthcyn, launched a counter-attack, capturing Ongentheow's queen; the Scylfings killed King Hæthcyn at Ravenswood; Hæthcyn's brother, Hygelac, counter-attacked

---

[1] For discussion of the sources behind these traditions, see pp. 4–5, 36, 49, 53, 141–42.

and killed King Ongentheow; Ongentheow was eventually succeeded by Onela, who married the daughter of the Scylding ruler, King Healfdene; Ohthere's two sons, Eanmund and Eadgils, sought refuge with the young Hrethling king, Heardred, son of Hygelac; King Onela attacked the Geats, killing his own brother's son, Eanmund, and the Hrethling king, Heardred; supported by the Geats, the surviving Scylfing exile, Eadgils, attacked and killed his uncle, Onela; Eadgils became king of the Swedes.

Hrethling tradition:

King Hrethel had three sons, Herebeald, Hæthcyn and Hygelac; King Hrethel fought against the Scylfings; Herebeald was accidentally killed by his own brother, Hæthcyn, in a childhood shooting accident; King Hrethel died of grief and was succeeded by Hæthcyn; King Hæthcyn attacked the Scylfings and died at Ravenswood; Hæthcyn was succeeded by Hygelac; King Hygelac married Queen Hygd; King Hygelac had a son, Heardred; King Hygelac died in a foolhardy raid on the Franks and his bones were preserved as relics on an island on the Rhine; Hygelac was succeeded by his young son, Heardred, but he was killed by Onela, King of the Swedes, leaving no successor; without a king to protect them, the Geats were confronted with the threat of invasion from the Scylfings, to the north, and the Merovingian Franks, to the south.

Working within these broad traditional parameters, the *Beowulf*-poet nonetheless exercised a considerable degree of poetic licence, making a number of both major and minor interventions in order to dramatize dynastic crises. This chapter will argue that the most important of these interventions was the shaping of a new hero, King Beowulf, through the combination of an existing tale about a famous swimmer with legends of Sigemund the dragon-slayer and the death of King Hygelac. In merging these stories for a new purpose, the poet appears to have drawn upon a number of further narrative traditions, including a Scandinavian variant of Panzer's Folktale Type 301B (also known as 'The Bear's Son Tale', 'The Three Stolen Princesses' or 'Two Trolls'), as well as legends of dragon-slaying saints. From these and other raw materials, the poet fashioned a new narrative in which the death of a dragon-slaying king signifies the end of a royal line and the collapse of a nation.

In the second part of this chapter, I argue that the poet opportunistically inserted the story of Scyld Scefing and Beow into the interregnum between the legendary Danish kings Heremod and Healfdene in order to provide structural and thematic balance for the new story of the death of King Beowulf and to serve as a prologue to his dynastic drama. In composing this mythical account of the (re)formation of a royal house, the poet combined the legend of Heremod's decline with a rich and suggestive array of Scandinavian, biblical, Anglo-Saxon and perhaps also classical traditions. The adventures of the fictionalized hero provide the essential link between these structurally apposed tales of the rise of the Scyldings and the fall of the Hrethlings.

Making New Songs from Old

Once the hero's victory over Grendel in Heorot has been made known, a Danish court-poet takes to the floor to celebrate in verse *sīð Bēowulfes*, 'Beowulf's exploit/adventure' (872a).[2] This *scop* (lit. 'shaper') starts his song of Beowulf, however, by way of allusion to two earlier legendary figures, Sigemund the dragon-slayer and the wicked King Heremod:

>   Hwīlum cyninges þegn,
> guma gilp-hlæden,   gidda gemyndig,
> sē ðe eal fela   eald-gesegena
> worn gemunde,[3]   word ōþer fand   870
> sōðe gebunden;   secg eft *ongan*
> sīð Bēowulfes   snyttrum styrian
> ond on spēd wrecan   spel gerāde,
> wordum wrixlan;   wēlhwylc gecwæð,
> þæt hē fram Sigemundes   secgan hȳrde   875
> ellen-dǣdum,   uncūþes fela,
> Wælsinges gewin,   wīde sīðas,
> *þāra þe gumena bearn   gearwe ne wiston*
> (867b–78). (Emphasis added).

[Sometimes the king's thane, a man well-stocked with glorious words, knowledgable in songs, the one who could remember from far back a great many ancient tales, found other words truly bound together. The man afterwards *began* to skilfully recite Beowulf's exploits and to successfully recount a tale, to mix words. He spoke a good deal that he had heard said about Sigemund's glorious deeds, many unknown things, [about] the battles of Wael's son, *about which the sons of men did not readily know*.]

The Danish court-poet's account of Sigemund's career culminates in the hero's glorious defeat of a great dragon and plundering of its treasure-hoard:

> Hæfde āglǣca   elne gegonen,
> þæt hē bēah-hordes   brūcan mōste
> selfes dōme;   sǣ-bāt gehlēod,

---

[2] For discussion of this passage, see Tolkien, 'Commentary', pp. 280–92; *CCB*, pp. 105–14.

[3] See Introduction, p. 7, on the appearance of similar lines in a late Anglo-Saxon manuscript, possibly in the form of a quotation from, or allusion to, this passage.

bær on bearm scipes   beorhte frætwa
Wælses eafera;   wyrm hāt gemealt.
(893–97).

[The awe-inspiring one had achieved glory, so that he could enjoy the ring-hoard to his own judgement; he loaded the sea-boat, bore into the bosom of the ship shining treasures, Wael's son; the serpent melted in heat.]

Legends about the hero Sigemund (ON Sigmundr), and his son Sigurd (ON Sigurðr) and nephew Fitela (ON Sinfjötli), were well-known among the Germanic peoples and appear to have circulated throughout the Anglo-Saxon period. The name Sigemund appears twice in the Durham *Liber Vitae*, a ninth-century Northumbrian confraternity book, providing some indication of the legend's popularity in the early Anglo-Saxon period.[4] Moreover, the Prosopography of Anglo-Saxon England database (PASE) records a further four individuals bearing this name living from the ninth to eleventh centuries. The survival of traditions about Sigemund in the later period of Anglo-Danish rule is attested by a stone carving from the Old Minster at Winchester appearing to depict Sigemund and a wolf.[5] In Scandinavian and wider Germanic tradition, however, it is Sigemund's son, Sigurd (ON Sigurðr, MHG Siegfried), who was the more celebrated figure.[6] Indeed, as Orchard notes, *Beowulf* 'is the only source which attributes a dragon-slaying to Sigemund, rather than to his son'.[7] It is possible that the Danish *scop* (or rather the *Beowulf*-poet), for reasons now obscure, has transferred the dragon-slaying episode from Sigurd to

---

[4] For the text of the *Liber Vitae*, see *The Oldest English Texts*, ed. H. Sweet, EETS o.s. 34 (London, 1885), pp. 153–66; and *Durham Liber vitae: London, British Library, MS Cotton Domitian A.VII: edition and digital facsimile with introduction, codicological, prosopographical and linguistic commentary, and indexes including the Biographical Register of Durham Cathedral Priory (1083–1539) by A. J. Piper*, 3 vols, ed. D. Rollason and L. Rollason (London, 2007), I. For discussion of connections with *Beowulf*, see Whitelock, *Audience*, pp. 66–67; Wright, *Cultivation of Saga*, p. 19; R. L. Kellogg, 'The Context for Epic in Later Anglo-Saxon England', in *Heroic Poetry in the Anglo-Saxon Period: Studies in Honor of Jess B. Bessinger, Jr.*, ed. H. Damico and J. Leyerle (Kalamazoo, MI, 1993), pp. 139–56, at 146–47; Wormald, 'Redating'; Neidorf, 'Beowulf before *Beowulf*'; and Neidorf, 'Germanic Legend'.

[5] D. Tweddle, M. Biddle and B. Kjølby-Biddle date the carving to 'c. 980/993–4 and 1093–4, probably 1017–35' ('Winchester (Old Minster) 88, Hampshire', CASSS, 12 vols, IV: *South-East England* [Oxford, 1996], http://www.ascorpus.ac.uk/catvol4.php?pageNum_urls=277&totalRows_urls=293, accessed 3 January 2019). For a recent discussion, see Thomson, *Communal Creativity*, pp. 36–37. For a possible Spanish connection, see A. Breeze, '*Beowulf* 875–902 and the Sculptures at Sangüesa, Spain', *NQ* 38 (1991), 2–13.

[6] Sigurd is celebrated in the Old Norse *Völsunga saga* (c. 1270), while Siegfried is the hero of the Middle High German *Niebelungenlied* (c. 1200).

[7] *CCB*, p. 108. See further M. Griffith, 'Some difficulties in *Beowulf*, lines 874–902: Sigemund reconsidered', *ASE* 24 (1995), 11–41.

Sigemund. However, it seems more likely that *Beowulf* reflects an earlier version of the legend, in which Sigemund rather than Sigurd was the dragon-slayer.[8] What is significant here is that the same elements of the Sigemund-legend that the *scop* chooses to focus on, namely his slaying of a dragon, his winning of glory and his acquisition of a great treasure-hoard, will prove pivotal in the story of Beowulf's own death.[9]

Following this tale of Sigemund, the *scop* turns to the cautionary tale of King Heremod, who was betrayed to his enemies because of his *swīð-fer-hþes sīð*, 'strongminded way' (908a):[10]

> Sē wæs wreccena   wīde mǣrost
> ofer wer-þēode,   wīgendra hlēo,
> ellen-dǣdum – hē þæs ǣr onðāh –   900
> siððan Heremōdes   hild sweoðrode,
> eafoð ond ellen.   Hē mid Ēotenum wearð
> on fēonda geweald   forð forlācen,
> snūde forsended.   Hine sorh-wylmas
> lemedon tō lange;   hē his lēodum wearð,   905
> eallum æþellingum   tō aldor-ceare
> (898–906).

---

[8] The name Sigurd is absent from both the Durham *Liber Vitae* and PASE. For the argument that *Beowulf* reflects an earlier tradition in which Sigemund, rather than his son Sigurd, was the dragon-slayer, see G. Neckel, 'Sigmunds Drachenkampf', *Edda* 13 (1920), 122–40; T. D. Hill, 'The Confession of Beowulf and the Structure of *Vǫlsunga saga*', in *The Vikings: Papers from the Cornell Lecture Series Held to Coincide with the Viking Exhibition 1980–1981*, ed. R. T. Farrell (London, 1982), pp. 165–75; and North, *Origins*, p. 70. See further Bonjour, *Digressions*, pp. 46–47. For the analogues, see Garmonsway, pp. 251–64. In *Vǫlsunga saga*, Sinfjötli (OE Fitela) is presented as Sigmund's incestuous son, a detail which goes unmentioned in *Beowulf*. For the suggestion that the Christian Anglo-Saxon poet suppressed the incestuous elements of this story, see J. W. Earl, 'The Forbidden *Beowulf*: Haunted by Incest', *PMLA* 125 (2010), 289–305. Again, however, it is possible that the story of Sinfjötli/Fitela's incestuous origins only became part of the legend after the composition of *Beowulf*.

[9] The dragon-fights of Sigemund/Sigurd and Beowulf are also linked through the theme of cursed treasure (cf. *Beo*, 3051–57). See *CCB*, pp. 153–55; and K4, p. 264; North 'Heathen Polity', pp. 73–77. In some versions of the legend, the dying dragon, Fáfnir, warns Sigurd (son of Sigemund) not to take treasures from its hoard as they are cursed, a warning he chooses not to heed. See, for example, *Fáfnismál* (in the Poetic Edda), chs 20–21; and *Vǫlsunga saga*, ch. 18. For a recent discussion of connections between Sigemund and Beowulf, see E. Sebo, 'Foreshadowing the End in *Beowulf*', *ES* 99 (2018), 836–47.

[10] Cf. K4, p. 171: '908. *sīð*, either "lot, fate" or, perhaps, "journey", referring to Heremōd's exile after his brother (Humblus in Saxo) was made king.' Heremod's lack of generosity with treasures is not mentioned in the *scop*'s account, which focuses on his descent into misery (*Hine sorh-wylmas/lemedon tō lange*), but this theme is brought to the fore later by Hrothgar (1709b–24a). See below, Chapter Four, pp. 211–20, for comparison of Heremod and Saul.

Shaping the Dynastic Drama

[He was the most famous of exiles, far and wide, throughout the people, protector of warriors, for glorious deeds – he had prospered because of them – after Heremod's strength declined, his might and glory. He was betrayed among the Jutes into the power of enemies, swiftly dispatched. Sorrow-surges oppressed him for too long; he became a deadly-affliction for his people, for all the nobles.]

Like Sigemund, Heremod is a traditional figure whose legend must have been known in some form to the poem's original audience. Although he is not mentioned elsewhere in the extant corpus of Old English heroic poetry, Heremod is presented as the 'father' of Sceldwa (i.e. Scyld) in ninth-century West Saxon royal genealogies.[11] Heremod is also widely attested as a personal name throughout the Anglo-Saxon period.[12] The *scop*'s association of Heremod with Sigemund is paralleled in Norse tradition, where the heroes Hermóðr and Sigmundr appear together as heroes in the service of Oðin.[13] In the late-tenth-century Old Norse poem *Hákonarmál*, Hermóðr is sent by Oðin to welcome a newcomer to Valhǫl, while Snorri describes how Oðin sent his son, Hermóðr, to plead with the goddess Hel for the release of Baldr (*Gylfaginning*, ch. 49).[14] It is unclear, however, if there is any connection between these legends of Hermóðr the servant of Oðin and Heremod the wicked king of *Beowulf*, or indeed the figure with the same name who appears in the West Saxon genealogy. A closer Norse parallel to *Beowulf*'s account of Heremod's decline is to be found in Saxo Grammaticus's description of a Danish king named Lother, son of Dan and father of Skjöldr (OE Scyld), who was deposed by his subjects and killed on account of his arrogance and crimes (*Gesta Danorum*, I.2.2).[15] I will argue below that just as the legend of Sigemund served as one inspiration for the story of Beowulf's death, so the tale of Heremod's fall provided the impetus for the poet's fashioning of a new myth of dynastic regeneration in the form of the Scyld-prologue.

---

[11] *CCB*, p. 107. For discussion of the Anglo-Saxon royal genealogies, see pp. 141–46.

[12] The name Heremod appears once in the Durham *Liber Vitae*, while PASE records some thirteen Anglo-Saxons named Heremod between the ninth and eleventh centuries, in addition to the Danish king who appears in the West Saxon genealogy and *Beowulf* ('Heremod, 1–14', PASE, accessed 12 September 2018).

[13] See, for example, the poem *Hyndluljóð*, recorded in the late fourteenth-century *Flateyjarbók*. See Garmonsway, pp. 116–18. See further *CCB*, p. 107. A further connection between Heremod and Sigemund/Sigurd may be suggested by the transformation of Fáfnir into a dragon as a punishment for coveting the wealth of his brothers (*Völsunga saga*, ch. 14).

[14] On connections between the slaying of Baldr and Herebeald, see above, Chapter One, pp. 88 n.195.

[15] *Saxo Grammaticus: Gesta Danorum, The History of the Danes*, 2 vols, ed. K. Friis-Jensen, trans. P. Fisher (Oxford, 2015), I, pp. 22–23. See further *CCB*, pp. 111–12.

As has often been noted, this portrait of a Danish oral poet creating a new tale from existing materials provides a meaningful analogue to the *Beowulf*-poet's own compositional technique.[16] Both poets use their knowledge of old tales beyond the memories of their audience to skilfully shape a new story from traditional materials.[17] Moreover, both the fictional *scop* and the *Beowulf*-poet depart from tradition in order to present their own unique versions of events, variations on tales *þāra þe gumena bearn gearwe ne wiston*, 'which the sons of men did not readily know' (878).[18] As Larry D. Benson comments, while later medieval authors such as Chaucer often paraded their respect for earlier *auctoritees*, it was common for poets in the early Anglo-Saxon period to freely and imaginatively reshape traditional materials, citing the Anglo-Latin poets Alcuin and Bede, as well as Cynewulf and the authors of the Old English biblical poems *Exodus*, *Genesis A*, and *Christ and Satan*.[19] The authors of classical epics likewise

---

[16] See N. E. Eliason, 'The "Improvised Lay" in *Beowulf*', *PQ* 31 (1952), 171–79; R. E. Kaske, 'The Sigemund-Heremod and Hama-Hygelac Passages in *Beowulf*', *PMLA* 74 (1959), 489–94; R. P. Creed, '"... wel-hwelc gecwæþ ...": The Singer as Architect', *Tennessee Studies in Literature* 11 (1966), 131–43; J. Opland, 'From Horseback to Monastic Cell: The Impact on English Literature of the Introduction of Writing', in *Old English Literature in Context*, ed. J. D. Niles (Cambridge, 1980), pp. 30–43. The question as to whether oral poets such as those depicted in these poems ever existed in Anglo-Saxon England has been much debated: see R. Frank, 'The Search for the Anglo-Saxon Oral Poet', *Bulletin of the John Rylands University Library of Manchester* 75 (1993), 28–36; J. D. Niles, 'The Myth of the Anglo-Saxon Oral Poet', *Western Folklore* 62 (2003), 7–61; and Thornbury, *Becoming a Poet*, pp. 11–36.

[17] See W. Parks, 'The traditional narrator and the "I Heard" formulas in Old English Poetry', *ASE* 16 (1987), 45–66; Schaefer, 'Rhetoric and Style', p. 120; Robinson, *Appositive Style*, p. 28; S. B. Greenfield, 'The Authenticating Voice in *Beowulf*', *ASE* 5 (1976), 51–62.

[18] The adverb *gearwe*, 'readily', is the headstave, bearing the alliteration of the line. Orchard comments: 'if the *Beowulf*-poet seems content to manipulate myth in the service of his story, so too he seems at times to play fast and loose with legend' (*CCB*, p. 105). Orchard is referring here, in the first instance, to the poet's apparent transference of the Scyld Scefing foundling story from Scef to Scyld, and in the second, to his seemingly novel treatment of the legend of Sigemund.

[19] Benson, 'Originality', p. 37. It is worth noting that later Anglo-Saxon poets could also take a free approach to source material. For a discussion of the *Judith*-poet's approach to the biblical narrative, for example, see Thomson, *Communal Creativity*, pp. 40–43. On the dating of *Beowulf* and other Old English poems, see pp. ix–x, 6, 237. For a consideration of the *Beowulf*-poet's technique in terms of classical rhetoric, see G. J. Engelhardt, '*Beowulf*: A Study in Dilation', *PMLA* 79 (1955), 825–52. The authors of the Latin biblical epics known to the Anglo-Saxons, Juvencus, Arator and Sedulius, also frequently embellished their biblical sources, amplifying or compressing episodes, in order to emphasize certain themes: see M. Lapidge, 'Versifying the Bible in the Middle Ages', in *The Text in the Community: Essays on Medieval Works, Manuscripts, and Readers*, ed. J. Mann and M. Nolan (Notre Dame, 2006),

augment heroic legends, creating new stories out of old materials. Homer seems to have introduced or amplified the role of heroes such as Patroclus and Achilles in his treatment of the Trojan legend, while Virgil often reduces or amplifies Homeric material in the *Aeneid*, for example conflating two characters into one and adding new scenes.[20] The *Beowulf*-poet was similarly inventive, juxtaposing previously disparate narrative elements, amplifying or embellishing ancient Scandinavian royal legends for a Christian Anglo-Saxon audience.

Folktale and Legendary Parallels to Beowulf's First Two Fights

While the *Beowulf*-poet appears to have taken his main inspiration for the hero's dragon-fight from the Sigemund-legend, numerous analogues and some possible sources have been identified for Beowulf's fights with Grendel and Grendel's mother.[21] The most intensively studied analogue is the fourteenth-century Icelandic outlaw tale, *Grettis saga*.[22] Beowulf's fight with Grendel has several parallels with Grettir's struggle with a troll named Glámr, who has been causing mischief by raiding farms and killing livestock at Thorhallsstad:

Beowulf's fight with Grendel (688–836, 2069b–2100)	Grettir's fight with Glámr (*Grettis saga*, chs 32–35)
Beowulf remains in the hall overnight and pretends to be asleep as Grendel attempts to grab him (688–90, 736b–66).	Grettir remains in the hall overnight and pretends to be asleep as the troll, Glámr, attempts to grab him.
Grendel is surprised by Beowulf's strength (718–19, 750–56, 764b–65a, 788b–90).	Glámr is surprised by Grettir's strength.

---

pp. 11–40; P. McBrine, *Biblical Epics in Late Antiquity and Anglo-Saxon England: 'Divina in Laude Voluntas'* (Toronto, 2017).

[20] See J. Hooker, 'Homer, Patroclus, Achilles', *Symbolae Osloenses* 64 (1989), 30–35, at 31, 34; W. Allan, 'Arms and the Man: Euphorbus, Hector, and the Death of Patroclus', *The Classical Quarterly* 55 (2005), 1–16; M. L. West, *The Making of the Iliad: Disquisition and Analytical Commentary* (Oxford, 2011), p. 42; G. N. Knauer, 'Virgil's *Aeneid* and Homer', *Greek, Roman, and Byzantine Studies* 5 (1964), 61–84, at 77.

[21] For connections with Sigemund, as well as hagiographical parallels, see Chapter Three, pp. 180–82.

[22] For detailed discussion of the extensive scholarship and further discussion of these and other connections, see Orchard, *Pride and Prodigies*, pp. 140–68; and K4, pp. xxxvi–xliii.

In the ensuing struggle the hall is damaged and benches are upturned (767–82a).	In the ensuing struggle the hall is damaged and benches are upturned.
Grendel attempts to flee but is prevented by Beowulf (762–66, 786–94a, 809–18a).	Glámr attempts to flee but is prevented by Grettir.
Beowulf (later) cuts off Grendel's head (1584b–90c).	The fleeing troll condemns Grettir as an outlaw, but Grettir recovers and cuts off the troll's head.

An even more striking series of parallels connects Beowulf's fights with both Grendel and Grendel's mother to Grettir's battle with two trolls at Sandhaugar:

Beowulf's fights with Grendel and Grendel's mother	**Grettir's fights with two trolls at Sandhaugar (*Grettis saga*, chs 64–66)**
Beowulf hears of a monster attacking a hall and travels to challenge it (194–228).	Grettir hears of a troll attacking a hall and travels to challenge it.
During a struggle in the hall, Beowulf cuts off Grendel's arm before he flees to his cave under a mere (809–36).	During a struggle in the hall, Grettir cuts off the giantess's arm before she flees into a waterfall.
Beowulf later descends into the mere where he discovers a cave in which he defeats Grendel's mother (and cuts off Grendel's head) (1492–1590).	Grettir later descends into the waterfall, where he discovers a cave in which he defeats a male giant.
Seeing the Grendelkin's blood in the water, the Danes who had been waiting on the shore for Beowulf fear him dead and abandon him (1591–1605a).	Seeing the giant's blood in the water, a priest who had been holding a rope for Grettir fears him dead and abandons him.
Beowulf strikes Grendel's mother with a *hæft-mēce* (named Hrunting), lent to him by Unferth; the sword fails to kill its target (1455–72, 1518–33a).	The troll strikes Grettir with a *hepti-sax*; the sword fails to kill its target.

Beowulf reaches for a giant sword hanging on the wall of the cave (1557–69).	The troll reaches for a giant sword hanging on the wall of the cave.
Beowulf returns with treasures and presents Hrothgar with a giant's sword-hilt on which the story of God's victory over the giants is carved in runes (1677–99).	Grettir returns with treasures and presents the priest with a rune-staff on which are carved his own achievements in the watery cave.

Given the extent of these (and other) resemblances in plot, and the presence of the related hapaxes *hæft-mece* and *hepti-sax*, the possibility of a direct link between *Grettis saga* and *Beowulf* remains tantalizing, if beyond proof.[23] However, it is now recognized that Beowulf's fights with the Grendelkin and Grettir's Sandhaugar episode are variants of the common folktale known variously as 'The Bear's Son Tale', 'The Three Stolen Princesses' or 'The Two Trolls'. In this story, a hero, typically descended from or brought up by a bear, defends a dwelling against a monster or troll, wounding it before descending into a subterranean dwelling where he confronts another monster or troll, often of different gender.[24]

The bear-like qualities of Beowulf are hinted at by details such as his name, which some have taken to mean 'bee-wolf' (i.e. 'bear'), as well as his fondness for fighting without weapons, not only with Grendel

---

[23] North, *Origins*, p. 19. For a sceptical view of the possibility of direct influence, see Magnús Fjalldal, *The Long Arm of Coincidence: the Frustrated Connection between* Beowulf *and* Grettis saga (Toronto, 1998).

[24] F. Panzer, *Studien zur germanischen Sagengeschichte, I:* Beowulf (Munich, 1910), labelled this Type 301b. See further K3, pp. ix–xxix; Chambers, *Introduction*, pp. 62–68, 451–506; Wrenn-Bolton, *Beowulf*, pp. 46–51; N. K. Chadwick, 'The monsters and *Beowulf*', in *The Anglo-Saxons – Studies in some aspects of their history and culture presented to Bruce Dickins*, ed. P. Clemoes (London, 1959), pp. 171–203; G. V. Smithers, *The Making of* Beowulf: *Inaugural Lecture of the Professor of English Language Delivered in the Appleby Theatre on 18 May 1961* (Durham, 1961); T. A. Shippey, 'The Fairy-Tale Structure of *Beowulf*', NQ 214 (1969), 2–11; J. M. Stitt, Beowulf *and the Bear's Son: Epic, Saga, and Fairytale in Northern Germanic Tradition* (New York, 1992); Davis, *Demise of Germanic Legend*, pp. 159–62; Andersson, 'Sources and Analogues', esp. pp. 129–34; Niles, *Beowulf*, pp. 3–30; CCB, pp. 120–29. M. Fjalldal, '*Beowulf* and the Old Norse Two-Troll Analogues', *Neophilologus* 97 (2013), 541–53, argues that Beowulf's fights with Grendel and his mother are more closely related to Norse tales of animated corpses (*draugar* and *haugbúar*) than to tales of the Two-Trolls type. For a selection of northern folktale analogues to the fights with the Grendelkin, see Garmonsway, pp. 331–32; and K4, pp. 313–15. For parallels with the Irish folktale, 'The Hand and the Child', see J. Carney, 'The Irish Elements in *Beowulf*', in his *Studies in Irish Literature and History* (Dublin, 1955), pp. 77–128; and M. Puhvel, Beowulf *and Celtic Tradition* (Waterloo, ON, 1979), pp. 86–138. For Japanese parallels, see M. Ogura, '*Beowulf* and the *Book of Swords*: similarities and differences in scenes, features and epithets', *SELIM* 16 (2009), 7–22.

but also against the *Hūga cempan*, 'champion of the Hugas', Dæghrefn, whom he crushes to death in a *hilde-grāp*, 'battle-grip', during the ill-fated Frisian raid (2501–09).[25] One particular variant of 'The Bear's Son Tale' that is of special significance to *Beowulf* is the tale of Bödvar Bjarki ('little bear'), preserved in a range of Scandinavian texts.[26] Only in the Bödvar Bjarki tradition and *Beowulf* do we find elements of 'The Bear's Son Tale' combined with Scylding dynastic legend. As a champion of King Hrólfr (OE Hrothulf), Bödvar Bjarki, son of Björn and Bera ('Bear' and 'Bear'), defends the Danish royal hall at Hleidargard (modern-day Lejre) against a winged beast whom weapons cannot harm. Like Beowulf, Bödvar questions the bravery of the hall's defenders and takes it upon himself to challenge the beast, though unlike Beowulf, the hero is accompanied in this task by a farmer's son named Hött, mocked by the court on account of his lowly status:

> Ok sem leið at jólum, gerðust menn ókátir. Böðvarr spyrr Hött, hverju þetta sætti. Hann segir honum, at dýr eitt hafi þar komit tvá vetr í samt, mikit ok ógurligt –, "ok hefir vængi á bakinu, ok flýgr þat jafnan. Tvau haust hefir þat nú hingat vitjat ok gert mikinn skaða. Á þat bíta ekki vápn, en kappar konungs koma ekki heim, þeir sem at eru einna mestir."
>
> Böðvarr mælti: "Ekki er höllin svá vel skipuð sem ek ætlaði, ef eitt dýr skal hér eyða ríki ok fé konungsins."
>
> Höttr sagði: "Þat er ekki dýr, heldr er þat mesta tröll."
>
> Nú kemr jólaaftann. Þá mælti konungr: "Nú vil ek, at menn sé kyrrir ok hljóðir í nótt, ok banna ek öllum mínum mönum at ganga í nokkurn háskva við dýrit, en fé ferr eftir því, sem auðnar. Menn mína vil ek ekki missa."
>
> Allir heita hér góðu um at gera eftir því, sem konungr bauð.
>
> Böðvarr leynndist í burt um nóttina. Hann lætr Hött fara með sér, ok gerir hann þat nauðugr, ok kallaði hann sér stýrt í bana. Böðvarr segir, at betr mundi takast. Þeir ganga í burt frá höllinni, ok verðr Böðvarr at bera hann, svá er hann hræddr.

---

[25] On Beowulf as bear, see W. W. Skeat, 'On the Signification of the Monster Grendel in the Poem of Beowulf; with a Discussion of lines 2076–2100', *The Journal of Philology* 15 (1886), 120–31. On 'bee-wolf', see H. Sweet, *Anglo-Saxon Reader in Prose and Verse* (Oxford, 1884), p. 202; J. Harris, 'Beowulf's Name', in *Beowulf: A New Verse Translation*, trans. S. Heaney, ed. D. Donoghue (New York, 2002), pp. 98–100; Fulk, 'Beowulf's Name'; C. Abram, 'Bee-Wolf and the Hand of Victory: Identifying the Heroes of *Beowulf* and *Vǫlsunga saga*', *JEGP* 116 (2017), 387–414. Orchard suggests a more plausible etymology is *Beow-wulf*, 'the wolf of (the god) Beow', citing the common ON name *Þórólfr*, 'the wolf of (the god) Þór' (*CCB*, p. 121 n. 117).

[26] The legend is attested by the tenth-century Old Norse poem *Bjarkamál*, a dialogue between Böðvar and his companion Hjalti, which is quoted in fragmentary form in Saxo's *Gesta Danorum* (Bk I.II.6.9–8.2); the fifteenth-century ballad, *Bjarkarímur*; and the fourteenth-century *fornaldasögur*, *Hrólfs saga kraka* (chs 24–52). For a plot-summary of *Hrólfs saga*, see Appendix B.

Nú sjá þeir dýrit mundu gleypa hann. Böðvarr bað bikkjuna hans þegja ok kastar honum niðr í mosann, ok þar liggr hann ok eigi með öllu óhræddr. Eigi þorir hann heim at fara heldr. Nú gengr Böðvarr móti dýrinu. Þat hæfir honum, at sverðit er fast í umgerðinni, ok nú fær hann brugðit umgerðinni, svá at sverðit gengr ór sliðrunum, ok leggr þegar undir bægi dýrsins ok svá fast, at stóð í hjartanu, ok datt þá dýrit til jarðar dautt niðr.

Eftir þat ferr hann þangat, sem Höttr liggr. Böðvarr tekr hann upp ok berr þangat, sem dýrit liggr dautt. Höttr skelfr ákaft.

Böðvarr mælti: "Nú skaltu drekka blóð dýrsins."[27]

[As Yuletime drew near, gloom settled over the men. Bödvar asked Hött what caused their dejection. Hött told him that a huge, monstrous beast had come there the past two winters. 'The creature has wings on its back and it usually flies. For two autumns now it has come here, causing much damage. No weapon can bite into it, and the king's champions, even the greatest among them, do not return home.'

Bödvar said, 'The hall is not so well manned as I had thought, if one animal alone could destroy the king's land and his livestock.'

Hött said, 'It is not an animal, rather it is the greatest of trolls.'

Then came Yule eve, and the king [i.e. Hrólfr] said, 'It is my wish that tonight men remain calm, making no noise, and I forbid any of my men to put themselves in danger with the beast. The livestock will be left to their fate, because I do not want to lose any of my men.'

Everyone faithfully promised the king to do as he wished.

Bödvar stole away in the night and took Hött with him. Hött went only after being forced to do so, declaring that he was being steered towards death. Bödvar said, 'Things will turn out for the better.' They now left the hall behind them, with Bödvar carrying Hött because he was so frightened.

They saw the creature, and immediately Hött started to scream as loudly as he could, crying that the beast would swallow him. Bödvar told the dog to be quiet and threw him down on the moor. There he lay, not a little scared, at the same time not daring to go home. Bödvar now went against the beast. He was hampered by his sword, which, as he tried to draw it, stuck fast in its scabbard. Determined, Bödvar urged the sword out until the scabbard squeaked. Then he grasped the scabbard and the sword came out of the sheath. Immediately he thrust it up under the beast's shoulder, striking so hard that the blade reached quickly into the heart. Then the beast fell dead to the ground.

After this encounter Bödvar went to the place where Hött was lying. He picked up Hött and carried him to where the beast lay dead. Hött was trembling violently.

Bödvar said, 'Now you will drink the beast's blood.'][28]

---

[27] 'Hrólfs saga kraka ok kappa hans', in *Fornaldr Sogür Norðurlanda* I, ed. Guðni Jónsson (Rejkjavik, 1950), pp. 1–105, at 66–67. Chapter numbers are cited from this edition.

[28] Trans. J. Byock, *The Saga of King Hrolf Kraki* (London, 1998), pp. 50–51. For the

With Bödvar's connivance and emboldened by the blood, Hött now 'kills' the beast in the view of King Hrólfr. Impressed by this sudden change in Hött's demeanour, the king renames him Hjälti (ch. 36). Later, in the climax of the saga, Hjälti and Bödvar die together as the Danish royal hall is attacked by Hjörvard (OE Heoroweard) (ch. 52).[29]

Despite these substantial parallels, in recent decades scholars have rarely explored the relationship of Beowulf and Bjarki.[30] Indeed, the matter has largely been considered closed since Larry Benson's influential 1970 essay, 'The Originality of *Beowulf*', which stressed that 'only in its latest developments [i.e. *Bjarkarímur*] does the Bjarki story look anything like the story of *Beowulf*, and the latest versions [...] do not look that much like our poem.'[31] However, the case was re-opened in 2006 by Richard North,

---

sake of consistency, I have added diacritics in ON names and adjusted the paragraphing of Byock's translation to match the ON text.

[29] Guðni Jónsson, pp. 104–05. Saxo incorporates a section of *Bjarkamál*, in which Hjälti tries to rouse Bödvar during this raid. See above, p. 67. A further connection between *Beowulf* and the Bödvar Bjarki tradition is found in the story of Eadgils/Aðils. In the Old English poem, Beowulf assists the exiled Swedish prince, Eadgils (2392–96), against his uncle, King Onela; in traditions derived from *Skjöldunga saga*, Bödvar Bjarki and Hjälti are numbered among twelve champions sent by Hrólfr to assist King Aðils of Uppsala – Hrólfr's stepfather – against King Áli (OE Onela) of Norway in a great battle at Lake Vænir. Arngrímur's recension of *Skjöldunga saga* (ch. 12) mentions Hrólfr's twelve champions, but it does not provide their names. Bjarki and Hjälti are named, however, among Hrólfr's champions by Snorri (*Skáldskaparmál*, ch. 54) and in *Bjarkarímur* (VIII, stanzas 17–18, 22–28). In Snorri's account, King Áli dies in the battle, but Aðils refuses to reward Hrólfr's men. Snorri provides further details of this conflict in his *Heimskringla* (*Ynglinga saga*, chs 28–29), where he explains how Aðils, son of King Óttarr (OE Ohthere), raided Saxland, taking much plunder, though not the slave-girl Yrsa, who later became Queen of Sweden; the Danish king Helgi, son of Hálfdan, attacks the Swedes, causing Aðils to flee, and marries Queen Yrsa; their son is Hrólfr; on discovering that Helgi is also her father, Yrsa leaves him for Aðils; Helgi dies in a raid and Hrólfr succeeds him as King of the Danes; Aðils subsequently fights the Norwegian king Áli at Lake Vænir, gaining the victory with Hrólfr's support and killing Áli; there follows an account of how King Aðils died after falling from his horse at a sacrifice to the goddesses. The conflict between Aðils and Áli is not mentioned in *Hrólfs saga kraka*. For the texts, see Garmonsway, pp. 216–21. For discussion, see North, *Origins*, pp. 45–46.

[30] For example, neither Bödvar Bjarki nor *Hrólfs saga* are mentioned in Orchard's *Pride and Prodigies* or CCB. K4, however, briefly mentions these parallels (pp. clxxxix–clxxxv) and includes short summaries of Saxo's account of Bjarki (Lat. Biarco) (p. 300), *Hrólfs saga* and *Bjarkarímur* (pp. 306–07). See Appendix for a plot summary of *Hrólfs saga*. See also T. A. Shippey, '*Hrólfs saga kraka* and the Legend of Lejre', in *Making History: essays on the Fornaldasögur*, ed. M. Arnold and A. Finlay (London, 2010), pp. 17–23.

[31] Benson, 'Originality', p. 48. Cf. O. L. Olson, 'The Relation of the *Hrólfs Saga Kraka* and the *Bjarkarímur* to *Beowulf*: A Contribution to the History of Saga Development in England and the Scandinavian Countries' (Unpubl. doctoral dissertation, University of Chicago, 1916); A. Olrik, *The Heroic Legends of*

who proposed that the Anglo-Saxon poet developed the figure of Beowulf by transferring legends originally associated with Bjarki from the court of King Hrólfr (OE Hrothulf) to that of his uncle, King Hróar (OE Hrothgar), before moving Hygelac into the position previously occupied by Hrólfr (OE Hrothulf) as Bödvar Bjarki/Beowulf's patron and close friend.[32]

It is, of course, impossible to prove what version of the Bjarki-story, if any, was known to the *Beowulf*-poet. Indeed, it may even be the case that the story of Bödvar Bjarki, champion of King Hrólfr and defender of the Danish royal hall against a monster, developed long after the composition of *Beowulf*. Moreover, there are numerous discrepancies between the hall-fights of Bödvar and Beowulf. For example, Bödvar does not travel to the Danish royal hall with the intention of ridding it of a monster, but rather to seek the service of King Hrólfr. Most significantly for this discussion, while Beowulf's fights with monsters in Heorot dramatize underlying dynastic tensions among the Scyldings, there is no obvious connection between Bjarki's fight with the winged beast and the Danish royal succession. Indeed, in *Hrólfs saga* the entire episode simply serves as an opportunity for Bjarki to prove himself worthy of a place among Hrólfr's champions, and to elevate the status of his companion, Hött. Hrólfr's wars with Adils and Hjörvard are not treated in any detail until long after the episode with the winged beast, and although Bjarki plays an important role in these conflicts as one of Hrólfr's bravest and most outspoken champions, he is never presented as a contender for the Danish throne.[33]

It seems safer to conclude, therefore, that in early Scandinavian tradition a version of the Bear's Son/Two Trolls Tale became associated with Scylding dynastic legends, and that some version of this story was known to the authors of both *Beowulf* and the Bjarki tradition.[34] This is effectively the position taken up by John D. Niles in the most recent review of the connections between *Beowulf* and *Hrólfs saga*. Rejecting the possibilities that these two texts originated independently or that the Icelandic saga was directly influenced by the Anglo-Saxon poem, Niles proposes that the

---

Denmark: Translated from the Danish and Revised in Collaboration with the Author, ed. and trans. L. M. Hollander, Scandinavian Monographs 4 (New York, 1919). For a summary of the arguments, see Andersson, 'Sources and Analogues', p. 132.

[32] North, *Origins*, pp. 36–65. North further suggests that the Geatish Hrethling dynasty is largely the invention of the *Beowulf*-poet, who transformed Bjarki's death in Hrólfr's burning hall into Beowulf's death in the dragon's fire, while developing the character of Wiglaf from Hjälti. See above, pp. 107–08, for the possibility that the *Beowulf*-poet transferred the dragon-slaying legend of Sigurd to his father, Sigemund.

[33] Before travelling to Hrólfr's court, Bödvar briefly rules the kingdom of the Uppdales in Norway and poses as ruler of Gautland in the absence of his brother, King Thorir (*Hrólfs saga*, chs 29–33).

[34] Cf. K4, p. xliii.

tale of the haunting of the Scylding hall and its deliverance by a non-Danish hero merged with a form of the Two-Troll type in early Scandinavia. A version of this story then came to Britain, whereupon the tale of the hero's death in a fight against a dragon was added. This composite story then took on the form of an Old English alliterative poem, during the composition of which personal names were anglicized (e.g. ON *Hrólfr* became OE *Hróðulf*, and ON *Hróarr* became OE *Hróðgār*), and characters were filled out and developed in new directions. Finally, the poem was endowed with Christian meaning through the addition of the stories of Creation, Cain and Abel and the Flood, producing *Beowulf* as we now have it.[35]

My approach in the next section differs from that of Klaeber, Tolkien, Niles and others in that instead of viewing the poem as, in essence, a folktale with a (relatively superficial) pseudo-historical setting, I propose that the poet utilized folktale elements in order to dramatize key moments in dynastic history.[36] Specifically, I argue that the *Beowulf*-poet's main inspiration was not the Two Trolls folktale or the story of Bjarki but rather the legend of King Hygelac's death.

Shaping a New Hero

While the basic plots of the hero's three monster-fights have many parallels in a wide range of folktales, saints' lives and other sources, the figure of Beowulf himself, prince of the Geats, son of Ecgtheow, nephew of King Hygelac, has no counterpart in northern royal legend or Germanic

---

[35] J. D. Niles, 'On the Danish Origins of the *Beowulf* Story', in *Anglo-Saxon England and the Continent*, ed. H. Sauer and J. Story, with the assistance of G. Waxenberger, Medieval and Renaissance Texts and Studies 394, ISAS Essays in Anglo-Saxon Studies 3 (Tempe, AZ, 2011), pp. 41–62, at 56–61. See further, J. D. Niles, '*Beowulf* and Lejre', in Beowulf *and Lejre*, Medieval and Renaissance Texts and Studies 323, ed. J. D. Niles and M. Osborn (Tempe, AZ, 2007), pp. 169–234. Roberta Frank similarly argued that a bilingual Anglo-Saxon poet translated the Scandinavian names in *Beowulf* from Old Norse into Old English during the Viking Age ('Skaldic Verse and the Date of *Beowulf*', pp. 124–25). See also E. G. Stanley, 'The Date of *Beowulf*: Some Doubts and No Conclusions', in Chase, ed. (1981), pp. 197–211, at 207. However, as Chambers comments, the names in the poem are 'the correct English forms which we would expect, according to English sound laws, if the names had been brought over in the sixth century and handed down traditionally' (*Introduction*, p. 323). For further objections to the theory of a philologically-minded Viking-Age poet, see K3, p. cxvii; Whitelock, *Audience*, p. 26; Bjork and Obermeier, 'Date, Provenance, Author, Audience', p. 27; R. D. Fulk, 'Dating *Beowulf* to the Viking Age', *PQ* 61 (1982), 341–59, at 343–44; Newton, *Origins*, p. 15; and now L. Neidorf and R. J. Pascual, 'Old Norse Influence on the Language of *Beowulf*', *Journal of Germanic Linguistics* 31 (2019), 298–322. On the question of the poem's date of composition and subsequent transmission, see Introduction, pp. 6–9, and Conclusion, pp. 237–46.

[36] For the views of Klaeber and Tolkien, see Introduction, pp. 5–6.

heroic tradition more generally. Beowulf's name does not conform with the pattern of alliterative name-giving which characterizes royal families in the poem, setting him apart from the other members of his own Hrethling dynasty.[37] Moreover, Beowulf is absent from records of Scandinavian royal tradition. The name, Beowulf, does occur, however, in several Anglo-Saxon contexts: a single 'Biuulf' is attested in the Durham *Liber Vitae*, while PASE records a 'Beulf' (Latin 'Beulfus') in the Domesday Book;[38] the first element of the hero's dithematic name, Beow-, appears as an ancient ancestor of the West Saxon royal house in genealogies, in some cases as the 'son' of Scyld/Sceldwa;[39] and we find a *Beowan ham* close to a *Grendles mere* in a tenth-century Anglo-Saxon charter, perhaps suggesting a link between Beow (if not Beowulf) and a mere-dwelling figure named Grendel.[40] As we saw in the previous chapter, a further clue that the hero has been inserted into Scandinavian royal legend is provided by the unusual number of details provided about his ancestry on his arrival in Denmark.[41] Further hints of Beowulf's fictionality, if any more were needed, are provided by his lack of siblings, queen and children. Although some stories about Beowulf may have circulated prior to the composition of our poem, it seems reasonable to conclude that Beowulf's involvement in the affairs of the Scyldings and Hrethlings is largely the invention of the *Beowulf*-poet.[42]

---

[37] Dobbie, ASPR IV, p. xxxiv; K4, pp. l–li. See also Sisam, *Structure*, p. 52; Frank, 'Germanic legend', pp. 94–95; Stanley, *In the Foreground*, pp. 14–15.

[38] 'Beulf 1', PASE, accessed 12 September 2018. On the *Liber Vitae* see Whitelock, *Audience*, pp. 66–67; Wormald, 'Redating'.

[39] On Anglo-Saxon royal genealogies, see below, Chapter Four. In the manuscript, as we have seen, Scribe A confuses this Beow, son of Scyld, with Beowulf, the hero of the poem; see p. 8.

[40] This connection was first noted by J. M. Kemble, *The Saxons in England: a history of the English commonwealth till the period of the Norman Conquest*, 2 vols (London, 1849), I, pp. 416–18, and was subsequently discussed in greater detail by Karl Müllenhoff, 'Zeugnisse und Excurse zur deutschen Heldensage', *Zeitschrift für deutsches Altertum* 12 (1865), 253–86, at 282–84. For the relevant extracts, see Shippey and Haarder, pp. 277–78, 341–42. The topic was taken up again by R. L. Reynolds, 'An Echo of *Beowulf* in Athelstan's Charters of 931-933 A.D.?', *MÆ* 24 (1955), 101–03. Benson, however, cautions that 'the charter provides no basis for believing that any story involving the Beo(w) of *Beowan ham* and Grendel had anything like the shape of the basic plot of our poem' ('Originality', p. 44). The ON name 'Bjólfr', which may be cognate with 'Beowulf', is recorded among the early settlers of Iceland: see *CCB*, p. 128. Philip Shaw is currently reassessing evidence for the geographical distribution of human names in *Beowulf*.

[41] See pp. 56–57.

[42] On the possible fictionality of the hero's involvement in the Hrethling dynasty, see Biggs, 'Politics of Succession', 710–11. Neidorf, 'Beowulf before *Beowulf*', 567, cautions against crediting the poet with inventing the figure of Beowulf, arguing that 'he belongs to a group of figures who are evidently unique to Anglo-Saxon heroic-legendary tradition'.

One such story that may have circulated about Beowulf before the poem is the swimming contest with Breca. On his arrival in Heorot, the hero claims to have bound five giants and an unspecified number of *niceras*, 'sea-monsters' (420b–22),[43] prompting Unferth to reply with an alternative version of events in which Beowulf lost out to Breca (506–28).[44] Noting the alliteration of *Beowulf*, *Breca* and *Bronding*, Benson has suggested that this story of Beowulf the great swimmer served as a kernel of tradition which the poet amplified, thereby producing 'an original work of art, based on a variety of traditional materials brought together in a new way for new and more sophisticated purposes'.[45] The plausibility of Benson's theory is supported by the fact that Beowulf's reputation as a great swimmer is alluded to on no less than three further occasions: first in the narrator's detailed account of his descent into and return from the haunted mere (1441–54, 1492–1650); then in the hero's own, embellished report of the same episode to Hygelac (2131–42); and finally, in the narrator's account of the hero's superhuman feat of swimming back to the Geats from Frisia carrying thirty suits of armour following Hygelac's death (2359b–68).[46] In order to bring this tale of Beowulf the swimmer into his dynastic drama, the poet needed a great event from royal legend in which to involve his hero. He found this in the legend of the death of Hygelac. In the next section, I propose that Beowulf is a fictionalization, or poetic double, of his legendary uncle, King Hygelac. In other words, the poetic fiction of

---

[43] MS *fife* has been emended by some to *fifel* (see K4, pp. 16, 141).
[44] Breca is mentioned in *Widsith* as a ruler of the Brondings (21a). Much later we learn that the Geats had in fact considered Beowulf lazy and cowardly (2187b–88a). This echo of the folktale motif of the 'unpromising youth', who exceeds expectations and makes a name for himself in adolescence, links Beowulf with another hero mentioned in the poem, Offa. See Leneghan, 'Offa Digression', 552–53.
[45] Benson, 'Originality', p. 69.
[46] On Beowulf's swimming prowess and connections with other Germanic/Norse legends, as well as the debate as to whether the contest with Breca involved swimming or rowing, see P. A. Jorgensen, 'Beowulf's Swimming Contest with Breca: Old Norse Parallels', *Folk-Lore* 89 (1978), 52–59; J. W. Earl, 'Beowulf's Rowing-Match', *Neophilologus* 63 (1979), 285–90; M. Puhvel, 'The Aquatic Contest in *Hálfdanar saga Brönufóstra* and Beowulf's Adventure with Breca: Any Connection?', *NM* 99 (1998), 131–38; *CCB*, pp. 125–28, 249–51; and D. Anlezark, 'All at Sea: Beowulf's Marvellous Swimming', in *Myths, Legends and Heroes: Essays on Old Norse and Old English Literature in honour of John McKinnell*, Toronto Old Norse-Icelandic Series, ed. D. Anlezark (Toronto, 2011), pp. 225–41. For Irish parallels, see Puhvel, *Celtic Tradition*, pp. 55–60. For comparison of Snorri's allusion to the rowing of Hymir and Thor (*Hymiskviða* stanzas 17–27) and the rowing of Grettir, Þorgeirr Hávarsson and Þormóðr Berson in *Grettis saga* ch. 50, see U. Dronke, ed. and trans., *The Poetic Edda, Volume III: Mythological Poems II* (Oxford, 2011), pp. 103–05. I am grateful to Heather O'Donoghue for this last reference. Grettir is also famed as a swimmer (see, for example, *Grettir's Saga*, ch. 50).

Beowulf's death in battle against the dragon is an elaborate poetic variation of the legend of Hygelac's death in Frisia.[47]

The Poetic Elaboration of the Death of Hygelac

No single event looms so large in *Beowulf* as Hygelac's death.[48] There are five direct references spread across the narrative (1197–1214a, 2201b, 2354b–72, 2497–2509, 2910b–21) as well as Hrothgar's prediction that Beowulf will make a worthy king of the Geats, should Hygelac die soon (1845–53a). Evidently, this particular episode of northern royal history was of special interest for our poet and his audience. Significantly, the historicity of Hygelac's death is corroborated by Gregory of Tours' sixth-century *History of the Franks* III.3, which records the death of a 'Danish' king named *Chlochilaichus* (= OE Hygelac) during the reign of the Merovingian King Theuderic (r. 511–33):

> His ita gestis, Dani cum rege suo nomen Chlochilaichum evectu navali per mare Gallias appetunt. Egressique ad terras, pagum unum de regno Theudorici devastant atque captivant, oneratisque navibus tam de captivis quam de reliquis spoliis, reverti ad patriam cupiunt; sed rex eorum in litus resedebat, donec navis alto mare conpraehenderent, ipse deinceps secuturus. Quod cum Theudorico nuntiatum fuisset, quod scilicet regio eius fuerit ab extraneis devastata, Theudobertum, filium suum, in illis partibus cum valido exercitu ac magno armorum apparatu direxit. Qui, interfectu rege, hostibus navali proelio superatis oppraemit omnemque rapinam terrae restituit.

> [When these things had thus transpired, the Danes, along with their king, by the name of Chlochilaich, approached Gaul over the sea with naval transport. Upon disembarking, they laid waste a district of the kingdom of

---

[47] J. M. Kemble, *Über die Stammtafel der Westsachsen* (Munich, 1836), pp. 28–20 suggests that Beowulf was a 'shadow-image of the earlier hero *Beowulf* [i.e. Beow the son of Scyld]' (printed in Shippey and Haarder, pp. 205–06, at 206). On the (probably scribal) confusion of Beow and Beowulf, see above, p. 8. I use the term 'fiction' here advisedly, in the sense of a story 'imaginatively invented' (*OED* s. v. *fiction* 3. B), rather than in the more specialized sense of '[t]he species of literature concerned with the narration of imaginary events and the portraiture of imaginary characters; fictitious composition' (*OED* s. v. *fiction* 4.a.). For debates as to the distinction between fiction and history in Anglo-Saxon literature, see Whitelock, *Audience*, pp. 71–72; Biggs, 'The Dream of the Rood and Guthlac A as a Literary Context for the Monsters in Beowulf', p. 297; Biggs, 'Politics of Succession', 710, n. 5; and L. Ashe, *Early Fiction in England: From Geoffrey of Monmouth to Chaucer* (London, 2015), pp. xvi–xvii.

[48] Brodeur, *Art*, pp. 78–79, terms Hygelac's death a *leitmotif*. For the similarly prominent theme of Beowulf's death, see below, p. 137. See further L. E. Fast, 'Hygelac: a Centripetal Force in *Beowulf*', *Annuale Medievale* 12 (1972), 90–99.

Theuderic, and with their ships freighted equally with captives and other spoils, they desired to return to their own country. But their king remained ashore until the ships should reach the high seas, whereupon he would follow. When this was reported to Theuderic, i.e. that his kingdom had been devastated by invaders, he directed his son to the area with a powerful and well-equipped army. Once he had killed the king, Theudebert crushed the overwhelmed enemy in a naval battle and restored all that had been taken from the land.][49]

Although Gregory identifies Chlochilaich (OE Hygelac) as a Dane rather than a Geat, there are enough similarities to indicate that we are dealing with the same event: both Scandinavian kings launch ill-fated seaborne attacks on the Merovingian realm in pursuit of plunder.[50]

Stories about Hygelac's death appear to have reached Anglo-Saxon England by the eighth century, if not before. Although he is not mentioned elsewhere in the extant corpus of Old English heroic poems treating Germanic legend, the name Hygelac appears four times in the Durham *Liber Vitae*,[51] while the PASE database records two figures named Hyglac in early Anglo-Saxon England.[52] Most pertinent to *Beowulf*, however, is an entry in the *Liber monstrorum*, a catalogue of strange human and

---

[49] Text and translation from K4, pp. 310–11 (cf. B. Krusch and W. Levison, eds, MGH, *Scriptorum Rerum Merovingicarum* I, i, 2nd edn [Hanover, 1951], 97–99), though I have given the English forms of personal names in the translation. The eighth-century *Gesta Francorum* (ch. 19) reproduces Gregory's account, adding the detail that the region that 'Chochilaicus' laid waste to was that of the 'Atuarii'. Saxo Grammaticus, in his thirteenth-century *Danish History*, mentions the victory of a Danish king, 'Hugletus', over the Swedish despots Hömothus and Högrimus in a naval battle (IV.117), but later tells the tale of one 'Hugletus', king of Ireland, 'prone to avarice' and given to patronising mimes and jugglers, who is slain by the hero Starkatherus (VI.185–86). The relevant sections are translated in Garmonsway, pp. 113–15.

[50] Cf. *Beo* 1202–1214a, 2354b–59a, 2910b–21.

[51] Also included in the *Liber Vitae* are the names Heremod (x1), Hereric (x1), Hrothulf (x3), Hunfrith (=Unferth) (x3), Wulfgar (x1), Heardred (x11), Herebeald (x8), Biuulf (x1), Wiglaf (x1), Eanmund (x8) and Eadgils (x1), Froda (x1), Ingeld (x16), and the Angle rulers Wærmund (x3) and Offa (x9) (cf. *Beo* 1931b–62). In *Beowulf*, Wermund is referred to as Garmund (1962a), but in the Mercian royal genealogies he appears as Wermund. For discussion, see Leneghan, 'Offa Digression'. Noticeably absent from the *Liber Vitae* are the Beowulfian Danish royal names Scyld, Scef, Healfdene, Hrothgar, and Hrothmund; the Geatish royal names Hrethel and Hæthcyn; and the Swedish royal names Ongentheow, Onela and Ohthere.

[52] 'Hyglac 1', an eighth-century lector and priest mentioned in Æthelwulf's early-ninth-century Latin poem, *De Abbatibus*; and 'Hyglac 2', the recipient of a mid eighth-century letter from one Alchfrith: PASE, accessed 12 September 2018. We should not be surprised at Hygelac's absence from the Anglo-Saxon royal genealogies, given the tradition recorded in *Beowulf* that his royal line died out soon after his death.

non-human creatures, probably produced in England or perhaps Ireland c. 650–750:[53]

> Et fiunt monstra mirae magnitudinis, ut rex Higlacus, qui imperauit Getis et a Francis occisus est, quem equus a duodecimo aetatis anno portare non potuit. Cuius ossa in Rheni fluminus insula, ubi in Oceanum prorumpit, reseuata sunt et de longinquo uenientibus pro miraculo ostenduntur. (I. 2).
>
> [And there are monsters of prodigious size, such as King Higlacus, who ruled the Getae and was killed by the Franks, whom, once he reached the age of twelve, no horse was able to bear. His bones are preserved on an island in the river Rhine where it empties into the sea, and they are shown to visitors from afar as a wonder.][54]

Here, as in *Beowulf*, Higlacus (OE Hygelac) is named as King of the Getae (i.e. Geats). However, in the Old English poem, of course, it is Beowulf, rather than Hygelac, who is famed for his prodigious strength.[55] Similarly, at the close of the poem, King Beowulf gives orders to Wiglaf to have his own barrow constructed on the coast, to serve as a monument visible to seafarers:

> Hātað heaðo-mǣre   hlǣw gewyrcean
> beorhtne æfter bǣle   æt brimes nōsan;
> sē scel tō gemyndum   mīnum lēodum
> hēah hlīfian   on Hrones Næsse,
> þæt hit sǣ-līðend   syððan hātan
> Bīowulfes Biorh   ðā ðe brentingas
> ofer flōda genipu   feorran drīfað.
> […]
> Geworhton ðā   Wedra lēode

---

[53] I follow Lapidge's dating: '*Beowulf*, Aldhelm, the *Liber Monstrorum* and Wessex', pp. 164–65. The work is preserved in five continental manuscripts dating from the ninth to eleventh centuries; for details, see Orchard, *Pride and Prodigies*, p. 86, n. 1.

[54] Text and translation from Orchard, *Pride and Prodigies*, pp. 254–317, also printed in K4, pp. 311–12. See also *Liber Monstrorum*, ed. F. Porsia (Bari, 1976), I.2, pp. 89–92. For discussion, see Chambers, *Introduction*, p. 4; Garmonsway, pp. 112–15; Whitelock, *Audience*, pp. 41–46; L. G. Whitbread, 'The *Liber Monstrorum* and *Beowulf*', *Mediaeval Studies* 36 (1974), 434–71; J. A. Leake, *The Geats of Beowulf: A Study in the Geographical Mythology of the Middle Ages* (Madison, WI, 1967); Lapidge, '*Beowulf*, Aldhelm, the *Liber Monstrorum* and Wessex'; Orchard, *Pride and Prodigies*, pp. 86–115; A. Orchard, 'The Sources and Meaning of the *Liber monstrorum*', in *I Monstra nell'Inferno Dantesco: Tradizione e Simbologie*, Atti del XXXIII Convegno storico internazionale, Todi, 13–16 ottobre 1996, ed. Enrico Menestò (Spoleto, 1997), pp. 73–106; and CCB, p. 134.

[55] For example, lines 196–97: *sē wæs moncynnes mægenes strengest/ on þǣm dæge þysses līfes*, 'he who was the strongest of all mankind in that day of this life'. Cf. lines 718–19, 750–54, 789–90, 1844–45a etc.

hlǣw on hōe,   sē wæs hēah ond brād,
wēg-līðendum   wīde gesȳne
(3156–58).

["Give orders to the battle-brave ones to build a barrow, shining over the funeral fire, at the water's edge; that must tower high over Whale's Cliff to the memory of my people, so that sea-travellers afterwards will call it 'Beowulf's barrow', those who drive their ships far over the darkness of the waves." [...] The people of the Geats then constructed a barrow on the headland, that was high and broad, visible to seafarers from afar.]

I would suggest, therefore, that the *Beowulf*-poet has transferred two elements of the Hygelac-legend, namely the Geatish king's prodigious qualities and seaside burial, to his fictionalized nephew, Beowulf.[56]

A much later account of this same figure, by now thought of as a Swedish king, is provided in *Ynglinga saga*, a *forneskjusaga* written by Snorri *c*. 1200:

Hugleikr hét son Álfs, er konungdóm tók yfir Svíum eptir þá brœðr, því at synir Yngva váru þá börn at aldri. Hugleikr konungr var engi hermaðr, ok sat hann at löndum í kyrrsæti; hann var auðigr mjök ok sínkr af fé. Hann hafði mjök í hirð sinni allskonar leikara, harpara ok gígjara ok fiðlara; hann hafði ok með sér seiðmenn ok allskonar fjölkunnigt fólk. Haki ok Hagbarðr hétu brœðr tveir, ok váru ágætir mjök. Þeir váru sjákonungar ok höfðu lið mikit, fóru stundum báðir samt, en stundum sér hvárr þeirra: margir kappar váru með hvárumtveggja þeirra. Haki konungr fór með her sinn til Svíþjóðar á hendr Hugleiki konungi, en Hugleikr konungr samnaði her fyrir; þá kómu til liðs við hann brœðr tveir, Svipdagr ok Geigaðr, ágætir menn báðir ok hinir mestu kappar. Haki konungr hafði með sér 12 kappa, þar var þá Starkaðr hinn gamli með honum; Haki konungr var ok hinn mesti kappi. Þeir hittust á Fyrisvöllum; varð þar orrosta mikil, féll brátt lið Hugleiks konungs. Þá sóttu fram kappariner Svipdagr ok Geigaðr; en kappar Haka géngu 6 á móti hvárum þeirra, ok urðu þeir handteknir. Þá gékk Haki konungr inn í skjaldborg at Hugleiki konungi, ok drap hann þar ok sonu hans tvá. Eptir þat flýðu Svíar, en Haki konungr lagði lönd undir sik ok

---

[56] For the argument that the *Beowulf*-poet drew directly on the *Liber monstrorum* and other literary accounts of Hygelac, see W. Goffart, '*Hetware* and *Hugas*: Datable Anachronisms in *Beowulf*', in Chase (1981), pp. 83–100; and North, *Origins*, pp. 39–45. Given the fact that in the early Anglo-Saxon period, before the conversion brought literacy to the educated elite, heroic legends must have circulated orally – and probably in the form of alliterative verse – it seems unnecessary to assume, however, that the *Beowulf*-poet must have learned the legend of Hygelac's death from the same literary sources that have come down to us. For a recent discussion of how the rules of alliterative versification ensured the transmission of heroic legend, see R. J. Pascual, 'Oral Tradition and the History of English Alliterative Verse', *SN* 89 (2017), 250–60.

gerðist konungr yfir Svíum. Hann sat þá at löndum 3 vetr, en í því kyrrsæti fóru kappar hans frá honum ok í víking ok féngu sér svá fjár.[57]

(*Ynglinga saga*, ch. 25, 'Fall Hugleiks konungs').

[It was the son of Álfr called Hugleikr who became king over the Svíar after the brothers, because Yngvi's sons were still children then. King Hugleikr was no warrior, and he stayed peaceably on his estates. He was very wealthy, and stingy with money. He had in his court a lot of all kinds of players, harpists and fiddlers. He also had with him sorcerers and all kinds of practitioners of magic. There were brothers called Haki and Hagbarðr who were very fine men. They were sea-kings and had many followers, travelling sometimes together, sometimes separately. They both had many champions with them. King Haki went with his force to Svíþjóð against King Hugleikr, and King Hugleikr assembled a force to meet them. Then two brothers, Svipdagr and Geigaðr, came to join his company, both outstanding men and great champions. King Haki had twelve champions with him. Starkaðr gamli (the Old) was with him. King Haki was also a great champion. They met at Fýrisvellir. A great battle took place there. Hugleikr's company fell quickly. Then the champions Svipdagr and Geigaðr advanced, but six of Haki's champions went against each of them, and they were taken captive. Then King Haki penetrated the shield wall against King Hugleikr and killed him and his two sons there. After that the Svíar fled, and King Haki took power over the lands and made himself king over the Svíar. He stayed in the lands for three years, and in this time of peace his champions left him and went raiding and so gained wealth for themselves.][58]

The parallels with *Beowulf* are faint, the Hygelac-legend having changed considerably over the centuries. Most strikingly, while in *Beowulf*, Hygelac is famed as a warrior and sets out for Frisia in pursuit of treasure, in Snorri, Hugleikr is *engi hermaðr*, 'no warrior', preferring to stay at home instead of attacking his neighbours. Moreover, Hugleikr's death as the victim of a sea-borne raid reverses the situation presented in *Beowulf*. One resemblance, however, is in the fact that in both accounts the king's death leads to the subjugation of his nation by a foreign invader, though, as we have seen, this event is postponed in *Beowulf* by the brief reign of Heardred and the uneventful fifty-year reign of Beowulf himself.[59] In Snorri's account, Hugleikr is cast as a relatively minor figure in Scandinavian royal history whose death results in only a brief interruption in the succession of the Ynglings.[60] *Beowulf*, on the

---

[57] *Snorra Sturlusonar: Heimskringla eða: Sögur Noregs konunga*, 3 vols. ed. N. Linder and H. A. Haggson (Uppsala, 1869–72), I, pp. 20–21.
[58] *Snorri Sturluson: Heimskringla, Volume I: The Beginnings to Óláfr Tryggvason*, trans. A. Finlay and A. Faulkes (London, 2011), p. 24.
[59] For debate as to whether the Geats were in reality conquered after the fall of their royal house, see Leake, *The Geats of* Beowulf.
[60] After Haki's three-year reign the Yngling line is restored with the accession of

other hand, presents Hygelac's death as an event of great significance, heralding the collapse of the Hrethlings.

The *Beowulf*-poet saw in the legend of Hygelac's death an opportunity to explore the question of kingly responsibility. With the story of Scyld, the poet provides the dictum that good kings must gain treasure by attacking their neighbours and forcing them *gomban gyldan*, 'to yield tribute' (11a). By returning so frequently to the theme of Hygelac's death, however, the poet continually invites his audience to reflect on whether kings themselves should risk their lives by fighting in the vanguard.[61] In a recent discussion, Fred Biggs argues that with each description of Hygelac's death, the poet gradually sought to introduce more fictionalized elements, allowing in the process for greater emphasis on Beowulf's role in the raid.[62] Biggs proposes that the poet added these fictional elements to allow for the story of the Hrethlings to continue beyond Hygelac's death with the reign of Beowulf, and to emphasize the theme of succession.[63] Building on Biggs's argument, in the discussion below I consider the various allusions to Hygelac's death alongside other references to Beowulf's uncle, in order to explore more fully how the poet worked up his hero from the legend of Hygelac's death.

From Hygelac to Beowulf

The possibility that the story of King Beowulf's death is a poetic embellishment or variation of the legend of Hygelac's fall in Frisia was raised

---

Hugleikr's cousin, Jörund (*Ynglinga saga*, ch. 23). Snorri's account of Jörund's death in a raid on Limfjord in the land of the Danes bears some similarities with Hygelac's death as recorded in *Beowulf*: 'Jǫrundr, son of King Yngvi, was king at Uppsalir. He then ruled the lands and often went raiding in the summer. One summer he went with his army to Danmǫrk. He raided around Jutland and in autumn went into Limafjǫrðr and raided there. He lay with his troop in Oddasund. Then Gýlaugr, king of the Háleygir, son of Guðlaugr who was mentioned above, arrived there with a large army. He engaged in battle with Jǫrundr, and when the local inhabitants realised this, they flocked there from all directions with ships both large and small. Then Jǫrundr was overpowered and his ship cleared. He jumped into the water, but was captured and taken ashore. Then King Gýlaugr had a gallows raised and led Jǫrundr to it and had him hanged. Thus ended his life.' (*Ynglinga saga*, ch. 24; Finlay and Faulkes, p. 26).

[61] On the idea of the king embodying the 'luck' of the people in Germanic kingship, see Chaney, *Cult of Kingship*, pp. 2–3, 12–17.

[62] Biggs, 'History and Fiction'. John McNamara argues that the poet had more freedom in his elaboration of Beowulf's character than with the more historically-rooted figure of Hygelac: 'Beowulf and Hygelac: Problems for Fiction in History', *Rice University Studies* 62 (1976), 55–63. Like Biggs, McNamara focuses almost entirely on the Frisian raid.

[63] Biggs, 'History and Fiction', p. 145.

almost a century ago by both R. W. Chambers and W. W. Lawrence.[64] Since then, however, the topic has barely been broached, despite its obvious importance to our understanding of the *Beowulf*-poet's compositional method. One reason for this oversight is the widespread belief that Beowulf is essentially a folktale figure placed in a historical setting. This section provides an alternative approach, arguing that the poet developed the fictional Beowulf out of his legendary uncle, Hygelac.

It is clear from the manner in which the hero is introduced that King Hygelac's reputation exceeded that of his young, relatively obscure nephew, whose name is not mentioned until line 343.[65] Hence, when first we meet Beowulf, at home in Geatland, he is described only as *Higelāces þegn* (194b). Similarly, on arriving in Denmark, the hero declares to the coastguard, *Wē synt gum-cynnes Gēata lēode/ ond Higelāces heorð-genēatas*, 'We are of the race of the Geatish people and Hygelac's hearth-companions' (260–61), before announcing to Hrothgar's court, *Wē synt Higelāces bēod-genēatas*, 'We are Hygelac's table-companions' (342b–43a). Much later in the work, some fifty years after Hygelac's death, King Beowulf fondly recalls how he was reared by his grandfather, Hrethel, alongside his three maternal uncles, with Hygelac singled out for special praise: *Herebeald ond Hæðcyn oððe Hygelāc mīn*, 'Herebald and Hæthcyn and my Hygelac' (2434).[66] Beowulf's closeness to Hygelac is again to the fore as he makes his first address to Hrothgar. This long speech, comprising forty-eight lines, is structured around three deferential references to Hygelac appearing in its opening, middle and closing lines:

> Wæs þū, Hroðgār, hāl!   Ic eom *Higelāces*
> *mǣg ond mago-ðegn*;   hæbbe ic mǣrða fela
> ongunnen on geogoþe. [...]
> [...] ic þæt þonne forhicge,   swā mē *Higelāc* sīe,

---

[64] Chambers, *Introduction*, p. 13; Lawrence, *Epic Tradition*, p. 104. Lawrence compares this poetic innovation with the addition of the fictional Roland to legends surrounding Charlemagne and the transformation of the British chief, Arthur, into the legendary king. See also Dobbie, *Beowulf and Judith*, p. xxxiv. Du Bois, 'Unity of *Beowulf*', 392–93, suggests that the poet invented the figure of Beowulf to represent the national strength of the Geats and its inevitable decline.

[65] See K4, p. 129, for discussion of the trope of withholding the hero's name. On the poem's original and subsequent audiences, see the Conclusion. Compare the dramatic postponement of the naming of Grendel until the b-verse of line 102 (*wæs se grimma gǣst Grendel hāten*, 'the fierce spirit was called Grendel'), blurring the narrative present with the mythic past of the *scop*'s song of Creation and thereby merging the figures of Grendel and the serpent, who in the biblical account is described immediately after the Creation of the world (Gen. 3.1).

[66] Brodeur describes Beowulf's love for Hygelac as his 'strongest and most enduring emotion' (*Art*, p. 80). For a less positive view of this relationship, see Goldsmith, *Mode and Meaning*, p. 212. On Hygelac's role in the poem more generally, see *CCB*, pp. 98–99, 134–35 and 210.

mīn mon-drihten   mōdes blīðe,
þæt ic sweord bere   oþðe sīdne scyld [...].

Onsend *Higelāce*,   gif mec hild nime
beadu-scrūda betst   þæt mīne brēost wereð,
hrægla sēlest;   þæt is *Hrǣdlan lāf*,
Wēlandes geweorc.   Gǣð ā wyrd swā hīo scel.
(407–09a, 435–37, 452–55). (Emphasis added).

[Greetings to you, Hrothgar! I am *Hygelac's kinsman and young thane*; I have achieved a great deal of fame in my youth. [...] I scorn that I should carry a sword or a broad shield, so that *Hygelac, my liege lord*, will be pleased with me at heart [...]. Send to *Hygelac*, if battle should take me, the best of war-shirts that my breast wears, the finest of mail-coats; that is *Hrethel's heirloom*, Weland's workmanship. Fate always goes as it must.]

Beowulf is presented here as the servant of two masters: on the one hand, we witness the young opportunist, eager to prove his monster-slaying credentials to the Scylding king, Hrothgar; on the other, Beowulf announces his status as a Hrethling, recipient of King Hrethel's mail-coat, loyal servant of Hygelac.[67] As we have seen in the previous chapter, this scenario is further complicated when Hrothgar begins to entertain the notion of adopting Beowulf as his own son and potential heir after the hero's successes against Grendel and Grendel's mother. In addition to *Hrǣdlan lāf*, 'Hrethel's heirloom', Beowulf will soon receive dynastic treasures of the Scyldings, among them the armour of King Heorogar, and (possibly) the sword of Hrothgar's father, King Healfdene (1020b).[68] In this way, the poet positions Beowulf as the fulcrum of his dynastic drama, as a young ætheling destined for the throne in one of these two royal houses.[69]

The first of the various allusions to Hygelac's death appears soon after Beowulf's introductory speech in Heorot (1202–14a). The mention of Wealhtheow's gift of *heals-bēaga mǣst*, 'the greatest of neck-rings' (1195b), sparks off two interlinked digressions, the first analeptic, the second proleptic. First, the narrator muses that never had he heard of a better necklace since the legendary Hama carried off the *Brōsinga mene*, 'necklace of the Brosings' (1199), and fled Eormanric,[70] before remarking that Hygelac would wear this same necklace on the day of his death in Frisia (1202–05a). This dilatory method of narration is, of course, typical of the *Beowulf*-poet. Nevertheless, the effect here is particularly striking, as in the space of a

---

[67] On Beowulf's poor standing among the Geats as a youth, see pp. 132–33.
[68] See above, pp. 19, 64–65, 84–85.
[69] On Beowulf's connections to the third major royal dynasty, the Swedish Scylfings, see above, pp. 93–102, and below, pp. 180–93.
[70] The Gothic legend of Hama and Eormanric is mentioned in *Deor* (21–26) and *Widsith* (8, 88–92 and 111–30). See *CCB*, pp. 115–16; K4, p. 193.

few lines we move from the narrative present of Wealhtheow's gift to the legendary Germanic past of Hama and Eormanric before looking forward to Hygelac's death. In this single moment, the poet deftly links Beowulf's adventures among the Danes with the 'timeless' heroes of the Germanic heroic age and the legendary Hygelac.

Our first encounter with King Hygelac in-the-flesh is occasioned by his nephew's return home to the Geats. As the hero's ship lands on the shore, the young but nonetheless battle-hardened ruler sits distributing rings in his stronghold, waiting for news of his nephew:

> Hī sīð drugon
> elne geēodon,   tō ðæs ðe *eorla hlēo,*
> *bonan Ongenþeoes*   burgum in innan,
> *geongne gūð-cyning   gōdne* gefrūnon
> hringas dǣlan.   Higelāce wæs   1970
> sīð Bēowulfes   snūde gecȳðed,
> þæt ðǣr on worðig   *wīgendra hlēo,*
> *lind-gestealla*   lifigende cwōm,
> heaðo-lāces hāl   tō hofe gongan.
> Hraðe wæs gerȳmed,   swā *se rīca* bebēad,   1975
> fēðe-gestum   flet innanweard.
> (1966b–75).

[They had survived the journey, went with glory to where they knew *the protectors of warriors, slayer of Ongentheow, young war-king,* within the stronghold, gave out rings *with goodness.* Swiftly Beowulf's exploit was made known to Hygelac, that there in the enclosures *the protector of warriors, shield-companion,* had returned alive, safe and sound from the battle-play, coming home. Quickly the hall was cleared, as *the mighty one* instructed, for the foot-guests.]

The close identification of uncle and nephew is suggested by the overlapping lexical terms used to describe them in this scene: hence Hygelac is *eorla hlēo* while Beowulf is *wīgendra hlēo*.[71]

This long linking section, often referred to as 'Beowulf's Return', was considered suspect by many early scholars due to the repetition of material and the presence of unusual vocabulary.[72] In the mid-twentieth

---

[71] The term *hlēo*, 'cover, shelter, protection', occurs on twelve occasions in *Beowulf*, most frequently in the collocations *eorla hlēo* (used of Beowulf: 791b; Hrothgar: 1035a, 1866a, 2142a; and Hygelac: 1967b, 2190a), and *wīgendra hlēo* (used of Hrothgar: 429b; Sigemund: 899b; Beowulf: 1972b, 2337b), as well as the compound *hlēo-burh*, 'sheltering town, stronghold' (912a, 1731b). Orchard notes that the terms used to describe Hygelac 'suggest a flattering comparison with the recently lauded Offa' (*CCB*, p. 223).

[72] Levin Schücking, for example, saw this passage as a clumsy attempt to join what were originally two separate poems, one on Beowulf's adventures among the Danes, the other on the dragon-slaying (*Beowulfs Rückkehr*, p. 72). Schücking

century, Francis P. Magoun, Jr., for example, described the passage as a recapitulation or 'folk-variant' on the Danish section, citing as evidence of its separate authorship various factual inconsistencies between the earlier version of events and Beowulf's account on his return to Hygelac's court, among them the mention of Grendel's *glōf* (2085b) and the naming of Grendel's victim, *Hondsciō* (2076a).[73] More recent interpretations, however, have accounted for these inconsistencies by drawing attention to the poetic technique of variation or pointing to the presence of multiple narrators in the text.[74] When viewed from a dynastic perspective, the structural significance of the 'Return' becomes clear: having established himself as a strong candidate for kingship in Denmark, Beowulf must now consolidate his position within his own royal house, the Hrethlings, by realigning himself with Hygelac.

Beowulf's report also provides the poet with a final opportunity to reflect on dynastic intrigue among the Scyldings, a subject that must have been of considerable interest to his audience, through his description of the previously unmentioned figure of Hrothgar's daughter, Freawaru (2020–24a). The hero's remarkably detailed prognosis of her anticipated marriage to Ingeld (2024b–69a) reintroduces the theme of the feud between *āþum-swēoran*, 'father-in-law and son-in-law' (81b–85), that will soon destroy Heorot.[75] In the light of this information, Hrothgar's attempted adoption of Beowulf starts to make considerably more sense. Beowulf may well have hoped to win the hand of a Scylding princess in return for ridding Heorot of Grendel.[76] For comparison, we may note that Hygelac

---

regarded lines 1888–2200 as comprising the 'Return', but excludes the story of Freawaru and Ingeld (2026–70) from his discussion. Schücking observed that a number of phrases and formulas occurred only in this passage and two further passages sometimes regarded as 'suspect', namely the Scyld-prologue, which he treats as lines 1–63, and the story of Offa's bride. For a summary and translation of Schücking's arguments, see Shippey and Haarder (1998), pp. 507–11. See also Chambers, *Introduction*, pp. 117–20. On the significance of the Scyld-prologue and tale of Offa's bride to the dynastic drama, see above, Chapter One, pp. 39–46 and 78–82, and Chapter Three, pp. 179–80.

[73] Magoun, '*Béowulf A*': a Folk-Variant', 96.
[74] See K3, pp. lvii–lviii; Sisam, *Structure*, pp. 46–50; A. Brodeur, '*Beowulf*: One Poem or Three?', *Medieval Literature and Folklore Studies: Essays in Honor of Francis Lee Utley*, ed. J. Mandel and B. A. Rosenberg (New Brunswick, 1970), pp. 3–28; J. W. Schwetman, 'Beowulf's Return: the Hero's Account of His Adventures among the Danes', *Medieval Perspectives* 13 (1998), 136–48. Kevin Kiernan cited damage to fol. 179 in support of Schücking's argument that 'Beowulf's Return' joins together two originally separate poems (Beowulf *Manuscript*, pp. 243–70, esp. p. 252). For recent discussions of 'Beowulf's Return' which treat the passage as integral, see *CCB*, pp. 222–27; and J. M. Hill, *Narrative Pulse*, pp. 65–69.
[75] For discussion of this feud between Hrothgar and Froda, King of the Heathobards, and father of Ingeld, see Chapter One, pp. 52–53.
[76] In medieval romance, of course, the hero is often rewarded for his achievements with the king's daughter's hand in marriage. North notes that in the

rewarded his warrior, Eofor, for killing Ongentheow with marriage to his *āngan dohtor*, 'only daughter' (2998b).[77] The hero's lowly standing among the Geats, and his weak claim to the Hrethling throne, would certainly make such a prestigious match desirable for an ambitious young prince. With Hrothgar's only daughter's future already settled, the Danish king offers to accept Beowulf as a son. As we have seen, the king's gesture was not well-received by Queen Wealhtheow, who feared that the adoption of Beowulf, and by implication his potential stake in the Danish succession, would endanger her sons and lessen their chances of kingship.[78] With Wealhtheow's instruction that Hrothgar should restrict the succession to his own immediate kin, and no Scylding princess available for him to marry, the chance of Beowulf attaining a prominent position in Heorot – at least by peaceful means – effectively disappears. With the hero's path to kingship among the Danes now blocked, the focus shifts to his close relationship with Hygelac and his status as a Hrethling.

Hygelac's statement that he had long tried to dissuade Beowulf from such a dangerous task in Denmark (1994b–97b) seems to contradict both the narrator's earlier comment that the wise men of the Geats did not dissuade Beowulf from travelling to Denmark (202b–04) and Beowulf's own statement that the same *snotere ceorlas* had in fact encouraged him to seek out Hrothgar (415–18). Some have taken this inconsistency to be an indication of Hygelac's lack of wisdom, in that his advice runs counter to that of the *snotere ceorlas* (202b).[79] Louviot, on the other hand, has warned against reading irony into this passage, emphasizing that each of these individual statements has a 'purely local function'.[80] The most immediate local function of Hygelac's claim that he had tried to prevent his nephew from risking his life is to further underline their close friendship and to highlight their equally headstrong natures.[81] Hence both Hygelac and Beowulf are described elsewhere as seeking out glory in foreign lands *for wlenco*, 'out of daring *or* pride'.[82] First, on the hero's entrance into Heorot, Wulfgar declares: *Wēn' ic þæt gē for wlenco nalles ne for wræc-sīðum/ ac for*

Scandinavian analogues, Bjarki is rewarded for his bravery with a bride, the daughter of Hrólfr, and suggests therefore that the hero's lengthy prognostication on the prospects of Freawaru and Ingeld masks his own disappointment at not being the one to marry her (*Origins*, pp. 111–15).

[77] For the argument that Hygelac's reward of Eofor was excessive, see Hall, 'Hygelac's only daughter'; for a more positive assessment of this gesture and of Hygelac's character more generally, see now L. Neidorf, 'Hygelac and His Daughter: Rereading *Beowulf* Lines 2985–2998', *MÆ* (forthcoming).

[78] On Wealhtheow's response to Hrothgar's offer of adoption, see pp. 72–76.

[79] See, for example, A. Bammesberger, 'Who Advised Beowulf to Challenge Grendel?', *ANQ* 24 (2011), 244–48; and *CCB*, p. 204, n. 6.

[80] Louviot, *Direct Speech*, p. 216.

[81] See further K. Malone, 'Beowulf the Headstrong', *ASE* 1 (1972), 139–45.

[82] On the ambivalence of *wlenco* in the poem, see Gwara, *Heroic Identity*, pp. 21–25.

hige-þrymmum Hrōðgār sōhton, 'I expect that you have sought out Hrothgar out of daring, not because of exile, but with greatness of heart' (338–39).[83] Later, we learn that Hygelac similarly *for wlenco wēan āhsode,/ fæhðe tō Frȳsum,* 'out of pride *or* arrogantly (?) sought out woe, a feud among the Frisians' (1206–07a).[84]

Continuing this close identification of the two characters, the hero respectfully frames his long report by acknowledging his fealty and kinship to Hygelac: *Þæt is undyrne, dryhten Hygelāc,* 'That is clear, lord Hygelac' (2000); *ic lȳt hafo/ hēafod-māga nefne, Hygelāc, ðec,* 'I have few close kin except for you, my Hygelac' (2150b–51).[85] Further opportunities for mutual expressions of loyalty and esteem between uncle and nephew arise during the exchange of treasures, in which Beowulf explains the history of the armour he received from Hrothgar before presenting it to Hygelac as a sign of loyalty with the instruction: *Brūc ealles wel!,* 'Make good use of it all!' (2162b).[86] The harmonious relationship of uncle and nephew echoes the portrait of Hrothgar and Hrothulf seated together in Heorot:

> Hygelāce wæs
> nīða heardum   nefa swȳðe hold,
> ond gehwæðer ōðrum   hrōþra gemyndig.
> (2169b–71).
>
> [His nephew was very dear to Hygelac, fierce in battle, and each to the other mindful of benefits.]

However, just as that scene of family unity in Heorot was overshadowed by the threat of future conflict, so too the poet quietly hints at the troubles that lie ahead for the Hrethlings through mention of Beowulf's gift to Hygelac's queen, Hygd, of the great necklace that he had received from Wealhtheow (2172–74a). We have already learnt that this same treasure will fall into the hands of the Franks after Hygelac wore it on his fatal attack on Frisia (1202–14a). Through this subtle allusion to Hygelac's death, the poet keeps the audience's attention on the question of succession during the exchange of treasures, gradually preparing the ground for Beowulf to assume his uncle's role as king.

Alert to the dramatic transformation of this *æþeling un-from,* 'noble of unpromising origins' (2188a), into a prince with strong royal credentials,

---

[83] The apposition of the parallel dative constructions *for wlenco* and *for hige-þrymmum* encourages us to read the former in a positive sense, as 'out of high spirit, daring'. Wulfgar himself is introduced as a *wlonc hæleð,* 'proud warrior' (331b).

[84] The collocation of *wēan* and *fæhðe* might perhaps suggest a less positive sense of *for wlenco* in this instance.

[85] Cf. *CCB,* p. 226. Compare the similar structure of Beowulf's speech to Hrothgar (407–55), discussed above at pp. 127–28.

[86] See J. M. Hill, *Narrative Pulse,* pp. 65–74.

Shaping the Dynastic Drama

Hygelac matches Beowulf's gift of Heorogar's armour with ancestral treasures of the Hrethlings, as well as a vast estate:[87]

> Hēt ðā eorla hlēo   in gefetian   2190
> heaðo-rōf cyning   *Hrēðles lāfe,*
> golde gegyrede;   næs mid Gēatum ðā
> sinc-māðþmum sēlra   on sweordes hād;
> þæt hē on Bīowulfes   bearm ālegde,
> ond him gesealde   seofan þūsendo,[88]   2195
> bold ond brego-stōl.   Him wæs bām samod
> on ðām lēodscipe   lond gecynde,
> eard ēðel-riht,   *ōðrum swīðor*
> *sīde rīce   þām ðǣr sēlra wæs.*
> (2190–99). (Emphasis added).

[Then the protector of warriors, the battle-brave king, ordered *Hrethel's heirloom* to be fetched, gold-adorned; there was no better treasure-gift among the Geats in the form of a sword; he placed that in Beowulf's lap, and gave to him seven thousand hides, a hall and princely seat. Together they both held inherited land among that people, land right and territory, *though the broader kingdom was reserved for the one who was senior* (i.e. Hygelac).]

Although Hygelac's seniority as ruler is emphasized, Beowulf has now taken a major step towards the Geatish throne. The narrator then moves swiftly from Hygelac's death to the 'reign' of the dragon, passing over the brief reign of Heardred and Beowulf's uneventful fifty-year occupation of the throne in the space of a few lines:[89]

> Eft þæt geīode   ufaran dōgrum   2200
> hilde-hlæmmum,   syððan Hygelāc læg,
> ond Heardrēde   hilde-mēceas
> under bord-hrēoðan   tō bonan wurdon,
> ðā hyne gesōhtan   on sige-þēode
> hearde hilde-frecan,   Heaðo-Scilfingas,   2205
> nīða genǣgdan   nefan Hererīces:
> syððan Bēowulfe   brāde rīce
> on hand gehwearf;   hē gehēold tela
> fīftig wintra   — wæs ðā frōd cyning,
> eald ēþel-weard —   oð ðæt ān ongan   2210
> deorcum nihtum   draca rīcsian
> (2200–11).

---

[87] Biggs, 'Geatish Succession', suggests that Hygelac effectively makes Beowulf a sub-king, if not co-ruler. See, however, North, 'Heathen Polity', p. 96.
[88] Cf. K4, p. 237: 'The amount of land given to Bēowulf would therefore be the equivalent to that of North Mercia.'
[89] See below, pp. 180–94, on the integration of the dragon into the dynastic drama.

[After that it came to pass, through the clashing of battles, at a certain time after Hygelac lay dead, and battle-blades under shield-coverings had become the slayer to Heardred, when those fierce war-chiefs sought him out among the victorious people, laid low the nephew of Hereric (i.e. Heardred) through hostility: afterwards the broad kingdom passed into the hands of Beowulf; he held it well for fifty years – he was an experienced king, ancient guardian of the homeland – until a certain one began to reign on dark nights, a dragon.]

By glossing over Heardred's reign so briefly, the poet effectively presents Beowulf as Hygelac's true successor. In this passage, we are presented with another variation on the bloodless Scylding succession, with each stage determined by the violent death of a king. By condensing the reigns of Heardred and Beowulf into a few short lines, the poet has effectively overlaid the legend of Hygelac's death in Frisia with the deadly struggle between his fictional nephew and the *draca*.

The narrator returns to the theme of Hygelac's death as King Beowulf prepares to face his own fate against the dragon. In this penultimate account of the Frisian raid, the poet deftly transforms Hygelac's defeat into another opportunity for Beowulf to demonstrate his swimming prowess and to further underline his own royal credentials. Hence, while Hygelac's attempt to plunder the Franks ends in disaster, Beowulf swims home with his own spoils of battle:

```
          Nō þæt læsest wæs
hond-gemōta   þǣr mon Hygelāc slōh,                2355
syððan Gēata cyning   gūðe rǣsum,
frēa-wine folca   Frēslondum on,
Hrēðles eafora   hioro-dryncum swealt,
bille gebēaten.   Þonan Bīowulf cōm
sylfes cræfte,   sund-nytte drēah;                 2360
hæfde him on earme   ealra þrītig
hilde-geatwa   þā hē tō holme þrong.⁹⁰
Nealles Hetware   hrēmge þorfton
fēðe-wīges,   þē him foran ongēan
linde bǣron;   lȳt eft becwōm                      2365
fram þām hild-frecan   hāmes nīosan.
Oferswam ðā sioleða bigong   sunu Ecgðeowes,
earm ān-haga   eft tō lēodum
```
(2354b–68). (Emphasis added).

---

[90] S. H. Horowitz, 'Beowulf, Samson, David and Christ', *Studies in Medieval Culture* 12 (1978), 17–23, compares Beowulf's return from Frisia with the biblical tale of Samson's return from Ashkelon with the armour of thirty men (Iud. XIV.19). Orchard notes that Grendel similarly snatches thirty thanes on his first visit to Heorot (123a) (*CCB*, p. 145).

[That was no lesser hand-combat than when men killed Hygelac, after the king of the Geats, lordly friend of the people, in the clashing of battle, Hrethel's son, died in the land of the Frisians through the drinking of swords, beaten down with blades. *From there* Beowulf escaped, through his own skill, endured a long swim; he had on his shoulders the battle-gear of all of thirty, when he plunged into the sea. Not at all did the Hetware have need to rejoice in that foot-battle, when they carried shields against him; few came back to seek out their homes from that war-chief. The son of Ecgtheow swam over the going of waves, wretched exile, back to his people.]

With the transitional adverb *þonan*, 'thence', and the dramatic postponement of his name, Beowulf emerges triumphantly from the disaster of Hygelac's defeat in Frisia.

The two remaining references to the Frisian raid confirm this impression of the poet's use of Hygelac's legend as the basis for the story of King Beowulf. During the course of Beowulf's speech at Hronesnæss, discussed in the previous chapter, the hero once more speaks of his close relationship with his late uncle:[91]

'[...] *Ic him* þā māðmas, þe *hē mē* sealde,	2490
geald æt gūðe, swā *me* gifeðe wæs	
lēohtan sweorde; *hē mē* lond forgeaf,	
eard, ēðel-wyn. Næs *him* ǣnig þearf	
þæt *hē* to Gifðum oððe tō Gār-Denum	
oððe in Swīo-rīce sēcean þurfe	2495
wyrsan wīg-frecan, weorðe gecȳpan;	
symle *ic him* on fēðan beforan wolde,	
āna on orde,[92] ond swā tō aldre sceall	
sæcce fremman, þenden þis sweord þolað	
þæt mec ǣr ond sīð oft gelǣste,	2500
syððan ic for dugeðum Dæghrefne wearð	
tō hand-bonan, Hūga cempan –	
nalles hē ðā frætwe Frēs-cyninge,	
brēost-weorðunge bringan mōste,	
ac in campe gecrong cumbles hyrde,	2505
æþeling on elne; ne wæs ecg bona,	

---

[91] The collocations *ic him* and *hē mē* are not uncommon in *Beowulf* outside of this passage (*ic him* also occurs at lines 560b, 601b, 963a, 968b, 243a, 2816b, 2877a; *hē mē* also occurs at lines 446b, 472b, 681b, 762b, 1832b, 2089a, 2134b, 2146b) or elsewhere in the Old English poetic corpus. However, nowhere else do we find them in such close proximity or appearing with such frequency.

[92] Beowulf's boast that he had always fought before Hygelac, *āna on orde*, 'alone in the vanguard' (2498a), recalls his earlier decision to fight Grendel single-handed (424b–26a: *ond nū wið Grendel sceal,/ wið þām āglǣcan āna gehēgan/ ðing wið þyrse*, 'and now I will contend with Grendel alone, against that terrible one, meet with the giant') as well as his resolve to take on the dragon *alone* (2345a–47a, 2529–37).

> ac him hilde-grāp heortan wylmas,
> bān-hūs gebræc. Nū sceall billes ecg,
> hond ond heard sweord, ymb hord wīgan.'
> (2490–2509). (Emphasis added).

[*I repaid* him *in battle for the treasures* he *gave to* me, *as it was granted to me, with a gleaming sword.* He *gave* me *land, territory, a joyous homeland.* He *did not have any need to seek out a worse war-chief from among the Gifthas or the Spear-Danes or from the Swedish kingdom, to purchase one with wealth. I would always go before* him *on foot,* alone *in the vanguard, and so for as long as I live, I must perform in battle, for as long as this sword lasts, that before and since has always served me, in front of the troops, I became the hand-slayer of Dæghrefn, champion of the Hugas. Not at all was he able to bring that treasure to the Frisian king, the breast-garment [of Hygelac], but he fell in the throng, protector of the standard, the nobleman in glory. Nor was a sword the killer, but a battle-grip broke his bone-house, the welling of the heart. Now the edge of the blade, hand and fierce sword, must fight for the hoard.*]

The poet's imaginative linking of Hygelac's fatal pursuit of treasure, Sigemund's plundering of the dragon's *bēah-hord* (894a) and Beowulf's impending dragon-fight comes into sharper focus in the closing lines of the speech, in which the hero now declares his own intention to fight for a *hord* (2509a). The motivating factors behind Beowulf's decision to fight the dragon are, of course, more numerous than simply the desire for treasure or glory or revenge for the burning of his own hall (2333–36). As king of the Geats, Beowulf now has a duty to defend his people from the merciless attacks of the terrible dragon who, left unopposed, would leave nothing living (2312–36). Nevertheless, it is striking that in Beowulf's last account of Hygelac's fall, the hero closely aligns his own fate with that of his uncle.[93] Through this recurrent pattern of echoes and allusions, we are consistently invited to view the fictional hero's dragon-fight as a poetic amplification or variation of the legend of Hygelac's death in Frisia.

The final reference to the Frisian raid comes in the long speech of the Geatish Messenger (2910b–21), in which Beowulf's own death-scene is once again placed in apposition with that of his uncle:

> Wīglāf siteð
> ofer Bīowulfe, byre Wīhstānes,
> eorl ofer ōðrum unlifigendum,
> healdeð hige-mǣðum hēafod-wearde
> lēofes ond lāðes. 2910

---

[93] Indeed, the narrator's subsequent epitaph for Beowulf might just as well have served for Hygelac: *Bīowulfe wearð/ dyrht-māðma dǣl dēaðe forgolden*, 'a portion of that lordly treasure was purchased with death by Beowulf' (2842b–43).

> Nū ys lēodum wēn
> orleg-hwīle,   syððan underne
> Froncum ond Frȳsum   *fyll cyninges*
> wīde weorðeð.   Wæs sīo wrōht scepen
> heard wið Hūgas,   syððan Higelāc cwōm
> faran flot-herge   on Frēsna land,   2915
> þǣr hyne Hetware   hilde genǣgdon,
> elne geēodon   mid ofer-mægene,
> þæt se byrn-wiga   būgan sceolde,
> fēoll on fēðan;   nalles frætwe geaf
> ealdor dugoðe.   Ūs wæs ā syððan   2920
> Merewīoingas   milts ungyfeðe.
> (2906b–21). (Emphasis added).

[Wiglaf, the son of Weohstan, sits over Beowulf, unliving, one nobleman above the other, keeps guard with brave thoughts over the beloved one (i.e. Beowulf) and the hated one (i.e. the dragon). Now is the expectation of a time of strife for this people, once *the death of the king* is revealed, becomes widely known among the Franks and Frisians. That feud was begun fiercely among the Hugas when Hygelac came sailing with a fleet into the land of the Frisians, where the Hetware overcame him in battle, gloriously dispatched him with a superior force, so that the mail-coated warrior had to retreat, fall among the foot-troops; not at all did the lord give treasure to the retainers. Ever since that we have received no favour from the Merovingians.]

Although the hero is the subject of the genitive construction *fyll cyninges*, the Messenger silently elides the deaths of Beowulf and Hygelac, moving seamlessly from one to the other. What now becomes clear is that Beowulf's uneventful fifty-year occupation of the throne and the brief reign of Heardred have merely postponed the inevitable consequences of the *wrōht*, 'quarrel, strife', that began with Hygelac's ill-fated expedition to Frisia.

Running parallel to these various allusions to Hygelac's fall are a series of intimations of Beowulf's own impending death scattered over some six hundred lines before the event itself is finally described in lines 2817–20.[94] This retardation of the narration of Beowulf's death allows the poet to weave the hero's personal tragedy into the wider dynastic drama, merging it with the legend of the fall of Hygelac and positioning it as the final episode in the Scylfing-Hrethling wars.[95] Fittingly, it is in the description of King Beowulf's funeral rites that the poet provides his final and most sophisticated elaboration on the theme of the death of Hygelac, the kernel

---

[94] Direct or indirect hints of Beowulf's approaching death appear at lines 2208b–11, 2309b–11, 2341b–43, 2397–2400, 2419b–24, 2534b–36, 2573–75, 2589–91a, 2709b–11a and 2724–28.

[95] See Robinson, *Appositive Style*, p. 60, on the poet's 'retarding style'.

of this section of the narrative. We have seen above how the construction of Beowulf's barrow as a marvel visible to seafarers recalls the legend of Hygelac's relics, as preserved in the *Liber monstrorum*.[96] Another common factor in the deaths of Beowulf and Hygelac is the pursuit of treasure. Contrary to Beowulf's own wish that the treasures he has gained with his life will benefit his people, the lordless Geats return them to the earth from which they once came:

> Hī on beorg dydon   bēg ond siglu,
> eall swylce hyrstra,   swylce on horde ǣr
> nīð-hēdige men   genumen hæfdon;
> forlēton eorla gestreon   eorðan healdan,
> gold on grēote,   þǣr hit nū gēn lifað
> eldum swā unnyt,   swā hyt ǣror wæs.
> (3163–68).

> [They placed in the barrow rings and jewels, all such treasures as hostile men had previously taken from the hoard; they let the earth hold the treasure of warriors, gold in the grit, where it still lives now, as useless to men as it was before.]

Some scholars have taken this gesture to symbolize a rejection of the entire pagan, heroic culture embodied by Beowulf, with its reckless pursuit of treasure and glory, others as a critique of the hero himself.[97] However, when approached from a dynastic perspective, it becomes possible to view the poem's ending in a more optimistic light: in commemorating the fall of the Hrethlings, this section mirrors the opening account of the rise of the Scyldings; the implication is that the Geats will now suffer a period of lordlessness, just as the Danes had, until such a time as God intervenes in human history by sending a ruling dynasty who will begin the circulation of treasure again.[98] There is little evidence within the work to support the view that the poet set out to critique the pursuit of treasure in and of itself. Indeed, the narrator consistently expresses admiration not only for those who win and circulate treasure, but for treasures themselves, which are lovingly described.[99] Nor does the poet overtly condemn kings

---

[96] See pp. 122–24.
[97] See, for example, E. G. Stanley, 'Hæthenra Hyht in *Beowulf*', in *Studies in Old English Literature in Honor of Arthur Gilchrist Brodeur*, ed. S. B. Greenfield (Eugene, OR, 1963), pp. 136–51; Goldsmith, *Mode and Meaning*. For further discussion of the poem's contentious closing lines, see Introduction, p. 16, and Chapter Four, pp. 228–31.
[98] For similar views of the poem's cyclical structure, see B. S. Cox, 'From Dane to Dane, Comfort to Comfort, Funeral to Funeral', in her *Cruces of Beowulf* (The Hague and Paris, 1971), pp. 154–73, at 172; and Owen-Crocker, *Four Funerals*, pp. 238–39.
[99] A. Faulkner, 'The Language of Wealth in Old English Literature: from the

for risking their lives in pursuit of treasure and wealth. In the opening section of the poem, Scyld Scefing restores the fortunes of the Danes by winning treasure from the neighbouring peoples, attacking their meadhalls and forcing them to pay tribute (4–11). With Hygelac's fatal raid on Frisia, the poet problematizes the idea of the king risking his own life in order to win treasure for his people. By dying without a suitable heir in place, Hygelac places the Hrethling dynasty in jeopardy and exposes the Geats to foreign attack. Following the death of the fictionalized Beowulf, the full consequences of his legendary uncle Hygelac's untimely fall in Frisia are finally brought into the foreground. Although Beowulf hopes the treasure he has won will help the *lēoda þearfe*, 'need of the people' (2801a), with their ruling dynasty extinct the Geats now find themselves in the same state of *fyren-ðearfe*, 'terrible need', and lordlessness (14–16a) that the Danes had suffered in the poem's opening section. Like Scyld, Beowulf has succeeded in winning a great treasure for his people, but like Hygelac, the pursuit of treasure has resulted in his death. In this way, the fictional hero draws together the two structurally apposed narratives of the rise and fall of dynasties that frame the work. The loading of treasures onto Beowulf's funeral pyre clearly echoes the piling of Scyld's 'funeral' ship with the spoils of his victories (37b–48).[100] Crucially, however, unlike Scyld, Beowulf has failed to secure the succession. With neither a king nor an heir to distribute it, the great treasure-hoard that Beowulf has gained from the dragon can be of no use to the Geats.

Shaping a New Myth of Dynastic Origins: Scyld Scefing and Beow

This chapter has so far argued that the legend of Hygelac's fall provided the poet with the main inspiration for the story of the death of King Beowulf. In this final section, I propose that, in order to provide structural

---

Conversion to Alfred' (Unpubl. doctoral dissertation, University of Oxford, 2019), demonstrates how the authors of the early Old English biblical epics, *Genesis A* and *Daniel*, shared with the *Beowulf*-poet a profound respect for treasure and wealth, viewing it as a suitable reward for heroic endeavour. For discussion of complex attitudes to wealth and treasure in *Beowulf* and other Old English literature, see E. Leisl, 'Gold und Manneswert im *Beowulf*', *Anglia* 71 (1952), 259–73, trans. J. D. Niles, with the assistance of S. A. Dubenion-Smith, as 'Gold and Human Worth in *Beowulf*', in Niles, *Old English Literature*, pp. 173–83; E. Tyler, *Old English Poetics: The Aesthetics of the Familiar in Anglo-Saxon England* (Cambridge, 2006); North, 'Heathen Polity'; and W. Rudolf, 'The Gold in *Beowulf* and the Currencies of Fame', in *Gold in der Heldensage*, Reallexikon der germanischen Altertumskunde, Ergänzungsband, ed. W. Heizmann, V. Millet und H. Sahm (Berlin, 2018), pp. 115–41.

[100] See above, Chapter One, pp. 40–46, for discussion of how Scyld's funeral-scene avoids mentioning his death.

balance for this story, the poet turned to legends surrounding the neighbouring Danish royal house, the Scyldings (ON Skjöldungr). As noted in the previous chapter, this decision to merge tales of two separate royal houses into a single narrative universalizes the dynastic drama, extending its scope beyond that of the more narrowly-focused *forneskjusögur* and *fornaldarsögur*.[101] The poet introduces the Danish royal foundling, Scyld Scefing, and his son Beow, in such a highly allusive manner that many scholars have assumed that the audience was already familiar with some version of this story.[102] However, the fact that the names Scyld Scefing and Beow do not follow the pattern of *H*-alliteration which characterizes all the other members of Hrothgar's dynasty gives us reason to suspect that, like Beowulf himself, they are in fact interlopers in royal legend.[103] Indeed, a review of the analogues indicates that these figures originated not in Scandinavia but in Anglo-Saxon England.[104] In what follows, I propose

---

[101] This feature of the poem makes it unlikely that the poem was composed to appeal to any one particular Anglo-Saxon ruling family with Scandinavian roots. For the argument that genealogical connections between the East Anglian dynasty and the Swedish and Danish dynasties mentioned in the poem suggest an East Anglian provenance, see Newton, *Origins*. For the argument that other Anglo-Saxon kingdoms had equally strong connections with Sweden, see J. Hines, *The Scandinavian Character of Anglian England in the pre-Viking Period*, BAR 124 (Oxford, 1984), p. 289. Close connections between the poem's material culture and that of sixth-century Sweden – in particular the prevalence of gold – have recently been adduced in B. Gräslund, *Beowulfkvädet: Den nordiska bakgrunden*, Acta Academiae Regiae Gustavi Adolphi 149 (Uppsala: Kungl. Gustav Adolfs Akademien för svensk folkkultur, 2018). Others have argued that the presence of the Offa digression points to a connection with the court of Offa of Mercia: for a summary of the arguments, see Leneghan, 'Offa Digression'. The presence of names corresponding to Scyld Scefing and Beow in the West Saxon royal genealogy has given rise to speculation that the poem was composed for Alfred or one of his descendants: see pp. 143–46, 240–44. Finally, Kevin Kiernan (*Beowulf Manuscript*), and most recently Helen Damico (*Beowulf and the Grendel-kin*) have proposed that the poem was composed to honour the Anglo-Danish rulers of England in the eleventh century.

[102] For example, Judy King comments that this passage constitutes 'less a portrait of Scyld than the poet's summary of what is known about him from poetry or song' ('Launching the Hero', 457). See also Niles, *Beowulf*, p. 207; D. Clark, 'Relaunching the Hero'. For more general discussion of the poet's allusive style, see Whitelock, *Audience*, pp. 34–44.

[103] The same is true of all the 'Half-Danes' mentioned in the Finnsburg episode: Hoc, Hnæf, Hildeburh and Hengest. For the suggestion that Hengest was a Jute, see Orchard, *CCB*, p. 183. On Beowulf's name and his association with the Hrethlings, see above pp. 118–19. In the West Saxon royal genealogies, Heremod appears as the father or ancestor of Scyld, and most commentators would therefore place Scyld Scefing's arrival among the Danes during the interregnum that resulted from Heremod's deposition, before the reign of Healfdene.

[104] This is also the conclusion of C. E. Anderson, 'Scyld Scyldinga: Intercultural Innovation at the Interface of West and North Germanic', *Neophilologus* 100 (2016), 461–76, at 471–72. For translations of the relevant sections of the Scandinavian analogues, see Garmonsway, pp. 118–23.

that rather than viewing the Scyld-prologue as a summary of a well-known Danish royal legend, we should regard it as another innovation of the *Beowulf*-poet.[105] As discussed below, the poet was so successful in passing off this intervention in Danish royal legend as tradition that it eventually found its way into the West Saxon royal genealogy.[106]

Several of the chief Scandinavian sources mention an early ruler of the Danes named Skjöldr (OE Scyld), but in none of these texts is this figure associated with a foundling legend or ship funeral, or indeed with Scef or Beow. For example, Saxo Grammaticus's *History of the Danes* (c. 1216) traces the origin of the Danish people back to Dan and Angul, the sons of Humblo, who rose to power through their outstanding courage and virtue but who were not thought of as kings.[107] Dan's son, Humbli, was elected king by the people only to be usurped by his brother Lother. As discussed above, the strong parallels between Saxo's account of Lother and *Beowulf*'s Heremod suggest both are variants of the same royal legend: Lother's abuse of power provokes a popular uprising and results in his death; he is succeeded by Skyoldus (OE Scyld), who restores the family's good name and achieves fame by overcoming a bear in his youth.[108] Saxo notes that it was from Skyoldus that the Danish kings took the title of Skioldungs.[109] Like *Beowulf*'s Scyld, Skyoldus leaves his kingdom to a son (Gram), who inherits his father's good qualities as a respected ruler.

Skjöldunga saga (c. 1200), attested by Arngrímur Jónsson's sixteenth-century Latin abstract, presents a more mythological version of the origins of Scandinavian kingship, tracing its inception back to the arrival of Odinus (ON Oðinn, OE Woden) from Asia.[110] After conquering much of northern

---

[105] This section builds on my essay, 'Reshaping Tradition: the Originality of the Scyld Scefing Episode in *Beowulf*', in *Transmission and Generation in Medieval and Renaissance Literature: Essays in Honour of John Scattergood*, ed. K. Hodder and B. O'Connell (Dublin, 2012), pp. 21–36. My argument here broadly agrees with that of Richard North, who proposes that the *Beowulf*-poet created the figure of Scyld Scefing by merging Scandinavian legends about Scyld (ON Skjöldr), the first king of the Scyldings/Skjöldungs, with the Anglo-Saxon folkloric association of the shield and the sheaf (*Origins*, pp. 36–39). North proposes that the poet drew here on Virgil's genealogy for King Latinus (*Aeneid* VII.45–49).

[106] For a later example of such an intervention in royal legend, compare Geoffrey of Monmouth's refashioning of the story of the Trojan Brutus into a British foundation legend, and its subsequent assimilation into Anglo-Norman historiography and beyond. See, for example, T. Summerfield, 'Filling the Gap: Brutus in the *Historia Brittonum*, *Anglo-Saxon Chronicle* MS F, and Geoffrey of Monmouth', *The Medieval Chronicle* 7 (2011), 85–102.

[107] This section of Saxo's text is based on the Old Danish *Bjarkamál*.

[108] For connections between *Beowulf* and 'The Bear's Son Tale', see pp. 113–18.

[109] Friis-Jensen, I, pp. 22–23. See *CCB*, pp. 111–12; Bruce, *Scyld and Scef*, pp. 134–40.

[110] For a plot-summary of *Skjöldunga saga*, see Appendix A. For the text, see 'Danasaga Arngríms Lærða', ed. Guðnason, pp. 3–38; and Miller, 'Fragments of Danish History', 10.

Europe, Odinus divides his realm between his sons, assigning Denmark to Scioldus and Sweden to Ingo. From these first rulers are derived the tribal names Skiolldungar and Inglingar (ch. 1). Scioldus establishes the Danish royal seat at Hledra (i.e. modern-day Lejre) and is succeeded by Leifus I, Frodo I, Leifus II (Herleifus) and various other rulers including Dan, down to Frodo IV, who has two sons, Halfdanus (OE Healfdene) and Ingialldus (OE Ingeld), born of different mothers (ch. 9), who rule for a time together. Halfdanus produces a daughter, Signya, and two sons, Roas (ON Hroar, OE Hrothgar) and Helgo (ON Helghi, OE Halga). However, Ingialldus, out of greed for the kingdom, leads a surprise attack against his brother, Halfdanus, and kills him (ch. 10). As children, Roas and Helgo go into hiding, but once they are grown, they avenge their father's death by killing Ingialldus. The brothers then rule together, with Roas marrying an English princess and Helgo abducting and raping a Swedish princess, Yrsa, who bears him a son, Rolfo (ON Hrolf, OE Hrothulf), nicknamed Krag (or Krake). The account of Rolfo's career in *Skjöldunga saga* broadly agrees with *Hrólfs saga*: Rolfo's uncle, Roas (OE Hrothgar), is killed by his cousins, Rærecus (OE Hrethric) and Frodo (OE Froda), sons of Ingialldus; Rolfo then succeeds his father, Helgo, as king and presides over a great court which includes the champion Bödvar Bjarki; Rolfo is killed by Hiørvardus (OE Heoroweard), who is himself killed by Woggerus, a warrior who had promised to avenge Rolfo's death; Hiørvardus is succeeded by Rærecus (OE Hrethric), the paternal cousin of Rolfo's father Helgo, who fights against Walldarus; at this time the kingdom of Denmark is divided, with Rærecus ruling at Sælandia and Walldarus at Skane.[111]

Sven Aggesen's twelfth-century *Brief History of the Kings of Denmark* also presents Skiold as the first ruler of the Danes, explaining that he was so named 'because he admirably guarded all the boundaries of the kingdom by the protection which his defence afforded'.[112] In Sven's account, Skiold has two sons, Halfdan (OE Healfdene) and Frothi (the dragon-slayer),[113] who contest the succession; Halfdan kills Frothi and takes the kingdom; Halfdan is succeded by his son Helghi (OE Halga), famed for his piracy; Helghi is succeeded by Rolf (OE Hrothulf) Kraki, who is killed – Sven does not say by whom – at the royal residence at Lejre; Rolf is succeeded by Rokil Slagenback and Frothi the Bold.[114]

---

[111] Miller, 'Fragments of Danish History', 16.
[112] Garmonsway, p. 120.
[113] Roas (OE Hrothgar) is absent from Sven's account of the early Danish kings, with Frothi standing in his place.
[114] For translations of the relevant sections, see Garmonsway, pp. 125, 143–44, 157–58.

These sources demonstrate that traditions concerning an early Danish ruler named Scyld (ON Skjöldr, Latin Scioldus/Skyoldus), from whom the Scyldings (ON Skjlödungar) took their name, were current in Scandinavia from the twelfth century, and perhaps much earlier. It is possible, therefore, that the audience of *Beowulf* knew something of an early Danish king by the name of Scyld. However, the names Scef and Beow, as well as the foundling legend and the royal funeral that accompany Scyld in *Beowulf*, are all strikingly absent from the Scandinavian accounts of early Danish kingship, with all the evidence pointing instead to their origin in Anglo-Saxon England.[115]

The sole Scandinavian source that does feature these names, the twelfth-century Icelandic *Langfeðgatal*, betrays clear signs of Anglo-Saxon influence. This geneaology traces the ancestry of the Scandinavian kings back beyond Odin to the biblical Noah, via classical gods including Saturn and Jupiter and the kings of Troy, incorporating the sequence *Sescef, Beðvig, Athra, Itermann, Heremotr, Scealdua, Beaf, Eat, Goðulfi, Finn, Frealaf, Voden*.[116] Far from providing an authentic witness to early Scandinavian traditions, however, these generations are clearly dependent on a version of the pedigree created for King Æthelwulf of Wessex, as preserved in the long *ASC* entry for the year 855, with *Seskef/ Sescef* representing a garbled rendering of OE *se Scef*, 'that Scef':[117]

> Beaw Sceldweaing, Scyldwa Heremoding, Heremod Itermoning, Itermon Hraðraing, Hraðra Hwalaing, Hwala Bedwiging, Bedwig Sceafing; id est filius Noe, se wæs geboren on þære earce Noes; Lamech, Matuasalem, Enoc, Iared, Malalehel, Camon, Enos, Seth, Adam primus homo, et pater noster, id est Christus.[118]
>
> (*ASC*, MS B *s.a.* 855)

> [Beaw the son of Sceldwa, Sceldwa the son of Heremod, Heremod the son of Itermon, Itermon the son of Hrathra, Hrathra son of Hwala, Hwala the son of Bedwig, Bedwig the son of Scef. That Scef was Noah's son, and he was born in the ark; Lamech, Methuselah, Enoch, Jared, Mahalaleel, Cainan, Enos, Seth, Adam the first man, and our father, who is Christ.]

Æthelwulf's genealogy certainly presents a much closer analogue to *Beowulf* than anything contained in the extant Scandinavian sources. Yet,

---

[115] As R. W. Chambers comments, it is unlikely that the Danes would have utterly forgotten 'so striking a story, concerning the king from whom their line derived its name' (*Introduction*, p. 86).
[116] *Alfræði Íslensk: Islandsk Encyklopædisk Litteratur*, 3 vols (Copenhagen, 1917–18), III, ed. Kr. Kålund, p. 58.
[117] See A. Faulkes, 'Descent from the gods', *Mediaeval Scandinavia* 11 (1978–79), 92–125, at 94.
[118] *The Anglo-Saxon Chronicle MS B*, The AS Chronicle: a Collaborative Edition 4, ed. S. Taylor, (Cambridge, 1983), p. 33.

while the poem presents Scyld as the 'son' of Sce(a)f, in the *ASC* these figures are separated by Itermon, Hrathra, Hwala and Bedwig, names that do no feature anywhere in *Beowulf* or other royal legends. The suspicion that Æthelwulf's pedigree, like *Langfeðgatal*, is a learned scholarly fabrication rather than a reliable witness to early Scandinavian royal legend is confirmed by the transformation of Sceaf into the ark-born son of Noah.[119]

An even closer parallel to *Beowulf* is preserved in Æthelweard's *Chronicon*, a late-tenth-century Latin translation of the *ASC*. Here we find the same forms of the personal names as in *Beowulf*, arranged in the same genealogical sequence: *Scef-Scyld-Beo(w)*. Moreover, in place of the *ASC*'s story of Sceaf's birth in Noah's ark is a royal foundling legend remarkably similar to that preserved in the Old English poem:

> [...] Geat, sextus decimus Tetuua, septimus decimus Beo, octauus decimus Scyld, nonum decimus Scef. Ipse Scef cum uno dromone aduectus est in insula oceani que dicitur Scani, armis circumdatus, eratque ualde recens puer, et ab incolis illius terrae ignotus. Attamen ab eis suscipitur, et ut familiarem diligenti animo eum custodierunt, et post in regem eligunt; de cuius prosapia ordinem trahit Aðulf rex.

> [Geat, his sixteenth (ancestor) Tetwa, his seventeenth Beow, his eighteenth Scyld, his nineteenth Scef. And this Scef arrived with one light ship in the island of the ocean which is called Skaney, with arms all around him. He was a very young boy, and unknown to the people of that land, but he was received by them, and they guarded him with diligent attention as one who

---

[119] On early medieval royal genealogies as scholarly fictions based on biblical models, see D. N. Dumville, 'Kingship, Genealogies and Regnal Lists', in Sawyer and Wood (1977), pp. 77–104, at 90–96. See further, Chapter Four, pp. 201–03. D. Anlezark, 'Sceaf, Japheth and the Origins of the Anglo-Saxons', *ASE* 31 (2002), 13–46, attributes the invention of the story of Sceaf's birth in Noah's ark to the Alfredian court-circle, noting that it 'privileged the West Saxons among all northern peoples' (45). Tolkien comments that this move 'gave the northern kings a place in an unwritten chapter (as it were) of the Old Testament' ('Commentary', p. 161). In Chapter Four, I explore the possibility that *Beowulf* itself performed a similar task, inviting the Anglo-Saxons to think of their Scandinavian royal ancestors as analogous to the ancient kings of Israel. On the avoidance of classical (and in particular Trojan) ancestors as a distinguishing feature of the Anglo-Saxon genealogies, setting their royal houses apart from continental dynasties, see E. Tyler, 'Trojans in Anglo-Saxon England: Precedent without Descent', *RES* 64 (2013), 1–20. A Lombard king named Sceafa appears in the king-lists of *Widsith* (32b), alongside the Beowulfian figures Breca, Finn, Hnæf, Ongentheow, Offa, Hrothgar and Hrothulf. According to Paul the Deacon, the Lombards came from the island of *Scadinavia*, though he does not mention Sceafa/Sceaf: *Paul the Deacon, History of the Langobards*, trans. W. D. Foulke (Philadelphia, 1907), I, 1–7. We cannot, therefore, identify the Lombard Sceafa of *Widsith* with the Anglo-Saxon tradition of a Danish foundling named Scyld or Sce(a)f with any confidence.

belonged to them, and elected him king. From his family King Æthelwulf derived his descent.][120]

Although the foundling legend is here attributed to Scef, rather than Scyld, the description of the infant's mysterious arrival by boat, his subsequent acceptance by the people and rise to kingship all recall the opening of *Beowulf*, as does the location of Skaney.[121] Æthelweard's *Chronicon* dates from the latter part of the tenth century, but he is thought to have used a now-lost copy of the *ASC* predating the ninth-century archetype that lies behind all other extant versions.[122] Audrey Meaney has proposed that this same hypothetical early version of the *ASC* was the source for the foundling story and genealogy common to both *Beowulf* and Æthelweard.[123] Michael Lapidge, on the other hand, finds it more plausible that an early version of the West Saxon royal pedigree was indebted to 'a poem resembling (if not identical with) our *Beowulf*'.[124] A third possibility is that Æthelweard's *Chronicon*, compiled around the time of the copying of the Nowell Codex, was itself influenced by *Beowulf*.[125] However, in a recent essay, Dennis Cronan has downplayed the connection between *Beowulf*

---

[120] *The Chronicle of Æthelweard*, ed. A. Campbell (London, 1962), pp. 32–33. I follow Campbell's translation, though I have altered 'Sceaf' to 'Scef' to reflect the spelling of the Latin and to indicate its closeness to *Beowulf*. For a discussion of the authenticity of the *Chronicon*, see A. Lutz, 'Æthelweard's *Chronicon* and Old English poetry', *ASE* 29 (2000), 177–214, at 177–81. Sisam, 'Genealogies', 320–21, n. 3, suggests it is the work of a 'Celtic-trained secretary' commissioned by Æthelweard. See also A. C. Murray, '*Beowulf*, the Danish Invasions, and Royal Genealogy', in Chase, ed. (1981), pp. 101–11, at 106–07; J. M. Bately, *The Anglo-Saxon Chronicle: Texts and Textual Relationships*, Reading Medieval Studies 3 (Reading, 1991), p. 46.

[121] Cf. *Beowulf* 19b: *Scyldes eafera Scedelandum in*, 'Scyld's son (i.e. Beow) in Scedeland (i.e. Skaney)'. On the concept of the 'stranger king', see above, p. 42.

[122] F. M. Stenton, 'The South-Western Element in the Old English Chronicle', in *Preparatory to Anglo-Saxon England: Being the Collected Papers of Frank Merry Stenton*, ed. D. M. Stenton (Oxford, 1970), pp. 106–15, at 114; E. E. Barker, 'The Anglo-Saxon Chronicle Used by Æthelweard', *Bulletin of the Institute of Historical Research* 40 (1967), 74–91, at 77–79.

[123] Meaney, 'Scyld Scefing', 37. See also A. Campbell, 'The Use in *Beowulf* of Earlier Heroic Verse', in *England Before the Conquest: Studies in Primary Sources presented to Dorothy Whitelock*, ed. P. Clemoes and K. Hughes (Cambridge, 1971), pp. 283–92, at 290, who argues that the story of Scyld Scefing's arrival in the land of the Danes is a product of bookish learning, deriving from 'an annotation to a genealogy'. Newton suggests that both *Beowulf* and Æthelweard's *Chronicon* are dependent on 'a common Old English source, perhaps a genealogy maintained in verse' (*Origins*, p. 76). See also Niles, 'Locating *Beowulf* in Literary History', 95.

[124] Lapidge, '*Beowulf*, Aldhelm, the *Liber Monstrorum* and Wessex', 187. See also Fulk, 'Eddic Analogue', 320.

[125] See Bately, *Texts and Textual Relationships*, p. 46, n. 315; Tolley, '*Beowulf*'s Scyld Scefing Episode', 12. Sisam suggests that Æthelweard may have known, and

and the West Saxon genealogies, noting that the non-West Saxon, archaic forms of the names Sceld-*wa* and Tæt-*wa* in the *ASC* are 'suggestive of a complex and perhaps long textual history' distinct from that represented by *Beowulf*.[126] In the following discussion, I propose that the story of the foundling Scyld Scefing/Sceaf was not the creation of an inventive West Saxon genealogist but rather another innovation of the *Beowulf*-poet. In fashioning a dynastic foundation myth to serve as a prologue to his work, the poet appears to have drawn together a rich and suggestive array of folktale, biblical and perhaps classical imagery, all of which he brought to bear on royal legends of the Scyldings.

Scholars have long recognized that the Scyld-prologue contains elements of an agricultural myth. As Andy Orchard notes, the significance of the royal names Scyld Scefing ('Shield with the Sheaf' or 'son of Scef') and Beow ('Barley') would have been readily apparent to an Anglo-Saxon audience.[127] The veneration of the sheaf was an important feature of early northern harvest rituals and in some instances the corn-god was represented by the figure of a boy.[128] Moreover, there is evidence to suggest the ritualistic association of the shield and the sheaf in an Anglo-Saxon context. The thirteenth-century *Chronicle of Abingdon* relates how the monks settled a land dispute during the reign of Edmund (941–46) by placing a sheaf of wheat on a shield and allowing it to float downriver, marking out territory as it went. A miracle occurred, enabling the shield to travel against the current and encircle a flooded island which was then claimed as the property of the monastery.[129] Although this story survives only in a post-conquest account, the detail of the round shield suggests its authenticity. The *Beowulf*-poet may have been influenced by this Anglo-Saxon folk-tradition in developing the story of the royal foundling, Scyld Scefing.[130]

---

rejected, the fanciful story of Sceaf's birth in Noah's ark and descent from Adam ('Genealogies', 320).

[126] D. Cronan, '*Beowulf* and the Containment of Scyld in the West Saxon Royal Genealogy', in Neidorf (2014), pp. 112–37, at 123. Moreover, Cronan points to the fact that Alfred's family sought to diminish the significance of their Danish ancestor, Scyld, by 'containing' him within Christian tradition, whereas in the Old English poem Scyld is 'uncontained in every way' as the founder of a great royal line (p. 137).

[127] *CCB*, pp. 102–03. See further F. C. Robinson, 'The Significance of Names in Old English Literature', *Anglia* 86 (1968), 14–85.

[128] See Chambers, *Introduction*, pp. 6–8, 68–86 and 292–304; Harris, 'The Dossier on Byggvir'; Fulk, 'Eddic Analogue'.

[129] For the text see *Chronicon Monasterii de Abingdon*, ed. J. Stevenson (London, 1858), vol. 1, p. 89; trans. in *CCB*, pp. 102–03.

[130] One might compare the personification of objects such as swords, mail-coats and helmets elsewhere in the poem. See further, for example, G. Clark, 'Beowulf's Armor', *ELH* 32 (1965), 409–41; C. Brady, '"Weapons" in *Beowulf*:

In the imaginative linking of the shield and the sheaf within the context of a royal foundation myth, the poet may also have had in mind pairs of legendary founder-figures with alliterating names, such as Hengest and Horsa, Cerdic and Cynric, and even Romulus and Remus.[131] Another possible inspiration for the foundling legend, however, is biblical tradition. As Gale Owen-Crocker notes, the story of an abandoned infant who rises to become the saviour of an embattled people recalls the story of Moses.[132] Like Scyld, Moses was sent by God to rescue an afflicted people (Ex. 2.1–10; 3.7–10) in recognition of their suffering (Ex. 2.23–25; 3.7–9; 3.16), and there are interesting parallels between their respective funerals:[133]

mortuusque est ibi Moses servus Domini in terra Moab iubente Domino
et sepelivit eum in valle terrae Moab contra Phogor *et non cognovit homo sepulchrum eius usque in praesentem diem*

an Analysis of the Nominal Compounds and an Evaluation of the Poet's Use of Them', *ASE* 8 (1979), 79–141; Robinson, *Appositive Style*, p. 71.

[131] For Hengest and Horsa, see Bede, *HE* I.15; and *ASC* MS A, *s. a.* 449. For Cerdic and Cynric, see *ASC* MS A, *s. a.* 495 (*ASC MS A*, ed. Bately, pp. 17–19). Newton suggests that Hroðmund and Hryp, two names contained in the genealogy of King Ælfwald of East Anglia (c. 713–49) and perhaps connected with Hrothgar's sons, Hrothmund and Hrethric, were thought of as East Anglian founder figures during the reign of Ælfwald (*Origins*, pp. 77–81). On this tradition, see M. Salvador Bello, 'The Arrival of the Hero in a Ship: A Common Leitmotif in Old English Regnal Tables and the Story of Scyld Scefing in *Beowulf*', *SELIM* 8 (1998), 205–21. Such legends were common among the Germanic-speaking peoples. Paul the Deacon, for example, records the story of Ibor and Aio, ancestors of the Lombards, who opposed the aggression of the Vandal kings Ambri and Assi; see Foulke, ed., *History of the Langobards*, I. 7, pp. 11–15. On legends of Romulus and Remus in Anglo-Saxon England, including their depiction on the Franks Casket, see M. Hunter, 'Germanic and Roman antiquity and the sense of the past in Anglo-Saxon England', *ASE* 3 (1974), 29–50, at 32 and 38–40; and C. L. Neuman de Vegvar, 'The Travelling Twins: Romulus and Remus in Anglo-Saxon England', in *Northumbria's Golden Age*, ed. J. Hawkes and S. Mills (Stroud, 1999), pp. 256–67.

[132] Owen-Crocker, *Four Funerals*, p. 18. For detailed discussion of connections between biblical rulers and the kings of *Beowulf*, see Chapter Four. For connections between Beowulf and Moses, see G. R. Wieland, '*Manna mildost*: Moses and Beowulf', *Pacific Coast Philology* 23 (1988), 86–93. See also Owen-Crocker, *Four Funerals*, pp. 18–19 and 103–04; T. D. Hill, 'Scyld Scefing', p. 43. The possibility that the poet modelled some aspects of Scyld's career (and indeed that of his predecessor, Heremod) on the biblical figure of King Saul is explored in Chapter Four, pp. 197, 210–11, 219–23.

[133] Cf. *Beowulf* 14b: *fyren-ðearfe ongeat*, 'He (i.e. God) recognized their terrible need'. Compare, for example, the text of the Old English Heptateuch: *Æfer langre tide Egipta cyning forðferde and Israela bearn clypodon geomriende for þan weorcum. And hira clypung com to Gode fram þam weorcum and he gehirde heora geomrungæ and gemunde þara getreowþa þe he behet Abrahame and Isaace and Iacobe, and beseah to Israhela bearnum and alysde hig* (Ex. 2.23–25) (*The Old English Heptateuch and Ælfric's Libellus de veteri testament et novo*, 2 vols, EETS o.s. 30, ed. R. Marsden [Oxford, 2008], I, p. 91).

Moses centum et viginti annorum erat quando mortuus est *non caligavit oculus eius nec dentes illius moti sunt*
fleveruntque eum filii Israhel in campestribus Moab triginta diebus et conpleti sunt dies planctus lugentium Mosen
Iosue vero filius Nun repletus est spiritu sapientiae quia Moses posuit super eum manus suas et oboedierunt ei filii Israhel feceruntque sicut praecepit Dominus Mosi

(Deut. 34.5–9). (Emphasis added).

[And Moses the servant of the Lord died there, in the land of Moab, by the commandment of the Lord. And he buried him in the valley of the land of Moab over against Phogor: *and no man hath known of his sepulchre until this present day*. Moses was a hundred and twenty years old when he died: *his eye was not dim, neither were his teeth moved. And the children of Israel mourned for him in the plains of Moab thirty days: and the days of their mourning in which they mourned for Moses were ended.* And Josue the son of Nun was filled with the spirit of wisdom, because Moses had laid his hands upon him. And the children of Israel obeyed him, and did as the Lord commanded Moses.]

Like Moses, Scyld departs with his strength still intact (27: *fela-hrōr fēran on frēan wǣre*, 'he departed into the Lord's keeping, very strong'), while the Danes, ignorant of their ruler's final resting place, mourn his passing:[134]

        him wæs geōmor sefa,
murnende mōd.   Men ne cunnon
secgan tō sōðe,   sele-rǣdende,
hæleð under heofenum,   hwā þǣm hlæste onfēng.
(49b–52).

[They were sad in mind, grieving in spirit. Men cannot truly say, counsellors in the hall, warriors under heavens, who received that cargo.]

This link with the funeral of Moses supplements the array of analogues and possible sources already identified for Scyld's ship-funeral, among them the Sutton Hoo ship-burial,[135] an account of the funeral of Saint

---

[134] Both Moses and Scyld are succeeded by leaders of the people, Josue and Beow, both of whom inherit the qualities of their predecessors.

[135] See, for example, S. Lindquist, 'Sutton Hoo and *Beowulf*', Antiquity 22 (1948), 131–40; H. R. Ellis Davidson, 'Archaeology and *Beowulf*', in Garmonsway (1971), pp. 350–64, at 59–60. In the light of Sutton Hoo, Francis P. Magoun, Jr. suggested that the story of Hygelac's raid on Frisia came to Anglo-Saxon England through the 'gateway' of East Anglia ('Béowulf and King Hygelác in the Netherlands: Lost Anglo-Saxon Verse Stories about this event', *ES* 35 [1954], 193–204, at 203–04). For a recent discussion of archaeological and genealogical links between the poem and East Anglia in this period, see Newton, *Origins*, esp. pp. 30–53, 105–31. For a sceptical review of the connection, see R. Frank, '*Beowulf* and Sutton Hoo: The Odd Couple', in *Voyage to the Other*

Gildas in a *Vita* by a monk of Rhen,[136] and various descriptions of Viking and other Scandinavian royal ship-funerals.[137]

There is, of course, widespread material and documentary evidence for the practice of ship-burial throughout the early northern world, from as early as the Bronze Age.[138] An author as inventive and imaginative as the *Beowulf*-poet, therefore, would not have needed a specific source, literary or otherwise, in order to sketch the story of Scyld's departure.[139] Indeed, as Gale Owen-Crocker notes, in many respects Scyld's funeral stands apart from the various accounts of Norse ship-funerals, which typically feature cremation and human or animal sacrifice.[140] The poet may have suppressed such details on account of his audience's Christian sensibilities, yet cremation, if not sacrifice, does feature in the other two funeral set-pieces in the poem, those of Hildeburh's kin and King Beowulf.[141]

A more plausible explanation for the absence of cremation at Scyld's funeral is the *Beowulf*-poet's keen sense of structure and alertness to the principle of contrast. As early as 1924, Carl Wilhelm Von Sydow suggested that the story of Scyld's arrival and departure is a variant on the folktale motif of the foundling who returns alive to the unknown world from whence he arrived.[142] Moreover, as we saw in Chapter One, Scyld's funeral stands in apposition with that of King Beowulf at the poem's conclusion, framing the work with contrasting images of dynastic

---

World: The Legacy of Sutton Hoo, Medieval Cultures 5, ed. C. B. Kendall and P. S. Wells (Minneapolis, MN, 1992), pp. 47–64. See, however, Owen-Crocker, *Four Funerals*, pp. 27–34.

[136] For the text, see *Vita Gildae Auctore Monacho Ruiensi (Vita I)*, in *Gildae De Excidio Britanniae, Fragmenta, Liber de Paenitentia*, Cymmrodorion Record Series 3, ed. H. Williams (London, 1899), pp. 317–89, cited in Meaney, 'Scyld Scefing', 29. This parallel was first noted by A. F. Cameron, 'Saint Gildas and Scyld Scefing', *NM* 70 (1969), 240–46. See further Meaney, 'Scyld Scefing', 29–40; Meaney, 'Postscript', pp. 59–61.

[137] The ship funerals of the Norse kings Sigvardus, Baldr and Haki are described in *Skjöldunga saga*, *Gylfaginning*, and *Ynglinga saga* respectively, while the Arab traveller Ibn Fadlān describes an inland ship-inhumation that took place among a Swedish tribe in the Volga region in the early-tenth century. For the texts, see Garmonsway, pp. 341–49; Ibn Fadlān, *Ibn Fadlān and the Land of Darkness: Arab Travellers in the Far North*, trans. P. Lunde with an Introduction by C. Stone (London, 2012), pp. 50–54. See further Ellis Davidson, *Gods and Myths*, p. 52.

[138] See G. Jones, *A History of the Vikings* (Oxford, 1968; repr. London, 1975), p. 19.

[139] Indeed, the association between ships and the 'voyage to the other world' is at least as old as the pyramids. See H. R. Ellis Davidson, *Gods and Myths of Northern Europe* (Harmondsworth, Middlesex, 1964), p. 137.

[140] Owen-Crocker, *Four Funerals*, p. 123.

[141] L. G. Whitbread proposes emending line 56a *aldor of earde*, 'lord away from the land', to *aldor ofer āde*, 'lord above the pyre', in order to arrive at 'the more satisfying implication that the funeral ship had drifted away ablaze': '*Beowulf* and Archaeology: Two Further Footnotes', *NM* 69 (1968), 63–72, at 65–66. However, this emendation has not found favour with modern editors.

[142] C. W. Von Sydow, 'Scyld Scefing', *Namn och Bygd* 12 (1924), 63–95.

progression and failure.[143] Having developed the story of Scyld Scefing and Beow from a diverse range of sources, including folktales, biblical tradition and Anglo-Saxon and perhaps classical foundation myths, the *Beowulf*-poet found a convenient lacuna in Danish royal tradition in the form of the interregnum between Heremod and Healfdene. Into this gap he inserted this new story of Scyld Scefing, thereby providing his work with a suitably mythical introduction that emphasizes the role of God in shaping the fortunes of dynasties and nations. By suppressing the story of Heremod's decline until a more apposite moment in the narrative, the poet was able to position this new hero, Scyld Scefing, with his mysterious arrival and departure, as effectively the founder of the Danish royal line that continues down to Hrothgar. However, as we shall see in the final part of this discussion, the legend of Heremod itself may have played a key role in the poet's shaping of Scyld Scefing and Beow.

As discussed in the beginning of this chapter, the Danish *scop* presents Heremod as a young prince to whom the Danes had looked for comfort (909: *sē þe him bealwa tō bōte gelȳfde*), hoping that he would receive (or inherit)[144] his father's nobility and rule the kingdom well (912: *fæderæþelum onfōn, folc gehealdan*). However, despite a promising childhood, Heremod fails to prosper (910b: *geþēon*) before losing his privileged position at the royal court: *Hē mid ēotenum wearð/ on fēonda geweald forð forlācen*, 'He was banished into the power of enemies, among the Jutes (or giants?)' (902b–03);[145] finally, he descends into wickedness: *hine fyren onwōd*, 'evil entered him' (915).[146] Hrothgar provides a similar assessment of Heremod's decline, explaining to Beowulf: *ne gewēox hē him tō willan, ac tō wæl-fealle/ ond tō dēað-cwalum Deniga lēodum*, 'he did not grow in accordance with their wishes, but for their destruction, and became a death-killer to the Danish people' (1711–12), *lēod-bealo longsum*, 'a lasting life-affliction to the people' (1722a). Both accounts emphasize Heremod's failure to prosper, highlighting his spectacular fall from grace after promising beginnings.

In the story of Scyld Scefing and Beow, we find the legend of Heremod's decline reversed to produce a royal foundation legend suitable for the poem's opening. Hence Scyld miraculously transcends his destitute origins and abandonment as a child (7a, 43–46), flourishing as a youth (8: *wēox under wolcnum weorð-myndum þāh*), before rising to become a great king who is feared by all of his neighbours (5–11) but dear to the Danish

---

[143] See Bonjour, *Digressions*, pp. 9–11.
[144] OE *fōn* is the verb most commonly used to denote the act of royal succession, e.g. X *fēng to rīce*, 'X took/succeeded to the kingdom'.
[145] On the meaning of MS *eotenum*, see K4, p. 171.
[146] See Chapter Four, pp. 211–13, 217–19, for comparison with the evil spirit of Saul.

people (30b: *Wine Scyldinga*; 31a: *lēof land-fruma*; 34b: *lēofne þēoden*), who grieve at his departure (49b–50a). Moreover, before Scyld's death, God recognizes the 'dire need' (*fyren-ðearfe ongeat*) of the Danes and blesses Scyld with a son, *folce tō frōfre*, 'as a comfort to the people',[147] Beow, who in turn provides an example to the audience of how any young warrior (20a: *geong guma*) should prosper (*geþeon*) through praiseworthy deeds (24b: *lof-dǣdum*). In stark contrast to Heremod, Beow proves himself worthy to succeed his father through his good deeds (20b: *gōde gewyrcean*), becoming a *lēof lēod-cyning longe þrāge*, 'beloved people-king for a long time' (54). Of course, it is possible that the *Beowulf*-poet's account of Heremod is itself an inversion of the Scyld Scefing story. However, given the presence of the Lother analogue in the Scandinavian accounts, and the absence of the Scyld Scefing-Beow story from all other records of early Danish kingship, this seems much less likely.[148] I would suggest therefore that the *Beowulf*-poet, with his fondness for dramatic reversals of fortune (*edwenden*) and contrast, shaped a new story of dynastic origins out of the legend of Heremod's decline in much the same way that he developed the story of King Beowulf from the legend of Hygelac's fall. In transforming the fall of Heremod into the rise of Scyld, the poet imaginatively drew together a rich array of folkloric and mythical themes, in addition, perhaps, to certain biblical and classical traditions. Through these innovations, the poet shaped his dynastic drama, repurposing ancient Scandinavian royal legend for a Christian Anglo-Saxon audience.

Conclusion

In this chapter I have argued that the author of *Beowulf* was an original artist who brought his own imagination to bear on a traditional body of royal legends. The poet's inventive handling of royal traditions is demonstrated by his willingness to introduce new characters and episodes into legendary settings. Borrowing the terminology used by Martin L. West in his discussion of the integration of Achilles into the Trojan legend, I propose that we can now identify eight discrete stages in the evolution of the tale of King Beowulf:[149]

Stage 1. In Scandinavian royal tradition, a version of the Bear's Son Tale comes into contact with legends of the Scyldings.

---

[147] On the Christological associations of this phrase, and its implications for our understanding of the characterization of Beowulf and the other kings of the poem, see Chapter Four.
[148] See pp. 109, 141.
[149] Cf. West, *Making of the* Iliad, pp. 44–47.

Stage 2. A Germanic legend exists involving a hero named Beowulf who competes with Breca in a swimming contest.

Stage 3. Scandinavian royal legends concerning King Hygelac's fall in Frisia come to Anglo-Saxon England some time in the sixth or early-seventh century.

Stage 4. Scandinavian royal legends concerning the deposition of King Heremod and the ensuing interregnum also arrive in Anglo-Saxon England at some point.

Stage 5. Legends about Sigemund the dragon-slayer come into contact with Christian tales of dragon-slaying saints in early Anglo-Saxon England.

Stage 6. Beowulf the great swimmer is transformed into the nephew of King Hygelac, thereby making him the last of the Hrethlings.

Stage 7. Scyld Scefing and Beow are inserted into Danish royal tradition between Heremod and Healfdene.

Stage 8. Beowulf is transformed into a great hero who defeats monsters in the Scylding court and dies fighting a dragon in defence of his people.

The order in which Stages 1–5 took place is unclear and, for our purposes, relatively unimportant. However, Stages 6–8 are, in my view, to be most readily explained as innovations of the *Beowulf*-poet, though it is of course possible that some of these elements had already begun to coalesce prior to the composition of our poem. The next chapter will explore in more detail how the poet integrated the monsters into his dynastic drama.

3

The Role of the Monsters in the Dynastic Drama

Unlike royal legends, which can only be productive within a specific set of cultural circumstances, monsters have a universal appeal. Indeed, it was probably Grendel, Grendel's mother and the dragon that brought *Beowulf* to the attention of the compilers of the Nowell Codex, and it is this element of the poem that most fascinates modern readers.[1] The *Beowulf*-poet was alert to the universalizing power of monsters and made imaginative use of them in order to bring his drama of ancient *þēod-cyningas* and *æþelingas* to life in the minds of his Anglo-Saxon audience. One productive area of study has been the search for analogues and possible sources for these three *āglǣcan*, 'awe-inspiring ones'.[2] Another approach is to explore connections between the hero, himself also referred to as an *āglǣca* (2592a), and the monsters he challenges.[3] Others have considered

---

[1] On the compilation of the Nowell Codex, see Introduction, pp. 7–9. Modern critics have generally shown more interest in Grendel, and to a lesser extent Grendel's mother, than the hero's third and greatest adversary, the dragon. Orchard, for example, focuses primarily on Grendel and Grendel's mother (*Pride and Prodigies*; *CCB*, pp. 187–202), and in discussing the dragon, concentrates on the presentation of its adversaries, Beowulf and Wiglaf (*CCB*, pp. 256–60). For an overview of the vast body of scholarship, see K4, pp. xxxvi–li. For an unusually detailed analysis of the hero's dragon-fight, see Gwara, *Heroic Identity*, pp. 239–310.

[2] See, for example, R. E. Kaske, '*Beowulf* and the Book of Enoch', *Speculum* 46 (1971), 421–31; R. Mellinkoff, 'Cain's monstrous progeny in *Beowulf*: part I, Noachic tradition', *ASE* 8 (1979), 143–62; R. Mellinkoff, 'Cain's monstrous progeny in *Beowulf*: part II, post-diluvian survival', *ASE* 9 (1981), 183–97; D. Williams, *Cain and Beowulf: A Study in Secular Allegory* (Toronto, 1982); D. Anlezark, 'Grendel and the Book of Wisdom', *NQ* 53 (2006), 262–69. On the dragon, see esp. Rauer, *Dragon*.

[3] See esp. S. L Dragland, 'Monster-Man in *Beowulf*', *Neophilologus* 61 (1977), 606–18; S. B. Greenfield, 'A touch of the monstrous in the hero, or Beowulf re-Marvellised', *ES* 63 (1982), 294–300, repr. in Greenfield (1989), pp. 67–73; and Orchard, *Pride and Prodigies*. Soper has recently argued that the dragon symbolizes the 'unproductive use of life experience', contrasting it with the 'well-performed elderliness' of kings Hrothgar and Beowulf ('A Count of Days', pp. 230–31). The precise meaning of the poetic term *āglǣca* has been much debated. Cf. *DOE* s. v. *āglǣca*: 'awesome opponent, ferocious fighter'. In *Beowulf* it is used to refer either to Sigemund or the dragon he kills (893a), as well as Grendel (645b, 816a) and the dragon that Beowulf fights (2529a); in other

how the monsters embody specific fears that the audience of the poem might have felt,[4] or explored the sophisticated narrative strategies that the poet uses in order to make the monsters appear more terrifying.[5] In the Introduction, I discussed how scholars had tended to marginalize the monsters or treat them as unwelcome guests in the text prior to Tolkien's 'Monsters and the Critics'.[6] So successful was Tolkien in defending the centrality of the monsters, however, that for many modern readers the monsters *are* the poem, while the royal legends that surround them are regarded as extraneous period-detail that the poem would perhaps be better off without.

However, as we have seen in the previous chapters, the poet carefully constructed his work around the idea of the dynastic life-cycle, and fully expected his audience to share his deep interest in ancient royal legends. Moreover, as this chapter will demonstrate, in contrast to the monstrous foes of Grettir and Bjarki, who have no obvious connection to wider political concerns and serve simply as foils for the hero, all three of the monsters of *Beowulf* are carefully integrated into the wider dynastic drama. A number of scholars have previously connected the monsters – in particular Grendel – to some of the poem's political concerns.[7] Notably, Fred Biggs has consistently argued that the monsters are used by the poet to explore the theme of royal succession – more specifically, the tension he identifies between Germanic and Christian models of succession.[8]

Old English poems the term appears most frequently in reference to the devil (e.g. *Jul* 268b; *And* 1312a) or demons (*Guth A* 575a), but also in the sense of a formidable adversary (e.g. *And* 1131b), where it is used by the Meremodonians to refer to the saint. For discussion and further references, see *CCB*, p. 90.

[4] For J. D. Niles, for example, the monsters are terrifying 'because they destroy the hall and with it the possibility of communal life' (*Beowulf*, p. 233), while for Andrew Scheil '[m]onstrosity serves as the epiphenomenon of a more profound engagement with the unfolding of human lives in time and history' ('Historiographic dimension', 284).

[5] See, for example, A. Renoir, 'Point of View and Design for Terror in *Beowulf*', *NM* 63 (1962), 154–67; Lapidge, 'Beowulf and the Psychology of Terror'; *CCB*, pp. 189–202.

[6] See above, pp. 5, 10.

[7] Davis, for example, argues that Beowulf's adversaries are 'primarily political monsters' used 'to isolate and demonize [...] kindred solidarity' (*Demise of Germanic Legend*, pp. x–xi).

[8] For example, in his most recent exploration of this topic, Biggs argues that Grendel and Grendel's mother 'express the conflicts likely to occur when there are too many successors for the throne' (i.e. the Scylding crisis), while the dragon, 'hoarder of treasure, articulates the end of a royal line where there is no heir to the kingdom' (i.e. the crisis affecting the Hrethlings) ('History and Fiction', p. 139). Hence, Biggs connects both these aspects of the monsters with the hero, noting that Beowulf himself is also a contender for the Danish throne and embodies the problem of dying without a son (*ibid.*). See also esp. Biggs, '*The Dream of the Rood* and *Guthlac A* as a Literary Context for the Monsters in

Building on the work of Biggs and others, this chapter explores how the poet imaginatively employed monsters as portents of dynastic and national crises.[9] The first section offers a new solution to the notorious *gif-stōl* crux (168–69), reading Grendel's attempt to seize power in Heorot as an allusion to the Fall of the Angels. I then explore the presentation of Grendel's mother as an anti-type of the poem's ideal royal women and an opponent of the institutions of marriage and dynasty. Scholars have rarely considered connections between the dragon and royal institutions.[10] In the final section of this chapter, I therefore present an integrated reading of the simultaneous narration of the Swedish wars and the dragon-fight, arguing that these two narrative threads are mutually dependent.

The Monsters as Portents of Dynastic Crises

The medieval understanding of monsters as portents or warnings of national or royal crises has its roots in patristic thought. Famously, Augustine explained that the root of the noun *monstrum* is the verb *monstrare*, 'to show':

> Monstra sane dicta perhibent a monstrando, quod aliquid significando, demonstrent; et ostenta ab obstendendo; et portenta a portendendo, id est praeostendendo; et prodigia, quod porro dicent, id est, futura praedicant.[11]
>
> (*City of God*, 21.8).

> [A *monstrum* (from *monstrare*, to point out) means a marvel that points to some meaning. So, *ostentum* (from *ostendere*, to show) and *portentum* (from *portendere* or *praeostendere*, to show ahead of time) and *prodigium* (from *porro dicere*, to declare things a long way off) all mean a marvel that is a prediction of things to come.][12]

Beowulf, p. 300; Biggs, 'Beowulf's Fight with the Nine Nicors'; and now, for a similar approach, J. Olesiejko, 'The Grendelkin and the Politics of Succession at Heorot: the Significance of the Monsters in *Beowulf*', *Studia Anglica Posnaniensia* 53 (2018), 45–65. On Biggs's theory of contrasting modes of succession, see above, Introduction, pp. 20–21.

[9] See B. F. Huppé, *Doctrine and Poetry: Augustine's Influence on Old English Poetry* (New York, 1959), pp. 232–33.

[10] Niles, for example, observes that the dragon, unlike Grendel, is an animal who 'stands aloof from human institutions', serving instead as 'an agent of universal doom' (Review of C. Davis, *Beowulf and the Demise of Germanic Legend*, *Speculum* 73 [1998)], 497–99, at 498). Niles' reading of the dragon is indebted to that of Tolkien, who compares it to the world-serpent that defeats Thor at *Ragnarök*, as well as Fáfnir ('Monsters', pp. 59–60, 64–67).

[11] *PL* 41, col. 722.

[12] G. G. Walsh *et al.*, trans., *Augustine: City of God*, Fathers of the Church Series 24 (Washington, D.C., 1963), p. 362.

Isidore offers an alternative but complementary etymology, connecting *monstrum*, 'omens', with the verb *monere*, 'to warn':[13]

> *Prodigia* quod *porro dicant*, id est, futura praedicant. *Monstra* vero a *monitu* dicta, quod aliquid significandum demonstrent, sive quod statim monstrent quid appareat, et hoc proprietatis est.[14]
>
> (*Etymologies*, XI.iii.3).

> [Prodigies (*prodigium*) are so called, because they 'speak hereafter' (*porro dicere*), that is, they predict the future. But omens (*monstrum*) derive their name from admonition (*monitus*), because in giving a sign they indicate (*demonstrare*) something, or else because they instantly show (*monstrare*) what may appear (...).][15]

Isidore lists as portents 'certain monstrous races, like the Giants, the Cynocephali (i.e. 'dog-headed people'), the Cyclopes, and others' (*Etymologies*, XI.iii.12).[16] Many of the monsters of the Nowell Codex fit well with Isidore's category of 'portents [...] or unnatural beings' (XI.iii.7), including not only humanoid creatures such as Grendel and his mother, who are descended from biblical *gigantas* (113a), but also cynocephali, such as St Christopher and many of the beings in *Wonders*. As we shall see below, the advent of Grendel augurs both the feud between the Scyldings and Heathobards that will destroy Heorot (83b–85) and the *fācen-stafas*, 'acts of malice' (1018b), that will arise within the Danish royal house itself after Hrothgar's death.

Isidore places dragons in a separate category to monsters and portents, explaining how they are of a different nature as part of the race of serpents (*serpentes*):

> XII.iv.4–5: *Draco* major cunctorum serpentium, sive omnium animantium super terram. Hunc Graeci δράκοντα vocant. Unde et derivatum est in Latinum ut diceretur *Draco*; qui saepe a speluncis abstractus fertur in aerem, concitaturque propter eum aer. Est autem cristatus, ore parvo, et arctis fistulis, per quas trahit spiritum, et linguam exerit. Vim autem non in dentibus, sed in cauda habet, et verbere potius quam rictu nocet. Innoxius autem est a venenis, sed ideo huic ad mortem faciendam venena non esse necessaria,

---

[13] See J. J. Cohen, *Of Giants: Sex, Monsters, and the Middle Ages*, Medieval Cultures 17 (Minneapolis, 1999), p. xiv. See also the useful discussions of L. Verner, *The Epistemology of the Monstrous in the Middle Ages* (New York, 2005); and A. S. Mittman and S. M. Kim, 'Monsters and the Medieval Exotic', in *The Oxford Handbook of Medieval Literature in English*, ed. E. Treharne and G. Walker (Oxford, 2010), pp. 677–706.

[14] PL 82, col. 0419C.

[15] *The Etymologies of Isidore of Seville*, trans. S. A. Barney, W. J. Lewis, J. A. Beach and O. Berghof (Cambridge, 2006), p. 244.

[16] Barney *et al.*, p. 244.

quia si quem ligaverit, occidit. [...] Gignitur autem in Aethiopia, et India in ipso incendio jugis aestus.[17]

[The dragon (*draco*) is the largest of all the snakes, or of all the animals on earth. The Greeks call it δρακωυm [*drakoum*] whence the term is borrowed into Latin so that we say *draco*. It is often drawn out of caves and soars aloft, and disturbs the air. It is crested, and has a small mouth and narrow pipes through which it draws its breath and sticks out its tongue. It has its strength not in its teeth but in its tail, and it causes injury more by its lashing tail than with its jaws. Also, it does not harm with poison; poison is not needed for this animal to kill, because it kills whatever it wraps itself around. [...] It is born in Ethiopia and India in the fiery intensity of perpetual heat.][18]

Dragons do, nevertheless, serve in medieval chronicles as portents of disaster. The *ASC* entry for 793 (MSS E and F), for example, famously reports the appearance of *reðe fore-becena*, 'terrible portents', among them *fyrene dracan*, 'fiery dragons', prior to a great famine and the Viking sack of Lindisfarne:

793. Her wæron reðe forebecena cumene ofer Norþanhymbra land ond þet folc earmlice bregdon: þet wæron ormete ligræscas, ond wæron geseowene fyrene dracan on þam lyfte fleogende. Þam tacnum sona fyligde mycel hunger, ond litel æfter þam þæs ilcan geares on vi idus Ianuarii earmlice heðenra manna hergung adiligode Godes cyrican in Lindisfarenaee þurh reaflac ond mansleht.[19]

[793. In this year terrible portents appeared throughout the land of the Northumbrians and dreadfully afflicted that people: there were frightening fire-rushes, and fiery dragons were seen flying in the sky. A great hunger soon followed after those signs, and soon after that in the same year, on the 8th of January, the miserable attacks of heathen men destroyed God's church in Lindisfarne through plunder and manslaughter.]

From the later medieval period, chronicles recording the turbulent political upheavals of early-fifteenth-century England mention a number of strange omens and portents, among them dragons and monsters, as well as comets and eclipses of the sun and moon.[20] Behind all such medieval

---

[17] *PL* 82, cols 0442B–0443A.
[18] Barney *et al.*, p. 255. Isidore's definition of the dragon clearly lies behind Eusebius's Aenigma 42.
[19] *The Anglo-Saxon Chronicle MS E*, The Anglo-Saxon Chronicle: a Collaborative Edition 7, ed. S. Irvine (Cambridge, 2004), p. 42. See further M. Cesario, '*Fyrene dracan* in the Anglo-Saxon Chronicle', in *Textiles, Text, Intertext: Essays in Honour of Gale R. Owen-Crocker*, ed. M. Clegg Hyer and J. Frederick (Woodbridge, 2016), pp. 153–70.
[20] See C. Given-Wilson, *Chronicles: The Writing of History in Medieval England* (London and New York, 2004), pp. 30–31.

references to dragons as portents stands the figure of the great dragon, Satan, who appears as one of the signs of Judgement Day:

> et visum est aliud *signum* in caelo
> et ecce *draco magnus rufus* habens
>   capita septem et cornua decem
> et in capitibus suis septem diademata
> et cauda eius trahebat tertiam partem stellarum caeli
> et misit eas in terram
> et draco stetit ante mulierem quae erat paritura
> ut cum peperisset filium eius devoraret [...]
> et factum est proelium in caelo
> Michahel et angeli eius proeliabantur cum dracone
> et draco pugnabat et angeli eius
> et non valuerunt neque locus inventus est eorum amplius in caelo
> *et proiectus est draco ille magnus serpens antiquus qui vocatur Diabolus et Satanas*
> qui seducit universum orbem
> proiectus est in terram et angeli eius cum illo missi sunt [...].
> (Rev. 12.3–4, 7–9). (Emphasis added).

> [And there was seen another *sign* in heaven: and behold *a great red dragon*, having seven heads, and ten horns: and on his head seven diadems: And his tail drew the third part of the stars of heaven, and cast them to the earth: and the dragon stood before the woman who was ready to be delivered; that, when she should be delivered, he might devour her son. [...]. And there was a great battle in heaven, Michael and his angels fought with the dragon, and the dragon fought and his angels: And they prevailed not, neither was their place found any more in heaven. *And that great dragon was cast out, that old serpent, who is called the devil and Satan*, who seduceth the whole world; and he was cast unto the earth, and his angels were thrown down with him.][21]

As this chapter will demonstrate, the dragon in *Beowulf* functions in this way, as an apocalyptic sign of dynastic and national doom.[22] When the dragon is understood in the light of Satan, the dragon of Revelation,

---

[21] See below, pp. 162–73, for connections between Grendel's attempt to seize power in Heorot and the Fall of the Angels. Cf. *Solomon and Saturn I: worpað hine dēofol on dōm-dæge, draca egeslīce*, 'He will overthrow the devil on Judgement Day, the terrible dragon' (24b–25).

[22] Cf. Rauer, *Dragon*, p. 27: 'in all cases a monster's death is followed by a looming catastrophe of national proportions (in the form of Grendel's mother, internecine strife at the Danish court and further wars with the Swedes and Franks).' Jeffrey Jerome Cohen comments on the tendency for monsters to arise at times of crisis within a society more generally in 'Monster Culture (Seven Theses)', in *Monster Theory: Reading Culture*, ed. J. J. Cohen (Minneapolis, 1996), pp. 3–25, at 6–7. For an interesting application of this thesis to the time of the Nowell Codex's copying, see L. Viljoen, 'The *Beowulf* manuscript reconsidered: Reading *Beowulf* in late Anglo-Saxon England', *Literator* 24 (2003), 39–57. See also Powell, 'Meditating on Men and Monsters'.

an underlying typological link with Grendel begins to emerge: while Grendel's attempt to seize power in Heorot echoes Lucifer's failed revolt in heaven and the subsequent Fall of the Angels, so the advent of the dragon evokes the return of Satan in the lead-up to Judgement Day. Both Grendel and the dragon are Satanic figures who serve as portents of dynastic and national crises, and would have been readily perceived as such by the poem's Christian Anglo-Saxon audience.

Grendel and Cain

Grendel's dramatic entrance into the narrative interrupts the steady progression of the Danish royal house from the reign of Scyld and coincides with an allusion to the imminent destruction of Heorot in a family feud:

> Sele hlīfade
> hēah ond horn-gēap;   heaðo-wylma bād,
> lāðan līges;   *ne wæs hit lenge þā gēn,*
> *þæt se ecg-hete   āþum-swēoran*
> *æfter wæl-nīðe   wæcnan scolde.*
> *Ðā se ellen-gǣst   earfoðlīce*
> *þrāge geþolode,   sē þe in þȳstrum bād*
> þæt hē dōgora gehwām   drēam gehȳrde
> hlūdne in healle.
> (81b–89a). (Emphasis added).

[The hall towered, high and horn-gabled; *it was not long after* that *the sword-hatred between father-in-law and son-in-law would awaken after deadly slaughter. Then the famous spirit wretchedly suffered for a time, the one who dwelt in the shadows,* when he heard every day the joy, loud in the hall.]

Such suggestive juxtapositions of disparate narrative elements are, of course, typical of the *Beowulf*-poet's style.[23] The link between the as-yet

---

[23] Compare the *scop*'s tale celebrating Beowulf's victory over Grendel, which shifts in subject from Beowulf (871b–74a) to Sigemund (874b–900) to Heremod (901–13a) and then back to Beowulf (913b–15a) before finally, it seems, returning to Heremod (915b). For the suggestion that the final half-line, *hine fyren onwōd*, 'evil entered him' (915b), might in fact refer to Beowulf rather than Heremod, see *CCB*, p. 113. Another example is the second account of Beowulf's accession to the Geatish throne, in which the subject first shifts from Beowulf (2384b–86) to the Swedish king, Onela (2487–91a), and then, as some critics would see it, back again to Beowulf (2491b). On this passage, see S. B. Greenfield, 'Beowulf and the Judgement of the Righteous', in *Learning and Literature in Anglo-Saxon England: Studies Presented to Peter Clemoes on the Occasion of His Sixty-Fifth Birthday*, ed. M. Lapidge and H. Gneuss (Cambridge, 1985), pp. 393–407, at 399. On this passage, see further pp. 94–96. On this stylistic feature of *Beowulf* see further E. G. Stanley, 'Ἀπό Κοινοῦ, Chiefly in *Beowulf*', in *Anglo-Saxonica:*

unnamed *ellen-gæst*, resentful at his exclusion from the revelry in Heorot, and the family feud that will soon bring about this same hall's destruction remains implicit. In the lines that follow, the poet provides further clues as to the relationship between this figure and the world of Heorot by merging the narrative present of Danish royal history with the deep, biblical past:

>   Þǣr wæs hearpan swēg,
> swutol sang scopes.   Sægde sē þe cūþe
> frum-sceaft fīra   feooran reccan,
> cwæð þæt se ælmihtiga   eorðan worhte,
> wlite-beorhtne wang,   swā wæter bebūgeð,
> gesette sige-hrēþig   sunnan ond mōnan,
> lēoman tō lēohte   land-būendum,
> ond gefrætwade   foldan scēatas
> leomum ond lēafum,   līf ēac gesceōp
> cynna gehwylcum   þāra ðe cwice hwyrfaþ.
> Swā ðā driht-guman   drēamum lifdon
> ēadiglīce,   *oð ðæt ān ongan*
> *fyrene fremman   fēond on helle;*
> wæs se grimma gǣst   Grendel hāten
> mǣre mearc-stapa,   sē þe mōras hēold,
> fen ond fæsten;   fīfel-cynnes eard
> won-sǣlī wer   weardode hwīle,
> siþðan him scyppen   forscrifen hæfde
> in Cāines cynne –   þone cwealm gewræc
> ēce drihten,   þæs hē Ābel slōg
> (89b–108). (Emphasis added).

[There was the sound of the harp, the clear song of the *scop*. He who knew about the first creation of men spoke, recalled from afar, he said that the Almighty made the earth, the splendid expanse, also the water that encircles it, he fixed victoriously the sun and moon, as lights to men, land-dwellers, and adorned the surface of the earth with branches and leaves, created all life for each kind of those that move about alive. So that lordly-troop lived in joys, blessedly, *until a certain one began to perform crimes, an enemy from hell*; that fierce spirit was called Grendel, famous border-stepper, he who held the moors, fen and stronghold; the joyless man occupied the land of monstrous races for a time, since the Shaper had condemned him in Cain's kin – he avenged that feud, the Eternal Lord, when he slew Abel.]

As Malcolm Godden has observed, a network of biblical allusions in this passage to the Creation (Gen. 1), the Fall (Gen. 3) and Cain and Abel

---

Beiträge zur Vor- und Frühgeschichte der englischen Sprache und zur altenglischen Literatur: Festschrift für Hans Schabram zum 65. Geburtsdag, ed. K. R. Grinda and C. D. Wetzel (Munich, 1993), pp. 181–207; B. Mitchell, '*apo koinou* in Old English Poetry?', NM 100 (1999), 477–97; and Cronan, 'Narrative Disjunctions'.

(Gen. 4) invites the audience to connect the menacing presence of Grendel with the primordial sins of both Satan and Cain, and to link the hall-joys of Hrothgar's retainers with the pre-lapsarian bliss of Adam and Eve.[24] Moreover, the *scop*'s paraphrase of Genesis 1, with its images of growth (*līf ēac gesceōp; cwice hwyrfaþ, drēamum lifdon/ ēadiglīce*),[25] underscores the theme of dynastic development foregrounded in the opening of the work.[26] The underlying connection between Grendel and the anticipated *ecg-hete āþum-swēoran* that will soon check the dynasty's progress begins to emerge, however, with the revelation of the monster's Cainite ancestry. Here a series of verbal and syntactic echoes invite the audience to think of Grendel's cursed race of *un-tȳdras* as a monstrous rival dynasty to the Scyldings themselves:

>Þanon un-tȳdras ealle onwōcon,
>eotenas ond ylfe ond orcneas,
>swylce gīgantas, þā wið Gode wunnon
>lange þrāge; hē him þæs lēan forgeald.
>(111–14).

>[From there were born all cursed creatures, giants and elves and orcs, also those giants who fought against God for a long time; He gave them requital for that.][27]

Not only are the Cainite and Scylding genealogies linked, as Orchard notes, through the recurrence of forms of the verb *onwæcnan*,[28] but also through the use of the parallel triple naming-formula, *eotenas ond ylfe ond orcneas* (112), recalling *Heorogār ond Hrōðgār ond Hālga til* (61).[29] However,

---

[24] Godden, 'Old Testament', pp. 223–24. See further *CCB*, pp. 137–38. For parallels with *Cædmon's Hymn*, see Niles, *Beowulf*, pp. 78–79. For parallels with Virgil's *Aeneid*, I, 740–46, in which the Trojan minstrel Iopas sings a song in praise of creation to the accompaniment of the chitara, see F. Klaeber, 'Aeneis und Beowulf', *Archiv für das Studium der neuren Sprachen und Literaturen* 126 (1911), 40–48 and 339–59, at 343; T. B. Haber, *A Comparative Study of the Beowulf and the Aeneid* (Princeton, NJ, 1931), p. 132; Niles, *Beowulf*, pp. 74–79; and North, *Origins*, pp. 12–13. For a list of parallels with Christian tradition and Old English literature, see Klaeber, 'Christian Elements', pp. 1–2. Klaeber is, however, sceptical about parallels with *Cædmon's Hymn* ('Christian Elements', p. 2).

[25] On the dynastic resonance of the term *ēadig*, see above, pp. 88–90, in the discussion of Beowulf's speech at Hronesnæss.

[26] See Chapter One, pp. 38–50. For debate as to where precisely the *scop*'s song ends, see C. J. E. Ball, '*Beowulf* 99–101', *NQ* 18 (1971), 163. On the style of this passage, *CCB*, pp. 62–64. For verbal parallels with the advent of the dragon, see below, pp. 185–86.

[27] Cf. lines 1265b–66: *þanon wōc fela/ geōsceaft-gāsta; wæs þæra Grendel sum*, 'thence were born many cursed spirits; Grendel was one of them.'

[28] *CCB*, p. 64.

[29] Beowulf himself later employs a variant on this formula when describing his maternal uncles: *Herebeald ond Hæðcyn oððe Hygelāc mīn* (2434). For discussion

while the Scylding dynasty was sent by God *folce tō frōfre*, 'to comfort the people' (12–19),[30] *Cāines cyn* wage war with their Creator and threaten the survival of royal houses by perpetuating the sin of fratricide.[31] It is within this rich network of biblical allusions, then, that Grendel first appears as a portent of the troubles that lie ahead for the Scyldings.

Grendel, Lucifer and the Fall of the Angels

Envious of the revelry in the hall, Grendel begins his twelve-year reign of terror against the Danes, seizing control of the royal hall of Heorot. As the poet is careful to explain, Grendel now effectively 'rules' in place of the legitimate monarch, King Hrothgar:[32]

Swā rīxode   ond wið rihte wan,
āna wið eallum,   oð þæt īdel stōd

---

of this passage, see pp. 87–88. As K4 notes, the lists of young Scyldings and Hrethlings correspond to 'an ancient idiom well known from Homer' in which 'the last of three coordinate nouns in particular proper names, is marked by the addition of an epithet or some qualifying element' (p. 117). Cf. 1189: *Hrēðric ond Hrōðmund, and hæleþa bearn*. F. Klaeber, 'Eine kleine Nachlese zum *Beowulf*', *Anglia* 56 (1932), 421–31, at 425–29, also notes parallels with *Widsith* and various other Old English, Old Norse, Germanic and classical texts as well as examples from early Middle English.

[30] See Chapter Four on the distribution of this and related collocations in Old English verse and its Christological associations.

[31] Cf. Gen. 6.4–6, cited in the discussion below (pp. 172–73). See further M. Osborn, 'The Great Feud: Scriptural History and Strife in *Beowulf*', *PMLA* 93 (1978), 973–81, repr. in Baker (1995), pp. 111–25; Anlezark, *Water and Fire*.

[32] As Gwara notes, the verb *rīcsian* is only used in *Beowulf* here and in reference to the dragon (*Heroic Identity*, p. 247). On the dragon's 'reign', see below, pp. 185–86. Elsewhere, Grendel is referred to several times as holding/ruling the moors. For example: *sē þe mōras hēold,/ fen ond fæsten*, 'the one who ruled the moors, fens and stronghold' (103b–04a); *sinnihte hēold/ mistige mōras*, 'sinfully he ruled over the misty moors' (161b–62a); *micle mearc-stapan mōras healdan*, 'great border-steppers rule over the moors' (1348). Similar terminology is used to describe how each of the Scylding kings ruled over the Danes in turn. For example, Healfdene *hēold þenden lifde/ gamol ond gūð-rēouw glæde Scyldingas*, 'he ruled while he lived, old and warlike, the gracious Scyldings (57b–58). For further examples in the context of royal succession, see lines 465–67a, 911b, 1852b–53a, 1959b–60a, 2208b–09a, 2372b–73a. The verb *healdan* is also used three times to refer to the dragon's 'reign': *þrēo-hund wintra/ hēold on hrūsan hord-ærna sum*, 'for three hundred years ruled over a certain treasure-house in the earth' (2278b–79); *þēah ðe hord-welan hēolde lange*, 'although he ruled that hoard-wealth for a long time' (2344); *lift-wynne hēold*, 'he ruled the skies' (3043b). Cf. *DOE* s. v. *healdan* A.10.c.: 'to hold, maintain power over, govern (a territory *acc.*, as a surrogate authority).' As examples of this usage, *DOE* cites only the Old English *Bede* and *Orosius*. Another poetic example is *Maxims II*: *Cyning sceal rīce healdan*, 'the king must rule the kingdom' (1a).

hūsa sēlest. Wæs sēo hwīl micel:
twelf wintra tīd   torn geþolode
wine Scyldinga,   wēana gehwelcne,
sīdra sorga.
(144–49a). (Emphasis added).

[*So he ruled* and contested against righteousness, one against all, until the best of houses stood empty. That was a long time: for twelve years the friend of the Scyldings suffered grief, every kind of woe, far-reaching sorrows.]

Despite emptying Hrothgar's once joyous hall of its former occupants, Grendel's 'rule' of Heorot is, however, incomplete in one crucial aspect. The monster is unable to occupy the seat of royal power:[33]

Nō hē þone gif-stōl   grētan mōste,
māþðum for metode,   nē his myne wisse.
(168–69).

[He was not permitted to touch (*or* approach) that throne (i.e. to assume royal power *or* to be involved in the succession), those treasures, because of God; nor did he (i.e. Grendel) know His (i.e. God's) intention.]

The translation offered above is necessarily speculative, and will require some justification. Indeed, these lines have been described by Robert E. Kaske as 'the most difficult single crux in the poem'.[34] Although Tolkien would reject the passage as an interpolation, the majority of scholars treat these lines as authentic, if problematic, and a wide range of interpretations have been proposed.[35] Most scholars agree that the pronoun *hē*

---

[33] Compare the poet's equally enigmatic statement that Grendel could not drag away any more Danes under the shadows *þā metod nolde*, 'when the Creator did not allow it' (706b), and Beowulf's report to Hrothgar that although he attempted to stop the wounded Grendel from fleeing the hall, *ic hine ne mihte, þā metod nolde*, 'I could not prevent him, when the Creator did not wish for it' (967).

[34] R. E. Kaske, 'The *Gifstol* Crux in *Beowulf*', *Leeds Studies in English* n.s. 16 (1985), 142–51, at 142. Klaeber similarly comments: 'When all is said, the passage appears singularly awkward' (K3, p. 135).

[35] Tolkien, 'Monsters', p. 96, n. 34; Tolkien, 'Commentary', p. 186. For an overview, see F. C. Robinson, 'Why is Grendel's Not Greeting the *Gifstol* a *Wræc Micel?*', in *Words, Texts and Manuscripts: Studies in Anglo-Saxon Culture Presented to Helmut Gneuss on the Occasion of His Sixty-Fifth Birthday*, ed. M. Korhammer (Cambridge, 1992), pp. 257–62, at 257. Robinson offers two translations: 'By no means did he (Grendel) have to show respect for the throne; he despised the precious thing, did not feel love for it'; and 'By no means was he (Grendel) compelled by God to show respect for the throne, that precious thing, nor did he feel love for it' (pp. 261–62). Alfred Bammesberger proposes 'he (= Grendel) could not approach the throne (= Hroðgar's throne), he despised treasure, nor did he feel its (= the treasure's) love (= he felt no love for treasure)' ('Five Beowulf Notes', in Korhammer [1992], pp. 239–56, at 248). Both Robinson and

in 168a refers to Grendel, who is the subject of the preceding four lines (165b: *oft gefremede*; 166b: *Heorot eardode*), rather than Hrothgar.³⁶ It also seems clear that *māþðum* in 169a stands in apposition with *gif-stōl* in 168a. The connotations of the compound *gif-stōl* and the verb phrase *grētan mōste* are less clear.³⁷ As Murray McGillivray has shown, *gif-stōl* is used in Old English verse to invoke a broad range of symbols of royal power, rather than simply a literal 'gift-throne/seat'.³⁸ Hence in *The Wanderer*, the narrator recalls how in former times *gief-stōlas brēac*, 'he enjoyed the treasure-giving' (44b), while in *Maxims I (A)* the same term could refer to either a throne or, more generally, a royal hall: *Hond sceal hēofod inwyrcan, hord in strēonum bīdan,/ gif-stōl gegierwed stondan, hwonne hine guman gedǣlen*, 'the head must work the hand, the hoard wait in its treasures, the *gif-stōl* stand ready, when men deal it out' (66b–67). Elsewhere in *Beowulf*, *gif-stōl* is used to denote both King Beowulf's actual physical throne and, by metonymy, the royal hall of the Hrethlings:

Þā wæs Bīowulfe brōga gecȳðed
snūde tō sōðe, þæt his sylfes hām,

Bammesberger follow Pogatscher in reading MS *for metode* as the unattested verb *formetian*, 'despised': 'Zu Beowulf 168', *Beiträge zur Geschichte der deutschen Sprache und Literatur* 19 (1894), 544–45. See also Engelhardt, 'Dilation', 832. The editors of K4 suggest 'Grendel could not approach the throne, nor might he (as one of the seed of Cain) know his (God's) love (or perhaps: nor was he [Grendel] permitted his desire)' (K4, p. 126).

³⁶ Cf. Bammesberger, 'Five *Beowulf* Notes', p. 244. Though for an alternative reading, see Brodeur, *Art*, pp. 200–04: 'because Grendel haunted Heorot every night, Hrothgar could not aproach his own throne – on account of the Lord, whose love (or favor) Hrothgar did not know.' Cf. A. E. Dubois, 'Gifstol', *MLN* 69 (1954), 546–49, at 549: 'Hroþgar could not serve his people with gifts for the Lord, or make known his inclination to [...] *or* Hroþgar could not serve gods with gifts because of God's prohibition, or know God's will [...] *or* Hroþgar could not worship God with gifts, or know his own mind.'

³⁷ DOE gives the primary sense of *gyf-stōl*, *gif-stōl* as 'throne from which gifts are dispensed' (with examples from *Beo* 166a, 2327a, *Maxims I A* 67a), with secondary senses of 'a throne in heaven' (*Christ II* 572a) and 'perhaps in transferred sense: ceremony of gift-giving' (*Wanderer* 44b). The verb *grētan* occurs on eight further occasions in the poem: Beowulf announces that the Geats wish *to meet with* Hrothgar (347b); weapons cannot *touch/harm* Grendel (802b); Beowulf returns victorious from the mere with Grendel's head, *to meet/greet* Hrothgar (1646b); Hrothgar predicts that, following Beowulf's achievements, the Danes and Geats will henceforth *greet* each other in good spirits over the seas (1861a); Beowulf tells Hygelac how he came *to greet* Hrothgar after his victory over Grendel (2010b); the narrator comments that *wyrd* would soon *meet with* old King Beowulf, as he approaches the dragon (2421b); as he lies dying, Beowulf reflects with satisfaction that no neighbouring *folc-cyning* had dared to *meet* the Geats in battle during his long reign (2735b); and finally, Wiglaf reports to the Geats that Beowulf had ordered him *to greet* them and gave instructions for his funeral (3095b).

³⁸ M. McGillivray, 'What Kind of Seat is Hrothgar's *Gifstol*?', *SP* 105 (2008), 265–83.

bolda sēlest, bryne-wylmum mealt,
gif-stōl Gēata.
(2324–27a). (Emphasis added).

[Then the terror was made known to Beowulf, revealed as a truth, that his own home, the best of dwellings, was melted with burning flames, *the gift-throne of the Geats.*]

However, the use of the same compound in *Christ II* in reference to the heavenly 'throne of souls' (572a: *gǣsta gief-stōl*) has encouraged some scholars to search for religious significance in the *Beowulf*-passage. Hence, in 1909 Klaeber identified *gif-stōl* with 'the divine throne of grace', and proposed reading 169b, *nē his myne wisse*, as 'nor did he (God) take thought of him'.[39] Robert Estrich similarly argued that Grendel is forbidden from touching the *gif-stōl* 'because, as a symbol of semi-divine royalty, it was sacrosanct'.[40] Citing a passage in Gregory's *Morals on the book of Job* in which God is said not to recognize sinners at the Last Judgement, Kaske proposed that these lines describe how Grendel is denied access into the heavenly kingdom by God because of his crimes against Hrothgar in the earthly kingdom.[41] In a similar vein, Betty S. Cox argued for a link between the *gif-stōl* of 168a and the mercy-seat on the ark of the covenant (Ex. 25.10–22), noting that those who violate the ark in the Old Testament are sometimes associated with Cain (Jude 11).[42] Turning to the evidence of Anglo-Saxon lawcodes, William Chaney suggested that Grendel, as a criminal and fugitive, is denied access to royal asylum (*grið*) on the grounds that he is polluted by the sin of murder and described in the preceding lines as refusing to accept financial compensation (*fēa þingian*) from men (156b).[43] Finally, Murray McGillivray revived Richard Wülker's

---

[39] F. Klaeber, 'Textual notes on the *Beowulf*', *JEGP* 8 (1909), 254–59, 254–55.
[40] R. M. Estrich, 'The Throne of Hrothgar—*Beowulf*, ll. 168–169', *JEGP* 43 (1944), 384–89. Estrich therefore suggests that 'although Grendel dwelt in the gold-decked hall during the dark nights, still "he [Grendel] could not approach [or attack] the throne, the treasure, because of God; he did not know God's love"' (384). Cf. J. L. Baird, '"for metode": *Beowulf* 169', *ES* 49 (1968), 418–23: 'He (Grendel) might not at all approach the giftstool [throne], with treasures before [in the presence of] the ruler [i.e. the giftstool of Heorot; i.e. Hrothgar], nor know his [Hrothgar's] love.'
[41] Kaske, '*Gifstol*', 147. Kaske paraphrases: 'Heorot he held, the treasure-adorned hall [including, of course, its gift-throne], in the dark nights; but never could he [Grendel] have approached that other gift-throne, that treasure before God – nor did God even know him.'
[42] B. S. Cox, 'The *Gifstol* and the ark', in her *Cruces*, pp. 56–79, at 59. Cf. Huppé, *Doctrine and Poetry*, p. 233.
[43] W. Chaney, 'Grendel and the *Gifstol*: A Legal View of Monsters', *PMLA* 77 (1962), 513–20, at 51819. Chaney therefore suggests a translation of the passage as follows: 'he (Grendel) could not approach the throne (of Hrothgar), that precious object, because of God; he did not know God's favor (or love)' (520).

suggestion that Grendel was prevented from harming the gift-giving hall of Heorot because of the Lord.[44]

The interpretation presented above for lines 168–69 broadly accords with these readings in that it takes the *gif-stōl* itself as an allusion to the sanctity of kingship. However, given the emphasis on royal succession up to this point in the narrative, I propose that we take the prohibition against Grendel approaching the *gif-stōl* as referring to his failure to assume the office of king and, more specifically, his exclusion from the royal succession on the grounds of illegitimacy.[45] This reading makes sense within the context of the immediately surrounding text and, as we shall see, accords well with developing attitudes towards eligibility for kingship in early Anglo-Saxon England.

The suggestion that *gif-stōl* signifies as much the office of kingship as the physical throne in Heorot is supported by the appearance of two further *-stōl* compounds in this sense in *Beowulf*.[46] Queen Hygd offers the throne to Beowulf, *bēagas ond brego-stōl; bearne ne truwode,/ þæt hē wið ælf-ylcum ēþel-stōlas/ healdan cūðe*, 'rings and throne; she did not trust her son, that he would be able to rule the ancestral seats against foreigners' (2370–72a). Similarly, after Heardred's death, the Scylfing ruler Onela *lēt ðone brego-stōl Bīowulf healdan,/ Gēatum wealdan*, 'let Beowulf rule that princely seat, govern the Geats' (2389–90a).

Shortly before the *gif-stōl* crux, we are given to believe that Grendel is involved in a power-struggle with Hrothgar:

> Forðām gesȳne wearð
> ylda bearnum,   undyrne cūð
> gyddum geōmore   *þætte Grendel wan*
> *hwīle wið Hrōþgār*,   hete-nīðas wæg,
> fyrene ond fæhðe   fela missera,
> singāle sæce
> (149b–54). (Emphasis added).

[Afterwards it was made visible to the sons of men, clearly revealed in sad songs *that Grendel contested for a time against Hrothgar*, performed hateful attacks, crimes and feuds, many miseries, a continual quarrel.]

---

[44] McGillivray, 'Gifstol', 279–82.
[45] Noting a parallel with the early medieval Irish concept of the *geis*, 'a prohibition forbidding a person to do, or enjoining him to do, certain things' (189), Margaret W. Pepperdene suggests that Grendel 'cannot approach the throne of Hrothgar, the symbol of the king's lawful and God-given right to rule his people': 'Grendel's geis', *The Journal of the Royal Society of Antiquaries of Ireland* 85 (1955), 188–92.
[46] For detailed discussion of *-stōl* compounds in both Old English prose and verse, see McGillivray, '*Gifstol*'.

This *sæce*, 'quarrel', between Grendel and Hrothgar is clearly to be thought of in terms of a manifestation of the primordial conflict between Grendel's ancestors, the biblical giants, and their Creator: *þā wið Gode wunnon/ lange þrāge*, 'they contested against God for a long time' (113b–14a).[47] I would suggest that underlying the war between the giants and God and Grendel's conflict with Hrothgar is another biblical paradigm, that of Lucifer's revolt in heaven and the subsequent Fall of the Angels.

This tradition has as its basis several passages in the Old Testament, notably Israel's rebuke of the King of Babylon after the captivity in the Book of Isaiah:

> quomodo cecidisti de caelo lucifer qui mane oriebaris
> corruisti in terram qui vulnerabas gentes
> qui dicebas in corde tuo
> in caelum conscendam super astra Dei exaltabo solium meum
> sedebo in monte testamenti in lateribus aquilonis
> ascendam super altitudinem nubium ero similis Altissimo
> verumtamen ad infernum detraheris in profundum laci […].
> (Is. 14.12–15).

> [How art thou fallen from heaven, O Lucifer, who didst rise in the morning? How art thou fallen to the earth, that didst wound the nations? And thou saidst in thy heart: I will ascend into heaven, I will exalt my throne above the stars of God, I will sit in the mountain of the covenant, in the sides of the north. I will ascend above the height of the clouds, I will be like the most High. But yet thou shalt be brought down to hell, into the depth of the pit.][48]

As we saw at the beginning of this chapter, the war in heaven between the archangel Michael and Lucifer-Satan is also referred to in the Book of Revelation, where the devil returns in the form of a great red dragon as one of the signs of Judgement Day (12.7–9).[49] The Fall of the Angels appears frequently in Anglo-Saxon literature and visual culture, nowhere more so than in the poems and illustrations in MS Junius 11.[50] *Genesis A* describes Lucifer's failed attempt to establish his own

---

[47] Cf. 811b: *hē wæs fāg wið Gode*, 'he (i.e. Grendel) contested against God'. See further Osborn, 'Great Feud'.

[48] See also Job 1.6–7; Ezekiel 28.12–17. The Fall of the Angels is treated more expansively in the apocryphal Book of Enoch; see below, pp. p. 172 n.58.

[49] See above, pp. 156–59. For further New Testament allusions to the Fall of the Angels, see Epistles 2 Peter and Jude. For links between another dragon-fight associated with St Michael and Beowulf's last battle, see below, pp. 181–82.

[50] For another Anglo-Saxon illustration of the Fall of the Angels, compare MS Cotton Claudius B.iv ('The Old English Illustrated Hexateuch') fol. 2r. For a comprehensive overview of the tradition of the Fall of the Angels in Anglo-Saxon England, see now J. Fitzgerald, *Rebel Angels: Space and Sovereignty in Anglo-Saxon England* (Manchester, 2019).

high throne (*hēah-setl*) in the kingdom of heaven, and his subsequent banishment to hell:[51]

> Him þǣr sār gelamp,
> æfst and ofer-hygd,   and þæs engles mōd
> þe þone un-rǣd *ongan*   ǣrest fremman,
> wefan and weccean.   Þā hē worde cwæð,
> nīþes ofþyrsted,   *þæt hē on norð-dǣle*
> *hām and hēah-setl   heofena rīces*
> *āgan wolde*,   þā wearð yrre god
> and þām werode wrāð   þe hē ǣr wurðode
> wlite and wuldre.   Sceōp þām wēr-logan
> wræclicne hām   weorce tō lēane,
> helle-hēafas,   hearde nīðas.
> (*Genesis A*, 28b–38). (Emphasis added).

[Suffering and pride sorely befell them there, and that angel's pride, he who first *began* to weave (malice) and to incite through bad counsel. Then he spoke a word, thirsty with envy, *that he would possess a home and high-seat in that northern part of the kingdom of heaven*; then God became angry and enraged at that people, whom he had previously honoured with his countenance and glory. He appointed for those faithless ones an exiles' home, in payment for the deed, lamentations in hell, fierce punishments.]

Accompanying this text are two illustrations depicting Lucifer's rebellion.[52] The first, at the bottom of page 2, presents God, enthroned, confronting Lucifer, while the facing page features an elaborate, full-page illustration depicting the dramatic Fall of Lucifer and his Rebel Angels in four stages. In the image at the top of the page, we see Lucifer gesturing towards a throne, and looking back to his rebel angels who are offering him crowns; moving down the page, the second panel depicts Lucifer wearing a wreath surrounded by angels; the third section presents God, holding spears and surrounded by His angels; while the fourth panel, at the bottom of the page, presents the climax of the story, in which Lucifer and his rebel angels fall together with his throne into the mouth of hell, where they are bound in chains.[53]

---

[51] See further D. F. Johnson, 'The Fall of Lucifer in *Genesis A* and Two Anglo-Latin Royal Charters', *JEGP* 97 (1998), 500–21; Doane, ed., *Genesis A*, pp. 290–91.

[52] As A. N. Doane notes, these illustrations in fact fit better with the account of the Fall of the Angels in *Genesis B*, discussed below: *Genesis A: A New Edition, Revised* (Tempe, AZ, 2013), p. 29; cf. B. C. Raw, 'The Probable Derivation of Most of the Illustrations in Junius 11 from an Illustrated Saxon *Genesis*', *ASE* 5 (1976), 133–48.

[53] For discussion of these images and their possible sources, see Raw, 'Illustrations in Junius 11'; T. H. Ohlrgen, ed., *Anglo-Saxon Textual Illustration: Photographs of Sixteen Manuscripts with Descriptions and Index* (Kalamazoo, MI, 1992), pp. 88–89; C. E. Karkov, *Text and Picture in Anglo-Saxon England: Narrative Strategies in the*

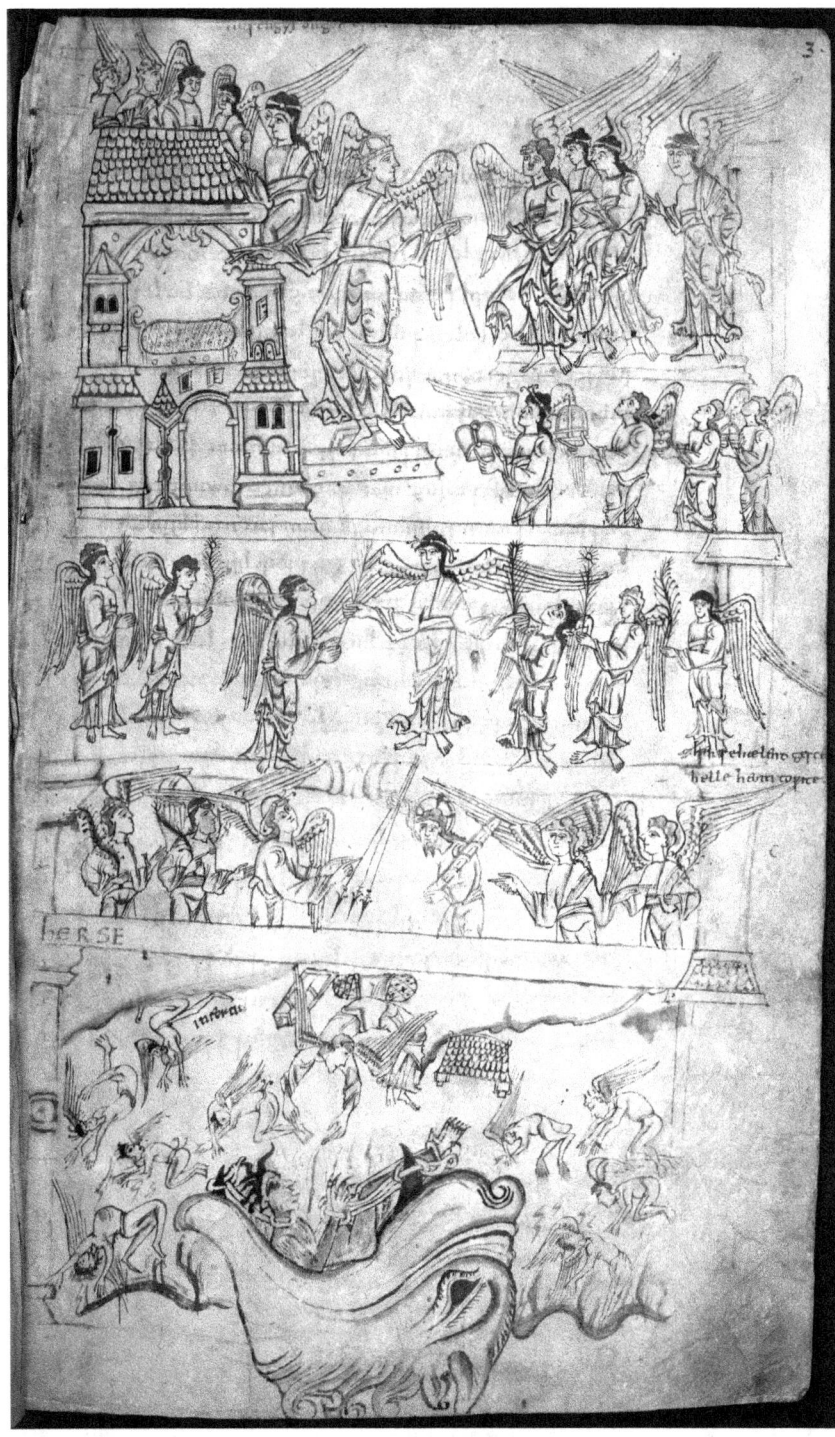

The Fall of the Angels; Oxford, Bodleian Library MS Junius 11, p. 3

A similar account of Lucifer's attempt to establish a rival throne in heaven appears in *Genesis B*:[54]

Ac hē āwende hit him tō wyrsan þinge,   *ongan* him winn up āhebban
wið þone hēhstan heofnes waldend,   *þe siteð on þām hālgan stōle.*
[...]
     Þohte þurh his *ānes cræft*
hū hē him strenglicran *stōl geworhte,*
hēahran on heofonum; cwæð þæt hine his hige spēone
þæt hē west and norð wyrcean ongunne,
trymede getimbro; cwæð him twēo þuhte
þæt hē gode wolde geongra weorðan.
(*Genesis B*, 259–60, 272b–77). (Emphasis added).

[But he turned this into a worse thing, *began* to raise up trouble against Him, against that highest ruler of heaven, *who sits on that holy throne.* [...] He thought through his *singular skill, how he could make a stronger throne for himself,* higher in heaven; he said that his mind spanned so far that he, west and north, would begin to construct, build with timbers; he said that he thought it disagreeable to him that he should become God's underling.]

In Lucifer's subsequent speech, which takes up the bulk of *Genesis B*, he makes clear his intent to seize (*fōn*) power from God in heaven, with the support of his loyal retainers, and build a better throne (*stōl*) for himself:

    Ic hæbbe geweald micel
tō gyrwanne *gōdlecran stōl,*
hēarran on heofne. [...]
Bigstandað mē strange genēatas, þā ne willað mē æt þām strīðe geswīcan,
hæleþas heard-mōde. Hīe habbað mē tō hearran gecorene,
rōfe rincas; mid swilcum mæg man ræd geþencean,
fōn mid swilcum folc-gesteallan. Frȳnd synd hīe mīne georne,

Junius 11 Manuscript, CSASE 31 (Cambridge, 2001), pp. 49–51; E. Coatsworth, 'The Book of Enoch and Anglo-Saxon Art', in Powell and Scragg (2003), pp. 135–51, at 137–39. In the manuscript's first illustration, on p. 1, God is depicted enthroned above Chaos. The illustration on p. 20 of MS Junius 11 depicts how Satan continued his feud with God by sending his messenger in the form of a serpent up into the Garden of Eden to tempt Adam and Eve.

[54] See T. D. Hill, 'The Fall of Angels and Man in the Old English *Genesis B*', in *Anglo-Saxon Poetry: Essays in Appreciation for John C. McGalliard*, ed. L. E. Nicholson and D. W. Frese (Notre Dame, 1975), pp. 279–90; and D. Thomas, 'Revolt in Heaven: Lucifer's Treason in *Genesis B*', in *Treason: Medieval and Early Modern Adultery, Betrayal, and Shame*, ed. L. Tracy (Leiden, 2019), pp. 147–69. For further reflections on this theme in Junius 11, see *Christ and Satan* (19–24, 81–88). The story also appears in *Solomon and Saturn II* (441–66): see D. Anlezark, 'The Fall of the Angels in *Solomon and Saturn II*', in *Apocryphal Texts and Traditions in Anglo-Saxon England*, ed. K. Powell and D. G. Scragg (Cambridge, 2003), pp. 121–34.

holde on hyra hyge-sceaftum.   Ic mæg hyra hearra wesan,
rædan on þis rīce.
(*Genesis B*, 280b–81a, 284–89a). (Emphasis added).

[I have it in my great power to build *a better throne*, higher in heaven. [...] Alongside me are strong retainers, they do not wish to betray me in that struggle, warriors fierce in mind. They have chosen me as leader, brave warriors; with such a man may take counsel, *with such comrades-in-arms (he) may seize (power)*. They are my eager friends, loyal in their intentions. I may become their leader, rule in this kingdom.]

As we have seen, the *Beowulf*-poet consistently invites his audience to identify Grendel not only with Cain but also with Lucifer/Satan and the serpent in the Garden of Eden. As Betty Cox notes, Satan is typically presented in Old English poetry as a miserable outcast from the joys of heaven, envious of both God in the act of Creation and man – in other words, any Anglo-Saxon would readily have identified Grendel with Satan.[55] Nowhere is this identification of Grendel with the devil more clear than in the lines immediately prior to the *gif-stōl* crux, where Grendel is referred to variously as *sē þe in þȳstrum bād*, 'the one who dwelt in darkness' (87b), *fēond on helle*, 'enemy in hell' (101b), *se grimma gæst*, 'the fierce spirit' (102a), *Wiht unhǣlo/ grim ond grǣdig*, 'unholy creature, fierce and greedy' (120b–21a), *þǣm fēonde*, 'that enemy' (143b), one who *wið rihte wan/ āna wið eallum*, 'contended against right, one against all' (144b–45a), a *deorc dēaþ-scua, duguþe ond geogoþe/ seomade ond syrede*, 'a dark death-shadow [who] lay in wait and ambushed the old and the young' (160–61a),[56] one of the *hel-rūnan*, literally those 'skilled in the mysteries of hell' (163a), who move or glide about (*hwyrftum scrīþað*), and *fēond mancynnes*, 'the enemy of mankind' (164b).[57] These associations condition the audience to think

---

[55] Cox, 'Old English Satan'. Cox notes that Grendel's envy of God in the act of Creation is triggered by the *scop*'s song, with its echoes of Genesis 1. See also O. F. Emerson, 'Grendel's Motive in Attacking Heorot', *MLR* 16 (1921), 113–19.

[56] In *Christ I*, the devil is referred to as *dēor dǣd-scua* (257b), translated by Mary Clayton as 'fierce agent of darkness' (*Old English Poems of Christ and His Saints*, DOML 27 [Cambridge, MA, 2013], p. 19). On the meaning of the verb *seomade*, see K4, p. 126.

[57] On the meaning of this line, see the note in K4, p. 126. Elsewhere, Grendel is described as the one who *Godes yrre bær*, 'bore God's anger' (711b), and is referred to by a range of further Satanic epithets, including *sceadu-ganga*, 'shadow-walker' (703a), *se scyn-scaþa*, 'the shining ravager' (707a), *se mān-scaða*, 'the wicked ravager' (712a), *fyrena hyrde*, 'guardian of crimes' (750b), *man-cynnes fēond*, 'mankind's foe' (1276a), and *Godes ansaca*, 'God's enemy' (1682b). Niles comments that Grendel's fury 'seems grounded in that same spirit of ferocious and ultimately self-destructive envy that led to Lucifer's revolt and Cain's act of fratricide' (Review of Craig Davis, *Beowulf and the Demise of Germanic Legend*, *Speculum* 73 (1998), 497–99, at 498). On Grendel and the devil, see B. S. Cox, 'The Old English Satan and Grendel's Motive', in her *Cruces*, pp. 80–101; L.

of the prohibition against Grendel approaching the *gif-stōl* in terms of Lucifer's failed attempt to usurp the heavenly throne.

Further support for reading the *gif-stōl* passage within this biblical context comes from the traditional association of Lucifer's fallen angels with those 'sons of God' who, according to Genesis 6, begat the race of giants with the 'daughters of men' in the time before the Flood:[58]

> cumque coepissent homines multiplicari super terram et filias procreassent videntes *filii Dei* filias eorum quod essent pulchrae acceperunt uxores sibi ex omnibus quas elegerant
> dixitque Deus non permanebit spiritus meus in homine in aeternum quia caro est eruntque dies illius centum viginti annorum
> *gigantes* autem erant super terram in diebus illis postquam enim ingressi sunt filii Dei ad filias hominum illaeque genuerunt isti sunt *potentes a saeculo viri famosi*
> videns autem Deus quod multa malitia hominum esset in terra et cuncta cogitatio cordis intenta esset ad malum omni tempore
> paenituit eum quod hominem fecisset in terra et tactus dolore cordis intrinsecus [...].
> (Gen. 6.1–6). (Emphasis added).

Malmberg, 'Grendel and the Devil', *NM* 78 (1977), 241–43; J. B. Russell, *Lucifer: The Devil in the Middle Ages* (Ithaca and London, 1984), pp. 147–49; K4, p. lxxvii. On the devil in Old English more generally, see P. Dendle, *Satan Unbound: The Devil in Old English Narrative Literature* (Toronto, 2001). A further connection between Grendel and Lucifer, 'the morning star' (Isaiah 14.12), may be found in the *ligge gelicost lēoht unfæger*, 'ugly light, most like fire' (727), that shines from Grendel's eyes as he enters Heorot. Anlezark connects this detail with giants that appear in the Book of Wisdom ('Grendel and the Book of Wisdom').

[58] On the importance of the biblical Flood in *Beowulf* and Anglo-Saxon England more generally, see Anlezark, *Water and Fire*. Cf. 1 Enoch 6.1–2: 'And it came to pass when the children of men had multiplied that in those days were born unto them beautiful and comely daughters. And the angels, the children of the heaven, saw and lusted after them, and said to one another: "Come, let us choose wives from among the children of men and beget us children."' Cf. 1 Enoch 7.1–6: 'And all the others together with them took unto themselves wives, and each chose for himself one, and they began to go in unto them and to defile themselves with them, and they taught them charms and enchantments, and the cutting of roots, and made them acquainted with plants. And they became pregnant, and they bore great giants, whose height was three thousand ells, who consumed all the acquisitions of men. And when men could no longer sustain them, the giants turned against them and devoured mankind. And they began to sin against birds, and beasts, and reptiles, and fish, and to devour one another's flesh, and drink the blood. Then the earth laid accusations against the lawless ones.' Text cited from *The Book of Enoch the Prophet: Being a Book wherein secret mysteries are revealed including the lost Books of Noah, the Prophecies of Enoch, particulars of Demonology and Angelology, and visions of the Apocalypse*, trans. R. H. Charles (San Francisco, 2003), pp. 5–6. See further Mellinkoff, 'Cain's monstrous progeny, part I', esp. 146–48; and Kaske, '*Beowulf* and the Book of Enoch'.

The Role of the Monsters in the Dynastic Drama

[And after that men began to be multiplied upon the earth, and daughters were born to them. *The sons of God* seeing the daughters of men, that they were fair, took to themselves wives of all which they chose. And God said: My spirit shall not remain in man forever, because he is flesh, and his days shall be a hundred and twenty years. Now *giants* were upon the earth in those days. For after the sons of God went in to the daughters of men, and they brought forth children, these are *the mighty men of old, men of renown*. And God seeing that the wickedness of men was great on the earth, and that all the thought of their heart was bent upon evil at all times, it repented him that he had made man on the earth.]

The *Beowulf*-poet carefully explains how Grendel and his mother are sprung from the same Cainite race of *gigantes* (OE *gigantas*) (111–14, 1258b–67a).[59] Within this expanded biblical context, it becomes possible to read the *gif-stōl* passage as an allusion not only to the Fall of the Angels but also to the demonic origins of the race of monsters from whom Grendel and his ilk descended.

This association of Grendel with Lucifer is reinforced as *se ellor-gāst*, 'the alien spirit' (808b), now defeated and mortally wounded, makes his way *on fēonda geweald*, 'in the protection of enemies *or* demons' (808a), *sēcan dēofla gedræg*, 'to seek out the company of devils' (756a) before his heathen soul is finally received into hell:[60]

Dēað-fǣge dēog   siððan drēama lēas
in fen-freoðo   feorh ālegde,
hǣþena sāwle;   þǣr him hel onfēng.
(850–52).

[Death-doomed he hid when, deprived of joy, he gave up his life in the fen-refuge, his heathen soul; hell received him there.]

Although Grendel effectively ruled in Heorot during his twelve years of terror, he was never able to occupy the legitimate seat of royal power, the *gif-stōl*, because of his lack of royal blood. Like that of his biblical counterpart, Lucifer, Grendel's attempt to usurp the throne will result in his damnation.[61]

---

[59] See above, pp. 58, 159–62.
[60] Beowulf predicts that the fratricidal Unferth will suffer damnation in *helle* (587–89). For the emendation of MS *helle* to *healle*, however, see Robinson, *Appositive Style*, pp. 129–30; *CCB*, pp. 252–53; and K4, p. 154.
[61] Scholars have long recognized that the vivid description of Grendel's mere (1357b–82) is itself modelled on the image of hell depicted in the *Visio Pauli*. For a summary of the arguments and key references, see K4, pp. 200–01.

Grendel and Royal Illegitimacy in Anglo-Saxon England

Although the audience is twice made aware of Grendel's Cainite ancestry (106–14, 1258b–68), the pagan Danes remain ignorant of his paternal lineage, as Hrothgar himself later explains to Beowulf:

>   nō hīe fæder cunnon,
> hwæþer him ǣnig wæs ǣr ācenned
> dyrna gāsta.
> (1355b–57a)

[They do not know of a father, whether any of the secret spirits was born before him.]

This lack of clearly defined paternal ancestry (*ryht-fæderencyn*) effectively makes Grendel a bastard.[62] Margaret Clunies Ross argues that Anglo-Saxon men seem to have been polygynous prior to the conversion, extending 'the privileges of inheritance to acknowledged illegitimate sons'.[63] Pre-Christian kings might therefore take a large number of concubines or wives as an expression of power, while any acknowledged son, even a bastard, could then be considered for the succession.[64] After the conversion, however, the Church sought to restrict the rights of inheritance and succession solely to those children born within wedlock. So concerned was the papacy with the moral laxity of Anglo-Saxon rulers that it sent legates to England in 786 to initiate reform. At a council held in an unknown location, the legates received assurances from King Offa of Mercia and King Cynewulf of Wessex that they would reform their vices. A synod was then held in Northumbria in the presence of King Ælfwold at which a capitulary was issued. The twelfth item expressly forbids children born

---

[62] *DOE* records that the Old English terms for a bastard (*dōc*) and bastard son (*hornung-sunu*) both appear just once, in the same gloss for Latin *nothus*, in MS Cotton Otho E.i; OE *dōc-incel* occurs as a gloss to *nothus* in a copy of Bede's *Metrical Life of Cuthbert*, in a passage referring to Aldfrith, the illegitimate brother of Ecgfrith. In his homily on Cuthbert, Ælfric refers to the same Aldfrith as Ecgfrith's *cyfesborena broðor*, 'brother born of a concubine'. Aldfrith's mother was the Irish princess, Fin; his father was King Oswiu of Northumbria. Aldfrith's illegitimate birth was not an obstacle to his succession in 685, following the death of his brother, Ecgfrith. However, by the end of the eighth century, Aldfrith would have been ruled out of the succession, at least in the eyes of the Church (pp. 174–76). OE *bastard*, derived from Old French *bastard*, appears in *ASC* MS D s. a. 1066, in reference to *Wyllelm Bastard*.
[63] Clunies Ross, 'Concubinage', p. 273.
[64] See Clunies Ross, 'Concubinage', p. 266; P. Stafford, *Queens, Concubines and Dowagers: The King's Wife in the Early Middle Ages* (Athens, GA, 1983, repr. Leicester, 1998).

outside of wedlock from assuming the office of kingship:[65]

> XII. Duodecimo sermone sanximus, ut in ordinatione regum nullus permittat pravorum praevalere assensum, sed legitime reges a sacerdotibus et senioribus populi eligantur, et non de adulterio vel incaestu procreati: quia sicut nostris temporibus ad sacerdotium secundum canones adulter pervenire non potest, sic nec christus Domini esse valet, et rex totius regni, et heres patriae, qui ex legitimo non fuerit connubio generatus.[66]

> [*Chap. 12:* In the twelfth chapter we decreed that in the ordination of kings no one shall permit the assent of evil men to prevail, but kings are to be lawfully chosen by the priests and elders of the people, and are not to be those begotten in adultery or incest; for just as in our times according to the canons a bastard cannot attain to the priesthood, so neither can he who was not born of a legitimate marriage be the Lord's anointed and king of the whole kingdom and inheritor of the land.][67]

Taking the prohibition against Grendel approaching the *gif-stōl* as a reflection of his illegitimacy brings us closer to a solution for 169b: *nē his myne wisse*.[68] The rare OE noun *myne* is usually taken to mean 'mind, thought, intention', while *wisse* is the third person singular present indicative form of the verb *witan*, 'to know'.[69] Scholars have debated as to whether the subject of *wisse* is Grendel, God or Hrothgar.[70] Grendel seems by far the

---

[65] See J. Story, *Carolingian Connections: Anglo-Saxon England and Carolingian Francia, c. 750–870* (Aldershot, 2003), pp. 55–92, 135–68.

[66] *Alcuini Sive Albini Epistolae*, ed. E. Dümmler, Epistolae Karolini Aevi II, MGH Epist. 4 (Berlin, 1895), 19–29, at 23–24 (no. 3).

[67] D. Whitelock, ed. and trans., *English Historical Documents, I: c. 500–1042*, 2nd edn (London, 1979), p. 771 (§191).

[68] A close parallel appears in *The Wanderer* 27b, where the MS reads *mine wisse*. Various emendations have been proposed for this half-line: in 1909, Klaeber suggested *mē mine wisse*, 'feel love for me' ('Textual notes on the *Beowulf*', 254), a reading accepted by R. F. Leslie in his edition (*The Wanderer* [Manchester, 1966], pp. 70–71); Krapp and Dobbie, on the other hand, emend to *min mine wisse* (*The Exeter Book*, ASPR III [New York, 1936], p. 134), while T. P. Dunning and A. J. Bliss emend to *minne myne wisse*, 'would know my thought': *The Wanderer* (London, 1969), p. 61–64, 109. R. E. Bjork retains the MS reading, and translates as 'who might understand my feeling' (*Old English Shorter Poems, II: Wisdom and Lyric*, DOML 32 [Cambridge, MA, 2014], pp. 4–5. Kenneth R. Brooks, however, argues for retaining the MS reading, but taking *mine* as *mīne* (with a long vowel), thereby producing the reading: 'might know of my people' (Review of R. F. Leslie, ed., *The Wanderer*, MLR 63 [1968], 157–59, at 158). See further A. L. Klinck, ed., *The Old English Elegies: A Critical Edition and Genre Study* (Montreal and Kingston, 1992), pp. 110–11.

[69] B-T, s.v. *myne*: 'the mind; purpose, desire'.

[70] The case for Hrothgar (*wine Scyldinga*) seems the weakest, although he does become the subject of the next line, and, as we have seen, abrupt changes in subject are common in the poem. For arguments in favour of taking God as the subject, see Klaeber, 'Textual Notes on the *Beowulf*', 255; K3, p. 135.

best candidate, reading 169b as part of a *no ... ne* construction in apposition with 168a: *Nō hē þone gif-stōl grētan mōste, [...] nē his myne wisse.*[71] Indeed, such a reading has the advantage of transforming 169b into the climax of a long section focused on Grendel's power struggle with Hrothgar, beginning some twenty lines earlier with that statement that *Grendel wan/ hwīle wið Hrōþgār*, 'Grendel fought for a time against Hrothgar' (151b–52a), and culminating in his failure to occupy the seat of legitimate power due to his ignorance of God's laws governing succession.

Further support for this reading of 169b is provided by the lines describing the pagan Danes' ignorance of God that follow shortly after. Here we find the same collocation of *metod* and *witan*, and its variant *cunnan*: *metod hīe ne cūþon,/ dǣda dēmend, ne wiston hīe drihten God*, 'they did not know the Creator, Judge of Deeds, nor did they know the Lord God' (180b–81).[72] A plausible reading of 169b would therefore be: 'he (Grendel) did not know God's wish (*or* intention).' In other words, because of ignorance of the laws of the Creator, Grendel usurped power in Heorot through illegitimate means. Usurpation, either by legitimate or illegitimate contenders, was a constant threat to the stability of royal houses in Anglo-Saxon England.[73] Through this imaginative association of Grendel with Lucifer and the Fall of the Angels, the *Beowulf*-poet issued a stern warning to his audience concerning the hellish fates of those who seize power by illegitimate means.[74]

---

[71] See K4, p. 126.

[72] To my knowledge, these lines have not been cited in the many discussions of the various cruces surrounding 168–69.

[73] For a detailed analysis of one particular Anglo-Saxon rebellion, see R. Lavelle, 'The Politics of Rebellion: The Ætheling, Æthelwold and West Saxon Royal Succession, 89–902', in *Challenging the Boundaries of Medieval History: the Legacy of Timothy Reuter*, ed. P. Skinner (Turnhout, 2010), pp. 51–80. One prominent example of the violent seizure of power by an individual with seemingly no royal ancestry is the accession of Offa of Mercia in 757. As D. P. Kirby comments, '[n]one of Offa's immediate forebears had been king of the Mercians and Offa himself is another example (like Æthelbald) of an ætheling competing successfully for the kingship from outside the innermost core of royal power': *The Earliest English Kings* (London, 1991), p. 134. See further B. Yorke, *Kings and Kingdoms of Early Anglo-Saxon England* (London, 1990), pp. 100–27; Brooke, *Saxon and Norman Kings*, pp. 96–97. For Alcuin's comments on Offa's execution of rival claimants, see *Alcuini Sive Albini Epistolae*, ed. Dümmler, 178–80, at 179 (no. 122). For a review of the arguments connecting *Beowulf* with Offa's reign, see Leneghan, 'Offa Digression'.

[74] Both Grendel and his mother are associated with images of seizing and grasping: see, for example, lines 122b–23a, 740–41a, 1501–02a, 1541–42. On the Grendelkin's 'steely claws', see M. Cavell, 'Constructing the Monstrous Body in *Beowulf*', *ASE* 43 (2014), 155–81, at 163–72.

Grendel's Mother and the Dynastic Theme

If Grendel's role in the dynastic drama is clear, what part does his mother play in the poem's politics? The absence of any reference to Grendel's mother prior to Beowulf's victory over her son (1255b–59, 1345–82) and the number of resemblances between the fights in the water-hall and Heorot led some early scholars to argue that this entire episode is simply a variation of the first fight, composed in order to flesh out the text for an audience who wanted more of the same.[75] Certainly some elements of this episode recall the story of Grendel. For example, the description of her night-time advance on Heorot (*Cōm þā tō Heorote*, 1279a) recalls the more elaborate narration of Grendel's own stalking of the same hall (*Cōm on wanre niht* [...] *Ðā cōm of more* [...] *Cōm þā tō recede*, 702b–27). However, the recognition that the hero's two fights in Denmark follow the pattern of the Two Trolls folktale, in which a hero overcomes two monsters, often of different sex, has resulted in the general acceptance of the structural integrity – and indeed centrality – of the Grendel's-mother episode.[76] In Klaeber's estimation the second fight is in fact 'vastly more interesting [than the first] by reason of its elaborate, romantic scenery, the variety and definiteness of incidents, [and] the dramatic quality of the battle'.[77] Like her son, she is a deeply ambiguous character who elicits revulsion for her acts of violence,[78] while also evoking sympathy through her presentation as a bereaved mother who is hunted down and killed while defending her own 'hall'.[79] On the one hand, her femininity is foregrounded through the

---

[75] W. A. Berendsohn, *Zur Vorgeschichte des 'Beowulf'* (Copenhagen, 1935), pp. 62–68, for example, argued that the Grendel's mother episode was the work of an Anglian interpolator. Cf. Sisam, *Structure*, p. 4: 'If [...] *Beowulf* had a life outside books [...] it could be adapted to a shorter time by reducing speeches or omitting episodes and digressions. The extant form suggests a serial in three instalments.' As we saw in Chapter One, Tolkien struggled to find a place for Grendel's mother in his bipartite theory of the work's structure. Cf. 'Monsters', p. 52: 'I shall confine myself mainly to the monsters – Grendel and the Dragon.'

[76] See esp. Rogers, 'Beowulf's Three Great Fights'; and Owen-Crocker, *Four Funerals*, pp. 217–33. See further Chapter One, pp. 33–34.

[77] K3, p. lii. Klaeber draws attention to the careful 'gradation' of the three fights, noting that as the difficulty of the challenge increases so does the hero's reliance on weapons. Bonjour reads this section as 'a transition between the two great crises' affecting the Danes and Geats: 'Grendel's Dam and the Composition of *Beowulf*', *ES* 30 (1949), 113–24; repr. in Bonjour (1962), pp. 29–50, at 34.

[78] For example, the narrator describes her as *gīfre ond galg-mōd*, 'ravenous and gallows-minded' (1275a), while Hrothgar refers to her as a *wæl-gǣst wæfre*, 'deadly slaughter-guest' (1331a) and *mihtig mān-scaða*, 'mighty guilty ravager' (1339a).

[79] The narrator comments *gegān wolde/ sorhfulne sīð sunu dēoð wrecan*, 'she wished to go on a sorrowful journey to avenge her son's death', 1277b–78), while

use of the female personal pronoun, *hēo*, no less than six times in one short passage describing her assault on Heorot (1292–1306a), yet elsewhere she is referred to in terms suggestive of masculinity, with Hrothgar, for example, describing her as a *secg*, 'man' (1379a). Although on the whole Grendel's mother has attracted less critical interest than her son or indeed the dragon, Jane Chance, Stacy Klein and others have shown how she acts as a destabilizing presence, inverting roles traditionally associated with royal women in the poem – such as peaceweaving and diplomacy – and taking on the traditionally masculine role of vengeance.[80] What remains relatively unexplored is the connection between Grendel's mother and the theme of succession. In this section, I will therefore briefly explore how the *Beowulf*-poet integrated the ogress of the Two Trolls folktale into his dynastic drama.

The first thing we note is the special emphasis the poet places on her status as a mother.[81] Indeed, seven of the eight instances of the word *mōdor* in the poem refer to her (1258b, 1275b, 1282a, 1538b, 1683b, 2118b, 2139b).[82] Moreover, in a reversal of the natural pattern of succession, Grendel's mother is presented as a parent who outlives her child:

> Þæt gesȳne wearþ,
> wīd-cūþ werum,   þætte wrecend þā gȳt
> lifde æfter lāþum,   lange þrāge,
> æfter gūð-ceare
> (1255b–58a). (Emphasis added).

[That became visible, widely known to men, that an avenger *lived still after the hateful one*, for a long time, after the war-care.]

This image of the bereaved parent recalls the story of Hildeburh, witness to the cremation of her son(s) (1063–1159a), recently recited by the *scop* in Heorot, while foreshadowing Beowulf's reflections on the grief of Hrethel and the *gomelum ceorle* at the loss of their respective sons on the eve of his own, childless death (2426–72). Where Grendel's mother differs dramatically from all these characters, of course, is that instead of simply

---

Hrothgar tells Beowulf *wolde hyre mæg wrecan*, 'she wished to avenge her kin' (1339b).

[80] Chance, 'Problem of Grendel's Mother'; Chance, *Woman as Hero*, pp. 95–109; Klein, *Ruling Women*, pp. 87–124. See also Overing, *Language, Sign, and Gender*, pp. 101–12; M. Dockray-Miller, 'The Masculine Queen of *Beowulf*', *Women and Language* 21 (1998), 31–38; M. W. Hennequin, 'We've Created a Monster: The Strange Case of Grendel's Mother', *ES* 89 (2008), 502–23; and K4, pp. cxxvi–cxxvii.

[81] As the editors of K4 note, the ogress of the Two Trolls folktale is sometimes depicted as the mother of the wounded male troll (pp. xxxvii–xliv, 196). On parallels with the Two Trolls folktale more generally, see above, pp. 111–18.

[82] The exception is the reference to *Onelan mōdor ond Ōhtheres* (2932a).

mourning her loss, she avenges herself on the Danes by taking the life of Æschere, Hrothgar's most beloved warrior (1292–99a).[83] Throughout the poem, royal women are presented as the preservers and perpetuators of royal lines, as mothers, peaceweavers and advisors.[84] Indeed, Grendel's mother is herself introduced by way of a genealogy that identifies her as a member of the race of Cain:[85]

> *Grendles mōdor,*
> *ides āglǣc-wīf yrmþe gemunde,*
> *sē þe wæter-egesan wunian scolde,*   1260
> *cealde strēamas, siþðan Cāin wearð*
> *tō ecg-banan āngan brēþer,*
> *fæderen-mǣge; hē þā fāg gewāt,*
> *morþre gemearcod man-drēam flēon,*
> *wēsten warode. Þanon wōc fela*   1265
> *geōsceaft-gāsta; wæs þǣra Grendel sum,*
> *heoro-wearh hetelic, sē æt Heorote fand*
> *wæccendne wer wīges bīdan.*
> (1258b–68). (Emphasis added).

[Grendel's mother, *a lady, an awe-inspiring woman, remembered hardship*, the one who had to dwell in water-terror, frozen streams, after Cain became a sword-slayer to his own brother, paternal relative; he went from that killing, marked by murder, fled the joys of men, occupied the wasteland. *Thence was born a great many cursed spirits; Grendel was one of those*, hateful fierce outcast; he who had found a waking warrior, ready for war at Heorot.]

By incurring the vengeance of Beowulf, however, Grendel's mother ironically brings about the extinction of this particular branch of the house of Cain. Her fate thereby anticipates the theme of the dying out of royal lines that will come to dominate the poem's final section.

Another aspect of the female monster that is given special emphasis in *Beowulf* is her unmarried status. The poet utilized this traditional feature of the ogress to dramatize the danger that a violent and unmarried woman can present to a royal court, a theme he will return to in the tale of the

---

[83] In Hrethel's case, the loss is so great that it causes his death (2468–71). For discussion of the legality of Grendel's mother's attack in terms of Anglo-Saxon practice, see K. O'Brien O'Keeffe, 'Body and law in late Anglo-Saxon England', *ASE* 27 (1998), 209–32; and H. Appleton, 'The Role of Æschere's Head', *RES* 68 (2017), 428–47.

[84] As Klein notes, the identities and energies of the 'two central queenly figures in *Beowulf*, Wealhtheow and Hygd', are fully 'invested in the issue of succession' (*Ruling Women*, p. 17). See further, Chance, *Woman as Hero*, pp. 1–11.

[85] For parallels with the Scylding genealogy, see above, pp. 161–62.

unqueenly conduct of Offa's bride. Like Grendel's mother, she captures innocent men in a deadly *mund-gripe*, 'hand-grip' (1938a):[86]

> Ne bið swylc cwēnlic þēaw
> idese tō efnanne, þēah ðe hīo ǣnlicu sȳ,
> þætte freoðu-webbe fēores onsǣce
> æfter lige-torne lēofne mannan.[87]
> (1940b–43).

[That is not a queenly custom for a lady to perform, though she may be peerless, that a peace-weaver should deprive a well-loved man of his life because of a pretended insult.]

As we have seen, royal women in *Beowulf* are invariably defined in terms of their marital relations: Healfdene's daughter is *Onelan cwēn/ Heaðo-Scilfingas heals-gebedda*, 'Onela's queen, the bed-companion of the Battle-Scylfing' (62b–63); Wealhtheow is *cwēn Hrōðgāres*, 'Hrothgar's queen'; Freawaru *gehāten is,/ geong gold-hroden, gladum suna Frōdan*, 'is promised, young and gold-adorned, to the gracious son of Froda' (2024b–25); and Offa's bride herself is redeemed by marriage. Through her lack of a spouse, as much as her advocacy of vengeance, Grendel's mother therefore provides a troubling counterpart to the hero himself, whose failure to marry and produce a son will have fatal consequences for his own dynasty and nation. In order to dramatize the final act of his dynastic drama, the fall of the Hrethlings, however, the poet needed a monster even more terrifying than Grendel's mother, something that could stand above human affairs. In turning to the age-old story of the dragon, the poet was able to link Germanic and Christian traditions with a symbol of universal doom.

The Swedish Wars and the Dragon-Fight

The modelling of Beowulf's fictional dragon-fight on the legend of Sigemund's dragon-fight alluded to by the Danish *scop* (874b–902a) is indicated by a series of verbal echoes: both heroes confront *dracas* who live *under hārne stān*, 'under a grey stone' (887b, 2553b, 2774b); when Sigemund strikes the fatal blow, *draca morðre swealt [...] wyrm hāt gemealt*, 'the dragon

---

[86] For discussion of the tale of Offa's bride, see above, pp. 78–82. Compare Grendel's mother, who grasps towards Beowulf *atolan clommum*, 'with terrible clutches' (1502a), and *grimmam grāpum* 'fierce grips' (1542a). Grendel and Beowulf himself, of course, are similarly identified as having strong hand-grips.

[87] This reference to the victims of Offa's bride as *lēofne mannan*, 'beloved men' (1943b), echoes the description of Grendel's mother's victim, Æschere, as Hrothgar's *hæleþa lēofost*, 'most beloved warrior' (1296), and *aldor-þegn [...] þone dēorestan*, 'the dearest chief thane' (1308–09a).

perished with murder [...] the serpent melted with heat' (892b, 897b), just as Beowulf's dragon *morðre swealt*, 'perished with murder' (2782b), *wæs se lēg-draca/ grimlic gryre-fāh glēdum beswǣled*, 'the fire-dragon was grimly decorated, consumed in flames' (3040b–41).[88]

In adapting this aspect of the Sigemund-legend for his dynastic drama, however, the *Beowulf*-poet appears to have drawn on various other dragon-fights.[89] Certain features of Beowulf's last battle, such as the motivating presence of treasure and the description of weapons, are common elements in northern dragon-slaying legends.[90] However, as scholars have noted, several other aspects of Beowulf's dragon-fight, notably the presentation of the beast as the enemy of the entire population and its destruction of the local region, are rare in northern legend but appear in accounts of the dragon-fights of Christian saints.[91] Christine Rauer has highlighted a particularly striking series of parallels between Beowulf's battle with the *wyrm* and the dragon-fights of St Samson of Dol, preserved in the mid-ninth century *Vita II Samsonis*, and St Michael the archangel, copied in the ninth- or tenth-century Homiliary of Saint-Pére.[92] Samson is accompanied to the dragon's cave by an army and a group of monks, whom he instructs

---

[88] For a list of further parallels, see K4, p. xlvi. Further echoes of the Sigemund-legend appear in the account of Wiglaf's plundering of the dragon's hoard (2773–82).

[89] For connections with the dragon-fight of Frötho (OE Froda), presented by Saxo as the father of Halfdan (OE Healfdene), see Rauer, *Dragon*, pp. 42–51; K4, pp. xlv–xlvii. For parallels with Thor, see U. Dronke, 'Beowulf and Ragnarök', *Saga-Book* 17 (1969), 302–25. See further Chambers, *Introduction*, pp. 92–97; Davis, *Demise of Germanic Legend*. For a recent discussion of the relationship between Beowulf and Old Norse myth more generally, see H. O'Donoghue, *English Poetry and Old Norse Myth: A History* (Oxford, 2014), pp. 16–24.

[90] In *Völsunga saga*, for example, Fafnir's brother, Regin, tells Sigurd: 'Fafnir became so ill-natured that he set out into the wilds and allowed no one to enjoy the treasure but himself. He has since become the most evil serpent and lies now upon this hoard. [...] Sigurd said: "Make a sword now with your skill so that its equal has never been made. Do this and I will be able to work great deeds if courage helps, and if you want me to kill this dragon"' (chs 14–15; trans. Byock, p. 59). The sword breaks and Regin fashions a second one, which similarly breaks; Sigurd then commands Regin to fashion a third sword from the fragments of Gram, a sword formerly owned by his father, Sigemund. After Sigurd has struck a mortal blow on Fafnir, the dragon warns him that 'this gold that was mine will be your death' (ch. 18; Byock, p. 64); Sigurd does not heed the warning and, after drinking the dragon's blood and eating its heart, takes the gold (chs 18–20); Sigurd is later murdered while sleeping by Guttorm (ch. 32).

[91] Goldsmith, *Mode and Meaning*, pp. 130–45; Lapidge, '*Beowulf*, Aldhelm, the *Liber Monstrorum* and Wessex', 278–82; P. Sorrell, 'The approach to the dragon-fight in *Beowulf*, Aldhelm, and the "traditions folkloriques" of Jacques Le Goff', *Parergon* 12 (1994), 57–87, at 77.

[92] Rauer, *Dragon*, pp. 89–124. See also *CCB*, pp. 149–51. For St Michael's battle against the great dragon Lucifer-Satan, see above, p. 158.

to wait outside while he deals with the beast alone; the saint bridles the dragon and commands it to go into the sea, where it drowns; the people rejoice at the saint's victory. Similarly, Michael confronts a fire-breathing dragon occupying a high mountain, from which it kills all within reach, devastating the local, pagan population; using a fiery sword, Michael splits the dragon into twelve parts; the beast is dragged into the sea by a team of oxen; the people build a church in Michael's honour, rejoicing and praising God.[93] By fusing these Germanic and hagiographical paradigms, the *Beowulf*-poet invites his Christian Anglo-Saxon audience to view his hero as both a pagan warrior who fights to win treasure and glory and as a saintly figure who fights a dragon in order to protect his people.[94]

However, two distinguishing features set Beowulf's dragon-fight apart from those of his Germanic and hagiographical counterparts: first, its positioning as the last of a carefully graded sequence of three monster-fights of increasing difficulty, following the two combats with male and female trolls;[95] second, its status as the final act in a narrative concerning the rise and fall of dynasties.

Scholars have often expressed dissatisfaction about the poet's decision to interrupt the potentially exciting narration of the dragon-fight with repeated allusions to the dynastic conflicts between the Hrethlings and the Scylfings, the so-called 'Swedish wars'. Klaeber, for example, wrote of the 'grave structural defects characteristic of the dragon fight', describing the Swedish wars as 'interesting' but of little relevance to the 'main story':

> Unlike the Danish element of the first part, which was no doubt familiarly associated with the central contests, the heroic traditions of Geatish-Swedish history were *entirely separate from the main story*, and *the author*, desirous though he was of availing himself of that interesting subject-matter for the purpose of epic enlargement, *failed to establish an organic relation between the two sets of sources*.[96] (Emphasis added).

---

[93] For the texts, see Rauer, *Dragon*, pp. 150–61.

[94] On Christological themes in *Beowulf*, and on the presentation of the hero as an idealized proto-Christian ruler, see Chapter Four, pp. 227–35.

[95] On the gradation of the monster-fights, see above, p. 177 n.77. G. V. Smithers proposed that the dragon-fight and the Grendel-fight were already linked prior to the composition of *Beowulf* (*Making*, pp. 12–16), pointing to an episode in *Grettis saga* in which the hero rescues treasure from a mound guarded by the ghost of its previous owner, Kar. After being lowered into the mound by a friend holding a rope, Grettir takes the treasure but is attacked by a troll; killing the troll, Grettir discovers that his friend has abandoned him; Grettir then makes his own way out of the mound with the treasure, including a valuable sword (*Grettis saga*, ch. 18). Benson, however, notes that the guardian of the mound here is not a dragon but a troll, a common folktale motif in Scandinavian tradition ('Originality', pp. 58–59). On the Fall of the Angels as a typological link between Grendel and the dragon, see above, pp. 158–59.

[96] K3, p. cvi. For similar views, see S. B. Greenfield, 'Geatish History, Poetic Art

The Role of the Monsters in the Dynastic Drama

In the previous chapter, I proposed that Beowulf's battle against the dragon is a fictional variation or amplification of the legend of Hygelac's death in pursuit of treasure in Frisia.[97] This section aims to demonstrate that the dragon-fight and the Swedish wars stand in apposition to one another, as parallel narratives in the dynastic drama.

When arranged in chronological sequence, the main events of the Swedish wars as presented in the poem can be summarized as follows:[98]

1. Herebeald, son of the Geatish King Hrethel, is killed in a shooting accident by his brother Hæthcyn (2147–33);[99] consumed by grief, Hrethel is unable to take vengeance on his son's slayer and dies (2444–71); Hæthcyn succeeds his father, Hrethel, as King of the Geats.

2. Ohthere and Onela, sons of the Swedish King Ongentheow, attack the Geats; the Geats launch a counter-attack in which both kings, Hæthcyn and Ongentheow, are killed; Hygelac now succeeds his brother, Hæthcyn, as king of the Geats; Onela becomes king of the Swedes (2472–89).[100]

3. Some years later, Hygelac dies in a raid on the Franks; Hygelac's widow, Queen Hygd, offers the Geatish throne to Beowulf, who declines and chooses to act instead as protector to Hygelac's young son, Heardred (2354b–79a).

4. Ohthere's two sons, Eanmund and Eadgils, seek refuge from their uncle, King Onela, at the court of the young Geatish king, Heardred (2379b–84a).[101]

---

and Epic Quality in *Beowulf*, Neophilologus 47 (1963), 211–17, repr. in Fulk (1991), pp. 120–26; and E. G. Stanley, 'The Narrative Art of *Beowulf*', in *Medieval Narrative: A Symposium*, ed. H. Bekker-Nielsen, P. Foote, A. Haarder and P. Meulengracht Sørensen (Odense, 1979), pp. 58–81, repr. in his *A Collection of Papers with Emphasis on Old English Literature*, Publications of the Dictionary of Old English 3 (Toronto, 1987), pp. 170–91. See also Benson, 'Originality', p. 61; Niles, 'Locating *Beowulf* in Literary History', pp. 100–01.

[97] See pp. 121–39.
[98] For further summaries of the Swedish wars, see K3, pp. xxxviii–xlv; K4, pp. lix–lxiv; Bonjour, *Digressions*, pp. 32–43. For a comparison with Saxo Grammaticus's account of the same conflict, see R. North, 'Saxo and the Swedish Wars in *Beowulf*', in *Saxo Grammaticus tra storiografia e letteratura*, ed. C. Santini (Rome, 1992), pp. 175–88.
[99] For the possibility that this legend is itself a variant of the myth of Baldr's death, see p. 88 n.195.
[100] It is unclear whether Onela's brother, Ohthere, first took the throne on Ongentheow's death; see pp. 94–95.
[101] For parallels with the legend of the exiled Danish princes, Roas/Hroar (Hrothgar) and Helgo/Helgi (OE Halga), see appendices.

5. Onela attacks and kills Heardred; one of the exiled Scylfing princes, Eanmund, is killed by a Wægmunding warrior, Weohstan, father of Wiglaf; Onela allows Beowulf to rule the Geats (2384b–90, 2611–68).

6. The surviving Swedish exile, Eadgils, attacks and kills his uncle, King Onela, with Beowulf's assistance (2391–96).

7. After Heardred's death, Beowulf rules the Geats for fifty years (2207–10a); following Beowulf's death, a Messenger predicts that various enemies surrounding the Geats, among them the Franks, Frisians and Swedes, will attack with devastating consequences (2900–3027).

Laid out in this manner, the outline of the Swedish wars seems relatively straightforward. However, as Michael Lapidge comments, in the poem itself 'the story [of the Swedish wars] is narrated, confusingly, in very nearly the reverse order from that in which the narrated events took place'.[102] The effect is startling: as the narration of the dragon-fight moves slowly forward, so we are simultaneously taken further and further back to the origins of the Swedish wars. The purpose of this highly unusual, contrapuntal narrative method only becomes fully apparent in the aftermath of the dragon-fight, when it emerges that the hero's uneventful fifty-year reign has merely postponed the inevitable consequences of Hygelac's raid on Frisia and the series of skirmishes with the Swedes.[103] With no royal house to protect them, the Geats are now exposed to attack and face annihilation.

Despite the poet's careful and consistent interweaving of these two narrative threads across the final third of the work, previous studies have invariably focused on either the Swedish wars or the dragon-fight in isolation.[104] In the most recent exploration of this topic, for example, James W. Earl provides a helpful survey of 'a tangle of questions' that surround the Swedish wars, before concluding that the poet and his audience shared in the conviction that these episodes from northern history 'provide a meaningful backdrop to the main action of the dragon fight'.[105] Two

---

[102] Lapidge, 'Beowulf and Perception', 72. Lapidge notes that the Swedish wars are narrated from a variety of perspectives (the narrator, Wiglaf, Beowulf, the Geatish Messenger), allowing for what Gerard Genette calls 'multiple internal focalisation'.

[103] On Beowulf as a variation on Hygelac, see Chapter Two, pp. 121–39.

[104] On the dragon-fight, see K. Sisam, 'Beowulf's Fight with the Dragon', RES 9 (1958), 129–40; Sorrell, 'The approach to the dragon-fight in Beowulf, Aldhelm, and the "traditions folkloriques" of Jacques Le Goff'; Rauer, Dragon; and Orchard, Pride and Prodigies. On the Swedish wars, see esp. Bonjour, Digressions, p. 42; Farrell, Beowulf, Swedes and Geats; and Earl, 'Swedish Wars'.

[105] Earl, 'Swedish Wars', 55.

important exceptions are essays by John Leyerle and Linda Georgianna, both of which consider how the royal material and dragon-fight work together in this section of the poem. Leyerle observes that the repeated allusions to the Swedish wars serve as an 'ominous warning' concerning the dangers that lie ahead for Beowulf's people should he fail to return from the dragon's cave: 'in this way the poet undercuts Beowulf's single-minded preoccupation with the dragon.'[106] Georgianna takes a similar view, arguing that Beowulf's recollection of episodes from the Swedish wars during his long speech at Hronesnæss distances the audience from the dragon-fight, thereby 'undermining the value and effectiveness of heroic action at precisely the moment when the hero is most relying on it'.[107] In both these readings, the Swedish wars and the dragon-fight are viewed as antithetical, the former realistic and historical, the latter heroic and implicitly fictional.[108] In this section, however, I consider the contrapuntal narration of these two stories as an example of the poet's appositional technique. In particular, I propose that the poet constructed his dragon-fight out of northern and hagiographical models in order to magnify the final act of his dynastic drama, the fall of the Hrethlings.[109] Just as the rise of a dynasty was presented as a miraculous result of divine intervention through the poet's insertion of the myth of Scyld Scefing and Beow into a gap in the Danish royal line, so the fall of a royal house is transformed into an awe-inspiring event, a *wundor*, 'astonishing thing', through the simultaneous narration of the hero's fatal struggle with the dragon.[110]

The political significance of the dragon is made clear from the moment of its first appearance in the narrative. Echoing the earlier depiction of Grendel as an anti-ruler who attempted to usurp legitimate royal authority in Heorot, the dragon is now ironically presented as King Beowulf's 'successor', a figure whose 'reign' signals the end of the royal line of Hrethel and serves as a portent of the fall of the Geatish nation:[111]

Eft þæt geīode   ufaran dōgrum
hilde-hlæmmum,   syððan Hygelāc læg,
ond Heardrēde   hilde-mēceas

---

[106] Leyerle, 'Interlace', p. 153.
[107] Georgianna, 'King Hrethel's Sorrow', 831.
[108] Cf. Bonjour, *Digressions*, p. 71: 'by keeping continuously in touch with "historical" events, [the digressions and episodes] represent the realistic note serving as a highly appropriate foil to the transcendental interest of the main theme with its highly significant symbolic value.'
[109] See more generally Robinson, *Appositive Style*.
[110] On the deaths of both Beowulf and the dragon as a *wundor*, see below, pp. 192–93.
[111] On Grendel as a failed usurper and Grendel's mother as an anti-type of the good queen, see above, pp. 162–76 and 177–80. On monsters as portents, see above, pp. 154–59.

under bord-hrēoðan   tō bonan wurdon,
ðā hyne gesōhtan   on sige-þēode
hearde hilde-frecan,   Heaðo-Scilfingas,
nīða genǣgdan   nefan Hererīces:
syððan Bēowulfe   brāde rīce
on hand gehwearf;   he gehēold tela
fīftig wintra – wæs ðā frōd cyning,
eald ēþel-weard – oð ðæt ān ongan
deorcum nihtum   draca rīcsian,
sē ðe on hēaum hofe   hord beweotode,
stān-beorh stēarcne
(2200–13a). (Emphasis added).

[Afterwards it came to pass, in later days, through the clashing of battles, once Hygelac lay dead, and battle-blades had become the slayer of Heardred, under the covering of shields, when the War-Scylfings, fierce battle-chiefs, sought him out among the victory-people, laid low with hostility the nephew of Hereric: afterwards the broad kingdom passed into Beowulf's hands; he ruled it well for fifty winters – he was then a wise king, *old guardian of the homeland – until a certain one, a dragon, began to reign on dark nights, the one who watched over the hoard* on the high heaths, steep stone-barrows.]

The half-line *oð ðæt ān ongan* links this portentous dragon with both Grendel and the devil, recalling the intrusion of the serpent-like *fēond on helle*, 'enemy in hell' (101b), into the Edenic world of Heorot some two thousand lines earlier.[112] Moreover, the appositional presentation of both Beowulf (*eald ēþel-weard*, 2210a) and the dragon (*sē ðe* [...] *hord beweotode*, 2212) as guardians invites the audience to compare them, just as the hero had previously been shown to resemble in certain ways both Grendel and Grendel's mother.[113] Over the next thousand or so lines, the poet will consistently exploit the traditional image of a dragon as both defender of its hoard (as we have seen, a common motif in northern dragon-slaying legends) and aggressor towards the local population (a feature of saintly dragon-fights). The fusion of the Germanic and hagiographical dragon-slaying archetypes allows the poet to position Beowulf's last monster-fight as a mirror to the conflict between the Hrethlings and Scylfings

---

[112] A similar construction is used in *Andreas* to describe how an unnamed Mermedonian reacts to the flood (1555b–56: *Þā þǣr ān ongann,/ feasceaft hæleð, folc gadorigean*). On connections between *Andreas* and *Beowulf*, see Introduction, p. 6, and Conclusion, pp. 241–44. The dragon is repeatedly identified as a *wyrm*, 'serpent' (e.g. 2221b, 2287a, 2307a).

[113] The dragon is subsequently described, like Beowulf, in terms of its age: *Swā se ðēod-sceaða þrēohund wintra/ hēold on hrūsan hord-ærna sum/ ēacen-cræftig*, 'So the ravager of the people held a certain hoard-treasure in the earth for three-hundred years, exceedingly powerful' (2278–80a). Later both Beowulf and the dragon are referred to as *āglǣcan*, 'awe-inspiring ones' (2592a). For links between Beowulf and the Grendelkin, see above, p. 153.

which similarly revolves around a series of attacks and counter-attacks and in which neither side has the moral high ground.[114]

The origins of the Swedish wars can be traced back at least to the abduction of Ongentheow's queen by the Geats, as summarized in the Geatish Messenger's speech at Beowulf's funeral:

Nē ic te Swēo-ðēode sibbe oððe trēowe	
wihte ne wēne, ac wæs wīde cūð	
þætte Ongenðīo ealdre besnyðede	
Hæðcen Hrēþling wið Hrefna Wudu,	2925
þā for onmēdlan ǣrest gesōhton	
Gēata lēode Gūð-Scilfingas.	
Sōna him se frōda fæder Ōhtheres,	
eald ond egesfull ond-slyht āgeaf,	
ābrēot brim-wīsan, brȳd āhredde,	2930
gomelan iōmeowlan golde berofene,	
Onelan mōdor ond Ōhtheres,	
ond ðā folgode feorh-genīðlan	
oð ðæt hī oðēodon earfoðlīce	
in Hrefnes Holt hlāfordlēase.	2935
(2922–35)	

[Nor do I expect peace or truce from the Swedish people, but it was widely known that Ongentheow ended the life of Hæthcyn son of Hrethel, at Ravenswood, when *the Geatish people arrogantly first sought out the War-Scylfings*. Quickly the old father of Ohthere (i.e. Ongentheow), *ancient and terrible, repaid the attack*, the old warrior chopped down the sea-captain, took back his bride, deprived of gold,[115] Onela's mother and Ohthere's, and then pursued his deadly enemies, until they got away from there with difficulty, to Ravenswood, lordless.]

The moral equivalence of the Geats and Swedes – and by implication Beowulf and the dragon – is brought sharply into focus in this passage. As with the account of Onela's dealings with Heardred and Beowulf, the Swedes are presented in a largely sympathetic light; in fact, the Messenger

---

[114] Cf. C. R. Davis, 'Theories of History in Traditional Plots', in *Myth in Early Northwest Europe*, Arizona Studies in the Middle Ages and the Renaissance 21, ed. S. O. Glosecki (Tempe, AZ, 2007), pp. 31–45, at 45, cited in Earl, 'Swedish Wars', 56: '[t]he poet deliberately ambiguates the rights and wrongs of the Geatish-Swedish feud through multiple moral equivalences.' On the generally positive presentation of the Swedes, see Farrell, *Beowulf, Swedes and Geats*, pp. 3–6. For the likelihood that Beowulf himself has Swedish blood through his Wægmunding father, Ecgtheow (cf. Ongen-theow), see Wardale, 'The Nationality of Ecgðeow'; Bryan, 'The Wægmundings – Swedes or Geats?'; Eliason, 'Beowulf, Wiglaf and the Wægmundings'; Lehmann, 'Ecgþeow the Wægmunding'; and Shaull, 'Ecgþeow, Brother of Ongenþeow'.

[115] It is unclear whether the gold in question belonged to Ongentheow himself or his queen.

blames his own people, the Geats, for arrogantly (*for onmēdlan*) first seeking out the *Gūð-Scilfingas*. Aggrieved and enraged by the theft of both his gold and his bride, Ongentheow, *eald ond egesfull*, 'old and terrible', stands in apposition with the ancient and equally terrifying dragon.[116] These parallels are consolidated a few lines later with the image of Ongentheow, *se gōda*, 'the good one', returning home, dragon-like, *eald under eorð-weall*, 'old under the earth-wall', to keep watch over his treasure-hoard:[117]

>Gewāt him ðā *se gōda*   mid his gædelingum,
>frōd fela-geōmor   fæsten sēcean,   2950
>eorl Ongenþīo   ufor oncirde;
>hæfde Higelāces   hilde gefrūnen,
>wlonces wīg-cræft;   wiðres ne truwode,
>þæt hē sæ-mannum   onsacan mihte,
>heaðo-līðendum   *hord forstandan*,   2955
>bearn ond brȳde;   bēah eft þonan
>*eald under eorð-weall*.
>(2949–57a). (Emphasis added).

>[Then *the good one* (i.e. Ongentheow) took himself with his kinsmen, old and very sad, to seek out his stronghold, the warrior Ongentheow turned away; he had heard about Hygelac's proud war-skill, and did not trust the resistance that he might call upon against the strength of the sea-warrior, *to defend his hoard* against the naval attackers, children and bride; he turned away from there, *old under the earth-wall*.]

Onela's subsequent killing of Heardred follows a similar pattern: the Swedish ruler is provoked by his Geatish counterpart's decision to provide refuge for the exiled Scylfing princes, Eanmund and Eadgils (2379b–90); Beowulf himself then sides with Eadgils in a retaliatory strike against Onela (2391–96).

It is within this context of dynastic feuding and cross-generational incursions into rival territory that the dragon's devastating assault on the land of the Geats is made meaningful for the Anglo-Saxon audience. Hence, the poet makes it clear that the dragon was itself provoked by the actions of a thief who disturbed its hoard:

>   Þǣr on innan gīong
>nīðða nāthwylc,   sē ðe nēh geþrong
>hǣðnum horde;   hond ēðe gefēng

---

[116] Cf. J. Gardner, 'Guilt and the World's Complexity: The Murder of Ongentheow and the Slaying of the Dragon', in *Anglo-Saxon Poetry: Essays in Appreciation for John C. McGalliard*, ed. L. E. Nicholson and D. W. Frese (Notre Dame, IN, 1975), pp. 14–22.
[117] Cf. Wiglaf's account of how he went *inn under eorð-weall*, 'in under the earth-wall' (3090a), as he explored the dragon's cave.

searo since fāh.   Nē hē þæt syððan bemāð,
þēah ðe hē slǣpende   besyred wurde
þēofes cræfte: þæt sīe ðīod onfand,
būfolc biorna,   þæt hē gebolgen wæs.[118]
(2214b–20).

[A certain man went inside there, he who pressed forward near to the heathen hoard; with his hand he easily found a cup decorated with treasure. He (i.e. the dragon) did not conceal that afterwards, although he had been deceived by the thief's skill while sleeping: because of that, the people living nearby discovered that he was enraged.]

This ambiguation of the theme of plunder continues as Beowulf, having witnessed the destruction of his own hall by the dragon (2324–27a), resolves to seek out the monster and win its hoard:

Ofer-hogode ðā   hringa fengel   2345
þæt hē þone wīd-flogan   weorode gesōhte,
sīdan herge;   nō hē him þā sæcce ondrēd,
nē him þæs wyrmes wīg   for wiht dyde,
eafoð ond ellen,   forðon hē ǣr fela
nearo nēðende   nīða gedīgde,   2350
hilde-hlemma,   syððan hē Hrōgāres,
sigor-ēadig secg,   sele fælsode,
ond æt gūðe forgrāp   Grendeles mǣgum
lāðan cynnes.
                      Nō þæt lǣsest wæs
hond-gemōta   þǣr mon Hygelāc slōh,   2355
syððan Gēata cyning   gūðe rǣsum,
frēa-wine folca   Frēslondum on,
Hrēðles eafora   hioro-dryncum swealt,
bille gebēaten.
(2345–59a). (Emphasis added).

[The protector of rings *proudly scorned that he should seek out that far-flyer with a troop, a large army*; he did not fear *that feud*, nor did the serpent's war concern him at all, its strength and courage, because he had previously survived many battles, escaping with his life, in the clashing of war, after he, the victory-rejoicing man, had cleansed Hrothgar's hall, and in battle crushed Grendel's kin, hateful race.

Nor was that the least of hand-to-hand battles when men killed Hygelac, after the king of the Geats, in the rush of war, the lord of the people, Hrethel's heir, perished with the blood of battle in Frisian lands, smashed by blades.]

---

[118] Fol. 179 is badly damaged, with the result that the text is heavily reconstructed here. I follow the text and translation of K4.

The comparison with Hygelac's ill-fated raid on Frisia invites the audience to question the wisdom of the king's decision to take on this challenge alone, while the verb *ofer-hogode* raises the question of whether Beowulf has succumbed to the sin of pride (*ofer-hygd*, 1740b) about which Hrothgar had warned him.[119] However, with the hagiographical – and indeed Christological – model in mind, the poet is careful to demonstrate that the hero acts not only out of desire to obtain the dragon's treasure, and the glory that comes with it, but also as a king who selflessly lays down his life in defence of his people, instructing them to stay behind:[120]

> Gebīde gē on beorge   byrnum werede,
> secgas on searwum,   hwæðer sēl mæge
> æfter wæl-ræse   wunde gedȳgan
> uncer twēga.   Nis þæt ēower sīð,
> ne gemet mannes   nefne mīn ānes,
> þæt hē wið āglǣcean   eofoðo dǣle,
> eorlscype efne.   Ic mid elne sceall
> gold gegangan,   oððe gūð nimeð,
> feorh-bealu frēcne   frēan ēowerne.
> (2529–37).

[You wait on the barrow, wearing mail-coats, warriors in armour, to see which of the two of us will better bear wounds after the slaughter-rush. That is not your journey, nor fitting for any man except me alone, that he should try his strength against that awe-inspiring one, perform a noble deed. I must win gold through glory, or battle will take your lord, terrible life-affliction.]

A further connection between the Swedish wars and the hero's last battle is provided by the revelation that the sword which Wiglaf carries to Beowulf's aid was *Ēanmundes lāf*, 'Eanmund's heirloom' (2611b), before it was given to Wiglaf's father, Weohstan, as a reward for killing the exiled Swedish prince (2610–25). Later Wiglaf will use this same sword to inflict a mortal wound on the dragon (2694–2702a). Bonjour proposes that this sword might later have served a similarly pivotal role in the Swedish wars as the sword that Beowulf predicts will reignite the feud between the Danes and Heathobards (2032–56), while R. E. Kaske argues that the narrator relates the sword's ancestry to provide an example of good retainership through the figure of Weohstan, emulated by the

---

[119] For Hrothgar's earlier warning to Beowulf against the sin of pride, see Chapter Four, pp. 217–20. See further, Orchard, *Pride and Prodigies*; and *CCB*, pp. 260–61. For the Geats' judgement of Beowulf's character in his funeral-scene, see Chapter Four, pp. 227–31.

[120] Cf. Matt. 14.34: 'And he saith to them: My soul is sorrowful even unto death; stay you here, and watch.' For further Christological echoes, see Chapter Four, pp. 231–35.

exemplary loyalty of his son, Wiglaf, towards Beowulf.[121] I would suggest that another function of this sword is to provide a physical link between the two sides in the Geatish-Swedish wars and the antagonists of the dragon-fight: Weohstan, a Wægmunding warrior loyal to the Swedish king, Onela, used this sword to kill the exiled Swedish prince, Eanmund, who was under the protection of both the Geatish king, Heardred, and Beowulf, son of Ecgtheow, a Wægmunding who had himself endured a period of exile at the court of Hrothgar; now Weohstan's son, Wiglaf, will use the same sword to defend the dying Geatish king, Beowulf, against the dragon.

As the narrative draws to a close, the Geatish Messenger anticipates the destruction of the Geatish nation by the combined might of the Franks, Frisians, Merovingians and Swedes:

>   Nū ys lēodum wēn   2910
> orleg-hwīle,   syððan underne
> Froncum ond Frȳsum   fyll cyninges
> wīde weorðeð.
> [...]
>   Ūs wæs ā syððan   2920
> Merewīoingas   milts ungyfeðe.
> Nē ic te Swēo-ðēode   sibbe oððe trēowe
> wihte ne wēne
> [...]
> Þæt ys sīo fæhðo   ond se fēondscipe,
> wæl-nīð wera,   ðæs ðe ić wēn hafo,   3000
> þē ūs sēceað tō   Swēona lēoda,
> syððan hīe gefricgeað   frēan ūserne
> ealdorlēasne,   þone ðe ǣr gehēold
> wið hettendum   hord ond rīce
> æfter hæleða hryre,   hwate Scilfingas,[122]   3005
> folc-rēd fremede,   oððe furður ġēn
> eorlscipe efnde.
> (2910b–13a, 2920b–23a, 2999–3007a).

[Now is the expectation for the people of a time of hardship, once the fall of the king is clearly made known to the Franks and Frisians. [...] Ever since that (i.e. Hygelac's raid) the mercy of the Merovingian was never shown to us. Nor do I expect truce or peace at all from the Swedish people. [...] That is the feud and enmity, deadly slaughter of men, that I expect to befall us, when the Swedish people seek us out, once they discover that our lord is

---

[121] Bonjour, *Digressions*, pp. 37–39; R. E. Kaske, 'Weohstan's Sword', *MLN* 75 (1960) 465–68. See further above, pp. 98–102.

[122] MS *Scyldingas* is usually emended to *Scilfingas*: see K4, p. 262; Neidorf, *Transmission*, pp. 83–84.

lifeless, he who before protected the hoard and kingdom against enemies, after the fall of warriors, the proud Scylfings, acted for the people's benefit, and furthermore performed noble deeds.]

The accuracy of the Messenger's prophecy is confirmed by the narrator, who prefaces this speech with the statement that *hē sōðlīce sægde ofer ealle*, 'he spoke truthfully above everyone' (2899), and finds an echo in the lament of the unnamed *Gēatisc meowle*, who similarly expresses her fear of *wæl-fylla worn, werudes egesan*, 'a great many slaughters, terror of troops' (3154). These two prophetic passages underline the dragon's role as a portent of dynastic and national disaster.

The equivalence of Beowulf and the dragon, twin symbols of entropy, culminates in the scene inside the barrow that immediately follows the Messenger's prophecy. Having set out to recover their king's corpse, the Geatish search-party finds instead the bodies of both Beowulf and the dragon, lying side-by-side:

> Fundon ðā on sande   sāwullēasne
> hlimbed healdan   þone þe him hringas geaf
> ǣrran mǣlum;   *þā wæs ende-dæg*   3035
> *gōdum gegongen*,   þæt se gūð-cyning,
> Wedra þēoden   *wundor-dēaðe swealt*.
> Ǣr hī þǣr gesēgan   syllicran wiht,
> wyrm on wonge   wiðer-ræhtes þǣr
> lāðne licgean;   wæs se lēg-draca   3040
> grimlic gryre-fāh   glēdum beswǣled;
> sē wæs fīftiges   fōt-gemearces
> lang on legere;   lyft-wynne hēold
> nihtes hwīlum,   *nyðer eft gewāt*
> *dennes niosian*;   wæs ðā dēaðe fæst,   3045
> hæfde eorð-scrafa   ende genyttod.
> (3033–46). (Emphasis added).

[They found then on the sand the soulless body laid out to rest, the one that had given them rings on previous occasions; *then the end of days had come to pass for the good one*, when the war-king, prince of the Weders, *died a wondrous death*. Before that they saw a more marvellous creature, a loathsome serpent lying on the ground there across from him; the fire-dragon was grimly stained with gore, burned by flames; he was fifty feet long, stretched out; once he had enjoyed flying at night, *and afterwards he went down to seek out his den*; he was secure in death, he had reached the end of his earth-cave dwelling.]

The parallel 'wondrous deaths' of Beowulf and the dragon serve as a powerful symbol of the rapidly approaching climax of the Swedish wars: the anticipated invasion and conquest of the lordless Geats by their powerful neighbours to the north and south. In a recent article, Eric Stanley favours translating *wundor-dēað* along the lines of Thorkelin (*portentosa morte obierat*, 'perished by a monstrous death/by death against a monstrous being') and Grundtvig (*Under-Værk*, 'wonder + work; pain suffering'), rather than Kemble's 'wondrous death', on the grounds that 'Beowulf's death was cruel, atrocious, horrendous: a horrid event for him and for his people' (345).[123] However, as we have seen, Hrothgar uses the term *wundor* in the sense of 'awe' at the beginning of his 'sermon', when describing the manner in which God sometimes grants royal power to a young warrior (1724b: *Wundor is tō secganne*, 'It is a wonder to relate'). Indeed, I would suggest that by using this compound *wundor-dēað* to describe Beowulf's demise, the poet sought to convey to his audience that the removal of royal power – and resultant collapse of a nation – is an equally wondrous and awe-inspiring event, to the divine gift of a dynasty with which the poem opened.[124] As the numerous allusions to the Swedish wars that intersperse the narration of the dragon-fight have persistently hinted, and as the Messenger's prophecy soon makes plain, the wondrous deaths of these two *āglǣcan*, 'awe-inspiring ones', serve as a portent to the larger tragedy of the fall of the Geatish nation.

Conclusion

This chapter has argued that all three of the monsters are themselves conceived in royal terms and play a central role in the dynastic drama: Grendel's 'rule' in Heorot can be understood as an attempted usurpation by an illegitimate contender from outside the royal kin; Grendel's avenging mother serves as an anti-type to the poem's various royal women who work to ensure the survival of royal families; and the dragon, in defending its hoard and destroying the royal seat of the Hrethlings, symbolizes the complexities of cross-generational dynastic feuding between the Geats and the Swedes. In the final section of the dynastic drama, the poet skilfully weaves together the central fable of the struggle between men and monsters with a deeper and more troubling narrative concerning the intertwined fates of royal families and nations. All three monsters serve as portents of dynastic and national crises, stories already well-known to the audience, that will take place 'off-stage': the feud between the Scyldings and the Heathobards and the strife between the grandsons of Healfdene; the fall of the Geats after the collapse of their ruling house.

---

[123] E. G. Stanley, 'Beowulf's *Wundordeað*', NQ 63 (2016), 343–45.
[124] Stanley has repeatedly emphasized the importance of wonder in Old English poetry: see *In the Foreground*, pp. 244–46; and 'Wonder-Smiths and Others: *smið* Compounds in Old English Poetry – With an Excursus on *hleahtor*', *Neophilologus* 101 (2017), 277–304.

By inserting these three monsters into two carefully-chosen moments of northern royal history, the poet brought these dynastic crises vividly and terrifyingly to life. The next chapter will consider how the poet drew on biblical paradigms of kingship in order to align his account of the fortunes of pre-Christian rulers with the narrative of salvation history.

4

Beowulf and Biblical Kingship

It is no longer in doubt that *Beowulf* is a thoroughly Christian poem, informed by a knowledge of both the Old and New Testaments.[1] Yet, the relevance of Christian themes to the poem's meaning remains a matter of considerable debate. Reading *Beowulf* as a Christian allegory in which the hero is brought down by avarice or pride is no longer in fashion,[2] and investigations of the poet's use of certain biblical paradigms, in particular stories from the Old Testament, have proved a more fruitful line of inquiry.[3] Marijane Osborn has analyzed how the poet uses the tradition of the war between God and the giants as a mythical context for the hero's monster-fights.[4] Robert E. Kaske, Ruth Mellinkoff, O. F. Emerson and others have examined connections between Grendel's descent from Cain and traditions of the pre- and post-diluvian giants.[5] Nicholas Howe has argued for the relevance of the Exodus story to the poem's presentation of pre-migratory Germanic peoples,[6] while Daniel Anlezark has argued that the organizing principle of the poem's structure is the Christian tradition of two great floods, the first being Noah's watery flood, the second the

---

[1] For useful overviews of the debate, see Irving, 'Christian and Pagan Elements'; and Cavill, 'Christianity and Theology in *Beowulf*'.
[2] Perhaps the most sustained attempt to read *Beowulf* as a Christian allegory is Goldsmith's *Mode and Meaning*. Assuming the poet's knowledge of Sulpicius Severus's *Vita S. Martini*, Goldsmith argues that the hero is brought down by cupidity in his pursuit of gold (see esp. pp. 65–96). Goldsmith's approach is informed by D. W. Robertson Jr.'s arguments for the pervasiveness of Augustinian doctrine on medieval thought: *A Preface to Chaucer: Studies in Medieval Perspectives* (Princeton, 1962). For criticism of the application of this approach to *Beowulf*, see E. John, '*Beowulf* and the Margins of Literacy', *Bulletin of the John Rylands University Library* (1974), 388–422, repr. in Baker (1995), pp. 51–77, at 56–57.
[3] For a recent study, see L. Besserman, *Biblical Paradigms in Medieval English Literature* (New York, 2012), esp. p. 18. See further Godden, 'Old Testament', p. 223; *CCB*, pp. 137–49.
[4] Osborn, 'The Great Feud'.
[5] Kaske, '*Beowulf* and the Book of Enoch'; Mellinkoff, 'Cain's monstrous progeny in *Beowulf*: part I'; Mellinkoff, 'Cain's monstrous progeny in *Beowulf*: part II'; O. F. Emerson, 'Legends of Cain, especially in Old and Middle English', *PMLA* 21 (1906), 831–929, at 879–916; N. Peltola, 'Grendel's Descent from Cain Reconsidered', *NM* 73 (1972), 284–91; Williams, *Cain and Beowulf*; Niles, *Beowulf*, pp. 66–95 and 181–82; Orchard, *Pride and Prodigies*, pp. 58–85; *CCB*, pp. 130–68.
[6] Howe, *Migration and Mythmaking*.

fiery conflagration of the Last Judgement.⁷ Most recently, Tristan Major has explored the poet's engagement with the story of Babel.⁸ In the previous chapter, I proposed that the Fall of the Angels provides a typological link between Beowulf's first and last great adversaries, Grendel and the dragon.⁹ Others have noted parallels between the hero and various Old Testament figures, including Moses, Samson, Judas Maccabeus and David.¹⁰ Fred C. Robinson has noted the presence of a 'double perspective' whereby the narrator and his audience understand events in the light of revealed Christianity but the pagan characters lack this insight.¹¹ Through comparison with early Irish material, Charles Donahue has suggested that the poet presents good pagan kings such as Hrothgar as noble monotheists, equivalent to the patriarchs, Abraham, Isaac and Jacob, who lived under the 'natural law' and could therefore be saved.¹²

Despite the prevalence of Old Testament themes, Paul Cavill has argued persuasively for the orthodox nature of the poet's Christianity and the pervasive influence of New Testament theology on the work more generally, as revealed, for example, in the various references to Judgement.¹³ Indeed, as Eric Auerbach explains, in the Middle Ages the Bible was understood even by laymen as a series of *figurae*, with events in the Old Testament typologically foreshadowing the New Testament: the figurative imagination sees all events in terms of the sequence Creation—Fall—Redemption—Last Judgement.¹⁴ This figurative understanding of scripture was instilled in the minds of medieval Christians through the

---

[7] Anlezark, *Water and Fire*, pp. 291–67.
[8] Major, *Undoing Babel*, pp. 209–10, 239–44.
[9] See above, pp. 58–59, 162–76 and 180–93.
[10] Wieland, '*Manna mildost*'; M. E. Goldsmith, 'The Christian Theme in *Beowulf*', *MÆ* 29 (1960), 81–101, at 81; Horowitz, 'Beowulf, Samson, David and Christ'; Getz, cited in *CCB*, pp. 142–47.
[11] Robinson, '*Beowulf*', p. 149.
[12] Donahue, '*Beowulf*, Ireland and the Natural Good'. See also Tolkien, 'Commentary', p. 160; Bloomfield, 'Patristics and Old English Literature'; B. S. Cox, 'Heaven for Heathens: Old Testament Christianity in *Beowulf*, in Cox (1971), pp. 12–32; T. D. Hill, 'The Christian Language and Theme of *Beowulf*', in Aertsen and Bremmer (1994), pp. 63–77; C. M. Cain, '*Beowulf*, the Old Testament, and the "Regula Fidei"', *Renascene: Essays on Value in Literature*, 49 (1997), 227–40; and G. Russom, 'Historicity and Anachronism in *Beowulf*', in *Epic and History*, ed. D. Konstan and K. A. Raaflaub (Chichester, 2010), pp. 243–61, at 244, 257.
[13] Cavill, 'Christianity and Theology in *Beowulf*', p. 38. See below, pp. 231–34, for Christological echoes.
[14] E. Auerbach, 'Typological Symbolism in Medieval Literature', *Yale French Studies* 9 (1952), 3–10. Auerbach explains that whereas in the allegorical or symbolic mode at least one element is a 'pure sign', in the figurative mode both signifier and signified are real facts or events.

liturgy, broadly conceived, and visual culture, such as church carvings, as well as the more rarefied pursuit of the study of books.[15]

The Bible provided a wellspring of new ideas about kingship and dynasty for early medieval Christians, not least the Anglo-Saxons. The four Books of Kings (= 1–2 Samuel, 1–2 Kings), and the supplementary material in 1–2 Paralipomenon (= 1–2 Chronicles), chart the introduction, development and eventual demise of dynastic kingship among the tribes of Israel and Judah.[16] In particular, the first three kings of Israel, Saul, David and Solomon, served as archetypes of medieval kingship. Saul typifies the warrior king, whereas David is chosen as king not for his countenance, height or stature but for his heart (1 Kings 16:7), and sets a standard of mildness and clemency against which all subsequent biblical kings are judged. In addition to his unparalleled success in war and acquisition of tribute from neighbouring rulers (3 Kings 4:21), Solomon receives the gift of wisdom from God (3 Kings 3:28).[17] David and Solomon were routinely identified figuratively as types of Christ, the King of Kings, while the everlasting dynasty promised to David was interpreted by the Church Fathers as the eternal kingdom won for humankind by Christ's sacrifice.[18] As Patrick Wormald notes, this narrative 'would have been familiar for anyone exposed to basic Judeo-Christian teaching' in the early medieval period.[19] Under the influence of this biblical model, medieval kings eventually came to see themselves not simply as war leaders but also as moral shepherds of their peoples. Despite the general recognition that *Beowulf* is a Christian poem that engages deeply with Old Testament themes, scholars have yet to explore in any detail the possibility that the poem's presentation of early Scandinavian kingship might be shaped by the biblical succession narrative. This chapter therefore assesses the evidence for the impact of biblical paradigms of kingship and dynasty on *Beowulf*. Part of the reason for this hesitancy to connect *Beowulf* and the Books of Kings is that, unlike the various allusions to Genesis, it has not been possible to establish a concrete textual link. Nowhere does the poet directly compare a Scandinavian pagan king to an Old Testament ruler in the way he connects Grendel with Cain, for example. However, this chapter

---

[15] On the importance of church carvings as a source of biblical iconography, see P. Portnoy, 'Verbal Seascapes in Anglo-Saxon Verse', in *The Maritime World of the Anglo-Saxons*, Medieval and Renaissance Texts and Studies 448, Essays in Anglo-Saxon Studies 5, ed. S. Klein, W. Schipper and S. Lewis-Simpson (Tempe, AZ, 2014), pp. 247–73.

[16] See A. E. Cundall, 'Sacral Kingship – the Old Testament Background', *Vox Evangelica* 6 (1969), 31–41, at 34.

[17] Cf. Proverbs 16:12: 'They that act wickedly are abhorrent to the king: for the throne is established by justice.'

[18] See below, pp. 222–23.

[19] Wormald, 'Kings and Kingship', p. 571.

aims to demonstrate that the cumulative force of what might otherwise be seen to simply share commonplaces between these texts is more likely to be the product of a shared cultural milieu in which all earthly kingship was understood in terms of the narrative of salvation history. Like other thinkers of his age such as Bede and Gregory of Tours, the *Beowulf*-poet, this chapter argues, understood earthly kingship through the lens of the Bible, in which Old-Testament rulers serve as figures of Christ, the King of Kings. The chapter begins by highlighting the profound impact of the biblical succession narrative on the development of dynastic kingship in the medieval West. The following section outlines some parallels and differences between Beowulfian and biblical kingship, before comparing the *Beowulf*-poet's vision of monarchy with that of the Venerable Bede.[20] The chapter concludes with a re-assessment of underlying Christological themes in the poem.

The Influence of Biblical Kingship in the Medieval West

The Israelite monarchy lasted some four centuries, from the time of Saul (*c.* 1050 BC) to the Babylonian captivity (*c.* 587 BC).[21] Neighbouring regions such as Mesopotamia and Egypt regarded their rulers as guarantors of fertility, order and security, and in many cases treated them as a god or a representative of a deity on earth. In Hebraic tradition, by contrast, earthly rulers were expected to act not as gods themselves but as viceroys of Yahweh, who is himself commonly referred to as a lord or king (Hebrew מֶלֶךְ, 'melek'; Greek βασιλέα, 'basileus'; Lat. 'dominus', 'rex').[22] The messianic theme is introduced at the beginning of the biblical succession narrative with the Song of Hannah:[23]

> arcus fortium superatus est
> et infirmi accincti sunt robore [...]
> Dominus mortificat et vivificat
> deducit ad infernum et reducit
> Dominus pauperem facit et ditat
> humiliat et sublevat
> suscitat de pulvere egenum et de stercore elevat pauperem
> ut sedeat cum principibus et solium gloriae teneat

---

[20] As Bonjour stresses, an investigation of the relationship between any given work and a putative source or analogue should pay as much attention to differences as it does to parallels: '*Beowulf* et le démon de l'analogie', first printed in Bonjour (1962), pp. 173–89, at 189.

[21] See K. W. Whitelam, 'Kings and Kingship', in *The Anchor Bible Dictionary*, 6 vols, ed. D. N. Freedman *et al.* (New York, 1992), IV, pp. 40–48.

[22] For example, Num. 23:21; Judg. 8:23. See Cundall, 'Sacral Kingship'.

[23] See below, pp. 231–34, for hints of messianic kingship in *Beowulf*.

> Domini enim sunt cardines terrae et posuit super eos orbem [...]
> Dominum formidabunt adversarii eius super ipsos in caelis tonabit
> Dominus iudicabit fines terrae et dabit imperium regi suo
> et sublimabit cornu christi sui [...].
> (1 Kings 2:4, 6–8, 10).

> [The bow of the mighty is overcome, and the weak are girt with strength. [...] The Lord killeth and maketh alive, he bringeth down to hell and bringeth back again. The Lord maketh poor and maketh rich, he humbleth and he exalteth. He raiseth up the poor from the dust, and lifteth up the poor from the dunghill: that he may sit with princes, and hold the throne of glory. For the poles of the earth are the Lord's, and upon them he hath set the world. [...] The adversaries of the Lord shall fear him: and upon them shall he thunder in the heavens. The Lord shall judge the ends of the earth, and he shall give empire to his king, and shall exalt the horn of his Christ.][24]

For the Church Fathers, the 'judgement of the Lord' was taken to signify the Second Coming or the return of God to heaven, while the granting of the empire to the king prefigured the eternal kingdom of Christ.[25] As John Chrysostom explains, the purpose of Hannah's exaltation of the Lord is to throw into relief the transience of earthly glories:

> Hence the exaltation is secure, having a firm and permanent root: while glory from human beings corresponds to the baseness of those glorifying, and so is liable to disappear, God's glory is not like that, remaining forever permanent. (John Chrysostom, *Homilies on Hannah* 4).[26]

In biblical tradition, earthly kingdoms are thus to be understood as imperfect types of the eternal glory of the heavenly kingdom, while even the best of the kings of Israel, David and Solomon, are shown to be imperfect types of Christ.

While modern biblical scholarship has identified certain elements of the succession narrative as anti-monarchical,[27] the medieval Church used 1–4 Kings extensively in its efforts to reform barbarian kingship and bring it into line with Christian moral standards. In the tradition of patristic

---

[24] The interpretation of the phrase 'the horn of his Christ' considerably exercised the Church Fathers. See, for example, *Bedae Venerabilis Opera*, Pars II, Opera Exegetica 2, *In Primam Partem Samuhellis Libri IIII; In Regum Librum XXX Quaestiones*, ed. D. Hurst, CCSL 119, p. 25.

[25] Eusebius of Caesaria, *Proof of the Gospel* 1.4.16; Augustine, *City of God* 17.4. See Franke *et al.*, pp. 202–04.

[26] Franke *et al.*, p. 203. For the Greek text, see *PG* 64, cols 675–708. For evidence of the circulation of Chrysostom's writings in Anglo-Saxon England, see 'John Chrysostom', in *Sources of Anglo-Saxon Literary Culture. Volume 5: Julius Caesar to Pseudo-Cyril of Alexandria*, ed. T. N. Hall (Kalamazoo, MI, forthcoming).

[27] See D. M. Howard, Jr., 'The Case for Kingship in the Old Testament Narrative Books and the Psalms', *Trinity Journal* 9 (1988), 19–35.

exegesis inherited by the Anglo-Saxons, the Old Testament demonstrates that kings who follow God's commandments will tend to enjoy His favour while those who disobey stand to lose their authority and incur divine retribution on themselves and their people. Hence Isidore of Seville writes, 'You will be a king (*rex*) if you act rightly (*recte*), if you do not, you will not be' (*Etymologies* IX.iii.4),[28] while Gregory the Great explains how 'the merits of rulers and people are so mutually connected that frequently the conduct of the people is made worse from the fault of their pastors and the conduct of pastors is changed according to the merits of their people' (*Morals on the Book of Job* 25.16).[29] Gregory in particular viewed kingship as both a spiritual and earthly office, identifying David and Solomon and models of the ideal Christian ruler who is not only victorious in war but also a *rector*, 'teacher', who sets a standard of wisdom, justice and clemency for his subjects.

The origins of early medieval dynastic kingship, such as we find described in *Beowulf*, can be traced to the great Christian dynasties of early Byzantium. Although there was no clear constitutional position on hereditary succession until as late as the eleventh century, Byzantine emperors vigorously promoted the dynastic principle and typically crowned their sons to ensure their succession. Royal marriages became increasingly important as a means of producing legitimate heirs and the practice of primogeniture had become common by the time of the Isaurian dynasty (717–812). Nevertheless, the threat of usurpation remained, and some Byzantine dynasties lasted no more than two or three generations.

The eastern empire also took the lead in forging a new, theocratic model of power. In temporal terms, the authority of the *basileus* was still firmly invested in his martial success, but imperial office eventually came to be equated with priestly and apostolic authority. Constantine and his descendants saw themselves as ruling on behalf of God as the temporal and spiritual protectors of the people. Though still essentially warrior rulers, Byzantine emperors came to model themselves on David and Solomon as well as Melchizedeck, the priest-king of Genesis 14:18–20, taking an active role in church affairs, caring for the poor and cultivating the love of wisdom.[30] For Eusebius, Constantine was an 'interpreter of

---

[28] Barney et al., p. 200. Cf. J. Canning, *A History of Medieval Political Thought 300–1450* (London, 1996), p. 20.

[29] *Ancient Christian Commentary on Scripture: Joshua, Judges, Ruth, 1–2 Samuel*, Old Testament IV, ed. J. R. Franke et al. (Downers Grove, IL, 2005), p. 397. For evidence of the wide circulation of Gregory's *Morals on Job* and Isidore's *Etymologies* in Anglo-Saxon England, see M. Lapidge, *The Anglo-Saxon Library* (Oxford, 2006), pp. 305–06, 311.

[30] See A. Louth, 'The Eastern Empire in the Sixth Century', in Fouracre (2005), pp. 93–117; Wormald, 'Kings and Kingship', pp. 576–80; Halsall, *Barbarian Migrations*, pp. 488–90; G. Dagron, *Emperor and Priest: The Imperial Office in*

the Word of God', responsible for directing his subjects to the heavenly kingdom.[31] As well as commissioning the construction of the Church of Holy Wisdom, Hagia Sophia, and reconquering Roman territories in the West, Justinian I (r. 527–65) issued coins with the image of the emperor on the reverse and Christ on the obverse and produced a monumental law code that sought to homogenize Roman law and presented the emperor as a Solomonic legislator. The so-called 'David plates', depicting scenes from David's accession based on 1 Kings 16–18, were probably commissioned by Heraclius (r. 610–41), consolidating the emperor's image as a 'new David' after his victory over the Persians.[32]

In the late Roman West, by contrast, imperial power had effectively been transferred into the hands of the army. By the late-fourth century, the emperor was usually a general elected (and often executed) by the army on account of his military capabilities, rather than his lineage.[33] Eugenius (392–94), himself elected by the Frankish Master of the Soldiers, Arbogast, was deposed by the eastern emperor, Theodosius, in 394, and subsequent Roman 'emperors' were often child rulers or puppets of barbarian masters.[34] In 476, the barbarian chieftain Odovacer deposed the last child emperor, Romulus Augustus, and declared himself King of Italy. Post-imperial Germanic rulers such as Theoderic, however, were alert to the advantages of adopting the triumphal militaristic style of their Roman predecessors.[35] Moreover, as Ian Wood notes, on entering into the empire, the powerful families of the leading Germanic tribes set about 'stressing their earlier royal pre-eminence'.[36] One way in which this was achieved was through the invention of elaborate royal genealogies, tracing a ruler's ancestry back to divine or semi-divine progenitors via

---

Byzantium, trans. J. Birrell (Cambridge, 2003), esp. pp. 13–53; and C. Rapp, 'Old Testament Models for Emperors in Byzantium', in *The Old Testament in Byzantium*, ed. P. Magdalino and R. S. Nelson (Harvard, 2010), pp. 175–98. For the association of Melchizedeck and David, see Ps. 110.4.

[31] Eusebius Pamphilus, 'The Oration of Eusebius Pamphilus in Praise of the Emperor Constantine, Pronounced on the Thirtieth Anniversary of his Reign', I.4, in *Nicene and Post-Nicene Fathers*, Series II, Vol. 1, ed. and trans. P. Schaff (New York, 1890), p. 583. For the Greek text, see *PG* 20, cols 1315–1438.

[32] As argued by S. S. Alexander, 'Heraclius, Byzantine Imperial Ideology, and the David Plates', Speculum 52 (1977), 217–37. Heraclius was first to formally adopt the Greek title *basileus* in place of the Latin *imperator*.

[33] Diocletian, himself elected by the army in 284, instituted the system of tetrarchy, involving two senior rulers termed 'augustus' and two junior 'caesars' who, in theory, were to be promoted on the death of an 'augustus'. See R. Gerberding, 'The Later Roman Empire', in Fouracre (2005), pp. 13–34.

[34] Gerberding, p. 25.

[35] See M. McCormick, *Eternal Victory: Triumphal Rulership in Late Antiquity, Byzantium and the Early Medieval West* (Cambridge, 1986); Halsall, *Barbarian Migrations*, p. 290.

[36] Wood, 'Kings, Kingdoms and Consent', p. 8.

generations of legendary heroes and kings. These documents are clearly literary fictions inspired by biblical models and cannot be taken at face-value as reliable evidence for the antiquity of Germanic ruling dynasties in the pre-migratory period.[37] Indeed, there is in fact no evidence for a cult of royal genealogy among the Germanic peoples before the sixth century.[38] Claiming descent from a long line of illustrious, royal ancestors enabled barbarian kings to style themselves as the scions of ancient dynasties rather than as merely the aristocratic leaders of war-bands.[39] Royal genealogies also played an important role in ethnogenesis in this period, providing a point of geographical and temporal origin for an emerging *gens*, 'people', centred on the *cyning*. Hence Jordanes traced the origin of the Gothic peoples back to the emergence of King Berig from the Scandinavian island of Scandza, a 'womb of nations' (*Getica*, IV.25), while Paul the Deacon states that the Lombards were descended from Ibor and Aio, who came from an island which he calls 'Scadinavia' and opposed the aggression of the Vandal kings Ambri and Assi.[40] Jordanes also provides a long, Old Testament-style genealogy for the Amalings, from whose house sprang the Ostrogothic rulers of Italy, Theoderic and his grandson Athalaric (*Getica*, XIII.78–IX.81), tracing their descent from generations of 'heroes', among them *Ermanaricus* (OE *Eormenric*)[41] and the progenitor Gapt (from proto. Germ. **Gautaz*), a Scandinavian war god who features in the royal genealogies of the Anglo-Saxons (OE *Geat*) and

---

[37] The Anglo-Saxon royal genealogies in the Anglian Collection, for example, follow the fourteen-generation model of Mat. 1:12–17. See Dumville, 'Kingship, Genealogies and Regnal Lists', pp. 90–96. Dumville makes an important distinction between the genealogy, essentially an ideological statement, and the regnal list, a more factual statement of succession, often including the length of kings' reigns. On King Æthelwulf's genealogy and its links with *Beowulf*, see above, pp. 143–45, and below, pp. 240–41.

[38] Dumville, 'Kingship, Genealogies and Regnal Lists', p. 96. Studies have confirmed that expansive genealogies are a product of the transition from orality to literacy such as we witness among the Germanic peoples in the early medieval period: see, for example, W. J. Ong, *Orality and Literacy: The Technologizing of the Word* (London and New York, 1982), pp. 66–67; D. E. Thornton, 'Orality, literacy and genealogy in early medieval Ireland and Wales', in *Literacy in Medieval Celtic Societies*, ed. H. Pryce (Cambridge, 1998), pp. 83–98, at 89; and H. Kennedy, 'From Oral Tradition to Written Record in Arabic Genealogy', *Arabica: Journal of Arabic and Islamic Studies* 44 (1997), 531–44, at 532.

[39] See P. Heather, 'Cassiodorus and the Rise of the Amals: Genealogy and the Goths under Hun Domination', *Journal of Roman Studies* 78 (1989), 103–28.

[40] Foulke, I.7, pp. 11–15. *Beowulf* locates the origin of the Scyldings in the same region, a tradition that seems to have been incorporated into the West Saxon royal genealogy in the ninth and tenth centuries.

[41] Eormanric is mentioned in *Beowulf* (2001a), *Widsith* (7–9a) and *Deor* (21–23).

other Germanic peoples.[42] Through this genealogy, Jordanes effectively claims that the Amalings had ruled the Goths for centuries.[43]

The Anglo-Saxons also devised impressive-looking royal pedigrees to elevate the prestige of their ruling dynasties. In most cases, these documents trace the origins of a royal house to Woden via legendary founder figures such as Hengest and Horsa (for Kent) and Cerdic and Cynric (for Wessex).[44] By the late ninth-century, the West Saxons had extended the list of their ancestors beyond Woden to incorporate a multitude of legendary Scandinavian kings, among them figures such as Heremod, Scyld, Scef and Beow, before ultimately merging their pedigree with the biblical line of Noah, Adam and Christ.[45] In the Conclusion, I consider how *Beowulf* itself may have served as an inspiration for the extension of the West Saxon royal pedigree and the transformation of the Danish royal foundling, Scyld Scefing/Scef, into the ark-born son of Noah.[46]

The Merovingians and the Cult of Royal Blood

The first great Christian dynasty to emerge in the post-Roman West was that of the Merovingians. In his sixth-century *History of the Franks*, Gregory of Tours (d. 594) describes how this family of Austrasian Franks, led by Clodio and his descendants, Childeric, Clovis and Merovech (d. c. 456), from whom the dynasty took its name, had brought most of the former Roman province of Gaul under their control by the turn of the sixth century. A century later, they had extended their influence further south into Visigothic Spain and Ostrogothic Italy, east into Swabia,

---

[42] See H. Moisl, 'Anglo-Saxon Royal Genealogies and Germanic Oral Tradition', *Journal of Medieval History* 7 (1981), 215–48, at 219–22. See also Sisam, 'Genealogies', pp. 313–14; Faulkes, 'Descent from the gods', 93; North, *Heathen Gods*, pp. 133–35. *Gaut* is also one of the many names for Odin in the Norse sagas. In several annotations to the Anglo-Saxon royal genealogies, *Geat* or *Geot* is mentioned as a cult figure whom the heathens worshipped as a god. North, *Heathen Gods*, p. 134, suggests that Geot/Geata is derived from the OE verb *geotan*, 'to pour' or 'to cut open', which may indicate an association of the name with religious sacrifice. The West Saxon genealogy for Æthewulf in the *ASC* has *Geat* as the 'father' of Godwulf, 'son' of Tætwa. Geat is also included at the head of the genealogy for the Northumbrian king Ida in *ASC* s. a. 547, *ibid.* p. 16. The genealogy for the Lindsey kings contained in MS Vespasian B VI, ff. 104–09 ends with Geat.
[43] The Ostrogothic kingdom came to an end shortly after the completion of the *Getica* with defeat by the eastern emperor, Justinian I, in 553.
[44] On the Indo-European myth of the 'divine twins', see Ward, *Divine Twins*; Meletinsky, *Poetics of Myth*, p. 471; Newton, *Origins*, pp. 79–80. See further p. 146.
[45] See pp. 143–45.
[46] See Conclusion, pp. 240–41.

Thuringia and Bavaria, and north into Frisia, encountering resistance from Saxons and Danes. The rise of the Merovingians contributed to the break-up of the Saxon confederation and the subsequent migration of continental Saxons and others to Britain. These migrating Saxons may have carried with them to Britain legends of a Scandinavian king who dared to challenge the might of the Merovingians, Hygelac, whose defeat by Theudebert, son of Theuderic (r. 511–c. 533), is recorded by Gregory, as we saw in Chapter Two.[47] Indeed, the extent of Merovingian power in this period is hinted at in *Beowulf* itself, with the Messenger's observation that since Hygelac's ill-fated raid on Frankish territory the Geats have never experienced *Merewīoingas milts*, 'the mercy of the Merovingians' (2921).[48]

Following the conversion of Clovis *c.* 486, and his baptism by Remigius in 508, Merovingian rulers vigorously promoted Christianity, founding monasteries and working closely with increasingly powerful bishops. These developments were in part due to the efforts of influential clerical writers such as Gregory of Tours and Venantius Fortunatus (d. *c.* 600), both bishops with close connections to the royal court, who drew on the Old Testament paradigms of David and Solomon to praise or chastise Merovingian kings.[49] As Raymond Van Dam observes, the tension between the Germanic warrior ethos and new Christian standards of rule was resolved through the Byzantine model of the emperor (*basileus*), 'who combined the Christian faith with an ideology of military victory.'[50] Hence Gregory describes Clovis as a 'new Constantine' during the description of his baptism (*Hist.* II.31), while praising Theudebert, who repelled the raid of Chlochilaich (OE Hygelac), for his justice, generosity and piety:

---

[47] See above, pp. 121–22.

[48] The meaningless MS reading *mere wio ingasmilts* is conventionally emended to *merewioingas milts*; for alternative emendations, such as *merewicingas*, see K4, pp. 99, 259–60. See further Neidorf, *Transmission*, pp. 88–91; Thomson, *Communal Creativity*, pp. 34–35, 218. This reference to the Merovingians as a feared dynasty has been considered by some as an indication of a date of composition before 751, when the Merovingians were replaced by the Carolingians and their memory expunged from history. See, for example, L. E. Wright, '*Merewioingas* and the Dating of *Beowulf*: A Reconsideration', *Nottingham Mediaeval Studies* 24 (1980), 1–6; Goffart, 'Datable Anachronisms', p. 88; T. Shippey, 'The Merov(ich)ingian again: *damnatio memoriae* and the *usus scholarum*', in *Latin Learning and English Lore: Studies in Anglo-Saxon Literature for Michael Lapidge*, 2 vols, ed. K. O'Brien O'Keeffe and A. Orchard (Toronto, 2005), I, pp. 389–406; and W. Goffart, 'The Name "Merovingian" and the Dating of *Beowulf*', *ASE* 36 (2007), 93–101.

[49] For the circulation of Venantius in Anglo-Saxon England, see R. W. Hunt, 'Manuscript evidence for knowledge of the poems of Venantius Fortunatus in late Anglo-Saxon England', *ASE* 8 (1979), 279–95.

[50] R. Van Dam, 'Merovingian Gaul and the Frankish Conquests', in Fouracre (2005), pp. 193–231, at 207.

At ille in regno firmatus, magnum se atque in omni bonitate praecipuum reddidit. Erat enim regnum cum iustitia regens, sacerdotes venerans, eclesias munerans, pauperes relevans et multa multis beneficia pia ac dulcissima accommodans voluntate. Omne tributo, quod in fisco suo ab eclesiis in Arvernum sitis reddebebatur, clementer indulsit. (*Hist.* III.25).

[Once he was firmly established on the throne, he proved himself great, distinguished by every virtue. He ruled his kingdom with justice, respecting his bishops, making gifts to the churches, relieving the poor and distributing many benefits with piety and the friendliest goodwill. He generously remitted all the tribute which was payable to his treasury from the churches in Auvergne.][51]

As we shall see below, *Beowulf* presents a comparable synthesis of Germanic and Christian models of kingship, particularly in the ruler portraits of Hrothgar and Beowulf.[52]

Like the great Gothic dynasties, the Amalings and Baltings, the Merovingians initially ruled solely on account of their military victories, rather than their ancestry. Indeed, as Guy Halsall notes, the Merovingian royal house itself 'had no deep roots'.[53] However, with the expansion of the Merovingian realm and the steady influx of tribute came an enhanced sense of kingly worth and an increasing obsession with royal blood. Ian Wood identifies the equal division of the Merovingian kingdom among Clovis's four sons after his death in 511 as a key moment in Frankish history, marking the emergence of a new type of Western hereditary kingship, part barbarian, part Roman, in which the kingdom was now thought of as the personal property of the ruling family.[54] Merovingian blood came to be symbolized by the conspicuous wearing of distinctively long hair and through the common Germanic practice of alliterative name-giving.[55] The dynasty also promoted a narrative of its antiquity through the fabrication of an elaborate royal genealogy.[56] While Gregory of Tours simply states, 'Some say that Merovech, the father of Childeric, was descended from Clodio',[57] the late-seventh-century Chronicle of Fredegar records that Clodio's wife was swimming in a river when she was impregnated by a

---

[51] MGH, *Scriptorum Rerum Merovingicarum* I, i, 123.
[52] See below, pp. 210–31.
[53] Halsall, *Barbarian Migrations*, p. 291.
[54] Wood, 'Kings, Kingship and Consent', pp. 26–27. On the prohibtion against Hrothgar controlling the *folc-scare*, see above, pp. 51–52.
[55] The names of most members of the Merovingian dynasty began with either *Ch–* or *Th–*.
[56] Seventh-century Merovingian royal genealogies and regnal lists are printed in *Rerum Merowingorum Genealogia*, MGH SS II. 1, ed. G. Pertz (1829), pp. 304–08.
[57] *Gregory of Tours: The History of the Franks*, trans. L. Thorpe (London, 1974), p. 125.

Minotaur-like creature.[58] The Merovingians' profound respect for royal blood, however, would ultimately prove self-defeating. So strong was their attachment to the dynastic principle that any male descendant of a Merovingian was technically eligible for the throne. Yet the absence of a restricting measure such as primogeniture meant that the succession was rarely smooth and a claimant needed the support of powerful magnates and, ideally, the incumbent ruler in order to guarantee his accession. A further complicating factor was the widespread practice of concubinage among the Merovingians, meaning that any number of princes, even those of dubious parentage, could seek election.[59] Chronic family feuding meant that by the eighth century a series of child-rulers and ineffective 'do-nothing kings' (*roi fainéants*) had gradually conceded power to the Mayors of the Palace, magnates who effectively carried out the duties of the kings but lacked the requisite royal blood. We find an analogous situation, of course, in *Beowulf*, in which the hero chooses to act as a protector to the child-king, Heardred, rather than disrupt the practice of patrilineal succession (2369–79a).[60] The influence of these magnates was so great that they themselves formed aristocratic, if not royal, dynasties such as the Pippinids, who had effectively gained control of Austrasia by the late-seventh century. This weakening of Merovingian authority culminated in 751 with the deposition of Childeric III by Pippin III on the grounds that he had no real 'kingly power' and was therefore not worthy of the name.[61]

In some ways, the Merovingians' strong attachment to the dynastic principle ran contrary to the practicalities of early medieval kingship, which was still essentially martial in character. But the achievements of this dynasty were remarkable, both in uniting the Frankish provinces under a single ruling family, and in forging a new Frankish ethnicity based on the common Christian faith which transcended ethnic differences. The legacy of the Merovingians was to ensure that subsequent rulers in the medieval West, among them the descendants of Charles Martel and Pippin, the Carolingians, would always seek to bolster their claim to royal legitimacy through familial ties, no matter how fictitious or

[58] Fredegar's Chronicle survives in an early-eighth-century copy by the monk Lucerius, MS Paris Bibliotheque Nationale Latin 10910, printed as *Fredegarii et aliorum chronica*, ed. B. Krusch, MGH script. rer. Merov. 2 (Hannover, 1888), II, Ch. III, 9. See J. M. Wallace-Hadrill, *The Long-Haired Kings* (Toronto, 1962; repr. 1989), pp. 68, 71–94, 158 and 221; Wallace-Hadrill, *Early Germanic Kingship*, pp. 17–19 and 51; Moisl, 'Anglo-Saxon royal genealogies', p. 224. For comparison with the mythical account of the foundation of a dynasty in the opening of *Beowulf*, see above, pp. 139–51.

[59] For example, the case of Gundovald, whose claims to be the son of Chlothar I were rejected by Childebert; see Wood, 'Kings, Kingship and Consent', p. 15.

[60] See above, pp. 19, 21, 91–92 and 133–34.

[61] See P. Fouracre, 'Francia in the seventh century', in Fouracre (2005), pp. 397–70.

fanciful. The *Beowulf*-poet's deep concern with royal blood, and the preservation of royal dynasties, should therefore be viewed within the context of these developments in post-Roman Europe. The events of 751 provide a useful window into the realities of royal succession: though in principle kingship should be restricted to those of the royal blood, election could override the dynastic principle if the heir was considered unsuitable. In other words, hereditary succession had become a model to be aspired to, though incessant warfare and the need for strong military leadership meant that at times a more pragmatic solution would prevail. The extent to which the dynastic principle had become intertwined with Germanic kingship is reflected by the fact that with Pippin's accession one dynasty simply replaced another: the Carolingians, like their Merovingian predecessors, similarly restricted the succession to their direct descendants. However, by the turn of the ninth century, barbarian kings had also come to style themselves as Christian emperors ruling 'by the grace of God'.

The Carolingians and Sacral Kingship

Ancestry combined with military success remained key factors in determining eligibility for kingship under the Carolingians. Within a decade or so of the deposition of Childeric, Paul the Deacon's *History of the Bishops of Metz* (c. 766) traced the origins of this new ruling dynasty back to St Arnulf of Metz, a Frankish bishop (d. 640) with close ties to the Merovingian court.[62] Following the coronation of Charlemagne as Holy Roman Emperor in 800, new Roman and Trojan ancestors were added to the royal pedigree, reflecting the ambitious and confident nature of Carolingian rule.[63] However, the Carolingians' major contribution to the development of early medieval kingship was the heightened emphasis on the king's role as a spiritual leader. Again, the inspiration was biblical, in particular the exemplary figures of David and Solomon. As Walter Ullmann comments, for the Carolingians, rulership 'was a gift from God, and no king should

---

[62] MGH SS. II. 3, *Domus Carolingicae Genalogia*, pp. 308–10. See further R. McKitterick, *Carolingian Culture: Emulation and Innovation* (Cambridge, 1993), p. 211.

[63] For example, a genealogy made for the Emperor Lothar I (d. 855) includes details of the migration of Priam and Antenor's descendants into the Germanic regions: *Priamus et Antenor egressi a Troia venerunt in Secambria, et inde in Pannonia, et inde in Meotides paludes, et inde iuxta ripas fluminis reni in extrema parte germaniae. Isti fuerunt princeps Marchomire et Sonone de genere Priami et Antenoris. Faromundus primus rex de ipso genere, et Clodio filius ipsius rex. Post Clodium Meroveus rex. Post Meroveum Hilderincus rex. [...] Pippinus [...] Carlomannus – Pippinus [...] Karolus Imperator [...] Ludovic – Karolus – Lodovicus – Lotharius* (MGH SS II. 3, *Domus Carolingicae Genalogia*, pp. 310–12).

therefore believe that his kingdom had come from his ancestors'.⁶⁴ While sixth- and seventh-century churchmen had urged Merovingian kings to imitate the models of the Old Testament, ninth-century clerics such as Remigius and Hincmar of Rheims were more successful in persuading their kings of the value of imitating biblical examples. Charlemagne instigated a wholesale revival of learning, while ruler portraits of Charles the Bald (d. 877) depict him as a new David or Solomon, crowned by the hand of God, dispensing justice and wisdom to his subjects in imitation of Christ.⁶⁵ The symbolism of these portraits, like the Byzantine David plates, reflects a twofold development in the institution of medieval kingship: by appealing to biblical precedent, Carolingian rulers associated themselves with the glories of Rome and its now-Christian empire, while also positioning themselves as figureheads of the Church. Like the Byzantine *basileus*, Carolingian emperors claimed responsibility for the temporal and spiritual well-being of their people.

Early Anglo-Saxon Dynasties

The growth of dynastic kingship in early Anglo-Saxon England was largely shaped by these continental developments. Following the migrations of Germanic-speaking peoples in the fifth and sixth centuries – around the time of King Hygelac's fatal raid on Merovingian territory – a network of small kingdoms began to emerge, with all but the East Saxons claiming descent from Woden.⁶⁶ From time to time, one *cyning* would extend his dominion over neighbouring kingdoms, an office Bede refers to as *imperium*.⁶⁷ The increasing power of these early Anglo-Saxon rulers is reflected by the construction of a number of large timber halls in the late-sixth and early-seventh centuries, perhaps comparable with the great Danish royal hall of Heorot as described in *Beowulf* (67b–82a). This period also saw a marked increase in princely burials, most famously the spectacular barrow- and ship-funeral of an East Anglian ruler, possibly King Rædwald (r. 599–624), discovered at Sutton Hoo in 1939. The main

---

⁶⁴ W. Ullmann, *The Carolingian Renaissance and the Idea of Kingship: The Birkbeck Lectures, 1968–9* (London, 1969), p. 55.

⁶⁵ See Wallace-Hadrill, *Early Germanic Kingship*, esp. p. 198; J. L. Nelson, *Charles the Bald* (London, 1992), pp. 15, 85.

⁶⁶ For this summary of the early Anglo-Saxon dynasties, I follow the discussion of Yorke, *Kings and Kingdoms*, pp. 1–22, 157–78.

⁶⁷ See P. Wormald, 'Bede, Bretwaldas and the Origins of the *Gens Anglorum*', in *Ideal and Reality in Frankish and Anglo-Saxon Society: Studies Presented to J. M. Wallace-Hadrill*, ed. P. Wormald (Oxford, 1983), pp. 99–129, repr. in Wormald (2006), pp. 106–134; S. Fanning, 'Bede, Imperium, and the Bretwaldas', *Speculum* 66 (1991), 1–26.

criterion for rule was still military leadership but, as on the continent, ancestry too played its part. By the eighth century, Anglo-Saxon kings, like the rulers of other Germanic peoples, were beginning to cultivate connections with ancient continental heroes and kings celebrated in poems such as *Beowulf* via increasingly elaborate royal genealogies.[68] Links with continental dynasties were particularly strong in the south: for example, the first Anglo-Saxon ruler to convert to Christianity, Æthelbert of Kent (r. c. 589–616), was married to a Merovingian princess, Bertha, the daughter of Charibert I. Early Anglo-Saxon kingdoms and dynasties, like those of *Beowulf*, were often short-lived; the death of a king in battle without a suitable successor could easily result in the annexation – and even disappearance – of an entire kingdom.

As in *Beowulf*, membership of an Anglo-Saxon dynasty was often expressed through the use of a common initial name-element. Patterns of succession varied from kingdom to kingdom, sometimes limited to close relatives of the king, sometimes permitting the accession of more distant claimants, depending on circumstances. As Barbara Yorke comments, a period of stability during which the succession was strictly limited to closely related members of the dynasty 'might be followed by a much more unsettled phase in which a ruler was characteristically succeeded by a distant cousin'.[69] Despite the seeming absence of the status of heir-apparent, successful rulers not only increased their kingdoms but ensured the succession of their descendants.[70] Under increasing pressure from the Church, Anglo-Saxon royal succession became more strictly limited to the direct and legitimate descendants of the king, a development which naturally led to more royal lines dying out due to a lack of heirs.[71] As is the case in *Beowulf*, in Anglo-Saxon England kingship passed through the male line, at least in principle. Hence, only one queen, Seaxburh of Wessex, appears in the regnal lists of this period. Under normal circumstances, Anglo-

---

[68] See Sisam, 'Genealogies'; Dumville, 'Kingship, Genealogies and Regnal Lists'.
[69] Yorke, *Kings and Kingdoms*, p. 168. We might envisage such a scenario taking place after Beowulf's death, if Wiglaf were to eventually take the throne: although he is related to Beowulf via the latter's father, Wiglaf has no direct blood-ties to the Hrethlings, of whom Beowulf, via the maternal line, is the last surviving member. As we have seen, however, the *Beowulf*-poet does not explore this possibility as he structures his poem around the life-cycle of an archetypal dynasty, beginning with the rise of the Scyldings and ending with the fall of the Hrethlings.
[70] One significant exception, in which an heir was officially designated, is the case of Ecgfrith, who was anointed by his father, King Offa of Mercia (r. 757–796). See Story, *Carolingian Connections*, pp. 175–79. As Story notes, in this period Anglo-Saxon England, as far north as Northumbria, was probably considered by some as part of the Carolingian *imperium* (pp. 161–66).
[71] For comparison of the mode of kingship and the practice of succession described in *Beowulf* and early Anglo-Saxon customs, see Girvan, *Seventh Century*, pp. 42–48. On the visit of the papal legates in 786, see pp. 174–75.

Saxon royal women could not inherit the throne themselves, though they could pass their royal blood on to their descendants.[72] In the Conclusion to this book, I argue that the political realities of early Anglo-Saxon England provide a plausible historical backdrop to the dynastic drama of *Beowulf*. Given the profound and lasting impact of the biblical succession narrative on early medieval kingship, the discussion that follows will assess the evidence for the influence of the Books of Kings on *Beowulf*.

Beowulf *and the Biblical Succession Narrative*

In the opening lines of *Beowulf*, God recognizes the *fyren-ðearfe*, 'terrible need', of the Danes, who had been *aldorlēase/ lange hwīle*, 'lordless for a long time' (14b–16a), by granting them a powerful ruler in the figure of Scyld Scefing who strikes fear into the surrounding peoples, before favouring Scyld by sending him a son *folce tō frōfre*, 'as a comfort to the people' (14a).[73] This passage finds a close parallel in the biblical succession narrative, in which the Israelites beg God for a king who can provide them with military protection against the Philistines (1 Kings 8). However, while in *Beowulf* kingship is itself presented as a gift from God (12–19), in the biblical narrative, the Israelites displease both Samuel and God by requesting a king. Indeed, God warns them that by doing so they are turning away from Him (1 Kings 8:5–7),[74] while Samuel predicts that the king they desire will cause them suffering (1 Kings 8:11–18). The Israelites persist in their demands, ignoring Samuel's warning; God responds by providing them with Saul, a man of the tribe of Benjamin. Saul's election as the first king of the Israelites is symbolized by his anointing by the prophet, Samuel:

> tulit autem Samuhel lenticulam olei et effudit super caput eius
> et deosculatus eum ait
> ecce unxit te Dominus super hereditatem suam in principem et liberabis populum eius de manibus inimicorum eius qui in circuitu eius sunt et hoc tibi signum quia unxit te dominus in principem [...].
> (1 Kings 10:1).

---

[72] Indeed, Yorke cites the literary example of Beowulf's accession via his mother as an example of how just such a situation might arise: *Kings and Kingdoms*, pp. 171–72. However, as we have seen, Beowulf's accession is very much a last resort in the case of the Hrethlings, and only becomes a viable option in the hero's eyes once all the other paternal descendants of Hrethel are dead; see above, pp. 83–93, 132–33.
[73] On the Christological resonance of this passage, see below, pp. 231–34.
[74] See further 1 Kings 12:12–15.

[And Samuel took a little vial of oil, and poured it upon his head, and kissed him, and said: 'Behold, the Lord hath anointed thee to be prince over his inheritance, and thou shalt deliver his people out of the hands of their enemies that are round about them. And this shall be a sign unto thee, that God hath anointed thee to be prince.'][75]

This ritual of royal anointing was to take on great significance in the medieval West from the late-eighth century onwards, symbolizing the sacrosanct, priestly nature of kingship and the ruler's duty to uphold the laws of God.[76] Nevertheless, within the succession narrative itself Saul serves chiefly as an example of charismatic kingship, 'a choice and goodly man' (1 Kings 9:1), of great height. Indeed, despite leading the Israelites to victories over their enemies, Saul is found to lack the moral qualities required of an ideal ruler, displeasing God for his failure to heed His commandments. Samuel informs Saul that God would have established his kingdom over Israel eternally, had he not sinned; as a result, the 'everlasting kingdom' will now pass to a man 'according to his own heart' (1 Kings 13:13–14), who is soon identified as David. Augustine would later explain this passage in terms of the eternal kingdom foreshadowed in Hannah's prophecy, rather than the earthly kingdom of David (*City of God*, 17.6).[77] With the anointing of David by Samuel, 'the spirit of the Lord departed from Saul, and an evil spirit from the Lord troubled him' (1 Kings 16:13–14).

Saul's descent into depression, culminating in his suicide after defeat by the Philistines, is loosely paralleled in *Beowulf* in the twice-told tale of King Heremod. According to the Danish *scop*, Heremod lost the warlike qualities required of a ruler (901b–02a: *hild sweðrode/ eafoð ond ellen*, 'his war-strength declined, might and courage') with the result that he was swiftly deposed and sent into exile (902b–04a), sinking into despair (904b–05a: *Hine sorh-wylmas/ lemedon tō lange*, 'sorrow-surges oppressed him for too long'), and becoming afflicted by evil: *hine fyren onwōd*, 'evil entered him' (915b). Hrothgar later uses the example of Heremod to illustrate to Beowulf the dangers that can beset a ruler. Predicting that the young Geat will one day become a lasting *frōfor*, 'comfort', to his people (1706b–08a), the old Scylding remarks:

                Ne wearð Heremōd swā
eaforum Egwelan,   Ār-Scyldingum;   1710
ne gewēox hē him tō willan   ac tō wæl-fealle

---

[75] For the career of Scyld Scefing, see above, pp. 39–46.
[76] See esp. J. L. Nelson, 'National Synods, Kingship as Office, and Royal Anointing: An Early Medieval Syndrome', *Studies in Church History* 7 (1971), 41–49, repr. in her *Politics and Ritual* (1986), pp. 239–58.
[77] Franke *et al.*, p. 243.

ond tō dēað-cwalum   Deniga lēodum;
brēat *bolgen-mōd*   bēod-genēatas,
eaxl-gesteallan,   oþ þæt hē āna hwearf,
mǣre þēoden   mon-drēamum from.   1715
(1709b–15). (Emphasis added).

[Heremod did not become so to the sons of Ecgwala, the Glory-Scyldings; nor did he grow according to their wishes, but he became a murderous death-killer to the Danish people; *angry in mind*, he killed his companions, table-companions, shoulder-companions, until alone he turned, the glorious prince, from the joys of men.]

In the course of his 'sermon', Hrothgar goes on to explain to the young king-in-waiting that although God had once exalted Heremod *ofer ealle men*, 'above all men' (1717b), his spirit grew bloodthirsty (*blōd-rēow*) as he neglected his duty to distribute treasures (1719b–20a) and became miserable (*drēamlēas gebād*, 1720b), a long-lasting affliction to the people (1722a).[78] As we shall see below, the possibility that the *Beowulf*-poet was influenced by this biblical paradigm in shaping the story of Heremod is increased by the fact that the Church Fathers used the story of Saul's downfall to illustrate the perils of office.[79]

Like Saul before him, David's royal authority ultimately rests on his martial strength. David's suitability for kingship is first publicly demonstrated when, like Beowulf, he also proves himself a valiant fighter by overcoming the Philistine giant, Goliath, in single-handed combat, scorning the weapons offered him by Saul. Indeed, Sylvia Horowitz has noted a number of close correspondences between David's fight with Goliath and Beowulf's battle with Grendel: for example, both heroes strip themselves of their armour before confronting their monstrous adversaries (1 Kings 17:39; *Beowulf*, lines 669–74); both battle alone and without a sword (1 Kings 17:39, 42, 50; *Beowulf*, lines 710–837); and both decapitate their foe, returning with the severed head (1 Kings 17:51, 54; *Beowulf*, lines 1584b–90, 1612–17).[80] I would suggest that a broader connection between Beowulf and David lies in the similar impact that their respective monster-fights have in terms of underlining their royal credentials. In the biblical account, David provokes Saul's jealousy when he is publicly recognized as the better warrior and therefore a better candidate for the throne:[81]

---

[78] For a recent study of Heremod's depression in the light of Anglo-Saxon attitudes towards death, see J. M. Morey, 'The Fourth Fate of Men: Heremod's Darkened Mind', in *Darkness, Depression and Descent in Anglo-Saxon England* (Kalamazoo, MI, 2019), ed. R. Wehlau, pp. 155–66.
[79] See below, pp. 218–20.
[80] Horowitz, 'Beowulf, Samson, David and Christ'. See further *CCB*, pp. 142–47.
[81] For the Danes' acclamation of Beowulf as an ideal candidate for kingship, see above, pp. 60–61.

porro cum reverteretur percusso Philistheo David
egressae sunt mulieres de universis urbibus Israhel
cantantes chorosque ducentes in occursum Saul regis
in tympanis laetitiae et in sistris
et praecinebant mulieres ludentes atque dicentes
percussit Saul mille et David decem milia
iratus est autem Saul nimis
et displicuit in oculis eius iste sermo
dixitque dederunt David decem milia et mihi dederunt mille
quid ei superest nisi solum regnum
non rectis ergo oculis Saul aspiciebat David ex die illa et deinceps
post diem autem alteram invasit spiritus Dei malus Saul [...].
(1 Kings 18:6–10).

[Now when David returned, after he slew the Philistine, the women came out of all the cities of Israel, singing and dancing, to meet king Saul, with timbrels of joy, and coronets. And the women sung as they played, and they said: Saul slew his thousands, and David his ten thousands. And Saul was exceedingly angry, and this word was displeasing in his eyes, and he said: They have given David ten thousands, and to me they have given but a thousand: what can he have more but the kingdom? And Saul did not look on David with a good eye from that day and forward. And the day after, the evil spirit from God came upon Saul.]

As discussed in Chapter One, after Beowulf's victory over Grendel, the Danes likewise declare Beowulf's throne-worthiness (856b–61), while simultaneously praising their own king, Hrothgar. Unlike Saul, however, Hrothgar is not angered by this elevation of a potential rival, although this development may have provided impetus for his plan to adopt the Geat as his son and appoint him as his successor.[82]

Like their Beowulfian counterparts, the kings of the biblical succession narrative typically consolidate their power by waging wars of conquest and exacting tribute from their neighbouring peoples.[83] David's civilizing influence is symbolized by the construction of walls, a 'house for David', built by carpenters and masons who come from afar (2 Kings 5:9–12), while Solomon takes advantage of a relatively peaceful period to build the Temple (3 Kings 5–6); likewise, Hrothgar's glorious reign culminates in his construction of the great royal hall of Heorot (64–82a). Moreover, both *Beowulf* and the Books of Kings share a concern with the dangerous consequences of rulers engaging in battle and not heeding the advice

---

[82] See above, Chapter One, pp. 63–64, 72–78.
[83] Compare, for example, the conquests of Scyld and his successors, Beow, Healfdene and Hrothgar (*Beowulf*, lines 9–11, 53–67a), with the conquests of David (2 Kings 8:1–14).

of their subjects.[84] Hence, for example, while David's men warn that he should not go out into battle 'lest thou put out the lamp of Israel' (2 Kings 21:17),[85] Wiglaf alludes to the fact that the Geats tried to dissuade Beowulf from confronting the dragon alone:

> Oft sceall eorl monig ānes willan
> wræc ādrēogan, swā ūs geworden is.
> Ne meahton wē gelǣran lēofne þēoden,
> rīces hyrde rǣd ǣniġne,   3080
> þæt hē ne grētte gold-weard þone,
> lēte hyne licgean þǣr hē longe wæs
> wīcum wunian oð worulde-ende;
> hēold on hēah-gesceap.
> (3077–84a).

[Often the will of one will cause many a warrior to suffer affliction, as has now happened to us. We could not advise the beloved prince, guardian of the kingdom, with any counsel, that he should not meet with that gold-protector, let him lie where he had been for a long time, remain in the stronghold until the world's end; he held to his high destiny.]

Another way in which *Beowulf* can be compared with the biblical succession narrative is in the manner the poem charts the development of kingship as an institution, from the warrior-king Scyld Scefing to the wise Hrothgar and the mild and generous Beowulf. As noted above, David is chosen by God as king because of his inner qualities rather than his prowess:

> et dixit Dominus ad Samuhel
> ne respicias vultum eius neque altitudinem staturae eius
> quoniam abieci eum
> nec iuxta intuitum hominis iudico
> homo enim videt ea quae parent
> Dominus autem intuetur cor [...].
> (1 Kings 16:7).

[And the Lord said to Samuel: Look not on his countenance, nor on the height of his stature: because I have rejected him, nor do I judge according to the look of man: for man seeth those things that appear, but the Lord beholdeth the heart.]

John Chrysostom interpreted David's act of sparing his persecutor Saul's life on encountering him in a cave (1 Kings 24) as a demonstra-

---

[84] See below, pp. 225–27, for parallels with Bede's account of the death of King Ecgfrith of Northumbria.

[85] For connections between the legend of Hygelac's death and the fiction of Beowulf's death, see Chapter Two, pp. 121–39.

tion of his attainment of Christian values, despite having lived under the Old Law:

> You see, while there is nothing remarkable for anyone in the ages of grace to be found free of resentment, forgiving enemies their sins and sparing abusers – that is, after the death of Christ, after such wonderful forgiveness of sins, after the directives redolent of sound values – in the old dispensation, by contrast, when the law permitted an eye to be plucked out for an eye, a tooth for a tooth, and vengeance to be taken on the wrongdoer in equal terms, who amongst the listeners is not struck by someone found to surpass the norm of the commandments and attain to New Testament values?
>
> (John Chrysostom, *Homilies on David and Saul* I).[86]

With this new emphasis on kingly morality and virtue in the succession narrative comes an enhanced awareness of the king's personal responsibility for the welfare of his people. Although David sins on several occasions, he is aware of his own failings and sets a moral and spiritual example by displaying contrition. Hence, for example, David accepts personal responsibility for a pestilence which afflicts his people, remembering his adultery with Bathsheba and his engineering of Uriah's death, actions which anger God (2 Kings 11:27), acknowledging: 'It is I who have sinned' (2 Kings 24:17).[87]

Similarly, in a moment of uncharacteristic introspection, King Beowulf wonders whether he has offended God after he discovers that his hall has been burnt to the ground by the dragon:

> Þæt ðām gōdan wæs
> hrēow on hreðre,   hyge-sorga mæst;
> *wēnde se wīsa   þæt hē wealdende*
> *ofer ealde riht,   ēcean dryhtne*
> *bitre gebulge*;   brēost innan wēoll
> þēostrum geþoncum,   swā him geþȳwe ne wæs.
> (2327b–32). (Emphasis added).

[That was a cause of great pain in the spirit of that good one, the greatest of mind-afflictions; *the wise one thought that he had offended and bitterly angered the Eternal Lord, in contravention of some old law*; his breast surged within with dark thoughts, in a way that was not customary for him.]

---

[86] Franke et al., p. 244. For the Greek text with Latin translation, see *PG* 54, cols 675–708, at 677–78. In the final part of this chapter, I will argue that both the *Beowulf*-poet and Bede find similarly admirable qualities in pre-Christian rulers who attained to some New Testament values, despite living before Christ (pp. 223–35).

[87] For Hrothgar's personal misery at the suffering of the Danes at the hands of Grendel, see above, p. 54.

It has been suggested that the phrase *ofer ealde riht* may refer to the pre-Mosaic 'old law', the law of the Old Testament more generally, or any other ancient taboo.[88] Alternatively, this phrase might hint at Beowulf's Davidic sense of moral responsibility for his people's suffering. Pagan as he is, Beowulf cannot identify the cause of his worry; the poem's Christian audience, on the other hand, is invited to speculate as to just what sin, if any, Beowulf has committed in order to unleash the dragon's devastation.[89]

Another important aspect of kingship common to *Beowulf* and the Books of Kings is the practice of patrilineal succession, in other words the dynastic principle. In *Beowulf*, as we have seen, this model is established through the transference of power from the 'stranger king' Scyld, whose ancestry is unknown, to his son, Beow, and thence to his direct descendants (12–25, 53–63). In the biblical succession narrative, while David replaces Saul through divine election rather than birth-right, all of David's successors are chosen from his bloodline, beginning with Solomon, though there are numerous instances of contested successions:[90]

> Salomon autem sedit super thronum David patris sui
> et firmatum est regnum eius nimis […].
> (3 Kings 2:12).

> [And Solomon sat upon the throne of his father David, and his kingdom was strengthened exceedingly.][91]

One area where the Books of Kings and *Beowulf* differ, however, is in their approach to royal marriage. In the biblical narrative, kings routinely take multiple wives and concubines, but in *Beowulf* rulers are uniformly monogamous. As we have seen, this feature of Beowulfian kingship is unlikely to reflect the actual practice of pre-Christian Scandinavian dynasties, where rulers probably did in fact practise concubinage, but should rather be viewed as a reflection of Anglo-Saxon attitudes towards royal marriage and legitimacy that took hold in the early-eighth century in response to pressure from the Church.[92] In the absence of royal marriage in the biblical narrative, women wield considerably less political influence than in the courts of *Beowulf*. One notable exception is the figure of Bathsheba, who reminds David of his promise to make their son, Solomon, his heir when confronted with the competing claim of Adonias, son of David and Haggith (3 Kings 1:5). We might compare Bathsheba's actions here with

---

[88] See K4, p. 242.
[89] On the 'double perspective', see above, p. 196.
[90] For example, David's own sons compete for the throne as he grows old (3 Kings 1–2).
[91] Cf. 1 Chron. 29:23: 'And Solomon sat on the throne of the Lord as king instead of David his father, and he pleased all: and all Israel obeyed him.'
[92] See pp. 23–24, 174–75.

Wealhtheow's intervention to prevent Hrothgar from adopting Beowulf and thereby potentially endangering their young sons.[93]

In *Beowulf*, royal wisdom is typified by the Solomonic figure of Hrothgar, who is referred to as wise (and old) more frequently than any other character: *snotor hæleð*, 'wise warrior' (190b), *frōd ond gōd*, 'old/wise and good' (279a), *frōd cyning*, 'old/wise king' (1306b), *se snotera*, 'the wise one' (1313b, 1786b), *þone wīsan*, 'that wise one' (1318a), *Wīsa fengel*, 'wise chief' (1400b), *snotra fengel*, 'old/wise chief' (1475a, 2156a), *snotor guma*, 'old/wise man' (1384a) and *se wîsa*, 'the wise one' (1698b).[94] Hrothgar's wisdom is most evident in his 'sermon', during which he instructs the young hero to avoid the dangers of pride, lest he should suffer the same fate as the wicked King Heremod, and explains that all power, including that of kings, is granted and taken away by God:

> Wundor is tō secganne
> hū mihtig god   manna cynne   1725
> þurh sīdne sefan   synttru bryttað,
> eard ond eorlscipe;   hē āh ealra geweald.
> Hwīlum hē on lufan   lǣteð hworfan
> monnes mōd-geþonc   mǣran cynnes,
> seleð him on ēþle   eorþan wynne,   1730
> tō healdanne   hlēo-burh wera,
> gedēð him swā gewealdene   worolde dǣlas,
> sīde rīce,   þæt hē his selfa ne mæg
> *for his unsnyttrum   ende geþencean.*
> Wunað hē on wiste;   nō hine wiht dweleð   1735
> ādl nē yldo,   nē him inwit-sorh
> on sefan sweorceð,   nē gesacu ōhwǣr,
> ecg-hete eoweð,   *ac him eal worold*
> *wendeð on willan;   hē þæt wyrse ne con* —
> oð þæt him on innan   ofer-hygda dǣl   1740
> weaxeð ond wrīdað;   þonne se weard swefeð,
> sāwele hyrde;   bið se slǣp tō fæst,
> bisgum gebunden,   bona swīðe nēah,
> sē þe on flān-bogan   fyrenum sceoteð.
> (1724b–44). (Emphasis added).

---

[93] See pp. 72–76.
[94] Beowulf is also often referred to as old/wise: Hrothgar praises the young Beowulf for his strength and his wisdom (*ne hȳrde ic snotorlicor/ on swā geongum feore guman þingian./ Þū eart mægenes strang ond on mōde frōd, wîs word-cwida*, 'I never heard a warrior speak with more wisdom in one so young in life. You are strong in might and wise in mind, a wise word-speaker', 1842b–45a); King Beowulf is later described by the narrator as *frōd cyning*, 'old/wise king' (2209a; cf. 2625a), and *se wîsa*, 'the wise one' (2329a), by Wiglaf as *wîs ond gewittig*, 'wise and conscious' (3094a), and by himself as *frōd folces weard*, 'old/wise guardian of the people' (2513a).

[It is a wonder to relate how mighty God, through the generosity of His spirit, gives wisdom to mankind, land and nobility; He controls all power. Sometimes He allows, through love, the thoughts of a man of a great family to turn, gives to him the joy of the earth in the homeland, allows him to rule the stronghold of men, grants to him a portion of worldly joys, a broad kingdom, *so that he himself, because of his lack of wisdom, cannot think of an end*. He remains in delight, in no way does he consider disease or old age, nor does deep sorrow penetrate into his spirit, nor any strife, sword-hatred show itself, *for all the world turns according to his will; he knows of nothing worse – until a portion of pride grows and takes root within him; then the guardian sleeps, the soul's shepherd; that sleep will be too deep, bound with sorrows, the slayer very near, he who shoots fiery darts from his arrow-bow*.]

While some commentators regard this passage as an inauthentic interpolation on the grounds that its homiletic style is at odds with the rest of the poem, others see it as the moral centrepiece of the work.[95] Certainly, as Eric Stanley comments, 'Christian thought and phrasing are [...] more frequent and consistent in his "sermon" than elsewhere in the poem,'[96] and scholars have detected a wide range of biblical and homiletic parallels for its imagery and themes.[97] For example, the figure of the archer in Hrothgar's sermon has been compared by Mark Atherton to the depictions of the devil in Anglo-Saxon psalters.[98] In monastic tradition, the

---

[95] On the homiletic style of the passage, see P. Clemoes, 'Style as the Criterion for Dating the Composition of *Beowulf*', in Chase (1981), pp. 173–85, at 180–81. For the suggestion that this passage is an interpolation, see Sisam, *Structure*, pp. 78–79; Irving, 'Christian and Pagan Elements', pp. 189–90; M. Lapidge, 'The Archetype of *Beowulf*', *ASE* 29 (2000), 5–41, at 37–39; see also *CCB*, pp. 67–68. For an early argument in favour of its integrity on thematic grounds, see J. Earle, *The Deeds of Beowulf: an English epic of the eighth century done into modern prose* (Oxford, 1892), pp. lxiv–lxv. Leonard Neidorf has recently presented linguistic evidence for the authenticity of this passage: 'The Language of Hrothgar's Sermon', *SN* 91 (2019), 1–10. Similar questions have been raised about the integrity of the so-called 'Christian excursus' (171b–88); for a summary see *CCB*, p. 153. See also K3, p. 135; Tolkien, 'Monsters', pp. 101–03; Whitelock, *Audience*, p. 78; and A. J. Bliss, *The Metre of* Beowulf (Oxford, 1963), p. 140. For arguments in favour of the integrity of this passage, see Brodeur, *Art*, p. 207; Campbell, 'Time Element'; E. Carrigan, 'Structure and Thematic Development in *Beowulf*', *Proceedings of the Irish Academy* 66C (1967), 1–51, at 6; F. C. Robinson, '*Beowulf*', in *The Cambridge Companion to Old English Literature*, 1st edn, ed. M. Godden and M. Lapidge (1991), pp. 142–59, at 150; and Dean, '*Beowulf* and the Passing of Time', 199.

[96] Stanley, *In the Foreground*, p. 243.

[97] See Klaeber, 'Christian Elements', pp. 47–51; Orchard, *Pride and Prodigies*, pp. 47–53; and *CCB*, pp. 158–62; K4, p. 214. Margaret Goldsmith notes parallels with Ps. 14 (*Mode and Meaning*, p. 223) and Pss 18.12, 118.71–72: 'The Christian Perspective in *Beowulf*', *Comparative Literature* 14 (1962), 71–90, repr. Fulk (1991), pp. 103–19, at 109.

[98] M. Atherton, 'The Figure of the Archer in *Beowulf* and the Anglo-Saxon Psalter', *Neophilologus* 77 (1993), 653–57.

'noonday devil' of the Psalter was understood as a personification of the vice of *acedia*, 'dejection', the same sin to which Heremod and his biblical counterpart, Saul, succumb:

> scuto circumdabit te veritas eius
> non timebis a timore nocturno
> a sagitta volante per diem
> a negotio perambulante in tenebris
> a ruina et daemonio meridian [...].
> (Ps. 90.5–6).

[His truth shall compass you with a shield: you shall not be afraid of the terror of the night, of the arrow that flies in the day, of the business that wanders about in the dark, of a fall, or of the noonday devil.][99]

Just as Hrothgar uses the story of Heremod to warn Beowulf of the temptations that can distract the mind of a ruler, so Gregory the Great used the story of Saul's downfall to illustrate the dangers of high office in his *Pastoral Care*, a text which was widely circulated throughout the Anglo-Saxon period, both in its original Latin and in the Alfredian translation:[100]

> II.2. Sic Saul post humilitatis meritum *in tumorem superbiae culmine potestatis excrevit: per humilitatem quippe praelatus est, per superbiam reprobatus* [...] Caeterorum namque comparationi se praeferens, quia plus cunctis poterat, magnum se prae omnibus aestimabat. [...] Plerumque ergo dum ex subjectorum *affluentia animus inflatur*, in fluxum superbiae ipso potentiae fastigio lenocinante corrumpitur.[101] (Emphasis added).

[Thus Saul, after merit of humility, *became swollen with pride, when in the height of power: for his humility he was preferred, for his pride rejected* [...]. For preferring himself in comparison with others because he had more power than all, he esteemed himself great above all. [...] Thus commonly, while the mind is inflated from an affluence of subordinates, *it becomes corrupted to a flux or pride*, the very summit of power being pander to desire. (*Pastoral Care* II.6)].[102]

---

[99] The translation here is my own, rather than the Douay-Rheims used elsewhere, as the base of that text is the Gallican Psalter rather than the Romanum.

[100] On Gregory's profound influence on Anglo-Saxon England and early medieval Europe more generally, see D. Anlezark, 'Gregory the Great: Reader, Writer and Read', in *The Church and Literature*, ed. P. Clarke and C. Methuen (Woodbridge, 2012), pp. 12–34.

[101] *PL* 77, cols 35C–35D.

[102] Franke *et al.*, p. 256. The Old English version of the *Pastoral Care*, produced in the late-ninth century under the auspices of King Alfred, renders this passage 'word-for-word': *Swæ swæ Saul Israhela kyning ðurh eaðmodnesse he geearnode ðæt rice, ond for ðæs rices heanesse him weoxon ofermetto. For eaðmodnesse he wæs ahafen ofer oððre menn, ond for ofermettum he wæs aworpen. [...] Forðy he ongeat ðæt he ma meahte ðonne ænig oðer, ða wende he ðæt he eac mara wære. [...] Swæ oft*

Hrothgar's portrait of the un-vigilant ruler, who assumes his success will never come to an end, can also be compared with the words of the psalmist, King David, who in Psalm 29.7 says to God: *ego autem dixi in mea abundantia non movebor in aeternum*, 'and I said in my abundance: I will never be moved.' In the Alfredian *Prose Psalms*, David's words are transformed into warning about the dangers of pride (*wlenco*): *Ic cwæð on minum wlencum and on minre orsorhnesse: 'Ne wyrð þisses næfre nan wendincg'*, 'I said *in my pride* and in my prosperity: "this will never change"' (*Prose Psalms*, Ps. 29.6).[103] The wealth of biblical and patristic echoes that characterize Hrothgar's sermon serve to reinforce the impression that the Danish king is a Solomonic dispenser of wisdom, as well as a just ruler who is fully cognisant of the responsibilities that come with royal office.[104] As such, Hrothgar sets an example of royal conduct for the hero to aspire to in his future career as ruler.

A further, more troubling connection between Hrothgar and Solomon, however, lies in the association of both rulers with the practice of idol-worship. God punishes Solomon for his idolatry and excessive polygamy by raising up adversaries against him, Hadad, Razod and Jeroboam, warning that He will divide the kingdom during the reign of his son (3 Kings 11:14, 23, 26, 33). Although it is unclear whether Hrothgar himself participated in seeking relief from his great adversary, Grendel, from the *gāst-bona*, 'soul-slayer' (177a), the poet implies that such practices were customary among the Danes:

>   Swylc wæs þēaw hyra,
> hæþenra hyht;   *helle gemundon*
> in mōd-sefan,   *metod hīe ne cūþon,*
> dǣda dēmend,   *ne wiston hīe drihten God,*

ðonne ðæt mod aðintt on ofermettum for ðære menge ðæs folces þe him underðieded bið, hit bið gewemmed mid ðæs onwaldes heanesse. (*King Alfred's West-Saxon Version of Gregory's* Pastoral Care, ed. H. Sweet, EETS o.s. 45 and 50 [London, 1871], 2 vols, I, p. 112 [Cotton MS]). Orchard (*Pride and Prodigies*, pp. 56–57), following Stanley ('*Hæþenra hyht*', p. 148), compares Gregory's account of Saul with King Beowulf. I would suggest a more apt comparison is with Heremod. Indeed, the narrator makes it clear that Beowulf became *frēondum gefægra*, 'a better friend' (915a), to mankind than Heremod. For discussion of Stanley and Orchard's assessment of the poem's closing lines in the light of Gregory's discussion of Saul, see below, pp. 228–31.

[103] O'Neill, *Old English Psalms*, p. 94. Cf. Ps. 9.25–32. On the pervasive influence of the Psalms on Old English literature, see M. J. Toswell, *The Anglo-Saxon Psalter* (Turnhout, 2014); and Toswell, 'Psalm Genres in Old English Poetry'.

[104] On the possibility that Hrothgar's warning against pride is connected with, or even inspired by, his examination of the sword hilt, with its runic inscription describing the destruction of the giants in the biblical flood, see Anlezark, *Water and Fire*, pp. 329–31. Anlezark compares Hrothgar's advice with the instruction of Solomon in the Old English poem, *Solomon and Saturn II*, and imagery of the devil as archer who attacks the soul in Vercelli Homily 4 (pp. 331–33).

nē hīe hūru heofena helm   *herian ne cūþon,*
wuldres waldend.
(178b–83a). (Emphasis added).

[Such was *their custom*, the hope of heathens, they remembered hell in their minds; *they did not know the Creator*, Judge of Deeds, *nor did they know* the Lord God, *nor indeed did they know how to worship* the Protector of Heaven, Ruler of Glory.]

The kings of *Beowulf*, like their Old Testament counterparts, are thereby shown to be imperfect forerunners of the Christian rulers of the poet's own day.

After the exemplary, though far from perfect, reigns of David and Solomon, a general pattern of decline characterizes the remainder of the succession narrative, with a number of examples of bad kingship: for example, Solomon's son and heir, Roboam, oppresses his people, while his successor, Abiam, 'walked in all the sins of his father which he had done before him; and his heart was not perfect with the Lord his God, as was the heart of David' (3 Kings 15:3). Following the division of the twelve tribes of Israel into two rival kingdoms, Judah and Benjamin remain under the rule of David's descendants while the 'lost ten tribes' of Israel are ruled by Jeroboam and his descendants. As in *Beowulf*'s account of the fall of the Hrethlings, the collapse of these royal houses results in a period of captivity and exile for their subject peoples. The royal line of Israel comes to an end with the Assyrian captivity during the reign of Hoshea (Osee) (4 Kings 17:6), while the destruction of the kingdom of Judah is signalled by the Babylonian capture of Sedecias, the last reigning king, and the execution of his sons:

adprehensum ergo regem duxerunt ad regem Babylonis in Reblatha
qui locutus est cum eo iudicium
filios autem Sedeciae occidit coram eo et oculos eius effodit
vinxitque eum catenis et adduxit in Babylonem [...].
(4 Kings 25:6–7).

[So they (the Babylonians) took the king, and brought him to the king of Babylon to Reblatha, and he gave judgement upon him. And he slew the sons of Sedecias before his face, and he put out his eyes, and bound him with chains, and brought him to Babylon.]

The end of the monarchy of Judah is confirmed by the burning of Solomon's capital, referred to as the king's house, and the sacking of Jerusalem. Without a ruling dynasty to protect them, the tribe of Judah are taken into captivity in Babylon:

mense quinto septima die mensis ipse est annus nonusdecimus regis Babylonis

venit Nabuzardan princeps exercitus
servus regis Babylonis Hierusalem
*et succendit domum Domini et domum regis et domos Hierusalem
omnemque domum conbusit igni*
et muros Hierusalem in circuitu destruxit omnis exercitus Chaldeorum qui erat cum principe militum
*reliquam autem populi partem qui remanserat in civitate
et perfugas qui transfugerant ad regem Babylonis
et reliquum vulgus transtulit Nabuzardan princeps militia* [...]
et translatus est Iuda de terra sua [...].
(4 Kings 25:8–11, 21). (Emphasis added).

[In the fifth month, the seventh day of the month, that is, the nineteenth year of the king of Babylon, came Nabuzardan commander of the army, a servant of the king of Babylon, into Jerusalem. *And he burnt the house of the Lord, and the king's house, and the houses of Jerusalem, and every house he burnt with fire.*[105] And all the army of the Chaldees, which was with the commander of the troops, broke down the walls of Jerusalem round about. *And Nabuzardan the commander of the army, carried away the rest of the people that remained in the city, and the fugitives that had gone over to the king of Babylon, and the remnant of the common people* [...] so Judah was carried away out of their land.]

We find broad analogues here with both the dragon's burning of Beowulf's royal hall (2324–27a) and the fate of the Geats after the fall of their royal house (2910b–28, 2999–3007a, 3015b–27, 3148b–55). However, while the fates of the Hrethlings and the royal houses of Israel and Judah are in some ways comparable, the crucial difference lies in the interpretation of the fall of the Israelite monarchy as foreshadowing the coming of Christ, King of Kings. As a reward for David's loyalty, God promises him an eternal dynasty through the prophecy of Nathan:[106]

cumque conpleti fuerint dies tui et dormieris cum patribus tuis
suscitabo semen tuum post te quod egredietur de utero tuo
et firmabo regnum eius
ipse aedificabit domum nomini meo
et stabiliam thronum regni eius usque in sempiternum [...]

---

[105] The sacking of Jerusalem was connected with the image of the dragon in the prophecy of Jeremiah 9.11: 'et dabo Hierusalem in acervos harenae *et cubilia draconum* et civitates Iuda dabo in desolationem eo quod non sit habitator.' ('And I will make Jerusalem to be heaps of sand, and *dens of dragons*: and I will make the cities of Judah desolate, for want of an inhabitant.') (Emphasis added).

[106] Cf. Ps. 88.4–5, 36–39; Ps. 88.19–39; Ps. 131.11–12. This unconditional promise of an eternal dynasty is subsequently complicated by the conditional promise made by God to Solomon (3 Kings 9:4–7), with some interpreters arguing that Solomon's failure to keep God's commandments results in the extinction of his royal line.

et fidelis erit domus tua et regnum tuum usque in aeternum ante faciem tuam
et thronus tuus erit firmus iugiter [...].
(2 Kings 7:12–13, 16).

[And when thy days shall be fulfilled and thou shalt sleep with thy fathers, I will raise up thy seed after thee which shall proceed out of thy bowels, and I will establish his kingdom. He shall build a house to my name, and I will establish the throne of his kingdom for ever. [...] And thy house shall be faithful and thy kingdom for ever before thy face, and thy throne shall be firm for ever.]

Patristic exegetes were careful to explain that this eternal kingdom promised to David's 'seed' is not the same kingdom that was inherited by his son, Solomon, but rather the heavenly kingdom won for mankind by David's descendant, Christ.[107] This interpretation of Nathan's prophecy allowed medieval rulers to view themselves as God's viceroys and to envisage their earthly realms as preparation for the heavenly kingdom.

Given the extent of these parallels between *Beowulf* and the biblical succession narrative, it seems likely that the poet drew on this paradigm in order to shape certain aspects of the figures of Heremod, Scyld, Hrothgar and Beowulf.[108] In this respect, the poet can be compared with another Anglo-Saxon who drew extensively on the Books of Kings in order to instruct the rulers of his own day: the Venerable Bede.

Bede and Beowulf on Kings

Bede's abiding interest in the Books of Kings is attested by the remarkable range of works he devoted to their interpretation: in his lengthy commentary *On the First Part of Samuel, that is up to the Death of Saul in Four Books*, dedicated to Bishop Acca of Hexham, Bede explores the Christological significance of the biblical narrative of the reigns of Saul and David;[109] *Thirty Questions on the Books of Kings* explains complex theological issues

---

[107] Cf. Tertullian, *Against Marcion* 3.20; Augustine, *City of God* 17.8.
[108] For links between Hygelac and Beowulf, and Heremod and Scyld, see Chapter Two, pp. 129–36, 150–51.
[109] See now S. DeGregorio and R. C. Love, ed. and trans., *Bede: On First Samuel* (Liverpool, 2019). See G. H. Brown, 'Bede's Commentary on I Samuel', in *Biblical Studies in the Early Middle Ages*, ed. C. Leonardi and G. Orlandi (Florence, 2005), pp. 77–90; G. H. Brown, 'Bede's Neglected Commentary on Samuel', in *Innovation and Tradition in the Writings of the Venerable Bede*, ed. S. DeGregorio (Morgantown, 2006), pp. 121–42; 'Bede's Style in his Commentary on I Samuel', in Minnis and Roberts (2007), pp. 233–51. See also J. Black, '*De Civitate Dei* and the Commentaries of Gregory the Great, Isidore, Bede, and Hrabanus Maurus on the Book of Samuel', *Augustinian Studies* 15 (1986 for 1984), 114–27.

not covered by available authorities;[110] and *On the Temple of Solomon* emphasizes typological links between the Old and New Testament.[111] It is primarily in his *Ecclesiastical History*, however, that Bede uses Old Testament kingship as a model for the conduct of contemporary rulers.[112] Like the *Beowulf*-poet, Bede learnt from the Bible that the authority of kings rests on their ability to defend their people from attack and to win military victories against their enemies.[113] Hence, the military conquests of the pagan Northumbrian king, Æthelfrith, are favourably compared with those of Saul (*HE* I.34),[114] while the description of the unprecedented military successes and resultant peace of Edwin's reign (*HE* II.5, 9) appears to be closely modelled on that of Solomon.[115] Two recent essays have taken contrasting approaches to Bede's use of the Old Testament in shaping a theory of contemporary kingship: Conor O'Brien emphasizes Bede's 'morally neutral' view of kingship, arguing that, like Augustine before him, he viewed the institution as essentially secular rather than priestly or ministerial;[116] Sarah Foot, on the other hand, comments that Bede 'saw kings on Earth essentially as reflections of the majesty of the heavenly king'.[117] Foot emphasizes Bede's concern throughout the *Ecclesiastical History* with the stability and unity of kingdoms, the ancestry and legiti-

---

[110] Trans. by W. Trent Foley in *Bede: A Biblical Miscellany*, ed. W. T. Foley and A. G. Holder (Liverpool, 1999), pp. 81–144. See further S. DeGregorio, 'Bede and the Old Testament', in *The Cambridge Companion to Bede*, ed. S. DeGregorio (Cambridge, 2010), pp. 127–41.

[111] *Bede: On the Temple*, trans. S. Connolly, with an Introduction by J. O'Reilly (Liverpool, 1995).

[112] See Wallace-Hadrill, *Early Germanic Kingship*, pp. 75–77.

[113] See J. McClure, 'Bede's Old Testament Kings', in Wormald (1983), pp. 76–98, at 87. See further C. E. Stancliffe, 'Oswald, "Most Holy and Most Victorious King of the Northumbrians"', in *Oswald: Northumbrian King to European Saint*, ed. C. Stancliffe and E. Cambridge (Stamford, 2005), pp. 33–83.

[114] *Bede's Ecclesiastical History of the English People*, ed. and trans. B. Colgrave and R. A. B. Mynors, (Oxford, 1969; repr. 1979), pp. 116–17. See below, pp. 227–35, for comparison of Bede's portraits of Æthelfrith and Oswald with the eulogy for Beowulf in the poem's closing lines.

[115] Colgrave and Mynors, pp. 148–51, 162–63. See McClure, 'Old Testament Kings', p. 88; P. J. E. Kershaw, *Peaceful Kings: Peace, Power, and the Early Medieval Political Imagination* (Oxford, 2011), pp. 31–39. Alan Thacker shows how Bede's portrait of the heretical Britons at the end of his *Ecclesiastical History* closely parallels his depiction of the Philistines in his commentary on Samuel: 'Bede, the Britons and the Book of Samuel', in *Early Medieval Studies in Memory of Patrick Wormald*, ed. S. Baxter, C. E. Karkov, J. L. Nelson and D. Pelteret (Farnham, 2009), pp. 129–48.

[116] C. O'Brien, 'Kings and Kingship in the Writings of Bede', *EHR* 132 (2018), 1473–98, at 1482.

[117] S. Foot, 'Bede's Kings', in *Writing, Kingship and Power in Anglo-Saxon England*, ed. R. Naismith and D. A. Woodman (Cambridge, 2017), pp. 25–51, at 50. Cf. Wallace-Hadrill, *Early Germanic Kingship*, pp. 76–78. See further N. J. Higham, *(Re-)Reading Bede: The Ecclesiastical History in Context* (London, 2006), pp. 148–69.

macy of rulers, and their fatherly role both in dynasties and towards their subjects.[118] Hence, for example, Bede takes care to explain how the Kentish throne was restored to Wihtred, *legitimus rex*, after a period of chaos during which it was held by 'various usurpers or foreign kings' (*reges dubii uel externi*) following the death of Wihtred's father, King Ecgberht, in 685:

> Quo uidelicet anno, qui est ab incarnatione dominica DCLXXXV, Hlotheri Cantuariorum rex, *cum post Ecgberctum fratrem suum*, qui nouem annis regnauerat, ipse XII annis regnasset, mortuus erat VII idus Februarias. Vulneratus namque est in pugna Australium Saxonum, quos contra eum Edric *filius Ecgbercti* adgregarat, et inter medendum defunctus. Ac post eum idem Edric anno uno ac dimidio regnauit; quo defuncto, regnum illud aliquot temporis spatium *reges dubii uel externi disperdiderunt*, donec *legitimus rex* Uictred, id est *filius Ecgbercti, confortatus in regno*, religione simul et industria gentem suam ab extranea inuasione liberaret.

(HE IV.26). (Emphasis added).

> [On 6 February in this year of our Lord 685, Hlothhere, king of Kent, died after a reign of twelve years, *having succeeded his brother Ecgberht*, who had reigned nine years. He was wounded in battle with the South Saxons, whom Eadric, *son of Ecgberht*, had raised against him. He died while his wounds were being attended to, Eadric ruled for a year and a half after Hlothhere and, when Eadric died, *various usurpers or foreign kings* plundered the kingdom for a certain space of time until *the rightful king*, Wihtred, *son of Ecgberht, established himself on the throne* and freed the nation from foreign invasion by his devotion and zeal.][119] (Emphasis added).

As we have seen throughout this book, the *Beowulf*-poet shares this concern with royal legitimacy and the stability of royal families. Another theme common to *Beowulf* and the *Ecclesiastical History* is the potentially dire consequences of rash military raids conducted by foolhardy kings. While the *Beowulf*-poet uses the legend of the death of Hygelac to sustain this theme throughout his work, Bede provides the example of King Ecgfrith of Northumbria:

> Anno dominicae incarnationis DCLXXXIIII Ecfrid rex Nordanhymbrorum, misso Hiberniam cum exercitu duce Bercto, uastauit misere gentem innoxiam et nationi Anglorum semper amicissimam, ita ut ne ecclesiis quidem aut monasteriis manus parceret hostilis. At insulani et, quantum ualuere, armis

---

[118] Foot, 'Bede's Kings', pp. 34–39.
[119] Colgrave and Mynors, pp. 430–31. On the expulsion of rulers who were not of the proper stock (*eiectis principibus regis non proprii*) by Wulfhere, son of King Penda of Mercia, see *HE* III.24 (Colgrave and Mynors, p. 294). On the rebellion of the Deiran princes Alhfrith and Oethelwald against the legitimate king of Bernicia, Oswiu, see *HE* III.14 (Colgrave and Mynors, p. 254). On the presentation of Grendel as an illegitimate usurper, see Chapter Three, pp. 174–76.

arma repellebant, et inuocantes diuinae auxilium pietatis caelitus se uindicari continuis diu inprecationibus postulabant. Et quamuis maledici regnum Dei possidere non possint, creditum est tamen quod hi qui merito inpietatis suae maledicebantur, ocius Domino uindice poenas sui reatus luerunt. Siquidem anno post hunc proximo idem rex, cum temere exercitum ad uastandam Pictorum prouinciam duxisset, multum prohibentibus amicis et maxime beatae memoriae Cudbercto, qui nuper fuerat ordinatus episcopus, introductus est simultantibus fugam hostibus in angustias inacesessorum montium, et cum maxima parte copiarum, quas secum adduxerat, extinctus anno aetatis suae xlmo, regni autem xvmo, die tertio decimo kalendarium Iuniarum. Et quidem, ut dixi, prohibuerunt amici, ne hoc bellum iniret; sed quoniam anno praecedente noluerat audire reuerentissimum patrem Ecgberctum, ne Scottiam nil se laedentem inpugnaret, datum est illi ex poena peccati illius, ne nunc eos, qui ipsum ad interitu reuocare cupiebant, audiret.

Ex quo tempore spes coepit et uirtis regni Anglorum 'fluere ac retro sublapsa referri' [Virgil, *Aeneid*, II.169]. [...] Vbi inter plurimos gentis Anglorum uel interemtos gladio uel seruitio addictos uel de terra Pictorum fuga lapsos [...]. (*HE* IV.26)

[In the year of our Lord 684 Ecgfrith, king of Northumbria, sent an army to Ireland under his ealdorman Berht, who wretchedly devastated a harmless race that had always been most friendly to the English, and his hostile bands spared neither churches nor monasteries. The islanders resisted force by force so far as they were able, imploring the merciful aid of God and invoking His vengeance with unceasing imprecations. And although those who curse cannot inherit the kingdom of God, yet one may believe that those who were justly cursed for their wickedness quickly suffered the penalty of their guilt at the avenging hand of God. Indeed the very next year the king rashly sent an army to ravage the kingdom of the Picts, against the urgent advice of his friends and particularly of Cuthbert, of blessed memory, who had recently been made bishop. The enemy feigned flight and lured the king into some narrow passes in the midst of inaccessible mountains; there he was killed with the greater part of the forces he had taken with him, on 20 May, in the fortieth year of his age and the fifteenth of his reign. As I have said, his friends urged him not to undertake this campaign; but in the previous year he had refused to listen to the holy father Ecgbert, who had urged him not to attack the Irish who had done him no harm; and the punishment for his sin was that he would not now listen to those who sought to save him from his own destruction.

From this time the hopes and strength of the English kingdom began to 'ebb and fall away'. [...] Many of the English were either slain by the sword or enslaved or escaped by flight from Pictish territory [...].][120]

---

[120] Colgrave and Mynors, pp. 426–28. For discussion of this passage, see Foot, 'Bede's Kings', p. 39; N. J. Higham, 'Bede's Agenda in Book IV of the *Ecclesiastical*

Bede's damning critique of Ecgfrith can be compared not only with the *Beowulf*-poet's treatment of Hygelac's foolhardy raid on the Franks but also with Wiglaf's more ambivalent remarks concerning how Beowulf would not listen to attempts to dissuade him from facing the dragon alone (3077–84a).[121]

Comparison with Bede's use of Old Testament models of kingship may provide a solution to the notorious debate surrounding the interpretation of the closing lines of *Beowulf*, in which twelve Geatish warriors ride around Beowulf's barrow, praising their king for his many virtues:[122]

> Þā ymbe hlǣw riodan   hilde-dīore,
> æþelinga bearn,   ealra twelfe,   3170
> woldon care cwīðan   ond cyning mǣnan,
> word-gyd wrecan,   ond ymb wer sprecan;
> eahtodan eorlscipe   ond his ellen-weorc
> duguðum dēmdon – swā hit gedēfe bið
> þæt mon his wine-dryhten   wordum herge,   3175
> ferhðum frēoge,   þonne hē forð scile
> of līc-haman   lǣded weorðan.
> Swā begnornodon   Gēata lēode
> hlāfordes hryre,   heorð-genēatas;
> cwǣdon þæt hē wǣre   wyruld-cyninga   3180
> manna mildust   ond monð-wǣrust,
> lēodum līðost   ond lof-geornost.
> (3169–82).

[Then around the barrow rode battle-brave ones, sons of æthelings, twelve in all, they wished to lament their sorrow and mourn their king, to recite a song with words, and to speak about the man; they praised his nobility and his brave deeds, weighed up his achievements – so is it fitting that a man should praise his beloved lord with words, cherish him in the heart, when he must be led forth from the body-home. So the people of the Geats lamented the fall of their lord, hearth-companions. They said that he was of all the kings of the world the mildest of men and the gentlest, the kindest to the people and the most eager for glory.]

History of the English People: A Tricky Matter of Advising the King', *Journal of Ecclesiastical History* 64 (2013), 476–93. For comparison of Ecgfrith's dynasty, the Æthelfrithings, with the Hrethlings in *Beowulf*, see below, pp. 237–40.

[121] See Gwara, *Heroic Identity*, pp. 12, 51–52, 246, for discussion of Wiglaf's statement against a range of other opinions about Beowulf's motivation. Compare also Hygelac's remark to Beowulf that he had tried to dissuade him from travelling to Denmark to challenge Grendel (1994b–97b); for the apparent contradiction between this and other statements about the circumstances of Beowulf's departure for Denmark see above, Chapter Two, p. 131. For connections between Hygelac's raid and Beowulf's dragon-fight, see Chapter Two, pp. 134–39, and Chapter Three, pp. 185–86.

[122] For a summary of opinions, see K4, pp. 271–72.

Many scholars have argued that the last word of the poem, *lof-geornost*, ironically undercuts the list of positive virtues that precede it. For example, Eric Stanley translates it as 'vainglorious', citing Ælfric's use of the term to refer to the sin of *iactantia*, 'vainglory', and arguing that Beowulf, like the idol-worshipping Danes (175–88), must be damned on account of his heathenism.[123] Others, however, see *lof-geornost* as the natural conclusion to the list of the king's virtue: R. D. Fulk, for example, translates it as 'most honor-bound', while Alfred Bammesberger suggests that we take *lof-geornost* as complementing *lēodum*, citing parallels in *Christ III* 910–17, thereby producing the reading: 'they proclaimed that he was of world-kings, of (all) men the kindest and most harmonious, most lenient to and eager to gain fame *for* his people' (emphasis mine).[124] Bede admires this same

---

[123] Stanley, 'Hæthenra Hyht', pp. 136, 150–51. See, for example, his 'Memory of the Saints': *Se seofoða leahter is iactantia gecweden, þæt is ydelgylp on ængliscre spræce þæt is ðonne se man bið lofgeorn and mid licetunge færð, and deð for gylpe gif he hwæt dælan wile, and bið þonne se hlisa his edlean ðære dæde and his wite andbidað on ðære toweardan worulde*, 'The seventh sin is called *iactantia*, in English speech that is idle boasting, that is when a man is *eager for fame/glory* and goes about hypocritically, and does it boastfully, if he will share out anything at all, and then fame is the reward of his words and his punishment awaits in the next world' (Skeat, I, pp. 336–62, at 356–59) (emphasis added). Orchard quotes this passage, and the following discussion of *superbia*, 'pride', in the conclusion to his discussion of the last word of *Beowulf*, commenting: 'If such was the lot of the man who was "eager for glory" (*lofgeorn*), how much more so for the man who was, like Beowulf, "most eager for glory" (*lofgeornost*)?' (*Pride and Prodigies*, p. 171). See also Robinson, *Appositive Style*, p. 81. There is, however, at least one piece of evidence that not everyone in early Anglo-Saxon England shared the belief that all pagans were necessarily damned: in Ch. 29 of the late-seventh- or early-eighth-century *Vita* of Gregory the Great by an anonymous monk of Whitby, we read that the pope interceded for the pagan Roman Emperor Trajan on account of his kindness to a widow, weeping tears and offering prayers on his behalf, with the result that he was rescued from hell and admitted into heaven: *The Earliest Life of Gregory the Great*, ed. and trans. B. Colgrave (Cambridge, 1968), p. 129.

[124] Fulk, *Beowulf Manuscript*, p. 295; A. Bammesberger, 'The Last Line of *Beowulf*', NQ 59 (2012), 463–65, at 465. See also Burrow, *Poetry of Praise*, pp. 58–60. J. Toswell, 'Psalm Genres in Old English Poetry', in *The Psalms and Medieval English Literature: From the Conversion to the Reformation*, ed. T. Atkin and F. Leneghan (Cambridge, 2017), pp. 218–32, at 228–30, compares these lines with the language of the Praise Psalms. A further comparison might be made with the unambiguous praise of King Hrolf (OE Hrothulf) in *Hrólfs saga*: 'Svipdag asked, "What is King Hrolf like?" His father answered, "I have heard that King Hrolf is open-handed and generous and so trustworthy and particular about his friends that his equal cannot be found. He withholds neither gold nor treasure from nearly everyone who wants or needs them. He is handsome in looks, powerful in deeds and a worthy opponent. The fairest of men, Hrolf is fierce with the greedy, yet gentle and accommodating with the unpretentious and modest. Toward all those who do not threaten him, he is the most humble of men, responding with equal mildness to both the powerful and the poor. Hrolf is so great that his name will not be forgotten as long as the world

eagerness for fame in the pagan king of Northumbria, Æthelfrith, whom he compares favourably with Saul:

> His temporibus regno Nordanhymbrorum praefuit *rex fortissimus et gloriae cupidissimus* Aedilfrid, *qui plus omnibus Anglorum primatibus gentem uastauit Brettonum*, ita ut Sauli quondam regi Israheliticae gentis conparandus uideretur, excepto dumtaxat hoc, *quod diuinae erat religionis ignarus*. Nemo enim in tribunis, nemo in regibus plures eorum terras, exterminatis uel subiugatis indigenis, aut tributarias genti Anglorum aut habitabiles fecit. Cui merito poterat illud, quod benedicens filium patriarcha in personam Saulis dicebat, aptari: 'Beniamin lupus rapax; mane comedat praedam et uespere diuidet spolia.'
>
> (*HE*, I.34). (Emphasis added).[125]

> [At this time, Æthelfrith, *a very brave king and most eager for glory*, was ruling over the kingdom of Northumbria. *He ravaged the Britons more extensively than any other English ruler*. He might indeed be compared with Saul, who was once king of Israel, but with this exception, that Æthelfrith was *ignorant of the divine religion*. For no ruler or king had subjected more land to the English race or settled it, having first either exterminated or conquered the natives. To him, in the character of Saul, could fittingly be applied the words which the patriarch said when he was blessing his son, 'Benjamin shall ravin as a wolf; in the morning he shall devour the prey and at night shall divide the spoil.'][126]

As Colgrave and Mynors note, Bede's phrase *rex fortissimus et gloriae cupidissimus* echoes Old English terms such as *dōm-georn*, 'eager for glory', 'used in heroic poems […] to describe the typical heroic warrior.'[127] However, the parallel with *Beowulf* is particularly striking, as only here do we find an equivalent phrase used in the superlative mood (*lof-geornost*).[128]

---

remains inhabited. He has exacted tribute from all kings who are near him, for everyone is willing to serve him."' (Byock, p. 31). For the Old Norse text, see Guðni Jónsson, p. 40 (ch. 22). For connections between *Hrólfs saga* and *Beowulf* see above, Chapters One and Two, esp. pp. 114–18. Wieland notes that the collocation *manna mildost* only occurs here and in *Exodus* (550a), where it is used in reference to Moses ('Manna mildost').

[125] Cf. Old English *Bede*: *se strongesta cyning ond se gylpgeornesta* (*The Old English Version of Bede's Ecclesiastical History of the English People*, ed. and trans. T. H. Miller, 4 vols, EETS o.s. 95, 96, 110, 111 [London 1890–98], I, p. 92).

[126] Colgrave and Mynors, pp. 116–17.

[127] Colgrave and Mynors, p. 116, n. 1. As Orchard notes, *dōm-georn* does not in fact occur in *Judith*, despite Colgrave and Mynors's statement to the contrary (*Pride and Prodigies*, p. 56, n.137). Elsewhere, *dōm-georn* occurs four times in *Andreas* (693a, 878a, 959a, 1308a), once in *Elene* (1290a), once in *The Wanderer* (17a), and once in *Riddle 31* (16a).

[128] On the rarity of superlatives in Old English poetry, see E. G. Stanley, 'Old English Poetic Superlatives', *Anglia* 135 (2017), 241–73.

Developing this connection between Beowulf, Æthelfrith and Saul, Orchard notes that, for Gregory, Saul was a model of pride:[129]

> Beowulf, like Æthelfrith (and Saul), a heroic king and equally 'most eager for praise' (*lofgeornost*), is, also, like Æthelfrith, a pagan, and no amount of special pleading can save him [...]. It may well be that from a Christian perspective the doubtless heroic Beowulf, in the closing words of the poem which celebrates his mighty deeds, like Alexander and Hercules, would seem damned with feigned praise.[130]

However, as Sarah Foot has recently argued, Bede admires Æthelfrith's eagerness for glory, and the comparison with Saul is in fact a favourable one; like Beowulf, his only failing is his paganism.[131]

Turning to the list of less-contentious virtues preceding *lof-geornost*, Fred Robinson has asked why the *Beowulf*-poet should wish to so suddenly introduce these qualities of mildness, generosity and gentleness when previously Beowulf has been praised for his strength and bravery.[132] However, as we have seen, these virtues are associated with the biblical David, a model for all medieval Christian rulers and a king whose fight with Goliath may have inspired some elements of Beowulf's own contest with Grendel. Moreover, Bede identifies similar qualities in his portrait of Æthelfrith's son, the convert King Oswald:[133]

> sed et regna terrarium plus quam ulli maiorum suprum ab eodem uno Deo, qui fecit caelum et terram, consecutus est; [...]. *Quo regni culmine sublimatus,*

---

[129] For Gregory's use of Saul as an example of pride, and comparison with Hrothgar's account of Heremod, see above, pp. 217–20.

[130] Orchard, *Pride and Prodigies*, p. 57; cf. Stanley, 'Hæthenra Hyht', p. 150.

[131] Foot, 'Bede's Kings', p. 40. Foot draws on Georges Tugene in explaining that the allusion to Benjamin 'rests upon an understanding that it might also be applied to the apostle Paul (called Saul before his conversion): the wolf that devours in the morning by persecuting Christians distributes his prey in the evening by preaching the gospel to the gentiles'; cf. G. Tugene, 'L'histoire "ecclésiastique" du peuple anglais: réflexions sur le particularisme et l'universalisme chez Bede', *Recherches augustiniennes* 17 (1982), 129–72, at 163–64. See also A. Thacker, 'Bede's Idea of the English', *Bulletin of the John Rylands Library* 92 (2016), 1–26, at 11. It is likely that, in addition to Christian praise poetry such as *Cædmon's Hymn*, Bede also drew on secular vernacular heroic poems in composing his *historia*. It is therefore possible that he modelled his ruler portraits of Æthelfrith and Oswald, at least in part, on a poem resembling *Beowulf*, as well as the Old Testament. See further A. Crépin, 'Bede and the Vernacular', in *Famulus Christi: Essays in Commemoration of the 13th Centenary of the Birth of the Venerable Bede*, ed. G. Bonner (London, 1976), pp. 170–92.

[132] Robinson, *Appositive Style*, p. 142.

[133] For discussion of this passage, see Stancliffe, 'Oswald', p. 61; Foot, 'Bede's Kings', pp. 44–46. For discussion of the *basileus*, see above, pp. 204–05.

nihilominus (quod mirum dictum est) pauperibus et peregrinis semper humilis benignus et largus fuit. (HE III.6). (Emphasis added).[134]

[[...] and also Oswald gained from the one God who made heaven and earth greater earthly realms than any of his ancestors had possessed. [...] *Though he wielded supreme power over the whole land, he was always wonderfully humble, kind, and generous to the poor and to strangers.*][135]

Queen Wealhtheow has sought to instil these same qualities of mildness, gentleness and kindness in the young Beowulf during her speech in Heorot (1216–31).[136] King Beowulf's eulogy confirms the efficacy of the Danish queen's words of instruction, with the *æþelinga bearn* singling out those same virtues in their king that Bede identified in the pagan Æthelfrith and the Christian Oswald. Like Æthelfrith, Beowulf represents the best of pagan kingship, but in his attainment of what Chrysostom called 'New Testament values', despite effectively living 'before Christ', he anticipates the Christian kingship of Oswald.

What has Beowulf to do with Christ?

In the light of this discussion of parallels between *Beowulf* and biblical kingship, in the last part of this chapter I consider the import of several messianic hints in the poem, however slight, that might have caught the ear of an attentive Anglo-Saxon audience. In his 1922 edition of *Beowulf*, Klaeber detected 'features of the Christian Savior in the destroyer of hellish fiends, the warrior brave and gentle, blameless in thought and deed, the king that dies for his people'.[137] In support of this view, Klaeber highlighted an echo of the Gospel of Luke in Hrothgar's observation that the *eald-metod*, 'ancient creator', was kind to Beowulf's mother in *bearn-ge-byrdo*, 'child-bearing' (942–46a).[138] M. B. McNamee went a step further in reading *Beowulf* as 'an allegory of salvation' that 'echoes the Liturgy

---

[134] Cf. Old English *Bede* III.4: *þearfum ond elþeodigum symle eaðmod ond fremsum ond rummod wæs* (Miller, I, p. 165). K4, p. 271, notes a parallel with Bede's description of Abbot Eata, *omnium mansuetissimus ac simplicissimus* (HE IV.27); Old English *Bede*: *Se wæs milde wer and monþwær* (Miller, II, p. 362). For the collocation of *mildost ond monðwærost* in Old English homiletic literature, see M. P. Richards, 'A Re-examination of *Beowulf* ll. 3180–3182', *ELN* 10 (1973), 163–67.
[135] Colgrave and Mynors, pp. 230–31. Oswald's generosity is displayed in his treatment of beggars (HE III.6).
[136] See above, Chapter One, pp. 74–75.
[137] K2, p. lii.
[138] Klaeber, 'Christian Elements', p. 51. In the biblical story, a woman says to Christ: 'Blessed is the womb that bore thee, and the paps that gave thee suck' (Luc. XI.27). Orchard finds this parallel 'rather strained' (*CCB*, p. 147).

and reflects New Testament theological dogma',[139] while Allan Cabannis found echoes of both the Harrowing of Hell and the sacrament of baptism in the account of Beowulf's descent into and emergence from Grendel's mere (1494b–96, 1618–25).[140] Most recently, Thomas D. Hill has noticed a parallel between the description of Beow *on fæder bearme*, 'in the father's bosom' (21b), and the biblical phrase, *in sinu patris*, used, for example, in the Gospel of John to refer to Christ: *unigenitus Filius, qui est in sinu Patris*, 'the only begotten Son who is in the bosom of the Father' (John 1.18).[141]

Another hitherto unrecognized Christological echo appears in the account of Beow's birth:

> Đǣm eafera wæs   æfter cenned
> geong in geardum,   þone God sende
> folce tō frōfre;[142]   fyren-ðearfe ongeat —
> þæt hīe ǣr drugon   aldor-lēase
> lange hwīle.
> (12–16a). (Emphasis added).

[*To him a son was born afterwards*, young in the courts, *whom God sent as a comfort to the people*; He recognized their terrible need, that they had previously suffered lordlessness for a long time.]

In Christian tradition, the theme of the birth of a son (especially one 'sent by God') who brings comfort to mankind naturally evokes the Virgin Birth. In the Roman Rite, Isaiah's prophecy of the birth of a king is used as the first reading for the Christmas Liturgy: 'For *a child is born to us*, and a *son is given to us*, and the government is upon his shoulder: and his name shall be called, Wonderful, Counsellor, God the Mighty, the Father of the world to come, the Prince of Peace' (Isaiah 9.6) (emphasis added). In the New Testament, John the Evangelist declares that this prophecy is fulfilled with the birth of Jesus Christ:

---

[139] McNamee, 'Allegory of Salvation'.

[140] Cabannis, '*Beowulf* and the Liturgy'. For further New Testament parallels, see *CCB*, pp. 147–49. For an overview of scriptural and patristic parallels, see Andersson, 'Sources and Analogues', pp. 142–43.

[141] T. D. Hill, 'On fæder bearme: Beowulf, Line 21', *NQ* 66 (2019), 2–5, at 3. Hill concludes: 'In adapting a Biblical phrase *on bearme fæder* to the secular context of Germanic wisdom poetry, he [i.e. the poet] was emphasizing subtly, but clearly, the ideal of loving harmony between father and son – a harmony which the evangelist evoked in his account of the love which unfolds within the Trinity' (5).

[142] The same combination of the themes of royal birth and the comfort this brings to a people occurs during the account of the birth of Eomer, son of Offa, who will also grow to become a help to warriors, presumably as king: *þonon Ēomēr wōc/ hæleðum tō helpe*, 'then Eomer was born, as a help to warriors' (1960b–61a). See Chapter One, pp. 78–82.

By this hath the charity of God appeared towards us, because *God hath sent his only begotten Son* into the world, that we may live by him.
(I John 4.9).

For God so loved the world, *as to give his only begotten Son*; that whosoever believeth in him, may not perish, but may have life everlasting. *For God sent not his Son into the world*, to judge the world, but *that the world may be saved by him*.
(John 3.16–17). (Emphasis added).

In Paul's fourth letter to the Galatians, the birth of Christ the king is interpreted as the end of an age, the completion of the Old Dispensation and the beginning of the New: 'But *when the fulness of the time was come*, God sent his Son, made of a woman, made under the law' (Gal. 4.4).

While the half-line *hæleðum tō helpe* appears to have originated as a secular phrase which could be adapted for Christian purposes,[143] the collocation *folce tō frōfre* appears in exclusively Christian contexts in Old English verse outside of *Beowulf*.[144] Indeed, outside of *Beowulf* both phrases only occur in reference to Christ in the extant corpus of Old English poetry, though admittedly this corpus is dominated by explicitly Christian literature.[145] The phrase *folce tō frōfre*, in particular, appears in association with the Virgin Birth, for example, in the Old English *Baptismal Creed* preserved in MS Junius 121 (as part of the so-called 'Old English Benedictine Office'), which revolves around meditative poetic expansions of the Latin Creed:[146]

Et in Iesum Christum filium eius unicum, dominum nostrum.
Ic on *sunu* þīne   sōðne gelȳfe,
hælende cyning,   hider *āsende*
of ðām uplican   engla rīce
[...]
and hēo cūðlīce   cende swā mǣrne
eorð-būendum   engla scyppend,

---

[143] Cf. *Christ* 427/427b: *gumum tō helpe*; *Heliand* I.51: *managon te helpun* (also referring to birth of Christ). In his discussion of the half-line *wrāþum on andan* (*Beo* 708b), Klaeber comments: 'No doubt a stereotype combination belonging to a general rhetorical pattern which may be exemplified by *folce to frofre, hæleðum to helpe, geomrum to geoce, dryhtne to willan, werþeodum to wræce, him to teonan, halgum to teona*' ('Beowulfiana Minora', *Anglia* 63 [1939], 400–25, at 409).

[144] Similarly, Stephen Morrison notes that the Beowulfian collocation *frōfor ond fultum* is 'an alliterating word pair reserved for religious contexts', perhaps derived from the frequently occurring psalm-verse, *adiutor et protector*: '*Beowulf* 698a, 1273a: *frofor ond fultum*', *NQ* 27 (1980), 193–96, at 196.

[145] For the use of *hæleðum tō helpe* in reference to Christ, see *Elene* 679a, 1011a.

[146] For discussion, see S. L. Keefer, ed., *Old English Liturgical Verse: A Student Edition* (Toronto, 2010), pp. 83–96. The text printed here is from ASPR VI.

sē tō frōfre gewearð   fold-būendum,
and ymbe Bethleem   bodedan englas
þæt ācenned wæs   Crīst on eorðan.
(*Baptismal Creed*, 9–11, 20–24). (Emphasis added).

[*And in Jesus Christ your only son, Our Lord. I truly believe in the Saviour, your own true Son, Redeeming King, that you sent here, from that kingdom of the angels above* [...] *and she gave birth to that glorious Shaper of angels for earth-dwellers, who brought comfort to land-dwellers*, and around Bethlehem the angels declared that Christ was born on earth.]

The same collocation occurs in the Christ-poems of the Exeter Book, where Christ Himself declares: *Wearð ic āna geboren / folcum tō frōfre*, 'I alone was born as a comfort to the people' (*Christ III*, 1418b–21a). Similarly, the tenth-century calendar poem known as the Old English *Menologium* is structured around the feast of Christmas, when God the Father sent his only son to comfort the people:

Crīst wæs ācennyd   cyninga wuldor,
on midne winter,   mǣre þēoden,
ēce ælmihtig;   on þȳ eahteoðan dæg
Hǣlend gehāten,   heofon-rīces weard.
[...]
Þænne emb fēower niht   þætte fæder engla
his sunu sende   on þās sīdan gesceaft
folcum tō frōfre. Ne gē findan magon
hāligra tīda   þe man healdan sceal,
swā bebūgeð gebod   geond Bryten-rīcu
Sexna kyninges   on þās sylfan tīd.[147]
(*Menologium*, 1–4, 226–31). (Emphasis added).

[*Christ was born, the King of Glory*, in midwinter, glorious prince, eternal lord; on the eighth day the Healer was named, guardian of the kingdom of heaven. [...] Then, after four nights the father of angels *sent his son* into this vast creation, *to comfort the people*. Now you may find the times of the saints that people must hold, as the order was commanded throughout the British kingdom *by the Saxon kings* at this same time.]

In the light of the New Testament, the echoes of messianic kingship in the opening lines of *Beowulf*, like those in the Old Testament succession narrative itself, are not intended to suggest that Beow, or Beowulf, is a saviour-figure, but rather to point towards the birth of Christ, King of Kings, a figure conspicuous by His absence in *Beowulf*.[148]

---

[147] The text printed here is taken from *The Old English Metrical Calendar (Menologium)*, ed. K. Karasawa (Cambridge, 2015), though spelling has been standardized (ii = ī) and macrons added.
[148] Robert Hanning suggests that we view Beowulf as a 'displaced Christ figure',

Conclusion

This chapter has shown how the biblical succession narrative provided the main inspiration for ideas of dynasty and kingship throughout the early medieval period. It has argued that the *Beowulf*-poet, like other thinkers of his age, naturally drew on biblical paradigms of kingship in shaping his dynastic drama and in making pagan royal legend meaningful for a Christian audience. Rather than viewing the hero as a Christ-figure who dies for his people, or conversely, as a damned heathen, it has proposed that we should regard Beowulf, together with the other good and bad kings of the poem, in the light of the equally varied ruler portraits of the Old Testament, as imperfect forerunners both of Christ and of the Christian rulers of the poet's own day. Through comparison with Bede's portraits of Æthelfrith and Oswald, it has suggested that the closing lines of the poem point away from the primitive, warlike model of Scyld and towards the emergence of a new model of Christian kingship in early Anglo-Saxon England.

In the Preface to his *Ecclesiastical History*, Bede dedicates his work to his own king, Ceolfrith, and instructs his readers to imitate the good behaviour of the rulers he describes, while learning from the mistakes of those who fell from God's favour through their sins.[149] In the Conclusion, I briefly consider how *Beowulf* may also have served as a model for contemporary kingship at three important stages in the work's transmission: the seventh or eighth century, the most probable period of its composition; the age of Alfred, when the poem came to be read alongside tales of classical heroes and Christian saints; and the reigns of Æthelred and Cnut, when the text was copied into the Nowell Codex.

---

comparing him with King Arthur and other heroes of secular medieval literature who, like Christ, enter history from the unknown and return to the unknown, but who differ from Christ in that they fail to change history ('*Beowulf* as Heroic History', 86).

[149] Colgrave and Mynors, pp. 2–3.

Conclusion

Reading the Dynastic Drama in Anglo-Saxon England

This book has argued that *Beowulf* is a dynastic drama revolving around the fortunes of three great royal houses, in which the hero's three monster-fights play a central role. Chapter One demonstrated that the narrative structure, which for so long has puzzled critics, traces the life-cycle of an archetypal dynasty from youth to maturity and old age. Questions surrounding seemingly problematic or extraneous passages, such as the Scyld-prologue, the tale of Offa's bride, and 'Beowulf's Return', are resolved when they are considered as elements of this wider dynastic drama. Chapter Two argued that the poet introduced the figure of Beowulf into northern dynastic legend by combining tales of a great swimmer with the legends of the death of King Hygelac and Sigemund the dragon-slayer. With this new story of the death of King Beowulf, the poet mythologized the fall of a great royal house. Chapter Two also proposed that the poet transformed the legend of the demise of King Heremod into a mythological account of the rise of the Scyldings under Scyld Scefing and Beow that serves as a fitting prologue to his dynastic drama. Chapter Three focused on the role of the monsters as portents of dynastic and national crises. It suggested that in addition to biblical stories of Creation, the Fall, Cain and the Flood, the poet also utilized the tradition of the Fall of the Angels in casting Grendel as an illegitimate usurper. Grendel's mother was read as an antitype of the ideal dynastic queen and as a disruptive force in the survival of royal families. Finally, this chapter explored the appositional relationship between the dragon-fight and the accounts of the Swedish wars. Chapter Four explored the relationship between *Beowulf* and biblical kingship, arguing that the succession narrative of the Books of Kings served as a mythical paradigm for the poet's dynastic drama. Comparing the *Beowulf*-poet's ambivalent attitude to pre-Christian kingship with that of Bede, it argued that the poem charts the development of dynastic kingship as an institution, from a purely charisma-based office to one contingent on wisdom, kindness and generosity. In the figure of King Beowulf, the poet harmonized the qualities of pagan warrior-kingship with new, Christian standards of royal virtue.

By way of conclusion, I now offer some brief suggestions as to how the dynastic drama of *Beowulf* might have been read in Anglo-Saxon England during three key periods in its reception: first, the probable period of its composition, that is between the conversion and the first Viking Age (c. 650–c. 800); then, the time when the poem came to be read alongside the Old English version of *Alexander's Letter to Aristotle* and provided an inspiration for the authors of royal genealogies and verse hagiography, the age of Alfred and his successors (c. 871–930); and finally, the period of the manuscript's copying, the age of Æthelred and Cnut (c. 980–1020).

Mercia and Northumbria in the Age of Bede

As noted in the Introduction, a range of factors, including linguistic, metrical, stylistic and cultural evidence, strongly point to the composition of *Beowulf* in something close to its present form in an Anglian-speaking region, most likely Mercia, during the seventh or early-eighth centuries.[1] Michael Swanton, Peter Clemoes and, most recently, Fred Biggs have all shown how the model of kingship depicted in *Beowulf*, in particular the close relationship between a ruler and his people and the approach to different models of succession, maps especially well onto this early period of Anglo-Saxon history.[2] Turning to the historical records of Mercia and its chief rival, Northumbria, in this period, we find a patchwork of warring dynasties not dissimilar to that presented in the poem. Like the Scyldings and Hrethlings, these early Anglian royal houses typically rose and fell within a few generations, their kings constantly waging war in pursuit of plunder and, in the vast majority of cases, dying in battle. Indeed, the fluctuating fortunes of the Northumbrian and Mercian royal houses during this period present a plausible and attractive context for the composition of the dynastic drama of *Beowulf*.[3]

Bede's account of the fall of the Æthelfrithings, rulers of Bernicia, in particular, bears close comparison with the poem's account of the fall of the Hrethlings. The pagan Æthelfrith (r. c. 593–616), admired by Bede for

---

[1] See esp. R. D. Fulk, '*Beowulf* and Language History', in Neidorf (2014), pp. 19–36; and Fulk, *History of Old English Meter*, pp. 348–92. For further references, see above, pp. x n.11, 6.

[2] Swanton, *Crisis and Development*, pp. 152–53; P. Clemoes, *Interactions of Thought and Language in Old English Poetry*, CSASE 12 (Cambridge, 1995), pp. 3–67; Biggs, 'History and Fiction', p. 156. T. D. Hill has recently argued for dating the poem in the seventh or eighth century on the grounds of its 'peculiar spiritual atmosphere': '*Beowulf* and Conversion History', in Neidorf (2014), pp. 191–201, at 197.

[3] For the historical background to this discussion, I rely largely on the authoritative account of F. M. Stenton, *Anglo-Saxon England* (Oxford, 1943; 3rd edn 1971), pp. 74–95 ('Anglian Northumbria') and pp. 202–38 ('The Ascendancy of the Mercian Kings'). See also Kirby, *Earliest English Kings*, pp. 50–150; Yorke, *Kings and Kingdoms*.

his love of fame, was the first to rule over both the kingdoms of Bernicia and Deira.[4] Following his death in battle against King Rædwald of East Anglia in 616, Æthelfrith's sons fled into exile, and the Northumbrian kingdom came into the hands of the Deiran prince Edwin, son of Ælle, who had himself sought refuge from Æthelfrith at the court of Rædwald. After his conversion by Paulinus, as recorded in Bede's famous story of the sparrow's flight through the hall (*HE* II.9–13), Edwin ruled the united kingdom of Northumbria until 632. Although now a Christian, Edwin was nonetheless, in Stenton's phrase, 'a typical king of the Heroic Age', and his death in battle against Cadwallon in 632 resulted in 'not only the collapse of the confederation which he had founded but the extinction of his branch of the royal house'.[5] Following Edwin's death, Northumbria once more split into two kingdoms, only to be reunited soon afterwards under the reign of Oswald, son of Æthelfrith.[6] With Oswald's death at the hands of Penda of Mercia in 641, however, the kingdom was yet again divided. Like Edwin, Oswald was a convert king, who came to be regarded as a saint after defeating the King of Gwynned, Cadwallon, at Heavenfield in 633/34.[7] Following his death in battle against Penda, the pagan king of Mercia, at Maserfield in 641/42, Oswald was succeeded by his brother, Oswiu, who was in turn succeeded by his son, Ecgfrith, in 664.[8] After Ecgfrith's death at the Battle of Nechtansmere in 685, the power of the Æthelfrithings began to wane due to a lack of suitable male heirs. In an attempt to revive the dynasty's fortunes, Aldfrith, a half-brother of Ecgfrith, was summoned from Ireland, but he died in 704/05 while his sons were too young to succeed him. There briefly followed the reign of a usurper of unknown origin, Eadwulf, before the Æthelfrithing line was briefly restored by Aldfrith's eldest son, Osred, who ruled as a minor from 705 under the protection of influential kin. However, in 716 Osred was killed and succeeded by Cenred, a distant, collateral relative.[9] The rarity of royal minorities in England before the tenth century makes the parallels between the fates of the Northumbrian child-king, Osred, and Hygelac's son, Heardred, of particular interest.[10]

---

[4] Bede, *HE* I.34, II.12; Colgrave and Mynors, pp. 116–17, 180–81. For comparison with Beowulf, see above, pp. 228–30.
[5] Stenton, *Anglo-Saxon England*, pp. 79–81.
[6] On Oswald and Beowulf, see above, pp. 230–31.
[7] Bede, *HE* II.5, III.2–3, III.9–14; Colgrave and Mynors, pp. 148–50, 214–21, 240–55.
[8] On Ecgfrith's calamitous raid on the Picts, see above, pp. 225–27.
[9] Bede, *HE* V.18, V.22; Colgrave and Mynors, pp. 512–13, 552–53. On Osred's minority, see Yorke, *Kings and Kingdoms*, pp. 87–88.
[10] Yorke, *Anglo-Saxon Kingdoms*, p. 87, notes that this is the only such case recorded in England before 900. Bernicia's rival Northumbrian dynasty, Deira, suffered a similar fate due to a series of premature deaths, both in battle and by natural causes, and a lack of legitimate heirs. On Merovingian child kings, see Chapter Four, p. 106.

Conclusion

After Oswald's death at Maserfield, the balance of power swung south to Mercia, where Penda ruled until his defeat by Oswiu, king of Deira, in 654. Frank Stenton provides a terse assessment of Mercian politics during the late-seventh and early-eighth centuries:

> There was much fighting in this period. Individual provinces passed by war from one king to another, the younger members of a dynasty occasionally rose against its head, and the entertainment of exiles was a fertile source of trouble. [...] The Mercian kingdom [...] was not so much a state as a group of peoples held together by an illustrious dynasty.[11]

The sudden revival of the Mercian dynasty under Wulfhere, son of Penda, provides an interesting historical counterpart to the story of Scyld Scefing, whose miraculous arrival signals a remarkable *edwenden*, 'reversal', in the fortunes of the Danes. After his father's death, Wulfhere went into hiding until he was declared king by a group of ealdormen in 657. Under his strong military leadership, Mercia underwent another period of military expansion, shattering Oswiu's overlordship of the southern kingdoms. Wulfhere held *imperium* until his defeat by Ecgfrith, son of Oswiu, in 674. Mercian *imperium* was again restored under Æthelbald (r. 716–757). Following Æthelbald's murder by his own bodyguard there was another brief period of in-fighting among rival claimants before the emergence of Offa (r. 757–786), a ruler whose name evoked the legendary king of the continental Angles whose deeds are celebrated in *Beowulf* (1931b–72) and *Widsith* (35–44).[12]

A Mercian poet in this period, attached to a religious centre such as Lichfield and in the orbit of a royal court such as Tamworth, would have had ample opportunity to reflect on the contrasting fortunes of royal dynasties. One might imagine such a poet composing a work in the style of Old English heroic verse, that used the royal legends of ancient times as a mirror for the rulers of his own day.[13] An in-depth exploration of links between *Beowulf* and this period of Mercian history falls outside the scope of this study, though such an investigation would doubtless shed new light on the poem's intersection with early Anglo-Saxon culture and literature. However, the recent discovery of the Staffordshire Hoard,

---

[11] Stenton, *Anglo-Saxon England*, p. 202. For a range of recent perspectives on Mercian culture in this period, see Brown and Farr (2005). See also M. D. T. Capper, 'Contested Loyalties: Regional and National Identities in the Midland Kingdoms of Anglo-Saxon England, c.700–c.900' (Unpubl. doctoral dissertation, University of Sheffield, 2010).

[12] For connections between the Offa-digression in *Beowulf* and the reign of Offa of Mercia, see above, pp. 80, 140 n.101.

[13] On the physical proximity of religious centres and royal courts in this period, see I. N. Wood, 'Monasteries and the Geography of Power in the Age of Bede', *Northern History* 45 (2008), 11–25.

probably deposited in the earth after a major battle between the Mercians and Northumbrians that took place close to Lichfield some time in the seventh century, gives us further pause for thought. Among the items discovered in the Staffordshire Hoard are weapons and parts of what may have been a processional cross, as well as a gold strip bearing an inscription from Numbers 10.35, the words uttered by Moses as he lifted up the ark: *Surge Domine et dissipentur inimici tui et fugiant qui oderunt te a facie tua*, 'Arise, O Lord, and let thy enemies be scattered, and let them that hate thee, flee from before thy face.'[14] The same scriptural verse appears in Felix's *Life of Guthlac* (c. 730–40), in which the saint, himself a Mercian prince, addresses King Æthelbald and expresses his wish that he will vanquish his enemies.[15] The Staffordshire Hoard therefore presents a striking analogue to the various accounts of treasure-deposits that recur at key moments throughout *Beowulf*, from Scyld Scefing's ship-funeral (26–52) to the Lay of the Last Survivor (2231b–77) to King Beowulf's glorious obsequies (3137–82).[16] In its blending of biblical rhetoric and warrior-kingship, the Hoard hints at the same form of cultural syncretism that may have given rise to the dynastic drama of *Beowulf*.

Alfredian Wessex

Another period during which *Beowulf* appears to have enjoyed some popularity was the reign of Alfred of Wessex (871–99). Dorothy Whitelock found it improbable that a poem that celebrates the glory of ancient Danish kings in its opening lines could have been composed at a time when all of the English kingdoms of the heptarchy save Wessex had come under Danish control.[17] As we saw in Chapter Two, however, it was during this same period that the West Saxon royal house began to declare its descent from various Danish kings mentioned in *Beowulf*, among them Heremod, Scef, Scyld and Beow, in the form of an elaborate royal genealogy.[18] As noted above, Dennis Cronan has recently argued persuasively that Alfred might have sought to 'contain' such Danish royal ancestors

---

[14] Cf. Ps. 68.2. For discussion of the hoard and its connections with Mercian and Northumbrian kingship in this period, and in particular with Oswald, see Foot, 'Bede's Kings', pp. 30–31. See further D. Symons, *The Staffordshire Hoard* (Birmingham, 2014).
[15] *Felix's Life of Saint Guthlac*, ed. and trans. B. Colgrave (Cambridge, 1985), p. 19.
[16] On the acquisition and use of treasure in *Beowulf*, see esp. pp. 106–08, 136–39.
[17] Whitelock, *Audience*, pp. 24–25. See also K3, p. cvii. For alternative views, see N. Jacobs, 'Anglo-Danish Relations, Poetic Archaism and the Date of *Beowulf*: A Reconsideration of the Evidence', *Poetica* 8 (1977), 23–43; R. I. Page, 'The Audience of *Beowulf* and the Vikings', in Chase (1981), pp. 113–22.
[18] See pp. 143–46.

within the broader narrative of Christian history after his conversion of Guthrum in 878, by making Scyld a descendant of Noah and ultimately Christ.[19] It seems, therefore, that even at some considerable remove from its original composition, *Beowulf* continued to perform an important political role, acting as a link between Anglo-Saxon and Scandinavian dynastic traditions.

In addition to this genealogical link with the ancient kings of the Danes, there are a number of other ways that *Beowulf* intersects with the political, spiritual and cultural concerns of the Alfredian court circle. Among the various Latin works translated into English during this period are several texts that share with *Beowulf* a deep interest in the morality of rulers and the close relationship between kings and God, among them Gregory's *Pastoral Care*, Boethius's *Consolation of Philosophy*, the (first fifty) Psalms, and Orosius's *History Against the Pagans in Seven Books*. As we saw in Chapter Four, the *Pastoral Care*, available in England since the Augustinian mission in 597, provides a close analogue to parts of Hrothgar's sermon and, in particular, the Danish king's account of the fall of King Heremod. The Orosian *History* also bears comparison with *Beowulf* through its focus on the rising and falling of the world's four great world empires (Babylon—Macedon—Carthage—Rome) (II.1.3–5). In contrast to *Beowulf*, however, which presents a cyclical vision of dynastic history in a time effectively before Christ, for Orosius the cycle of earthly empires has already reached its conclusion with the birth of Christ during the Roman Empire (VI.22).[20] In the age of Alfred and his successors, the West Saxons, like the Carolingians before them, came to see themselves as heirs to Rome, believing that their kings were chosen and anointed by God and that they, as a race, were therefore numbered among God's chosen people.[21] *Beowulf*, as this book has argued, presents a far more ambivalent view of kingship, closer to that of Bede. Nonetheless, it is possible to see how some aspects of the poem, notably the portraits of the Davidic Beowulf and the Solomonic Hrothgar, might have appealed to the Alfredian court circle.[22]

A further connection between *Beowulf* and Alfredian literature is provided by the verse saint's life *Andreas*, now preserved in the late-tenth century Vercelli Book but according to its most recent editors probably

---

[19] Cronan, 'The Containment of Scyld'.
[20] See Leneghan, *'Translatio imperii'*.
[21] See esp. Pratt, *Political Thought of Alfred*.
[22] Cf. Anlezark, *Water and Fire*, p. 373: 'For the *Beowulf* poet, as for Alfred, the great lesson taught by the past is that kings must rule wisely: in *Beowulf* it is this wisdom which gives the character of the pagan Hrothgar an exemplary quality both for the young Beowulf and for Christian audiences. In both Alfred's 'Boethius' and *Beowulf* the warning for the powerful is not to be foolish like the giants. Heremod succumbed to this danger; I would argue Beowulf does not.'

composed in Wessex during the late-ninth century.[23] It is now widely recognized that the *Andreas*-poet made extensive use of *Beowulf*, as well perhaps as the poems of Cynewulf, in adapting his Latin source, a now-lost version of the apocryphal Acts of Matthew and Andrew, to the tastes of an Anglo-Saxon audience familiar with vernacular heroic poetry.[24] By importing heroic diction and imagery from these vernacular works, the *Andreas*-poet sought to present his evangelizing saint as a *miles christi*.[25] Another way in which *Andreas* engages with *Beowulf* is in its transformation of the secular poem's ambivalent portrait of pre-Christian dynastic kingship into a confident celebration of the glories of apostolic succession.[26] Hence, the *Andreas*-poet repurposes the opening lines of *Beowulf*, with its evocation of the might and glory of *þēod-cyningas* and *æþelingas* in ancient times (1–3), to celebrate the victories of the Lord's thanes:

> Hwæt, wē gefrūnan   on fyrn-dagum
> twelfe under tunglum   tīr-ēadige hæleð,
> þēodnes þegnas.
> (*Andreas*, 1–3a).[27]

[Listen! We have heard of twelve under the skies, victory-blessed warriors, the thanes of the lord, in ancient times.]

The twelve apostles also recall the twelve *æþelinga bearn ealra twelfe*, 'sons of æthelings, twelve in all' (3170), who ride around King Beowulf's barrow praising him as the best of earthly kings. In the closing lines of *Andreas*, this scene finds its echo in the Meremedonians' joyous hymn to the eternal glory of the King of Kings:

> Ān is *ēce* god   eallra gesceafta!
> Is his miht ond his æht   ofer middan-geard
> brēme gebledsod,   ond his blæd ofer eall
> in heofon-þrymme   hālgum scīneð,
> wlitige on wuldre   tō wīdan aldre,
> *ēce* mid englum;   þæt is æðele cyning!
> (*Andreas*, 1717–22). (Emphasis added).

---

[23] North and Bintley, eds, *Andreas*, pp. 97–115.
[24] For a summary of the arguments, see North and Bintley, pp. 57–81.
[25] See, for example, D. Hamilton, '*Andreas* and *Beowulf*: Placing the Hero', in *Anglo-Saxon Poetry: Essays in Appreciation for John C. McGalliard*, ed. L. E. Nicholson and D. W. Frese (Notre Dame, IN, University of Notre Dame Press, 1975), pp. 81–98; I. Herbison, 'Generic Adaptation in *Andreas*', in *Essays on Anglo-Saxon and Related Themes in Memory of Lynne Grundy*, ed. J. Roberts and J. L. Nelson, King's College London Medieval Studies 17 (Exeter, 2000), pp. 181–211.
[26] On the apostles in Old English literature, see H. Magennis, '*Cristes leorningcnihtas*: traditions of the apostles in Old English literature', in *Aspects of Knowledge: Preserving and reinventing traditions of learning in the Middle Ages*, ed. M. Cesario and H. Magennis (Manchester, 2018), pp. 97–115.
[27] Quotations of *Andreas* are taken from the 2016 edition by North and Bintley.

[There is one *Eternal* God of All Creation! His might and His power are widely blessed in renown over middle-earth and His glory shines over all in the might of heaven, splendidly in glory for all time, *eternal* with the angels; that is a Noble King!][28]

While *Beowulf* closes with the lordless Geats facing an uncertain future, *Andreas* ends on a more optimistic note, with a people liberated from the chains of paganism and looking forward to their place in the eternal heavenly kingdom. While *Beowulf* places paganism and Christianity in what Fred Robinson calls 'a brief, loving, and faintly disquieting apposition',[29] *Andreas* sharply juxtaposes the two cultures, leaving its audience in no doubt about the path they must follow to avoid damnation.

There is some evidence to support the view that it was during the Alfredian period that *Beowulf* first came to be read as a critique of pagan kingship, rather than as a mirror of both good and bad kings. As several scholars, most recently Simon Thomson, have noted, the version of *Beowulf* that eventually found its way into the Nowell Codex was probably circulated together with a copy of the Old English version of *Alexander's Letter to Aristotle* since the Alfredian period or thereabouts.[30] Indeed, as Orchard has argued, the author of the *Letter*, who probably worked in the late-ninth or early-tenth century, appears to have made use of the Old English heroic poem in adapting his Latin source for an English audience.[31] The suggestive juxtaposition of the *Letter* and *Beowulf* invites the reader to judge Beowulf and Alexander as two rulers whose overweening pride

---

[28] Compare the Latin and Old English analogues: Codex Casanatensis: *unus est deus, quem nobis manifestavit beatus andreas apostolus eius dominum nostrum iesum christum, cui est honor et gloria, in secula seculorum, Amen* (*Die lateinischen Bearbeitungen der Acta Andreae et Matthiae apud Anthropophagos*, Beihefte zur Zeitschrift für neutestamentliche Wissenschaften 12, ed. F. Blatt [Giessen, 1930], p. 95), 'God is one, whom the blessed Apostle Andrew manifested to us, his Lord our Jesus Christ, to whom be honor and glory, forever and ever. Amen.' (*The Acts of Andrew in the Country of the Cannibals: Translations from Greek, Latin, and Old English*, Garland Library of Medieval Literature, 70.B, ed. and trans. R. Boenig [New York and London, 1991], p. 55); Blickling Homily XXIX: *An is Drihten God, se is Hælend Crist, and se Halga Gast, þam is wuldor and geweald on þære Halgan þrynnysse þurh ealra worulda woruld soðlice a butan ende* (Morris, p. 249), 'There is one Lord God, He is Christ the Saviour, and the Holy Spirit, whom is glory and power in the Holy Trinity, through all of the world, truly world without end.' For comparison with *Beowulf* 11b (*þæt wæs gōd cyning*) see Chapter One, pp. 41–42. See further Leneghan, 'Departure of Hero'.

[29] Robinson, *Appositive Style*, p. 82. Cf. Tolkien, 'Monsters', p. 73: 'We get in fact a poem from a pregnant moment of poise, looking back into the pit, by a man learned in old tales who was struggling, as it were, to get a general view of them all [...]. He could view from without, but still feel immediately and from within, the old dogma: despair of the event, combined with faith in the value of doomed resistance.'

[30] Thomson, *Communal Creativity*, pp. 27–34.

[31] Orchard, *Pride and Prodigies*, pp. 23–25.

causes their downfall. However, as this book has argued, when read in isolation from the *Letter*, *Beowulf* offers a rather more balanced view of both the merits and defects of pre-Christian kingship than that suggested by its position in the Nowell Codex. The transmission of *Beowulf* together with the *Letter* arguably says more about negative Alfredian attitudes to pagan history than it does about *Beowulf* itself.[32]

As this brief overview demonstrates, *Beowulf* remained relevant during the age of Alfred, providing inspiration for royal genealogists and hagiographers. However, in the climate of the Viking wars, it became necessary to adapt the poem's nuanced and ambiguous portrait of pagan Scandinavian kingship for new political and cultural purposes. By setting Scyld Scefing and his relatives within the narrative of salvation history, by transforming the pagan Beowulf into an evangelizing saint, and by inviting readers to compare the hero with the great pagan emperor Alexander the Great, Alfredian writers ensured that *Beowulf* was preserved despite the dramatically shifting cultural landscape of Anglo-Saxon England.

The Nowell Codex

The third and final phase of the poem's reception considered here comes towards the end of the Anglo-Saxon period, at the time of the text's copying into the Nowell Codex. As Thomson has recently argued, the considerable care which the two scribes took in attempting to correct and emend this already challenging, ancient and relatively obscure text provides some indication of the poem's appeal and value during the late-tenth or early-eleventh centuries.[33] For a range of predominantly cultural reasons, Thomson places the manuscript's copying in the reign of King Cnut, rather than during that of his West Saxon predecessor, Æthelred, as has traditionally been the case.[34] It is equally possible, however, given

---

[32] On Alfredian attitudes to classical and Germanic paganism, see Tyler, 'Trojans in Anglo-Saxon England'; B. Yorke, 'King Alfred and Weland: Transformation at the Court of King Alfred', in *Transformation in Anglo-Saxon Culture: Toller Lectures on Art, Archaeology and Text*, ed. C. Insley and G. Owen-Crocker (Oxford, 2017), pp. 47–70. For possible connections between *Beowulf* and Athelstan's court, see S. Foot, *Athelstan: The First King of England* (New Haven and London, 2011), pp. 115–17.

[33] Thomson, *Communal Creativity*, esp. pp. 149–252. Neidorf, *Transmission*, emphasizes the extent to which the scribes garbled ancient heroic names.

[34] Thomson, *Communal Creativity*, esp. pp. 44–64. Helen Damico has recently unearthed a series of interesting parallels between the Danish part of the poem and texts from Cnut's reign, though rather than using this as evidence for the poem's possible influence on Anglo-Danish court, she proposes that at least this part of the poem was in fact composed at this time as a political allegory: *Beowulf and the Grendelkin*. Damico's argument builds on the earlier sugges-

the overlapping dates ascribed by paleographers to the respective hands, that the two scribes lived through both the calamitous latter years of Æthelred's reign and the early years of Cnut. In addition to *Beowulf*, three of the other four items copied in the manuscript, *The Passion of Saint Christopher*, *Alexander* and *Judith*, all deal with the toppling of powerful rulers who are either deemed unfit for purpose or who simply come to the end of their allotted time on earth.[35] In the pages of the Nowell Codex, an English reader at this time would have encountered an entertaining and edifying selection of prose and verse texts in their own tongue. For some readers the main appeal of this collection might have been its exciting tales of ancient heroes, strange monsters and exotic locations. Yet those who chose to look more closely would also find instructive tales concerning the value of royal counsel, the exemplary conduct of kings and queens in ancient times, the terrible consequences of foolhardiness and royal pride, and the awe-inspiring power of God over the fates of royal houses.

As we saw in Chapter Two, the late-tenth-century *Chronicon* of Æthelweard traces the inception of the West Saxon dynasty back to the same Danish royal origin-legend with which *Beowulf* begins.[36] Within this context, *Beowulf* would have spoken directly to the political concerns of the house of Æthelred around the time of the Nowell Codex's copying. With the brief exile of King Æthelred in Normandy during 1013–14, the West Saxon house lost its grip on power for the first time since the early-ninth century, as the Danish King Sweyn Forkbeard took the throne. Although Æthelred was restored to the throne on Sweyn's death in 1014, within two years he too was dead, with the result that England came under the rule of Cnut. The overthrow of the West Saxon house, which by now traced its origins back to the ancestral home of the Scyldings in *Scani*, by the Christian Danish emperor, Cnut, who styled himself *Skjöldung*, provides yet another context in which the dynastic drama of *Beowulf* assumed new meaning under changed political circumstances. It is a testament to the remarkable skill of the *Beowulf*-poet, *sē ðe eal fela eald-gesegena/ worn*

---

tion of Kiernan that Scribe B of the Nowell Codex was, in effect, the *Beowulf*-poet: *Beowulf Manuscript*. For arguments in favour of the poem's copying in Æthelred's reign on palaeographical grounds, see esp. D. N. Dumville, '*Beowulf* Come Lately: Some Notes on the Palaeography of the Nowell Codex', *Archiv für das Studium der Neuren Sprachen und Literaturen* 225 (1988), 49–63; D. N. Dumville, 'The *Beowulf* Manuscript and How Not to Date it', *Medieval English Student's Newsletter* 39 (1998), 21–27; and, on cultural and contextual grounds, see, for example, Powell, 'Meditating on Men and Monsters'; L. Neidorf, 'VII Æthelred and the Genesis of the *Beowulf* Manuscript', *PQ* 89 (2010), 119–39.

[35] Thomson, *Communal Creativity*, p. 100, suggests that *Wonders of the East* served as a linking piece between hagiographical texts which originally stood at the opening of the codex and the secular texts, *Alexander* and *Beowulf*.

[36] See pp. 144–45.

gemunde, 'he who recalled a great many old tales from afar' (869), that this still strange and fascinating Old English poem continues to inspire so many divergent critical readings, interpretations and adaptations to this day. By imaginatively combining the raw materials of folktale, heroic legend and hagiography with biblical paradigms of feuding and kingship, this remarkable poet provided the Anglo-Saxons with their very own *cyninga-boc*, an Old English Book of Kings.

Appendix A:
Plot Summary of *Skjöldunga saga*[1]

Odinus conquers northern Europe and leaves Denmark and Sweden to his sons, Scioldus and Ingo (chs 1–2):

After arriving from Asia, Odinus 'conquered the inhabitants of most of northern Europe' and assigned territory to his sons: Denmark goes to Scioldus, from whom the Danes took the name Skiolldungar; Sweden is given to Ingo, from whom the Swedes take their name Inglingar. Scioldus ruled at Hledra (i.e. Lejre) in Zealand; Scioldus has a son, Leifus I, who succeeds him as king and enjoys a remarkably peaceful reign.

Frodo I and Herleifus (chs 3–4):

Leifus is succeeded by his son, Frodo I, famous for his knowledge, who also enjoys a tranquil reign; Frodo I dies in a fire and is succeeded by his son, Leifus II, renamed Herleifus after his success in battle; Herleifus has many sons, the most prominent of whom are Havardus and Leifus III.

Havardus, Dan I, and Dan II (chs 5–7):

The kingdom passes from Herleifus to his son, Havardus, and thence to his brother, Leifus III. Each of Leifus's six sons rules in turn at Lethra (i.e. Lejre); after the reign of Leifus's sixth son, Gunnleifus, the kingdom passes to a cousin, Frodo II, and thence to his son, Vermundus; a magnate named Rigus comes to rule in Jutland and marries a girl named Dana; their son, Dan I, from whom the Danes took their name, becomes king of Jutland; the royal genealogy becomes unclear for a time, but it emerges that Dan II, a descendant of Dan I, eventually came to rule in Jutland and married Olafa, granddaughter of Frodo II, son of Havardus, king of Denmark; Dan II is an outstanding warrior and earns the nickname *hinn Mikelate* ('proud' or 'magnificent'); during his reign, the Danes abandon the practice of cremation and begin interring their dead along with grave goods; Dan II and Olafa have a son, Frodo III.

---

[1] Text and spellings based on Clarence Miller's 2007 translation of Arngrímur Jónsson's sixteenth-century abstract.

Frodo III (the peaceful) and Frideleifus II (chs 7–8):

Frodo III succeeds his father Dan II and marries Inga, daughter of Ingo, king of Sweden; after a peaceful reign, Frodo dies in a hunting accident, leaving two sons, Fridleifus and Halfdanus. Fridleifus succeeds his father, Frodo III, suppressing witchcraft and surrounding himself with a group of great champions, including Starcardus; Fridleifus has two sons, Alo and Frodo, born to different mothers.

Frodo IV and his sons, Halfdanus (OE Healfdene) and Ingialldus (OE Ingeld) (ch. 9):

Frodo IV succeeds his father Fridleifus, while Alo becomes a famous sea-raider; Frodo maintains a great court at Lethra and at Ringsted, placing Starcardus in charge of his warriors; Alo becomes king of Sweden; Frodo and Alo wage war against each other; acting on Frodo's behalf, Starcardus deceives Alo and kills him; Frodo has two sons, Halfdanus (OE Healfdene), born of the kidnapped daughter of the defeated King Iorundus of Sweden, and Ingialldus (OE Ingeld), born to a different mother and considered the king's legitimate heir. Ingialldus marries the daughter of Sverting, a Swedish baron whom Frodo had subdued and forced to pay tribute; Frodo is murdered by Iorundus, King of Sweden, and Sverting, in revenge for the killing of his brother, Alo.

Ingialldus and Halfdanus (ch. 10):

Sverting placates his son-in-law Ingialldus, but Halfdanus, who now rules at Skåne, kills twelve of Sverting's sons in revenge for the killing of his father, Frodo; Ingialldus gives Halfdanus a third of his kingdom; Ingialldus has a son named Agnarus; Halfdanus has a daughter, Signya, and two sons, Roas (OE Hrothgar) and Helgo (OE Halga), by a woman named Sigrida. Ingialldus becomes greedy for the kingdom and attacks and kills Halfdanus, with the result that he becomes sole ruler of Denmark; Ingialldus marries his brother's widow, Sigrida; the two sons of Halfdanus and Sigrida, Roas and Helgo, hide from Ingialldus on an island in Skane; later they avenge their father's death by killing Ingialldus.

Roas (OE Hrothgar) and Helgo (OE Halga) (ch. 11):

Roas and Helgo rule together, Roas initially living a quiet life at home, while Helgo goes out raiding; Helgo abducts and rapes Olava, queen or duchess of Saxony, who bears him a daughter, Yrsa; Helgo gives up raiding, swapping roles with his brother, Roas, who marries an English princess; Helgo then takes up raiding again, attacking the king of Sweden

Appendix A

and seizing Yrsa; despite Roas's warnings that Yrsa bears a family resemblance, Helgo marries her, not knowing that she is his own daughter; Yrsa bears Helgo a son, Rolfo (OE Hrothulf), nicknamed Krag (or Krake); Olava learns about the marriage and secretly travels to Denmark, where she meets Yrsa and tells her that Helgo is in fact her father; Yrsa leaves Helgo, who dies in battle five years later.

Rolfo (OE Hrothulf) Krag (ch. 12):

Rolfo succeeds his murdered father, Helgo, aged eight; a little later, his uncle, Roas, is killed by his own cousins, Ærecus (OE Hrethric) and Frodo, sons of Ingialldus; Rolfo 'was remarkable and famous for his virtues: for wisdom, power or wealth, bravery and decency and outstanding kindness; he was tall and thin'; Woggerus gives Rolfo the nickname Krag/Krake on account of his height, and promises to avenge him should he ever be murdered; Rolfo has two daughters, Driva and Skur, the first of whom marries Wisterchus, a Swedish warrior and giant-slayer, while the second marries Bodvarus (i.e. Bodvar Bjarki), a Norwegian warrior and one of Rolfo's champions who 'bore away from all the others the prize for bravery'; this Bodvarus kills Agnarus, cousin of Rolfo's father and son of Ingialldus, on Rolfo's behalf; Rolfo wages war against Hiørvardus (OE Heoroweard), king of Öland, husband of Scullda, the daughter of King Adillus (OE Eadgils) and Queen Yrsa of Sweden (hence Rolfo's sister on his mother's side); Rolfo defeats Hiørvardus and forces him to pay tribute.

Adillus, king of Sweden, fights a great battle against Alo, king of the Upplands in Norway, at Lake Waener, which is frozen over with ice; Rolfo sends twelve warriors and, with their help, Adillus has the victory; Adillus fails to reward Rolfo's champions for their service, so Rolfo travels to Sweden with his warriors; Rolfo's men are deceived by Adillus and trapped in a hall, where they are attacked with fire; Queen Yrsa intervenes, bringing the payment due to Rolfo's champions; Adillus attacks the Danes with a huge army, but Rolfo manages to escape by strewing gold in the paths of the Swedes; Rolfo refuses a gift of chain mail and a military cloak from Odinus, disguised as a peasant in a hut.

Encouraged by his wife, Sculda, sister of Rolfo, Hiørvardus attacks Rolfo under the pretence of paying tribute; Rolfo and his men bravely defend themselves, but after Odinus appears in the battle on the side of Hiørvardus, Rolfo is slain along with all his warriors, save Woggerus.

Hiørvardus (ch. 12):

The next day, Hiørvardus is hailed as king by the Danes, but Woggerus kills him during the oath-taking ritual: 'Among the kings of Denmark he alone ruled for scarcely six hours.'

Rærecus (OE Hrethric) and Waldarus (chs 14–15):

Hiørvardus is succeeded by Rolfo's kinsman, Rærecus, the paternal cousin of Rolfo's father, Helgo; Walldarus wages war against Rærecus; the kingdom of Denmark is then divided between them, with Rærecus ruling at Sælandia and Walldarus at Skane. 'At this point in the accounts of the Icelanders or Norwegians, the line of the Danish kings breaks off.'

Appendix B:
Plot Summary of *Hrólfs saga kraka*[1]

King Frodi (chs 1–5):

The saga opens with an account of the conflict between the brothers, King Frodi (OE Froda) and King Halfdan (OE Healfdene). Halfdan has three children; two boys, Hroar (OE Hrothgar) and Helgi (OE Halga), and a daughter, Signy, who marries Jarl Saevil. Jealous of his brother's success, Frodi attacks and kills Halfdan in his hall. Halfdan's two sons, Hroar and Helgi, escape and hide from Frodi.

Frodi attempts to track down Hroar and Helgi, but is thwarted by the efforts of Vifil, a friend of Halfdan, who hides the boys on his island. With the assistance of their foster father, Regin, Hroar and Helgi attack Frodi and burn his hall, killing him and their own mother, Sigrid; Hroar and Helgi succeed Frodi. Hroar is mild and easy-going; Helgi is the greater warrior and held in higher regard. Hroar marries Ogn, daughter of the king of England, and rules there.

Hroar and Helgi, sons of Halfdan (chs 6–17):

Helgi rules in Denmark; Helgi attempts to marry Queen Olof, ruler of Saxland, but she tricks him after a feast, drugging him and putting him in a sack; Helgi, disguised as a churl, then tricks Olof into venturing into a wood on the pretext of leading her to treasure; Helgi captures Olof and takes her with him to his ship, where he rapes her; Olof secretly bears a child, Yrsa, whom she scorns, telling her that she is of low birth; Helgi returns to Olof's kingdom in disguise and falls in love with Yrsa, not knowing that she is in fact his daughter; Helgi takes Yrsa home with him and marries her; Hroar visits Helgi and receives a valuable ring from him.

Hrok, son of Jarl Saevil, requests a third of the kingdom and the same ring from Helgi as a reward for his father's assistance of the princes when they were in hiding, but Helgi refuses; Hrok visits Hroar and takes the ring from him, casting it into the sea; Hroar punishes Hrok by cutting off his foot; Hrok attacks and kills Hroar and asks for the hand of his widow, Ogn; Ogn refuses on the grounds that she is bearing the late Hroar's

---

[1] Chapter numbers are from Guðni Jónsson's edition. Spellings of personal and tribal names are taken from Byock's translation.

child, and sends word to Helgi; Ogn gives birth to Hroar's son, Agnar; Helgi attacks and maims Hrok; Agnar grows to become a great hero, surpassing his father, Hroar; Agnar swims to the bottom of the lake to recover Hroar's ring.

Helgi and Yrsa (his daughter via Olof) have a son, Hrolf; Olof visits Helgi and Yrsa, revealing Yrsa's parentage; Yrsa leaves Helgi to live with her mother, Olof. Adils (OE Eadgils), king of Sweden, marries Yrsa; Helgi is visited by an elfin woman in disguise; after they sleep together, Helgi promises to meet her in a year's time and honour the child she will bear; Helgi forgets his promise; three years later, a girl, Skuld, is presented to Helgi as his daughter; Skuld is raised at Helgi's court; Helgi goes on foreign raids, leaving his son, Hrolf (OE Hrothulf), at home.

Helgi travels to Adils' kingdom to retrieve Yrsa, but is tricked into attending a feast while preparations are being made for his murder; on the way back to his ships, Helgi is ambushed and killed by Adils' berserkers; Yrsa is angry with Adils for the murder of Helgi and threatens to harm his berserkers; Adils offers Yrsa gifts to compensate for the death of Helgi.

Svipdag and the berserkers (chs 17–23):

A challenger of low birth, Svipdag, comes to Adils' court and, with Yrsa's support, challenges the king's berserkers, killing several of them and causing the survivors to be banished for their failure; Svipdag is honoured by King Adils and accompanies him in war against the berserkers, who are now attacking his lands; Svipdag, with the support of his brothers, kills all the remaining berserkers; Svipdag is displeased with Adils for not joining him soon enough in the battle, and seeks service at the court of King Hrolf; Hrolf is initially sceptical of Svipdag and his men because of their previous allegiance to Adils, but he is persuaded to accept them into his retinue; Svipdag wins the respect of the leader of Hrolf's berserkers and fights alongside him; Hrolf sends a message to his mother, Yrsa, requesting the treasures of his father, Helgi, that are now in the possession of Adils.

Hrolf builds a great retinue of warriors, winning many battles, exacting a great deal of tribute and establishing a splendid royal seat at Hleidargard (i.e. Lejre); King Hjorvard (OE Heoroweard) marries Hrolf's daughter, Skuld; Hrolf tricks Hjorvard into holding his sword while he is undoing his belt, thereby making him an underking; Hjorvard resents the trick but obliges Hrolf and pays tribute to him.

Bodvar and his brothers (chs 24–37):

King Hring of Norway has a son named Bjorn; after Hring's queen dies, he travels in search of a new bride, meeting Hvit, daughter of the king of the

Lapps; Bjorn falls in love with Bera, daughter of a farmer; Hvit becomes an overbearing queen, ruling in Hring's absence while he is out raiding, but favours Bjorn; Hring instructs Bjorn to rule in his absence, but Bjorn refuses; Hvit attempts to seduce Bjorn, but he rejects her advances; Hvit strikes Bjorn with her wolfskin gloves, cursing him to live as a bear; Bjorn takes to the woods; Bjorn, now taking on the shape of a bear by night, kills many of the king's cattle; Bera encounters Bjorn and follows him to a cave; Bera and Bjorn are reunited; King Hring hears of the disappearance of his son, Bjorn, and the attacks of the bear; Queen Hvit urges for the bear (i.e. Bjorn) to be killed; Bjorn, in the form of a bear, is hunted and killed by the king's men; Bera has three sons, one half-elk (Elk-Frodi), one half-dog (Thorir), and the third, half-bear, named Bodvar Bjarki, favoured among his brothers; these three brothers gain a reputation for fierceness; Elk-Frodi becomes a bandit; Thorir becomes king of the Gauts, on account of his great size; Bodvar, who had remained at home with his mother, learns of his father's murder and resolves to take vengeance against Hvit; Bodvar and Bera confront King Hring with Hvit's deceit; Hring offers Bodvar the title of *jarl* and rule of the kingdom on the condition that he will not harm the queen; Bodvar rejects the king's offer, and storms into Queen Hvit's bedchamber, where he places a leather bag over her head and kills her. Bodvar briefly rules Hring's kingdom of the Uppdales in Norway, but soon becomes dissatisfied and, after arranging for his mother to marry a local *jarl*, sets off in service of another lord.

Bodvar draws a sword from a stone, placed there by his father Bjorn; Bodvar seeks out his brother, Elk-Frodi; the brothers fight; Elk-Frodi advises Bodvar to seek out King Hrolf, owing to his reputation for keeping the greatest champions; Bodvar drinks some of Elk-Frodi's blood, thereby gaining strength; Bodvar sets off in search of his other brother, Thorir, king of Gautland; Thorir is away and Bodvar is mistaken for him and honoured as king in his place; Bodvar is put in bed with Thorir's wife but refuses to sleep with her, explaining to her his secret; on Thorir's return, the brothers are reunited; Thorir offers Bodvar half his kingdom, but Bodvar declines. Bodvar travels to King Hrolf's hall at Hleidargard (i.e. Lejre); on the way, he encounters an old woman, who complains that Hrolf's champions have humiliated her son, Hott, by throwing bones at him; Bodvar promises to help Hott; Bodvar arrives at Hleidargard, and there discovers Hott hiding in a pile of bones; Bodvar takes Hott up and washes him, placing him at the table; Hrolf's champions are impressed by Bodvar's bravery in placing Hott at the table, but continue to mock Hott, throwing bones at him and Bodvar; Bodvar kills one of Hrolf's champions who has thrown a bone at him; Hrolf's champions ask the king to have Bodvar killed, but Hrolf refuses and has the newcomer brought to him; Bodvar accepts Hrolf's offer to join his retinue in place of the man that he killed, on the condition that Hott is also afforded a place in the hall; Hrolf accepts, but Bodvar's presence causes resentment among Hrolf's champions.

Gloom descends on the hall due to the attacks of a winged troll that flies by night; Hott explains to Bodvar that this monster has attacked the hall for two winters, that no weapon can harm it, and that the king's champions dare not return home for fear; at Yule, King Hrolf has his men promise that they will not fight the troll and leave the livestock to their fate; Bodvar sneaks out, taking Hott with him; on encountering the troll, Hott becomes afraid; Bodvar attempts to injure the troll with his sword, but the weapon becomes stuck in its scabbard; Bodvar draws his sword and kills the troll. Bodvar makes Hott drink the troll's blood, telling him he will now gain great strength; Bodvar and Hott fight; Bodvar gives Hott credit for killing the troll; Hrolf suspects that Bodvar was the real slayer of the troll, but acknowledges Hott and renames him Hjalti.

King Hrolf's champions (chs 38–46):

Bodvar and Hjalti overcome the king's berserkers on their return to the hall; Bodvar is now honoured as Hrolf's most esteemed warrior, sitting at his right-hand side, with Hjalti next to him; Svipdag and other champions sit at Hrolf's left, the berserkers sitting below them; Bodvar distinguishes himself in contests and is rewarded with the hand of Hrolf's only daughter, Drifa. Hrolf and his champions enjoy a period of success.

Bodvar incites Hrolf to recover his inheritance from King Adils; Hrolf is cautious because of Adils' skill in the black arts, but Bodvar is eager to test his mettle against the Swedish king. Hrolf and Bodvar set out for King Adils' court, encountering a strange farmer along the way (later revealed to be Odin in disguise); Adils is warned of their approach; Hrolf arrives at Adils' court in disguise, accompanied by a party of twelve of his champions, including Svipdag, Bodvar and Hjalti; they are attacked by Adils' men in the hall but, led by Svipdag, defend themselves; Adils gives orders for his slain warriors to be cremated in the hall and attempts to discover which member of the party is Hrolf by exposing him to the flames; realizing the treachery, Bodvar, Svipdag and Hjalti seize Adils' warriors and throw them into the fire, but Adils escapes by using magic; a man of low rank named Vogg, sent by Yrsa to tend to Hrolf, gives him the name Kraki, on account of his thin looks; Hrolf rewards Vogg with an arm-ring; Vogg promises to avenge Hrolf should harm come his way; Adils sends a wild boar to attack Hrolf; Bodvar defends Hrolf against the boar; Adils attempts to burn the house in which Hrolf and his champions are staying; led by Bodvar, Hrolf and his champions escape from the burning house, attacking and killing many of Adils' men; Hrolf is reunited with his mother, Yrsa, who gives Hrolf his father's treasures; Hrolf and his champions are pursued from Uppsala by Adils and his men; Hrolf

Appendix B

delays Adils' men by strewing gold in their path; as Adils stops to pick up a gold ring, Hrolf strikes off his buttocks, forcing him to retreat; on the way home, Hrolf's party again encounter the farmer, this time realizing that he is Odin in disguise; they refuse Odin's offer of armour; Bodvar advises Hrolf not to engage in more battles; Hrolf and his champions enjoy a time of peace.

<u>Hjorvard and Hrolf (chs 47–52)</u>:

Resentful at having to pay tribute to Hrolf, Queen Skuld, sister of Hrolf, encourages Hjorvard (OE Heoroweard) to plot the king's downfall; Skuld and Hjorvard travel with an army to attack Hrolf during the Yule feast at Hleidargard, under guise of paying tribute; realizing the danger, Hjalti wakes Hrolf's champions after the feast, including Bodvar; after drinking, Hrolf and his champions leave the hall to confront their attackers, though Bodvar is nowhere to be seen; a great battle takes place outside the hall, in which Hrolf, assisted by a great bear, kills many of the attackers; returning to the hall, Hjalti discovers Bodvar sitting idly in the king's chamber and chastises him; Bodvar recounts his deeds to Hjalti; Bodvar joins the battle, killing many of Hjorvard and Skuld's men; Bodvar tells Hjalti that he has wounded Hjorvard severely in the fight; Hrolf, together with all his champions, falls in the battle; Hjorvard is also killed; Skuld takes the Danish throne for a brief and unhappy reign; Hrolf's brothers, Elk-Frodi and Thorir, supported by Yrsa, attack and capture Skuld with a force led by Vogg; a burial mound is raised for Hrolf and each of his champions, who are interred together with their weapons.

Bibliography

Concordances and Dictionaries

Bessinger, Jess B., ed., and Philip H. Smith, Jr., programmer, *A Concordance to Beowulf* (Ithaca and New York: Cornell UP, 1969).

———, *A Concordance to the Anglo-Saxon Poetic Records, with an Index of Compounds* compiled by Michael W. Twomey (Ithaca and New York: Cornell UP, 1978).

Cameron, Angus F., Ashley Crandell Amos and Antonette diPaolo Healey, eds, *Dictionary of Old English: A to I online* (pubd online 2019), http://tapor.library.utoronto.ca/doe/dict/index.html.

Gneuss, Helmut, and Michael Lapidge, eds, *Anglo-Saxon Manuscripts: A Bibliographical Handlist of Manuscripts and Manuscript Fragments Written or Owned in England up to 1100*, Toronto Anglo-Saxon Series 15 (Toronto/Buffalo/London: UTP, 2014).

Hall, Thomas N., ed., *Sources of Anglo-Saxon Literary Culture. Volume 5: Julius Caesar to Pseudo-Cyril of Alexandria* (Kalamazoo, MI: forthcoming), https://saslc.nd.edu/samples/c/chrysostom.pdf.

Healey, Antonette diPaolo, with John Price Wilkin and Xin Xiang, eds, *Dictionary of Old English Web Corpus* (Toronto: Dictionary of Old English Project 2009).

Ker, Neil R., ed., *Catalogue of Manuscripts Containing Anglo-Saxon* (Oxford: The Clarendon Press, 1957).

Roberts, Jane, and Christian Kay, with Lynne Grundy, eds, *A Thesaurus of Old English* (London: King's College London, Centre for Late Antique and Medieval Studies, 1995), 2 vols.

Toller, Thomas Northcote, ed., *An Anglo-Saxon Dictionary Based on the Manuscript Collections of the Late Joseph Bosworth* (Oxford: Clarendon Press, 1898); Supplement ed. Thomas Northcote Toller (Oxford: Clarendon Press, 1921); Revised and Enlarged Addenda, ed. Alistair Campbell (Oxford: Oxford UP, 1972).

Tweddle, Dominic, Martin Biddle and Birthe Kjølby-Biddle, eds, *The Corpus of Anglo-Saxon Stone Sculpture*, 12 vols, IV: *South-East England* (Oxford: OUP, 1996), http://www.ascorpus.ac.uk, accessed 15 September 2018.

Editions and Translations

Barney, Stephen A., W. J. Lewis, J. A. Beach and Oliver Berghof, trans., *The Etymologies of Isidore of Seville* (Cambridge: CUP, 2006).
Bately, Janet, ed., *The Anglo-Saxon Chronicle MS A*, The Anglo-Saxon Chronicle: a Collaborative Edition 3 (Cambridge: D. S. Brewer, 1986).
Bjork, Robert E., ed. and trans., *Old English Shorter Poems, II: Wisdom and Lyric*, DOML 32 (Cambridge, MA: Harvard UP, 2014).
Blatt, F., ed., *Die lateinischen Bearbeitungen der Acta Andreae et Matthiae apud Anthropophagos*, Beihefte zur Zeitschrift für neutestamentliche Wissenschaften 12 (Giessen: Töpelmann, 1930).
Boenig, Richard, ed. and trans., *The Acts of Andrew in the Country of the Cannibals: Translations from Greek, Latin, and Old English*, Garland Library of Medieval Literature, 70.B (New York and London: Routledge, 1991).
Byock, Jesse, trans., *The Saga of King Hrolf Kraki* (London: Penguin, 1998).
Campbell, Alistair P., ed. and trans., *The Chronicle of Æthelweard* (London: Thomas Nelson & Sons, 1962).
Charles, R. H., trans., *The Book of Enoch the Prophet: Being a Book wherein secret mysteries are revealed including the lost Books of Noah, the Prophecies of Enoch, particulars of Demonology and Angelology, and visions of the Apocalypse* (San Francisco: Weiser Books, 2003).
Clayton, Mary, ed. and trans., *Old English Poems of Christ and His Saints*, DOML 27 (Cambridge, MA: Harvard UP, 2013).
Colgrave, Bertram, ed. and trans., *The Earliest Life of Gregory the Great* (Cambridge: CUP, 1968).
———, *Felix's Life of Saint Guthlac* (Cambridge: CUP, 1985).
Colgrave, Bertram, and R. A. B. Mynors, eds and trans., *Bede's Ecclesiastical History of the English People* (Oxford: Clarendon Press, 1969; repr. 1979).
Connolly, Sean, trans., *Bede: On the Temple*, with an Introduction by Jennifer O'Reilly (Liverpool: Liverpool UP, 1995).
DeGregorio, Scott, and Rosalind C. Love, eds and trans., *Bede: On First Samuel* (Liverpool: Liverpool UP, 2019).
Doane, A. N., ed., *Genesis A: A New Edition, Revised* (Tempe, AZ: Arizona Center for Medieval and Renaissance Studies, 2013).
Dobbie, Elliot Van Kirk, ed., *The Anglo-Saxon Minor Poems*, ASPR VI (New York: Columbia UP, 1942; 3rd edn, 1968).
———, *Beowulf and Judith*, ASPR IV (New York: Columbia UP, 1954).
Donoghue, Daniel, ed., *Beowulf: A New Verse Translation*, trans. Seamus Heaney (New York: Norton, 2002).
Dronke, Ursula, ed. and trans., *The Poetic Edda, Volume III: Mythological Poems II* (Oxford: Clarendon Press, 2011).
Dümmler, Ernst, ed., *Alcuini Sive Albini Epistolae*, Epistolae Karolini Aevi II, MGH Epistolae 4 (Berlin: Weidmann, 1895), 19–29.

Dunning, Thomas Patrick, and Alan Joseph Bliss, eds, *The Wanderer* (London: Methuen, 1969).

Earle, John, trans., *The Deeds of Beowulf: an English epic of the eighth century done into modern prose* (Oxford: Clarendon Press, 1892).

Fadlān, Ibn, *Ibn Fadlān and the Land of Darkness: Arab Travellers in the Far North*, trans. Paul Lunde with an Introduction by Caroline Stone (London: Penguin, 2012).

Finlay, Alison, and Anthony Faulkes, trans, *Snorri Sturluson: Heimskringla, Volume I: The Beginnings to Óláfr Tryggvason* (London: Viking Society for Northern Research, 2011).

Foley, W. Trent, and Arthur G. Holder, eds and trans, *Bede: A Biblical Miscellany* (Liverpool: Liverpool UP, 1999).

Foulke, William D., trans., *Paul the Deacon, History of the Langobards* (Philadelphia: Philadelphia Dept. of History, University of Pennsylvania, 1907).

Franke, J. R. et al., eds, *Ancient Christian Commentary on Scripture: Joshua, Judges, Ruth, 1–2 Samuel*, Old Testament IV (Downers Grove, IL: Intervarsity Press, 2005).

Fulk, Robert D., Robert E. Bjork and John D. Niles, eds, *Klaeber's* Beowulf *and* The Fight at Finnsburg, *Fourth Edition* (Toronto: UTP, 2008).

Fulk, R. D., ed. and trans., *The* Beowulf *Manuscript*, DOML 3 (Cambridge, MA: Harvard UP, 2010).

Garmonsway, G. N. and Jacqueline Simpson, trans., Beowulf *and its Analogues*, including 'Archaeology and *Beowulf*' by Hilda Ellis Davidson (New York: Littlehampton, 1971).

Guðnason, Bjarni, ed., *Danakonunga Sogur: Skjoldunga Saga, Knytlinga Saga, Ágrip Af Sogu Danakonunga*, Islenzk Fornrit 35 (Reykjavik: Hid Islenzka Fornritafélag, 1982).

Heaney, Seamus, trans., Beowulf: *A New Verse Translation* (London: Norton & Co., 1999; repr. New York, 2001).

Himes, Jonathan B., ed., *The Old English Epic of* Waldere (Cambridge: Cambridge Scholars Publishing, 2009).

Hurst, D. ed., *Bedae Venerabilis Opera*, Pars II, Opera Exegetica 2, *In Primam Partem Samuhellis Libri IIII; In Regum Librum XXX Quaestiones*, CCSL 119 (1963).

Irvine, Susan, ed., *The Anglo-Saxon Chronicle MS E*, The Anglo-Saxon Chronicle: a Collaborative Edition 7 (Cambridge: D. S. Brewer, 2004).

Jónsson, Guðni, ed., 'Hrólfs saga kraka ok kappa hans', in *Fornaldr Sogür Norðurlanda* I (Rejkjavik: Íslendingasagnaútgáfan, 1950), pp. 1–105.

Karasawa, Kazutomo, ed. and trans., *The Old English Metrical Calendar (Menologium)* (Cambridge: D. S. Brewer, 2015).

Keefer, Sarah Larratt, ed., *Old English Liturgical Verse: A Student Edition* (Toronto: Broadview, 2010).

Kendall, Calvin B., trans., *Bede: On Genesis* (Liverpool: Liverpool UP, 2008).

Kiernan, Kevin, ed., *Electronic Beowulf: 4th edition* (London: British Library, 2015), http://ebeowulf.uky.edu/ebeo4.0/start.html.

Klaeber, Friedrich, ed., Beowulf *and the* Fight at Finnsburg, 3rd edn (Boston: Heath, 1936; supplemented 1941 and 1950).

Klinck, Anne L. ed., *The Old English Elegies: A Critical Edition and Genre Study* (Montreal and Kingston: McGill-Queen's UP, 1992).

Krapp, George Philip, ed., Andreas *and* The Fates of the Apostles, *Two Anglo-Saxon Narrative Poems* (Boston: Ginn and Co., 1906).

——, ed., *The Junius Manuscript*, ASPR I (New York: Columbia UP; London: Routledge and Kegan Paul, 1931; 3rd printing 1969).

——, ed., *The Vercelli Book*, ASPR II (New York: Columbia UP, 1932).

——, ed., *The Paris Psalter and The Metres of Boethius*, ASPR V (New York: Columbia UP, 1933).

——, and Elliot Van Kirk Dobbie, eds, *The Exeter Book*, ASPR III (New York: Columbia UP, 1936).

Krusch, B, ed., *Fredegarii et aliorum chronica*, MGH script. rer. Merov. 2 (Hannover, 1888), II, Ch. III, 9.

Leslie, R. F., ed., *The Wanderer* (Manchester: Manchester UP, 1966).

Linder, N., and H. A. Haggson, eds, *Snorra Sturlusonar: Heimskringla eða: Sögur Noregs konunga* (Uppsala: W. Schultz, 1869–72), 3 vols.

Liuzza, Roy M., trans., *Beowulf: second edition* (Toronto: Broadview, 2013).

Malone, Kemp, ed., *The Nowell Codex: British Museum Cotton Vitellius A. vx, Second MS*, Early English Manuscripts in Facsimile 12 (Copenhagen: Rosenkilde and Bagger, 1963).

Marsden, Richard, ed., *The Old English Heptateuch and Ælfric's Libellus de veteri testamento et novo*, 2 vols, EETS o.s. 30 (Oxford: OUP, 2008).

Migne, Jacques-Paul, *et al.*, eds, *Patrologia Latina*, 221 vols (Paris: Imprimerie Catholique, 1841–55).

——, *Patrologia Graeca*, 161 vols (Paris: Imprimerie Catholique, 1856–66).

Miller, T. H., ed. and trans., *The Old English Version of Bede's* Ecclesiastical History of the English People, 4 vols, EETS o.s. 95, 96, 110, 111 (London: N. Trübner & Co., 1890–98).

Morris, Richard, ed. and trans., *The Blickling Homilies of the Tenth Century*, EETS o.s. 58, 63, 73 (London: Trübner & Co., 1874–80).

North, Richard, and Michael D. J. Bintley, eds, *Andreas: An edition* (Liverpool, Liverpool University Press, 2016).

O'Donnell, Daniel, ed., *Cædmon's Hymn: a multimedia edition and archive* (Cambridge: D. S. Brewer, 2005), http://people.uleth.ca/~daniel.odonnell/caedmon/html/htm/edition/ylda/index.

O'Neill, Patrick P., ed. and trans., *Old English Psalms*, DOML 42 (Harvard: Harvard UP, 2016).

Pertz, Georg, ed., *Rerum Merowingorum Genealogia*, MGH SS II. 1 (Hannover, 1829).

Porsia, Franco, ed., *Liber Monstrorum* (Bari: Dedalo Libri, 1976).

Ring, Abram, ed. and trans., *Waltharius*, Dallas Medieval Texts and Translations 22 (Louvain: Peeters, 2016).

Rollason, David, and Lynda Rollason, eds, *Durham Liber vitae: London, British Library, MS Cotton Domitian A.VII: edition and digital facsimile with introduction, codicological, prosopographical and linguistic commentary, and indexes including the Biographical Register of Durham Cathedral Priory (1083–1539) by A. J. Piper* (London: British Library, 2007), 3 vols, I.

Schaff, Paul, ed. and trans., *Nicene and Post-Nicene Fathers*, Series II, Vol. 1 (New York: The Christian Literature Company, 1890).

Skeat, Walter William, ed. and trans., *Ælfric's Lives of Saints*, 4 vols, EETS o.s. 76, 82, 94, 114 (London, 1881–1900, repr. in 2 vols, 1966).

Stevenson, Joseph, ed., *Chronicon Monasterii de Abingdon* (London: Longman, Brown, Green, and Longmans, 1858).

Sweet, Henry, ed., *King Alfred's West-Saxon Version of Gregory's* Pastoral Care, EETS o.s. 45 and 50 (London: Trübner & Co., 1871).

——, ed., *The Oldest English Texts*, EETS o.s. 34 (London: Trübner & Co., 1885).

Taylor, Simon, ed., *The Anglo-Saxon Chronicle MS B*, The AS Chronicle: a Collaborative Edition 4 (Cambridge: D. S. Brewer, 1983).

Thorkelín, Grímur Jónsson, ed., *De Danorum Rebus Gestis Seculis III et IV: Poema Danicum Dialecto Anglosaxonica* (Copenhagen: T. E. Rangel, 1815).

Thorpe, Lewis, trans., *Gregory of Tours: The History of the Franks* (London: Penguin, 1974).

Tolkien, J. R. R., trans., Beowulf: *A Translation and Commentary, together with* Sellic Spell, ed. Christopher Tolkien (Boston: Houghton Mifflin Harcourt, 2014).

Walsh, Gerald G., trans., *Augustine: City of God*, Fathers of the Church Series 24 (Washington, D.C.: Catholic University of America Press, 1963).

Weber, Robert, ed., *Le Psautier Romain et les autres anciens Psautiers latins*, Collectanea Biblica Latina X (Rome: Abbaye Saint-Jérôme, 1953).

Weber, Robert, and Roger Gryson, eds, *Biblia Sacra: Iuxta Vulgatam Versionem*, 5th edn (Stuttgart: Deutsche-Bibelgesellschaft, 2007).

Whitelock, Dorothy, ed. and trans., *English Historical Documents, I: c. 500–1042*, 2nd edn (London: Eyre Methuen, 1979).

Williams, Hugh, ed., *Vita Gildae Auctore Monacho Ruiensi (Vita I)*, in *Gildae De Excidio Britanniae, Fragmenta, Liber de Paenitentia*, Cymmrodorion Record Series 3 (London: David Nutt, 1899).

Wrenn, Charles Leslie, ed., *Beowulf with the Finnesburg Fragment* (London: George G. Harrup, 1953); 3rd edn fully revised by Whitney F. Bolton (New York: St Martin's Press, 1973).

Zupitza, Julius, ed., Beowulf: *Autotypes of the Unique Cotton MS. Vitellius A. XV in the British Museum, with a Transliteration and Notes*, EETS o.s. 245 (London: Trübner & Co., 1882), 2nd edn, containing a new reproduction of the manuscript, with an introductory note by Norman Davis (London: OUP, 1959; reprinted 1967).

Criticism

Abels, Richard, 'Royal Succession and the Growth of Political Stability in Ninth-Century Wessex', *The Haskins Society Journal: Studies in Medieval History* 12 (2002), 83–97.

Abraham, Lenore, 'The Decorum of *Beowulf*', *PQ* 72 (1993), 267–87.

Abram, Chris, 'Bee-Wolf and the Hand of Victory: Identifying the Heroes of *Beowulf* and *Vǫlsunga saga*', *JEGP* 116 (2017), 387–414.

Acker, Paul, 'Part 1. "Fragments of Danish History" (*Skjöldunga saga*)', *ANQ* 20 (2007), 1–9.

Aertsen, Alexander, and Suzanne Spain, 'Heraclius, Byzantine Imperial Ideology, and the David Plates', *Speculum* 52 (1977), 217–37.

Aertsen, Henk, and Rolf H. Bremmer, Jr., eds, *Companion to Old English Poetry* (Amsterdam: VU UP, 1994).

Allan, William, 'Arms and the Man: Euphorbus, Hector, and the Death of Patroclus', *The Classical Quarterly* 55 (2005), 1–16.

Anderson, Carl Edlund, 'Scyld Scyldinga: Intercultural Innovation at the Interface of West and North Germanic', *Neophilologus* 100 (2016), 461–76.

Anderson, Earl A, 'A Submerged Metaphor in the Scyld Episode', *Yearbook of English Studies* 2 (1972), 1–4.

——, 'Beow the Boy-Wonder (*Beowulf* 12–25)', *ES* 89 (2008), 630–42.

Andersson, Theodore M., 'Sources and Analogues', in Bjork and Niles, eds (1997), pp. 125–48.

Anlezark, Daniel, 'Sceaf, Japheth and the Origins of the Anglo-Saxons', *ASE* 31 (2002), 13–46.

——, 'The Fall of the Angels in *Solomon and Saturn II*', in *Apocryphal Texts and Traditions in Anglo-Saxon England*, ed. Kathryn Powell and Donald G. Scragg (Cambridge: D. S. Brewer, 2003), pp. 121–34.

——, *Water and Fire: The Myth of the Flood in Anglo-Saxon England* (Manchester: MUP, 2006).

——, 'Grendel and the Book of Wisdom', *NQ* 53 (2006), 262–69.

——, 'All at Sea: Beowulf's Marvellous Swimming', in *Myths, Legends and Heroes: Essays on Old Norse and Old English Literature in honour of John McKinnell*, Toronto Old Norse-Icelandic Series, ed. Daniel Anlezark (Toronto: UTP, 2011), pp. 225–41.

——, 'Gregory the Great: Reader, Writer and Read', in *The Church and Literature*, ed. Peter Clarke and Charlotte Methuen (Woodbridge: Boydell & Brewer, 2012), pp. 12–34.

Appleton, Helen, 'The Role of Æschere's Head', *RES* 68 (2017), 428–47.

Archambault, Paul, 'The Ages of Man and the Ages of the World: A Study of Two Traditions', *Revue d'Études Augustiniennes et Patristiques* 12 (1966), 193–228.

Ashe, Laura, *Early Fiction in England: From Geoffrey of Monmouth to Chaucer* (London: Penguin, 2015).

Atherton, Mark, 'The Figure of the Archer in *Beowulf* and the Anglo-Saxon Psalter', *Neophilologus* 77 (1993), 653–57.

Auerbach, Eric, 'Typological Symbolism in Medieval Literature', *Yale French Studies* 9 (1952), 3–10.

Baird, Joseph L., '"for metode": *Beowulf* 169', *ES* 49 (1968), 418–23.

Baker, Peter, ed., Beowulf: *Basic Readings*, Basic Readings in Anglo-Saxon England 1 (New York: Garland, 1995).

———, *Honour, Exchange and Violence in* Beowulf, Anglo-Saxon Studies 20 (Cambridge: D. S. Brewer, 2013).

Ball, Christopher J. E., '*Beowulf* 99–101', *NQ* 18 (1971), 163.

Bammesberger, Alfred, 'Hidden Glosses in Manuscripts of Old English Poetry', *ASE* 13 (1984), 43–49.

———, 'Five *Beowulf* Notes', in *Words, Texts and Manuscripts: Studies in Anglo-Saxon Culture Presented to Helmut Gneuss on the Occasion of His Sixty-Fifth Birthday*, ed. Michael Korhammer (Cambridge: D. S. Brewer, 1992), pp. 239–56.

———, 'Who Advised Beowulf to Challenge Grendel?', *ANQ* 24 (2011), 244–48.

———, 'The Last Line of *Beowulf*', *NQ* 59 (2012), 463–65.

———, 'The meaning of Old English *folcscaru* and the compound's function in *Beowulf*', *NOWELE: North-Western European Language Evolution* 72 (2019), 1–10.

Barker, E. E., 'The Anglo-Saxon Chronicle Used by Æthelweard', *Bulletin of the Institute of Historical Research* 40 (1967), 74–91.

Bartlett, Adeline Courtney, *The Larger Rhetorical Patterns in Anglo-Saxon Poetry* (New York: Columbia UP, 1935; repr. 1966).

Bately, Janet M., *The Anglo-Saxon Chronicle: Texts and Textual Relationships*, Reading Medieval Studies 3 (Reading: University of Reading, 1991).

Beekman Taylor, Paul, 'The Language of Sacral Kingship in *Beowulf*', *Studia Neophilologica* 66 (1994), 129–45.

Benediktsson, Jakob, 'Icelandic Traditions of the Scyldings', *Saga-Book* 15 (1957–61), 48–66.

Benson, Larry D., 'The Originality of *Beowulf*', in *The Interpretation of Narrative: Theory and Practice*, Harvard English Studies 1, ed. Morton W. Bloomfield (Cambridge, MA: Harvard UP, 1970), pp. 1–43; repr. in *Contradictions: From Beowulf to Chaucer: Selected Studies of Larry D. Benson*, ed. Theodore M. Andersson and Stephen A. Barney (Aldershot: Ashgate, 1995), pp. 32–69.

Berendsohn, Walter A., *Zur Vorgeschichte des 'Beowulf'* (Copenhagen:

Levin and Munksgaard, 1935).
Besserman, Lawrence, *Biblical Paradigms in Medieval English Literature* (New York: Routledge, 2012).
Biggs, Frederick M., 'The Naming of Beowulf and Ecgtheow's Feud', *PQ* 80 (2001), 95–112.
——, 'Beowulf's Fight with the Nine Nicors', *RES* 53 (2002), 311–28.
——, '*Beowulf* and some fictions of the Geatish succession', *ASE* 32 (2003), 55–77.
——, 'Hondscioh and Æschere in *Beowulf*', *Neophilologus* 87 (2003), 635–52.
——, 'The Politics of Succession in *Beowulf* and Anglo-Saxon England', *Speculum* 80 (2005), 709–41.
——, '*The Dream of the Rood* and *Guthlac A* as a Literary Context for the Monsters in *Beowulf*', in *Text, Image, Interpretation: Studies in Anglo-Saxon Literature and its Insular Context in Honour of Éamonn Ó Carragáin*, ed. Alastair Minnis and Jane Roberts (Turnhout: Brepols, 2007), pp. 289–301.
——, 'History and Fiction in the Frisian Raid', in Neidorf, ed. (2014), pp. 138–56.
Bintley, Michael D. J., *Trees in the Religions of Early Medieval England* (Woodbridge: Boydell & Brewer, 2015).
Bjork, Robert E., 'Speech as Gift in *Beowulf*', *Speculum* 69 (1994), 993–1022.
——, 'Digressions and Episodes', in Bjork and Niles, eds (1997), pp. 193–212.
Bjork, Robert E., and John D. Niles, eds, *A* Beowulf *Handbook* (Exeter: University of Exeter Press, 1997).
Bjork, Robert E., and Anita Obermeier, 'Date, Provenance, Author, Audiences', in Bjork and Niles, eds (1997), pp. 13–34.
Black, Jonathan, '*De Civitate Dei* and the Commentaries of Gregory the Great, Isidore, Bede, and Hrabanus Maurus on the Book of Samuel', *Augustinian Studies* 15 (1986 for 1984), 114–27.
Bliss, Alan Joseph, *The Metre of* Beowulf (Oxford: Blackwell, 1963).
Bloomfield, Morton W, 'Patristics and Old English Literature: Notes on Some Poems', *Comparative Literature* 14 (1962), 36–43; repr. in *Studies in Old English Literature in Honor of Arthur G. Brodeur*, ed. Stanley B. Greenfield (Eugene, OR: University of Oregon Books, 1963), pp. 36–43.
Bolton, Whitney F., *Alcuin and* Beowulf: *An Eighth-Century View* (New Jersey: Rutgers UP, 1986).
Bond, George, 'Links Between *Beowulf* and Mercian History', *SP* 40 (1943), 481–93.
Bonjour, Adrien, 'Grendel's Dam and the Composition of *Beowulf*', *ES* 30 (1949), 113–24; repr. in Bonjour (1962), pp. 29–50.
——, *The Digressions in* Beowulf, Medium Ævum Monographs 5 (Oxford: Blackwell, 1950; repr. 1965).

———, 'Beowulf and Heardred', *ES* 32 (1951), 193–200; repr. in Bonjour (1962), pp. 67–76.

———, 'Monsters Crouching and Critics Rampant: or the *Beowulf* Dragon Debated', *PMLA* 68 (1953), 304–12; repr. in Bonjour (1962), pp. 97–113.

———, '*Beowulf* and the Snares of Literary Criticism', *Études Anglaises* 10 (1957), 30–36; repr. in Bonjour (1962), pp. 121–28.

———, '*Beowulf* and the Beasts of Battle', *PMLA* 72 (1957), 563–73; repr. in Bonjour (1962), pp. 135–49.

———, '*Beowulf* et le démon de l'analogie', first printed in Bonjour (1962), pp. 173–89.

———, *Twelve* Beowulf *Papers 1940–1960, with additional comments* (Neuchâtel: Faculte des lettres, Université de Neuchatel, 1962).

Braccini, Giovanni Princi, 'Perché Hroðgar Stod on Stapole (*Beowulf* 926a)', in *Echi di Memoria: Scritti di varia filologia, critica e linguistica in recordo di Giorgio Chiarini*, ed. Gaetano Chiappini (Florence: Alinea, 1998), pp. 139–57.

Bradley, Henry, '*Beowulf*', in *Encyclopedia Britannica*, 29 vols, III (London: CUP, 1910–11), pp. 758–61.

Brady, Caroline, '"Weapons" in *Beowulf*: an Analysis of the Nominal Compounds and an Evaluation of the Poet's Use of Them', *ASE* 8 (1979), 79–141.

Breeze, Andrew, '*Beowulf* 875–902 and the Sculptures at Sangüesa, Spain', *NQ* 38 (1991), 2–13.

Bremmer, Rolf H., Jr., 'The Importance of Kinship: Uncle and Nephew in *Beowulf*', *Amsterdamer Beiträge zur älteren Germanistik* 15 (1980), 22–38.

Brettler, Marc, 'Cyclical and Teleological Time in the Hebrew Bible', in *Time and Temporality in the Ancient World*, ed. Ralph M. Rosen (Philadelphia: UPenn Press, 2004), pp. 111–28.

Brodeur, Arthur Gilchrist, *The Art of* Beowulf (Berkeley: University of California Press, 1959).

———, '*Beowulf*: One Poem or Three?', in *Medieval Literature and Folklore Studies: Essays in Honor of Francis Lee Utley*, ed. Jerome Mandel and Bruce A. Rosenberg (New Brunswick: Rutgers UP, 1970), pp. 3–28.

Brooke, C. N. L., *The Saxon and Norman Kings* (Oxford: Wiley-Blackwell, 2001).

Brooks, Kenneth R., Review of R. F. Leslie, ed., *The Wanderer*, *MLR* 63 (1968), 157–59.

Brown, George Hardin, 'Bede's Commentary on I Samuel', in *Biblical Studies in the Early Middle Ages*, ed. Claudio Leonardi and Giovanni Orlandi (Florence: SISMEL, Edizioni del Galluzzo, 2005), pp. 77–90.

———, 'Bede's Neglected Commentary on Samuel', in *Innovation and Tradition in the Writings of the Venerable Bede*, ed. Scott DeGregorio (Morgantown: West Virginia UP, 2006), pp. 121–42.

———, 'Bede's Style in his Commentary on I Samuel', in *Text, Image,*

Interpretation: Studies in Anglo-Saxon Literature and its Insular Context in Honour of Éamonn Ó Carragáin, ed. Alastair Minnis and Jane Roberts (Turnhout: Brepols, 2007), pp. 233–51.

Brown, Michelle P., '*Beowulf* and the Origins of the Written Old English Vernacular', *SELIM* 20 (2013–14), 81–120.

Brown, Michelle P., and Carol F. Farr, eds, *Mercia: An Anglo-Saxon Kingdom in Europe* (London and New York: Leicester UP/Continuum Books, 2001; repr. 2005).

Brown, Phyllis R., 'Cycles and Change in *Beowulf*', in *Manuscript, Narrative, Lexicon: Essays on Literary and Cultural Transmission in Honor of Whitney F. Bolton*, ed. Robert Boenig and Kathleen Davis (Lewisburg, PA: Bucknell UP, 2000), pp. 171–92.

Bruce, Alexander M., *Scyld and Scef: Expanding the Analogues* (New York: Routledge, 2002).

Bruce-Mitford, Rupert, 'Sutton Hoo and the Background to the Poem', included as a supplement to Girvan (1971), pp. 85–98.

Bryan, W. F., 'The Wægmundings–Swedes or Geats?', *MP* 34 (1936), 113–18.

Bundy, Mildred, 'Deciphering the Art of Interlace', in *From Ireland Coming*, ed. Colum Hourihane (Princeton, NJ: Princeton UP, 2001), pp. 183–210.

Burrow, John A., *The Ages of Man: A Study in Mediaeval Writing and Thought* (Oxford: Clarendon Press, 1986).

———, *The Poetry of Praise* (Cambridge: CUP, 2008).

Butler, Emily, 'Alfred and the Children of Israel in the Prose Psalms', *NQ* 57 (2010), 10–17.

———, '"And Thus Did Hezekiah": Perspectives on Judaism in the Old English Prose Psalms', *RES* 67 (2016), 617–35.

Cabannis, Allan, '*Beowulf* and the Liturgy', *JEGP* 54 (1955), 195–201; repr. in Nicholson, ed. (1963), pp. 223–32.

Cain, Christopher M., '*Beowulf*, the Old Testament, and the "Regula Fidei"', *Renascene: Essays on Value in Literature* 49 (1997), 227–40.

Cameron, Angus F., 'Saint Gildas and Scyld Scefing', *NM* 70 (1969), 240–46.

Campbell, Alistair P., 'The Time Element of Interlace Structure in *Beowulf*', *NM* 70 (1969), 425–35.

———, 'The Use in *Beowulf* of Earlier Heroic Verse', in *England Before the Conquest: Studies in Primary Sources presented to Dorothy Whitelock*, ed. Peter Clemoes and Kathleen Hughes (Cambridge: CUP, 1971), pp. 283–92.

Canning, Joseph, *A History of Medieval Political Thought 300–1450* (London: Routledge, 1996).

Capper, Morn D. T., 'Contested Loyalties: Regional and National Identities in the Midland Kingdoms of Anglo-Saxon England, c.700–c.900' (Unpubl. doctoral dissertation, University of Sheffield, 2010).

Carney, James, 'The Irish Elements in *Beowulf*', in his *Studies in Irish*

Literature and History (Dublin: Dublin Institute for Advanced Studies, 1955), pp. 77–128.

Carrigan, Edmund, 'Structure and Thematic Development in *Beowulf*', *Proceedings of the Irish Academy* 66C (1967), 1–51.

Cavell, Megan, 'Constructing the Monstrous Body in *Beowulf*', *ASE* 43 (2014), 155–81.

———, *Weaving Words and Binding Bodies: The Poetics of Human Experience in Old English Literature* (Toronto: UTP, 2016).

Cavill, Paul, 'Christianity and Theology in *Beowulf*', in *The Christian Tradition in Anglo-Saxon England: Approaches to Current Scholarship and Teaching*, ed. Paul Cavill (Cambridge: D. S. Brewer, 2004), pp. 15–40.

Cesario, Marilina, '*Fyrene dracan* in the *Anglo-Saxon Chronicle*', in *Textiles, Text, Intertext: Essays in Honour of Gale R. Owen-Crocker*, ed. Maren Clegg Hyer and Jill Frederick (Woodbridge: Boydell & Brewer, 2016), pp. 153–70.

Chadwick, Hector Munro, *The Origin of the English Nation* (Cambridge: CUP, 1907).

———, *The Heroic Age* (Cambridge: CUP, 1912).

Chadwick, Nora K, 'The monsters and *Beowulf*', in *The Anglo-Saxons— Studies in some aspects of their history and culture presented to Bruce Dickins*, ed. Peter Clemoes (London: Bowes and Bowes, 1959), pp. 171–203.

Chambers, R. W., *Widsith: A Study in Old English Heroic Legend* (Cambridge: CUP, 1912; repr. New York: Russell & Russell, 1965).

———, '*Beowulf* and the "Heroic Age" in England', in his *Man's Unconquerable Mind: Studies of English Writers, from Bede to A. E. Housman and W. P. Ker* (London and Toronto: Jonathan Cape, 1939), pp. 53–59.

———, *Beowulf: An Introduction to the Study of the Poem with a Discussion of the Stories of Offa and Finn*, 3rd edn with a supplement by Charles L. Wrenn (Cambridge: CUP, 1959).

Chance, Jane, *Woman as Hero in Old English Literature* (Syracuse, NY: Syracuse UP, 1986).

———, 'The Structural Unity of *Beowulf*: the Problem of Grendel's Mother', in Damico and Olsen, eds (1990), pp. 248–61.

Chaney, William A., 'Grendel and the *Gifstol*: A Legal View of Monsters', *PMLA* 77 (1962), 513–20.

———, *The cult of kingship in Anglo-Saxon England: The transition from paganism to Christianity* (Manchester: Manchester UP, 1970; repr. 1999).

Chase, Colin, ed., *The Dating of* Beowulf (Toronto: UTP, 1981).

Clark, David, 'Relaunching the Hero: the Case of Scyld and Beowulf Re-opened', *Neophilologus* 90 (2006), 621–42.

———, *Between Medieval Men: Male Friendship and Desire in Early Medieval English Literature* (Oxford: OUP, 2009).

Clark, George, 'Beowulf's Armor', *ELH* 32 (1965), 409–41.

———, *Beowulf*, Twayne's English Authors Series 477 (Boston: Twayne

Publishers Inc., 1990).

———, 'The Hero and the Theme', in Bjork and Niles, eds (1997), pp. 271–90.

Clarke, M. G., *Sidelights on Teutonic History during the Migration Period* (Cambridge: CUP, 1911).

Clemoes, Peter, 'Action in *Beowulf* and Our Perception of It', in *Old English Poetry: Essays on Style*, ed. Daniel G. Calder (Berkeley and Los Angeles: University of California Press, 1979), pp. 147–68.

———, 'Style as the Criterion for Dating the Composition of *Beowulf*', in Chase, ed. (1981), pp. 173–85.

———, *Interactions of Thought and Language in Old English Poetry*, CSASE 12 (Cambridge: CUP, 1995).

Clover, Carol J., 'The Germanic Context of the Unferþ Episode', *Speculum* 55 (1980), 444–68; repr. in Baker, ed. (1995), pp. 127–54.

Clunies Ross, Margaret, 'Concubinage in Anglo-Saxon England', in *Anglo-Saxon History: Basic Readings*, Basic Readings in Anglo-Saxon England 6, ed. David A. E. Pelteret (New York: Garland, 2000), pp. 251–88.

———, *The Cambridge Introduction to Old Norse-Icelandic Saga* (Cambridge: CUP, 2010).

Cochelin, Isabelle, 'Introduction: Pre-Thirteenth Century Definitions of the Life Cycle', in *Medieval Life Cycles: Continuity and Change*, ed. Isabelle Cochelin and Karen Smyth (Turnhout: Brepols, 2013), pp. 1–54.

Cohen, Jeffrey Jerome, 'Monster Culture (Seven Theses)', in *Monster Theory: Reading Culture*, ed. Jeffrey Jerome Cohen (Minneapolis: University of Minnesota Press, 1996), pp. 3–25.

———, *Of Giants: Sex, Monsters, and the Middle Ages*, Medieval Cultures 17 (Minneapolis: University of Minnesota Press, 1999).

Cooke, William, 'Hrothulf: A Richard III or an Alfred the Great?', *SP* 104 (2007), 175–98.

Cox, Betty S., *Cruces of* Beowulf, Studies in English Literature 60 (The Hague: Mouton, 1971).

Creed, Robert P., '"… wel-hwelc gecwæþ …": The Singer as Architect', *Tennessee Studies in Literature* 11 (1966), 131–43.

Crépin, André, 'Bede and the Vernacular', in *Famulus Christi: Essays in Commemoration of the 13th Centenary of the Birth of the Venerable Bede*, ed. Gerald Bonner (London: SPCK, 1976), pp. 170–92.

Cronan, Dennis, '*Beowulf* and the Containment of Scyld in the West Saxon Royal Genealogy', in Neidorf, ed. (2014), pp. 112–37.

———, 'Narrative Disjunctions in *Beowulf*', *ES* 99 (2018), 459–78.

Crowne, David K., 'The Hero on the Beach: An Example of Composition by Theme in Anglo-Saxon Poetry', *NM* 61 (1960), 362–72.

Cundall, Arthur E., 'Sacral Kingship – the Old Testament Background', *Vox Evangelica* 6 (1969), 31–41.

Cunningham, Valentine, 'Goodbye to *Beowulf*', *Times Higher Education*

Supplement, 12 May 2000: https://www.timeshighereducation.com/news/goodbye-to-beowulf/151563.article, accessed 29 January 2018.

Dagron, Gilbert, *Emperor and Priest: The Imperial Office in Byzantium*, trans. Jean Birrell (Cambridge: CUP, 2003).

Damico, Helen, *Beowulf and the Grendel-kin: Politics and Poetry in Eleventh-Century England*, Medieval European Studies XVI (Morgantown: West Virginia UP, 2015).

Damico, Helen, and Alexandra Hennessey Olsen, eds, *New Readings on Women in Old English Literature* (Bloomington, IN: Indiana UP, 1990).

Davies, Anthony, 'The Sexual Conversion of the Anglo-Saxons', in *A Wyf Ther Was: Essays in Honour of Paule Mertens-Fonck*, ed. Juliette Dor (Liège: Dépt D'anglais, Université de Liège, 1992), pp. 80–102.

Davis, Craig, Beowulf *and the Demise of Germanic Legend in England* (New York: Garland, 1996).

———, 'Theories of History in Traditional Plots', in *Myth in Early Northwest Europe*, Arizona Studies in the Middle Ages and the Renaissance 21, ed. Stephen O. Glosecki (Tempe, AZ: Arizona Center for Medieval and Renaissance Studies and Brepols, 2007), pp. 31–45.

Dean, Paul, '*Beowulf* and the Passing of Time', *ES* 75 (1994), 193–209, 293–302.

DeGregorio, Scott, 'Bede and the Old Testament', in *The Cambridge Companion to Bede*, ed. Scott DeGregorio (Cambridge: CUP, 2010), pp. 127–41.

Dendle, Peter, *Satan Unbound: The Devil in Old English Narrative Literature* (Toronto: UTP, 2001).

de Vries, Jan, *Heroic Song and Heroic Legend* (London: OUP, 1963).

Dockray-Miller, Mary, 'Beowulf's Tears of Fatherhood', *Exemplaria* 10 (1998), 1–28.

———, 'The Masculine Queen of *Beowulf*', *Women and Language* 21 (1998), 31–38.

Donahue, Charles, '*Beowulf*, Ireland and the Natural Good', *Traditio* 7 (1949–50), 263–78.

Dragland, S. L., 'Monster-Man in *Beowulf*', *Neophilologus* 61 (1977), 606–18.

Dronke, Ursula, 'Beowulf and Ragnarök', *Saga-Book* 17 (1969), 302–25.

Drout, Michael D. C., 'Blood and Deeds: The Inheritance System in *Beowulf*', *SP* 104 (2007), 199–226.

Du Bois, Arthur E., 'The Unity of *Beowulf*', *PMLA* 49 (1934), 374–405.

———, 'Gifstol', *MLN* 69 (1954), 546–49.

Dumville, David N., 'The ætheling: a study in Anglo-Saxon constitutional history', *ASE* 8 (1979), 1–34.

———, 'Kingship, Genealogies and Regnal lists', in Sawyer and Wood, eds (1977), pp. 77–104.

———, '*Beowulf* Come Lately: Some Notes on the Palaeography of the Nowell Codex', *Archiv für das Studium der Neuren Sprachen und*

Literaturen 225 (1988), 49–63.

———, 'The *Beowulf* Manuscript and How Not to Date it', *Medieval English Students' Newsletter* 39 (1998), 21–27.

Earl, James W., 'Beowulf's Rowing-Match', *Neophilologus* 63 (1979), 285–90.

———, *Thinking about* Beowulf (Stanford: Stanford UP, 1994).

———, 'The Forbidden *Beowulf*: Haunted by Incest', *PMLA* 125 (2010), 289–305.

———, 'The Swedish Wars in *Beowulf*', *JEGP* 114 (2015), 32–60.

Eliason, Norman E., 'The "Improvised Lay" in *Beowulf*', *PQ* 31 (1952), 171–79.

———, '*Beowulf* Notes', *Anglia* 71 (1952–52), 438–55.

———, 'The "Thryth-Offa Digression" in *Beowulf*', in *Franciplegius: Medieval and Linguistic Studies in Honor of Francis Peabody Magoun, Jr.*, ed. Jess B. Bessinger Jr. and Robert P. Creed (New York: New York UP, 1965), pp. 124–38.

———, 'Healfdene's Daughter', in *Anglo-Saxon Poetry: Essays in Appreciation, for John C. McGalliard*, ed. Lewis E. Nicholson and Dolores Warwick Frese (London and Notre Dame: University of Notre Dame Press, 1975), pp. 3–13.

———, 'Beowulf, Wiglaf and the Wægmundings', *ASE* 7 (1978), 95–105.

———, 'Beowulf's Inglorious Youth', *SP* 76 (1979), 101–08.

———, 'The Burning of Heorot', *Speculum* 55 (1980), 75–83.

Ellis Davidson, Hilda R., *Gods and Myths of Northern Europe* (Harmondsworth, Middlesex: Viking, Penguin, 1964).

———, 'Archaeology and *Beowulf*', in Garmonsway (1971), pp. 350–64.

Emerson, O. F., 'Legends of Cain, especially in Old and Middle English', *PMLA* 21 (1906), 831–929.

———, 'Grendel's Motive in Attacking Heorot', *MLR* 16 (1921), 113–19.

Engelhardt, George J., 'On the Sequence of Beowulf's *Geogoð*', *MLN* 68 (1953), 91–95.

———, '*Beowulf*: A Study in Dilation', *PMLA* 79 (1955), 825–52.

Enright, Michael J., *Lady with a Mead Cup: Ritual, Prophecy and Lordship in the European warband from La Tène to the Viking Age* (Dublin: Four Courts, 1996).

Estrich, Robert M., 'The Throne of Hrothgar – *Beowulf*, ll. 168–169', *JEGP* 43 (1944), 384–89.

Fanning, Steven, 'Bede, *Imperium*, and the Bretwaldas', *Speculum* 66 (1991), 1–26.

Farrell, Robert T., *Beowulf, Swedes and Geats* (London: Viking Society for Northern Research, 1972).

———, '*Beowulf* and the Northern Heroic Age', in *The Vikings*, ed. Robert T. Farrell (London: Phillimore, 1982), pp. 180–216.

Fast, Lawrence E., 'Hygelac: a Centripetal Force in *Beowulf*', *Annuale Medievale* 12 (1972), 90–99.

Faulkes, Anthony, 'Descent from the gods', *Mediaeval Scandinavia* 11 (1978–79), 92–125.

Faulkner, Amy, 'The Language of Wealth in Old English Literature: from the Conversion to Alfred' (Unpubl. doctoral dissertation, University of Oxford, 2019).

Fitzgerald, Jill, *Rebel Angels: Space and Sovereignty in Anglo-Saxon England* (Manchester: MUP, 2019).

Fjalldal, Magnús, *The Long Arm of Coincidence: the Frustrated Connection between* Beowulf *and* Grettis saga (Toronto: UTP, 1998).

———, '*Beowulf* and the Old Norse Two-Troll Analogues', *Neophilologus* 97 (2013), 541–53.

Foley, John Miles, *Traditional Oral Epic: The* Odyssey, Beowulf, *and the Serbo-Croatian Return Song* (Berkeley: University of California Press, 1990).

Foot, Sarah, *Athelstan: The First King of England* (New Haven and London: Yale UP, 2011).

———, 'Bede's Kings', in *Writing, Kingship and Power in Anglo-Saxon England*, ed. Rory Naismith and David A. Woodman (Cambridge: CUP, 2017), pp. 25–51.

Fouracre, Paul, 'Francia in the seventh century', in Fouracre (2005), pp. 397–70.

———, ed., *The New Cambridge History of Medieval Europe, Vol. 1, c. 500–c. 700* (Cambridge: CUP, 2005).

Frank, Roberta, 'Skaldic Verse and the Date of *Beowulf*', in Chase, ed. (1981), pp. 123–49.

———, 'The *Beowulf* Poet's Sense of History', in *The Wisdom of Poetry: Essays in Early English Literature in Honour of Morton W. Bloomfield*, ed. Larry D. Benson and Siegfried Wenzel (Kalamazoo, MI: Medieval Institute Publications, 1982), pp. 53–65.

———, '*Beowulf* and Sutton Hoo: The Odd Couple', in *Voyage to the Other World: The Legacy of Sutton Hoo*, Medieval Cultures 5, ed. Calvin B. Kendall and Peter S. Wells (Minneapolis: University of Minnesota Press, 1992), pp. 47–64.

———, 'The Search for the Anglo-Saxon Oral Poet', *Bulletin of the John Rylands University Library of Manchester* 75 (1993), 28–36.

———, 'Germanic Legend in Old English Literature', in Godden and Lapidge, eds (2013), pp. 82–100.

Fulk, R. D., 'Dating *Beowulf* to the Viking Age', *PQ* 61 (1982), 341–59.

———, 'Unferth and his Name', *MP* 85 (1987), 113–27.

———, 'An Eddic Analogue to the Scyld Scefing Story', *RES* 40 (1989), 313–22.

———, ed., *Interpretations of* Beowulf: *A Critical Anthology* (Bloomington, IN: Indiana UP, 1991).

———, *A History of Old English Meter* (Philadelphia: UPenn Press, 1992).

———, 'The Name of Offa's Queen: *Beowulf* 1931–3', *Anglia* 122 (2004), 614–39.
———, 'The Etymology and Significance of Beowulf's Name', *Anglo-Saxon* 1 (2007), 109–36.
———, '*Beowulf* and Language History', in Neidorf, ed. (2014), pp. 19–36.
Gang, T. M., 'Approaches to *Beowulf*', *RES* 33 (1952), 1–12.
Gardner, John, 'Guilt and the World's Complexity: The Murder of Ongentheow and the Slaying of the Dragon', in *Anglo-Saxon Poetry: Essays in Appreciation for John C. McGalliard*, ed. Lewis E. Nicholson and Dolores Warwick Frese (Notre Dame: University of Notre Dame Press, 1975), pp. 14–22.
Gelling, Margaret, 'The Landscape of *Beowulf*', *ASE* 31 (2002), 7–11.
Georgianna, Linda, 'King Hrethel's Sorrow and the Limits of Heroic Action in *Beowulf*', *Speculum* 62 (1987), 829–50.
Gerberding, Richard, 'The Later Roman Empire', in Fouracre, ed. (2005), pp. 13–34.
Girvan, Richie, *Beowulf and the Seventh Century* (London: Methuen, 1935; repr. 1971).
Given-Wilson, Chris, *Chronicles: The Writing of History in Medieval England* (London and New York: A&C Black, 2004).
Glosecki, Stephen O., '*Beowulf* and the Wills: Traces of Totemism?', *PQ* 78 (1999), 15–47.
Godden, Malcolm, 'Biblical Literature: the Old Testament', in Godden and Lapidge, eds (2013), pp. 214–33.
Godden, Malcolm, and Michael Lapidge, eds, *The Cambridge Companion to Old English Literature*, 2nd edn (Cambridge: CUP, 2013).
Goering, Nelson, 'The linguistic elements of Old Germanic metre: phonology, metrical theory, and the development of alliterative verse' (Unpubl. doctoral dissertation, Univ. of Oxford, 2016).
Goffart, Walter, '*Hetware* and *Hugas*: Datable Anachronisms in *Beowulf*', in Chase, ed. (1981), pp. 83–100.
———, *The Narrators of Barbarian History (A.D. 550–800): Jordanes, Gregory of Tours, Bede, and Paul the Deacon* (Princeton, NJ: Princeton UP, 1988; repr. Notre Dame: University of Notre Dame Press, 2005).
———, 'The Name "Merovingian" and the Dating of *Beowulf*', *ASE* 36 (2007), 93–101.
Goldsmith, Margaret E., 'The Christian Theme in *Beowulf*', *MÆ* 29 (1960), 81–101.
———, 'The Christian Perspective in *Beowulf*', *Comparative Literature* 14 (1962), 71–90; repr. Fulk, ed. (1991), pp. 103–19.
———, *The Mode and Meaning of* Beowulf (London: Athlone Press, 1970).
Graeber, David, and Marshall Sahlins, *On Kings* (Chicago: Hau Books, 2017).
Gräslund, Bo, *Beowulfkvädet: Den nordiska bakgrunden*, Acta Academiae

Regiae Gustavi Adolphi 149 (Uppsala: Kungl. Gustav Adolfs Akademien för svensk folkkultur, 2018).

Green, Dennis Howard, *Language and history in the early Germanic world* (Cambridge: CUP, 1998).

Greenfield, Stanley B., 'Geatish History, Poetic Art and Epic Quality in *Beowulf*', *Neophilologus* 47 (1963), 211–17; repr. in Greenfield (1989), pp. 3–18; and in Fulk, ed. (1991), pp. 120–26.

———, 'The Authenticating Voice in *Beowulf*', *ASE* 5 (1976), 51–62; repr. in Greenfield (1989), pp. 43–54.

———, 'A touch of the monstrous in the hero, or Beowulf re-Marvellised', *ES* 63 (1982), 294–300; repr. in Greenfield (1989), pp. 67–73.

———, 'Beowulf and the Judgment of the Righteous', in *Learning and Literature in Anglo-Saxon England: Studies Presented to Peter Clemoes on the Occasion of His Sixty-Fifth Birthday*, ed. Michael Lapidge and Helmut Gneuss (Cambridge: CUP, 1985), pp. 393–407.

———, *Hero and exile: The art of Old English poetry*, ed. George Hardin Brown (London: Hambledon Continuum, 1989).

Griffith, Mark S., 'Convention and Originality in the Old English "Beasts of Battle" Typescene', *ASE* 22 (1993), 179–99.

———, 'Some difficulties in *Beowulf*, lines 874–902: Sigemund reconsidered', *ASE* 24 (1995), 11–41.

Gudeman, Alfred, 'The Sources of the Germania of Tacitus', *Transactions and Proceedings of the American Philological Association* 31 (1900), 93–111.

Gwara, Scott, *Heroic Identity in the World of* Beowulf, Medieval and Renaissance Authors and Texts 2 (Leiden: Brill, 2008).

Haarder, Andreas, Beowulf: *The Appeal of a Poem* (Viborg: Akademisk Forlag, 1975).

Haber, Tom Burns, *A Comparative Study of the Beowulf and the Aeneid* (Princeton, NJ: Princeton UP, 1931).

Hall, Alaric, 'Hygelac's only daughter: a present, a potentate and a peace-weaver in *Beowulf*', *SN* 78 (2006), 81–87.

Halsall, Guy, *Barbarian Migrations and the Roman West, 376–568* (Cambridge: CUP, 2007).

Hamilton, David, '*Andreas* and *Beowulf*: Placing the Hero', in *Anglo-Saxon Poetry: Essays in Appreciation for John C. McGalliard*, ed. Lewis E. Nicholson and Dolores Warwick Frese (Notre Dame, University of Notre Dame Press, 1975), pp. 81–98.

Hanning, Robert W., '*Beowulf* as Heroic History', *Medievalia et Humanistica* 5 (1974), 77–102.

Harbus, Antonina, *The Life of the Mind in Old English Poetry* (Amsterdam: Rodopi, 2002).

———, *Cognitive Approaches to Old English Poetry*, CSASE 18 (Cambridge: CUP, 2012).

Hardy, Adelaide, 'Historical Perspective and the *Beowulf* Poet',

Neophilologus 63 (1979), 431–49.

Harris, Joseph, '*Beowulf* in Literary History', *Pacific Coast Philology* 17 (1982), 16–23; repr. in Fulk, ed. (1991), pp. 235–41.

———, 'A Nativist Approach to *Beowulf*: the Case of Germanic Elegy', in Aertsen and Bremmer, eds (1994), pp. 45–62.

———, 'The Dossier on Byggvir, God and Hero: *Cur deus homo*', *ARV* 55 (1999), 7–23.

———, '*Homo necans borealis*: Fatherhood and Sacrifice in *Sonatorrek*', in *Myth in Early Northwest Europe*, ed. Stephen O. Glosecki (Tempe, AZ: Arizona Center for Medieval and Renaissance Studies, 2007), pp. 153–73.

———, 'Beowulf's Name', in Heaney (2002), pp. 98–100.

Hart, Thomas Elwood, 'Tectonic Design, Formulaic Craft, and Literary Execution; the Episodes of Finn and Ingeld in *Beowulf*', *Amsterdamer Beiträge zur älteren Germanistik* 2 (1972), 1–61.

Haudry, Jean, '*Beowulf* dans la Tradition Indo-Européene (1): Structure et Signification du Poèm', *Études Indo-Européene* 9 (1984), 1–56.

Heather, Peter, 'Cassiodorus and the Rise of the Amals: Genealogy and the Goths under Hun Domination', *Journal of Roman Studies* 78 (1989), 103–28.

Hedeager, Lotte, trans. John Hines, 'Kingdoms, Ethnicity and Material Culture: Denmark in a European Perspective', in *The Age of Sutton Hoo: The Seventh Century in North-Western Europe*, ed. Martin Carver (Woodbridge: Boydell & Brewer, 1992), pp. 279–300.

Hennequin, M. Wendy, 'We've Created a Monster: The Strange Case of Grendel's Mother', *ES* 89 (2008), 502–23.

Herbison, Ivan, 'Generic Adaptation in *Andreas*', in *Essays on Anglo-Saxon and Related Themes in Memory of Lynne Grundy*, ed. Jane Roberts and Janet L. Nelson, King's College London Medieval Studies 17 (Exeter: King's College London, Centre for Late Antique and Medieval Studies, 2000), pp. 181–211.

Higham, N. J., *(Re-)Reading Bede: The Ecclesiastical History in Context* (London: Routledge, 2006).

———, 'Bede's Agenda in Book IV of the *Ecclesiastical History of the English People*: A Tricky Matter of Advising the King', *Journal of Ecclesiastical History* 64 (2013), 476–93.

Hill, John M., 'Beowulf and the Danish Succession: Gift Giving as an Occasion for Complex Gesture', *Medievalia et Humanistica* 11 (1982), 177–97.

———, 'Current Trends in *Beowulf* Scholarship', *Literature Compass* 4 (2007), 66–88.

———, *The Narrative Pulse of* Beowulf: *Arrivals and Departures* (Toronto: UTP, 2008).

———, *The Cultural World in* Beowulf, 2nd edn (Toronto: UTP, 2015).

Hill, Joyce, '*Þæt wæs geomoru ides!* A female stereotype examined', in Damico and Olsen, eds (1990), pp. 235–47.

Hill, Thomas D., 'The Fall of Angels and Man in the Old English *Genesis B*', in *Anglo-Saxon Poetry: Essays in Appreciation for John C. McGalliard*, ed. Lewis E. Nicholson and Dolores Warwick Frese (Notre Dame: University of Notre Dame Press, 1975), pp. 279–90.

———, 'The Confession of Beowulf and the Structure of *Vǫlsunga saga*', in *The Vikings: Papers from the Cornell Lecture Series Held to Coincide with the Viking Exhibition 1980–1981*, ed. Robert T. Farrell (London: Phillimore, 1982), pp. 165–75.

———, 'Scyld Scefing and the *Stirps Regia*: Pagan Myth and Christian Kingship in *Beowulf*', in *Magister Regis: Studies in Honor of Robert Earl Kaske*, ed. Arthur Groos (New York: Fordham UP, 1986), pp. 37–47.

———, 'The Christian Language and Theme of *Beowulf*', in Aertsen and Bremmer, eds (1994), pp. 63–77.

———, '*Beowulf* and Conversion History', in Neidorf, ed. (2014), pp. 191–201.

———, 'On *fæder bearme*: *Beowulf*, Line 21', *NQ* 66 (2019), 2–5.

———, 'Hrothgar's Speech of Adoption: A Danish-Latin Analogue', *NQ* 66 (2019), 163–66.

Hines, John, *The Scandinavian Character of Anglian England in the pre-Viking Period*, BAR 124 (Oxford: BAR, 1984).

———, 'The *Benedicite* Canticle in Old English Verse: An Early Runic Witness from Southern Lincolnshire', *Anglia* 133 (2015), 257–77.

Hollis, Stephanie, '*Beowulf* and the Succession', *Parergon* 1 (1983), 39–54.

Hooker, James, 'Homer, Patroclus, Achilles', *Symbolae Osloenses* 64 (1989), 30–35.

Horowitz, Sylvia H., 'Beowulf, Samson, David and Christ', *Studies in Medieval Culture* 12 (1978), 17–23.

Howard, Jr., David M., 'The Case for Kingship in the Old Testament Narrative Books and the Psalms', *Trinity Journal* 9 (1988), 19–35.

Howe, Nicholas, *Migration and Mythmaking in Anglo-Saxon England* (New Haven, CT: Yale UP, 1989).

———, *Writing the Map of Anglo-Saxon England: Essays in Cultural Geography* (New Haven, CT: Yale UP, 2008).

Hume, Kathryn, 'The Concept of the Hall in Old English Poetry', *ASE* 3 (1974), 63–74.

———, 'The Theme and Structure of *Beowulf*', *SP* 72 (1975), 1–27.

Hunt, R. W., 'Manuscript evidence for knowledge of the poems of Venantius Fortunatus in late Anglo-Saxon England', *ASE* 8 (1979), 279–95.

Hunter, Michael, 'Germanic and Roman antiquity and the sense of the past in Anglo-Saxon England', *ASE* 3 (1974), 29–50.

Huppé, Bernard F., *Doctrine and Poetry: Augustine's Influence on Old English*

Poetry (New York: SUNY Press, 1959).
Irvine, Susan, 'Bawling and brawling', *Times Literary Supplement*, 16 February 2018, pp. 26–27.
Irvine, Susan, and Winfried Rudolf, eds, *Childhood and Adolescence in Anglo-Saxon England* (Toronto: UTP, 2018).
——, 'Introduction', in Irvine and Rudolf, eds (2018), pp. 3–14.
Irving, Jr., Edward B., *A Reading of* Beowulf (New Haven, CT: Yale UP, 1968).
——, *Rereading* Beowulf (Philadelphia: UPenn Press, 1989).
——, 'Christian and Pagan Elements', in Bjork and Niles, eds (1997), pp. 175–92.
Jacobs, Nicholas, 'Anglo-Danish Relations, Poetic Archaism and the Date of *Beowulf*: A Reconsideration of the Evidence', *Poetica* 8 (1977), 23–43.
Jakobson, Ármann, 'Royal Biography', in *A Companion to Old Norse-Icelandic Literature and Culture*, ed. Rory McTurk (Oxford: Blackwell, 2005), pp. 388–402.
Jewell, Helen M., *Women in Dark Age and Early Medieval Europe c. 500–1200* (London: Palgrave Macmillan, 2007).
John, Eric, 'Folkland reconsidered', in his *Orbis Britanniae and Other Studies*, Studies in Early English History 4 (Leicester: Leicester UP, 1966), pp. 64–127.
——, 'The Social and Political Problems of the Early English Church', in *Land, Church, and People: Essays Presented to Professor H. P. R. Finberg*, ed. Joan Thirsk (Reading: British Agricultural Society Museum of English Rural Life, 1970), pp. 39–63.
——, '*Beowulf* and the Margins of Literacy', *Bulletin of the John Rylands University Library* (1974), 388–422; repr. in Baker, ed. (1995), pp. 51–77.
Johnson, David F., 'The Fall of Lucifer in *Genesis A* and Two Anglo-Latin Royal Charters', *JEGP* 97 (1998), 500–21.
Jones, Christopher, 'From Heorot to Hollywood: *Beowulf* in its Third Millennium', in *Anglo-Saxon Culture and the Modern Imagination*, Medievalism 1, ed. David Clark and Nicholas Perkins (Cambridge: D. S. Brewer, 2010), pp. 13–30.
Jones, Gwyn, *A History of the Vikings* (Oxford: OUP, 1968; repr. London: Book Club Associates, 1975).
Jorgensen, Peter A., 'Beowulf's Swimming Contest with Breca: Old Norse Parallels', *Folk-Lore* 89 (1978), 52–59.
Joy, Eileen A., and Mary Kate Ramsey, eds, with the assistance of Bruce D. Gilchrist, *The Postmodern* Beowulf: *A Critical Casebook* (Morgantown, WV: West Virginia UP, 2006).
Jurasinski, Stefan, *Ancient Privileges:* Beowulf, *Law, and the Making of Germanic Antiquity* (Morgantown, WV: West Virginia UP, 2006).
Karkov, Catherine E., *Text and Picture in Anglo-Saxon England: Narrative Strategies in the Junius 11 Manuscript*, CSASE 31 (Cambridge: CUP, 2001).

Kaske, Robert E., 'Weohstan's Sword', *MLN* 75 (1960), 465–68.

———, '*Sapientia et Fortitudo* as the Controlling Theme of *Beowulf*', *SP* 55 (1958), 423–57; repr. in Nicholson, ed. (1963), pp. 269–310.

———, 'The Sigemund-Heremod and Hama-Hygelac Passages in *Beowulf*', *PMLA* 74 (1959), 489–94.

———, '*Beowulf* and the Book of Enoch', *Speculum* 46 (1971), 421–31.

———, 'The *Gifstol* Crux in *Beowulf*', *Leeds Studies in English* n.s. 16 (1985), 142–51.

Kellogg, Robert Leland, 'The Context for Epic in Later Anglo-Saxon England', in *Heroic Poetry in the Anglo-Saxon Period: Studies in Honor of Jess B. Bessinger, Jr.*, ed. Helen Damico and John Leyerle (Kalamazoo, MI: Medieval Institute Publications, 1993), pp. 139–56.

Kemble, John Mitchell, *Über die Stammtafel der Westsachen* (Munich: Privately Printed, 1836).

———, *The Saxons in England: a history of the English commonwealth till the period of the Norman Conquest*, 2 vols (London: Longman, Brown, Green, and Longmans, 1849).

Kendall, Calvin B., *The Metrical Grammar of* Beowulf, CSASE 5 (Cambridge: CUP, 1991).

Kennedy, Hugh, 'From Oral Tradition to Written Record in Arabic Genealogy', *Arabica: Journal of Arabic and Islamic Studies* 44 (1997), 531–44.

Ker, W. P., *The Dark Ages* (Edinburgh: W. Blackwood, 1923).

Kershaw, Paul J. E., *Peaceful Kings: Peace, Power, and the Early Medieval Political Imagination* (Oxford: OUP, 2011).

Kiernan, Kevin S., Beowulf *and the* Beowulf *Manuscript* (New Brunswick, NJ: Rutgers UP, 1981); repr. with a new foreword by Katherine O'Brien O'Keeffe (Ann Arbor, MI: University of Michigan Press, 1997).

Kightley, Michael R., 'The Brothers of *Beowulf*: Fraternal Tensions and the Reticent Style', *ELH* 83 (2016), 407–29.

King, Judy, 'Launching the Hero: the Case of Scyld and Beowulf', *Neophilologus* 87 (2003), 453–71.

Kinney, Clare, 'The Needs of the Moment: Poetic Foregrounding as a Narrative Device in *Beowulf*', *SP* 82 (1985), 295–314.

Kirby, D. P., *The Earliest English Kings* (London: Unwin, 1991).

Klaeber, Friedrich, 'Textual notes on the *Beowulf*', *JEGP* 8 (1909), 254–59.

———, 'Aeneis und Beowulf', *Archiv für das Studium der neuren Sprachen und Literaturen* 126 (1911), 40–48 and 339–59.

———, 'Die christlichen Elemente im *Beowulf*', *Anglia* 35 (1911–12), 111–36, 249–70, 453–82; *Anglia* 36 (1912), 169–99; trans. by Paul Battles as 'The Christian Elements in *Beowulf*', *Old English Newsletter*, Subsidia 24 (Kalamazoo, MI: Medieval Institute Publications, 1997).

———, 'Eine kleine Nachlese zum *Beowulf*', *Anglia* 56 (1932), 421–31.

———, 'Beowulfiana Minora', *Anglia* 63 (1939), 400–25.

Klein, Stacy, *Ruling Women: Queenship and Gender in Anglo-Saxon Literature* (Notre Dame: University of Notre Dame Press, 2006).

Knauer, Georg Nicolaus, 'Virgil's *Aeneid* and Homer', *Greek, Roman, and Byzantine Studies* 5 (1964), 61–84.

Köberl, Johann, *The Indeterminacy of* Beowulf (Lanham, MD: UP of America, 2002).

Langeslag, Paul S., 'Monstrous Landscape in *Beowulf*', *ES* 96 (2015), 119–38.

Lapidge, Michael, '*Beowulf*, Aldhelm, the *Liber Monstrorum* and Wessex', *Studi Medievali* 3rd ser. 23 (1982), 151–92.

———, 'Versifying the Bible in the Middle Ages', in *The Text in the Community: Essays on Medieval Works, Manuscripts, and Readers*, ed. Jill Mann and Maura Nolan (Notre Dame: University of Notre Dame Press, 2006), pp. 11–40.

———, '*Beowulf* and the Psychology of Terror', in *Heroic poetry in the Anglo-Saxon period: studies in honor of Jess B. Bessinger, Jr.*, ed. Helen Damico and John Leyerle (Kalamazoo, MI: Medieval Institute Publications, 1993), pp. 373–402.

———, 'The Archetype of *Beowulf*', *ASE* 29 (2000), 5–41.

———, '*Beowulf* and Perception', *PBA* 111 (2001), 61–97.

———, *The Anglo-Saxon Library* (Oxford: OUP, 2006).

Lavelle, Ryan, 'The use and abuse of hostages in later Anglo-Saxon England', *EME* 14 (2006), 269–96.

———, 'The Politics of Rebellion: The Ætheling, Æthelwold and West Saxon Royal Succession, 899–902', in *Challenging the Boundaries of Medieval History: the Legacy of Timothy Reuter*, ed. Patricia Skinner (Turnhout: Brepols, 2010), pp. 51–80.

Lawrence, William Witherle, Beowulf *and Epic Tradition* (Harvard: Harvard UP, 1928).

Leader, Zachary, *The Life of Kingsley Amis* (London: Vintage Books, 2007).

Leake, Jane Acomb, *The Geats of* Beowulf: *A Study in the Geographical Mythology of the Middle Ages* (Madison, WI: University of Wisconsin Press, 1967).

Lee, Alvin A., *Gold-Hall and Earth-Dragon:* Beowulf *as Metaphor* (Toronto: UTP, 1998).

Lehmann, Ruth Preston, 'Ecgþeow the Wægmunding: Geat or Swede?', *ELN* 31 (1994), 1–5.

Leisl, Ernst, 'Gold und Manneswert im *Beowulf*', *Anglia* 71 (1952), 259–73; trans. J. D. Niles, with the assistance of Shannon A. Dubenion-Smith, as 'Gold and Human Worth in *Beowulf*', in Niles (2016), pp. 173–83.

Leneghan, Francis, 'The Poetic Purpose of the Offa Digression in *Beowulf*', *RES* 60 (2009), 538–60.

———, 'Royal Wisdom and the Alfredian Context of *Cynewulf and Cyneheard*', *ASE* 39 (2009), 71–104.

———, 'Reshaping Tradition: the Originality of the Scyld Scefing Episode in *Beowulf*, in *Transmission and Generation in Medieval and Renaissance Literature: Essays in Honour of John Scattergood*, ed. Karen Hodder and Brendan O'Connell (Dublin: Four Courts, 2012), pp. 21–36.

———, '*Translatio imperii*: The Old English *Orosius* and the Rise of Wessex', *Anglia* 133 (2015), 656–705.

———, 'The Departure of the Hero in a Ship: the Intertextuality of *Beowulf*, Cynewulf and *Andreas*', *SELIM* 24 (2019), 105–34.

Lester, Graham A., '*Earme on eaxle* (*Beowulf* 1117a)', *SN* 58 (1986), 159–63.

Lévi-Strauss, Claude, 'The Structural Study of Myth', *Journal of American Folklore* 68 (1955), 428–44.

Leyerle, John, 'Beowulf the Hero and the King', *MÆ* 34 (1965), 89–102.

———, 'The Interlace Structure of *Beowulf*', *University of Toronto Quarterly* 37 (1967), 1–17; repr. in Fulk, ed. (1991), pp. 146–67.

Lindquist, Sune, 'Sutton Hoo and *Beowulf*', *Antiquity* 22 (1948), 131–40.

Louth, A., 'The Eastern Empire in the Sixth Century', in Fouracre, ed. (2005), pp. 93–117.

Louviot, Elise, *Direct Speech in* Beowulf *and Other Old English Narrative Poems*, Anglo-Saxon Studies 30 (Cambridge: D. S. Brewer, 2016).

Lucas, Peter J., 'The Place of *Judith* in the *Beowulf*-manuscript', *RES* 41 (1990), 463–78.

Lutz, Angelika, 'Æthelweard's *Chronicon* and Old English poetry', *ASE* 29 (2000), 177–214.

Magennis, Hugh, *Images of Community in Old English Literature*, CSASE 18 (Cambridge: CUP, 1996).

———, *Anglo-Saxon Appetites: Food and Drink and Their Consumption in Old English and Related Literature* (Dublin: Four Courts, 1998).

———, *Translating* Beowulf: *Modern Versions in English Verse* (Cambridge: D. S. Brewer, 2011).

———, '*Cristes leorningcnihtas*: traditions of the apostles in Old English literature', in *Aspects of Knowledge: Preserving and reinventing traditions of learning in the Middle Ages*, ed. Marilina Cesario and Hugh Magennis (Manchester: MUP, 2018), pp. 97–115.

Magoun, Jr., Francis Peabody, 'Béowulf and King Hygelác in the Netherlands: Lost Anglo-Saxon Verse Stories about this event', *ES* 35 (1954), 193–204.

———, 'The Theme of the Beasts of Battle in Anglo-Saxon Poetry', *NM* 56 (1955), 81–90.

———, '*Béowulf A*: a Folk-Variant', *ARV* 14 (1958), 95–101.

———, '*Béowulf B*: A Folk-Poem on Beowulf's Death', *Early English and Norse Studies Presented to Hugh Smith in Honour of His Sixtieth Birthday*, ed. Arthur Brown and Peter Foote (London: Methuen, 1963), pp. 127–40.

Major, Tristan, *Undoing Babel: The Tower of Babel in Anglo-Saxon Literature* (Toronto: UTP, 2018).

Malmberg, Lars, 'Grendel and the Devil', *NM* 78 (1977), 241–43.

Malone, Kemp, 'Hrethric', *PMLA* 42 (1927), 168–313.

———, 'The Daughter of Healfdene', in *Studies in English Philology: A Miscellany in honor of Frederick Klaeber*, ed. Kemp Malone and Martin B. Ruud (Minneapolis: University of Minnesota Press, 1929), pp. 135–58.

———, 'Time and Place in the Ingeld Episode of *Beowulf*', *JEGP* 39 (1940), 84–85.

———, 'Hygd', *MLN* 56 (1941), 356–58.

———, 'Beowulf the Headstrong', *ASE* 1 (1972), 139–45.

Marshall, Sophie, 'Digression, Coherence, and a Missing Cup in *Beowulf*', *Zeitschrift für Literaturwissenschaft und Linguistik* 48 (2018), 167–92.

McBrine, Patrick, *Biblical Epics in Late Antiquity and Anglo-Saxon England: 'Divina in Laude Voluntas'* (Toronto: UTP, 2017).

McCann, Kathrin, *Anglo-Saxon Kingship and Political Power: Rex gratia Dei* (Cardiff: University of Wales Press, 2018).

McClure, Judith, 'Bede's Old Testament Kings', in *Ideal and Reality in Frankish and Anglo-Saxon Society: Studies Presented to J. M. Wallace-Hadrill*, ed. Patrick Wormald (Oxford: Basil Blackwell, 1983), pp. 76–98.

McCormick, Michael, *Eternal Victory: Triumphal Rulership in Late Antiquity, Byzantium and the Early Medieval West* (Cambridge: CUP, 1986).

McGillivray, Murray, 'What Kind of Seat is Hrothgar's *Gifstol*?', *SP* 105 (2008), 265–83.

McKitterick, Rosamond, *Carolingian Culture: Emulation and Innovation* (Cambridge: CUP, 1993).

McNamara, John, 'Beowulf and Hygelac: Problems for Fiction in History', *Rice University Studies* 62 (1976), 55–63.

McNamee, M. B., '*Beowulf*: An Allegory of Salvation?', *JEGP* 59 (1960), 190–207.

Meaney, Audrey L., 'Scyld Scefing and the Dating of *Beowulf*—Again', *Bulletin of the John Rylands University Library of Manchester* 71 (1988), 7–40.

———, 'Postscript to "Scyld Scefing and the Dating of *Beowulf*—Again"', in *Textual and Material Culture in Anglo-Saxon England: Thomas Northcote Toller and the Toller Memorial Lectures*, ed. Donald G. Scragg (Cambridge: D. S. Brewer, 2003), pp. 54–73.

Meletinsky, Eleazar M., *The Poetics of Myth*, trans. Guy Lanoue and Alexandre Sadetsky (New York: Routledge, 2000).

Mellinkoff, Ruth, 'Cain's monstrous progeny in *Beowulf*: part I, Noachic tradition', *ASE* 8 (1979), 143–62.

———, 'Cain's monstrous progeny in *Beowulf*: part II, post-diluvian survival', *ASE* 9 (1981), 183–97.

Michelet, Fabienne L., 'Hospitality, Hostility and Peacemaking in *Beowulf*', *PQ* 94 (2015), 23–50.

Mitchell, Bruce, 'Literary Lapses: Six Notes on *Beowulf* and Its Critics', *RES* 43 (1992), 1–17.

——, 'apo koinou in Old English Poetry?', NM 100 (1999), 477–97.
Mittman, Asa Simon, and Susan M. Kim, 'Monsters and the Medieval Exotic', in *The Oxford Handbook of Medieval Literature in English*, ed. Elaine Treharne and Greg Walker (Oxford: OUP, 2010), pp. 677–706.
Mize, Britt, 'Manipulations of the Mind-as-Container Motif in *Beowulf*, *Homiletic Fragment II*, and Alfred's *Metrical Epilogue to the Pastoral Care*', *JEGP* 107 (2008), 25–56.
Moisl, Hermann, 'Anglo-Saxon Royal Genealogies and Germanic Oral Tradition', *Journal of Medieval History* 7 (1981), 215–48.
Moore, Bruce, 'The Thryth-Offa Digression in *Beowulf*', *Neophilologus* 64 (1980), 127–33.
Morey, James H., 'The Fates of Men in *Beowulf*', in *Source of Wisdom: Old English and Early Medieval Latin Studies in Honour of Thomas D. Hill*, ed. Charles D. Wright et al. (Toronto: UTP, 2007), pp. 26–51.
——, 'The Fourth Fate of Men: Heremod's Darkened Mind', in *Darkness, Depression and Descent in Anglo-Saxon England*, ed. Ruth Wehlau (Kalamazoo, MI: Medieval Institute Publications/De Gruyter, 2019), pp. 155–66.
Morgan, Gerald, 'The Treachery of Hrothulf', *ES* 53 (1972), 23–39.
Morrison, Stephen, '*Beowulf* 698a, 1273a: *frofor ond fultum*', *NQ* 27 (1980), 193–96.
Morrison, Susan Signe, *The Literature of Waste: Material Ecopoetics and Ethical Matter* (New York: Palgrave Macmillan, 2015).
Morrissey, Ted, *The* Beowulf-*Poet and his Real Monsters: A Trauma-Theory Reading of the Anglo-Saxon Poem* (Lampeter: Edwin Mellen, 2013).
Müllenhoff, Karl, 'Seugnisse und Excurse zur deutschen Heldensage', *Zeitschrift für desutsches Altertum* 12 (1865), 253–86.
——, 'Die innere Geschichte des Beowulfs', *Zeitschrift für deutsche Philologie* 14 (1869), 193–224.
Murdoch, Brian, *The Germanic Hero: Politics and Pragmatism in Early Medieval Poetry* (London: Bloomsbury, 1996).
Murray, Alexander Callander, '*Beowulf*, the Danish Invasions, and Royal Genealogy', in Chase, ed. (1981), pp. 101–11.
Neckel, Gustav, 'Sigmunds Drachenkampf', *Edda* 13 (1920), 122–40.
Neidorf, Leonard, 'VII Æthelred and the Genesis of the *Beowulf* Manuscript', *PQ* 89 (2010), 119–39.
——, 'The Dating of *Widsið* and the Study of Germanic Legend', *Neophilologus* 97 (2013), 165–83.
——, 'Beowulf before *Beowulf*: Anglo-Saxon Anthroponymy and Heroic Legend', *RES* 64 (2013), 553–73.
——, ed., *The Dating of* Beowulf: *A Reassessment*, Anglo-Saxon Studies 24 (Cambridge: D. S. Brewer, 2014).
——, 'Germanic Legend, Scribal Errors and Cultural Change', in Neidorf, ed. (2014), pp. 37–57.

———, 'Hildeburh's Mourning and *The Wife's Lament'*, *SN* 89 (2017), 197–204.

———, *The Transmission of* Beowulf: *Language, Culture and Scribal Behavior*, Myth and Poetics 2 (Ithaca, NY: Cornell UP, 2017).

———, 'Unferth's Ambiguity and the Trivialization of Germanic Antiquity', *Neophilologus* 101 (2017), 439–54.

———, '*Beowulf*', in *Books to Film: Cinematic Adaptations of Literary Works*, Vol. I, ed. Jim Craddock (Detroit: Gale, 2018), pp. 21–24.

———, '*Beowulf* as Pre-National Epic: Ethnocentrism in the Poem and its Criticism', *ELH* 85 (2018), 847–75.

———, 'The Language of Hrothgar's Sermon', *SN* 91 (2019), 1–10.

———, 'Hygelac and His Daughter: Rereading *Beowulf* Lines 2985–2998', *MÆ* (forthcoming).

Neidorf, Leonard, and Rafael J. Pascual, 'Old Norse Influence on the Language of *Beowulf*', *Journal of Germanic Linguistics* 31 (2019), 298–322.

Neidorf, Leonard, Madison S. Krieger, Michelle Yakubek, Pramit Chaudhuri and Joseph P. Dexter, 'Large-scale quantitative profiling of the Old English verse tradition', *Nature: Human Behaviour* 3 (2019), 560–67.

Nelson, Janet L., 'National Synods, Kingship as Office, and Royal Anointing: An Early Medieval Syndrome', *Studies in Church History* 7 (1971), 41–49; repr. in her *Politics and Ritual in Early Medieval Europe* (London: Hambledon Press, 1986), pp. 239–58.

———, *Charles the Bald* (London: Longman, 1992).

Neuman de Vegvar, Carol L., 'The Travelling Twins: Romulus and Remus in Anglo-Saxon England', in *Northumbria's Golden Age*, ed. Jane Hawkes and Susan Mills (Stroud: Sutton Publishing Ltd, 1999), pp. 256–67.

Neville, Jennifer, *Representations of the Natural World in Old English Poetry*, CSASE 27 (Cambridge: CUP, 1999).

———, 'Redeeming Beowulf and Byrhtnoth: The Heroic Idiom as Marker of Quality in Old English Poetry', in *Narration and Hero: Recounting the Deeds of Heroes in Literature and Art of the Early Medieval Period*, Ergänzungsbände zum Reallexikon der Germanischen Altertumskunde 87, ed. Victor Millet and Heike Sahme (Berlin: De Gruyter, 2014), pp. 45–69.

Newton, Sam, *The Origins of* Beowulf *and the Pre-Viking Kingdom of East Anglia* (Cambridge: D. S. Brewer, 1993).

Nicholson, Lewis E., ed., *An Anthology of* Beowulf *Criticism* (Notre Dame: University of Notre Dame Press, 1963).

Niles, John D., Beowulf: *The Poem and Its Tradition* (Cambridge MA: Harvard UP, 1983).

———, 'Locating *Beowulf* in Literary History', *Exemplaria* 5 (1993), 79–109.

———, 'Introduction: *Beowulf*, Truth, and Meaning', in Bjork and Niles, eds (1997), pp. 1–12.

———, 'Myth and History', in Bjork and Niles, eds (1997), pp. 213–32.
———, Review of Craig Davis, Beowulf *and the Demise of Germanic Legend*, *Speculum* 73 (1998), 497–99.
———, 'The Myth of the Anglo-Saxon Oral Poet', *Western Folklore* 62 (2003), 7–61.
———, '*Beowulf* and Lejre', in Beowulf *and Lejre*, Medieval and Renaissance Texts and Studies 323, ed. John D. Niles and Marijane Osborn (Tempe, AZ: Arizona Center for Medieval and Renaissance Studies, 2007), pp. 169–234.
———, 'On the Danish Origins of the *Beowulf* Story', in *Anglo-Saxon England and the Continent*, ed. Hans Sauer and Joanna Story, with the assistance of Gaby Waxenberger, Medieval and Renaissance Texts and Studies 394, ISAS Essays in Anglo-Saxon Studies 3 (Tempe, AZ: Arizona Center for Medieval and Renaissance Studies, 2011), pp. 41–62.
———, *Old English Literature: A Guide to Criticism with Selected Readings* (Chichester: Blackwell, 2016).
Nist, John A., 'The Structure of *Beowulf*', *Papers of the Michigan Academy of Science, Arts, and Letters* 43 (1958), 307–14.
North, Richard, 'Saxo and the Swedish Wars in *Beowulf*', in *Saxo Grammaticus tra storiografia e letteratura*, ed. Carlo Santini (Rome: Il Calamo, 1992), pp. 175–88.
———, *The Origins of* Beowulf: *From Vergil to Wiglaf* (Oxford: OUP, 2007).
———, 'Hrothulf's Childhood and Beowulf's: A Comparison', in Irvine and Rudolf, eds (2018), pp. 222–43.
———, 'Gold and the Heathen Polity in *Beowulf*', in *Gold in der Heldensage*, Reallexikon der germanischen Altertumskunde, Ergänzungsband, ed. Wilhelm Heizmann, Victor Millet und Heike Sahm (Berlin: De Gruyter, 2018), pp. 72–114.
O'Brien, Conor, 'Kings and Kingship in the Writings of Bede', *EHR* 132 (2018), 1473–98.
O'Brien O'Keeffe, Katherine, 'Diction, Variation, the Formula', in Bjork and Niles, eds (1997), pp. 85–104.
———, 'Body and law in late Anglo-Saxon England', *ASE* 27 (1998), 209–32.
O'Donoghue, Heather, 'What has Baldr to do with Lamech?', *MÆ* 72 (2003), 82–107.
———, *English Poetry and Old Norse Myth: A History* (Oxford: OUP, 2014).
Ogilvy, J. D. A., 'Unferth: Foil to Beowulf?', *PMLA* 79 (1964), 370–75.
Ogura, Michiko, '*Beowulf* and the *Book of Swords*: similarities and differences in scenes, features and epithets', *SELIM* 16 (2009), 7–22.
Olesiejko, Jacek, 'The Grendelkin and the Politics of Succession at Heorot: the Significance of the Monsters in *Beowulf*', *Studia Anglica Posnaniensia* 53 (2018), 45–65.
O'Loughlin, J. L. N., '*Beowulf*—its Unity and Purpose', *MÆ* 21 (1952), 1–13.

Olrik, Axel, *The Heroic Legends of Denmark: Translated from the Danish and Revised in Collaboration with the Author*, ed. and trans. Lee M. Hollander, Scandinavian Monographs 4 (New York: The American-Scandinavian Foundation, 1919).

Olsen, Alexandra Hennessey, 'Gender Roles', in Bjork and Niles, eds (1997), pp. 311–24.

Olson, Oscar L., 'The Relation of the *Hrólfs Saga Kraka* and the *Bjarkarímur* to *Beowulf*: A Contribution to the History of Saga Development in England and the Scandinavian Countries' (Unpubl. doctoral dissertation, University of Chicago, 1916).

Ong, Walter J., *Orality and Literacy: The Technologizing of the Word* (London and New York: Routledge, 1982).

Opland, Jeff, 'From Horseback to Monastic Cell: The Impact on English Literature of the Introduction of Writing', in *Old English Literature in Context*, ed. John D. Niles (Cambridge: D. S. Brewer, 1980), pp. 30–43.

Orchard, Andy, 'Artful Alliteration in Anglo-Saxon Song and Story', *Anglia* 113 (1995), 429–63.

———, 'The Sources and Meaning of the *Liber monstrorum*', in *I Monstra nell'Inferno Dantesco: Tradizione e Simbologie*, Atti del XXXIII Convegno storico internazionale, Todi, 13–16 ottobre 1996, ed. Enrico Menestò (Spoleto: Accademia Tudertina e del Centro di Studi sulla Spiritualità, 1997), pp. 73–106.

———, 'Both Style and Substance: The Case for Cynewulf', in *Anglo-Saxon Styles*, ed. Catherine E. Karkov and George Hardin Brown (Albany, NY: SUNY Press, 2003), pp. 271–305.

———, *Pride and Prodigies: Studies in the Monsters of the* Beowulf-*Manuscript* (Cambridge: D. S. Brewer, 1985; repr. Toronto: UTP, 2003).

———, *A Critical Companion to* Beowulf (Cambridge: D. S. Brewer, 2003).

———, 'Reading *Beowulf* Now and Then', *SELIM* 12 (2003–04), 49–81.

———, 'The Word Made Flesh: Christianity and Oral Culture in Anglo-Saxon Verse', *Oral Tradition* 24 (2009), 293–318.

———, 'The Originality of *Andreas*', in *Old English Philology: Studies in Honour of R. D. Fulk*, Anglo-Saxon Studies 31, ed. Leonard Neidorf, Rafael J. Pascual and Tom Shippey (Cambridge: D. S. Brewer, 2016), pp. 331–70.

Orton, Daniel, 'Royal Piety and Davidic Imitation: Cultivating Political Capital in the Alfredian Psalms', *Neophilologus* 98 (2014), 477–92.

Osborn, Marijane, 'The Great Feud: Scriptural History and Strife in *Beowulf*', *PMLA* 93 (1978), 973–81; repr. in Baker, ed. (1995), pp. 111–25.

Overing, Gillian R, *Language, Sign, and Gender in* Beowulf (Carbondale and Edwardsville: Southern Illinois UP, 1990).

———, '*Beowulf*: A Poem in Our Time', in *The Cambridge History of Early Medieval English Literature*, ed. Clare Lees (Cambridge: CUP, 2012), pp. 309–31.

Owen-Crocker, Gale R., 'Telling a Tale: Narrative Techniques in the Bayeux Tapestry and the Old English Epic *Beowulf*', in *Medieval Art: Recent Perspectives: A Memorial Tribute to C. R. Dowdell*, ed. Gale R. Owen-Crocker and Timothy Graham (Manchester: Manchester UP, 1998), pp. 40–59.

———, *The Four Funerals in* Beowulf *and the Structure of the Poem* (Manchester: Manchester UP, 2000).

Page, R. I., 'The Audience of *Beowulf* and the Vikings', in Chase, ed. (1981), pp. 113–22.

Panzer, Friedrich, *Studien zur germanischen Sagengeschichte, I:* Beowulf (Munich: Oscar Beck, 1910).

Parkes, Malcolm B, '*Rædan, areccan, smeagan*: How the Anglo-Saxons Read', *ASE* 26 (1997), 1–22.

Parks, Ward, 'The traditional narrator and the "I Heard" formulas in Old English Poetry', *ASE* 16 (1987), 45–66.

Pascual, Rafael J., 'Old English Metrical History and the Composition of *Widsið*', *Neophilologus* 100 (2016), 289–302.

———, 'Oral Tradition and the History of English Alliterative Verse', *SN* 89 (2017), 250–60.

Pasternack, Carol Braun, *The Textuality of Old English Poetry*, CSASE 13 (Cambridge: CUP, 1995).

Peltola, Niilo, 'Grendel's Descent from Cain Reconsidered', *NM* 73 (1972), 284–91.

Pepperdene, Margaret W., 'Grendel's *geis*', *The Journal of the Royal Society of Antiquaries of Ireland* 85 (1955), 188–92.

Phillpotts, Bertha Surtees, 'Wyrd and Providence in Anglo-Saxon Thought', *Essays and Studies* 13 (1928), 7–28; repr. in Fulk, ed. (1991), pp. 1–13.

Pogatscher, Alois, 'Zu Beowulf 168', *Beiträge zur Geschichte der deutschen Sprache und Literatur* 19 (1894), 544–45.

Porck, Thijs, *Old Age in Early Medieval England: A Cultural History*, Anglo-Saxon Studies 33 (Cambridge: D. S. Brewer, 2019).

Portnoy, Phyllis, *The Remnant: Essays on a Theme in Old English Verse* (London: Runetree Press, 2005).

———, 'Verbal Seascapes in Anglo-Saxon Verse', in *The Maritime World of the Anglo-Saxons*, Medieval and Renaissance Texts and Studies 448, Essays in Anglo-Saxon Studies 5, ed. Stacy Klein, William Schipper and Shannon Lewis-Simpson (Tempe, AZ: Arizona Center for Medieval and Renaissance Studies, 2014), pp. 247–73.

Powell, Alison, 'Verbal Parallels in *Andreas* and its Relationship to *Beowulf* and Cynewulf' (Unpubl. doctoral dissertation, University of Cambridge, 2002).

Powell, Kathryn, and Donald G. Scragg, eds, *Apocryphal Texts and Traditions in Anglo-Saxon England* (Cambridge: D. S. Brewer, 2003).

Powell, Kathryn, 'Meditating on Men and Monsters: A Reconsideration of the Thematic Unity of the *Beowulf* Manuscript', *RES* 58 (2006), 1–15.

Pratt, David, 'Persuasion and Invention at the Court of King Alfred', in *Court Culture in the Early Middle Ages: The Proceedings of the First Alcuin Conference*, ed. Catherine Cubitt (Turnhout: Brepols, 2003), pp. 190–94.

———, *The Political Thought of King Alfred the Great* (Cambridge: CUP, 2007).

Puhvel, Martin, *Beowulf and Celtic Tradition* (Waterloo, ON: Wilfrid Laurier UP, 1979).

———, 'The Aquatic Contest in *Hálfdanar saga Brönufóstra* and Beowulf's Adventure with Breca: Any Connection?', *NM* 99 (1998), 131–38.

Rapp, Claudia, 'Old Testament Models for Emperors in Byzantium', in *The Old Testament in Byzantium*, ed. Paul Magdalino and Robert S. Nelson (Harvard, 2010), pp. 175–98.

Rauer, Christine, *Beowulf and the Dragon: Parallels and Analogues* (Cambridge: D. S. Brewer, 2000).

Raw, Barbara C, 'The Probable Derivation of Most of the Illustrations in Junius 11 from an Illustrated Saxon *Genesis*', *ASE* 5 (1976), 133–48.

Remein, Daniel C., and Erica Weaver, eds, *Dating Beowulf: Studies in Intimacy* (Manchester: MUP, 2019).

Renoir, Alain, 'Point of View and Design for Terror in *Beowulf*', *NM* 63 (1962), 154–67.

Reynolds, Robert L., 'An Echo of *Beowulf* in Athelstan's Charters of 931–933 A.D.?', *MÆ* 24 (1955), 101–03.

Richards, Mary P., 'A Re-examination of *Beowulf* ll. 3180–3182', *ELN* 10 (1973), 163–67.

Riedinger, Anita, 'The Formulaic Relationship between *Beowulf* and *Andreas*', in *Heroic Poetry in the Anglo-Saxon Period: Studies in Honor of Jess B. Bessinger*, Studies in Medieval Culture 32, ed. Helen Damico and John Leyerle (Kalamazoo, MI: Medieval Institute Publications, 1993), pp. 283–312.

Risden, E. L., 'Heroic Humor in *Beowulf*', in *Humour in Anglo-Saxon Literature*, ed. Jonathan Wilcox (Cambridge: D. S. Brewer, 2000), pp. 71–78.

Robertson, Jr., D. W., *A Preface to Chaucer: Studies in Medieval Perspectives* (Princeton: Princeton UP, 1962).

Robinson, Fred C., 'The Significance of Names in Old English Literature', *Anglia* 86 (1968), 14–85.

———, 'Teaching the Backgrounds: History, Religion, Culture', in *Approaches to Teaching* Beowulf, ed. Jess B. Bessinger and Robert F. Yeager (New York: Modern Languages Association, 1984), pp. 107–22.

———, *Beowulf and the Appositive Style* (Knoxville: University of Tennessee Press, 1985).

———, '*Beowulf*', in *The Cambridge Companion to Old English Literature*, 1st edn, ed. Malcolm Godden and Michael Lapidge (1991), pp. 142–59.

———, 'Why is Grendel's Not Greeting the *Gifstol* a *Wræc Micel?*', in *Words, Texts and Manuscripts: Studies in Anglo-Saxon Culture Presented to Helmut Gneuss on the Occasion of His Sixty-Fifth Birthday*, ed. Michael Korhammer (Cambridge: D. S. Brewer, 1992), pp. 257–62.

Rogers, H. L., 'Beowulf's Three Great Fights', *RES* 6 (1955), 339–55; repr. in Nicholson, ed. (1963), pp. 233–56.

Rudolf, Winfried, 'The Gold in *Beowulf* and the Currencies of Fame', in *Gold in der Heldensage*, Reallexikon der germanischen Altertumskunde, Ergänzungsband, ed. Wilhelm Heizmann, Victor Millet and Heike Sahm (Berlin: De Gruyter, 2018), pp. 115–41.

Russell, Jeffrey Burton, *Lucifer: The Devil in the Middle Ages* (Ithaca and London: Cornell UP, 1984).

Russom, Geoffrey, 'Historicity and Anachronism in *Beowulf*', in *Epic and History*, ed. David Konstan and Kurt A. Raaflaub (Chichester: Wiley-Blackwell, 2010), pp. 243–61.

Sahlins, Marshall, 'The Stranger-King: Or Dumézil among the Fijians', *Journal of Pacific History* 16 (1981), 107–32.

Salvador Bello, Mercedes, 'The Arrival of the Hero in a Ship: A Common Leitmotif in Old English Regnal Tables and the Story of Scyld Scefing in *Beowulf*', *SELIM* 8 (1998), 205–21.

Sánchez-Martí, Jordi, 'Age Matters in Old English Literature', in *Youth and Age in the Medieval North*, ed. Shannon Lewis-Simpson (Leiden: Brill, 2008), pp. 205–26.

Sawyer, Peter H., and Ian N. Wood, eds, *Early Medieval Kingship* (Leeds: University of Leeds, School of History, 1977).

Schaar, Claes, 'On a New Theory of Old-English Poetic Diction', *Neophilologus* 40 (1956), 301–05.

Schaefer, Ursula, 'Rhetoric and Style', in Bjork and Niles, eds (1997), pp. 105–24.

Scheil, Andrew, '*Beowulf* and the Emergent Occasion', *Literary Imagination* 11 (2008), 83–98.

———, 'The Historiographic Dimensions of *Beowulf*', *JEGP* 107 (2008), 281–302.

Schmidt, Gary D., 'Unity and Contrasting Kingships in Beowulf', *Concerning Poetry* 17 (1984), 1–11.

Schrader, Richard J., 'Succession and Glory in *Beowulf*', *JEGP* 90 (1991), 491–504.

Schrøder, Ludvig Peter, *Om Bjovulfs-drapen: Efter en række foredrag på folke-höjskolen i Askov* (Copenhagen: Schønberg, 1875).

Schücking, Levin L., *Beowulfs Rückkehr: Eine kritische Studie*, Studien zur englischen Philologie 21 (Halle: M. Niemeyer, 1905).

———, 'Das Köningsideal im *Beowulf*', *Bulletin of the Modern Humanities Research Association* 3 (1929), 143–54; trans. as 'The Ideal of Kingship in

Beowulf', in Nicholson, ed. (1963), pp. 35–49.

——, 'Heldenstolz und Würde im Angelsächsischen, mit einem Anhang: Zur Charakterisierungstechnik im Beowulfepos', *Abhandlungen der Philologisch-historischen Klasse der sächsischen Akademie der Wissenschaften*, 42.5 (Leipzig: Hirzel, 1933).

Schwetman, J. W., 'Beowulf's Return: the Hero's Account of His Adventures among the Danes', *Medieval Perspectives* 13 (1998), 136–48.

Sears, Elizabeth, *The Ages of Man: Medieval Interpretations of the Life-cycle* (Princeton, NJ: Princeton UP, 1986).

Sebo, Erin, 'Foreshadowing the End in *Beowulf*', *ES* 99 (2018), 836–47.

Semper, Phillipa, '*Byð se ealda man ceald and snoflig*: Stereotypes and Subversions of the Last Stages of the Life Cycle in Old English Texts and Anglo-Saxon Contexts', in Cochelin, ed. (2013), pp. 287–318.

Shaull, Erin M., 'Ecgþeow, Brother of Ongenþeow, and the Problem of Beowulf's Swedishness', *Neophilologus* 101 (2017), 263–75.

Shaw, Philip A. *Beowulf and the Germanic World: Studies in Heroic Narrative Tradition* (London: Bloomsbury, forthcoming).

Shippey, T. A., and Andreas Haarder, eds, Beowulf: *The Critical Heritage* (Abingdon: Routledge, 1998).

Shippey, T. A., 'The Fairy-Tale Structure of *Beowulf*', *NQ* 214 (1969), 2–11.

——, *Old English Verse* (London: Hutchinson University Library, 1972).

——, 'Structure and Unity', in Bjork and Niles, eds (1997), pp. 149–74.

——, 'The Merov(ich)ingian again: *damnatio memoriae* and the *usus scholarum*', in *Latin Learning and English Lore: Studies in Anglo-Saxon Literature for Michael Lapidge*, 2 vols, ed. Katherine O'Brien O'Keeffe and Andy Orchard (Toronto: UTP, 2005), I, pp. 389–406.

——, 'Kemble, *Beowulf*, and the Schleswig-Holstein Question', in *The Kemble Lectures on Anglo-Saxon Studies, 2005–08*, ed. Alice Jorgensen, Helen Conrad O'Briain and John Scattergood (Dublin: Trinity College Dublin, 2009), pp. 64–80.

——, '"The Fall of King Hæðcyn": Or *Mimesis* 4a, the Chapter Auerbach Never Wrote', in *On the Aesthetics of* Beowulf *and Other Old English Poems*, ed. John M. Hill (Toronto: UTP, 2010), pp. 247–66.

——, '*Hrólfs saga kraka* and the Legend of Lejre', in *Making History: essays on the Fornaldasögur*, ed. Martin Arnold and Alison Finlay (London: Viking Society for Northern Research, University College London, 2010), pp. 17–23.

——, 'Names in *Beowulf* and Anglo-Saxon England', in Neidorf, ed. (2014), pp. 58–78.

Simon, Walter M., 'Herbert Spencer and the "Social Organism"', *Journal of the History of Ideas* 21 (1960), 294–99.

Sisam, Kenneth, *Studies in the History of Old English Literature* (Oxford: Clarendon Press, 1953).

——, 'Anglo-Saxon Royal Genealogies', *PBA* 39 (1953), 287–346.

——, 'Beowulf's Fight with the Dragon', *RES* 9 (1958), 129–40.
——, *The Structure of* Beowulf (Oxford: Clarendon Press, 1965).
Skeat, Walter William, 'On the Signification of the Monster Grendel in the Poem of Beowulf; with a Discussion of lines 2076–2100', *The Journal of Philology* 15 (1886), 120–31.
Sklute, John L., '*Freoðuwebbe* in Old English Poetry', in Damico and Olsen, eds (1990), pp. 204–10.
Smithers, G. V., *The Making of* Beowulf: *Inaugural Lecture of the Professor of English Language Delivered in the Appleby Theatre on 18 May 1961* (Durham: University of Durham, 1961).
Soper, Harriet, '*Eald æfensceop*: Poetic Composition and the Authority of the Aged in Old English Verse', *Quaestio Insularis: Selected Proceedings of the Cambridge Colloquium in Anglo-Saxon, Norse and Celtic* 17 (2016), 74–100.
——, '*A Count of Days*: The Life Course in Old English Poetry' (Unpubl. doctoral dissertation, University of Cambridge, 2018).
Sorrell, Paul, 'The approach to the dragon-fight in *Beowulf*, Aldhelm, and the "traditions folkloriques" of Jacques Le Goff', *Parergon* 12 (1994), 57–87.
Stafford, Pauline, *Queens, Concubines and Dowagers: The King's Wife in the Early Middle Ages* (Athens, GA: University of Georgia Press, 1983; repr. Leicester: Leicester UP, 1998).
——, 'Political Women in Mercia: Eighth to Early Tenth Centuries', in *Mercia: an Anglo-Saxon Kingdom in Europe*, ed. Michelle P. Brown and Carol A. Farr (Leicester: Continuum, 2001), pp. 35–49.
Stancliffe, Clare E., 'Oswald, "Most Holy and Most Victorious King of the Northumbrians"', in *Oswald: Northumbrian King to European Saint*, ed. Clare E. Stancliffe and Eric Cambridge (Stamford: Paul Watkins Publishing, 2005), pp. 33–83.
Stanley, Eric G., 'Hæthenra Hyht in *Beowulf*', in *Studies in Old English Literature in Honor of Arthur Gilchrist Brodeur*, ed. Stanley B. Greenfield (Eugene, OR: Russell & Russell, 1963), pp. 136–51.
——, *The Search for Anglo-Saxon Paganism* (Cambridge: Rowman and Littlefield, 1975).
——, 'The Narrative Art of *Beowulf*', in *Medieval Narrative: A Symposium*, ed. Hans Bekker-Nielsen, Peter Foote, Andreas Haarder and Preben Meulengracht Sørensen (Odense: Odense UP, 1979), pp. 58–81; repr. in his *A Collection of Papers with Emphasis on Old English Literature*, Publications of the Dictionary of Old English 3 (Toronto: UTP, 1987), pp. 170–91.
——, 'The Date of *Beowulf*: Some Doubts and No Conclusions', in Chase, ed. (1981), pp. 197–211.
——, 'Ἀπὸ Κοινοῦ, Chiefly in *Beowulf*', in *Anglo-Saxonica: Beiträge zur Vor- und Frühgeschichte der englischen Sprache und zur altenglischen*

Literatur: Festschrift für Hans Schabram zum 65. Geburtsdag, ed. Klaus R. Grinda and Claus-Dieter Wetzel (Munich: Wilhelm Fink Verlag, 1993), pp. 181–207.

———, *In the Foreground:* Beowulf (Cambridge: D. S. Brewer, 1994).

———, '*Beowulf*: Lordlessness in Ancient Times is the Theme, as Much as the Glory of Kings, if not More', *NQ* 52 (2005), 267–81.

———, 'Beowulf's *Wundordeað*', *NQ* 63 (2016), 343–45.

———, 'Old English Poetic Superlatives', *Anglia* 135 (2017), 241–73.

———, 'Wonder-Smiths and Others: *smið* Compounds in Old English Poetry—With an Excursus on *hleahtor*', *Neophilologus* 101 (2017), 277–304.

Stenton, Frank Merry, *Anglo-Saxon England* (Oxford: OUP, 1943; 3rd edn 1971).

———, 'The South-Western Element in the Old English Chronicle', in *Preparatory to Anglo-Saxon England: Being the Collected Papers of Frank Merry Stenton*, ed. Doris Mary Stenton (Oxford: OUP, 1970), pp. 106–15.

Stevick, Robert D., 'Representing the Form of *Beowulf*', in *Old English and New: Studies in Language and Linguistics in Honor of Frederic G. Cassidy*, ed. Joan H. Hall, Nick Doane and Dick Ringler (New York: Garland, 1992), pp. 3–14.

Stitt, Michael J., Beowulf *and the Bear's Son: Epic, Saga, and Fairytale in Northern Germanic Tradition* (New York: Garland, 1992).

Story, Joanna, *Carolingian Connections: Anglo-Saxon England and Carolingian Francia, c. 750–870* (Aldershot: Ashgate, 2003).

Summerfield, Thea, 'Filling the Gap: Brutus in the *Historia Brittonum, Anglo-Saxon Chronicle* MS F, and Geoffrey of Monmouth', *The Medieval Chronicle* 7 (2011), 85–102.

Swanton, Michael J., *Crisis and Development in Germanic Society 700–800:* Beowulf *and the Burden of Kingship* (Göppingen: Kümmerle, 1982).

Sweet, Henry, *Anglo-Saxon Reader in Prose and Verse* (Oxford: Clarendon Press, 1884).

Symons, David, *The Staffordshire Hoard* (Birmingham: Birmingham Museums Trust, 2014).

Tennenhouse, Leonard, '*Beowulf* and the Sense of History', *Bucknell Review* 19 (1971), 137–46.

Thacker, Alan, 'Bede, the Britons and the Book of Samuel', in *Early Medieval Studies in Memory of Patrick Wormald*, ed. Stephen Baxter, Catherine E. Karkov, Janet L. Nelson and David Pelteret (Farnham: Routledge, 2009), pp. 129–48.

———, 'Bede's Idea of the English', *Bulletin of the John Rylands Library* 92 (2016), 1–26.

Thieme, Adelheid L. J., 'The Gift in *Beowulf*: Forging the Continuity of Past and Present', *Michigan Germanic Studies* 22 (1996), 126–43.

Thomas, Daniel, 'Revolt in Heaven: Lucifer's Treason in *Genesis B*', in

Treason: Medieval and Early Modern Adultery, Betrayal, and Shame, ed. Larissa Tracy (Leiden: Brill, 2019), pp. 147–69.

Thomson, Simon C., *Communal Creativity in the Making of the* Beowulf *Manuscript: Towards a Reception History of the Nowell Codex*, Library of the Written Word 67 (Leiden: Brill, 2018).

Thornbury, Emily V., *Becoming a Poet in Anglo-Saxon England*, Cambridge Studies in Medieval Literature 88 (Cambridge: CUP, 2014).

Thornton, David E, 'Orality, literacy and genealogy in early medieval Ireland and Wales', in *Literacy in Medieval Celtic Societies*, ed. Huw Pryce (Cambridge: CUP, 1998), pp. 83–98.

Tolkien, J. R. R., '*Beowulf*: The Monsters and the Critics', *PBA* 22 (1936), 245–95; repr. in Nicholson, ed. (1963), pp. 51–103.

——, *Finn and Hengest: The Fragment and the Episode*, ed. Alan J. Bliss (New York: Houghton Mifflin Co., 1983).

Tolley, Clive, '*Beowulf*'s Scyld Scefing Episode: some Norse and Finnish Analogues', *ARV* 52 (1996), 7–48.

Tonsfeldt, H. W., 'Ring Structure in *Beowulf*', *Neophilologus* 61 (1977), 443–52.

Toswell, Jane, *The Anglo-Saxon Psalter* (Turnhout: Brepols, 2014).

——, 'Psalm Genres in Old English Poetry', in *The Psalms and Medieval English Literature: From the Conversion to the Reformation*, ed. Tamara Atkin and Francis Leneghan (Cambridge: D. S. Brewer, 2017), pp. 218–32.

Tripp, Jr., Raymond P., 'Fathers and Sons: Dynastic Decay in *Beowulf*', *In Geardagum* 16 (1995), 46–60.

——, 'Humor, Wordplay, and Semantic Resonance in *Beowulf*', in *Humour in Anglo-Saxon Literature*, ed. Jonathan Wilcox (Cambridge: D. S. Brewer, 2000), pp. 49–70.

Tugene, Georges, 'L'histoire "ecclesiastique" du peuple anglais: réflexions sur le particularisme et l'universalisme chez Bede', *Recherches augustiniennes* 17 (1982), 129–72.

Tyler, Elizabeth, *Old English Poetics: The Aesthetics of the Familiar in Anglo-Saxon England* (Cambridge: D. S. Brewer, 2006).

——, 'Trojans in Anglo-Saxon England: Precedent without Descent', *RES* 64 (2013), 1–20.

Ullmann, Walter, *The Carolingian Renaissance and the Idea of Kingship: The Birkbeck Lectures, 1968–9* (London: Methuen, 1969).

Van Dam, Raymond, 'Merovingian Gaul and the Frankish Conquests', in Fouracre, ed. (2005), pp. 193–231.

Van Meurs, J. C., '*Beowulf* and Literary Criticism', *Neophilologus* 39 (1955), 114–30.

Verner, Lisa, *The Epistemology of the Monstrous in the Middle Ages* (New York: Routledge, 2005).

Viljoen, Leonie, 'The *Beowulf* manuscript reconsidered: Reading *Beowulf* in

late Anglo-Saxon England', *Literator* 24 (2003), 39–57.
Von Sydow, Carl Wilhelm, 'Scyld Scefing', *Namn och Bygd* 12 (1924), 63–95.
Wallace-Hadrill, J. M., *The Long-Haired Kings* (Toronto: Methuen, 1962; repr. 1989).
——, *Early Germanic Kingship in England and on the Continent: The Ford Lectures Delivered in the University of Oxford in Hilary Term 1970* (Oxford: Clarendon Press, 1971).
Wardale, Edith E., '*Beowulf*: The Nationality of Ecgtheow', *MLR* 24 (1929), 322.
Wehlau, Ruth, *The Riddle of Creation: Metaphor Structures in Old English Poetry* (New York: Peter Lang, 1997).
Weiskott, Eric, 'The Meter of *Widsith* and the Distant Past', *Neophilologus* 99 (2015), 143–50.
West, Martin L., *The Making of the* Iliad: *Disquisition and Analytical Commentary* (Oxford: OUP, 2011).
Whitbread, L. G., '*Beowulf* and Archaeology: Two Further Footnotes', *NM* 69 (1968), 63–72.
——, 'The *Liber Monstrorum* and *Beowulf*', *Mediaeval Studies* 36 (1974), 434–71.
Whitelam, Keith W., 'Kings and Kingship', in *The Anchor Bible Dictionary*, 6 vols, IV, ed. David Noel Freedman *et al.* (New York: Doubleday, 1992), pp. 40–48.
Whitelock, Dorothy, '*Beowulf* 2444–2471', *MÆ* 8 (1939), 198–204.
——, *The Audience of* Beowulf (Oxford: Clarendon Press, 1951).
Wieland, Gernot R., '*Manna mildost*: Moses and Beowulf', *Pacific Coast Philology* 23 (1988), 86–93.
——, 'The Unferth Engima: The *þyle* between the Hero and the Poet', in *Fact and Fiction: From the Middle Ages to Modern Times, Essays Presented to Hans Sauer on the Occasion of his 65th Birthday*, Part II, Münchner Universitätsschriften, vol. 37, ed. Renate Bauer and Ulrike Krischke (Frankfurt: Peter Lang, 2011), pp. 35–46.
Williams, David, *Cain and* Beowulf: *a Study in Secular Allegory* (Toronto: UTP, 1982).
Wilson, R. M., *The Lost Literature of Medieval England* (London: Methuen, 1970).
Wood, Ian N., 'Kings, Kingdoms and Consent', in Sawyer and Wood, eds (1977), pp. 6–29.
——, 'Monasteries and the Geography of Power in the Age of Bede', *Northern History* 45 (2008), 11–25.
Wormald, Patrick, 'Bede, *Beowulf* and the Conversion of the Anglo-Saxon Aristocracy', in *Bede and Anglo-Saxon England: papers in honour of the 1300th anniversary of the birth of Bede, given at Cornell University in 1973 and 1974*, BAR 46, ed. Robert T. Farrell (Oxford: BAR, 1978), pp. 32–95; repr. Wormald (2006), pp. 30–105.

———, 'Bede, Bretwaldas and the Origins of the *Gens Anglorum*', in *Ideal and Reality in Frankish and Anglo-Saxon Society: Studies Presented to J. M. Wallace-Hadrill*, ed. Patrick Wormald (Oxford: Blackwell, 1983), pp. 99–129; repr. in Wormald (2006), pp. 106–34.

———, 'Kings and Kingship', in Fouracre, ed. (2005), pp. 571–604.

———, '*Beowulf*: the Redating Reassessed', first published as an appendix to 'Bede, *Beowulf* and the Conversion of the Anglo-Saxon Aristocracy', in Wormald (2006), pp. 71–105.

———, *The Times of Bede: Studies in Early English Christian Society*, ed. Stephen Baxter (Malden: Blackwell, 2006).

Wright, Cyril Ernest, *The Cultivation of Saga in Anglo-Saxon England* (Edinburgh: Oliver and Boyd, 1939).

Wright, Louise E., '*Merewioingas* and the Dating of *Beowulf*: A Reconsideration', *Nottingham Mediaeval Studies* 24 (1980), 1–6.

Yorke, Barbara, *Kings and Kingdoms of Early Anglo-Saxon England* (London: Taylor and Francis, 1990).

———, 'King Alfred and Weland: Transformation at the Court of King Alfred', in *Transformation in Anglo-Saxon Culture: Toller Lectures on Art, Archaeology and Text*, ed. Charles Insley and Gale Owen-Crocker (Oxford: Oxbow, 2017), pp. 47–70.

Index

Achilles 1, 111, 151
Adils/Aðils 116 n.29, 117, 252–55
  See also Eadgils
Advent Lyrics
  See under Christ I
Ælfric 24, 26 n.122, 147 n.133, 174 n.62, 228
Æthelbald 24 n.114, 176 n.73, 239, 240
Æthelfrith 224, 229–31, 235, 237–38
Æthelred
  possible copying of *Beowulf* during reign of 31, 235, 237, 244–45
Æthelweard
  Chronicon 144–45, 245
Æthelwulf
  genealogy of 143–45, 202 n.37
Alexander's Letter to Aristotle 6, 8, 25 n.120, 35 n.14, 237, 243–44
Alfred 24, 25 n.118, 31, 37, 140 n.101, 144 n.119, 146 n.126, 219
  Old English *Boethius* 24, 45, 241
  Old English *Orosius* 24 n.114, 241
  Old English *Pastoral Care* 52 n.81, 219–20 n.102
  Old English *Prose Psalms* 26 n.122, 220, 241
  transmission of *Beowulf* during reign of 31, 235, 237, 240–44
Áli 116 n.29
  See also Onela
Andreas 6, 10, 26 n.122, 42 n.47, 45–46 n.63, 51–52 n.81, 186 n.112, 229 n.127, 241–44
Anglo-Saxon Chronicle 24, 25 n.117, 42 n.48, 143–47, 157, 174 n.62, 203 n.42
Anlezark, Daniel 30, 33 n.6, 37 n.26, 44 n.59, 143 n.119, 172 n.57, 195–96, 220 n.104, 241 n.22
Atherton, Mark 218
Auerbach, Erich 196
Augustine of Hippo 37, 44 n.59, 199 n.25, 211, 223 n.107, 224
  on monsters 155

Baker, Peter 68, 85 n.184
Baldr 88 n.195, 109, 183 n.99

  See also Herebeald
Bammesberger, Alfred 47 n.68, 52 n.81, 163–64 n.35, 228
Baptismal Creed 233–34
Basileus 17, 198–201, 204–08, 227–31
Bathsheba 215–16
Bear's Son Tale 105, 113–18, 151
  See also Two Trolls Folktale
Bede 23, 31, 35, 45, 110, 147 n.131, 174 n.62, 198, 208
Ecclesiastical History
  influence of Old Testament kingship on 223–31, 235, 236
  on Mercian and Northumbrian dynasties 214 n.84, 237–40, 241
Benson, Larry D. 11–12 n.44, 110, 116, 119–20, 182 n.95
Beow 3, 8, 18 n.84, 25, 39–47, 54 n.88, 62 n.106, 80 n.168, 87 n.192, 90, 98, 100, 102, 103, 105, 119, 121 n.47, 139–52, 185, 203, 213 n.83, 216, 232, 234, 236, 240
Beowulf
  Beowulf's Return 32, 34 n.9, 80, 83–86, 91, 120, 129–30, 236
  Christianity of x, 9–11, 15 n.70, 20, 26, 30–31, 36–37, 108 n.8, 118, 149, 159–73, 180, 181–82, 195–98, 210–35, 236, 243
  critical reception of viii–x, 9–11
  date of x, 6, 20, 118 n.35, 204 n.48, 236–46
  digressions in 5, 9–12, 18, 31, 46 n.66, 128, 177 n.75
  See also Finnsburg Episode, Offa Digression, Swedish Wars
  ending of 3, 16, 37, 74, 75 n.155, 137–38, 209 n.69, 220 n.102, 227–31, 235, 242–43
  fictional elements in 14–15 n.66, 18 n.84, 57, 82, 86 n.188, 105, 106–11, 118–52
  Finnsburg Episode 11, 28, 44 n.56, 68–72, 78, 140 n.103
gif-stōl crux 10, 155, 162–76

293

manuscript of viii, 6–9, 16, 25 n.120, 31, 32 n.4, 35 n.14, 39 n.34, 130 n.74, 145, 153, 156, 358 n.22, 244–46
Offa Digression 28, 78–82, 99 n.226, 122 n.51, 140 n.101, 180, 232 n.142, 236, 239
provenance of x, 6, 80, 140 n.101, 237–40
Scyld Prologue 3 n.7, 27, 28, 38 n.32, 39–46, 71, 77, 80, 90, 91, 102, 105, 109, 129 n.72, 139–52, 236
Swedish wars 33 n.5, 49, 78, 83, 93–103, 155, 180–94, 236

Beowulf
assistance of Eadgils against Onela 97–8, 105, 116 n.29, 183–84, 188
as *basileus* 17, 204, 227–31
childlessness of 26 n.122, 38, 41, 81–82, 100–02, 119, 178
and Christ 231–35
commitment to dynastic principle 19, 91
and David 134, n.90, 196–231, 235, 240
death of 3, 4, 18, 21, 24, 27, 28, 30, 33, 38, 61, 83, 90–93, 102, 105, 108, 109, 117, 120–39, 178, 184, 185 n.111, 192–93, 209 n.69, 236
eulogy of 3, 16–17, 75 n.155, 223 n.114, 227–31
father of
See under Ecgtheow
fictionality of 14–15 n.66, 56–57, 82, 104–39, 151–52, 180–83
fight with dragon 16, 18, 27, 29, 30, 32, 38, 40, 61, 82, 83, 117, 153–59, 164 n.37, 214–16, 222, 227
links to Sigemund legend 106–11, 151–52, 236
links to Swedish wars 96, 98, 180–94
as elaboration of legend of Hygelac's death 120–39, 236
fight with Grendel 30, 32, 55–63, 111–18, 135 n.92, 182 n.95, 196, 212, 227 n.122, 230
fight with Grendel's mother 29, 33–34, 38, 49–50 n.75, 68, 69, 111–18
mother of xx n.1, 15, 18, 20, 26, 48 n.71, 86, 88, 231

relationship to Hygelac 118–39, 151–52
King 14–18, 151–52, 223–35
unpromising youth of 81 n.174, 103, 120 n.44, 132–33
wisdom of 34, 217 n.94
Bible, and related apocrypha
Old Testament
Deuteronomy 147–48
Enoch 153 n.2, 167 n.48, 168–70 n.53, 192 n.58, 195
Exodus 30, 147, 165, 195
Ezekiel 167 n.48
Fall of the Angels 159, 167–73, 176, 196, 236
Genesis 29–30, 50–51, 161, 197, 200
Cain and Abel 26, 37, 50, 58, 97, 118, 143, 153 n.2, 159–62, 164 n.35, 165, 171–74, 179, 195, 236
Creation and Fall 50–51, 127 n.65, 160–61
Noah's Flood 30, 33 n.6, 37, 44 n.59, 46 n.64, 118, 143–45, 172, 195–96, 203, 220 n.104, 236, 241
Origin of giants 172–74, 195
Isaiah 167, 172 n.57, 232
Job 167 n.48
Jude 165, 167
Kings
connections with *Beowulf* 210–35
influence on medieval kingship 198–210
Numbers 240
Psalms 1 n.1, 38, 39 n.33, 45 n.63, 201 n.30, 218, 218 n.97, 219, 220, 222 n.106, 228 n.124, 240 n.14, 241
New Testament
Acts of Matthew and Andrew 242
Galatians 36, 233
John 232–33
Luke 25, 82, 231
Matthew 25, 202 n.37
Revelation 37 n.26, 158, 167
Judgement Day 30, 101, 157–59, 165, 167, 196, 199
Biggs, Frederick M. 20–21, 76 n.159, 86, 90 n.200, 92 n.209, 102, 103 n.236, 119 n.42, 121 n.47, 126, 133 n.87, 154–55, 237

Index

Bjarkamál   67, 114 n.26, 116 n.29, 141 n.109
   See also Saxo Grammaticus
Bödvar Bjarki   114–18, 130–31 n.76, 142, 154, 249, 252–55
Bonjour, Adrien   3, 10, 27 n.127, 40, 44, 177 n.77, 185 n.108, 190, 198 n.20
Breca   58, 120, 144 n.119, 152
Brodeur, Arthur   10, 48, 121 n.48, 127 n.66, 164 n.36
Brosinga mene   128–29
Burrow, John   34, 55 n.90
Byzantium
   emergence of Christian dynasties in   200–01, 204

Cabannis, Allan   15 n.70, 232
Cædmon's Hymn   50–51, 161 n.24, 230 n.131
Cain and Abel
   See under Bible and related apocrypha, Genesis
Carolingians   92, 204, 206, 209, 241
   Development of sacral kingship among   207–08
Cerdic and Cynric   147, 203
Chambers, R. W.   80 n.168, 118 n.35, 127, 143 n.115
Chance, Jane   49 n.75, 74, 178
Chaney, William   126 n.61, 165
Chlochilaicus   121–22, 204
   See also Hygelac
Christ I (Advent Lyrics)   45 n.62, 46 n.63, 171 n.56
Christ II (Ascension)   165
Christ III (Christ in Judgement)   234
Christ in Judgement
   See under Christ III
Christ, Jesus
   connections with Beow   232–33
   connections with Beowulf   231–35
Chronicle of Abingdon   146
Chrysostom, John   199, 214–15, 231
Clark, David   78, 90 n.200
Clark, George   2, 88 n.196
Clemoes, Peter   237
Clovis   203–05
   See also Merovingians
Clunies Ross, Margaret   74 n.153, 174
Cox, Betty S.   138 n.98, 165, 171
Cronan, Dennis   145–46, 240–41
Cnut, King

   possible copying of *Beowulf* during reign of   244–46
Cunningham, Valentine   viii
Cynewulf   110
   use of by *Andreas*-poet   242
   possible knowledge of *Beowulf*   6–7
   Elene   10, 51 n.81, 229 n.127, 233 n.144
   See also Christ II

Dæghrefn   113, 135–36
Damico, Helen   x n.11, 28 n.130, 32 n.4, 140 n.101, 244 n.34
Dan (I and II)   109, 141–42, 247–48
David   24, 37 n.26, 196–223, 230, 241
Dockray-Miller, Mary   78
Deor   11, 69 n.135, 128 n.70, 202 n.41
Devil
   see under Lucifer
de Vries, Jan   32
Donahue, Charles   46 n.64, 196
Dragon
   biblical models for   157–58
   connections with accounts of Swedish Wars   180–94
   death of   192–93
   hagiographical models for   181–82, 185–86
   as portent   155–59, 185, 186, 192, 236
   as ruler   185–86
   See also Sigemund, St Samson, St Michael
Drout, Michael D. C.   21
Durham *Liber Vitae*   21 n.97, 107–09, 119, 122
Dynastic principle
   Beowulf-poet's preoccupation with   14, 18–28
   biblical background to   197–98, 216
   emergence of in medieval West   198–210
   lack of evidence for among early Germanic peoples   22–24

Eadgils   18 n.84, 92, 95, 97–98, 102, 105, 122 n.51, 183–84, 188, 249, 252
   See also Adils/Aðils, Eanmund
Eanmund   18 n.84, 92, 95, 96, 99, 102, 105, 122 n.51, 183–84, 188, 190, 191
   See also Eadgils
Earl, James W.   184
Ecgfrith of Mercia   209 n.70

295

Ecgfrith of Northumbria 174 n.62, 225–27, 238–39
Ecgtheow 15, 18 n.84, 28, 35, 40, 56, 63, 87, 92, 99, 103 n. 235, 118, 187 n.114, 191
Edwin 224, 238
Eofor 94, 96–97 n.217, 98, 131
　See also Wulf
Eomer 79–80, 232 n.142
Exodus 10, 51, 110, 229 n.124

Felix of Crowland
　Vita Guthlaci 24
Finn 65, 68–72, 143, 144 n.119
　See also Beowulf, Finnsburg Episode
Finnsburg Fragment 4, 11, 68–69
Fitela 61 n.105, 107–08
　See also Sigemund, Sigurd, Völsunga saga
Foot, Sarah 224–25, 230
Freawaru 40 n.37, 53, 80–81, 99 n.226, 104, 130, 180
Fremu
　See under Offa, Bride of
Froda (Frötho) 40, 53, 81, 122 n.51, 142, 180, 181 n.89, 251
Fulk, R. D. 3 n.6, 6 n.18, 228, 237 n.1

Genesis A 2 n.3, 25 n.120, 26 n.122, 50 n.76, 51 n.81, 59 n.98, 110, 138–39 n.99, 167, 168
Genesis B 26 n.122, 52 n.81, 170–71
Georgianna, Linda 185
Godden, Malcolm 160–61
Goldsmith, Margaret 16, 127 n.66, 181 n.91, 195 n.2, 218 n.97
Grendel 18–19, 30, 32, 38, 55–60, 127 n.65, 130
　genealogy of 58, 153 n.2, 156, 159–62
　as portent 53, 82, 153–62
　as Satanic usurper 29, 162–73, 176, 185, 193, 236
　　See also Bible, Old Testament, Fall of the Angels
　and Two Trolls tale 111–18
Grendel's Mother
　as antitype of royal women 29, 49–50 n.75, 72 n.145, 155, 177–80, 193, 236
　genealogy of 156, 173, 174–76, 179
　as grieving mother 68

　as portent 154 n.8, 156
　structural role of 33–34, 177–80
　and Two Trolls tale 111–18
Gregory the Great 165, 200, 219 n.100, 228
　Earliest Life of 228 n.123
　Morals on the Book of Job 165, 200
　Pastoral Care 219–20, 230, 241
Gregory of Tours
　History of the Franks 35, 121–22, 198, 203–05
Grettir
　See under Grettis saga
Grettis saga 111–13, 120 n.46, 154, 182 n.95
Gwara, Scott 16, 131 n.82, 153 n.2, 162 n.32, 227 n.121

Hæthcyn 19 n.88, 63, 87, 88, 90, 91, 93–94, 97–98, 104–05
Halga 18 n.85, 47–49, 52, 67, 87, 88, 104, 161
　See also Helgi (Helgo)
Halsall, Guy 22, 23 n.110, 205
Heaney, Seamus 1
Heardred 15, 19, 21, 48 n.71, 57, 86–87, 91–92, 95–97, 105, 122, 125, 133–34, 137, 166, 183–88, 191, 206, 238
Heathobards 27, 52 n.84, 53, 66, 80, 99 n.226, 104, 156, 190, 193
　See also Froda, Ingeld
Helgi (Helgo) 48–49, 53 n.86, 73, 116 n.29, 142, 248, 251
　See also Halga
Hengest 68–69, 140 n.103
Hengest and Horsa 147, 203
Heorogar 19, 21, 47–49, 52, 58 n.98, 65, 76 n.159, 84, 85, 87, 104, 128, 133, 161
Heoroweard 19 n.88, 21, 48–49, 63, 67, 84, 85 n.184, 104
　See also Hjörvard, Hiarwardus, Hiarvarthar
Herebeald 63, 87–91, 105, 122 n.51, 127, 161 n.29, 183
Heremod 16, 26, 29, 47, 61–63, 96 n.214, 104–09, 122 n.51, 141, 159 n.23
　and Scyld Scefing 46, 150–52, 236
　and Saul 211–12, 217–23, 241
　in West Saxon royal genealogy 42 n.48, 109, 140, 143, 203, 240
　See also Hermóðr, Lother

296

Hermóðr 109
  See also Heremod
Hiarvarthar
  See under Hjörvard
Hiarwardus
  See under Hjörvard
Hildebrandslied 11
Hildeburh 34 n.11, 68–72, 140 n.103, 149, 178
Hill, John M. 56 n.91, 76 n.159, 90 n.200
Hill, Thomas D. 63–64 n.112, 87–88, 232, 237 n.2
Hjörvard (Hiørvardus, Hiarvarthar, Hiarwardus) 65 n.114, 67, 116, 249, 252, 255
  See also Heoroweard
Hledra
  See under Lejre
Hleidargard
  See under Lejre
Hnæf 46 n.67, 68–71, 140 n.103, 144 n.119
Hollis, Stephanie 18, 21, 48
Homer 10 n.34, 110, 162 n.29
  See also Achilles
Howe, Nicholas 30, 36–37, 195
Hrethel 15, 18 n.84, 20, 56, 57, 63, 66 n.121, 87–88, 93, 101, 103 n.236, 105, 122 n.51, 127, 128, 133, 178, 185, 210 n.72
  death of 90, 105, 179 n.83, 183
Hrethlings
  See under Hrethel, Herebeald, Hæthcyn, Hygelac, Heardred, Beowulf
Hrethric 63, 67, 72, 73, 75–76, 84 n.179, 104, 142, 147 n.131
  See also Røricus
Hroar (Hróar)
  See under Roar
Hrolf (Hrólfr) 5, 36, 47–49, 53, 64–65 n.114, 114–18, 131 n.76, 142, 228–29 n.124, 251–55
  See also Hrothulf
Hrólfs saga kraka
  See under Hrolf
Hrothgar 15, 25 n.120, 34, 40 n.37, 47, 50–91, 100, 103 n.235, 104, 112, 121, 122 n.51, 127, 129 n.71, 140, 144 n.119, 147 n.131, 153 n.3, 156, 162, 177–78, 191, 196, 231

accession of 21, 48–49
attempted adoption of
  Beowulf 18–19, 27, 63–65, 72–78, 85, 128, 130–32, 217
power-struggle with
  Grendel 162–76
sermon of 150, 190, 193, 211–13, 217–20
and Solomon 213, 217–20, 241
  See also Roar
Hrothmund 63, 72–73, 84 n.179, 104, 122 n.51, 147 n.131, 162 n.29
Hrothulf 47–49, 52 n.83, 63, 104, 122 n.51, 132, 144 n.119
  'treachery' of 64–67, 72–73, 75 n.8, 88, 91
  See also Hrolf
Hugleikr 124–25
  See also Chlochilaichus, Hygelac
Hume, Kathryn 13
Hygd 79 n.166, 84 n.182, 105, 132
  offer of Geatish throne to
    Beowulf 15, 19, 21, 27, 48 n.71, 91–92, 166, 179 n.84, 183
Hygelac 14–18, 48, 55 n.89, 63, 66 n.120, 83–86, 104–05, 117, 161 n.29
  accession of 19 n.88, 90–91, 105, 183
  daughter of xx n.1, 49 n.75, 130–31
  death of 13, 19, 28, 57 n.94, 83, 87, 90–92, 105, 118–39, 148 n.135, 151–52, 183, 185–91, 204–05, 208, 225, 227
  as legendary model for Beowulf 28, 118–39, 151–52, 184, 225, 236
  See also Chlochilaichus, Hugleikr
  See also Beowulf, Beowulf's Return

Ingeld 66, 122 n.51
  marriage to Freawaru 40 n.37, 53 n.86, 80–81, 99 n.226, 104, 129–30 n.72, 130
  See also Ingialldus
Ingialldus 53 n.86, 142, 248–49
  See also Ingeld
Isidore of Seville 156–57, 200

Jordanes 35, 202–03
Judith 8, 10, 90 n.199, 110 n.19, 229 n.127, 245
  See also Nowell Codex
Junius 11, MS 167–70
  See also Genesis A, Genesis B

297

Kaske, Robert E.   13, 163, 165, 190, 195
Ker, W. P.   5, 10, 32 n.3
Klaeber, Friedrich   5–6, 10, 15 n.70, 39 n.34, 40 n.39, 71 n.143, 92 n.209, 118, 161 n.24, 162 n.29, 163 n.34, 165, 175 n.68, 177, 182–83, 218, 231, 233 n.143
Klein, Stacy   21 n.96, 81, 178, 179 n.84
Kinney, Clare   38

Langfeðgatal   143–44
Lapidge, Michael   11, 80 n.168, 123 n.53, 145, 184
Lawrence, W. W.   1 n.2, 126
Legates, Papal
   visit to England in 786 of   174–75
Lejre (Hleidargard, Hledra)   49, 114, 142, 247, 252–53, 255
Leyerle, John   12 n.46, 13, 16, 185
Liber monstrorum   4, 122–23, 138
Lindisfarne, sack of   157
Lother   109, 141, 151
Louviot, Elise   15–16 n.71, 74–75, 88 n.196, 131
Lucifer
   and Grendel   159, 162–76
   and the dragon   158–59, 167

Magoun, Francis P., Jr.   14 n.64, 33–34 n.9, 129–30, 148 n.135
McGillivray, Murray   164, 165–66
McNamee, M. B.   231–32
Meaney, Audrey   40, 145
Meletinsky, Eleazar   29
Menologium   234
Mercia, Kingdom of   6, 22, 80, 133 n.88, 140 n.101, 174, 176 n.73, 209 n.70, 225 n.119, 237–40
Merovingians   121–22
   in *Beowulf*   8, 105, 137, 191
   attachment to dynastic principle   203–08, 209
Messenger, Geatish
   prophecy of   90, 92, 93–94, 97–98, 102, 136–37, 184, 187–88, 191–93, 204
Michael, St   158, 167, 181–82
Modthryth
   See under Offa, bride of
Morey, James H.   4 n.9, 21, 38, 212 n.78
Morgan, Gerald   88
Moses   240

and Beowulf   147 n.132, 196, 229 n.124
and Scyld Scefing   147–48
Murdoch, Brian   17

Nabuzardan   221–22
Nathan
   prophecy of   222–23
Neidorf, Leonard   x, 2 n.3, 9 n.28, 22 n.97, 70 n.139, 119 n.42, 131 n.77, 218 n.95, 244 n.33
Niles John D.   4 n.11, 13, 33 n.5, 50–51, 117–18, 154 n.4, 155 n.10, 171 n.57
Nist, John   13
Noah   30, 46 n.64, 143–45, 195, 203, 241
   See also Bible, *under* Old Testament, Genesis, Noah's Flood
North, Richard   2 n.5, 28, 34 n.9, 80 n.168, 81 n.173, 90 n.200, 92 n.209, 116–17, 131 n.76, 133 n.87, 183 n.98
Northumbria, Kingdom of   49, 107, 157, 174, 203 n.42, 209 n.70, 224–31, 237–40
   See also Æthelfrith, Ecgfrith, Oswald
Nowell Codex
   See under Beowulf, manuscript of
   See also Alexander's Letter to Aristotle, Wonders (Marvels) of the East, Judith, Passion of St Christopher

O'Brien, Conor   224
Odin (Oðin)   41 n.46, 88 n.197, 109, 141–43, 203 n.42, 247, 249, 254–55
   See also Woden
Offa of Angeln   79, 82, 99 n.226, 120 n.44, 122 n.51, 129 n.71, 144 n.119, 232 n.142
   bride of   xx n.1, 28, 72 n.45, 78–82, 180, 236
Offa of Mercia   80, 140 n.101, 174, 176 n.73, 209 n.70, 239
Ohthere   18 n.84, 93–97, 104–05, 116 n.29, 122 n.51, 178 n.82, 183, 187
Onela   18 n.84, 95–99, 104–05, 116 n.29, 122 n.51, 183–84, 188, 191
   bride of   47, 83, 104, 180
   role in Beowulf's accession   92, 95–98, 159 n.23, 166, 184
   See also Áli
Ongentheow   8–9, 18 n.84, 25 n.120, 90, 92, 93–98, 104–05, 122 n.51, 129, 131, 144 n.119, 183, 187

bride of 83, 94, 105, 178 n.82, 187
and dragon 187–88
Orchard, Andy 3 n.7, 6–7, 16, 25–26 n.120, 64 n.114, 65 n.117, 66 n.122, 71 n.143, 74 n.154, 75, 99 n.225, 107, 110 n.18, 111 n.22, 114 n.25, 116 n.30, 134 n.90, 140 n.103, 146, 153 n.1, 161, 220 n.102, 228 n.123, 229 n.127, 230, 231 n.138, 243
Orosius, *History Against the Pagans in Seven Books* 241
   Old English *Orosius*
   See under Alfred
Oswald 224 n.114, 230–31, 235, 238–39, 240 n.14
Oðin
   See under Odin
Owen-Crocker, Gale 34, 42 n.47, 70 n.137, 147, 149

Paul the Deacon
   History of the Langobards 35–36, 144 n.119, 147 n.131, 202
   History of the Bishops of Metz 207
Penda 225 n.119, 238–39

Rædwald 208, 238
Rærecus
   See under Røricus
Rauer, Christine 158 n.22, 181
Ravenswood, Battle of 90–91, 93–94, 97–8, 104–05, 187
Roas (Hroar, Hróar, Roar) 48–49, 53 n.86, 64–65 n.114, 67, 73, 117, 142, 183 n.101, 248–49, 251–52
   See also Hrothgar
Roar
   See under Roas
Robinson, Fred C. 2 n.4, 10–11, 27 n.126, 81, 137 n.95, 163 n.35, 173 n.60, 196, 230, 243
Rogers, H. L. 33–4
Rolf (Rolvo)
   See under Hrolf
Røricus (Rærecus) 67, 142, 249–50
   See also Hrethric

Samson 134 n.90, 196
Samson, St 181–82
Samuel 210–11, 214
Satan
   See under Lucifer

Saul 197, 198, 210–14, 216, 223, 224
and Æthelfrith 228–31
and Heremod 211–13, 219–20
Saxo Grammaticus (*Gesta Danorum*) 4–5, 53 n.86, 63 n.112, 67, 108 n.10, 109, 114 n.26, 116 n.29, 122 n.49, 141, 181 n.89, 183 n.98
   See also Bjarkamál
Scef (Sceaf) 42, 80 n.168, 110 n.18, 122 n.51, 140–46, 203
   See also Scyld Scefing
Sceldwa (Scyldwa) 42 n.47, 109, 119, 143
Schücking, Levin L. 13, 15 n. 70, 32, 130 n.72, 130 n.74
Scyld Scefing 1, 8, 22, 25–27, 28, 38–46, 47, 61, 64, 72, 78, 80, 83, 93, 96, 102, 103, 119–20, 126, 130 n.72, 139, 159, 203, 210, 223, 236, 239, 241, 244
   death and funeral of 3, 27, 34 n.11, 44–45, 49, 53, 71, 90, 98, 240
   fictionality of 104–06, 110 n.18, 139–52, 185
   as stranger king 42, 91, 216
   as warrior king 213–14, 235
   and Wulfhere 239
   See also Sceldwa, Scioldus, Skjold (Skjöldr)
Scyldings
   See under Heremod, Scyld Scefing, Beow, Healfdene, Heorogar, Hrothgar, Halga, Heoroweard, Hrethric, Hrothmund, Hrothulf
Scyldwa
   See under Sceldwa
Scylfings
   See under Ongentheow, Ohthere, Onela, Eanmund, Eadgils
Shaw, Philip A. 119 n.40
Sigemund 61, 63, 105, 106–08, 111, 129 n.71, 136, 152, 153 n.3, 159 n.23, 180–81, 236
   relationship with Sigurd 107–08, 117 n.32, 181, 201
Sigurd
   See under Sigemund, relationship with Sigurd
Sisam, Kenneth x n.12, 5 n.15, 32, 34, 40, 145–46 n.125, 177 n.75
Skjöld (Scioldus, Skyoldus, Skjöldr) 40, 41 n.46, 109, 141–42, 247

See also Scyld Scefing
Skjöldunga saga   4–5, 36, 41 n.46, 47 n.68, 49, 53 n.86, 67 n.125, 116 n.29, 141–42, 147 n.137, 247–50
Snorri Sturluson   5, 109, 116 n.29, 120 n.46
   Ynglinga saga   36, 49 n.74, 116 n.29, 124–25, 149 n.137
Solomon
   and Hrothgar   213, 217, 220–23, 241
   as model for medieval kings   197, 200, 204, 207–08, 224
   as type of Christ   199
   as legislator   201
   accession of   216
Solomon and Saturn I   157 n.20
Solomon and Saturn II   170 n.54, 220 n.104
Spencer, Herbert   35
Staffordshire Hoard   239–40
Stanley, Eric G.   9 n.30, 13, 92 n.208, 193, 218, 219–20 n.102, 228
Stenton, Frank M.   237 n.3, 238, 239
Survivor, Last   34 n.11, 240
Sutton Hoo   148, 208
Swanton, Michael   13, 16 n.73, 20, 237
Sweyn Forkbeard   245
Sven Aggesen
   Brief History of the Kings of Denmark   53 n.86, 142
Svipdag   124–25, 228–29 n.124, 252, 254

Tacitus   22–23
Theudebert
   killing of Chlochilaich (Hygelac)   121–22
   virtues of   204
   See also Merovingians
Thomson, Simon C.   8 n.26, 9 n.28, 9 n.29, 35 n.14, 110 n.19, 243–44, 245 n.35
Thryth
   See under Offa, bride of
Tolkien, J. R. R.   viii n.2, x n.12, 5, 10, 12, 33–35, 39 n.34, 70 n.139, 103, 118, 144 n.119, 154, 155 n.10, 163, 177 n.75, 243 n.29

Tripp, Raymond P., Jr.   ix, 21
Two Trolls Folktale   105, 111–18, 177–78, 182
   See also Bear's Son Tale

Unferth   57–58, 72 n.146, 112, 119, 122 n.51, 173 n.60

Van Dam, Raymond   204
Venantius Fortunatus   204
Virgil   111, 141 n.105, 161 n.24, 226
Völsunga saga   107–09, 181
   See also Sigemund, Sigurd, Fitela
Von Sydow, Carl Wilhelm   149

Waldere   11
Wealhtheow   19, 58–66, 72–78, 91, 128, 131–32, 179 n.84, 180, 216–17, 231
Weohstan   96–7, 99, 102, 184, 190–91
Widsith   4, 11, 52 n.83, 66, 69 n.135, 72 n.145, 120 n.44, 128 n.70, 144 n.119, 162 n.29, 202 n.41, 239
Wiglaf, King of Mercia   80 n.168
Wiglaf, Wægmunding   2 n.4, 3, 61 n.105, 66 n.121, 82, 85 n.184, 96, 98–102, 117 n.32, 122 n.51, 123, 137, 153 n.1, 164 n.37, 181 n.88, 184, 188 n.117, 190–91, 209 n.69, 214, 217 n.94, 227 n.121
Wihtred   225
Woden   22, 41 n.46, 141, 203, 208
   See also Odin, Oðin
Wonders (Marvels) of the East   8, 156, 245 n.35
   See also Nowell Codex
Wood, Ian   23, 201, 205
Wormald, Patrick   2 n.5, 21 n.97, 22, 23 n.104, 197
Wulf   97–98
   See also Eofor
Wulfgar   56, 122 n.51, 131–32
Wulfhere   239

Ynglinga saga
   See under Snorri Sturluson
Yorke, Barbara   208 n.66, 209, 210, 238 n.10

Volume 40: Old English Lexicology and Lexicography: Essays in Honor of Antonette diPaolo Healey, *edited by Maren Clegg Hyer, Haruko Momma and Samantha Zacher*

Volume 41: Debating with Demons: Pedagogy and Materiality in Early English Literature, *Christina M. Heckman*

Volume 42: Textual Identities in Early Medieval England: Essays in Honour of Katherine O'Brien O'Keeffe, *edited by Jacqueline Faye, Rebecca Stephenson and Renée R. Trilling*

Volume 43: Bishop Æthelwold, his Followers, and Saints' Cults in Early Medieval England: Power, Belief, and Religious Reform, *Alison Hudson*

Volume 44: Global Perspectives on Early Medieval England, *edited by Karen Louise Jolly and Britton Elliott Brooks*

ANGLO-SAXON STUDIES

Volume 1: The Dramatic Liturgy of Anglo-Saxon England,
M. Bradford Bedingfield

Volume 2: The Art of the Anglo-Saxon Goldsmith: Fine Metalwork in Anglo-Saxon England: its Practice and Practitioners, *Elizabeth Coatsworth and Michael Pinder*

Volume 3: The Ruler Portraits of Anglo-Saxon England, *Catherine E. Karkov*

Volume 4: Dying and Death in Later Anglo-Saxon England, *Victoria Thompson*

Volume 5: Landscapes of Monastic Foundation: The Establishment of Religious Houses in East Anglia, c. 650-1200, *Tim Pestell*

Volume 6: Pastoral Care in Late Anglo-Saxon England, *edited by Francesca Tinti*

Volume 7: Episcopal Culture in Late Anglo-Saxon England, *Mary Frances Giandrea*

Volume 8: Elves in Anglo-Saxon England: Matters of Belief, Health, Gender and Identity, *Alaric Hall*

Volume 9: Feasting the Dead: Food and Drink in Anglo-Saxon Burial Rituals, *Christina Lee*

Volume 10: Anglo-Saxon Button Brooches: Typology, Genealogy, Chronology, *Seiichi Suzuki*

Volume 11: Wasperton: A Roman, British and Anglo-Saxon Community in Central England, *edited by Martin Carver with Catherine Hills and Jonathan Scheschkewitz*

Volume 12: A Companion to Bede, *George Hardin Brown*

Volume 13: Trees in Anglo-Saxon England: Literature, Lore and Landscape, *Della Hooke*

Volume 14: The Homiletic Writings of Archbishop Wulfstan, *Joyce Tally Lionarons*

Volume 15: The Archaeology of the East Anglian Conversion, *Richard Hoggett*

Volume 16: The Old English Version of Bede's *Historia Ecclesiastica*, *Sharon M. Rowley*

Volume 17: Writing Power in Anglo-Saxon England: Texts, Hierarchies, Economies, *Catherine A. M. Clarke*

Volume 18: Cognitive Approaches to Old English Poetry, *Antonina Harbus*

Volume 19: Environment, Society and Landscape in Early Medieval England: Time and Topography, *Tom Williamson*

Volume 20: Honour, Exchange and Violence in *Beowulf*, *Peter S. Baker*

Volume 21: *John the Baptist's Prayer* or *The Descent into Hell* from the Exeter Book: Text, Translation and Critical Study, *M.R. Rambaran-Olm*

Volume 22: Food, Eating and Identity in Early Medieval England, *Allen J. Frantzen*

Volume 23: Capital and Corporal Punishment in Anglo-Saxon England, *edited by Jay Paul Gates and Nicole Marafioti*

Volume 24: The Dating of *Beowulf*: A Reassessment, *edited by Leonard Neidorf*

Volume 25: The Cruciform Brooch and Anglo-Saxon England, *Toby F. Martin*

Volume 26: Trees in the Religions of Early Medieval England, *Michael D. J. Bintley*

Volume 27: The Peterborough Version of the Anglo-Saxon Chronicle: Rewriting Post-Conquest History, *Malasree Home*

Volume 28: The Anglo-Saxon Chancery: The History, Language and Production of Anglo-Saxon Charters from Alfred to Edgar, *Ben Snook*

Volume 29: Representing Beasts in Early Medieval England and Scandinavia, *edited by Michael D.J. Bintley and Thomas J.T. Williams*

Volume 30: Direct Speech in *Beowulf* and Other Old English Narrative Poems, *Elise Louviot*

Volume 31: Old English Philology: Studies in Honour of R.D. Fulk, *edited by Leonard Neidorf, Rafael J. Pascual and Tom Shippey*

Volume 32: 'Charms', Liturgies, and Secret Rites in Early Medieval England, *Ciaran Arthur*

Volume 33: Old Age in Early Medieval England: A Cultural History, *Thijs Porck*

Volume 34: Priests and their Books in Late Anglo-Saxon England, *Gerald P. Dyson*

Volume 35: Burial, Landscape and Identity in Early Medieval Wessex, *Kate Mees*

Volume 36: The Sword in Early Medieval Northern Europe: Experience, Identity, Representation, *Sue Brunning*

Volume 37: The Chronology and Canon of Ælfric of Eynsham, *Aaron J. Kleist*

Volume 38: Medical Texts in Anglo-Saxon Literary Culture, *Emily Kesling*

Volume 39: The Dynastic Drama of *Beowulf*, *Francis Leneghan*

www.ingramcontent.com/pod-product-compliance
Lightning Source LLC
Chambersburg PA
CBHW051600230426
43668CB00013B/1921